THE UNTOLD STORY OF THE FBI

DOJ
Volume 1

THE UNTOLD STORY OF THE FBI

Archives of a Wall Street Analyst

DOJ

Volume 1

John Wilson

Resource Capital Research
Sydney

Copyright © 2024 John Wilson

All rights reserved. No part of this book may be reproduced
or used in any manner without the prior written permission of the copyright owner,
except for the use of brief quotations in a book review. The author has asserted his moral
right to be identified as the author of this work.

To request permissions, contact the publisher at info@rcresearch.com.au

A catalogue record for this work is available from the National Library of Australia

Title: The Untold Story of the FBI, Archives of a Wall Street Analyst, DOJ Volume 1
Hardcover: ISBN **978-1-7635214-1-4**
Paperback: ISBN **978-1-7635214-0-7**
e-book: ISBN **978-1-7635214-2-1**
Subjects: Freeport Indonesia, Inc
Freeport-McMoRan Copper & Gold Inc
West Papua, Indonesia
Grasberg mine
Department of Justice – United States
National security – United States
National security - Australia
Federal Bureau of Investigation
Australian Security intelligence Organisation
Australian Secret Intelligence Service
Political
Memoir

First hardcover edition August 2024.

Resource Capital Research
Level 21, 68 Pitt Street,
Sydney NSW 2000
Australia

GPO Box 5030
Greenwich NSW 2065
Australia

rcresearch.com.au

"They went after high-ranking military officers; they went after members of Congress, both Senate and the House, especially on the intelligence committees and on the armed services committees and some of the – and judicial. But they went after other ones, too. They went after lawyers and law firms. All kinds of – heaps of lawyers and law firms. They went after judges. One of the judges is now sitting on the Supreme Court that I had his wiretap information in my hand. Two are former FISA court judges. They went after State Department officials. They went after people in the executive service that were part of the White House – their own people. They went after antiwar groups. They went after U.S. international – U.S. companies that that do international business, you know, business around the world. They went after U.S. banking firms and financial firms that do international business. They went after NGOs that – like the Red Cross, people like that that go overseas and do humanitarian work. They went after a few antiwar civil rights groups. So, you know, don't tell me that there's no abuse, because I've had this stuff in my hand and looked at it. And in some cases, I literally was involved in the technology that was going after this stuff."[1]

(NSA whistleblower Russell Tice)

---

[1] Washingtonblog, 20 June 2013, NSA Whistleblower: NSA Spying On – and Blackmailing – Top Government Officials and Military Officers
http://www.washingtonsblog.com/2013/06/nsa-whistleblower-nsa-spying-on-and-blackmailing-high-level-government-officials-and-military-officers.html

Contents

FOIA Attorney Pete Sorenson Comment 7
Preface 8
Introduction 9
    Backstory 9
    Who runs America? 25
    West Papua, Indonesia 35
    Conclusion 40
Archive Overview 45

Appendix 62

Section I   Department of Justice and the FBI 64
    I-1a   FBI conduct not in "good faith" 66
    I-1b   Background PI report: FBI operative Dr. Steve Garber 78

Section II   Letter to AUSA Mr. John Moustakas - 2023 84
    II-1a   Letter from Pete Sorenson to AUSA Mr. John Moustakas: 87
        I.   Background on the Matter 88
        II.   FBI/DOJ Acting in "Bad Faith" 89
        III. FBI/DOJ Misapplication of FOIA Exemptions 91
        IV. Assistance with Locating Responsive Records 91
        A. Documents Not Searched 92
            1)   Susan Holmes, or Susan Acker[son] Holmes 92
            2)   Dr Steven Garber, or Steve Garber 92
            3)   Wilson and people operating on behalf of the FBI or other DOJ elements 92
            4)   Freeport McMoran Copper and Gold Inc 92
            5)   S.G. Warburg and SBC Warburg - Wilson's work related to Freeport McMoran 92
            6)   All records of encounters and discussions between John Wilson and Susan Holmes 93
            7)   Susan Holmes: NYC, June 1999 disclosure of existence of Wilson FBI file 94
            8)   Susan Holmes - FBI work visit to Australia for background on Wilson – C.2002 94
            9)   Susan Holmes - NYC, Café Fiorello covert interview (2003) 95
            10) Susan Holmes: introduction 98
            11) Susan Holmes: NYC, Café Fiorello (cont.): Gaslighting – psychological attack. 100
            12) FBI knowledge of photographs of Wilson NYC, C1996-97 102
            13) Solicitation of Wilson by an undercover drug dealer, NYC, C.1996-97 104
            14) Steve Garber – New York records: C.1996-1998 105
            15) Steve Garber – Prescott, AZ records: 1999 106
            16) Steve Garber - vicinity of Central Park and Upper West Side, NYC: C.June 2004 108
            17) Steve Garber – vicinity of Union Square, NYC: C.Sept 2004 109
            18) Colorado rafting trip 1997 109
            19) Dave Foreman – New York records 109
            20) Dave Foreman – Colorado, Utah, Arizona records 110
        B. Documents Withheld Entirely 111
        C. Documents Redacted Inappropriately 111
    II-2a   Email exchange: AUSA Mr. John Moustakas: 114

Section III   Declarations of John Wilson **120**

    III-1a   John Wilson's second Declaration: 30 August 2022 123

    III-2a   John Wilson's first Declaration: 16 November 2021 200

Section IV   General Correspondence **296**

    IV-1   Correspondence 2004 to 2010/11 298

        FBI/DOJ 299

        Senator Charles Schumer 314

        Congressman Jerrold Nadler 340

        House Judiciary Committee (HJC) 358

        United Nations Human Rights Committee (UNHRC) 365

        Other 371

    IV-2   Correspondence 2010 to 2014 373

        House Judiciary Committee (HJC) 374

        Other 375

    IV-3   Correspondence 2015 to 2019 377

        FBI/DOJ 378

        Senator Charles Schumer 397

    IV-4   Correspondence 2020 to 2023 422

        FBI/DOJ 423

        Senator Charles Schumer 429

        Senator Kirsten Gillibrand 434

        Congressman Jerrold Nadler 437

Section V   FBI - Freedom of Information (FOIA) **440**

    V-1   FOIA requests, appeals and OGIS mediation: 2004 to 2005 442

    V-2   FOIA requests, appeals and OGIS mediation: 2013 to 2014 451

    V-3   FOIA requests, appeals and OGIS mediation: 2019 to 2020 564

    V-4   FOIA requests, appeals and OGIS mediation: 2021 to 2023 577

Section VI   FBI - FOIA Judicial Review **632**

    VI-1   First FBI - FOIA Judicial Review - BLHNY: 8 December 2020 634

        Complaint 635

        Judge's Report and Recommendation 641

    VI-2   Second FBI - FOIA Judicial Review - Sorenson: 8 October 2022 657

        Complaint 658

        Summary Declaration of John Wilson 666

        Expert Witness Report: 25-year veteran of the FBI—Jennifer Coffindaffer 681

INDEX **695**

Table of Exhibits

Section I - Department of Justice and the FBI

Exhibit 1: *April 2021.*   BLHNY—private investigator's report on FBI operative Steve Garber. _____ *78*
Exhibit 2: *8 April 2024.*   Email from DOJ to attorney Pete Sorenson – re FBI redaction policy._____ *80*

Section II - Correspondence with AUSA Mr. John Moustakas - 2023

Exhibit 3: *11 July 2023.*   Letter from Attorney Pete Sorenson to AUSA Moustakas outlining FBI abuse. __ *87*
Exhibit 4: *August 2023.*   DOJ, AUSA Moustakas: "Is this the mining expert? Or it that L____?" _____ *114*

Section III - Declarations of John Wilson

Exhibit 5: *30 August 2022.*   Second notarized Declaration of John Wilson. _____ *123*
Exhibit 6: *16 November 2021.*   First notarized Declaration of John Wilson. _____ *200*

Section IV - General Correspondence

Exhibit 7: *17 January 2005.*   Letter from John Wilson via Attorney Barry Fisher to DOJ, OIG_____ *299*
Exhibit 8: *16 April 2005.*   Letter from John Wilson via Attorney Barry Fisher to DOJ/OIG_____ *300*
Exhibit 9: *16 August 2005.*   Email from John Wilson to DOJ, Marvin Hernandez _____ *301*
Exhibit 10: *27 August 2005.*   Email from Barry Fisher to John Wilson re DOJ, Hernadez. _____ *302*
Exhibit 11: *10 February 2006.*   Letter from DOJ to Attorney Barry Fisher._____ *302*
Exhibit 12: *22 February 2006.*   Email from John Wilson to Barry Fisher re DOJ, Hernandez. _____ *303*
Exhibit 13: *22 February 2006.*   Email from Barry Fisher to John Wilson to re DOJ, Hernandez. _____ *304*
Exhibit 14: *22 February 2006.*   Email from John Wilson to Barry Fisher re DOJ, Hernandez – confirms "they are agents"._____ *305*
Exhibit 15: *22 February 2006.*   Email from John Wilson to DOJ, Marvin Hernandez – FBI denies agents are "employees", but does not deny they are "contractors"._____ *305*
Exhibit 16: *8 March 2006.*   Email from DOJ, Marvin Hernandez to John Wilson._____ *306*
Exhibit 17: *8 March 2006.*   Email from John Wilson to DOJ, Marvin Hernandez._____ *306*
Exhibit 18: *11 May 2006.*   Email from DOJ, Marvin Hernandez to John Wilson – FBI confirms one agent is an "employee". _____ *307*
Exhibit 19: *11 May 2006.*   Email from John Wilson to Barry Fisher re DOJ, Hernandez – DOJ backtracking on agent admission._____ *308*
Exhibit 20: *19 May 2006.*   Email from John Wilson to DOJ, Marvin Hernandez._____ *308*
Exhibit 21: *14 June 2006.*   Email from John Wilson to DOJ, Marvin Hernandez. _____ *309*
Exhibit 22: *23 August 2006.*   Letter from John Wilson via Barry Fisher to DOJ, OIG._____ *309*
Exhibit 23: *19 September 2007.*   Email from John Wilson to Attorney Barry Fisher re ABC reporter. ___ *311*
Exhibit 24: *7 December 2006.*   Letter from John Wilson via Attorney Barry Fisher to DOJ, OIG. _____ *312*
Exhibit 25: *22 April 2005.*   Letter from John Wilson via Attorney Barry Fisher to Senator Schumer.____ *314*
Exhibit 26: *25 May 2006.*   Letter from John Wilson via Attorney Barry Fisher to Senator Schumer. ___ *316*
Exhibit 27: *9 June 2006.*   Email from Barry Fisher to John Wilson. _____ *318*
Exhibit 28: *13 June 2006.*   Letter from Senator Schumer to DOJ. _____ *319*
Exhibit 29: *20 June 2006.*   Email from Barry Fisher to John Wilson._____ *320*
Exhibit 30: *9 August 2006.*   Letter from the DOJ, OIG to Senator Schumer. _____ *320*
Exhibit 31: *15 August 2006.*   Email from Barry Fisher to John Wilson _____ *321*
Exhibit 32: *23 August 2006.*   Letter from John Wilson via Attorney Barry Fisher to Senator Schumer. _ *321*
Exhibit 33: *1 January 2007.*   Letter from John Wilson via Attorney Barry Fisher to Senator Schumer.__ *326*
Exhibit 34: *20 February 2007.*   Letter from John Wilson via Attorney Barry Fisher to Senator Schumer. *327*
Exhibit 35: *3 April 2007.*   Letter from Senator Schumer to DOJ._____ *328*

Exhibit 36: *7 May 2007. Letter from the DOJ to Senator Schumer.* _____ 329
Exhibit 37: *7 June 2007. Letter from Senator Schumer to DOJ.* _____ 330
Exhibit 38: *7 June 2007. Letter from John Wilson via Attorney Barry Fisher to Senator Schumer.* _____ 331
Exhibit 39: *9 August 2007. Letter from the DOJ to Senator Schumer.* _____ 333
Exhibit 40: *6 September 2007. Letter from John Wilson via Attorney Barry Fisher to Senator Schumer.* 334
Exhibit 41: *27 February 2008. Letter from John Wilson via Attorney Barry Fisher to Senator Schumer.* 336
Exhibit 42: *12 June 2008. Letter from John Wilson via Attorney Barry Fisher to Senator Schumer.* ____ 339
Exhibit 43: *12 June 2007. Letter from John Wilson via Attorney Barry Fisher to Congressman Nadler.* _ 340
Exhibit 44: *19 September 2007. Email from John Wilson to Congressman Jerrold Nadler.* _____ 341
Exhibit 45: *2 September 2009. Letter from John Wilson via Barry Fisher to Rep. Jerrold Nadler.* _____ 343
Exhibit 46: *2009-2011. Email trail between John Wilson and Rep. Nadler's staffers.* _____ 344
Exhibit 47: *17 January 2005. Letter from John Wilson via Attorney Barry Fisher to Rep. Conyers, HJC.* _ 358
Exhibit 48: *16 April 2005. Letter from John Wilson via Barry Fisher to Rep. Conyers, HJC.* _____ 360
Exhibit 49: *26 July 2005. Letter from John Wilson via Attorney Barry Fisher to HJC.* _____ 361
Exhibit 50: *14 September 2005. Email from office of Rep. Scott, ranking member of the HJC to Wilson.* 363
Exhibit 51: *28 September 2005. Email from John Wilson to Mindy Barry, staffer, HJC.* _____ 364
Exhibit 52: *14 April 2007. Letter from John Wilson via Attorney Barry Fisher to UNHRC.* _____ 365
Exhibit 53: *24 April 2007. Letter from UNHRC to John Wilson via Attorney Barry Fisher.* _____ 367
Exhibit 54: *24 August 2007. Letter from UNHRC to John Wilson via Attorney Barry Fisher.* _____ 369
Exhibit 55: *2 May 2005. Letter from John Wilson via Attorney Barry Fisher to Senator Clinton.* _____ 371
Exhibit 56: *15 September 2010. Letter from John Wilson via Barry Fisher to HJC.* _____ 374
Exhibit 57: *25 February 2013. Email from John Wilson to United Steelworkers.* _____ 375
Exhibit 58: *27 February 2013. Email from United Steelworkers to John Wilson.* _____ 376
Exhibit 59: *9 March 2015. Letter from John Wilson to DOJ, Office of the Inspector General.* _____ 378
Exhibit 60: *9 March 2015. Fax from John Wilson to DOJ, Office of the Inspector General.* _____ 380
Exhibit 61: *2 October 2015. Email from John Wilson to Attorney Barry Fisher re DOJ/FBI.* _____ 381
Exhibit 62: *8 February 2016. Fax from Attorney Barry Fisher to DOJ/FBI.* _____ 382
Exhibit 63: *9 February 2016. Letter from DOJ, FBI to John Wilson.* _____ 392
Exhibit 64: *23 February 2016. Letter from John Wilson to DOJ, FBI.* _____ 393
Exhibit 65: *25 May 2016. Letter from DOJ, OIG to John Wilson's Attorney Barry Fisher.* _____ 395
Exhibit 66: *24 June 2016. Letter from Attorney Barry Fisher to the US Attorney General, DOJ and FBI.* 396
Exhibit 67: *14 March 2016. Online Casework Request from John Wilson to Senator Schumer.* _____ 397
Exhibit 68: *9 February 2017. Online and faxed Casework Request from John Wilson to Sen. Schumer.* _ 400
Exhibit 69: *15 March 2017. Letter from John Wilson to Senator Schumer re Casework Request.* _____ 410
Exhibit 70: *2017-2021. Email trail: John Wilson, Attorney Barry Fisher and Senator Schumer.* _____ 412
Exhibit 71: *1 March 2019. Emails: John Wilson and Senator Schumer's office re OGIS.* _____ 419
Exhibit 72: *5 June 2020. Letter from Attorney Barry Fisher to FBI, Director Wray.* _____ 423
Exhibit 73: *26 June 2020. Letter from FBI to Attorney Barry Fisher.* _____ 426
Exhibit 74: *18 March 2022. Letter from John Wilson to US Attorney General Garland.* _____ 427
Exhibit 75: *2021-2022. Various emails between John Wilson, attorneys and Senator Schumer.* _____ 429
Exhibit 76: *25 May 2022. Online Caseworker Request from John Wilson to Senator Gillibrand.* _____ 434
Exhibit 77: *2022. Various emails from John Wilson to Senator Gillibrand.* _____ 436
Exhibit 78: *26 May 2022. Copy of online Casework Request from John Wilson to Jerrold Nadler.* _____ 437
Exhibit 79: *26 May 2022. Automated email response from Congressman Nadler to John Wilson.* _____ 438

Section V – FBI - Freedom of Information Requests (FOIA)

Exhibit 80: *12 October 2004. FOIA letter from Attorney Rachel Minter to FBI.* _____ 444
Exhibit 81: *25 October 2004. FOIA letter from FBI to Attorney Rachel Minter.* _____ 445
Exhibit 82: *19 December 2004. FOIA appeal letter from John Wilson to FBI, cc Barry Fisher.* _____ 446
Exhibit 83: *30 December 2004. FOIA appeal letter from FBI to John Wilson.* _____ 448
Exhibit 84: *16 April 2005. FOIA appeal letter from FBI to John Wilson.* _____ 449
Exhibit 85: *6 September 2005. FOIA appeal letter from FBI to John Wilson.* _____ 450
Exhibit 86: *14 June 2013. FOIA letter from John Wilson to FBI.* _____ 453

Exhibit 87: *Jul-Nov 2013.   Emails between Wilson, FBI - Sobonya; and FOIA Attorney David Sobel.* _____ 454
Exhibit 88: *20 November 2013.   Letter from FBI to John Wilson (received circa December 2013).* _____ 460
Exhibit 89: *23 December 2013.   Appeal letter from John Wilson FOIA Attorney David Sobel to FBI.* _____ 462
Exhibit 90: *25 February 2014.   Appeal letter from FBI to Attorney David Sobel.* _____ 466
Exhibit 91: *14 June 2013.   FOIA letter from John Wilson to FBI.* _____ 469
Exhibit 92: *29 January 2014.   FOIA letter from FBI to John Wilson.* _____ 470
Exhibit 93: *20-25 March 2014.   Emails between John Wilson and Attorney David Sobel.* _____ 474
Exhibit 94: *26 March 2014.   FOIA Request email from John Wilson to FBI.* _____ 475
Exhibit 95: *6 May 2014.   Letter assigning FOIA No. from FBI to John Wilson.* _____ 483
Exhibit 96: *25 September 2014.   Letter and disc of released documents from FBI to John Wilson.* _____ 494
Exhibit 97: *25 September 2014.   Disc contents - released documents from FBI to John Wilson.* _____ 499
Exhibit 98: *6 November 2014.   FOIA Request Appeal letter from John Wilson to FBI.* _____ 510
Exhibit 99: *6 November 2014.   FOIA Appeal letter from John Wilson to FBI.* _____ 513
Exhibit 100: *23 February 2015.   FOIA Appeal decision letter from FBI to John Wilson.* _____ 514
Exhibit 101: *May 2017 - Nov 2018.   Emails between Wilson, Barry Fisher and OGIS – 2017-2019.* _____ 516
Exhibit 102: *8 June 2017.   Email from OGIS to John Wilson: Assigned case no. 201703007.* _____ 523
Exhibit 103: *16 August 2017.   Email from OGIS to John Wilson: Assigned case no. 201703993.* _____ 528
Exhibit 104: *2 November 2017.   Email from OGIS to John Wilson: Apology from OGIS for delays and confusion - Case no. "sent in error".* _____ 532
Exhibit 105: *18 December 2018.   OGIS mediation FOIA Appeal decision letter to John Wilson re case no. 201703007.* _____ 543
Exhibit 106: *12 April 2019.   Email letter from OGIS to John Wilson: Closing case no. 201703007.* _____ 548
Exhibit 107: *23 October 2019.   Website FOIA Request from John Wilson to FBI.* _____ 566
Exhibit 108: *29 October 2019.   FOIA Response from FBI to John Wilson.* _____ 568
Exhibit 109: *18 February 2020.   FOIA Request Appeal from John Wilson to FBI.* _____ 572
Exhibit 110: *21 February 2020.   FOIA Appeal confirmation letter to John Wilson from FBI, OIP.* _____ 573
Exhibit 111: *21 March 2020.   FOIA Appeal decision review letter to John Wilson from FBI, OIP.* _____ 575
Exhibit 112: *20 May 2022.   FOIA Request from Attorney Pete Sorenson for John Wilson to the FBI.* _____ 579
Exhibit 113: *13 June 2022.   FOIA response from the FBI to Pete Sorenson re John Wilson.* _____ 587
Exhibit 114: *1 September 2022.   FOIA Administrative Appeal to the OIP, DOJ from Pete Sorenson.* _____ 591
Exhibit 115: *1 September 2022.   FOIA Admin. Appeal receipt from the OIP, DOJ to Pete Sorenson.* _____ 599
Exhibit 116: *28 April 2023.   FOIA "litigation release" letter and disc sent to Attorney Pete Sorenson.* _____ 600
Exhibit 117: *28 April 2023.   Disc contents - released documents from FBI to John Wilson.* _____ 604

Section VI – FBI - FOIA Judicial Review

Exhibit 118: *8 December 2020.   Complaint: First FOIA litigation filed in the US District Court for the Southern District of New York by Attorney David Rankin.* _____ 636
Exhibit 119: *16 February 2022.   Report and Recommendation.* _____ 641
Exhibit 120: *8 October 2022.   Complaint: Second FOIA litigation filed in the United States District Court for the District of Columbia by Attorney Pete Sorenson.* _____ 659
Exhibit 121: *17 March 2014.   Summary Declaration of John Wilson* _____ 666
Exhibit 122: *17 March 2024.   Independent Expert's Report: Jennifer Coffindaffer - a 25 year veteran of the FBI.* _____ 681

Glossary

USA

AUSA	Assistant United States Attorney – US Department of Justice, attorneys who represent the federal government of the United States in civil and appellate litigation and in federal criminal prosecutions.
CIA	Central Intelligence Agency
DOJ	Department of Justice
FBI	Federal Bureau of Investigation
FOIA	Freedom of Information Act
NSA	National Security Agency
OGIS	The Office of Government Information Services – an FOIA mediation resource
OIG	Office of the Inspector General - responsible for conducting internal investigations of DOJ employees and programs, including allegations of criminal wrongdoing or administrative misconduct by DOJ employees.
OPIC	Overseas Private Investment Corporation

Australia

ASIO	Australian Security Intelligence Organisation
ASIS	Australian Secret Intelligence Service
IGIS	Inspector General of Intelligence and Security

FOIA Attorney Pete Sorenson Comment

It's been my extreme pleasure and honor to represent John Wilson on two Freedom of Information Act (FOIA) cases. Both cases are still pending in the District Court in Washington, DC. One case involves the FBI's hoarding and refusing to release records. The other involves the US State Department dragging its feet on a simple request for records of its investigation of US mining company Freeport-McMoRan. In the latter case, John is aware of and requested the interim and final reports by the State Department undertaken around 1996 following its investigation into the company which was launched after eyewitness allegations the company was involved with the killing of Indigenous protestors and other human rights abuses in the vicinity of its large Grasberg copper and gold mine in West Papua, Indonesia in the mid-1990s. John has pursued these cases, under FOIA, in an effort to exercise his rights to access justice in the USA in a struggle against these large and corrupt state bureaucracies that protect vested interests. He's also pursuing these cases to uncover the truth about the Federal Bureau of Investigation (FBI), the Department of Justice (DOJ) and the State Department's complicity in unwarranted persecution of US citizens at home and foreign nationals in far flung places like West Papua, Indonesia.

C. Peter Sorenson, Senior Attorney, Sorenson Law LLC

Preface

The documents in this archive tell the story of the US Department of Justice's (DOJ) and the Federal Bureau of Investigation's (FBI) corruption and evasion of accountability when targeting civil society "dissidents". It also tells of my efforts to hold the FBI and DOJ to account.

The official documents and correspondence appended in the archive paint the picture of the corrupt means by which these agencies crush and silence civil society in support of America's corporate behemoths. Their tactics are Orwellian and Kafkaesque. For the most part, my efforts from 2004 to the publication of this work in 2024, and those of my attorneys over the past twenty years, have been thwarted, compromised by hollowed out oversight agencies and regulators.

Intended as a historical record of official documents, appended are my notarized Declarations and court documents that include evidence of FBI malfeasance, oppressive surveillance, wiretaps, gaslighting and cancel culture. These Declarations contain detailed accounts of events, and disclosure of FBI methods targeting "dissidents". Agents are named, dates and locations provided, and details of events discussed. The archive comprises correspondence either directly by me, or my attorneys, with various FBI/DOJ departments, elected representatives including Senator Charles Schumer and Congressman Jerrold Nadler, and Freedom of Information requests (FOIA).

This preface provides backstory of the events that have occurred since my Wall Street analyst report came out in 1996 critical of US mining company Freeport-McMoRan's activities in West Papua, Indonesia. It sheds light on the travesty occurring in resource rich West Papua, Indonesia, backed by the US, where New York Stock Exchange (NYSE) listed Freeport-McMoRan has interests in the massive Grasberg copper and gold mine. The preface also contains background on the US surveillance state. It provides context for the complaint letters, included in the appended archive, I have sent over the years to the FBI and DOJ, among others, and outlines FBI retribution against me. Key points and timelines are provided in this volume, however, it is not intended as a narrative that offers a complete account of events. A narrative will be included in volume two.

At least seven other people in the USA were targeted for their criticism of Freeport-McMoRan around this time, including journalists and academics. Our intelligence agencies frequently covertly target professionals, those who speak out, or protest, against establishment interests, typically on business and human rights issues. As one agent, Steve Garber said to me, most people in America don't even realize they've been targeted.

This is part one of a four-part archive series. Volume one covers the DOJ, which is responsible for the FBI. As mentioned above, it comprises notes and reflections on disparate aspects of this story including the FBI's targeting of civil society, and the lack of effective oversight. Notes and reflections in the preface cover topics such as the FBI's personal attacks on me, the public's fear of authority, notes on Henry Kissinger's past close association with Freeport, corruption of Western intelligence agencies, the methods used to oppress civil society and target leaders, professionals, and anyone else with influence, and the Western backed atrocities against Indigenous people in West Papua, Indonesia and elsewhere, to access their natural resources.

Other archives planned for release are volume two, which is focused on the Department of State; volume three, on Australian partnering agencies to the FBI – Australian Security Intelligence Organisation (ASIO) and Australian Secret Intelligence Service (ASIS); and volume four, a detailed transcript of a covert interview conducted by the FBI in 2003 at Café Fiorello in New York City.

Introduction

Part A

Backstory

A Personal Reckoning

Of the passions of youth, finding a life partner and establishing a career path are prominent. Optimism and dreams—the energy that drives innovation and change, and the will to hold authority to account—brush up against establishment interests and a previous generation's way of doing things. Arriving in New York City in 1993 at the age of thirty, unknown to me at the time, I was about to embark on a journey that contained a copious mix of all these.

There is no hard and firm definition of what makes someone a dissident in the US, no red line one crosses on the journey as a regular citizen to becoming a political target of the State. However, once that line is crossed, one is sanctioned, "kneecapped", the silent, democratic way—in secret—isolated and cast aside socially and economically as effectively as if renditioned to a remote halfway house enroute to a gulag archipelago somewhere in Siberia. The "virtual gulags" of modern-day America and its allies are built on oppressive surveillance, interference with relationships, cancel culture, blacklisting and gaslighting.

In my case, I found where the line is drawn after publication of a standard work report to global fund managers and analysts that touched on the US mining company Freeport-McMoRan Grasberg mine deaths in West Papua, Indonesia, in the mid-1990s—killings of Indigenous protestors at the hands of the Indonesian military, written about by the *New York Times*. I thought my report could possibly meet with professional rebuke from within the corporate hierarchy and a chance I would lose my job if the world were truly corrupt, but that proved to be a gross understatement. It was yet another rite-of-passage, the choice to stand up for justice, or hunker down, remain silent and be complicit in the killings. A pang of guilt arose. It was an awful realisation, that in the worst case I might be forced to make the choice—my job or justice.

At the time, I was a young mining analyst, with a recent Wharton MBA working in the New York equity research division of SG Warburg (now part of UBS). My research report (published March 12, 1996: refer to the Appendix) had raised the issue of US mining company Freeport-McMoRan. According to media reports, it was under investigation by the US Department of State following widely reported eyewitness allegations it was involved in the killing of Indigenous protestors at its massive Grasberg gold and copper mine in remote West Papua, Indonesia. The company denied any role in human rights abuses, and allegations were not subsequently proven in court.

Freeport's problems weren't limited to eyewitness' allegations of company personnel being directly involved in human rights abuses, a notion "reinforced by overwhelming evidence" provided in two independent human rights reports in 1995 (ACFOA, and the Catholic Church).

The US government, concerned at the negative publicity, rescinded the company's Overseas Private Investment Corporation (OPIC) political risk insurance, intended as a slap on the wrist. OPIC is a US federal agency that supports US investment offshore. It canceled its US$100 million political risk insurance to Freeport citing environmental degradation in a letter dated October 10, 1995—the first time it had ever canceled a policy in its 25-year history. In setting out its reasons for doing so, OPIC implied the company had misled both it and the market on its environmental record. It was a major embarrassment for the company and potentially a significant liability.

In 1996, Henry Kissinger, former US Secretary of State, a board member of Freeport-McMoRan and company advisor was doing the rounds in Washington DC, along with former CIA Director and Freeport advisor James Woolsey, desperately attempting to have the rescinded OPIC insurance policy re-instated.

It appeared Freeport was highly sensitive and increasingly apprehensive about the prospects of a backlash and potential for shareholders (some with very deep pockets) to launch a lawsuit against the company for misrepresentation of its activities in West Papua, Indonesia. The last thing, it seemed, the FBI and Freeport wanted was Wall Street analysts to factor these issues into their valuations and publish details that are sent directly to fund managers around the world, despite commentary by the wider media within the US.

At the end of the day, the actual response my research report drew was vicious. I had not envisaged the full-on onslaught the US and its allied foreign intelligence agencies were inclined to launch against a regular citizen, led by the FBI. This story is about American power and the disturbing way it is deployed both at home and abroad. What happened to me could happen to any young professional doing their job if they come up against people in power who have something to hide.

In 1996 and 1997, the FBI launched an undercover wide-ranging attack against me in retribution that included targeting my career, relationships—both personal and professional, and oppressive surveillance. It targeted the long-term relationship between Susan Holmes (my girlfriend, undercover FBI agent and environmentalist) and me, on the cusp of a marriage engagement, used tactics to sow doubt and mistrust between us which contributed to our relationship break-up. We split up in late 1997 after dating for three years. FBI tactics included the deletion of critical phone messages between us, intervention to arrange "work" trips away for each of us at key times to derail efforts to get back together after we broke up (her FBI role was known by her employer at the Sierra Club who obliged the FBI's requests whenever possible, in my case the FBI interacted covertly with management), FBI honey traps, arranged for Susan, apparently as a honey trap, to visit a California US Congressional candidate, among other things (recounted in more detail in my Declaration in the appendix, and in a narrative to be published in volume two of this series).

After our split up in 1997 and my return to Australia in mid-1999, we both eventually found new partners. By 2003, Holmes was married, living in Washington D.C., and now complicit with the FBI in targeting me. However, evidently, she had lingering reservations about the FBI and divided loyalties concerning me. I assume this was on account of our long, personal history, and what she now knew about the true nature of the agency's activities.

Based on revelations by undercover FBI agents Susan Holmes to me in 2003 during a covert interview at Café Fiorello in New York City, and Dr. Steven Garber to me in 2004, the FBI has undertaken extensive surveillance of me and my contacts, turning and recruiting whoever they could, bugging my apartment, telephone, intercepting emails, and recording conversations (for more details refer to my sworn court Declarations in the Appendix). The agency has taken extraordinary pains to delve deeply into all aspects of my past. Over the course of my life, I have had many hundreds of friends, colleagues, and acquaintances. Several dozens of these I am now aware have been approached, and in cases interfered with and recruited. In addition to people I already knew, others have made themselves known to me, in cases befriending me, only later to reveal their involvement with an intelligence agency.

The intelligence agencies have no compunction about targeting their own agents or citizens when it suits their purposes, like Susan and the Christmas of 1997 when they targeted and undermined our anticipated engagement, or the West Papuans that so loyally served their interests giving vital support and land position to General Douglas MacArthur in the Pacific during WWII. The West Papuan's were blithely sacrificed to the Indonesians when it served American interests to do so in the 1960s. Virtually, anyone can be sacrificed, and replaced, when it suits the changing interests of those in power.

I have faced political and authoritarian demons I never contemplated I would encounter in my life. This story sheds as much light on the conduct of the Western intelligence agencies, under the leadership of the US, at home as it does the plight of Indigenous people caught in military conflict zones abroad. Innocent bystanders everywhere caught in wars: The hidden, secret places of the world, like West Papua, Indonesia; Nigeria; the Democratic Republic of Congo (DRC); Ecuador, and elsewhere, with domestic and foreign backers funding armed violence to secure resources, deserves much greater public attention. It is moral bankruptcy for the world's most powerful to target Indigenous people. They are easy military targets, no match for the US and allies with their modern weaponry. Targeting Indigenous people in this way is a war crime, as with targeting innocent civilians in any war—it's against everything just and noble the United States and West profess to stand for.

Undercover FBI agent Dr Steve Garber's disclosure to me in 2004 in New York City was in the days before mass social media networking and the FBI assumed this story would never be heard.

Dissidents on Wall Street—the "new cold war"

The research report I wrote on Wall Street on Freeport-McMoRan (dated March 12, 1996) followed international media reports of further killings and strike activity at the Grasberg mine. The 1994 Christmas Day massacre in which seven people were killed, and which was widely reported in the world media, represented just a small portion of the thirty-seven Indigenous protesters reported killed in the vicinity of the mine in 1994 and 1995.

Below is a paragraph from the March 12, 1996, report:

> Our view is that increased military presence poses potential for escalation of the violence in the mid term, heightening the political risk of Freeport's investment in Irian Jaya [West Papua, Indonesia]. Ultimately, Freeport needs to deal with the civil aspects of this situation to allay investors concerns, and possibly also those of the US Department of State. The timing is unfortunate for Freeport as it coincides with the arbitration over whether $100 million in OPIC political risk insurance should be rescinded. The company has increasingly come under scrutiny following reported human rights abuses in the area of the mine and also concerns over its environmental record. The latter was cited by OPIC last November as the basis for withdrawing the $100 million in insurance.

The report touched on the Grasberg killings and environmental concerns and indicated a civil, rather than a military, solution was preferable in resolving labor disputes at Grasberg. In the scheme of things, my comments offered a relatively mild rebuke, but the extremity of the response of the authorities shows how sensitive they were, and remain in the present, to the issues. With people like Henry Kissinger, a former US Secretary of State on the board, former American ambassadors to Indonesia, military advisers and company security department staffed with former US military personnel, CIA, and FBI agents, the company seemed to appreciate its tenuous position on the political and security fronts.

The mention of Freeport in the context of human rights and environmental abuses raised the company's profile with investors in a way that had potential to create a negative financial backlash against it. Indeed, over the years, substantial investment funds have dumped their holdings in Freeport amid global publicity on ethical concerns about the company's activities, including the large Government Pension Fund of Norway. It dumped and blacklisted Freeport's shares in 2006 citing environmental concerns. Other government funds to blacklist Freeport shares include New Zealand (2012) and Sweden (2013).

New Zealand's Superannuation Fund in September 2012 blacklisted Freeport-McMoRan from its investment funds citing human rights concerns. It was the first major fund to blacklist Freeport on grounds that specifically included human rights concerns, saying:

> Freeport McMoRan has been excluded [from the fund] based on breaches of human rights standards by security forces around the Grasberg mine, and concerns over requirements for direct payments to government security forces by the company in at least two countries in which it operates...[2]

The area around Freeport's concession areas in West Papua, Indonesia has had a long history of killings, ostensibly by the Indonesian military, which continues up to the present (2024). Many hundreds, indeed thousands, of deaths have been documented by human rights agencies. In 1994, the brutality seemed to be spiraling out of control with seven Indigenous protestors shot and killed in a short period around Christmas Day. Some of the protestors were reportedly killed at point-blank range, inside steel shipping containers on Freeport property. For a sensitive topic, it received unusually wide publicity and the US State Department had reportedly taken the unusual step of launching a formal investigation.

Little is known of the Indonesian province of West Papua (formerly called Irian Jaya), which is located on the western half of the island of New Guinea, just north of Australia. Indeed, many people confuse it with the adjacent independent country of Papua New Guinea (PNG), which is located on the eastern half of the same island. West Papua has been the subject of an official media blackout by the Indonesian government since its military invaded in 1962. It was not till the advent of the internet in the early 1990s that word of the plight of the Indigenous people and the atrocities inflicted on them reached the rest of the world, including the shocking reports of the 1994—95 massacre.

The FBI and Freeport were evidently nervous about the impact of this shift in media influence and the obvious potential for serious political and financial market backlash against the company—including in New York, where the financial community played a key role in the financing of Freeport's activities.

The human rights abuses committed against the Indigenous people of West Papua, Indonesia, ostensibly by the Indonesian military, are extensive and include arbitrary detention, torture, rape, and extra-judicial killings. Transmigration is also an insidious part of West Papuan history under Indonesian rule—an Indonesian government policy whereby large numbers of people, mostly ethnic Asians, from other parts of Indonesia are relocated to West Papua on a scale that makes the original Melanesian inhabitants minorities in the province, and which has prompted claims of genocide (including a report

---

[2] Jenny Denton, 18 October 2013 Swedish Pension Funds Divest Freeport McMoRan Holdings, Environmental News Service. http://ens-newswire.com/2013/10/18/swedish-pension-funds-divest-freeport-mcmoran-holdings/

by Yale Law School)[3]. Further, the new arrivals historically have received benefits and opportunities not available to the Indigenous people.

In 2003, Freeport publicly acknowledged it had been directly paying Indonesian military and police units and officials who were involved in maintaining security around the mine. As disturbing as the payments themselves was the startling scale of the amounts of money involved. In 2005, the *New York Times* reported that the company had paid US$20 million between 1998 and 2004 for these services including paying one individual US$150,000. The size of the payments to the military and police appears to have increased significantly over time (looking at years 2005 to 2011). For example, Freeport's Securities and Exchange Commission (SEC) filings indicate the spending on internal civilian security in 2011 was US$37 million, plus an additional US$14 million paid directly to the Indonesian government and military—a total of US$51 million spent in relation to Grasberg—just in 2011 alone.

It seems surprising that these payments pass muster with the US DOJ and are not in breach of the US Foreign Corrupt Practices Act which the US government aggressively enforces against foreign corporations. Indeed, the US United Steelworkers union in 2011 asked the DOJ to investigate Freeport's payments but the powerful union was fobbed off and heard nothing substantive back on the matter (refer to correspondence in the Appendix).

In an article published in 2011 to coincide with the fiftieth anniversary of Indonesian occupation of West Papua, anthropologist and academic Hugh Brody referred to the large sums of money and Freeport's close links to the Indonesian military as the "militarization of mining"[4]. Indeed, Freeport CEO Jim-Bob Moffett reported security matters relating to the mine as the "new cold war" and said there was "no alternative to our reliance on the Indonesian military and police…."

With the killings of 1994—96 attracting worldwide attention, Freeport's public relations machine went into overdrive. It paid for a full-page ad in the *New York Times*, made an infomercial, threatened to sue journalists and academics covering the matter and withdraw a financial donation made by the company to endow a chair in environmental communications at the local Loyola University in New Orleans.

But what is little known, and never reported is the role that the FBI played during this time to lower the profile of Freeport's controversial Grasberg operation and silence discussion in the US that included targeting Wall Street analysts.

The use of FBI power in this way is more disturbing given the agency's dual role in helping to identify and interview eyewitnesses to the alleged human rights abuses on location in West Papua, Indonesia. The killings in West Papua, Indonesia of Indigenous people have continued to the present day attributed to the Indonesian military. With the region virtually closed to foreigners and a media blackout enforced, little of what is happening there is reported by the mainstream media.

---

[3] Elizabeth Brundige, et al., Allard K. Lowenstein International Human Rights Clinic Yale Law School, April 2004, Indonesian Human Rights Abuses in West Papua: Application of the Law of Genocide to the History of Indonesian Control.
[4] Hugh Brody, 30 November 2011 December 1, 1961: Fly the flag of independence – West Papua and the Indonesian Empire, www.opendemocracy.net

Meeting with the FBI and Freeport—May 1996

A couple of months later after the publication of my March 12, 1996, report, I was in Freeport McMoRan's boardroom at its head office, then in New Orleans, at a briefing for Wall Street analysts. During the briefing Q&A, I asked the Chairman and CEO, James (Jim Bob) Moffett, a question about the US State Department's human rights investigation into the company's activities in West Papua, Indonesia. He affirmed that the investigation was ongoing. Unusual for a CEO of a major NYSE corporation, he became increasingly agitated and angry during a rambling, long-winded reply.

In response to the analyst report and question I asked during the analysts' briefing, the FBI's threat came promptly. The FBI was, in hindsight, ready and waiting. It was delivered by their man who had been sitting among the analysts in Freeport's boardroom, where Moffett had just conducted the annual analyst briefing and Q&A.

The FBI's man came up to me and threatened me in an icy tone that left no uncertainty as to its ill intent. He was around my age (early thirties) and dressed in a business suit. He had stood near me as I spoke briefly with Moffet in the boardroom alcove after the meeting. As I started to move away from Jim Bob, the FBI's man moved with me. Emerging from my shadow, he stepped squarely in front of me and without introducing himself addressed me using my first name.

"John, I respect you for asking that question," he said, referring to my question during the briefing. "But you might wish you hadn't."

Ignoring my own surprise that he knew my name, I replied, "So what? What do I care? What can they do to me?"

"You might not want to find out," he said firmly.

I held his gaze for a moment and then moved away.

It was a threat in no uncertain terms. More accurately, it was an absolute decree, a disclosure from which there was no turning back. It was as if a nest of tarantulas had awoken; the FBI and its agents, the supposed protector of democratic freedoms in the US, had emerged from its dark cover and was on the prowl.

At the time the FBI campaign commenced, supported by ASIO and ASIS, I was young—thirty-three years old—on the cusp of establishing a career and on the verge of committing to a life partner, an undercover FBI agent and professional environmentalist, with the intention of having a family. I was still new to Wall Street, a relatively unknown analyst with limited influence, which made me an easy target. Certainly, I had no connections into the political world at a level that could be called upon to pull strings and potentially haul the FBI into line on this issue. With former Secretary of State Henry Kissinger (of Vietnam, Cambodia, East Timor, Chile, and Nixon-era fame) on the board, former US ambassadors to Indonesia advising the company, and the US heavily involved in supplying and supporting Indonesia's military, the company's interests seemed well protected in Washington DC.

Almost as disturbing as what has, and continues to, unfold in West Papua, Indonesia, to the present day, are the US government's tactics in silencing dissent both at home and abroad, laying the foundation for atrocities with the FBI and CIA brooking no criticism, even to the mildest forms of protest.

What has unfolded since my March 1996 report has been a dystopian, Orwellian-Kafkaesque retribution unleashed by the FBI and their allied Western intelligence agencies against me (and Susan) using invasive tools and predatory instincts so well exposed in recent years by the likes of WikiLeaks and Edward Snowden. The agencies targeted my career, my family and friends, endeavored to undermine my credibility and call into question my sanity. In the years that followed, I have encountered and been targeted by a small battalion of FBI agents in the US, some flying to Australia, and ASIO /ASIS agents in Australia, some flying to New York City to target me. Moving beyond the surveillance powers of the state, the collection of data and invasion of privacy, I know firsthand what they can do with all that information, how that information has been used mercilessly to interfere in my life in surprising places and in astonishing ways, in places I assumed could never be compromised (refer to my sworn Declarations in the Appendix. I expect to publish more details in narrative form in volume two of this series).

I have come to see the wisdom of the Founding Fathers with a new, deeper appreciation wrought from the realization of the shortcomings of human nature from which flow the persistent character flaws and abuses of those in power. The separation of powers, heralded as fundamental to democracy and essential to reining in corrupt or selfish leaders and political agendas, has been eroded to a devastating extent in the US and the West more broadly.

Undercover FBI Operatives Holmes, Garber, etc: Silencing Domestic "Dissent"

Complicating things, at the time of my work on Freeport-McMoRan in 1996, my long-term girlfriend, Susan Holmes (from 1994 to 1997), was an environmentalist and undercover FBI agent. During the time we went out, she disclosed to me and discussed her role with the FBI many times, showed me her undercover FBI ID card, and other FBI work items. Included in her disclosures was the work the FBI does in targeting dissidents (see my Declaration of 2022 published in Section III in this volume). One of her dissident targets she was close to, was the high-profile environmental activist and co-founder of Earth First! Dave Foreman. Her close association with Foreman is particularly significant to this story. Susan always said Dave Foreman was no longer a primary concern of the FBI, but it was the people attracted to him and that hung out with him, who the FBI was concerned about.

After the FBI's campaign commenced against me in 1996 due to my Freeport-McMoRan work, it used Susan's close connection to Foreman to misrepresent me as a close contact and confidant of Foreman, an association that is a red flag marker for law enforcement. As detailed in my Declaration in the Appendix, Holmes naively, at the behest of the FBI, arranged for me to attend occasions with her where Foreman was present—a lecture in New York City in 1997, and a rafting trip down the Colorado River, in the summer of 1997. The rafting trip down the Colorado River was with Susan and twenty or so other activists and journalists, and I was placed in Foreman's dory with two others. These encounters were fully documented by the FBI according to what Susan later told me, including photos—all planned by the FBI. The intention was to make me appear a legitimate target of the FBI to both compromise and satisfy oversight agency screening processes. The screening processes were well understood by senior intelligence officials, people like Henry Kissinger and James Woolsey, who were then able to abuse and subvert them if they were inclined to. The trip organisers allocated me to Dave Foreman's dory for the duration of the trip of several days. Associating me with David Foreman, a person targeted by the FBI, seemed to be a well-planned and deliberate tactic by the FBI to falsify evidence and subvert oversight screening mechanisms intended to stop agency corruption.

In retrospect Susan seemed to have limited awareness, or misunderstood, who the FBI targeted under the term "dissident". One afternoon in 1997 in my apartment on Amsterdam Avenue, she tried to recruit me to work undercover for the FBI, explaining that the FBI wanted more undercover agents working on Wall Street. She gave me the full pitch but I had no interest in applying.

At the time of her disclosures in the mid-1990s about her work for the FBI when we dated, she fervently held, based on her training by the FBI, that dissidents were "really bad people" intent on destroying America and they deserved what they got from the FBI.

Had she been deceived? Susan said she had been taught and believed the FBI's political targets were wayward dissidents. She had been inculcated to believe they were obnoxious, loud, unrelenting, ungrateful malcontents intent on undermining America. Susan is an intelligent person, Dartmouth-educated, but she genuinely believed that. And she genuinely believed they deserved harsh treatment and got what they deserved.

Little did she realize at the time that she would soon experience the other side of this dissident suppression treatment. The authority and power of the FBI, combined with her privileged upbringing, may have resulted in blindsiding her critical reasoning about the agency's activities. Steve Garber once said that the FBI's recruitment screening process continued through training sessions over years—with agents often self-selecting out of the agency as more about the FBI's mission and methods were disclosed.

Other FBI agents seemed similarly indoctrinated to misunderstand what the agency was having them do to dissidents. In 2007, my elected representative in Sydney, Tanya Plibersek, MP, raised my complaint about ASIO and the FBI in federal Parliament. Shortly after, while I was visiting Arizona, I explained to a pesky young undercover FBI agent, Ben Worden, ensconced at the Diamond Mountain Buddhist retreat centre, that my complaint about the FBI/ASIO and the connection to Freeport-McMoRan had been raised in the Australian Parliament. I attempted to hand him the two-page transcript, but he refused to take it. I found other agents did likewise. FBI agents consistently refused to accept the transcript, whereas others I spoke with and offered it to, were invariably interested and accepted. Presumably, this behaviour is part of the FBI training to insulate inexperienced agents from the activities of the corrupt agency and hold them under the sway of FBI propaganda. I don't think many FBI agents, let alone regular Americans, have any understanding of the FBI's real intent and agenda. Susan seemed to have everything else going for her. Perplexed, I wondered why she would take on a job with the FBI. It was an unspoken sticking-point in our relationship.

By 1999, Susan's opinion seemed to have softened. We had broken-up by then but were contemplating getting back together. She told me, "You would not believe how surprised I was when I saw your name on the work files." Alluding to "work" was a euphemism for the FBI. We were having dinner at the South Sea Port in New York City, and she added cryptically, "I'm not going to let them do this to you!" It didn't click with me at the time what she was talking about, and she didn't elaborate when I asked her to explain.

It is not clear why anyone would want to help an agency do the things the FBI does. Susan learned this directly, when, as one of their own agents, she was ruthlessly targeted to get to me! But why would she still want to work for them after seeing this and learning what she had?

The FBI had interfered in our relationship in 1997, deliberately sabotaging it at a time we had been discussing marriage. She had invited me to her family home in Detroit that year for Christmas, which was intended as an opportunity to propose and announce our engagement. But it wasn't to happen. In 2003, when she subsequently covertly interviewed me for the FBI in New York City, she said she had vomited as she came to understand what had happened to me, and between us.

Defying the orders of authority is no easy task for most. Reference Stanley Milgram, the Yale University psychologist who famously demonstrated this in the 1960s with his electric shock experiment. So why would you put yourself in the position where you are required to follow the orders of what amounts to a veiled, secret-police-like agency to do who knows what to whomever they want it done? Why would you knowingly put yourself in the employ of someone, like the FBI or ASIO/ASIS, etc., that may demand you turn on friends and family?

What sort of people want to work for the FBI I wondered—hasn't everyone read Orwell, or Kafka? Why would someone choose to work there? Why do people select the careers they do? What does it say about their personal talents and aspirations given the alternative possibilities? Why would they choose the FBI as an employer, especially considering the political abuse they know they would be involved with? Is it a James Bond syndrome? Of course, crime fighting is noble, but what control does a recruit have over the decision to fight crime or "fix" political opponents. No control, I assumed. They were obedient, and they did what they were told like in any other job, or they left. Not so much the dashing, mythical James Bond figure as the hollowed-out Adolf Eichmann, the hapless Nazi bureaucrat convicted of war crimes at Nuremberg, whose insipid obedience to directives from the authorities inspired the term "the banality of evil".

The FBI identifies and sabotages as many of its targets' relationships and opportunities as it can. They spread smears cast by small army of undercover agents paid to do what they are told without asking questions. They spread or fabricate rumors and inuendo of socially derogatory traits, creating an echo chamber—whatever they can get traction with, illicit sex of all sorts including paedophilia, illicit drugs and alcohol abuse, anything that can be portrayed as abusive or sneaky, criminal or anti-social, modified and tailored to maximise damage to each target. The target at one time or another may be painted as gay, alcoholic, deficient in some core attribute and unemployable, or guilty of physical and sexual assault. The target is never directly confronted with the rumours, let alone the evidence, and they are given no chance to offer a counter narrative or challenge accusations.

In my case, I was surprised people in the rumor mill in most cases didn't seek independent verification from me, clarification or to provide context. As one fire burns out, another is lit by the agencies. The first I know of it is an odd reaction by someone, strange looks or a cryptic remark—in the work place, a friend over dinner, or from an acquaintance in the street. I don't know what their allegations are, I don't know which other agencies are involved, nor does there appear to be any way to bring it to a head, hold them to account, in any forum, let alone the courts.

The worst of human nature is easily preyed upon by the intelligence agencies. Susan told me in the mid-1990s that if Americans knew the true number of undercover operatives at work domestically, they would think they were living in a totalitarian state. In East Germany, the notorious Stasi secret police recruited around one in ten civilians to work as "spies"—recruiting from a broad cross section of society to penetrate all and every aspect of community and civil life. All kinds of people were hired, and the only commonality was a preparedness to work against their fellow citizen, inform on and betray their neighbors, work colleagues, friends and family in the name of the state's ideals and their own personal financial aspirations.

Who hasn't been readied for the head-to-head with the totalitarian hydra? As high school kids, we read George Orwell's *1984* and *Animal Farm*, Huxley's *Brave New World*, and Aleksandr Solzhenitsyn's *One Day in the Life of Ivan Denisovich*. Kafka, we read later. Each described dystopias, where personal relationships took second seat to priorities enforced by abstract State ideals. History and literature are replete with States where the worth of our human values was displaced and supplanted by the pressing abstract ideals of the government in vogue at the time. Many seem blind to these same forces, here and now, at home in our "liberal" West.

Freeport Critics Targeted

I don't regret having asked the questions about Freeport, but I do regret the aggression and violence of the FBI's response.

I am not the only one targeted for speaking out about Freeport around this time. Andrew Duff of the Austin Chronicle published a list of names of seven people, at least those he was aware of, who he said were targeted with threats of legal action by Freeport unless they desisted from making "false and damaging accusations". His list comprised journalists Robert Bryce and Daryle Slusher; university professors Steven Feld, a music ethnologist who had spent much time studying the people and tribes of West Papua, Indonesia; Alan Cline and Robert Boyer; and environmentalists Lori Udall and Bill Bunch.[5]

In an article for Mother Jones in 1996, Robert Bryce mentioned another Freeport threat. This one was against New Orleans based WWL-TV news anchor-man Bill Elder. Elder had accused Freeport CEO Jim Bob Moffett of lying to him on air during an interview about OPIC, and also subsequently accused Freeport of blocking his travel to West Papua, Indonesia, by not granting the Indonesian consulate permission for him to enter. Bryce reported that Freeport officials had visited WWL and made veiled threats to sue the station Elder worked for.[6]

But there were not just legal threats. According to reports, Freeport also demanded the return of funding, after a series of student protests, from Loyola University in New Orleans where it had funded a chair in environmental communication.

Other critics in the West were directly targeted by the intelligence agencies operating to protect Freeport's reputation in the fallout of the spate of negative human rights and environmental reports starting to emerge from West Papua, Indonesia.

Professor and author Tim Flannery is a renowned zoologist I heard speak on climate change at the Australian Museum in Sydney in 2016 and I spoke with him after. He has spent a lot of time working with the Indigenous people in West Papua, Indonesia, and has many friends there as recorded in his engaging book *Throwim Way Leg*. He ruefully commented when I asked him about Freeport and West Papua, Indonesia, that "A lot of dark things are happening up there in West Papua." He swallowed, anxiety and fear swept across his eyes, and he repeated, "It is very dark." He was humble and had deep empathy for the people there, clearly perturbed and opposed to what was happening on a human rights front there. His response was in stark contrast to the many FBI and ASIO/ASIS agents I have met who attempt to cover up the abuses there, using tactics I have described elsewhere—apologists for Freeport and US policy. I wondered to what extent Flannery had experienced pushback and undermining from the agencies; he certainly wasn't someone playing their game. There had been some adverse, unusual media and setbacks he had faced that are consistent with ASIO coercion, but, as usual, nothing was publicly confirmed by the agency.

I had been targeted by Freeport, too, it seemed. Not with legal action, but with an initial attempt to exclude me as a Wall Street mining analyst from their annual analyst briefing in 1996. The briefing, which I ended up attending after I requested an invitation several times and which I had attended in the past, was standard for all mining analysts from mainstream banks to be invited to.

---

[5] Denise Leith 2003, The Politics of Power Freeport in Suharto's Indonesia, University of Hawai'i Press. p7, footnote 10 p262.
[6] Robert Bryce, 1 September 1996 Spinning Gold, Mother Jones.

But what was not known previously was the role the FBI, a US federal government agency that is part of the DOJ, played. Unlike OPIC, the US federal government agency that provides political risk insurance for US corporations, whose activities are in the public domain, the FBI works without operational disclosure and is protected from public visibility. According to agents Holmes (in 2003) and Garber (in 2004), and consistent with the agency interference and threats I received, the FBI was secretly batting for Freeport, no matter what, mustering its huge resources and vast reach to defend the company from critics. The FBI's deployment and extra-judicial punishment is unconstitutional and undermines civil society, making it harder for civil society to hold public entities to account.

The FBI has threatened and attacked me from every angle: social, family, work, privacy, electronic, tracking and recruitment of friends, and gross interference in all my social and professional networks—as described elsewhere in this book—chilling professional commentary and civil society.

It had never occurred to me to become a dissident and spend my time defending against and attacking a central pillar of American power. I did not see opposition to the killing of Indigenous protestors as a dissenting opinion as such; I assumed that everyone saw the killing as wrong and took such a position for granted. The contentiousness of the issue seems related to working on Wall Street, toeing the line, and remaining silent even where investors would benefit to know how their money is being invested!

Fabricating enemies of the state, creating "evil doers" and "dissidents" gives the US cover to do what it wants, in the name of national security, or in political police activity at home—mass surveillance. As former US president Bill Clinton said shortly after leaving office, "Y' got to understand...there are some people in my country...who think America must always have enemies."[7] They create opponents, find unnecessary fights and set forth to always have an enemy to show those who might oppose a government policy on more important matters to US interests to be wary. Manufacturing issues and lying about evidence are repeated behaviors mastered by the intelligence agencies—behavior and tactics with "a distinct resemblance to the Bush administration's determination to invent a case that Saddam possessed weapons of mass destruction."

Why should the FBI try to link me to the "environmental terrorists" targeted by Susan in her work for the FBI? If I were a real enemy of the state, there would be no need to engineer a "problem" for which they offer the "solution". The answer is the FBI wanted cover for something else. Presumably, they show the manufactured adverse evidence to the oversight agencies to justify their interest in me. On the other hand, they show the treatment, banishment and abuse of an outspoken analyst to other public spokespeople with a view to intimidating and controlling their behavior.

It is not clear what word best describes someone targeted in the US for political "crimes", for speaking out, but "dissident" seems as good as any. Wikipedia describes dissidents as those who inform society "about violation of laws and human rights". The term "dissident" is frequently used by the US government to describe foreign citizens subjected to unconscionable acts by their governments for speaking out in opposition, and it was widely used from the 1940s to describe people opposed to totalitarian systems or policies of totalitarian governments, especially under the Soviets.

The US has always maintained in relation to other governments that it is necessary not only to protect dissidents but to encourage and facilitate opinion, debate and access to information to enable a strong democracy. It says tolerance of dissent and free speech is the foundation of a free and open society, and thereby a healthy and resilient government and people. I wish it would follow its own advice!

---

[7] Bob Carr, 7 December 2016 Donald Trump is finding new enemies where he should be seeing allies, The Sydney Morning Herald.

My newfound status as a state target seems to reflect the nervousness of government officials in the US involved with the Freeport issue than any objective risk posed by my note or question. Their response seems to reflect a new way of doing things in the US. It is a disturbing trend, a move away from democracy and the rule of law.

In 2012, US Senator Bernie Sanders (I-VT) stated that "[w]e are seeing our country move toward an oligarchic government." And another senator referred to the US as practicing a new form of fascism.

Domestic Surveillance—The FBI is Not Acting in "Good Faith"

The FBI is not acting in "good faith" as attested to in 2024 in a Declaration (see Appendix) by former FBI agent, a twenty-five-year veteran of the agency, and Expert Witness, Jennifer Coffindaffer. In her Declaration she points out multiple shortcomings of the FBI— skirting its obligations under FOIA— based on my request for information from the agency and suggests a number of key databases the agency neglected to search. Her conclusion is consistent with my experience of the agency's conduct in general since it commenced targeting me in 1996—that it's not acting in "good faith".

The FBI (and ASIO/ASIS) has thrown nets over all my communications, identifying and targeting family, friends, associates and colleagues. The presence of the FBI surveillance in the home, workplace, car, and other places regularly frequented by the target, and now via iPhone GPS tracking and remote activation of microphone and video, gives the agency potential for 24/7 near blanket surveillance capability.

The FBI targets all areas it identifies as important to the target—means of making a living, interests, friends, family, and spiritual life, to name a few. The FBI attacks in silence, inflicting life-changing interference to careers and relationships, among other things. It identifies and recruits agents or informants in all these areas to inflict material and psychological damage. Its target "dissidents" are frequently not even aware the FBI is responsible for sabotaging some key aspects of their life. The FBI, and other intelligence/security agencies lie and deceive seamlessly to shore-up their own reputations while diminishing their target's—to make any good features of their target seem bad, and bad features monstrous.

Emails, telephone, internet browsing, you name it—anything with an electronic footprint is picked up and stored. Many members of the public declare that they have nothing to fear from this, that they have done nothing wrong. But it is misplaced confidence, a judgement that mistakes the risk of this kind of intrusion. Make no mistake, if you give someone unfettered access to all aspects of your life, and they are of a mind to do so, they will use this information in a way that will harm you. Its potential uses are diverse—to interfere and manipulate, to embarrass the target, or help their adversaries. It is naïve to simply say you have nothing to hide.

The public now knows from Ed Snowden's National Security Agency (NSA) leaks in 2013 that the government has undertaken illegal mass surveillance, without specific warrants or meaningful oversight, of domestic and foreign telephone calls, email, online chats and browser histories. Another NSA whistleblower, Russell Tice said, among all the officials the NSA secretly targeted, there was a big push to target lawyers: "They [the NSA] went after lawyers and law firms. All kinds of–heaps of lawyers and law firms. They went after judges." [8] (The full quote from Tice is in the next section, and upfront

---

[8] Washingtonblog, 20 June 2013, NSA Whistleblower: NSA Spying On – and Blackmailing – Top Government Officials and Military Officers

in this book). I have found many of my lawyers, but not all, compromised at some level. Some have gone as far as trying to undermine my case. It certainly makes a mockery of "conflict of interest", "attorney client privilege", and any notion of "justice" or the "separation of powers". (I filed a detailed complaint with an Australian regulator against a lawyer in Sydney, where the same level of agency interference occurs as in the USA. The regulator found against the lawyer, Rocco Ardino, and sanctioned him, though stopped short of saying he was compromised by a law enforcement or intelligence agency. The regulator drolly said I had not provided sufficient evidence to prove that link.)

According to the NSA leaks, the government spies on contacts with up to three degrees of separation: That would mean targeting my contacts, their contacts, and, in cases, their contacts.[9] As FBI agent Susan Holmes said, they maliciously connect to virtually everyone the target knows. It is a process that takes time, power, and money, and requires extensive intrusive and illegal surveillance. An excellent opinion piece in the *New York Times* (June 15, 2013) "I Know What You Think of Me" discusses the damage that can be done when someone else takes control to record and selectively disclose your information.

Where the Constitution or national legislation precludes invasive wiretaps and data harvesting, by whichever country, whether it be Australia, America, or any other allied country, it is simply outsourced out of the jurisdiction of the oversight agencies and courts. As journalist and whistleblower Annie Machon, a former intelligence officer for MI5, the UK security service, wrote in articles that appeared in newspapers around the world:

> If the capability continues to exist to watch the rest of the world, how can Americans be sure that the NSA et al won't stealthily go back to watching them once the scandal has died down— or just ask their best buddies in GCHQ to do their dirty work for them?
>
> I'm sure that the UK's GCHQ will be happy to step into the breach. It is already partially funded by the NSA, to the tune of $100 million over the last few years; it has a long history of circumventing US constitutional rights to spy on US citizens (as foreigners), and then simply passing on this information to the grateful NSA....In fact, this is positively seen to be a selling point to the Americans from what we have seen in the Snowden disclosures.[10]

If democracy fails in the US or its institutions fail in major part, as some already have, like the media, it won't be the fault of the president of the USA or some adversary like the Russians or the Chinese. The culprits will be sitting under our very noses, right at home in Washington or Canberra or London— our home-grown autocrats, secretive domestic intelligence agencies.

The Stanley Milgram Experiment

So, each of us is expected to co-operate with our government—with every level of government, every policy and regulation it produces—and never challenge anything? What is co-operation? Co-operation

---

http://www.washingtonsblog.com/2013/06/nsa-whistleblower-nsa-spying-on-and-blackmailing-high-level-government-officials-and-military-officers.html

[9] James Risen and Laura Poitras, 28 September 2013 N.S.A. Gathers Data on Social Connections of U.S. Citizens, The New York Times. http://www.nytimes.com/2013/09/29/us/nsa-examines-social-networks-of-us-citizens.html?smid=fb-nytimes&WT.z_sma=US_NGD_20130928&_r=0

[10] Annie Machon, 5 October 2013 Intel union: Spy agency heads won't roll with US and UK allied, RT. http://rt.com/op-edge/nsa-gchq-prosecute-spy-leaders-770/

is defined as individuals working together to achieve a common goal or benefit. How deep is this singularity in outlook expected to run?

Why are "common" people, Joe citizens, so ready to do what is wrong and so easily recruited by their government for misguided missions? The Stanley Milgram experiments conducted in the 1960s while he was a professor of social psychology at Yale University showed even regular people, let alone "divinely chosen leaders", were capable of torture and execution of innocent people if they believed they were acting on the orders of those in authority. In what was widely hailed as a landmark study of social psychology, Milgram showed committing abuses and atrocities against others was not something unique to the Nazi's personal constitution or some other idiosyncratic feature of totalitarian states but a common trait of human nature. This lack of personal moral responsibility was a resource that could be tapped by any state with devious intentions.

In the Milgram Experiment, the "victims" were actors pretending to be innocent subjects. The perpetrators, whose actions were being studied, were directed to administer electrical shocks to them. The perpetrators were directed by authority figures and believed they were delivering real electric shocks (they weren't, in fact), directed to hurt and in cases kill the subjects (who acted the appropriate pain or death scene response). The experiment proved people were prepared to do harm and, in cases, kill if directed to do so by those they deemed to hold legitimate authority.

Milgram demonstrated that regular people abdicate moral responsibility if they believe they are acting on state orders. Knowing the difference between right or wrong was irrelevant to their action. As Milgram himself concluded: "The social psychology of this century reveals a major lesson: often it is not so much the kind of person a man is as the kind of situation in which he finds himself that determines how he will act."[11]

Some people will do anything to endear themselves to authority and enhance their own standing selfishly and ruthlessly against the interests of the group. All authority need do is ask. Status of "authority" itself is sufficient grounds to command obedience and sideline questions of personal responsibility, moral right or wrong. People, like machines, are reduced to obedient minions of authority capable of even the worst atrocities without moral compunction. No personal responsibility. Armies of such people, manipulated by this basic instinct to blindly obey authority, can participate in atrocities most individuals would never dream of committing alone.

The interests of those in power are not always clear. The rich seek protection from the poor, and the poor seek protection from their circumstances. Their goals are inconsistent and changeable.

Irrespective of whether you are rich or poor, deep down, most of humankind lives with anxiety that comes from knowing we are only temporary residents of this earth. There is no eternal tether to here, and we are no more permanently tethered to our bodies than we are to this time or the land we live in. At some point not of our choosing, we will lose it all, every bit of "me and mine" stripped away by inexorable forces. States are fighting an enemy they can't defeat. People attempt to assuage this existential anxiety with a variety of tonics and measures, many of which lead to gross injustices for others as they attempt to postpone their own day of reckoning. This anxiety and fear will never be extinguished by deceit, bullets and war, but by the insights of the great social and religious reformers

---

[11] Kendra Cherry, undated, The Milgram Obedience Experiment: The Perils of Obedience, psychology.about.com, downloaded 10 February 2014.
http://psychology.about.com/od/historyofpsychology/a/milgram.htm

of history whose profound teachings later founded Christianity, Buddhism, and other great world religions.

"How Much Evil Must We Do in Order to Do Good?"[12]

Vietnam War US Secretary of Defense, Robert McNamara, oversaw the greatest debacle of American ideology put into practice: around 58,000 American soldiers killed, nearly 3.5 million North and South Vietnamese soldiers and civilians killed. It was a huge death toll for a war that America ultimately deemed to be a mistake. He asks in an apologetic, confessional tone in the documentary *The Fog of War*, "How much evil must we do in order to do good?"

My "friends" in the modern-day intelligence agencies, like their ilk through history, are siloed, told only what will motivate them to act in accord with the agencies' desired outcome. They doubt their superiors' justification is always for "good". They know they may have been being lied to. They know they may be causing harm to others. They know that they may be the perpetrators of human rights abuse against their fellow citizens. But they do it anyway. They know that their own motivation may be financial gain and their means of acquiring it deception at the expense of those around them. With averted looks and avoidance of contact, agents reveal their shame, guilt and, ultimately fear, a foreboding of the unknown: What will become of them without the money or the status that position and inclusion bring them? They attempt to take control of my life, my former girlfriend Susan's, West Papuan's, and others', not out of greater ability to divine right from wrong, but on account of holding power. Simply because they can.

Some people believe they are not, as individuals, responsible for the decisions they make, nor do they feel they have any responsibility for the decisions their government makes. They tell themselves lies so often they have forgotten the truth. They tell themselves that their power to oppose this colossus is meaningless, therefore there is no moral need to stand against injustice enacted in our name no matter how obscene: no personal guilt. But the reality is not that they are powerless to speak out, but that they are cowards or indifferent to the suffering of others. We have used our military for the good of the world on occasion. There have also been times our country has gone to war on false pretences, corrupt intelligence agencies or politicians fabricating threats and deceiving the public. Not prepared to make a certain sacrifice, some people express no opposition as they watch their bombs fall on the innocent families of Iraq, in West Papua, Indonesia, Chile, Cambodia, Vietnam, Nigeria, and Ecuador, among others. There are rivers that burn, sometimes conduits for the bodies of the dead, invisible emissions that clog the skies, and untold other acts of barbarity committed around the world and at home. As we enjoy the comforts of our homes, neighborhoods and standing in the world, we proclaim we are without guilt.

Henry Kissinger, Freeport-McMoRan, and US Foreign Policy – West Papua, Indonesia

Former US Secretary of State, Henry Kissinger, warned at the time of the defeat in 1991 of the communist bloc that the greatest threat to world peace was now American unilateralism. It was a prophecy from a man whose ruthless ambition, power, and history of deployment of military violence well understood the threat posed to the world by the unbridled passions of men like himself. Indeed,

---

[12] Quote from former US Secretary of Defense, Robert McNamara from 1961 to 1968, who was a key architect of the Vietnam War, in the 2004 documentary The Fog of War.

the new America he played a high-profile role in helping to shape seems in his time to have abandoned the noble principles enshrined in the Declaration of Independence and the Constitution.

Kissinger's integrity and judgement have long been in question. He stands accused of undermining the Vietnam peace accord, delaying it by years at the cost of thousands of US lives, and many more Vietnamese lives, motivated by self-interest to further Nixon's and his own political career, among other things. As unlikely as it seemed in 1996, our paths were unfortunately to cross. He was also involved politically in the US decision that cleared the way for the military annexation of West Papua by Indonesia.

Kissinger was National Security Advisor from January 20, 1969, to November 3, 1975, under President Richard Nixon and then President Gerald Ford when Nixon was impeached in 1974. Renowned and internationally acclaimed journalist Christopher Hitchens, in his scorching book *The Trial of Henry Kissinger*, provided evidence and advocated that Kissinger be put on trial for war crimes and crimes against humanity. Here, I focus on Kissinger's role as expounded by Hitchens in US atrocities in Indochina because it demonstrates a similar pattern of destruction, obfuscation and deceit seen in West Papua, Indonesia, where Kissinger's involvement has helped shape the destruction of the Indigenous Melanesian people who inhabit the region:

> There is no evidence of Henry Kissinger, as national security advisor or secretary of state, ever seeking even such modest assurances [to take prudent measures to protect the civilian population during the bombing of Cambodia]. Indeed, there is much evidence of his deceiving Congress about the true extent to which such assurances as were offered were deliberately false. Others involved, like Robert McNamara, McGeorge Bundy and William Colby, have since offered varieties of apology or contrition or at least explanation: Henry Kissinger never.

General Taylor described the practice of air strikes against hamlets suspected of "harboring" Vietnamese guerrillas as "flagrant violations of the Geneva Convention on Civilian Protection, which prohibits 'collective penalties' and 'reprisals against protected persons' and equally in violation of the Rules of Land Warfare."

Within Kissinger's sphere of influence arose US mining company Freeport-McMoRan of which he in time became an influential adviser and director. Freeport-McMoRan manages the Grasberg copper and gold mine in Indonesia through its subsidiary PT Freeport Indonesia (PT-FI). PT-FI is held 48.76% by Freeport-McMoRan after it partially divested its stake in recent years to PT Mineral Industri Indonesia, a state-owned enterprise (which holds 51.24%), that is wholly owned by the Indonesian government. The Grasberg mine is one of the world's largest and most valuable deposits of copper and gold, located in the once pristine, glacier clad mountains of equatorial West Papua, Indonesia.

Historically, the company controlled the mining and exploration leases from the 1960s when US-backed Indonesian dictator General Suharto came to power and the US-backed Indonesia's military annexation of the territory. The annexation followed a corrupt Indonesian military-controlled plebiscite in 1969. West Papua had declared independence from Dutch Colonial rule December 1, 1961, but was occupied shortly after by Indonesia. Under Indonesian occupation, the death toll of the traditional owners has been breathtaking, entire hamlets and villages targeted and families slaughtered. At others, the chiefs were tortured and thrown from helicopters. Strings of villages and subsistence smallholdings have been destroyed in tactics reminiscent of the Vietnam War with napalm, aerial strafing, infantry and cluster munitions. United Nations reports estimate 100,000 Indigenous people have been killed as a direct result of military assault, and many more displaced, livelihoods destroyed and destitute.

Because of what I experienced at the hands of the FBI, I read more widely about dystopian secret police forces and their state backers, and I looked more deeply into what was happening in West Papua, Indonesia. In the next two sections, I provide comments on the USA, and the FBI in particular, and some background on events in West Papua, Indonesia, where the massive Grasberg gold and copper mine is located.

Part B

Who runs America?

Separation of Powers - Undermined by US Intelligence Agencies

Research from Princeton University professor Martin Gilens[13] and Pew Research indicate America is a plutocracy—a government run by the rich and influential. Parochially, this is the "1 percent"—"the establishment". The practical aspects of how this is achieved and maintained is considered here. I contend that it is the intelligence agencies' systematic undermining of the separation of powers, and their deep, coercive intrusions into individuals' private space that makes this possible.

The US agencies have incredible leeway to snoop at home and interfere with any individual they choose. As NSA analyst and whistleblower Edward Snowden told *The Guardian* newspaper in 2013, "I, sitting at my desk, certainly had the authority to wiretap anyone, from you or your accountant, to a federal judge, to even the President."[14]

The intelligence agencies in the West, like their kin in parts of the world with more notorious reputations, use their powers "strategically" for institutional advancement or to embellish individual career paths, but not necessarily to protect and advance American (and Western) values—values that we still like to think of as truth, justice and human rights. These values have been surrendered to the political expediency of realpolitik by wealthy and political oligarchs. As MIT professor Noam Chomsky said, "The governments seek to extend power and domination and to benefit their primary domestic constituencies—in the US, primarily the corporate sector ... We see that all the time." [15]

Banyan Tree Model of Secret Power

Through the deep penetration of undercover intelligence agents and their comprehensive networks of informants and collaborators, anthropologist and sociologist Eben Kirksey accounts for how the "architecture of power" is constructed using the metaphor of the banyan tree. This is a strangler fig

---

[13] Tom McKay, 21 March 2022 Princeton Study Discovers What Our Politicians Really Think About Us, New York Progressive Action Network,
https://nypan.org/about/news-and-updates/2022/3/21/princeton-study-discovers-what-our-politicians-really-think-about-us
[14] Mark Hosenball, 12 June 2013 Edward Snowden Search Began Days Before NSA surveillance Program Reports Went Public, Reuters. www.reuters.com/article/2013/06/12/us-usa-security-snowden-hunt-idUSBRE95B1A220130612
[15] Noam Chomsky 17 August 2013, Chomsky: The U.S. behaves nothing like a democracy, Salon. http://www.salon.com/2013/08/17/chomsky_the_u_s_behaves_nothing_like_a_democracy/

from Indonesia that grows on its host as a parasite, then as it matures, chokes, and kills it.[16] This alternative "architecture of power", as Kirksey describes it, sheds light on the construction and institutional growth of alternative power structures right over the top of existing structures. It is a model of political "subversion, replication, and domination" which describes the Indonesian subjugation of West Papua, Indonesia as an example. It also aptly describes the way our Western intelligence agencies have subsumed, infiltrated, and hollowed out our own democratic institutions.

Applying the Banyan Tree Model of Secret Power to the US, the domestic intelligence agencies secretly unite disparate, notionally independent institutions and link them together by recruiting individuals at all levels, especially "individuals occupying high ranking positions in different institutions".

Individuals in positions of power who are secretly joined together can include "journalists, professors, pastors, corporate executives, and development workers". The list is extended to include any individual, organization or institution in a position to influence public opinion, from bureaucrats, lawyers, members of the judiciary, the executive, legislators and their staffers, civil society leaders, academics, bankers and scientists, to folk singers, actors, poets and writers. Their secret "latticed network of connections" constructed "inside key structures of power" is a powerful tool of subversion. Their links enable coordinated control by the chain of command they secretly report to—the intelligence agencies—and "quietly working together" use "subtle tactics to influence the agenda of the national dialogue" and beyond.

The network, connected via "unofficial channels", is invisible to outsiders. Together, "these people form[ed] a latticed network of connections ... that are difficult to disrupt". In the US, this network is vast, billions of dollars are invested annually to maintain it, and over three million people reportedly have security clearance representing a complete cross section of society.

The increased power of intelligence agencies has diminished the political relevance of elected officials, public opinion and political debate. In this new system, much more is achieved through hidden channels than the public forums of earlier times, and the human rights of the governed are increasingly ignored and difficult to defend.

Journalist Kurt Opsahl of Electronic Frontier Foundation reports:

> "The administration keeps on attempting to justify the NSA spying by claiming there is oversight from the other branches of government. But, as Pentagon Papers whistleblower Daniel Ellsberg noted in the Why Care About NSA Spying[17] video, spying makes a mockery of that separation. How can that oversight be meaningful if the NSA's huge storehouse of information contains the private...habits of every senator, representative, and judge? When the only protection against abuse is internal policies, there is no serious oversight."[18]

This vast latticed network of secretly interconnected individuals and the ever-expanding power of technology gives our intelligence agencies easier and deeper reach to collect information, influence, and control us—as private individuals and as public officials. It is a system in which duty is redefined, personal morality and human relationships are surrendered to a different loyalty: The people running the intelligence agencies—are the self-decreed masters of the state.

---

[16] Eben Kirksey, 2012 Freedom in Entangled Worlds: West Papua and the Architecture of Global Power, Duke University Press, p68-p73.
[17] Brian Knappenberger, 25 November 2013 Why Care About NSA Spying, The New York Times. www.nytimes.com/video/opinion/100000002571435/why-care-about-the-nsa.html
[18] Kurt Opsahl, 27 November 2013 The NSA is Tracking Online Porn Viewing to Discredit "Radicalizers", Electronic Frontier Foundation.

NSA whistleblower Russell Tice revealed to the *New York Times* in 2005 that the NSA was targeting a broad spectrum of society from key US officials to NGOs and civil society groups. Below is an interview excerpt with Tice, in which he discusses the extent to which the NSA targeted officials from judges to oversight committees, with the intent of blackmailing them, coercing, and controlling them:

> They went after high-ranking military officers; they went after members of Congress, both Senate and the House, especially on the intelligence committees and on the armed services committees and some of the—and judicial. But they went after other ones, too. They went after lawyers and law firms. All kinds of—heaps of lawyers and law firms. They went after judges. One of the judges is now sitting on the Supreme Court that I had his wiretap information in my hand. Two are former FISA court judges. They went after State Department officials. They went after people in the executive service that were part of the White House— their own people. They went after antiwar groups. They went after US international—US companies that that do international business, you know, business around the world. They went after US banking firms and financial firms that do international business. They went after NGOs that—like the Red Cross, people like that that go overseas and do humanitarian work. They went after a few antiwar civil rights groups. So, you know, don't tell me that there's no abuse, because I've had this stuff in my hand and looked at it. And in some cases, I literally was involved in the technology that was going after this stuff.[19]

Who is ultimately calling the shots in our political system now? Domestic spying makes a mockery of the separation of powers that is the keystone of democracy. The security forces have gone way beyond using their power to protect legitimate democratic national security interests and undermined democracy by targeting the judiciary, media and legislators. The intelligence agencies have discarded protections and freedoms, we are told, in the name of "national security", but really, they have abandoned them, and in their place set their sights on the high economic growth achieved in recent decades in countries like China and Singapore. Now elements of the Chinese model, notably elements of authoritarian control, are deemed advantageous to business, reducing business risk, increasing certainty and predictability of earnings and reduced investment timeframes, but at the loss of civil liberties. A unilateral decision has been made on our behalf to dispense with the purely "democratic experiment" in favor of more authoritarian government. It is a change that underwrites greater freedom for business, but with the necessary trade-off being less freedom for individuals with ever greater state controls and coercive powers over civil society.

In championing this transition of power to the secret realm of the intelligence agencies, they claim it serves the "national interest". Indeed, they say, no matter what they do, it serves the "national interest". "National interest" amounts to anything they want it to mean, and which perversely is the reason they claim they don't need strong oversight. Of course, they are also acting in their self-interest, elevating their stature and power as the natural alternative authority to Parliament, Congress, or other legislative body, the media, and the courts.

If the public remains apathetic and passive as the intelligence agencies move our political system away from democratic values to a non-representative model of government, the general population will likely find it has a heavy burden to carry. History has shown how authoritarian, non-representative governments respond in times of great social stress with ruthless treatment of individuals, undesirable

---

[19] Washingtonblog, 20 June 2013, NSA Whistleblower: NSA Spying On – and Blackmailing – Top Government Officials and Military Officers
http://www.washingtonsblog.com/2013/06/nsa-whistleblower-nsa-spying-on-and-blackmailing-high-level-government-officials-and-military-officers.html

outcomes which democracies are designed to prevent. Populations that desire the benefits of centralized control in the good times, give up the benefits of being part of a democracy in difficult times. No system is perfect, or near perfect, but democracy offers powerful checks and balances. As Churchill said, "Democracy is the worst form of government, except for all those other forms that have been tried from time to time."

It is the ability to constructively tap the power of the masses that gives democracy its strength; and in undermining this, government abuses abound and freedom withers. Our leaders' choices as to what level and type of force, violence not excluded, to inflict against individuals, including against asylum seekers and dissidents, are ultimately constrained by exposure and potential public sanction.

Budgets of the intelligence agencies have ballooned in recent years. For example, in Australia, ASIO, reflects this shift in self-appointed rulership, and has built itself a massive headquarters in a prominent position in the nation's capital, Canberra, competing with Parliament House and the other key democratic institutions of the nation for public prominence.

The transition involving the erosion of our rights has been a gradual spiral downward, like the rise of apartheid in South Africa. Armed with coercive powers and capabilities enhanced continuously with new and incremental legislation—legislative creep—they breach trust, break the law, circle and constrict the heart of democratic government. In doing so they act without fear of being caught, without fear of accountability, unconstrained by public scrutiny.

As the infamous and hubristic Henry Kissinger declared: "The illegal we do immediately; the unconstitutional takes a little longer." He craved power, indeed was addicted to it, going so far as to say, "Power is the ultimate aphrodisiac." His decisions and influence, often conducted in secret, directly impacted the lives of hundreds of millions, if not billions, of people. Was his high worth the global pain?

Privacy and Power

In a gross perversion of the Constitution, in twenty-first century America, these tactics have become a staple of mainstream power. The government and executive impose ever greater sanctions against those citizens and others who expose their secrets and violate their "privacy", while simultaneously enabling ever greater ease of access to and weakening the right to privacy of the governed.

One of the most troubling aspects of the NSA, as revealed by Snowden and reported by Glenn Greenwald in *The Guardian* was the effort the agency went to in hiding its true intent and ambitions regarding its mass collection and use of personal information from congress and the American people:

> The general revelation that the objective of the NSA is literally the elimination of global privacy: ensuring that every form of human electronic communication—not just those of The Terrorists™—is collected, stored, analyzed and monitored.

> The NSA has so radically misled everyone for so long about its true purpose that revealing its actual institutional function was shocking to many, many people, and is the key context for understanding these other specific revelations.[20]

---

[20] Katie Rogers, 2 October 2013 Glenn Greenwald and Janine Gibson: 10 highlights from their Reddit AMA, Guardian. http://www.theguardian.com/world/2013/oct/01/glenn-greenwald-janine-gibson-reddit-nsa

Greenwald went further in a 2013 article, pointing out that James Clapper, the Director of National Intelligence (2010—2017), "repeatedly deceived the American people", lied to congress and his agency appeared to be complicit in the CIA's spying on the Senate Intelligence Committee. Despite this, he was not prosecuted. On the contrary, he was shielded, protected, and defended by Washington:

> Indeed, if I had to pick the single most revealing aspect of this entire NSA scandal—and there are many revealing ones about many different realms—it would be that James Clapper lied to the faces of the Senate Intelligence Committee about core NSA matters, and not only was he not prosecuted for that felony, but he did not even lose his job, and continues to be treated with great reverence by the very Committee which he deliberately deceived. That one fact tells you all you need to know about how official Washington functions.[21]

The agencies have the surveillance tools to access and threaten people where they are most vulnerable: their private lives. It is the most fundamental door to power—to understand people's desires and fears in relation to wealth, power, influence, intimate relationships, status, the protection of family—and be able to collect information to threaten or enhance these outcomes. As J Edgar Hoover demonstrated, targeting and revealing individuals' privacy is the realm where real power resides; the files that allow its keepers to coerce presidents and senators, indeed anyone who gets in the way. The protection of privacy is key.

The separation of private and public life ensures power is distributed and kept in check. Attacking people's privacy is a key weapon of abuse, as Kurt Opsahl of Electronic Frontier Foundation reports:

> As Cato Fellow Julian Sanchez points out, there is a lengthy and disturbing history of abuse. FBI Director 'J. Edgar Hoover maintained a notorious "Sex Deviate" file filled with salacious bits of information on the sexual proclivities of prominent Americans: actors, columnists, activists, members of Congress, and even presidents.' Hoover used that information to ensure appropriations for the FBI and expand his political power.[22]

Author and journalist Richard Kessler describes how Hoover opened fissures and breached privacy at the FBI, establishing a way of doing business that today is still very much a part of the FBI's modus operandi:

> "The moment [Hoover] would get something on a senator," said William Sullivan, who became the number three official in the bureau under Hoover, "he'd send one of the errand boys up and advise the senator that 'we're d[o]ing an investigation, and we by chance happened to come up with this data on your daughter. But we wanted you to know this. We realize you'd want to know it.' Well, Jesus, what does that tell the senator? From that time on, the senator's right in his pocket."

> Lawrence J. Heim, who was in the Crime Records Division, confirmed to me that the bureau sent agents to tell members of Congress that Hoover had picked up derogatory information on them.

> "He [Hoover] would send someone over on a very confidential basis," Heim said. As an example, if the Metropolitan Police in Washington had picked up evidence of homosexuality,

---

[21] Glenn Greenwald, 27 September 2013 Sen. Ron Wyden: NSA 'repeatedly deceived the American people', Guardian. http://www.theguardian.com/commentisfree/2013/sep/27/ron-wyden-nsa-systematically-deceived
[22] Kurt Opsahl, 27 November 2013 The NSA is Tracking Online Porn Viewing to Discredit "Radicalizers", Electronic Frontier Foundation.

he [Hoover] would have him say, 'This activity is known by the Metropolitan Police Department and some of our informants, and it is in your best interests to know this.' But nobody has ever claimed to have been blackmailed. You can deduce what you want from that." [23]

Kessler goes on to say that President Truman, a month after taking office in 1945, sounded the alarm bells about Hoover's FBI: "We want no Gestapo or Secret Police. FBI is tending in that direction. They are dabbling in sex life scandals and plain blackmail." He followed this up two years later adding, "All Congressmen and Senators are afraid of him." [24]

The NSA leaks might be news, but none of what is described is new. This kind of political targeting has been going on for decades, ever since Hoover perfected the techniques to support his and the agency's agenda. He gradually turned the intelligence agencies from crime fighters and technocrats defending the national security into king makers and political henchmen. It's a legacy that continues to this day. Kurt Opsahl continues:

> [While the intelligence agencies] support using surveillance to tarnish the reputation of people the NSA considers "radicalizers," US officials have in the past used similar tactics against civil rights leaders, labor movement activists and others. Under J. Edgar Hoover, the FBI harassed activists and compiled secret files on political leaders ....[25]

Further, NSA documents released by Snowden exemplify how individuals' "personal vulnerabilities" can be learned through electronic surveillance, and then exploited to undermine a target's credibility, reputation and authority." [26] Private information gathered through surveillance, including collection of communications content, metadata (the time, duration, location of communications, but not its content) is exploited to neutralise targets, by leaking that information publicly, or to a select network of friends, work and industry colleagues, peers and associates of the target specially recruited at great effort by the agencies for that purpose; or the target might be blackmailed depending on what the information is. Once they have the information, the agencies have multiple options in how it can be used. The excerpt below is from an article by Glenn Greenwald, quoting Jameel Jaffer of the American Civil Liberties Union:

> Jameel Jaffer, deputy legal director of the American Civil Liberties Union, said these revelations give rise to serious concerns about abuse. "It's important to remember that the NSA's surveillance activities are anything but narrowly focused—the agency is collecting massive amounts of sensitive information about virtually everyone," he said.
>
> "Wherever you are, the NSA's databases store information about your political views, your medical history, your intimate relationships and your activities online," he added. "The NSA says this personal information won't be abused, but these documents show that the NSA probably defines 'abuse' very narrowly."[27]

---

[23] Ronald Kessler, 2011 The Secrets of the FBI, Crown Publishers, NY as reported by Jay Stanley, 15 October 2013 On the Prospect of Blackmail by the NSA, American Civil Liberties Union.
[24] Jay Stanley, 15 October 2013 On the Prospect of Blackmail by the NSA, American Civil Liberties Union.
[25] Kurt Opsahl, 27 November 2013 The NSA is Tracking Online Porn Viewing to Discredit "Radicalizers", Electronic Frontier Foundation.
[26] Glenn Greenwald, Ryan Gallagher, Ryan Grimryan, 26 November 2013 Top-Secret Document Reveals NSA Spied On Porn Habits As Part Of Plan To Discredit 'Radicalizers', Huffington Post.
[27] Glenn Greenwald, Ryan Gallagher, Ryan Grimryan, 26 November 2013 Top-Secret Document Reveals NSA Spied On Porn Habits As Part Of Plan To Discredit 'Radicalizers', Huffington Post.

The methods of the intelligence agencies are highly susceptible to abuse. How can the government justify, among other things, the targeted collection of video surveillance of innocent Americans in their bedrooms—the targeting of "embarrassing sexually explicit information"? This is not a tactic reserved only for high profile leaders—like Dr. Martin Luther King Jr., it extends to everyone.

With the wall of privacy dismantled the most valuable things to an individual, things that have no price tag and no market value, are accessible to government interference: our relationships are no longer protected from interference; our memories can be scandalized and exploited; and the government manipulates our careers, reputations and status. Once the agencies have the information on a target, they control the timing and extent of the leaks. With it, they maliciously poison their personal environment—stirring up domestic, professional, and social problems, causing conflict on multiple fronts, economic and potentially legal problems, to produce instability and insecurity.

Maligning reputations and making people out to be predators, deviants, abusers, addicts or possessing some other cocktail of socially undesirable traits does not protect the state's military interests. The claims to secrecy around these domestically targeted "techniques and methods" is fraudulent, made to protect the agencies' techniques and methods in the war of propaganda and control at home—creating heroes and villains and encouraging behavioral norms that serve their goals. With these techniques—video, secret recordings, dodgy dossiers, and the like—they influence workplace culture, public policy, and broader society to reflect the interests of the wealthy and politically connected.

Psychological Torment

While in Tasmania in 2010, I chanced to visit the notorious Australian convict prison Port Arthur. The prison represented a shift in the penal system away from physical punishment toward psychological punishment, from hard labor to extended periods of solitary confinement. A quote from Charles Dickens appears on a wall plaque at Port Author today:

> "I hold this slow and daily tampering with the mysteries of the brain to be immeasurably worse than any torture of the body; and because its ghastly signs and tokens are not so palpable to the eye and sense of touch as scars upon the flesh; … and it exerts few cries that human ears can hear; therefore I the more denounce it…" (American Notes, 1842)

Dickens comments pertained to the effects of solitary confinement at Eastern State Penitentiary in Philadelphia, which he visited in 1842. Since the mid-nineteenth century, considerable advances in the psychological tools of punishment have taken this to a new level of sophistication and incapacitation.

Today's psychological war chest deployed by our intelligence agencies against civil society is sophisticated and secretive, intentionally inflicting various forms of psychiatric injury, including heightened stress, anxiety, paranoia, and psychosis—with practices generically known as cancel culture, gas lighting, and industrial smear campaigns. While the injuries inflicted are readily visible to observers, the causes are not. Chillingly, it is not by accident that our agencies have developed means of attack that don't leave physical evidence that might implicate them. They leave no calling card by which they may be held to account, and in Australia they (ASIO/ASIS) conceal even the locations of their outposts for fear of reprisal attacks, as has occurred from time to time in the USA against the FBI by citizen vigilantes.

Our agencies have taken their oppressive craft from that practiced and refined in recent European history, shaping it to fit their own time and culture. The eastern European oppression under the Stasi and other notorious secret police regimes has found its way to the modern-day West where it thrives in arbitrary bubbles of totalitarian dystopia thrown around the lives of specific targets.

Silencing Dissent

The sophisticated methods of the West's intelligence and security agencies' domestic operations, in particular those of the Five-Eyes anglosphere intelligence alliance—the USA, UK, Canada, Australia and NZ—came into sharper focus as I read about security and police state organizations like the FBI, CIA, ASIO and ASIS and their brethren. Again, as on the topic of Freeport-McMoRan and West Papua, Indonesia, I read widely about oppressive domestic intelligence agencies.

I read some interesting books, including *Dirty Secrets: Our ASIO Files* by Australian academic Meredith Burgmann which is about ASIO's targeting of civil society in Australia (contrary to ASIO's strident denials that it targets civil society). Leading Australians who are, or were, targeted by ASIO recount their experiences. Many were writers, journalists, academics, and other members of civil society who were in the public eye. A blurb about the book describes it as:

> Stories of leading Australians—including Mark Aarons, Phillip Adams, Nadia Wheatley, Michael Kirby, Peter Cundall, Gary Foley and Anne Summers—who were under surveillance by ASIO. Writers from across the political spectrum have opened their ASIO files, read what the state's security apparatus said about them and confronted their pasts. Reflecting on the interpretations, observations and proclamations that anonymous officials make about your personal life is not easy. Yet we see outrage mixed with humour, not least as ASIO officers got basic information wrong a lot of the time and many of the writers had to contend with personal betrayal. [T]hose who were spied on now look right back at the watchers.

I read *Stasiland* by Anna Funder, a revealing and engaging book about "individuals who resisted the East German regime, and others who worked for its secret police, the Stasi". Other books and authors I read that stand out include *The Castle* by Franz Kafka, *Silencing Dissent* by Clive Hamilton, books by Naomi Wolf, Noam Chomsky, Hannah Arendt, George Orwell, Aldous Huxley, and Aleksandr Solzhenitsyn. There was a 2006 movie, *The Lives of Others,* written and directed by Florian Henckel von Donnersmarck, a suspenseful story of a writer targeted by the Stasi in East Germany. Another excellent 2006 movie, *The Good Shepherd* – a thriller set in the 1960s about the CIA, revealing and critical of the agency, starring Matt Damon and Angelina Jolie, directed by Robert De Niro. I read an interesting play by Henrik Ibsen, *An Enemy of the People*. I perused ground-breaking articles by Yale University psychologist Stanley Milgram (described earlier). I read articles by journalists and whistle-blowers such as Julian Assange and Edward Snowden, articles about the American Senate's Church Commission in 1975, which investigated intelligence agency abuses including assassinations; and journalist reports disclosing the US NSA's watchlists which contained thousands of names of prominent and powerful Americans.

So many books, movies and articles speak to the corrupt secret police powers that shape and control societies—including the USA today.

Worlds Collide - *The Castle,* by Franz Kafka

There are strong parallels between Kafka's characters and the way modern day "dissidents" are targeted and punished silently by the likes of the FBI and ASIO in the West today.

The Castle tells of the protagonist, "K.", a regular member of civil society, who tried to arrange a meeting with the mysterious, out of reach authorities to clear up what he felt must have been an unfortunate misunderstanding. K. sought to meet the authorities to resolve what he thought must be an error in their classification and mistreatment of him as a dissident and enemy of the state. While Kafka started the book in 1922 and died in 1924 before finishing it, he indicated the intention was K., despite his various efforts, would wait a lifetime and still not succeed in his mission—neither being granted a meeting by the authorities (the government officers and secret police/security agencies who control "the Castle"), nor resolve his problem.

A timeless book, Kafka superbly captures the human impact of these agencies' intrusions on the life of the target. He describes the mysterious and surreal impact to the life of a target that has offended and subsequently fallen out of favor with the authorities. The modern-day Western intelligence agencies' equivalent efforts diminish, and silence ("de-platform") targets include gas lighting, industrial level cancel culture and oppressive surveillance.

The quote below is from Kafka's *The Castle*:

> We all knew there would be no specific punishment; people just avoided us, people from the village as well as from the Castle. But while of course we noticed that the people from the village avoided us, there was no sign from the Castle. But then we hadn't seen any sign of help from the Castle before, so how could we have noticed any change of attitude now? This silence was the worst, far worse than the people here avoiding us; they hadn't done it out of conviction, perhaps they didn't have anything against us at all, there was none of the contempt they have today, they had only acted out of fear, and now they were waiting to see how things would develop ....

> "How can I explain?" said Olga. "We weren't afraid of what was going to happen, we were already suffering, we were in the process of being punished....They were all sorry for what they had done—when a family respected in the village is suddenly completely ostracised like that, everyone losses out in the same way; they had only thought they were doing their duty by avoiding us, we would have done just the same in their place. And they hadn't even known exactly what it was all about ... but again, it wasn't out of hostility towards us at all, it was simply out of duty, just as it would have been anyone else's in the same situation."

The authorities never formally notify K. of his new status, but K. experiences new mysterious blocks, locked out of a system and relationships he once took for granted. From afar, the authorities in *The Castle* attempt to destroy him by derailing his career, relationships and hopes, to isolate and effectively remove him from the "normal" workings of society.

Indeed, the authorities in the Castle interfered in the lives of the subjects freely without official notification, as in the West today, certainly in Australia and the USA. As agent Steve Garber of the FBI said to me, most people never realize they've been targeted or interfered with.

Waiting for months, then years, and eventually decades for the DOJ, FBI and ASIO and ASIS to respond to my requests for information, for records, to explain their interference parallels the timeframes and frustrations of K. All the while, questions remain unanswered and unacknowledged. The public interest and accountability of our agencies is not served by their actions: I have never been formally notified I was under investigation for any crime, or for any other reason, let alone formally questioned or charged. Formal requests, even FOIA lawsuits, encounter evasive or non-responsive responses, a brick wall of untestable exemptions and unchallengeable denials put forward by today's occupants in the Castle.

In *The Castle*, as with the FBI and ASIO/ASIS, protagonists are silently blacklisted, ostracized, and their relationships are maliciously and meticulously targeted and undermined. In one case, Kafka's authorities went so far as to ensure the extended family lost its business, collateral damage, in the authorities' efforts to remove the last supporting network available to the target. These are disturbingly consistent with agent Steve Garber's disclosures to me about how and why the FBI (and ASIO/ASIS) targets dissidents in the USA (and more broadly, in the West) today, to smear and damage them socially and professionally, gradually and meticulously removing their support networks till the target collapses in a breakdown. The FBI uses the metaphor of the kids game "Kerplunk", in which sticks holding up balls are gradually removed by the players till the balls collapse.

Kafka describes what could pass for the experience of the agencies' timeless interference tactics. Ostracism by recruiting one's peers—peers who meekly oblige the authorities' requests but have no awareness of the background circumstances; blacklisting to diminish economic means and social status; gaslighting and entrapment. These are cornerstone features of the FBI and ASIO/ASIS's approach to marginalizing and isolating targeted citizens today.

Widespread collection of metadata, electronic surveillance of all kinds and variety, give the intelligence agencies vast access to our lives today and with that great power over every individual they personally target. It is the most sophisticated system of control and influence likely ever devised and implemented. Friends, family and other people with influence over the target are recruited, scripted, sometimes with tainted advice, and sent unannounced, as a powerful tools of FBI sabotage.

Like K., eventually, the target finds they are living in a world in which there is no such thing as a "normal" interaction, trust is undermined, and any meaningful interaction is rare. One can be ambushed at any moment by friend or stranger, and frequently is. The agencies use this enormous trove of electronic data and other surveillance material to fortify and buttress their attacks—for any purpose—they are not required to specify—and against any individual—including the most powerful, those lower down and even against those within their own ranks.

There is pain for the targets in having friends and family betray them, bought out by the agencies with cash or other rewards. At least American agencies, too, know the pain of betrayal and the problems it causes. They, too, know the relatively low cost paid by foreign agencies to recruit and "turn" their own agents. Some high-profile US moles, recruits and defectors include Robert Hanssen of the FBI, Aldrich Ames of the CIA, and Ed Snowden—high profile defectors.

Modern-day "Virtual Gulag"

The US offered safe-haven to Nazis after WWII, to individuals from whom there was something to be gained in return—rocket technology, military, science, and access to spy networks developed by the German spy agencies throughout Russia. With their entry to the US, baggage arrived in the form of knowledge and know-how in notorious police state tactics.

The extent to which these German war criminals shaped American agencies like the FBI and CIA isn't clear. Irrespective of whether the methods were imported or homegrown, insights offered by Czech writer Franz Kafka in works like *The Castle*, *The Trial*, and *Metamorphosis* about the subtle and horrifying impact of secret government police agencies remain chillingly prescient for the West today.

In summary, I have seen firsthand how our intelligence agencies, spearheaded by the vast powers given to agencies like the FBI, ASIO/ASIS and the CIA, have abused the separation of powers intended as the bulwark of accountability and foundation of our democratic system. Centralized and secretive, the agencies' vast powers and secret surveillance are potent tools of social and political control. Through the banyan tree analogy of the strangler fig, our intelligence agencies have undermined the separation of powers, compromised the independence of democratic institutions like the media, oversight agencies, regulators, legislators and civil society. Their stranglehold renders redress all but impossible without political backing. And into this space American and Western "dissidents" are gathered, marginalized or removed, like a virtual gulag. In the modern-day virtual gulags of the West, given its secret and isolated targeting of individuals, there is no brotherhood, no bonding within a community of similarly designated "dissidents", no sense of solidarity.

The agencies continue to do all this, their multitude of non-public programs, intrusions, surveillance and interference, in secret. They pull down the shutters and claim national security privilege. No meaningful response from the FBI, DOJ, various inspector's general and oversight agencies despite multiple efforts at accountability, detailed complaint letters, requests under Freedom of Information Act, approaches from lawyers. Stonewalled and still waiting. Years of prolonged harassment and interference met with repeated and disingenuous denials; the Western government's omerta - bound by a brotherhood of silence, with the unofficial mantra deny, deny, deny.

In the next section, I provide comments about West Papua, Indonesia, why American authorities are so sensitive about the region, its military annexation by Indonesia and rising adverse publicity.

Part C

West Papua, Indonesia

Militarised Mining

West Papua, Indonesia, is a region that possesses vast resource wealth, is populated by militarily weak Indigenous populations, and people with strong connections in Washington take an avid interest in it.

Denise Leith provides deep and disturbing insights into corporate America's relationships to US intelligence agencies and military, and to foreign governments that intersect with the personal details of my story. She details the company Chairman and CEO Jim Bob Moffett's motive and background for his emergency flight to West Papua, Indonesia, on March 12, 1996, the same day my contentious report was published. She put in sharp focus the motivation for silencing not only me, but at least seven other professionals in the USA she names (named earlier).

As the reality in West Papua, Indonesia, and the FBI's response at home to control and silence dissent sunk in, I read more widely and deeply to find perspective. Initially, I did not fully appreciate how dire and unjust was the situation of the Indigenous people in West Papua, Indonesia, in 1996, and that continues to the present day, nearly thirty years later in 2024. Descriptions of the military attacks backed and enabled by Western governments led by the USA were shocking, as were the pernicious deployment of Western intelligence agencies to chill civil society and hide these evil acts from the public at home.

As I learned more about why these agencies reacted the way they did in response to my 1996 work report and subsequent question to Freeport Chairman and CEO Jim Bob Moffett at the company briefing for Wall Street analysts at its headquarters in New Orleans, the insights of writer Hermann Hesse could not have rung more true or timely as I reread *Steppenwolf*, one of my favorite books from youth:

> Every age, every culture, every custom and tradition has its own character, its own weakness and its own strength, its beauties and cruelties; it accepts certain sufferings as matters of course, puts up patiently with certain evils. Human life is reduced to real suffering, to hell, only when two ages, two cultures and religions overlap.[28]

Hesse's insight well describes the forces at work in West Papua following the military annexation by Indonesia. Anthropologist and academic Hugh Brody, Canada Research Chair in Aboriginal Studies at the University of the Fraser Valley, wrote in 2011 directly of the military annexation of West Papua by Indonesia backed by the USA as a betrayal of its former WWII ally:

> What we have to understand is that Indonesia invaded an independent country. It did so with the help of UN confusions and many forms and levels of trickery, and with US collusion. This invasion depended on a profound disregard for the rights and aspirations of the people of Papua.
>
> The flow of political turmoil in Jakarta, the resultant deals with US military interests and the unleashing of unrestricted mining in West Papua—this set of events was the underlying cause of the oppression, imprisonment and murder of horrifyingly large numbers of tribal people, as well as the total destruction of many of their homes and villages.[29]

The history of the Indonesian military, not only under Suharto but since, reveals the military authority in Indonesia acts with a culture of impunity, is responsible for gross human rights abuses, including murder, rape, and torture. The country has one of the worst human rights records in the world. The Indigenous people have never had much of a chance in defending themselves with primitive weapons against an army supplied with modern US weapons, technology and supported by US military advisers. The death toll in West Papua, Indonesia, has been horrendous. While it is difficult to pin down firm numbers, Australian observers estimated in 2005 that 100,000 West Papuans have been killed by the military since 1969, and other sources indicated another 100,000 or more people displaced.

The brutality of the Indonesian military in West Papua is documented only sporadically. The province is all but closed to foreign visitors, and it remains under media blackout. Nonetheless, enough information has emerged to paint a clear picture of the devastating consequences for the traditional Papuan landowners, and particularly the original inhabitants of the Freeport concession area, dominated by the Amungme and Kamoro, but also the Moni, Nduga and other peoples. Though closed to the official media, news reports of ongoing human rights abuses in West Papua, Indonesia, still find their way into the Western media via NGOs and the internet.

Colonial history is repeating in West Papua, Indonesia, in the twentieth and twenty-first centuries. Large numbers of traditional landowners have been killed in recent decades in an undeclared war that has wiped out villages, entire communities, their livestock—all trace of them gone. It is the frontline of another interminable war financed and supported by America and the West in the jungles of Southeast Asia. Unlike colonial wars in Australia and the war in Vietnam, this war is on-going, part of a grim "general silence that surround[s] the process of occupation."[30]

A Yale Law School report for the Indonesia Human Rights Network (April 2004) described the secret war in West Papua, Indonesia, targeting the Indigenous people:

---

[28] Hemann Hesse, 1927 Steppenwolf, Penguin Group 2009, translated by Martin Secker and Warburg Ltd 1929, p28.

[30] Judith Wright, 1981 The Cry for the Dead, Oxford University Press,

Strafing and bombing missions killed numerous West Papuan villagers and caused thousands to flee their homes into the jungles. In May 1977, OV-10 Broncos dropped antipersonnel "Daisy Cluster" bombs near the village of Ilaga, located on the other side of the Puncak Jaya mountain chain from Freeport's mine. At the end of August, two OV-10 Bronco Bombers shelled the region of Akimuga. Soldiers also destroyed most of the food gardens belonging to Papuans in the region. As a result, many Papuan children suffered severe malnutrition.[31]

A footnote stated:

> "Daisy Cluster" or "Cluster bombing" is a high-altitude delivery of a 15,000-pound conventional bomb designed to kill everyone present within a huge area. Originally it was designed to create an instant clearing in the jungle.

The Politics of Power: Freeport in Suharto's Indonesia by Australian academic Denise Leith was one of the most confronting books I read of the atrocities of modern-day West Papua, Indonesia. Leith describes the operation against the Indigenous people in and around the Freeport concession:

> American Broncos and helicopter gunships carpet bombing, strafing, and reputedly napalming the surrounding villages. This operation was aimed at punishing the perpetrators and deterring further attacks on the mine.[32]

The Amungme people from the highlands near the mine were especially targeted by the military to clear them from the area of the mine. Those that survived this napalm-fueled fire were forced to move to the lowlands where many died from malaria, a pervasive disease to which highland people had little or no resistance.[33]

The tribal chiefs and leaders were singled out for special treatment. As if further intimidation were required, the US advised military captured the headmen at different villages in the Baliem Valley, took them up in helicopters and hurled them to their deaths into the jungles or sea below. It was a chilling tactic of fearsome colonial domination.[34] Eerily, the tactic is reminiscent of Chile's US backed dictator General Augusto Pinochet who dealt in a similar way with dissidents in the 1970s and 1980s—kidnapped, drugged and pushed from helicopters far out at sea. It is a strange and frightening common thread of military dictatorships supported by the West, and the USA in particular, a cold-blooded campaign of murder intended to neutralize opposition to the regime. Disturbingly, the once feted and now infamous US statesman and businessman Henry Kissinger's (who died in 2023) name is closely associated with both regimes during the reign of these particularly heinous dictators. Later, a systematic campaign of state sanctioned assassination of West Papuan political leaders occurred.

The Indonesian government, Freeport-McMoRan and the US government are taking no chances in West Papua, Indonesia, with the heavy militarization of the mine site in significant part, at times, paid for by Freeport. In addition, Freeport has, at times, provided logistical support to the Indonesian military; and in the US, Freeport's extensive, high level political connections help protect it at home. Washington delivers a US-government-backed flanking maneuver initiated by the FBI to silence commentators that might otherwise raise the public profile of the project and potentially jeopardize

---

[31] Elizabeth Brundige, et al., Allard K. Lowenstein International Human Rights Clinic Yale Law School, April 2004, Indonesian Human Rights Abuses in West Papua: Application of the Law of Genocide to the History of Indonesian Control, p23.
[32] Denise Leith 2003, The Politics of Power Freeport in Suharto's Indonesia, University of Hawai'i Press. P227
[33] Ben Bohane, Liz Thompson, and Jim Elmslie, 2003 West Papua Follow the Morning Star, Prowling Tiger Press, p100.
[34] Ed. Alan Whittaker, 1990 West Papua: Plunder in Paradise, Anti-Slavery International, p15.

the company's legitimacy in the USA and elsewhere. The US government wants no repeat of the nationalist Bougainville Revolutionary Army's successful shutdown of Bougainville Copper Ltd.'s Panguna copper mine (owned by CRA, now part of Rio Tinto) in 1989 in the neighboring independent country, Papua New Guinea (PNG).

The economic returns to Freeport in profits, and to the US and Indonesian governments in taxes and royalties, have been huge, but are still utterly insignificant compared to the US's overall massive GDP. Encouraged and empowered by support from their countries, these men seemingly have had the ability to control West Papua, Indonesia, and have used every means at their disposal to do so. Perversely, the moral toll of the craven blood money taken at such a reputational cost to Western authority and human cost to innocent West Papuans in Indonesia is borne by the general population while a small coterie of powerful figures become rich in the process. At every level, it is a travesty of governance, a betrayal of the people and of democracy.

The American electorate would be aghast if it knew the killings of Indigenous people in West Papua, Indonesia backed by the US government and corporate-funded Indonesian military, had underwritten and maximized the profits and dividend streams to Freeport's shareholders. The governments responsible contend there are no available alternatives to military action: No possibility of a moratorium on mining; no possibility of conducting operations in line with international environmental and social standards as per those in the US; no possibility of the expense of paying higher royalty payments to traditional owners in line with royalty payments paid to landowners in the US; and certainly no possibility of uniting the ethnically aligned Melanesians in West Papua, Indonesia, with neighboring PNG to unite the Indigenous cultures on the island of New Guinea.

With a neocolonialist worldview running deep in the West, it seems unlikely things are going to improve any time soon for the West Papuans living under the military annexation and oppressive rule of Indonesia.

The West's Long History of Colonialism

Ongoing colonialist attitudes are evident in a long tradition of Western governments that continue to surreptitiously target Indigenous communities for their wealth in out of the way places.

In writing this section, I read with alarm histories of Australian atrocities directed against its Indigenous communities during colonial rule. Among these was an especially confronting account by Judith Wright in *The Cry for the Dead,* with echoes in West Papua, Indonesia today, that documented the horrifying extent and brutality of the atrocities, the dispersal and destruction of the Aboriginal people by the white settlers and governments of the nineteenth and early-twentieth centuries. These were the Black Wars in which pastoralists and governments through "an unwritten law made men keep silence" on these events.

Equally eye opening to Wright's historical account was Senior Crown Prosecutor Mark Tedeschi, QC's *Murder at Myall Creek*, to which he brings a forensic legal mind focused on a single event—the 1838 massacre of Indigenous People at Myall Creek by white settlers, and subsequent efforts by the authorities and community to bury and silence complaints. In 1838, twelve stockmen murdered twenty-eight Aboriginal men, women and children who were camped peacefully at the Myall Creek station in northern New South Wales. In an extraordinary story of legal courage and persistence in standing up to the establishment interests and powers of the day, then attorney general of NSW John

Plunkett took to trial and won the conviction of seven of the stockmen responsible for the murders; they were subsequently hanged.

The techniques of the colonial powers recounted by Tedeschi and Wright closely echo the current-day methods used by the modern governments of the USA and Australia, among others. Indeed, the parallels are haunting in how they bury the evidence to silence, discredit, isolate and marginalize those of their own ilk and kind who speak out to expose their crimes. These methods include the extraordinarily long official delays in response to complaints, denials, ostracism, gaslighting, a system of captive regulators, reprisals that sabotage careers, and interference in social, family and professional networks—the modern-day definition of cancel culture. Nothing has changed in 150 years. It is even more affronting given the new deference with which governments now claim to hold local Indigenous people. Unfortunately, this support is all too hollow, spoken by an unrepentant political-military-industrial complex endlessly intent on wealth accumulation, careers and power. The Australian, British and US governments continue to fund, aid, and abet the slaughter of Indigenous groups and destroy their culture in hidden places like West Papua, Indonesia, the Niger Delta in Nigeria, Ecuador, and parts of the Amazon.

These days, people still "keep silence", even in the face of outrageous abuses in places like West Papua, Indonesia, fearful of "security" agency retribution. Nothing has changed from colonial days except the level of sophistication, the physical and psychological torment of extra-judicial punishment to "deplatform" and cancel opponents, and chill civil society.

Leith, Wright and Tedeschi's accounts have demonstrated the power, reach and importance of the written word and spurred my own determination to persist in telling this story.

West Papua, Indonesia: Weake – Life, Death and Human Rights

Author Peter Matthiessen[35] poignantly captures the human face of tragedy in West Papua, Indonesia. He distils the many thousands of deaths through a single lens, recounting that of a young West Papuan boy named Weake, and the impact his death had on his friends, family, and village. While Weake was not a direct casualty of a colonial landgrab, through him Matthiessen conveys the beauty and sophistication of Melanesian Indigenous culture. It is rich, sensitive, and caring, with elaborate ritual, mourning and grieving for the loss of loved ones.

He was ambushed near a river where he and a couple of his young friends were playing. Weake suffered more than twenty puncture wounds, Matthiessen describes how the boy cries out in deep pain with each breath. His friends helped him back to his village. All those with him in a room there try to comfort him but are powerless to change the outcome. He describes the elaborate funeral that follows, the personal impacts on family and friends, and the days of mourning.

The impotency these people felt in the face of Weake's death echoes my own feelings at the death of a good school friend of mine. Diagnosed with leukemia when we were fifteen years old, he died within twelve months. His doctors, family, and friends looked on too, powerless to change the outcome. The daily observance of physical decline, his courage, questions, angst and hope resonate deeply. It was a different coming-of-age ritual, an unusual and secret initiation into the adult world, a reality few adults in the Western world had even experienced. They lacked wisdom and knew nothing of the suffering

---

[35] Peter Mathiessen, 1962 Under the Mountain Wall: A Chronicle of Two Seasons in Stone Age New Guinea, Penguin Group, p151-172.

in the loss of a child. Their collective response revealed a societal failing and existential angst that undermined their authority, and precipitated a loss of faith in their wisdom and leadership.

Our society invests so heavily in healthcare to save lives, so how perverse it is that, with the mere flick of a pen, the same society tortures and destroys innocents in distant places like West Papua, Indonesia, knowing the personal distress and devastation it causes. Why would people, our countrymen, so maliciously inflict this suffering and pain on a community of innocent, defenseless people, and do so repeatedly? I feel ashamed and aggrieved. The moral collapse of the perpetrators is yet to be reckoned with, and also of our society that gives them safe harbor and is thereby complicit in these deeds.

Part D

Conclusion

What values lie behind the notions of realpolitik and exceptionalism? State secrecy goes way beyond the common sense understanding of national security to include suppression of information about the government's skullduggery in places like West Papua, Indonesia, where atrocities are regularly committed in support of business interests, such as the massive US mining company Freeport-McMoRan, to the spy agencies' intrusions into our everyday lives at home. There are large unresolved questions around whom the government represents, whom it is targeting behind this veil of secrecy and why, and what exactly it hides. Capitalism is a brilliant, efficient system of organizing markets, production and services—but it requires effective regulation and political oversight to ensure it operates in the best interests of society.

Our leaders—Western governments—re-commit the tactics and injustices of past generations, secretly inflicting great harm on Indigenous people in out of the way places to take their land and wealth. Their tactics are cruel, inhumane, and devastating to Indigenous communities that face unspeakable trauma and loss. Nothing really has changed from colonial times when major power imbalances were abused in secret.

America is a country I deeply love, and I am grateful to be rooted in its people and places. In what has become an unfortunate rite-of-passage for many young professionals, one is unofficially presented with a bleak choice, to be complicit in the suffering of others by remaining silent, or face career impediment, rebuke and sanction (at the hands of our intelligence agencies). Under duress, opting for "contentment with guilt" seems to be the preferred option of many faced with that bleak choice—they conclude there is no point challenging the US government. It seems leading a "perfect" life is premised on accepting a tacit social contract of silence and complicity, no matter how egregious the abuse. Some likely repress the memory of their decision to be complicit, while others recalibrate their moral compass to allow for the infliction of suffering on others, reasoning that it is unavoidable, or possibly, that those afflicted deserve it. Some wilfully harm others if the benefits to self and others are sufficient—the utilitarian approach—maximum good for the maximum number of people. They reject the argument that intrinsic human rights should be equally respected for all people.

Personal Consequences of FBI Interference

The payback for speaking out against Freeport-McMoRan has been going on for over twenty years. For the first eight years, I didn't realize the FBI was involved till confirmed by undercover FBI agent

Steve Garber in 2004. At the same time, I have been getting on with the rest of my life. Through my consulting business when it was operating, then my wife's professional roles, we have fortunately had sufficient income. It may not have been the career I expected, but then careers frequently, for many, are not.

I have been fortunate to have greater involvement with raising our two beautiful young children too. My wife and I have now been married going on twenty years (since 2005), despite the background issues described in this volume of intelligence agency interference and the pressures that places on relationships and the family.

My uprooting has not been as abrupt nor as painful as for many, like those ripped from earth in sudden early death, as those in West Papua, Indonesia. However, for me personally, lots has changed at the hands of agency intervention: new country, new vocation, new partner.

I moved countries to get away from the FBI's abuse in the US, only to encounter the same allied abuses from ASIO/ASIS in Australia operating as seamless extensions of the US intelligence agencies. The FBI interfered with my career, my relationship with my then long-term girlfriend—Susan Holmes, an undercover FBI operative—my friends, and various networks.

Ironically, despite the persistence of the agencies'-imposed constraints on my social and professional life, and my loss of privacy through oppressive surveillance, I am, to use Nietzsche's phrase, freer of the constraints of the "they"—the forces of peer and societal pressure—than I ever had been or would have been. Indeed, I have been grateful for this time, freedom and space. I have discovered a great deal about my government and myself, have been surprised by what I have encountered, and have taken time to rethink my closest held beliefs, personal and otherwise. It has at times, been a challenging journey, but overall wonderful.

I have come to see the wisdom of great religious figures, with their extraordinary transformative spiritual insights into life, death, and society. I am not saying I am better off overall because of FBI interference, though I might be. It is impossible to know for certain. As I have been forced to let go of former aspirations and opportunities, a new work-life balance opened. In their place, I have a new life with rich and rewarding insights and interests. Aside from my former small boutique research business and other consulting work, these benefits include more time for family and personal interests—like hiking, traveling, religion, contemplation, reading, writing, and more recently soccer. I am also more engaged in political and environmental activism.

Goals in Publishing

A key motivation for writing this book and accompanying archives is to shed light on the media blackout and injustice in both the military annexation of West Papua, Indonesia, and the cruel and unusual methods of our intelligence agencies to silence civil society at home in the West.

This story is in part an exposé of the corruption of our democratic institutions, the undermining of the separation of powers, and the hollowing out of these key institutions through pervasive infiltration of the intelligence agencies on the pretext of providing greater "security". I am also seeking justice on a personal level.

The plight of, and atrocities committed against, the First Nations people of West Papua, Indonesia, and elsewhere, are acts of modern-day colonialism. It is my hope that one day West Papuans will achieve independence or form a unified nation on the island of New Guinea with their neighbor Papua

New Guinea (PNG) free of Indonesian and US backed violence, to live with the safety, security, and dignity all people are entitled to, and to find peace and prosperity in their land.

Efforts to achieve transparency and accountability of the agencies and some semblance of justice in the USA through the proscribed oversight channels has been stymied at every turn for around twenty years. Writing a book to publicize the abuses both in West Papua, Indonesia, and domestically, seemed a last resort. Intriguingly, the agencies continue to interfere even in this process, at times over the years compromising advisors and editors. I am hopeful that something fruitful and positive will come of my written endeavors here but accept that this story may never end and give no more satisfaction than the telling of it.

At the end of the day, human potential is to be celebrated. All through history, across all civilizations, we have seen this blossom in extraordinary ways, irrespective of the system that claims credit for nurturing it. This book is not about criticizing the undeniable fruits of civilization. It is about bringing criminals to account, those individuals a neocolonialist system might have corruptly backed and did back in some clear cases. Simply, they are murderers and plunderers—modern day pirates—educated and armed with mighty military technology—taking what is rightfully the property of others. Their actions diminish not only their victims, but all of us, and they add nothing to the amazing scientific renaissance blooming in the modern world. They act contrary to our laws, values, and conventions, and not least, the United Nations Declaration on the Rights of Indigenous Peoples (UNDRIP).

As with mainstream journalists, people in the public eye such as celebrities, scientists, academics, artists, all potential opinion leaders, there are things mainstream analysts are apparently not allowed to mention. There is a personal sense of justice, of healthy self-esteem and power in exposing the tactics of this self-serving bully. For this I am grateful. I feel in a small way I have helped expose an abusive, secretive intelligence agency culture that uses ruthless tactics at home and abroad.

Unresponsive Oversight

The FBI abuses at home have not abated in the ensuing decades but intensified. My efforts to access justice and to hold the FBI accountable through regulatory, judicial, and media oversight channels have been thwarted at every turn through each of the successive presidencies of George W. Bush, Barack Obama, Donald Trump and now Joe Biden.

I applied to the FBI/DOJ under FOIA for my personal records. Despite all the details disclosed to me by agents Holmes in 2003 and Garber in 2004 that revealed the FBI's extensive access to my personal information spanning decades, and the agency's coordinated gaslighting efforts which require detailed agency record keeping, nothing was released. The inability to find the records reminded me of Holmes' questions to me during an FBI covert interview at Café Fiorello in NYC in 2003 in which she raised the "shell game" analogy—a game run by a con artist—an apt analogy for trying to access personal records under FOIA from a government agency.

"Did you ever play the shell game?" she asked. "You know, where someone has three cups facing down and they place a ball under one of the cups. They then shuffle the cups and ask you to guess which is the cup with the ball under it?"

ChatGPT describes the game as a trick: The trick is performed in a way that makes it seem easy to keep track of the ball, but the operator of the game uses sleight of hand to manipulate the shells to keep the ball hidden. This makes it very difficult for the player to correctly identify which shell the ball is under. The shell game is typically used by con artists to cheat people out of their money, as the operator often has various tactics to ensure that the player loses.

The analogy to FOIA requests is obvious to people who have filed one – trying to identify where the records are held, only to be told there is nothing there. In the case of FOIA requests, records can be moved between agencies, filed under unspecified names or categories, held in unspecified or undisclosed databases the location of which can change or remain secret. There are lots of ways agencies can deceptively manipulate how and where the records are held to frustrate the applicant. Citizens do not have access to a fair process, and intentionally so.

I have turned to writing this archival volume after having no meaningful response from a multitude of official channels—captive regulators and ineffective oversight—including the DOJ, FBI, various offices of inspectors general, Freedom of Information requests, media, elected representatives, human rights NGOs and so on. All these have been infiltrated and compromised at some level.

As a result of ineffectual oversight, in this volume, as well as previously, I have named FBI agents and Australian intelligence agents. Naming and shaming are an important part of the accountability for people and agencies that have done the wrong thing, especially where there is no alternative effective oversight that deserves the name.

One agent in Australia told me that my efforts to address agency abuses had made a significant impact, precipitating amendments to agency protocols in targeting of dissidents. Other amendments seemed to be directed solely at strengthening the opaqueness of their work, such as new legislation that prohibits the naming of ASIO and ASIS agents, among other agencies, (a change that occurred after my meeting with, and disclosures to, former Australian Attorney General Philip Ruddock in 2013). The agent mentioned also the impact made by my having the matter raised in the Australian Parliament on several occasions though my elected representatives, publication of letters to various parliamentary enquiries critical of, and detailing, agency abuses, various prominent advertisements outing agency abuses, and social media coverage, among other things.

However, in the absence of my accessing the courts, I am skeptical there will ever be any tangible results on transparency and accountability, let alone justice. Unfortunately, a standing Royal Commission to oversee the intelligence community in Australia, a powerful fulcrum for obtaining justice and accountability, was never implemented, despite it being one of the key recommendations from Justice Hope in his Royal Commission into intelligence agency abuses in the 1970s.

Obstacles to Publication

Having little joy with official oversight channels, I decided to write a book as a way to get the story out. As the various drafts unfolded, I found the task confronting and challenging, deciding what to tell, what not to tell, thinking about what was relevant to the public, what may be relevant to my family, and eventually to my then young children. In 2009, when I first thought about writing a book, the personal aspects of the story were still raw for me—the betrayals and psychic wounds. The story was still unfolding in West Papua, Indonesia, too and potentially for Freeport-McMoRan in the US courts. I was awaiting any meaningful response from regulators and oversight authorities in the USA and Australia to my complaints—thinking, naively, that oversight might be independent and effective. Writing was frustrating and slow, as I recalled events, pieced together notes and joined the dots. The story became more complex, more nuanced, more personal.

At the very least, potential publication of this story, and others in the series, has been delayed years by agency interference and thereby, in the meantime, readers denied a chance to read a book critical of the central powers in our new Western style of government. My efforts in the first instance to retain the services of an experienced writer or ghost writer to take on the task were met with a wall of intelligence agents or collaborators coming forth to "help", but, in fact, were spoilers. If I found someone that was independent, they were promptly compromised. Over the years, I retained some writers/editors for short standalone sections of the book, and their tactics were almost always the same: interminable delays for every draft, no matter how many pages, from individual chapters or articles of ten to twenty pages, to an entire book, stretching from an estimated several weeks to eventually take up to six months to deliver—one excuse after the next for delays. The draft eventually delivered would invariably be riddled with newly introduced inaccuracies of every kind: basic facts wrong, events turned around, ideas of benefit to the agencies introduced and accolades for their work included, meaningful events removed, errors introduced into citations and quotes. Drafts were unusable, or virtually so, and usable only with significant effort from me to re-edit them.

In writing this, I have faced threats to my business, which have been subsequently carried out by the agencies. Since 1996, I have also received veiled and not-so-veiled threats of blackmail and death threats. The blackmail threats relate to release of any personal information that the agencies have collected on me through surveillance or other means, legal or illegal, that may cause embarrassment to me. One agent said threateningly, "If you publish, they're [the intelligence agencies] not going to like it. You know what to expect. They will hit back." In relation to death threats, comments from agent provocateurs, such as, "You are lucky to still be alive;" and, "How long do you think you will live?" have been directed at me with menace. "You might want to be careful. You might find your water laced with something!" They instill a sense of fear or uncertainty as to what their intentions are. And further threats in the form of "friendly advice" from inside "friends": "You might want to be careful. These are dangerous people." A comment left on my association Facebook page in 2013 read, "Sorry dude but you're a dead man walking sorry man its just avmatter of time." (sic).

It takes a special skill to write a book that would tell the story in a way that would attract wide readership and get the story out to a wider public—an artform. Sure, I could write it report style, reliably document, annotate and provide supporting references where available. I could philosophize, ruminate and provide personal background. I put it out on Facebook and WordPress. As mentioned, attempts to retain or team with co-writers, ghost writers, researchers and editors has been widely interfered with by the agencies. One qualified, accomplished and published author in Australia interested in probing and challenging the lies of government declined to help, citing concerns he held for his wife and small son.

In conclusion, I would like to thank all the wonderful people and beings in my life, my family, parents, and children in particular. All the beings I cherish, those who are friends, those that are neutral, and those that have been adversaries; we have all served each other in different ways. Thank you.

John Wilson

Sydney August 2024

Archive Overview

This archival volume contains twenty years of my correspondence and court documents in the USA. The letters and emails, starting in late 2004 and continuing to the publishing of this volume in 2024, comprise correspondence either directly by me or my attorneys with various FBI/DOJ departments, as well as elected representatives including Senator Charles Schumer and Congressman Jerrold Nadler. It also includes emails, freedom of information requests (FOIA), details of administrative reviews, two notarized Declarations I made, and two court challenges under FOIA for release of records.

Together, they tell the story of my efforts to gain FBI and DOJ accountability in the USA, efforts which for the most part have been thwarted. This follows interference since 1996 and disclosures to me by the FBI in 2003 and 2004 that I have been the subject of a "payback" operation following my March 12, 1996, analyst report published while working as a mining analyst on Wall Street for a major UK investment bank, SG Warburg (now UBS Warburg). My work as a mining analyst involved covering NYSE listed US mining companies, and one of my reports on Freeport-McMoRan came to the attention of the "authorities". It touched on controversies surrounding Freeport and the region's human rights record.

Freeport-McMoRan, through its associate, PT Freeport Indonesia, owns and operates the massive Grasberg copper and gold mine in West Papua, Indonesia. Today, it retains a large interest in the project of around 49% and has a special permit to operate the mine until 2041. At the time of my report in 1996, the company was reportedly under investigation by the US State Department following a series of eyewitness allegations it was involved in the killing of Indigenous protestors in and around the mine site. The company denied any role in human rights abuses and eyewitness reports were never proven in court.

Since commencing operations there, the company has surrounded itself with heavy hitter Washington insiders, retaining them as employees, consultants or board members, including former secretary of state Henry Kissinger who was both on the board and also was a consultant to the company. According to Denise Leith (author of *Power of Politics: Freeport in Suharto's Indonesia*) Kissinger, around the time my report was published, was running around Washington trying desperately to get the company's rescinded US$100M political risk insurance (OPIC) policy re-instated. It's cancelation by the US government agency had cited environmental concerns, however, according to an FBI source, the "real" reason had been intended as a slap on the wrist for the bad press coming out of West Papua concerning allegations of Freeport human rights violations. At least seven other people in the USA were targeted for their criticism of Freeport around this time, including journalists and academics.

The archive, in aggregate, tells the story of a pervasive corrosion of justice in the USA, marked by political influence, "captive" regulators, corrupt DOJ/FBI and the power of money.

I am a dual Australian and USA citizen. I moved to the USA from Sydney in 1991 to attend The Wharton School of the University of Pennsylvania where I graduated with an MBA in 1993 and moved to New York City. I retained the ephemeral benefits of political representation in the USA, registered as a Federal Voter in NYC, after I returned to Australia in 1999. This move followed a period of sustained harassment and interference from the FBI in my personal life and career since 1996.

Two undercover FBI agents disclosed the FBI's involvement to me. The first was my former girlfriend from 1994 to 1997, Susan Holmes, in 2003. She was an environmentalist closely involved with the Sierra Club, living in NYC and an undercover FBI agent. The other disclosure in 2004 was from Dr. Steven Garber, a Sierra Club volunteer and biologist living in NYC, and an undercover FBI agent. These disclosures are detailed by my attorney Pete Sorenson in a letter to the DOJ, AUSA John Moustakas in 2023, and in my 2021 and 2022 notarized Declarations, both included in this volume one of my archives.

The letters and court documents reveal anything but "good faith" patterns of behavior by the FBI/DOJ to thwart accountability. These methods include their repeated refusal to officially confirm or deny the involvement of FBI operatives. The DOJ/FBI's lack of "good faith" was evident across a range of activities, including suppression of dissent, misuse of surveillance powers, evasive and misleading responsiveness to allegations of abuse of power, attempted entrapment, political suppression, tainted records and planted evidence. Their methods echo those used by British colonialism in Australia (and by extension elsewhere) to conceal the murder of Indigenous inhabitants and supress dissent described by Mark Tedeschi in *Murder at Myall Creek*.

It is hoped that this book will be of value to a wide audience, including current and future citizens of the USA, UK and Australia as they seek to learn about their countries' governance and history.

Introduction to the Archives

This is the first of an intended four volume archive; and potentially a related, though separate extended exposé and memoir narrative.

Volume 1: (2024) is focused on the backstory and accountability of the FBI/DOJ in the USA. The appendix contains court records and correspondence with the DOJ/FBI and others—emails and letters.

Volume 2: (Target release date 2024) is directed at the US State Department. The appendix contains court records, emails and letters primarily concerning the State Department. It contains a discussion of Freeport-McMoRan's activities in West Papua, Indonesia. It will likely also include a wider ranging discussion of my story.

Volume 3: (Target release date 2024). This is a transcript based on my notes and recollections of the FBI covert interview of me in 2003 at Café Fiorello in NYC. It amounts to around four hundred pages of transcript and commentary.

Volume 4: (Target release date 2025). This is focused on efforts to seek accountability in Australia with partnering agencies of the FBI and CIA. The appendix contains emails and letters primarily concerning Australian intelligence agencies ASIO and ASIS.

At some point, I may endeavor to publish a detailed exposé-style memoir detailing the entanglement of my personal life while dating an undercover FBI agent who was an articulate, well-educated environmentalist, my work as a Wall Street analyst covering Freeport-McMoRan, and the State, whose agencies are primed to defend and promote corporate behemoths. It is an unholy alliance that apparently creates and protects wealth irrespective of the source, with flagrant disregard of the Constitution and laws, prompting one US senator decades ago to describe it as "a new form of fascism".

Volume one of the archives is set out broadly in chronological order with the oldest material dating from 2004 up front to the FOIA court documents of 2024 at the end.

A summary of each section follows:

Section I: DOJ/FBI - US Law Enforcement and Intelligence Agencies

FBI conduct not in "good faith": One of the lawyers I retained in NYC early on, Rachel Minter, filed an FOI request on my behalf to the FBI in 2004. She exclaimed upon hearing my story, words to the effect, "Mr Wilson, if the FBI is involved, you can't believe a word they say!" Such is their reputation in New York and among the legal fraternity more broadly.

In this section, with the assistance of ChatGPT, is a summary of how the FBI/DOJ fails to act in "good faith". I have then provided specific instances from my experience where the FBI has failed to act in "good faith"—including attempted entrapment, misuse of surveillance power and political suppression.

Undercover FBI operative – contractor Dr. Steve Garber: In 2021, I retained New York City law firm BLHNY to commence litigation against the FBI. BLHNY retained, at their instigation, the services of a private investigator to provide background reports on various undercover FBI operative – contractors involved in my long running complaint against the FBI, including Steve Garber. A redacted, abridged report on Steve Garber is included in the appendix.

Complete Social Security Numbers (SSN) for the subjects were identified but practice is not to include the complete number, nor DOB in public documents, a policy outlined and followed by the FBI. An email from Assistant United States Attorney Tabitha Bartholomew to my attorney Pete Sorenson in 2024 explains the DOJ's policy in redacting the personal identifiers of subjects when making documents public – a practice I followed here (email excerpt below):

DOJ email from AUSA Tabitha Bartholomew:

> *Per our local rules, the only personal identifiers that must be redacted (unless the court orders otherwise) is SSNs, DOBs, names of minor children, and financial account numbers. ...I note that ... "other private information" are not subject to our local rule....*

Section II: Correspondence with DOJ, AUSA John Moustakas - 2023

Letter to Assistant United States Attorney John Moustakas: This section contains a letter to Assistant United States Attorney Mr. John Moustakas. My attorney Pete Sorenson sent an extensive letter to the AUSA Moustakas concerning the search concerns we have with our FOIA request to the FBI intended as a good faith collaboration and negotiation with the FBI.

In the letter, Pete Sorenson outlines the evidence and circumstances supporting the assertion that the FBI holds records on me. Much of the material comes from my notarized sworn Declaration dated August 30, 2022, included in Section III of this volume. It includes some extra material, concerning efforts by the FBI to "gaslight" me, a form of psychological attack that necessarily involves the active use and retention of records by the FBI.

An excerpt from the letter on gaslighting explains (for full details and context see the letter and Declarations in the appendix):

> *Mr. Wilson believes, and has stated, that the FBI collected distinct descriptions and scenarios from Wilson in the 2003 interrogation of Wilson by Holmes at Café Fiorello, NYC and engaged in subsequent efforts using those descriptions and scenarios to gaslight Wilson as a form of psychological attack. Mr. Wilson is prepared to state that this suggests the FBI is hiding and withholding records that Wilson is entitled to.*
>
> *During Holmes' questioning of Wilson, she would periodically ask Wilson to describe specific scenarios about the future, imaginative events, and stories. When Wilson had no response to many of her requests, Holmes would implore him to "say anything. It doesn't matter. Just say anything. Make it up," she said repeatedly.*
>
> *In this vein, Holmes asked Wilson about 25 or 30 different topics and scenarios and Wilson gave brief answers, many of which subsequently were presented to Wilson in various ways at various times years later, gaslighting him as a form of psychological attack. Examples are below.*

This information was provided to AUSA Moustakas in addition to details concerning evidence of FBI entrapment, misuse of surveillance powers, suppression of dissent, abuse of power, and so on.

The long delay by AUSA Moustakas in responding, and what he said when he did respond, was hard to interpret as being in "good faith". When, after three weeks, there had been no response from Moustakas, my attorney sent him a follow-up email on August 3, stating "We sent that letter to you on July 11, 2023, and we would like the FBI's response in a timely fashion."

The next day, August 4, Moustakas responded, "Have you received any response whatever? Is the search completely done? Is this the mining expert? Or it that L_____?" The FBI/DOJ provided no further response to the letter. It's unlikely that anyone would interpret this as a government agency acting in "good faith"!

Six weeks later, evidently disillusioned with working for the DOJ, AUSA, John Moustakas resigned. He emailed my attorney Pete Sorenson, and forthrightly declared late on September 12, 2023, at ten minutes to midnight, "Friday I am interviewing for another position to get the f out of here", (excerpt of email in Section II). While my attorney and Moustakas did not always see eye-to-eye, they nonetheless seemed to have a close professional relationship.

A few months later, John Moustakas departed, and this case was passed on to AUSA Tabitha Bartholomew. Both Moustakas and Bartholomew seemed to be serially behind in their work commitments, frequently requesting extensions of time to meet their obligations to the court (refer to emails in Section II). I mention these details in the summary, as it reflects on the culture and corruption of the DOJ, adding another perspective that helps put in context the struggle I faced with holding it to account.

Section III: John Wilson Declarations – 2021 and 2022

This section contains my notarized Declarations.

The first declaration, dated November 16, 2021, deals largely with the issues surrounding my targeting following my work as an analyst on Freeport-McMoRan in 1996, including the work by my then long-term girlfriend Susan Holmes, who was an undercover FBI agent, threats made to me by a federal agent in Freeport's boardroom alcove, threats and payback to at least seven other professionals critical of Freeport at the time, and Freeport's activities in West Papua, Indonesia.

One of the annexures (Exhibit 3) includes the names of alleged Australian agents listed in an email I sent on June 14, 2013, to the former Australian Attorney General Philip Ruddock, whom I met with on three occasions in his electoral office to discuss my complaint. Names included:

- <u>Robert Sadleir</u>: Sydney; son of former ASIO Director General David Sadleir (1992-96);
- <u>Dr Trent Allen</u>: Sydney, stockbroking analyst;
- <u>Michael and Claudia Hackman</u>: Sydney business people;
- <u>Deborah Bye</u>: Melbourne, former lawyer;
- <u>Daniel Aitken</u>: Central Coast, NSW, and Boston, USA;
- <u>Richard Kaan</u>: Sydney, former business consultant; and
- <u>Fabian Babich</u>: Sydney, former stockbroking analyst

Other alleged Australian agents named in the Declaration include Charlie Cropper (formerly of the Eastern Suburbs, Sydney). Agent Susan Holmes in 2003, during the FBI's covert interview in New York City at Café Fiorello, went further in her discussion of Cropper. She suggested he was part of a small coterie of 1980s college boys which the FBI referred to as the "rat pack", some of whom were recruited to work for an Australian intelligence agency. (The original "rat pack" of the 1960s was an informal group of singers Frank Sinatra, Dean Martin, Sammy Davis Jr., Peter Lawford, and Joey Bishop, known for their sordid, wild carousing). She said that via this group, Australian agencies had been influenced by a would-be rival of mine who had "white-anted" (undermined) me. Holmes used the allegory of ancient Roman justice in relation to modern-day intelligence agency processes, where authorities gave the crowds a say in the punishment of "offenders" Barabbas and Jesus. She alluded to the thumbs up or thumbs down nature of a populist process – a nod, she said, to the role small cogs play in the modern-day intelligence agency process of who can end up on a watchlist, watchlists intended to chill civil society. She alluded to the, at times, arbitrary nature of ASIO/ASIS assessments, capricious and lacking in professionalism, and that they would have been consulted in the process of the FBI launching an attack on me.

Also mentioned in the Declaration are Richard Maish (formerly of ANZ and Warrama Consulting, Sydney), and Mark B. Wilson (formerly of Avalon, Sydney). There are more names of alleged Australian agents I could provide, but this list provides enough for the record to substantiate my claims of agency interference with me.

If there is a standing Royal Commission into our agencies at some point in the future, as recommended by Justice Hope in his two Royal Commissions of the Australian intelligence agencies in 1974 and 1983, this list of names is sufficient to establish the truth of my allegations and provide a basis for the Commissioner to dig deeper. Establishing a standing Royal Commission into the intelligence agencies was a key recommendation of the Hope Royal Commission. It was a key part of a two-step oversight process. The other was an internal regulator, the Inspector General of Intelligence and Security (IGIS), which was subsequently established. However, without establishing the Royal Commission to bring judicial rigour, independence and public accountability to the oversight process, oversight of Australia's intelligence community remains deeply flawed and open to wide abuse.

While Justice Hope designed a complete system of oversight for independence, rigor, accountability and justice, the politicians sought ultimate control of the oversight process and intentionally built it without the essential Royal Commission—a huge flaw that gives politicians backdoor control. The act of excluding the Royal Commission deprives members of the public a powerful judicial pathway for addressing grievances and a remedy for injustice.

A separate annexure (Exhibit 2) includes the name of FBI agents (operatives) I encountered through the late 1990s and 2000s in various letters sent to the DOJ/FBI over time including March 9, 2015, and February 23, 2016. Names included:

> Michael Mills: the FBI agent who moved into my apartment in NYC at Apt 906, 170 West 74th Street, NY, NY 10023 in 1999 and occupied it for several years when I sublet it before my return to Australia.
>
> Kathleen Walton: former mining analyst at Merrill Lynch in NYC.
>
> Matthew Levey: – Kroll Associates, Inc (New York City midtown office): consulting work case manager 2003 and 2004. Former State Department employee.
>
> Jeffrey S Robards: corporate finance, formerly Ernst & Young (E&Y) NYC. Now working for C.W. Downer & Co—a boutique M&A firm in Boston.
>
> Susan A. Holmes (formerly resident in New York City in the 1990s); Sierra Club NYC volunteer; Dartmouth College; resides Washington, DC.
>
> Stephan Chenault: volunteer Sierra Club NYC Group since 1990s.
>
> John Klotz: volunteer Sierra Club NYC Group since 1990s.
>
> Ben Worden, Rob Haggerty and Allison Dey (Tucson area): FBI agents involved with Diamond Mountain Buddhist group in southern Arizona and California.
>
> George Schneider and Livingston Sutro (Sierra Vista, AZ); Jennifer Conner (NYC): Associated with Diamond Mountain Buddhist group in southern Arizona.
>
> Paul Whitby: (Tucson): biologist.
>
> Leigh Freeman: Cherry Creek, Denver based head-hunter. Downing Teal.
>
> Robert Schultz: Albuquerque based head-hunter. MRC Mining Search.
> http://www.miningsearch.com/mining-search/our-team/
>
> Steven D. Garber: (wife Andrea—collaborator) additional details: biologist; lived in Manhattan for much of the 1990s before taking a two-year posting to teach biology at Embry Riddle in Prescott, AZ, before returning to the New York area (White Plains). Books authored include *The Urban Naturalist* (New York. John Wiley and Sons. 1987). PhD in Ecology, Environmental Sciences—Rutgers, The State University of New Jersey-Newark. BS in Natural Resources, Cornell University.

First Declaration 2021: This first Declaration was submitted to the court in 2021 as part of the evidence in my first FOIA court case against the FBI. It subsequently was appended to my second Declaration.

Second Declaration 2022: My second notarized sworn Declaration, dated August 30, 2022, was submitted to the FBI as part of my new FOIA request in the administrative appeal.

This second Declaration includes much additional material about my relationship with undercover FBI agent Susan Holmes from 1994 to 1997 in part to ward off comments that she was not a real girlfriend but part of the later (post-1996) FBI operation against me. The Declaration includes disclosures from Holmes to me, disclosures about her work for the FBI that an undercover operative would not make to their target. Our relationship lasted for three years, including an invitation to her parents' home in Detroit for Christmas in 1997 to get engaged. It commenced in 1994, well before the threats and interference I started to receive in 1996 on account of my work on US mining company Freeport-McMoRan. Her disclosures to me include, on multiple occasions, details of her work for the FBI, her mother's disclosures of the same, showing me her FBI ID card, FBI apparel like T-shirts and jacket, disclosure of multiple aspects of various operations she was involved with for the FBI and techniques used by the FBI. All these details are readily independently verifiable should there ever be an opportunity through the court to subpoena witnesses, including Holmes and Garber, FBI officials or find an independent regulator that is not "captive".

Interestingly, Holmes also mentioned techniques used by the DOJ/FBI to evade accountability, including the mischaracterization of FBI operatives as "employees" or some other misclassification. She said she was not technically an employee of the FBI but worked for them in a role akin to an "independent contractor" like many other undercover FBI agents, which was denoted by the black background of her FBI ID card. This contrasted with the white background of FBI employees. Retaining the services of operatives as "independent contractors" as opposed to "employees" is a legal maneuver intended to shield the FBI from legal accountability for these agents conduct.

I found, as mentioned in my Declaration and also contained in the correspondence of Section IV, the DOJ/FBI repeatedly misclassified Holmes, Garber, Sutro and other FBI operatives I complained about. The DOJ/FBI created a strawman, misclassified them, then denied they were "Special Agents" or "employees" of the FBI, but never whether they were operatives of the DOJ/FBI. Despite multiple attempts by myself and attorney Barry Fisher over nearly two decades to get a response to this issue from the DOJ/FBI and US Attorney General, there were only ever evasions or non-responses from them. Never did they address the substance of the relationship of the DOJ/FBI to the operatives and thereby make themselves accountable for their conduct.

Also of interest, as transcribed in my Declaration August 30, 2022, when we were dating, Holmes and I were walking home late one evening in summer 1996 through NYC after an Irish folk music concert she invited me to. On our walk, she outlined various FBI tactics to me, recounted here over about fifteen pages, including those used to target dissidents, the use of FBI "honeytraps", training, oversight, fishing expeditions, her FBI target David Foreman, etc. Some excerpts are below:

> *"It's a big fishing expedition," I remarked indignantly.*
>
> *"Yes. A witch hunt," Susan confirmed.*
>
> *"But how do they get away with that," I challenged circling back. "Doesn't the FBI get accused of bullying or unethical behaviour? Isn't there some kind of oversight process?"*
>
> *"Yes, but it doesn't stop it. So, it doesn't look like a witch hunt, the FBI waits till they find some legitimate reason to investigate the target, or can manufacture a reasonably plausible reason, to justify their investigation, make it less obvious that it is vindictive," she said. "Judges don't like witch hunts, and there is a backlash against the agency if this is what it looks like. So, they conceal it, try to make it appear legitimate, like a discovery that came out of a routine, impartial investigation. Not a stitch-up. But some judges are motivated by ambition, not integrity, and are complicit."*

"What else does the FBI do to them?" I asked, assuming there must be a lot of things they could do to their targets, things they wouldn't like.

"They try not to do physical things, not leave a physical trail to get the police and courts involved," she said.

"Another thing they do is smear them with sexual assault or complaints of abuse. They undertake a major fishing expedition," she continued. "They look back to peoples' college days— they almost always find something. And if they don't find it there, they look wider, they go back through the teen and tween years, if need be, till something comes up. Somewhere they overstepped the mark, it doesn't need to be rape or anything like that, it doesn't matter how innocent or slight, so long as it was not welcome or out of line. The FBI can find something like this on virtually all men, and even many women."

"You would be surprised," she said continuing, again as a matter of fact. "Every male has something. The FBI always finds something. They even find something on a lot of females. If it is not in college, they look closely in later years' and go back to high school years or earlier. They recruit people close to the person in that time or place they are looking at, find the people and ask them the questions. "Did so and so ever do anything inappropriate to you. Just curious. I heard something, I don't know if it is true, and am just asking around. It doesn't matter, they eventually find someone where something has happened. They can get someone to say something. Anything at all that could be construed as sexual assault; an unwanted kiss, an inappropriate hug, or something more."

"But does this work? What does this do? Does anybody listen or care if it is a minor thing? High school, or puberty age, everyone seems a bit awkward, unsure, looking for boundaries," I responded trying to understand what damage the FBI could do with this tactic.

"Yes. You can always get someone to listen, someone they [the dissident] cares about. It always has an impact somewhere, no matter how small." Susan continued. "If it is college age, 18 or over, it is sexual assault. It is relatively easy to get someone to make a formal complaint about it to the police, even years later. They just encourage them to do it for the record. If it is a relatively minor thing, or at a younger age in high school, or even primary school, it still takes a toll on the target. There can still be a police report, the information leaked or given to people around the target to embarrass them. It still takes a toll, no matter what. But if it is serious, the person could go to jail. If they have done something wrong, they will get them a long sentence, the harshest punishment permissible. And sex offenders are treated as the scum of the scum in jail and prison life is very unsafe and hard for them."

"If they find something to prosecute them for and the matter goes to court, the FBI gets a reporter friendly to the agency to cover the case, someone they are close to, maybe on the payroll, maybe gets preferential treatment from the FBI. They put it in the newspaper, whatever newspapers they can get to carry it, local, state, national - whatever level of coverage they can get for it. It doesn't matter. They try to destroy them in the public eye."

Section IV: General Correspondence—DOJ, FBI, Elected Reps

This section comprises emails and letters primarily between me or Barry Fisher, my long-term personal attorney on this matter from 2005 to 2022, and the FBI/DOJ. It also includes discussion between me and Barry assessing responses from the DOJ, FBI, OIG Senators, and Congressmen and looking at options for moving forward. Barry Fisher was a senior partner at Fleishman and Fisher, lawyers in Los Angeles, an esteemed constitutional lawyer who was referred to me by a friend from California. He was a valuable sounding board and advocate who also kindly offered his services to me on a generous reduced fee and pro bono basis. The responses we received to complaints we sent to the FBI, DOJ, and OIG were form letters, perfunctory in tone and substance, repetitive and they disingenuously side-stepped accountability.

The section is broken broadly into four chronological parts. In places, boundaries are moved slightly to maintain continuity of strands of correspondence. The four chronological parts are: 2004—2011; 2010—2014; 201—2019; and 2020—2024.

Correspondence includes that with my NYC congressman Jerrold Nadler, my New York senator, Chuck Schumer, as well as other representatives at various times over the span of nearly two decades, the House Judiciary Committee around 2005—2010, in addition to the DOJ, FBI, and the Office of the Inspector General (OIG) for the DOJ. The OIG has responsibility for conducting investigations of DOJ/FBI employees and programs. My correspondence campaigns waxed and waned over this time, sometimes with intervals of five years or more, but in aggregate I contacted agencies and representatives multiple times over the span of around two decades from 2004 to the time of publication of this volume in 2024. I mention a few notable highlights below.

House Judiciary Committee: Around 2005, I directly contacted the House Judiciary Committee (HJC), which has oversight responsibility for the FBI, with details of my complaint. Jason Cervenak called me back and interviewed me at length, for around 1.5 hours and followed up with a second call to me with further questions. He was oversight counsel with the House Judiciary Committee and his number was 202 225 3926/6793(d). It was unusual for a staffer to act in this direct way, as I learned later, normally the Committee acts only upon representation and request from a member of Congress. Nothing came of his extensive interview. At his request, I gave him a detailed statement outlining FBI abuse, including names of individuals involved and he said he would contact them. My efforts to follow-up were stonewalled. His boss Mindy Barry became involved, speaking with and emailing me on several occasions. Still, nothing transpired. Eventually, both Cervenak and Barry were transferred into other departments. Some years later, in an attempt to rekindle the complaint, I contacted the Committee office but staffers could find no record of the complaint or interview file notes.

DOJ, Investigative Specialist, Marvin Hernandez: In 2006, DOJ employee, "Investigative Specialist" Marvin Hernandez acknowledged in an email to me on May 11, 2006, that one of the people I named without specifying which (from the list of Holmes, Garber, Sutro) was an employee of the FBI:

Good afternoon John,

Per our conversation, I wanted to let you know that the FBI, acknowledged on out of the three individuals as being employees. Unfortunately, the other 2 individuals, are not, and have not been employed with the FBI.

I will let you know, what else can be done.

He later retracted this. I believe he did so under duress. Marvin subsequently advised me that the DOJ management had told him to not correspond or talk with me any further. I believe he was correct in making his original disclosure to me and his subsequent retraction is unreliable. This subsequently was stone walled by the DOJ/FBI and went nowhere.

Senator Charles Schumer: As a Federal Voter (US citizen residing overseas) registered in NYC, I approached my elected federal representative Senator Chuck Schumer, for help, via my attorney Barry Fisher. Senator Schumer followed up with the DOJ/OIG about my complaint, but the DOJ/OIG merely responded to him with similar shallow blow-off statements from their form letters. As Barry Fisher emailed me after receiving a copy of the DOJ/OIG letter dated August 9, 2006, sent to Senator Schumer, "John-here is the response to Shumer. not very helpful. Barry". Despite my requests to take the matter further and probe the FBI/DOJ evasive and non-responses to the substance of the complaint, Senator Schumer took the matter no further and stopped corresponding with myself and Barry Fisher.

Over the years, I approached other elected reps for assistance too, including my second NY federal senator, **Senator Hillary Clinton**, in May 2005 (and later in 2022, I contacted her successor, **Senator Kirsten Gillibrand**). At the behest of Congressman Nadler's staffers, I contacted **Congressman Scott**, the ranking member of the House Judiciary Committee later that year. Nothing budged on any front. There was no discernible action anywhere to hold the FBI/DOJ accountable on the matters comprising my complaint.

The United Nations Human Rights Council (UNHRC): In 2007, having met only dead ends with requests for accountability from the FBI/DOJ in the USA, I sent a complaint via Barry Fisher to UNHRC on April 14, 2007. The UNHRC responded August 20, 2007, that they did not have jurisdiction over FBI/DOJ abuses as the USA is not a signatory to the International Covenant on Civil and Political Rights (ICCPR).

Congressman Jerrold Nadler: In 2009, I circled back to my NYC Congressman, Jerrold Nadler. In September 2009, I met with Congressman Nadler's staffer Celine Mizrahi in the federal office building in NYC. During the meeting, a large security guard made his presence known, constantly wandering the corridors by the congressmen's offices with loud clanging keys, chains, handcuffs and weapons, as if transported from a scene in a Dickens novel. While the meeting with Celine went well and she said she would talk to the Congressman about my case and act on a number of fronts, nothing was ever acted on. Her promised action points on behalf of Congressman Nadler, all which came to zero, included:

> *1. Follow up with the House Judiciary Committee over their staffer's previous interviews with me and records of enquiries they made; ascertaining the Committee's powers and rights with respect to the FBI/DOJ in relation to investigating the specifics of the allegations I have raised; ascertaining the steps/process for further enquiry/investigation.*
>
> *2. Direct follow up with the FBI/DOJ to broaden the terms of reference.*
>
> *3. Follow up with Senator Schumer's office to ascertain status of my complaint with regards to the Senate Judiciary Committee.*
>
> *4. Celine offered to undertake/discuss further action that may be appropriate.*

Over the following two years from November 2009 to November 2011, I sent emails and made multiple telephone calls to her or her boss, Ellen Wallach, most of which went unanswered. In the end, there was no follow-up by Congressman Nadler on anything. My last email in relation to the meeting was sent November 10, 2011, to Celine Mizrah and cc'd to Ellan Wallach:

> *Hi Celine,*

I have not heard back from you since December 2010 – nearly 12 months, despite a number of attempts to contact you. At that time you confirmed that Congressman Nadler, a member of the House Judiciary Committee - a Committee which has oversight responsibility for the FBI, would raise my concerns with staffers at the Committee and you would provide me with feedback.

As a registered Federal Voter in Congressman Nadler's NYC district I initiated dialogue with his NYC office over two years ago. I would like to bring closure to this matter of prolonged FBI interference with myself (ongoing for 15 years) and I seek my Congressman's help in this regard. I am concerned that there has been no further communication from you and would appreciate any clarification of the status of your enquiries into this matter.

Thanks and regards.

John

It's a pity nothing moved forward from my personal point of view, the point of view of the Indigenous people of West Papua, Indonesia, living under military oppression, and strengthening the authenticity of democratic channels in America.

The United Steelworkers Union (USW): Allied concerns: I was not the only one seeking clarity and being rebuffed about what was happening in West Papua, Indonesia. In addition to at least seven other professionals already mentioned that had been targeted after speaking out on Freeport, the powerful United Steelworkers Union (USW) in the USA was also rebuffed by the DOJ. The USW made a request to the DOJ to investigate allegations, reported in The Wall Street Journal, that Freeport made direct payments to Indonesian police in contravention to the Corrupt Foreign Practices Act. In February 2013, I emailed the USW to see what response they received from the DOJ (news item and my email below). The DOJ fobbed the USW off, saying it wouldn't comment and suggested instead, it follow-up directly with the Indonesian government.

> *Hi,*
> *I am a former Wall Street analyst doing some work on Freeport. Where did your complaint to the DOJ get to concerning the below issue about Freeport? Are there any letters/documents you can share? [See article below]*
>
> *Mining News: US DOJ investigation.*
>
> *Grasberg at 5% capacity: report, 7 November 2011*
>
> *"...... the recent revelations that Freeport made payments to Indonesian police have resulted in a United Steelworkers request for investigations from the US Department of Justice.*
>
> *"The Indonesian police have recently been quoted in the local media acknowledging that they accepted millions of dollars from Freeport-McMoRan's Indonesian subsidiary PT Freeport to provide security for the miner's operations in Papua, Indonesia," the major US union said.*
>
> *"The Foreign Corrupt Practices Act bans companies from paying foreign officials to do or omit to do an act in violation of his or her lawful duty."*
>
> *A spokesman from the US Department of Justice declined to comment on the matter, according to the Wall Street Journal."*

http://www.miningnews.net/StoryView.asp?StoryID=2491536Mining News: US DOJ investigation.

Regards.
John Wilson

The USW responded with the DOJ's response:

We received an initial response from the DOJ on April 27, 2012 saying that they reviewed the allegations, but "cannot comment publicly on whether we are pursuing a particular matter." The letters also encouraged us to bring the events of October 10, 2011, to the attention of appropriate authorities in Indonesia. That was the last we heard.

Unfortunately, "That was the last we heard" is an oft repeated sentiment from individuals and groups after attempting to hold US corporations and government agencies to account.

Section V: Freedom of Information Requests (FOIA), Administrative Appeals, and OGIS Mediation

This section comprises applications and correspondence over multiple attempts to access FBI records on myself through Freedom of Information (FOI) requests. These efforts from 2004 to 2022 resulted in no significant releases, despite Holmes and Garber stating the existence of an FBI file on me, outlining some specific contents, and the ongoing interference in my life as outlined in the 2023 letter to AUSA John Moustakas, included earlier in this volume.

In 2014, the FBI released one disc of documents which ostensibly comprised correspondence concerning my FOI requests. A second disc was released by the FBI in 2023, again related to correspondence around FOI. The FBI refused to release certain documents claiming either "criminal" investigation exemption (in 2014) or "other than criminal" exemption (2023)—an inconsistency in application of exemptions without explanation.

I appealed the FOI findings to no avail, and mediation services through the Office of Government Information Services (OGIS), National Archives and Records Administration, to no avail around 2017—2019.

Subsequently, I retained FOIA lawyers and filed two lawsuits against the FBI/DOJ.

From 2004 to 2024, various FOIA attorneys have made requests for accountability from the FBI/DOJ through FOIA. These include Rachel Minter, David Sobel, David Rankin and Peter Sorenson. At the time of publication of this volume, Peter Sorenson is litigating against the FBI/DOJ on my behalf under FOIA.

One of the FOIA attorneys whom I retained from a large firm some years ago in NYC left me with cause to wonder if one or more of the team advising me had been compromised. They acted, at times, in a way consistent with what FBI operative Susan Holmes disclosed years prior as being FBI techniques intended to weaken or undermine legal action. This included sending me key documents at the twelfth hour to review and edit with no prospect for me to respond meaningfully in time. I was instructed verbally over the phone by an associate to exclude quotations in my Declaration—contrary to what other lawyers advised was good practice—statements that form the basis of evidence and credibility. I felt taunted by the partner on several occasions who explained that being co-opted by the FBI was only an issue if they were caught doing so and then held to account; that I was way too naïve in having confidence in democratic processes to resolve my complaint in a just way; and long-winded phone conversations where they frequently skirted the substance of issues. Having said that, there were also moments of seemingly genuine effort and input on their part.

As with the previous section, Section IV, I have included email trails of communication with different lawyers, in part to illustrate different approaches, strategizing as to who to talk to, which reps, and so on. It is included also partly as a record of correspondence with elected reps and other officials. It also shows the large amount of accumulated time and effort over the years (spread intermittently over two decades) not just be me, but attorneys as well, giving the illusion that the wheels of justice are turning whereas, in reality, there was no progress in that direction whatsoever. Indeed, the incessant time and delays undermine justice, weaken memories and corrode evidence. As one well-placed person said, "It is not by accident that there is no way through this," alluding to the legislation and captive regulators that make the system a brick wall to most.

Office of Government Information Services (OGIS): The OGIS offers FOIA mediation services between federal agencies in the USA and the public. Following my initial approach to them, Barry Fisher emailed and called them. However, disappointingly, their processes were not discernibly different to the FBI's—no transparency, no follow through with witnesses, and long, inexplicable delays. On October 24, 2017, Barry emailed me in palpable frustration the response he received from OGIS to the message he left them months before: "I received this today as a response to my email and call months ago." OGIS's response was boilerplate, including the unhelpful message: "Your case is in our queue pending assignment." Six months later, after further efforts to engage OGIS, Barry emailed me April 10, 2018: "[n]ever possible to reach someone by phone??and if live person, someone knowledgeable or simply registering concern?"

On June 11, 2018, after over twelve months of attempting to engage OGIS, I emailed Barry seeking alternative avenues to address FBI abuses and lack of accountability: "This [] FOIA appeal review has now been sitting with OGIS for over a year - one could reasonably wonder if there is any real hope of resolution here...." On June 16, 2018, I emailed Barry a sampling of various dead ends we had hit in seeking accountability:

> [T]he complaint is shifting from FBI abuse, to lack of any viable means for individuals abused by which the FBI can be held accountable, i.e. oversight channels compromised or ineffective - based on loss of my complaints, interview records and files by the House Judiciary Committee (you spoke with a couple people there at one point about my case); no access to records via FOI; inordinate delays (in the vicinity of 12 months) in their correspondence and refusal to address the substance of complaints; year/s in delays to address appeals; no follow through from congressman (Nadler) and senators (Schumer) in seeking accountability. You have been involved in much of this over the years and know firsthand the number of avenues we have tried and the nature of meaningless or incorrect answers and in cases no response at all. There is probably more I could add, but this gives you the gist of it.
>
> Whether the channels lack independence, are compromised or underfunded is not the point. It is that they are not effective - in effect system leaves people in my position without any rights regards justice/fairness, etc.

Barry responded: "yes, corrupt system. inspector general Horowitz justice department jumps to trump/republican requests but connected to you, others, including imprisoned oppressed client of mine, a dead ear, unmoving hand. and getting worse"

Alternatives Options: There are few ways through, it seems: a careless fragment left by the intelligence agencies in the form of physical evidence could be their undoing in court; or access to a well-connected individual with the influence to make things "happen" within the agencies. Who knows, maybe one day one of the courts will call the FBI/DOJ's "bad faith" conduct by name, subpoena witnesses and allow cross examination to get to the truth.

Despite the intent of the US Constitution and separation of powers, the US system has subverted justice to the point that the federal government's totalitarian-like intelligence agencies are able to get away with whatever their counterparts in totalitarian states elsewhere in the world can.

Irrespective of the David and Goliath power indifference, I pushed ahead with judicial review. With next to no expectation of justice, it seemed, at least, a way to create a permanent record of events. A record that removes control of the narrative from the intelligence agencies with their incessant deceptions, manipulations and propaganda, and offers an opposing point of view.

On May 9, 2019, I asked Barry what we should do next given the FBI had justified its incursions into my life for matters concerning "criminal" investigation. What that was about or what I was accused of was never disclosed, merely hidden behind FBI-claimed exemptions in their response to FOIA request:

> *Can I re-engage your services to help with a renewed effort to get to the bottom of whether I am a suspect or have been "legitimately" investigated by the FBI for some possible or alleged crime? It is now over 20 years since the interference began, and over 5 years since the last FOI request was responded to (in 2014). The implication of 552a (j)(2) in the FBI FOI response appears to be that I am or have been a suspect or investigated by the FBI for some possible or alleged crime - is that correct? How do I find out what it is the FBI has suspected me of, or investigated me for?*
>
> *As you are aware FOI requests went nowhere and previous requests to the internal inspector general at DOJ provided no useful information.*
>
> *Recent OGIS emails re my request for arbitration are below - but ultimately the process went nowhere.*

Barry recommended I commence an FOI lawsuit working with a specialist attorney in that area. In an email to me June 26, 2019, he re-affirmed his view:

> *the judicial and legislative branches of the government are the only separate one that might look at what the executive branch, DOJ, State etc., have or have not done. Nothing has resulted from direct complaints to the executive and legislative branches. perhaps if there was implication of Clinton and/or Obama administrations, this executive regime or the republican controlled senate might take interest. otherwise, the judicial branch.*

Given the expected high costs and doubtful prospects of victory, litigation had not been an approach I wished to pursue. But my view changed in 2020.

Section VI: FOIA Judicial Review

Since 2020, I have filed two lawsuits under FOIA against the FBI.

The first lawsuit was filed in New York by David Rankin of BLHNY (based in NYC) in December 2020. We had a technical victory that forced the FBI to conduct further searches, but no new documents were released. (Costs were partially awarded, the bulk of which were assumed by BLHNY, and which they intended to appeal at their expense).

The second lawsuit was filed in Washington, DC, by Peter Sorenson of Sorenson Law LLC (based in Oregon) in October 2022 (ongoing at time of publication of this volume in 2024). In an apparent coincidence, Pete disclosed he was also the attorney to David Foreman, the environmental activist and co-founder of Earth First! targeted in the mid-1990s by my then girlfriend, FBI agent Susan Holmes.

In both cases, testimony was provided by an expert witness, Jennifer Coffindaffer, a former FBI agent and veteran of twenty-five years.

Overall, the court documents, based on sworn Declarations tell the detailed story of FBI retribution against me for work I undertook as a Wall Street mining analyst covering NYSE listed US mining behemoth Freeport-McMoRan's activities, through its associate PT Freeport Indonesia, at its Grasberg mine in West Papua, Indonesia. The company was reportedly under investigation by the US Department of State at the time, following eyewitness allegations it was involved in the killing of Indigenous protestors and other human rights and environmental abuses. (As mention, the company denied these claims and they were not subsequently proven in court.)

These documents are from FBI filings in an FOIA case against the FBI in United States District Court for the District of Columbia. The case is ongoing as of May 2024.

Declaration of FBI Veteran, Expert Witness Jennifer Coffindaffer—FOIA Case

Excerpts from the Declaration of former FBI agent, Expert Witness, a 25-year veteran of the FBI, Jennifer Coffindaffer are below, in support of the Plaintiff, John Wilson. She attests the FBI is not acting in "good faith" and suggests a number of key databases the agency neglected to search. As former FBI Special Agent, Senior Supervisory Resident Agent ("SSRA"), and Supervisory Special Agent ("SSA") Jennifer Coffindaffer explains in her Declaration:[36]

> 2. I was retained by counsel for the Plaintiff to review and evaluate the totality of the records provided by the Federal Bureau of Investigation ("FBI") pursuant to Mr. Wilson's Freedom of Information Act ("FOIA") Request No. 1548515-000 and to give my expert opinions thereafter as to the adequacy of the search conducted by the FBI and any Exemptions asserted by the FBI with respect to the records requested.

> 3. In developing my opinions, I have relied on my knowledge, training, skill, education and experience developed during my 25 years as FBI Special Agent, Senior Supervisory Resident Agent ("SSRA") and Supervisory Special Agent ("SSA") with the FBI, including specific experience in the areas of conducting electronic searches, and finding and retrieving documents within the FBI's databases, including: the Central Records System ("CRS"), Automated Case Support system ("ACS"), Sentinel Electronic Surveillance files ("ELSUR"), Informant Databases ("DELTA") as well as other FBI databases. I have also relied on the experience of fellow agents and clerks in the FBI related to searches within the same FBI databases.

> 20. In short, there is no reason for any records to remain hidden more than 20 years after the documents were created and using GLOMAR as an excuse to not produce the records undermines the legitimate use of GLOMAR to withhold records under FOIA.

> 21. Based on the FBI's track record of unresponsiveness concerning the production of records regarding the Plaintiff's FOIA responses, and a court ordered recommendation, it is my

---

[36] Jennifer Coffindaffer's full Declaration is contained in Section IV of the Appendix in this volume.

opinion that the FBI's assertion that they have acted in "Good Faith" and have been responsive is not accurate. Specifically, initially the FBI responded they had no records. Then, the FBI responded they had one record. Then the FBI responded they had 22 records but provided limited production of the 22 records. Then the FBI asserted they had 35 records, yet again limited the production. With each request, the FBI's answer has changed.

22. Based on each of the points cited above, it is my opinion that the FBI has not in good faith conducted responsive searches pertaining to the Plaintiff's FOIA requests.

Appendix

Section I

Department of Justice and the FBI

Section I

Department of Justice and the FBI

I-1   **FBI conduct not in "good faith"**

        a)   The FBI is not acting in "good faith": A conversation with ChatGPT.

        b)   Background report – FBI operative Dr. Steve Garber

I-1a FBI conduct not in "good faith"

A conversation with ChatGPT

* * * * *

"Good Faith" – 2023

Demonstrating lack of FBI "good faith": Wilson's notarized Declaration of 30 August 2022 offers evidence of records held by the FBI. The FBI has also demonstrated a pattern of behavior in evasive or non-responses to Wilson and his lawyer's repeated complaint about FBI operatives Holmes, Garber, etc.

The letter from Wilson's attorney Pete Sorenson to Assistant United States Attorney (AUSA) Moustakas of 11 July 2023 (largely drawn from Wilson's Declaration 30 August 2022) summarizes multiple violations by the FBI to follow proper investigative procedures. These include that the FBI targeted Wilson for political reasons on account of his work as a mining analyst covering US mining company Freeport-McMoRan's activities in West Papua, Indonesia, where it was alleged Freeport had been involved with the killing of Indigenous protestors and other human rights violations and environmental abuses.

Among other things, the letter to Moustakas, includes details illegal surveillance of Wilson's phone and electronic payments where no warrants have been produced despite requests by Wilson's attorney Pete Sorenson; and theft of property comprising Freeport-McMoRan branded corporate promotion items Wilson NYC apartment, among other things.

A summary of the FBI not acting in good faith in Wilson's case is detailed below. Category headings are from ChatGPT.

1. **Evidence in Wilson's case that the FBI is not acting in "good faith"**

    (a) **Suppression of dissent and political bias in investigations:** Wilson, as outlined in the Sorenson letter to Moustakas and Wilson's Declaration 30 August 2022, has stated and provided multiple details of FBI threats, retaliation and disclosures – as suppression of dissent. These were confirmed by Holmes and Garber concerning FBI interference with Wilson on account of his work as a Wall Street mining analyst covering US mining company Freeport-McMoRan which was under investigation following allegations of killing Indigenous protestors and other human rights violations at its massive Grasberg mine in West Papua, Indonesia. Wilson's work included a 12 March 1996 report critical of the company and subsequent question on human rights to the company's Chairman Jim Bob Moffett at an analyst briefing in New Orleans in May 1996 following which threats and retribution targeting Wilson commenced.

    (b) **Entrapment/fabrication:** i) FBI operative Holmes was aware of the attempted NYC undercover police drug sting on Wilson. (Reference: Letter to Moustakas – page 20, para 13; plus references in Moustakas letter to Wilson's notarized Declaration 30 August 2022).

(ii) Multiple efforts and comments from FBI operatives to link Wilson to David Foreman, the high-profile eco-activist and co-founder of Earth First! that FBI operative Holmes was targeting for the FBI. (Reference - examples include: Letter to Moustakas: page 15, para 10e – photos of Wilson in Foreman's dory; pages 27-28, para 19-20; plus references in Moustakas letter to Wilson's notarized Declaration 30 August 2022).

(iii) There were many perverse questions from Holmes and Garber to Wilson with no apparent reason about Wilson's work with and knowledge of explosives as a mining engineer in operations for major global mining company BHP. FBI skewed questions and connotations to imply Wilson has an interest in illegal application of explosives to damage dams and other infrastructure. (Reference - examples include: Letter to Moustakas: page 22-23, para 14d-h).

(c) **Misuse of surveillance powers** – (i) re Holmes' disclosure of details of Wilson's NYC home phone calls and records of my credit card purchases. Garber's revelations concerning Wilson's Arizona based calls. (Reference: Letter to Moustakas: Holmes' disclosures re NYC home phone calls page 14-15, para 10; Garber's revelations re Arizona wiretaps page 25, para 16d; plus references in Moustakas letter to Wilson's notarized Declaration 30 August 2022).

(ii) The FBI, during the period in question, has a history of deliberately deceiving regulators. A newspaper article in the Sydney Morning Herald from August 25, 2002 titled "Court Reveals FBI Deceit" details FBI and DOJ deceit in falsifying more than 75 applications for search warrants and wiretaps in prior years. Wilson Decl., appendix Exhibit 5 p. 180-182.

(d) **Lack of transparency in asset forfeiture:** Theft of Freeport-McMoRan company merchandise given to analysts at analyst briefings such as bags, small flashlights and other token items. These items were removed from Wilson's apartment in NYC by the FBI without a warrant or permission sometime around 1997-99 - as disclosed with Wilson by FBI operative Holmes – Wilson Declaration 30 August 2022.

(e) **Allegations of FBI abuse of power** - (i) stemming from Wilson's Freeport-McMoRan research report and questions to the CEO including threats, intimidation and harassment. (Examples include multiple references in Moustakas letter: page 9, para 3c – threats in Freeport boardroom alcove; pages 16-19, para 11 - gaslighting; and Wilson Declaration).

ii) FBI operatives Susan Holmes and Steve Garber disclosed to Wilson in 2003 and 2004 respectively, in NYC that Wilson was the target of an FBI campaign of intimidation, surveillance, and harassment in retribution for his work as a mining analyst in 1996 on Freeport-McMoRan. They revealed many private details of Wilson's life collected from surveillance and interviewing peers. Garber's June 2004 disclosures, Wilson Decl. 162 to 185, p. 66-73 and September 2004 disclosures, Wilson Decl. 202-212, p.78-81 to Wilson of the FBI campaign targeting him.

iii) The FBI collected distinct descriptions and scenarios from Wilson in the 2003 interrogation of Wilson by Holmes at Café Fiorello, NYC, and engaged in subsequent efforts over the coming years to use those descriptions and scenarios to gaslight Wilson as a form of psychological attack.

The FBI is hiding and withholding records that Wilson is entitled to and is not acting in "good faith".

2. **Evidence in Wilson's case: the FBI is not acting in "good faith" – specific to FOIA**

   (f) **Evasive or non-responsive responses; Inadequate or misleading responses:** The FBI/DOJ has failed to respond on multiple occasions to requests they confirm whether Holmes, Garber, et al, are operatives of the FBI. The FBI and DOJ repeatedly evade the question, neither confirming nor denying if they are operatives of the FBI. They repeatedly either do not respond or offer evasive answers such as saying only that the people named are not classified as "employees" or "special agents" of the FBI but not whether they are operatives or in some other category (contractors, or "persons having access to FBI facilities" in FBI parlance (phrase is from an FBI letter to Wilson 29 January 2014). Responses were neither prompt nor substantive. (Reference: Examples include letter to Moustakas – pages 4-7, paras 1-5).

   (g) **Unjustified withholding of information:** Unjustified targeting of Wilson by the FBI renders all information collected and held on him by the FBI unjustified, and therefore any exemptions relied upon by the FBI in Wilson's case are unjustified.

   (h) **The FBI's delay** in responding to the FOIA appeal filed 1 September 2022 by Wilson's attorney Pete Sorenson.

   (i) **Public interest and accountability:** Wilson has never been formally notified he was under investigation for any crime, or for any other reason, let alone formally questioned or charged.

   (j) **Public's right to know:** the details of Wilson's complaint against the FBI as disclosed in his Declaration of 30 August 2022 and the Moustakas letter provide details of FBI reprisal due to Wilson's work as a Wall Street mining analyst covering US mining company Freeport-McMoRan which was accused of killing Indigenous protestors and other human rights violations in West Papua, Indonesia.

   (k) **Reasonable search methods:** The FBI is expected to consult with personnel who may have knowledge of the requested information. Despite multiple requests and evidence provided by Wilson over nearly two decades, and his attorney, the DOJ/FBI has failed to address whether Holmes, Garber, etc are operatives of the FBI, working as contractors, etc,. The FBI has evaded answering this question and therefor skirted its obligation to reveal and consult with these personnel in fulfilling the agencies obligations under FOIA. The role of these individuals is outlined in detail in Wilson's Declaration 30 August 2022 and letter to Moustakas.

   (l) **Consultation and collaboration:** Did the FBI's FOIA search include consultation with other agencies, potentially the CIA, NYPD, etc – potential collaborators with the FBI given certain details outlined in the Moustakas and letter and Wilson's Declaration. If specific agencies were consulted, the FBI made no mention of this. "Good faith requires the FBI to engage in such consultation and collaboration as necessary to fulfill its obligations under FOIA."

(m) **Balancing interests; Public interest and accountability:** Wilson has never been formally notified he was under investigation for any crime, or for any other reason, let alone formally questioned or charged. Yet on multiple occasions two or more operatives of the FBI have revealed compelling details of surveillance and interference of Wilson by the FBI attributed to his work as an analyst on US mining company Freeport-McMoRan.

(n) **Best practices and guidance:** The public has no idea of what databases exist in the FBI, nor what search terms define or signify. The FBI has provided no guidance in this area. Therefor the public has no meaningful way to assess whether the FBI has acted in a manner consistent with its obligations.

(o) **Evidence of the existence of additional records:** "Challenging the agency's good faith: Requesters who believe that the FBI did not act in good faith can challenge the agency's assertions by presenting evidence that demonstrates a lack of thoroughness, inconsistencies, or other indications of improper handling of the FOIA request. This can involve submitting evidence of the existence of additional records or showing that the agency's search methods were inadequate." Wilson's Declaration 30 August 2022 and Moustakas letter sets out in details evidence of the existence of further records from discussion on gaslighting to detailed revelations by Holmes and Garber concerning surveillance of Wilson and records of his association with David Foreman.

3. ChatGPT[37]: When is the FBI not acting in "good faith" in general circumstances.

Q: What constitutes the FBI not acting in "good faith"?

A: ChatGPT

The concept of "good faith" refers to the honest and sincere intention to act in a fair and just manner, without any ulterior motives or improper conduct. When it comes to the Federal Bureau of Investigation (FBI), not acting in "good faith" would typically involve instances where the agency or its representatives engage in misconduct, negligence, or unethical behavior that undermines the principles of fairness, justice, or the rule of law. Here are a few examples of what could be considered as the FBI not acting in "good faith":

1. **Fabricating evidence:** If the FBI knowingly creates or alters evidence to falsely implicate someone or to manipulate the outcome of an investigation, it would be a clear violation of acting in good faith. This includes manufacturing false documents, tampering with witness statements, or presenting misleading information.

2. **Withholding exculpatory evidence:** The FBI has a legal obligation to disclose evidence that could be favorable to the defense in criminal cases. Intentionally failing to disclose such evidence, known as Brady violations, would be acting in bad faith and undermining the defendant's right to a fair trial.

3. **Engaging in illegal surveillance:** If the FBI conducts surveillance or wiretapping without proper legal authorization, such as obtaining warrants based on false information or bypassing required procedures, it would be an example of acting in bad faith.

4. **Targeting individuals based on personal or political bias:** The FBI is expected to conduct investigations impartially, without being influenced by personal or political biases. If it is discovered that the agency selectively targets individuals or groups based on their race, religion, ethnicity, or political affiliations, it would be considered acting in bad faith.

5. **Coercion or intimidation tactics:** If the FBI employs coercive methods, intimidation, or threats to elicit information from witnesses, suspects, or individuals unrelated to an investigation, it would be acting in bad faith and potentially violating their constitutional rights.

6. **Failure to follow proper investigative procedures:** The FBI is expected to follow established protocols and guidelines in its investigations. If agents deviate from these procedures, such as conducting searches without warrants, conducting unauthorized surveillance, or engaging in unauthorized activities, it would be considered acting in bad faith.

7. **Entrapment:** If the FBI induces or coerces individuals into committing illegal acts that they would not have otherwise committed, it could be seen as acting in bad faith. Entrapment occurs when law enforcement officers, including FBI agents, actively

---

[37] Generated by ChatGPT, an AI language model developed by OpenAI.

encourage or facilitate criminal behavior that the individual would not have engaged in without such encouragement.

8. **Misrepresentation or perjury:** If FBI agents provide false information or lie under oath during investigations, court proceedings, or when presenting evidence, it would be acting in bad faith. Misrepresentation or perjury undermines the credibility of law enforcement and the justice system.

9. **Retaliation or harassment:** If the FBI targets individuals or groups for retaliation or harassment due to their exercise of protected rights, such as freedom of speech or association, it would be considered acting in bad faith. This includes targeting whistleblowers or individuals who expose misconduct within the agency.

10. **Abuse of power:** If FBI agents misuse their authority or engage in actions that exceed their legal powers, it would be considered acting in bad faith. This could include using excessive force during arrests, conducting unlawful searches or seizures, or engaging in corrupt practices such as accepting bribes or engaging in illegal activities.

11. **Violation of privacy rights:** The FBI has the responsibility to respect individuals' privacy rights while conducting investigations. If the agency engages in warrantless surveillance, invasive monitoring, or collects personal information without proper legal justification, it would be seen as acting in bad faith and violating constitutional rights.

12. **Lack of transparency:** If the FBI operates without transparency, intentionally withholding information from the public or impeding efforts to hold the agency accountable, it will raise concerns about acting in good faith. Transparency is essential for maintaining public trust and ensuring proper oversight.

13. **Political manipulation:** If the FBI becomes politicized and uses its investigative powers to target or harass individuals or groups based on their political beliefs, affiliations, or activities, it would be seen as acting in bad faith. The FBI should remain impartial and independent, avoiding partisan motivations or interference.

14. **Suppression of dissent:** If the FBI engages in the suppression of legitimate dissent or peaceful protests by targeting activists, monitoring lawful political activities, or using surveillance to intimidate individuals exercising their First Amendment rights, it would be seen as acting in bad faith. The agency should respect and protect the constitutional rights of individuals.

15. **Targeting journalists or undermining press freedom:** If the FBI targets journalists, conducts surveillance on media organizations, or engages in actions that undermine press freedom or the protection of confidential sources, it would be seen as acting in bad faith. Freedom of the press is a fundamental pillar of democracy.

These additional points highlight further considerations related to the FBI not acting in "good faith." Upholding the principles of fairness, justice, and accountability is essential for maintaining public trust in law enforcement agencies.

4. **ChatGPT: When is the FBI not acting in "good faith" re FOIA**

Q: What constitutes the FBI not acting in "good faith" in relation to FOIA searches?

A: ChatGPT

In the context of the Freedom of Information Act (FOIA), the term "good faith" generally refers to the requirement that government agencies, including the Federal Bureau of Investigation (FBI), conduct searches for requested records in a diligent and honest manner. While the concept of "good faith" can be subjective, there are certain factors that may indicate the FBI is not acting in good faith during FOIA searches. Examples include:

1. **Failure to conduct an adequate search:** The FBI is expected to make a reasonable effort to locate all responsive records within their possession, control, and scope. If it becomes evident that the FBI has not taken reasonable steps to search for relevant documents or has deliberately excluded certain sources, it may be considered a lack of good faith.

2. **Unjustified withholding of information:** Under FOIA, government agencies can withhold certain information based on specific exemptions, such as national security, personal privacy, law enforcement techniques, or confidential business information. However, if the FBI withholds information without providing a valid and lawful justification, it may indicate a lack of good faith.

3. **Failure to fulfill statutory obligations:** The FBI, like other government agencies, has specific obligations under FOIA, including providing access to requested records, applying exemptions appropriately, and facilitating the appeals process. Failure to fulfill these obligations in a consistent and lawful manner may indicate a lack of good faith.

4. **Presumption of good faith:** There is a general presumption that government agencies, including the FBI, act in good faith when processing FOIA requests. This means that they are presumed to be making a genuine effort to locate and disclose responsive records in accordance with the law.

5. **Burden of proof:** If a requester believes that the FBI has not acted in good faith, the burden of proof typically rests on the requester to provide evidence supporting their claim. This evidence could include specific instances of inadequate searches, unjustified withholding, delays, or misleading responses.

6. **Evasive or non-responsive responses:** If the FBI provides evasive or non-responsive answers to FOIA requests, such as by providing incomplete or misleading information, it could suggest a lack of good faith in fulfilling its obligations.

7. **Challenging the adequacy of the search:** Requesters can challenge the adequacy of the FBI's search by presenting evidence that suggests the agency did not make a reasonable effort to locate responsive records. This evidence could include inconsistencies in the agency's responses, indications of missing or overlooked records, or information suggesting the existence of additional relevant documents.

8. **Importance of documentation and record-keeping:** Agencies like the FBI are expected to maintain proper documentation of their search efforts, decision-making processes, and justifications for withholding or redacting information. Clear and well-documented records can play a role in demonstrating good faith and ensuring transparency in the FOIA process.

9. **Reasonable search methods:** The FBI is expected to employ reasonable search methods to locate responsive records. This may involve utilizing electronic databases, conducting manual searches in relevant file systems, consulting with personnel who may have knowledge of the requested information, or employing advanced search technologies as appropriate. The agency should employ methods that are likely to result in the discovery of responsive records.

10. **Application of exemptions:** The FBI, like other government agencies, can withhold certain information under FOIA exemptions. However, the application of these exemptions must be done in good faith. The agency should provide specific justifications for applying each exemption, explaining how the release of the requested information would harm a protected interest. Exemptions should not be used as a blanket response to avoid disclosure.

11. **Documentation and record-keeping:** The FBI is expected to maintain proper documentation of its search efforts, decision-making processes, and justifications for withholding or redacting information. Clear and well-documented records help demonstrate the agency's good faith in conducting the search and provide transparency in the FOIA process.

12. **Public interest and accountability:** The concept of good faith is closely tied to the public interest and the importance of holding government agencies accountable. Courts may consider the potential impact on the public's right to know when evaluating whether the FBI acted in good faith. The agency's commitment to transparency and responsiveness can play a role in demonstrating its good faith efforts.

13. **Challenging the agency's good faith:** Requesters who believe that the FBI did not act in good faith can challenge the agency's assertions by presenting evidence that demonstrates a lack of thoroughness, inconsistencies, or other indications of improper handling of the FOIA request. This can involve submitting evidence of the existence of additional records or showing that the agency's search methods were inadequate.

14. **Best practices and guidance:** The FBI can establish and promote best practices and internal guidance to ensure consistent and effective handling of FOIA requests. This can include providing clear instructions to personnel involved in the search and review processes, disseminating standardized search protocols, and sharing lessons learned to improve future FOIA operations.

It's essential to note that the specific application of "good faith" in FOIA cases can vary depending on the circumstances, legal interpretations, and jurisdiction. If you have a particular scenario or question in mind, please provide more details, and I'll do my best to assist you further!

[Note: ChatGPT, is an online artificial intelligence "large language model-based chatbot" able to search large tracts of information across the internet and compile cohesive summaries. It was asked to compile a) what constitutes the FBI not acting in "good faith" in general, and; b) what constitutes the FBI not acting in "good faith" specifically in freedom of information (FOIA) cases.]

5. ChatGPT: Historical examples of the FBI not acting in "good faith"

Q: Give examples of where the FBI did not act in "good faith".

A: ChatGPT

Acting in "good faith" refers to the principle of conducting oneself honestly, sincerely, and with a genuine intent to fulfill one's duties or obligations. In the context of the FBI (Federal Bureau of Investigation) or any law enforcement agency, acting in good faith means that its officials and agents are expected to carry out their responsibilities diligently, ethically, and lawfully, with an honest belief in the correctness and legality of their actions.

When the FBI acts in good faith, it implies that its agents are operating within the bounds of the law, adhering to established regulations and guidelines, and pursuing their investigations or operations with integrity. Acting in good faith requires agents to gather evidence, conduct interviews, and make decisions based on objective facts and the best information available to them at the time. It entails avoiding biases, personal agendas, or any malicious intent.

However, it is important to note that the concept of acting in good faith is subjective and can be interpreted differently in various situations. Disagreements or controversies may arise regarding whether the FBI's actions were truly in good faith, particularly if there are allegations of misconduct, abuses of power, or violations of civil liberties. In such cases, independent oversight bodies or the courts may assess the actions of the FBI to determine whether they were in line with the principles of good faith and the applicable laws.

There have been instances where the actions of the FBI have raised concerns about acting in "good faith". Here are a few examples:

1. **Misuse of surveillance powers:** If the FBI unlawfully obtains or misuses surveillance warrants, such as through deliberate omissions or misrepresentations to the court, it would be considered a violation of acting in good faith. For example, the controversy surrounding the surveillance of Carter Page, a former Trump campaign advisor, raised questions about the FBI's application process for Foreign Intelligence Surveillance Act (FISA) warrants.

2. **Political bias:** If there is evidence to suggest that FBI officials or agents acted with political bias, favoring or targeting individuals or groups based on their political beliefs, it would undermine the principle of acting in good faith. The text messages exchanged between FBI employees Peter Strzok and Lisa Page, which revealed anti-Trump sentiments during the investigation into Russian interference in the 2016 election, raised concerns about potential bias.

3. **Withholding exculpatory evidence:** If the FBI fails to disclose or intentionally withholds evidence that could be favorable to the accused, it would be seen as acting in bad faith. This issue came to light in cases such as the prosecution of former Senator Ted Stevens, where the FBI was found to have withheld evidence that could have exonerated him.

4. **Entrapment or overstepping investigative boundaries:** If the FBI engages in entrapment, where they induce or coerce individuals into committing crimes they would not have otherwise committed, it would be considered acting in bad faith. Similarly, if the FBI exceeds its investigative authority or violates constitutional rights during the course of an investigation, it will raise concerns about acting in good faith.

5. **Failure to address internal misconduct:** If the FBI fails to address or adequately investigate allegations of misconduct within its ranks, such as corruption, abuse of power, or cover-ups, it will undermine the perception of acting in good faith. Instances of agents engaging in illegal activities or unethical behaviour without appropriate consequences can erode public trust in the organization.

6. **Anthrax investigation (2001):** Following the 2001 anthrax attacks, where letters containing anthrax spores were sent through the mail, the FBI launched an investigation. The case faced criticism for its handling, including the targeting of scientist Steven Hatfill as a suspect. Hatfill was later exonerated, and the FBI settled a lawsuit with him. The investigation's handling raised concerns about acting in good faith and the potential impact on innocent individuals.

7. **Hillary Clinton email investigation (2015-2016):** The FBI's investigation into the use of a private email server by former Secretary of State Hillary Clinton drew criticism and raised concerns about political bias. Critics argued that the FBI's handling of the case, including the decision not to recommend charges, was influenced by political considerations and favouritism.

8. **James "Whitey" Bulger (1994-2011):** The FBI's relationship with notorious Boston mobster James "Whitey" Bulger raised serious concerns about acting in good faith. It was revealed that Bulger had been an FBI informant while simultaneously engaging in criminal activities. Critics alleged that the FBI protected Bulger and turned a blind eye to his crimes, which included murder, drug trafficking, and extortion. This case exposed corruption within the FBI and damaged public trust in the agency.

9. **Michael Flynn investigation (2017-2020):** The FBI's investigation into former National Security Advisor Michael Flynn's contacts with Russian officials during the transition period led to controversy. Flynn pleaded guilty to lying to the FBI but later sought to withdraw his plea, alleging misconduct by the FBI. Concerns were raised about the circumstances surrounding Flynn's interview, including allegations of entrapment and the withholding of exculpatory evidence. The investigation's handling garnered significant attention and raised questions about acting in good faith.

10. **Operation Varsity Blues (2019-present):** The FBI's investigation into a college admissions scandal, which involved parents bribing college officials and manipulating the admissions process, raised concerns about acting in good faith. Critics questioned whether the FBI was focusing on the most significant threats to society and argued that resources could have been better allocated elsewhere. The case also prompted discussions about fairness in the college admissions process and the role of law enforcement in addressing such issues.

These examples demonstrate instances where the FBI's actions, investigations, or handling of cases have faced scrutiny, leading to concerns about acting in good faith, integrity, and adherence to established protocols. It is important to note that ongoing investigations and legal proceedings may provide further insights and outcomes in these cases.

It's important to note also, that these examples are not exhaustive, and each case should be evaluated based on the specific circumstances and available evidence.

6. What constitutes "Adequate Search" under FOIA in the Supreme Court

Attorney Pete Sorenson emailed further conversations with ChatGPT.

Q: Has the Supreme Court of the United States ever said what constitutes an adequate search under the Freedom of Information Act?

A: ChatGPT

The Supreme Court of the United States has not specifically defined what constitutes an adequate search under the Freedom of Information Act (FOIA). FOIA is a federal law that provides the public with the right to request access to government records, subject to certain exemptions. While the Supreme Court has ruled on various FOIA-related cases and principles, it has not issued a definitive ruling that lays out a precise standard for what constitutes an adequate search.
However, lower federal courts have developed a body of case law that addresses the adequacy of searches conducted by government agencies in response to FOIA requests. These lower courts have established some general principles and guidelines for evaluating whether a search is adequate.

Some factors that courts often consider when determining the adequacy of a FOIA search include:

1. **Agency's Good Faith Effort:** Courts typically look at whether the agency made a good faith effort to locate and retrieve responsive records. Agencies are expected to use reasonable methods and resources to conduct their searches.

2. **Scope of the Request:** The complexity and scope of the FOIA request can impact the adequacy of the search. Agencies are not required to search for records that fall outside the scope of the request.

3. **Search Terms and Techniques:** Courts may examine the search terms and techniques used by the agency to determine if they were appropriate and likely to uncover responsive documents.

4. **Exemption Claims:** If an agency withholds documents under one of the FOIA's exemptions, courts will assess whether the agency has provided a lawful and sufficiently detailed explanation for the withholding.

5. **Affidavits and Declarations:** Agencies often submit affidavits or declarations explaining their search efforts and justifying any redactions or withholdings. Courts may review these documents to evaluate the adequacy of the search.

6. **Requester's Input:** Courts may also consider any input from the FOIA requester regarding the adequacy of the search.

While there is no one-size-fits-all standard for what constitutes an adequate search under FOIA, these factors provide some guidance for evaluating the sufficiency of an agency's efforts in responding to FOIA requests. Ultimately, whether a search is deemed adequate may depend on the specific circumstances of each case and the legal arguments presented by the parties involved.

Q: How does a Plaintiff show that the FBI fails to act in good faith when searched for records under the Freedom of Information Act?

A: ChatGPT

To show that the FBI fails to act in good faith when searching for records under the Freedom of Information Act (FOIA), a plaintiff would typically need to demonstrate the following:

1. **Inadequate Search Effort:** The plaintiff must provide evidence or arguments suggesting that the FBI's search for records was inadequate or cursory. This could involve showing that the search terms used were too narrow, that relevant locations or databases were omitted, or that the search was not comprehensive enough to locate responsive documents.

2. **Evidence of Concealment:** The plaintiff can attempt to present evidence indicating that the FBI intentionally concealed or withheld records. This might include instances where the FBI improperly redacted information, classified documents unnecessarily, or failed to release documents that should have been accessible under FOIA.

3. **Unjustified Delays:** If the FBI has unreasonably delayed responding to the FOIA request or has not met statutory deadlines, the plaintiff can argue that these delays are indicative of a lack of good faith. However, it's important to note that FOIA allows for certain permissible delays, so the plaintiff must demonstrate that the delays were unjustified or excessive.

4. **Patterns of Non-Compliance:** If the plaintiff can show a pattern of non-compliance with FOIA requests by the FBI, it may bolster the argument that the agency is not acting in good faith. This could involve providing examples of other cases where the FBI failed to provide requested records or engaged in similar behavior.

5. **Inadequate Explanations:** If the FBI provides inadequate or implausible explanations for withholding or redacting information in response to a FOIA request, the plaintiff can use this as evidence of bad faith. Challenging the justifications offered by the agency can be a key element of demonstrating bad faith.

It's important to remember that FOIA litigation can be complex, and the burden of proof is generally on the plaintiff to establish that the agency acted in bad faith. Plaintiffs often work with legal counsel experienced in FOIA litigation to build their case and navigate the legal process effectively. Additionally, FOIA litigation can take time, and agencies have certain legal defenses they can employ, so it's essential to be prepared for a potentially lengthy legal battle when pursuing a FOIA case.

I-1b   Background PI report: FBI operative Dr. Steve Garber

FBI operative Dr. Steve Garber

*   *   *   *   *

In 2021, I retained New York City law firm BLHNY to commence litigation against the FBI. At their instigation, BLHNY retained the services of a private investigator to provide background reports on various FBI operative – contractors involved in my long running complaint against the FBI, including Steve Garber.

Complete Social Security Numbers (SSN) for the subjects were identified but practice is not to include the complete number, nor DOB in public documents, a policy outlined and followed by the FBI. An email from Assistant United States Attorney Tabitha Bartholomew to my attorney Pete Sorenson in 2024 below explains the DOJ's policy in redacting the personal identifiers of subjects when making documents public. I extended the same courtesy to the FBI in redacting personal information of operatives. (Except, I took the additional step of redacting Garber's street address).

Report excerpts on Garber are provided below.

*   *   *   *   *

Exhibit 1: April 2021.   BLHNY—private investigator's report on FBI operative Steve Garber.

Steven Daniel Garber

DOB: June X, 1954

SSN: XXX-XX-XXXX

Address: ███████, Stamford, CT 06905

Garber appears to be currently self-employed, possibly as a consultant. He owned Garber Home Inspections, LLC, a domestic limited liability company registered in Connecticut, from June 2012 until he recently dissolved the company on February 3, 2021. We believe that Garber was previously the President of Worldwide Ecology in Stamford, CT, from 2006-2016. He claims to be licensed by the US Army Corps of Engineers for Hazardous Materials/Waste Handling and also to be licensed to teach in CT. He worked for the Department of Homeland Security from April 2, 2017 through March 30, 2019, and also as an adjunct instructor at Berkeley College from April 1, 2013 through June 30, 2014. Both of these jobs were exact matches with his SSN. In the 1990s Garber was living in NYC and in 1999 he moved to Arizona to teach at Embry-Riddle Aeronautical University but was back in the northeast no later than 2003.

Garber sued Embry-Riddle on August 26, 2001 and claimed that his contract was not renewed in retaliation for advocating on behalf of a student with a disability and because he threatened to contact environmental authorities to report illegal dumping of fuel on the tarmac at Love Field (Dallas, TX). Garber v. Embry-Riddle Aeronautical University, Case No. 3:2001cv00746, filed on August 26, 2001 in the Arizona District Court (Prescott Division). He demanded $750,000; however, the Court granted the Defendant's motion of summary judgment on April 30, 2003, and the complaint was dismissed. Garber got nothing.

According to Garber's profile on LinkedIn, he claims to have a PhD from Rutgers, an MBA from NYU, an M.A. from the University of Kansas and a B.S from Cornell. He did not provide the dates that the degrees were awarded and at this time, we have not verified his degrees.

Steven Daniel Garber (continued)

Facebook link: https://www.facebook.com/stevegarber.net

Litigation

In addition to suing Embry Riddle Aeronautical University in 2001, we found the following cases associated with Garber.

Steven Garber v. City of White Plains, Index No. 80050/2011, filed on March 9, 2011 in the Supreme Court of the State of New York, Westchester County. This was a Small Claims Assessment Review in which Garber asked for a reduction in the tax assessment in order to reduce his property taxes. At the time, the property taxes on his residence at 12 Cedarwood Road, White Plains, NY, were $18450 and Garber wanted that amount reduced to $12,100. On August 3, 2011, the property taxes were reduced by $3,325 for a total of $15,125 and the case was closed.

Garber, Steven D. vs. Garber, Andrea aka Lightman, Andrea, Index No. 0030481/2010, filed on April 6, 2011 in the Supreme Court of the State of New York, Westchester County. This was a contested divorce which finally settled on January 11, 2012; however, Ms. Lightman brought an action for contempt on April 9, 2014 which was decided on September 22, 2014. Documents pertaining to the dissolution of a marriage in New York State are not available on-line.

Kuhrt et al vs. Garber et ux, Case No. P-1300-cv-20020417, filed on June 20, 2002 in the Yavapi County (AZ) Superior Court. Kenneth Kuhrt and Regina Kuhrt sued Steven Garber and his wife, Andrea Lightman aka Andrea Garber. The case settled on October 16, 2002 and the case was dismissed on November 19, 2002, but no other information is available on-line. On-line access to case documents is available only for cases filed after July 1, 2010; however, a document retriever can be sent to the courthouse to obtain the case file.

We searched the indices of the Superior Court and Small Claims Courts of Connecticut, all counties, and found no cases associated with Steven Garber or his business.

Professional Licenses

We confirmed with the Connecticut State Department of Education that Steven D. Garber currently holds the following professional licenses.

Certificate Type:	Initial Educator
Status:	Active
Curriculum:	.041-Vocational Agriculture, Grades 7-12
Term of License:	April 1, 2020-March 31, 2023

Certificate Type:	Provisional Educator
Status:	Active
Curriculum:	.030-Biology, Grades 7-12
Term of License:	January 14, 2017-January 13, 2025

Certificate Type:	Provisional Educator
Status:	Active
Curriculum:	.034-General Science, Grades 7-12
Term of License:	January 14, 2017-January 13, 2025

In addition, we confirmed with the Occupational & Professional Licensing Division of the Connecticut Department of Consumer Protection that Steven Garber was previously licensed as a Home Inspector. License No. H0I.000069/1 was issued on July 1, 2013 and expired on June 30, 2015. The license was in Mr. Garber's name and at the time he was operating Garber Home Inspections, LLC.

Ex-Spouse

Andrea Shelley Lightman formerly known as Andrea S. Garber
Address: White Plains, NY 10605

* * * * *

Exhibit 2: *8 April 2024.   Email from DOJ to attorney Pete Sorenson – re FBI redaction policy.*

On Mon, Apr 8, 2024 at 12:35 PM Bartholomew, Tabitha (USADC) <Tabitha.Bartholomew@usdoj.gov> wrote:

Hi Pete –

Thanks for your message. Per our local rules, the only personal identifiers that must be redacted (unless the court orders otherwise) is SSNs, DOBs, names of minor children, and financial account numbers. I am going back to check our filing to see if any of these items were inadvertently left unredacted, but I note that Mr. Wilson's residence and unidentified "other private information" are not subject to our local rule. As there is no protective/seal order in the case, I am not certain of the basis for redacting information not subject to LCvR 5.4(d). Happy to discuss if I am missing something here, ahead of our next deadline.

On that subject, could you please let me know if I should indicate June 7th as plaintiff's reply date? I plan to file my motion by 5pm. Many thanks,

Best,

Tabitha Bartholomew | Assistant U.S. Attorney
(202) 252-2529 (o) | (202) 809-0411 (c)
Email: Tabitha.Bartholomew@usdoj.gov

* * * * *

Section II

Letter to AUSA Mr. John Moustakas - 2023

Section II

Correspondence between DOJ, Assistant United States Attorney (AUSA) Mr. John Moustakas and attorney Pete Sorenson – 2023

II-1. Letter to DOJ AUSA Mr John Moustakas: 11 July 2023

    a)   Letter from attorney Pete Sorenson outlining FBI abuse.

II-2. Email trail between DOJ AUSA Moustakas and Pete Sorenson: August 2023

    a)   Emails of 3-4 August 2023.

II-1   Letter to DOJ AUSA Mr John Moustakas: 11 July 2023

II-1a   Letter from Pete Sorenson to AUSA Mr. John Moustakas:

Letter to DOJ Assistant United States Attorney (AUSA) Mr John Moustakas from attorney Pete Sorenson outlining FBI abuse: 11 July 2023

* * * * *

Exhibit 3: *11 July 2023.   Letter from Attorney Pete Sorenson to AUSA Moustakas outlining FBI abuse.*

July 11, 2023 - 11:45 EDT

John Moustakas
Assistant United States Attorney
601 D Street, NW
Washington, DC 20530

(202) 252-2518

john.moustakas@usdoj.gov

Re: Wilson v FBI, Case No. 22-3062-ABJ (Plaintiff's Further Explanation of FBI Failures to Conduct an Adequate Search and Release Responsive Records

Dear Mr. Moustakas,

   Thank you for the opportunity to present information to you and the FBI issues concerning the search and withholding of records in this case.

We are, of course, very interested in what the FBI has done to search for and release records responsive to Mr. Wilson's Freedom of Information Act ("FOIA") Request No. 1548515-000. For ease of reference, Mr. Wilson's Request is attached as Exhibit 101.

We view this effort as a part of our good faith effort to meet and confer concerning issues that are likely to go to Court. We request the declaration of the FBI official who has searched for responsive records. Additionally, we would request a Vaughn Index, showing the precise records that have been withheld in full, or in part.

I.   Background on the Matter

John Wilson ("Plaintiff" or "Mr. Wilson") has submitted numerous Freedom of Information Act ("FOIA") Requests in hopes of receiving responsive records. As part of his Administrative Appeal, Mr. Wilson has provided a very thorough Declaration, dated 30 August 2022 that is part of the record of this case. This Declaration will be referenced throughout this letter.

Mr. Wilson is both an Australian and US citizen. He completed his MBA in 1993, at The Wharton School of the University of Pennsylvania. Following his graduation from Wharton, Mr. Wilson worked on Wall Street for a major British investment bank, S.G. Warburg (now part of UBS Warburg), as a securities analyst covering US mining companies. ¶ 16, p. 6 Declaration of Mr. John Wilson ("Wilson Decl."). On March 12, 1996, Mr. Wilson authored a report flagging concerns about NYSE listed Freeport McMoran Copper and Gold Inc. ("Freeport"), one of the world's largest and most valuable copper companies. ¶ 17, p. 6 Wilson Decl. At the time, Freeport owned the Grasberg copper and gold mine in West Papua, Indonesia and was under investigation by the US State Department following eyewitness allegations it was involved in the killing of Indigenous protesters and other human rights abuses. *Id.*

Following the publication of the report which touched on human rights issues and Freeport's loss of OPIC political risk insurance, Mr. Wilson received a backlash from Freeport, his employer S.G. Warburg and the FBI. ¶ 18, p. 7 Wilson Decl. In his Declaration, Mr. Wilson has stated that FBI and partnering agencies interfered in his career, professional, social and family networks, and attempted to entrap him in a failed drug sting, DUI and other offenses. ¶ 111, p. 52-53; appendix 16, p. 99 Wilson Decl. Mr. Wilson has stated that at least seven other professionals who made disclosures in the mid-1990s related to Freeport McMoran, including academics and journalists, have described a backlash, including being threatened, blacklisted, and in other ways intimidated for their work. ¶ appendix 21, p. 88-89 Wilson Decl. The experiences of these other professionals are detailed in Denise Leith's The Politics of Power Freeport in Suharto's Indonesia. *Id.*

Mr. Wilson further states that he gained detailed knowledge of the FBI's interest in him through his long-term relationship with Ms. Susan Holmes, who claimed to work undercover for the FBI in some capacity. Ms. Holmes "showed [Mr. Wilson] her black background FBI ID card," on multiple occasions. ¶ 12, p. 2 Wilson Decl.

During his time working in New York, through the work of Ms. Holmes, Mr. Wilson states he was associated with environmental activists in the United States. ¶ 12, p. 2 Wilson Decl. One such activist, Dave Foreman, was known for involvement with environmental extremism; Mr. Foreman founded *Earth First!* was a well-known advocate for the conservation of wildlife and wildlands, often encouraging other activists to utilize aggressive tactics in response to governmental actions that harmed the environment. ¶ 12, p. 3 Wilson Decl. Mr. Wilson believes that the interest that the FBI took in him from mid 1996 is confirmed and furthered by interactions and relationships in Mr. Wilson's personal life. ¶ 12, p. 2 Wilson Decl. According to Mr. Wilson, Susan Holmes, Mr. Wilson's long-term girlfriend from 1994 to 1997, informed Mr. Wilson on many occasions that she worked in some capacity for the FBI, and provided detailed of her work for the FBI including that she targeted environmental extremists in the eastern half of the USA that included the founder of Earth First! Dave Foreman, while her FBI counterpart in the western USA targeted the Unabomber. ¶ 79-80, p. 24-25 Wilson Decl.

In his Declaration, Mr. Wilson stated that in 1997, Mr. Wilson was invited by Ms. Holmes on a rafting trip down the Colorado River. ¶ 114, p. 53 Wilson Decl. Mr. Wilson, Ms. Holmes, and Mr. Foreman, were all present on this trip, along with around 20 other people, mainly high-profile US environmentalists, and including media personnel. *Id*. Mr. Wilson believes his inclusion on the trip and placement in Foreman's dory was part of the FBI ploy to portray Mr. Wilson as a close associate of Dave Foreman in order to create the appearance of the FBI's justified interest in Mr Wilson. *Id*.

Mr. Wilson has stated that in 2003, agent Holmes confirmed to Mr. Wilson the FBI's interest in him, and this was verified by agent Steve Garber in 2004. Furthermore, Mr. Wilson has stated that Ms. Holmes subjected him to an extended detailed interview in 2003. ¶ 33, p.11 Wilson Decl. Mr. Wilson states that he had multiple conversations and connections with Steve Garber, who began befriending him following publication of Mr. Wilson's March 12, 1996 work report, and subsequently in July 1997 he was introduced by the FBI through agent Holmes' work to Dave Foreman. ¶ 24, p. 8 Wilson Decl. Mr. Wilson has stated, in his Declaration, that in 2004 Steve Garber confirmed that Mr. Wilson was the subject of an FBI investigation as a result of Mr. Wilson's earlier report and work on Freeport McMoran. ¶ 12, p. 37 Wilson Decl.

Mr. Wilson has stated that since around mid-1996, Mr. Wilson has been targeted, investigated and interfered with, by the FBI based on disclosures from FBI agents Holmes and Garber, consistent with the timing of threats made to him and interference experienced. Attached to this letter is the Declaration of Mr. John Wilson dated 30 August 2022. Mr. Wilson now seeks records held by the FBI relating to him. He also seeks confirmation and an explanation from the FBI as to the reasons for, and instances in which, FBI operatives have targeted him.

II.   **FBI/DOJ Acting in "Bad Faith"**

Mr. Wilson is prepared to assert that the FBI is acting in "bad faith" for the following reasons:

1. The DOJ in 2006 acknowledged one of the people Mr Wilson named without specifying which (from the list of Holmes, Garber, Sutro) was an agent/employee of the FBI. Mr. Wilson has stated that this was acknowledged May 11, 2006, by Marvin Hernandez of the DOJ who confirmed in an email to John Wilson one of the individuals Wilson named was an employee of the FBI. While this was later retracted by Marvin Hernandez, Mr. Wilson believes that it warrants further explanation. Mr. Wilson states that he was advised by Marvin Hernandez that DOJ management had revoked Hernandez's authority to correspond with or talk with him about anything. Mr. Wilson believes and is prepared to state that Hernandez was correct in making his original disclosure to Wilson and his subsequent retraction is unreliable.

2. In his Declaration, Mr. Wilson has stated that the FBI has been disingenuous in repeatedly misclassifying the people named as FBI operatives, misclassifying them in categories of employees or special agents, but never including contractors or other categories of FBI operatives in their denials. John Wilson, Barry Fisher and others have made repeated requests and clarifications to the FBI/DOJ to correct their misclassifications and respond more broadly to the assertion the people named are operatives of the FBI working as contractors or in some other arrangement with the FBI. However, in a sign of bad faith, the FBI/DOJ have never responded to this request for a broader search and response.

Wilson is prepared to state that he has a long list of many letters, to and from the DOJ/FBI, where the FBI/DOJ repeatedly misclassified the FBI's association with Garber, Holmes and others to avoid answering the substance of his complaint. Wilson Decl., appendix Exhibit 8, p 155-158).

Mr. Wilson is prepared to allege that repeated misclassification is an act of "bad faith" on the part of the FBI/DOJ. Mr. Wilson believes that this is consistent with disclosures made to Wilson by FBI agent Holmes in 1997 concerning techniques used by the FBI/DOJ to evade transparency and accountability. The detailed disclosure from Holmes to Wilson is part of the transcript provided in Mr. Wilson's declaration.

Mr. Wilson is prepared to state that the FBI/DOJ has deliberately not responded to Wilson's allegations concerning Holmes, Garber and others as operatives of the FBI by misclassifying them as "employees" or "special agents," and thereby excluding other categories of FBI operatives from their response, because Wilson's allegations are substantially correct – these people are operatives of the FBI, performing duties at the official direction of the FBI.

Mr. Wilson, in future declarations, is prepared to state that the reason the FBI has evidently fastidiously and deliberately avoided responding to this is because the FBI is illegitimately targeting Wilson for his work on Freeport McMoran. As such, Mr. Wilson is prepared to state that the FBI is deliberately not reporting and releasing records/files Wilson is entitled to.

3.   Mr. Wilson has stated that FBI operatives Susan Holmes and Steve Garber disclosed to Wilson in 2003 and 2004 respectively, in NYC that Wilson was the target of an FBI campaign of intimidation, surveillance, and harassment in retribution for his work as a mining analyst in 1996 on Freeport McMoran. Garber's June 2004 disclosures, Wilson Decl. 162 to 185, p. 66-73 and September 2004 disclosures, Wilson Decl. 202-212, p.78-81 to Wilson of the FBI campaign targeting him.

4.   Mr. Wilson is prepared to state that the FBI, during the period in question, has a history of deliberately deceiving regulators. A newspaper article in the Sydney Morning Herald from August 25, 2002 titled "Court Reveals FBI Deceit" details FBI and DOJ deceit in falsifying more than 75 applications for search warrants and wiretaps in prior years. Wilson Decl., appendix Exhibit 5 p. 180-182.

5.   Mr. Wilson believes, and has stated, that the FBI collected distinct descriptions and scenarios from Wilson in the 2003 interrogation of Wilson by Holmes at Café Fiorello, NYC and engaged in subsequent efforts using those descriptions and scenarios to gaslight Wilson as a form of psychological attack. Mr. Wilson is prepared to state that this suggests the FBI is hiding and withholding records that Wilson is entitled to.

For the above reasons, Mr. Wilson believes the FBI/DOJ is acting in "bad faith" in denying Wilson his FBI records, in the FBI's claims of the adequacy of their search, and in their applied Exemptions.

III.   **FBI/DOJ Misapplication of FOIA Exemptions**

According to FBI operatives Holmes in 2003 and Garber in 2004 Wilson was targeted by the FBI in retribution for his work on US mining company Freeport McMoran in 1996. The FBI falsely associated Wilson as an associate of Dave Foreman, an environmental activist of interest to the FBI and co-founder of Earth First!, and a work subject of Holmes who targeted environmental extremists in the eastern half of the USA undercover for the FBI.

As such, reliance on the FOIA exemptions used by the FBI in relation to Mr Wilson dating back to 1996 are not justified.

IV.   **Assistance with Locating Responsive Records**

We have structured our letter to assist the FBI in finding additional responsive records. There are three major parts to this letter. Part (A) is a review of the records that we believe that the FBI has, but has not released or even searched for - these will be referred to as Documents not Searched. This is a partial list based on Mr Wilson's 30 August 2022 Declaration and other documents and is not intended to represent a full list of reports held by the FBI on Mr Wilson. Part (B) is documents withheld under an inappropriately applied exemption - these will be referred to as Documents Withheld Entirely. Part (C) is documents that were found and provided, but were partially or fully redacted - these will be referred to as Documents Redacted Inappropriately.

A. Documents Not Searched

We want to make you aware of some specific records that, while included within the four corners of Plaintiff's request, the FBI hasn't provided. For the following search terms, there has been no indication of any search by the FBI to find responsive records:

1) **Susan Holmes, or Susan Acker[son] Holmes,** and any positions that Ms. Holmes may have held with the FBI, as an operative, informant, independent contractor, any other relationship or capacity.

2) **Dr Steven Garber, or Steve Garber,** and any positions that Dr. Garber may have held with the FBI, as an operative, informant, independent contractor, any other relationship or capacity.

3) **Wilson and people operating on behalf of the FBI or other DOJ elements**: All records describing or documenting interactions therewith - in particular, Susan Ackerson Holmes and Steve Garber from 1993 to the present.

4) **Freeport McMoran Copper and Gold Inc.:** All records regarding Mr. Wilson and Freeport McMoran from March 1996 and after.

5) **S.G. Warburg and SBC Warburg - Wilson's work related to Freeport McMoran**: The following further explains documents and reasons why these records are believed to be held by the FBI. Mr. Wilson has stated, or is prepared to state, the following:

   a) <u>1996 - Analyst report on Freeport</u>: Mr. Wilson authored a work investment report on March 12, 1996 while working for S.G. Warburg as a mining analyst in NYC which was published and distributed to investors and to clients.
   b) <u>1996 – Freeport analyst briefing</u>: Notes of attendance for John Wilson in May 1996 to the analyst briefing at Freeport McMoran's HQ in New Orleans.
   c) <u>1996 - Threats in Freeport McMoran HQ</u>: Freeport McMoran's corporate headquarters in New Orleans: May 1996. Wilson was threatened in Freeport McMoran's boardroom alcove after he asked a question to the company's CEO and Chairman Jim Bob Moffett about the State Department interim report and ongoing investigation of eyewitness allegations concerning human rights abuses at Freeport McMoran's massive Grasberg copper and gold mine in West Papua, Indonesia.

Wilson's question was part of a work briefing Q&A with Freeport senior management and other Wall Street analysts in New Orleans in May 1996 after which Wilson was threatened in the boardroom alcove by an individual who appears to have been a federal agent. ¶ 19, p. 7 Wilson Decl.,

d) <u>C.2000-2003 - Operative connects to Freeport Chairman</u> - personal details: Early to mid 2000s: After moving back to Australia from the USA in 1999, on regular short trips back to the US Mr. Wilson was subjected to surveillance and interference. One example from around early to mid 2000s he stayed at the Road Runner backpackers in downtown Tucson, AZ where a federal agent or operative was placed in his bunk room and revealed many distinctive personal details about Mr. Wilson. The operative insisted Mr. Wilson tell him whenever Mr. Wilson logged into his email account on the public computer. This was the time before laptops and smartphones were ubiquitous, and Mr. Wilson would often use computer cafes or accommodation provided computers to login into email and other accounts. The operative was persistent and noticed when Mr. Wilson did login and came and sat next to him. The operative insisted he wanted to show Mr. Wilson something "cool" online. Mr. Wilson gave him the mouse and keyboard and the operative navigated onto the political donations website on the computer, the site where campaign finance contributions are reported and contributor details disclosed. The operative located Freeport CEO Jim Bob Moffet's name and home address and showed Mr. Wilson, asking him what he thought of the information and about Freeport.

e) <u>Circa 2003-2004 – Multiple FBI operatives question Wilson about Freeport</u>: Focused interest in Mr. Wilson's 1996 Freeport report from multiple people: FBI operatives Susan Holmes in 2003 and Steve Garber in 2004 asked Mr. Wilson multiple questions about his 12 March 1996 research report on Freeport McMoran. In addition, around June 2004, other operatives independently asked Mr. Wilson about Freeport McMoran and his 12 March 1996 report, namely Matthew Levey of Kroll Consulting, ¶ 32, p. 10 Wilson Decl., (who approached and retained Mr. Wilson to undertake consulting work looking into environmental and human rights issues with Freeport McMoran in West Papua, Indonesia), Julie Androshick and Kathleen Walton in NYC – making a total of at least 5 people to raise and ask Mr. Wilson about the report.

Reference to, or a record of, these encounters and conversations in Tucson, or other parts of the USA, including between Mr. Wilson and Holmes in NYC, would be held by the FBI.

6) **All records of encounters and discussions between John Wilson and Susan Holmes – from 1993 to present.**

Mr. Wilson has provided some background information on his relationship with Susan Holmes. As stated by Mr. Wilson in his Declaration:

a) Susan Holmes and John Wilson were in a long-term relationship from mid 1993 till late 1997 living and working in NYC. At the time, Susan Holmes was an environmental advocate and worked undercover as an operative of the FBI. John Wilson was employed in investment banking working in mining finance on Wall Street. ¶ 14-16, p. 6 Wilson Decl.

b) During the time they went out, Holmes made multiple detailed disclosures to Mr Wilson about her work for the FBI and showed Mr Wilson her FBI ID work card on 2 occasions. ¶ 15, p. 6 Wilson Decl. Mr. Wilson provides this information to establish that Holmes and Wilson were in an intimate relationship and Wilson, in 1993, was not at that time the subject of FBI interest and target of Holmes' FBI work; and that no FBI operative would make such detailed candid disclosures about their work to a target.

c) According to FBI disclosures to Wilson from Garber, ¶ 37, p. 12 Wilson Decl., in 2004 and Holmes, ¶ 28, p. 9 Wilson Decl., in 2003 (details below), Wilson came to the interest of the FBI after publication of his 12 March 1996 work report on Freeport McMoran.

d) Holmes was informed by the FBI of its interest in Wilson only at some point after they broke up in late 1997 at which time Holmes was falsely led to believe by the FBI that Wilson was of interest on account of his involvement in some non-disclosed criminal activity. ¶ 28, p. 9; 83, p.42 Wilson Decl.,

7) **Susan Holmes: NYC, June 1999 disclosure of existence of Wilson FBI file**

As stated by Mr. Wilson, in June 1999, in NYC, Holmes told Wilson she had seen his FBI file – "work files". ¶ 28, p. 9 Wilson Decl. During June 1999, before Wilson left the USA to move back to Australia for work, Holmes and he met up many times. *Id.* Holmes told him that "You would not believe how surprised I was when I saw your name on the work files." *Id.* Mr. Wilson states that alluding to "work" was a euphemism for the FBI. *Id.* Furthermore, Mr. Wilson states that while Holmes and Wilson were having dinner at the South Sea Port in NYC, Ms. Holmes said, "I'm not going to let them do this to you," referring to her knowledge of the FBI campaign against Wilson which she later disclosed to him in 2003, and agent Garber formally disclosed to Wilson in 2004. *Id.*

Mr. Wilson has stated that files concerning Wilson would be in existence as of, and prior to, Holmes' disclosure at this date in June 1999.

8) **Susan Holmes - FBI work visit to Australia for background on Wilson – C.2002**

Mr. Wilson has stated that, in 2002, an Australian agent, Mark Wilson, an IT specialist formerly of Avalon, Sydney, a former high school friend of Mr. Wilson, informed Mr Wilson around 2002 while they were walking down Kent St in Sydney that Susan Holmes was visiting Sydney for work and asked whether she had tried to contact him while she was in Sydney. ¶ 30, p. 10 Wilson Decl.

9) **Susan Holmes - NYC, Café Fiorello, Holmes interrogation of Wilson: - 2003**

   a) Mr. Wilson is prepared to, in future Declarations, state the following: Ms. Holmes subjected Mr. Wilson to a detailed interview at Café Fiorello, which she stated were on behalf of a US government agency, and included many private and confidential details and specific information about Mr. Wilson's life, events and people he knew from Australia, USA and elsewhere. The information she had included clear and distinct records of school and university reports, assignment grades, study group details, personal details of friends and associates of Mr Wilson all the way back to primary school, university and various career roles. It was evident from Holmes' immediate recall of physical details such as stature and height of these people and comments that she had met with some or all of the people she mentioned, including Ian Porter, Bruce Burgess, Mark Wilson, Chris Stenhouse, Scott Kirby, Scott Blamey, Charles Cropper, Andrew Martin, among others. She said things like "so and so didn't seem too bad," or "so and so was quite tall" conveying the impression she had met them. She spoke at length about Charles Cropper, his attempt at a legal career in London which was cut short, an announced family business contract with the US military and she insinuated his, and others, connection to an Australian intelligence agency – variously ASIS and ASIO. Holmes did not disclose the specific source of her information despite requests from Wilson to say where she had got so much information about him from.

   b) The FBI would hold references or records pertaining to Mr. Wilson of this information. Each of the matters raised below indicates the existence of an FBI file reference or record. The clear and details Holmes recounted included but were not limited to information regarding Wilson's background collected through her own work channels reaching back to early childhood. Through Holmes' revelations, the FBI had knowledge, for example, of specific content of various official private and state records pertaining to Wilson; and multiple personal and workplace events including details of people involved, locations and approximate dates. ¶ appendix 52-77, p. 96-102 Wilson Decl.

   c) As the disclosures continued over about a 2.5 hour dinner, Holmes' questions and statements revealed she knew many of the events and intricate details of Wilson's life, indicating the extensive resources, capability and reach of the organization required to prepare such a record, requiring the backing of a powerful institution. Eventually when asked by Wilson during the interview specifically who she was working for in doing this Holmes confirmed she was undertaking the work for a US government agency, understood to be the FBI. But she did not provide any further details when asked. ¶ appendix 53, p. 87 Wilson Decl.

d) Some of the things Holmes raised are listed below and speak to file references or records that would be held by, or accessible, to the FBI. The list is intended as a summary or to provide a flavor of the sort of information she had, with further **details available in Wilson's Attached Declaration and other notes available upon** request. ¶ appendix 52-77, p. 96-102 Wilson Decl.

e) Holmes raised details of Mr. Wilson's Freeport McMoran Report and his question to the CEO in 1996, and indicated his work on Freeport was the cause of the interference he had been facing. ¶ 34, p. 11; 133, p.59 Wilson Decl.

f) Holmes knew specific details of personal conversations Wilson had with current and former work peers and colleagues going back decades; ¶ appendix 52-77, p. 96-102 Wilson Decl.

g) Holmes knew details of phone calls Wilson had made on his private home phone;

h) Holmes knew specific details of Wilson's minor traffic offenses (dates, location, vehicle, offense) incurred in Australia, some going back decades; ¶ 34, p. 11; 84, p. 44 Wilson Decl.

i) Holmes knew intimate and private details of work records from various companies Wilson had worked at over the years, including details of colleagues and specific events and details of certain work assignments in each workplace.
She mentioned around 10 or 15 things from each workplace and in doing so disclosed she had access to Wilson's workplace records there and had information passed along from one or more of his work colleagues. The below is a partial list of matters she raised by way of example. ¶ appendix 72, p. 100-101 Wilson Decl. (Details in Mr. Wilson's 2003 interview transcript available on request).

DKB: This includes, but is not limited to, by way of example, private discussions at DKB in NYC around 1997 of hiring a Tibetan secretary, details of a work email someone had tampered with and sent Wilson, and an event involving HR in 1998.

BHP: She knew details of discussions at BHP Wilson was involved with around 1989, for example, of a pit wall technical issue, a mine site traffic accident involving contractors, a new type of gold mineralisation for the region Wilson was involved with identifying, a briefing on mine design parameters Wilson gave to the regional exploration team, details of a casual exchange in the men's room, details of a walk around Melbourne Wilson had with an Indigenous elder associated with a development project in the NT and private or confidential feedback and various other discussions or incidents concerning Wilson.

Warburg: She knew details of a specific equity research presentation Wilson made on Kaiser Aluminum at Warburg around 1995 and the details of a report of a merger assessment he made around the same time with details of accolades he received from sales and corporate finance teams, and details of a large block trade that went through on one of Wilson's companies in 1996.

Multiplex, Sydney: She knew specific details from Wilson's work at Multiplex in Sydney around 1999-2000 including specific content of conversations and events concerning Richard Maish of Warrama Consulting and Tony Cooper geologist with client firm Comet Resources who both inexplicably and falsely smeared and maligned Wilson. Holmes knew the details of private conversations between them and Wilson, and the repercussions and indicated they had been co-opted by an FBI partnering agency in Australia such as ASIO or ASIS, a missing work report from Wilson's desk, personal effects on Wilson's desk including the name of a public figure in a photo, and details of a search of legal records for a work matter.

j) Holmes knew specific records of Wilson's school and university grades – for example she mentioned Wilson's Wharton various levels of grade performance in finance, accounting and DSCI, good results of a year 7 term test in maths at high school; records of state tests; medical history; and camping records at US national parks – including specific details at Glacier National Park of a ranger discussion. This discussion with Wilson, for example, around 1998-99 involved a spring melt river crossing Wilson made to Red Feather Lake so that it turned out he was the first person to access a region of the park for that season. Holmes said it was a big deal as rangers were always meant to be the first in to camp sites each season and asked Wilson questions about how he had done it (due to his height at 6'4" fording the river was possible) and whether there had been any signs of anyone using the camp sites there, pointing out that fugitives sometimes hide in such places over winter. (Details in Mr. Wilson's 2003 interview transcript available on request)..

k) Holmes knew private, insider details of an outplacement service Wilson used after leaving DKB in 1998, including specifics of correspondence he sent out, details of a flashing red phone light at the 5 O'Clock Club psychologist Ellis Chase he had met with there, and a former Warburg salesperson he also met there. She knew the minute details of the office and some of the things that had transpired there, including that on one occasion Ellis Chase had left the room for a while during one of their consultations and Holmes inexplicably knew and asked about the fact he had left Wilson's personnel file on top of his desk. (Details in Mr. Wilson's 2003 interview transcript available on request).Holmes knew details of interviews in NYC Wilson had around 1998-99, including going three rounds for an investment banking role in which she knew details of the US firm and of people discussing such roles near him in the Utopia Diner the morning of the final interview – she knew the location, the content of their discussion, what stage Wilson was in the interview process; she knew the details of a Canadian bank equity analyst role he interviewed for around this time too, including specific details of the odd behavior of the interviewer who was on the phone with his wife. ¶ (Details in Mr. Wilson's 2003 interview transcript available on request).

10) **Susan Holmes: NYC, Café Fiorello, 2003 (cont.):**

Surveillance - FBI knowledge of Wilson's phone calls content, movements, and purchases

<u>Wiretaps C.1997-2000</u>

   a) Mr. Wilson states that Holmes had knowledge of specific phone calls Wilson had received or made from his home phone a year or two after they had split up. She mentioned at least 3 in detail during the NYC 2003 interrogation of Wilson, calls made or received on Wilson's home phone around 1998 and 1999, not just metadata – date, time, number, owner of the number – but she knew the content of the call –s well and went through each call with Wilson in explicit detail as to why the other person on the call asked or made certain specific comments, or reacted the way they did. ¶ appendix 67-70, p. 99-100 Wilson Decl.

   b) For example, Holmes asked: "You received a call from some girl asking you if you wanted to go out on a date. A trader. Who was she, how did you know her and why didn't you want to go out?" Wilson recalled the conversation from some years before and then answered. ¶ appendix 68, p. 100 Wilson Decl.

   c) Holmes then asked, "You made a call enquiring about possibly joining a yoga class. Who was the person you spoke to - did you know them? Why were they so rude?" It's true, the person was surprisingly rude. Wilson didn't know her and had never spoken to her before. "Who knows!?" he exclaimed. But again, Holmes knew the details of the call. ¶ appendix 69, p. 100 Wilson Decl.

   d) Holmes also knew the details of a call Wilson made around June 1999, shortly before he left the US permanently, in the context of "courtesy calls" he made to a few people he didn't know that well but had been loosely associated with to let them know he was leaving. Again, the call had had a distinctive quality, something unexpected, which Holmes was aware of and assumed that Wilson would likely remember as she made mention of it. ¶ appendix 70, p. 100 Wilson Decl.

Mr. Wilson has stated that these wiretaps occurred between 1997 and 2000.

FBI photos of John Wilson in Dave Foreman's dory 1997

e) During the NYC 2003 interrogation at Café Fiorello, she told Wilson that she has photos of him with David Foreman including the Colorado rafting trip in 1997 in her "work" files. ¶ 34, p. 11-12 Wilson Decl.

Wilson Credit/Debit card purchase records C.1997-1999

f) Mr. Wilson is prepared to state that Holmes knew details of electronic purchases made by Wilson including specific details of an artwork, a collage by Maggie Taylor titled "Don't pester me". She queried whether he had purchased it because of the title to which he said "No. I hadn't even noticed it till later." She mentioned a dental product he purchased around 1999, location and product description. Other purchase transactions she mentioned included a backpacking first aid kit he purchased out west and a set of native American cards – again she knew the details of both, location, date, cost, product description. ¶ 84, p. 44 Wilson Decl.

FBI Wilson human surveillance C.1997-1999

g) As one example of FBI human surveillance, Mr. Wilson is prepared to state that the FBI was aware of Wilson's movements. Holmes asked Wilson during the 2003 NYC interview about an incident on his walk to work at Warburg around late 1996-97, "One morning, directly across the street from the office as you waited to cross Park Avenue, you looked over the street very intently at the office. You seemed to be looking at the second story window. What were you looking at?" It was true, Wilson agreed he had done what she described, but how would she know that he wondered? Her question of course was very revealing, a fact she no doubt was aware of. "I was looking to see if I could see any of my colleagues in the corporate finance department. They typically worked back late at night and didn't normally start work till after 9am. I didn't expect to see any of them there yet," he replied. Wilson says he must have looked intently, as someone else had made a remark about his searching look that same morning in the office when he arrived at work. Now, years later Wilson asked Holmes how she knew this. But she gave no answer.

(A full transcript of the 2003 NYC Café Fiorello interrogation of Wilson by Holmes based on Wilson's detailed notes and recollections is available upon request).

11) Susan Holmes: NYC, Café Fiorello, 2003 (cont.): Gaslighting – psychological attack.

According to his Declaration, Mr. Wilson had a lengthy discussion with Susan Holmes at Cafe Fiorello in New York City in 2003. Mr. Wilson has informed me that he is prepared, if this matter goes to briefing, that the FBI has failed to search for and provide him with records regarding this conversation. To illustrate the memory of, and notes he has on, this conversation, Mr. Wilson will state under oath some of the more specific details of the conversation. These include:

a) During Holmes' questioning of Wilson she would periodically ask Wilson to describe specific scenarios about the future, imaginative events, and stories. When Wilson had no response to many of her requests, Holmes would implore him to "Say anything. It doesn't matter. Just say anything. Make it up," she said repeatedly.

b) In this vein, Holmes asked Wilson about 25 or 30 different topics and scenarios and Wilson gave brief answers, many of which subsequently were presented to Wilson in various ways at various times years later, gaslighting him as a form of psychological attack. Examples are below.

c) Rembrandt costume: Holmes asked: "What would be a weird or outlandish thing to wear to a business meeting, if you were to wear something to make fun of the person, to mock, or to show you weren't taking them seriously? Just come up with anything, it doesn't matter", she said. Wilson intentionally offered ridiculous and absurd imagery he said intrigued and to play along with what he found to be Holmes' odd conduct that evening. Wilson described a distinctive baggy Rembrandt type costume, oversize floppy shoes, a very baggy suit, loose white shirt with frills and a broad brimmed, large floppy hat.

d) In 2010, Wilson who owned a boutique equity research business at that time in Sydney, states he interviewed a well credentialed job applicant. In September, 2011 Wilson received an email from someone claiming to be a Wharton MBA who gave his name as Peter Benda. Wilson had never met him. Benda said he was involved with the mining industry and in Sydney from the USA on business. Benda, the applicant, arrived at Wilson's offices wearing the distinctive Rembrandt costume and turned out to be a fake candidate.

e) Mr. Wilson has stated that he had a second, similar experience. Holmes asked Wilson to imagine he was interviewing someone for some position in the future. "Describe something odd or unusual they might do while waiting for you," she requested. "It doesn't matter. Just say anything!" Perplexed and intrigued about Holmes' odd behavior and questions, Mr. Wilson states that he described someone in a dated business suit - Indiana Jones style, wearing a fedora or similar hat, reading an archaic technical book on maritime navigation for sailors, someone who was planning to undertake an epic round the world sailing odyssey.

f) Wilson further stated that, in 2010, Wilson, who owned a boutique equity research business at that time in Sydney, interviewed another well credentialed job applicant. The applicant, Fabian Babich, a well-known former Sydney equity analyst and someone who Wilson had been warned of by operative Andrew Martin now worked for an Australian intelligence agency, arrived at Wilson's offices an hour early and needed to wait. wearing the distinctive clothing described by Wilson to Holmes, and reading an archaic maritime navigation manual in prelude to an epic sailing trip he said he was planning. Again, Babich turned out to be a fake job applicant.

g) Additionally, Mr. Wilson has stated that Holmes asked, "Describe a trip you would like to do or wish you had done. Suggest anything; what souvenirs or artifacts would you have purchased?" Wilson suggested a trip into West Papua, Indonesia. "How would you do it, how would you organize it, what would you bring back? Just say anything," she encouraged. What was the point of all this Wilson wondered, sensing these were questions whose answers she didn't really care about. She repeated the refrain: "It doesn't matter, just say anything. Make it up."

h) Wilson described an epic trip into Papua New Guinea, a river trip up the Fly River, taking river boats or canoes to different villages along the river and returning with some crafts from the area. "What crafts?" she insisted. Wilson said jokingly "three massive totem poles". "How would you arrange or plan such an expedition?" she continued. Wilson replied, "I would ask a seller of PNG arts and crafts in the Sydney suburb of Paddington for their travel connections, agencies and ideas on where to go and how to proceed."

hh) C.2008, in Sydney, Graeme Jolly, a lawyer Wilson knew from years' ago bumped into Wilson in the street and invited him back to see his legal offices. There, three massive West Papuan totem poles lined the entrance and Jolly outlined where he had got them outlining all the same details Wilson had provided to Holmes in 2003, as well, Jolly's name and details had come up during the conversation. Jolly had no interest in adventure travel, no particular interest in indigenous communities and his story seemed fake to Wilson. Furthermore, Jolly was aware of recent private events concerning Wilson, suggesting he had been "gotten to" by a partnering Australian agency.

i) 4. House furniture: Continuing, Holmes asked Wilson, "What furniture would you like for your house one day?". Holmes pushed for answers. "Just say anything off the top of your head. It doesn't matter. Just make it up!" Wilson flippantly described some bizarre furniture using small off-cuts of wood or any available building material to make a rustic, hodge podge bar, stools and chairs of assembled and overlapping off-cuts in a basement room.

j) In 2005, Mr. Wilson was introduced to Clark and was shown his home renovation in Balmain, a suburb of Sydney. In his basement, he had the same bar, stools and chairs as Wilson had described to Holmes in 2003. Clark said he had personally made using offcuts. It was out of keeping with the rest of the furnishings in the house and style of the renovations. Clark's behavior was odd, he seemed uncertain, and his explanation seemed fake.

k) There were other scenarios Holmes asked Wilson to describe which over time were brought to the attention of Wilson in Sydney, or elsewhere, in the years after 2003. These included an introduction to a composer's musical composition; a short film synopsis, details of a kids' school skit, an outlandish party, distinct details of a eulogy for a parent, distinct odd comments at a high school reunion, distinctive odd tailor-made toys, and so on.

l) The creative scenarios on many of the topics Susan had asked Wilson to describe to her in 2003 gradually over the years appeared in his life. They manifested in unexpected places, at unexpected times, and with unexpected people. It soon became clear why she had kept pushing him for answers, no matter the content, saying, " It doesn't matter. Just say anything. Make it up."

Mr. Wilson believes that reference to, or a record of, these questions, answers and encounters would be held by the FBI.

(A full transcript of the 2003 NYC Café Fiorello interrogation of Wilson by Holmes based on Wilson's detailed notes and recollections is available upon request).

12) **FBI knowledge of photographs of Wilson NYC, C1996-97**

At dinner at Café Fiorello, NYC in 2003, Mr. Wilson has stated that Holmes disclosed to Wilson intimate details of various strange or unusual events targeting Wilson starting in 1996.

Mr. Wilson is prepared to state that the following are additional incidents where Mr. Wilson believes the FBI was photographing him:

a) Holmes asked Wilson whether he remembered the photographer at the crossing and the hotdog he ate at Papaya as he walked home from work at Warburg to his apartment on the Upper West Side one evening around late 1996. He did remember and she asked him to describe what happened, and what he thought was the reason for it.

b) Most evenings after work Wilson would take the subway home and walk several blocks along Amsterdam Avenue to 74th Street. One evening, around late 1996, he made an uncustomary stop at Gray's Papaya, a fast-food shop on the corner near the 72nd Street subway stop that sold hot dogs and fruit juices. It was the first time he had done so. He bought a hot dog with various accouterments and ate it nearby before continuing the short journey home. As he waited at the traffic lights to cross 72nd street at Amsterdam, he noticed a photographer on the other side of the pedestrian crossing wielding a camera with a massive telephoto lens, celebrity caliber, pointed directly at him.

c) Wilson recounted the details, paraphrasing, "The photographer was prominent, conspicuous, standing in front of the other pedestrians on the other side of the street and made no effort to conceal his activities. As I crossed, the camera followed me, and he moved too, always training the lens on me, finger on the trigger. He moved around, different angles, squatted, stood up, but all the time had the camera steadily locked on me. As I got closer I could see his finger clicking away. A few people crossing also looked at me to see if I was some sort of celebrity or public figure they might recognise. I was nothing of the sort. It was, of course, strange, why would he have singled me out to photograph? Who was this guy and why was he photographing me? But it was New York and easy to be blasé about such things. Strange but so what I thought. Maybe this guy was looking for a generic photo to illustrate some business or NYC story for some magazine or paper somewhere in the world – who knows and I didn't really care".

d) Wilson commented that in late1997 or early 1998, about a year or so later, he got a taste of how the photos might be used. But at the time he had no reason to suspect it was the FBI.

e) Again, paraphrasing Wilson: "After I had started a new job at DKB on Wall Street around late 1997, one of the young banker's made an off-the-cuff remark to me, as if randomly, about me taking a big bite into a hotdog in front of Grays Papaya on my way home from work. Very specific. But he didn't mention why he was saying this to me or where the information had come from. I asked him what he was talking about but he gave only a blank silence in return. It was a strange comment from him but without any further information forthcoming it was difficult to put it in context. There was no reason at that point for me to link it to the guy who had been photographing me; in any event, even if the photographer had been top of my mind, a year later, how or why could there be a link between him and this banker?"

f) But Holmes knew the details of it all, both the photographer and of the subsequent questions from the young banker. Holmes did not disclose to Wilson how she knew either the details or made the connection between these events.

g) Mr. Wilson believes that Holmes disclosure of these incidents could reasonably be concluded to be part of the FBI's intimidation and interference campaign as alleged.

(Reference to, or a record of, these encounters would be held by the FBI.]

(A full transcript of the 2003 NYC Café Fiorello interrogation of Wilson by Holmes based on Wilson's detailed notes and recollections is available upon request).

13) **Solicitation of Wilson by an undercover drug dealer, NYC, C.1996-97**

Mr. Wilson has stated that at dinner at Café Fiorello, NYC in 2003, Holmes disclosed to Wilson intimate details of various strange or unusual events targeting Wilson starting in 1996.

Wilson has stated he was targeted by an undercover drug dealer. ¶ appendix 66, p. 99 Wilson Decl. Mr. Wilson has explained this in his Declaration, and is prepared to state the following details in future Declarations.

a) During the 2003 NYC interview, Holmes asked Wilson about a drug dealer who solicited him as he walked home around late 1996-97, in the same period as the episode involving the photographer at the crossing, and around 6 months or so after his 12 March 1996 report on Freeport McMoran was distributed. ¶ 66, p. 99 Wilson Decl.

b) Holmes asked Wilson, "There was a black man on your street corner under your apartment you spoke to one evening on your way home from work. He was a dealer selling drugs. Do you remember?" she asked. "Yes," Wilson said. "Why did you make eye contact with him, then walk over and talk to him?" she asked.

c) Wilson explained, "I was curious. He was nearby on the edge of the footpath and as I walked by he indicated he had something to say. Inquisitive, I stopped and looked at him. He asked if I wanted to buy any drugs. I was surprised, I had never seen a drug dealer in the neighborhood and never been propositioned the whole time I had lived in New York. Except then. Mr. Wilson said cordially, "no thanks," and he nodded pleasantly in acceptance of my response as I moved on."

d) "Then a short while later you came back down and made eye contact again. Why?" she asked. Continuing, Wilson said, "I went home, changed into my running gear and a short while later emerged back out on the street headed to Central Park for a run. As I went by, I noticed he was still there. Again, he made focused eye contact and as I went by, he made me another offer. This time I kept going. He was never there again, nor was any other dealer, at least that I noticed."

e) "Didn't you think it was odd there was a drug dealer at your building, after all it wasn't a neighborhood that attracted street dealers," she said, referring to 74th Street and Amsterdam on the Upper West Side. She was right, Wilson was surprised. Again, she asked, "Why did you make eye contact with him? Were you tempted to buy marijuana from him?"

f) Holmes knew a lot about the interaction, all the nitty details, down to eye contact and conversation. Again, she refused to divulge the source of her information.

g) Wilson responded, "No, I didn't know what he was doing there. I was curious to find out what he wanted, and I thought he was the one that made eye contact. I had absolutely no interest in drugs, let alone buying any." Holmes knew Wilson had no interest in drugs, something she already knew well having gone out with him for 3 years. "Did it ever occur to you that the fellow might have been an undercover police officer?" she asked rhetorically.

h) Wilson only made the connection to a personally targeted law enforcement sting with Steve Garber's revelation to him in September 2004 at the Blue Water Grill in Union Square, NYC that Wilson was the target of an FBI campaign in retribution for his work on Freeport McMoran (details below).

i) Given Holmes detailed knowledge of the exchange with the dealer, it seems he was not just a random undercover drug dealer but targeting Wilson directly. The FBI, or partnering law enforcement agency, had evidently orchestrated the sting. Holmes' highly detailed knowledge suggested the FBI had debriefed directly with the dealer on his interaction with Wilson. Holmes' revealed familiarity with many of the details of the exchange Wilson had with him, Wilson's expression, aspects of the conversation, the fact that Wilson had held his eye contact.

j) The comments by Holmes were not those of a casual observer. The FBI it seems had tried to entice Wilson, directly or through association with a partnering agency, to do something illegal, buy drugs, presumably under video surveillance with a view to entrapping and prosecuting him. A prosecution for drugs would be a good way to destroy someone's professional career trajectory, certainly on Wall Street.

(Reference to, or a record of, these encounters would be held by the FBI.]

(A full transcript of the 2003 NYC Café Fiorello interrogation of Wilson by Holmes based on Wilson's detailed notes and recollections is available upon request).

14) **(a) Steve Garber – New York records: C.1996-1998**

Mr. Wilson has declared the following details:

a) Wilson has stated he initially regarded Garber as an acquaintance of Holmes, having met him through her at the Sierra Club, NYC in 1994, and later, that she worked with Garber undercover for the FBI. Between 1994 and mid-1996, Wilson saw Garber infrequently, around 2 or 3 times.

b) In Mid-1996, two years' after Wilson first met Garber, he started to make concerted effort to befriend him after publication of Wilson's report at SG Warburg and question to Freeport CEO Jim Bob Moffett that had touched on allegations of Freeport McMoran related killings in West Papua, Indonesia.

c) In this period Garber invited Wilson to join him on various day trips, and at one point around late 1997 surreptitiously entered his apartment building. ¶ 26, p. 8-9; 120, p. 55 Wilson Decl.

d) Late 1997; NYC - Garber intensified interactions with Wilson, making frequent calls and requests to Wilson to meet. He started calling Wilson regularly at work at DKB in 1997 and 1998. Garber invited Wilson for a walk to Central Park after work one day notionally for birdwatching (Garber was a PhD naturalist), around late 1997, after the Colorado rafting trip Holmes, Wilson and Foreman all attended that summer, Garber asked Wilson numerous questions that Wilson found ridiculous, strange and odd about big dams, dams like on the Colorado, and how Wilson thought they could be sabotaged or blown up. It was late afternoon, and Garber wanted to know how Wilson would blow up a dam wall. He knew Wilson had started his career as a mining engineer and had some work experience with explosives in the mining industry.

e) Wilson, in hindsight, believes Garber's intention in asking Wilson these things was to help the FBI construct a more elaborate illusion; misinformation about Wilson to justify their interference with him in relation to his work on Freeport McMoran..

f) As time passed and they were back on 72nd Street near the end of the walk, Garber's questions became increasingly ludicrous and personal – wanting to know if Wilson had ever thought about blowing up a dam, dreamt about it, what mining industry technology could be applied, even hypothetically, he prodded Wilson. He asked hopefully, "just imagine something," he said, "think of anything." It was hypothetical he said but he pushed for firm answers. Surely there was something Garber insisted eventually in frustration at Wilson having no answer. ¶ 130, p. 58 Wilson Decl.

g) Wilson said to Garber, "I assume you're trying to stop this sort of thing," to which Garber said "yes." He implored Wilson with words to the effect: "Just say anything, make it up, it doesn't matter." In frustration at Garber's doggedness, Wilson came up with a Walt Disney "Roadrunner" inspired cartoon slapstick scenario, knowing it to be a completely implausible response and told Garber as much, but Garber seemed satisfied and moved on. ¶ 131, p. 58-59 Wilson Decl.

h) Holmes in 2003, NYC at Café Fiorello during her interrogation of Wilson, asked Wilson if he remembered that walk with Garber in late 1997 and his questions about blowing up dams. Holmes reminded Wilson of the details of that conversation and how impractical the idea he had mentioned to Garber. She asked Wilson that evening in 2003 whether he couldn't imagine something more practical on the same topic of blowing up dams. It seemed to Wilson that the FBI had done some research following the 1997 discussion with Garber and determined conclusively the scenario "devised" was implausible and impractical. Given Holmes' familiarity with these details years later, it seems the FBI holds records, file notes, or similar on Wilson. ¶ 131, p. 58-59 Wilson Decl.

i) Reference to, or a record of, these encounters, phone calls and conversations between Wilson and Garber would be held by the FBI.

15) **(b) Steve Garber – Prescott, AZ records: 1999**

Mr. Wilson has stated that:

a) Around April or May 1999 Wilson visited Steve Garber, Andrea, his wife and their two kids at their home in Prescott, AZ for two days and nights with the intention of hiking with Steve. Steve had moved to Prescott from NYC several months before having taken a teaching job at

Embry Riddle Aeronautical University; he said he was lecturing on the local eco-system, a topic of interest to Wilson. Holmes warned Wilson not to visit Garber in the prior weeks saying it was a trap, but she didn't explain how. It turned out to be an FBI trap in which Garber secretly recorded two evenings of conversation amounting to several hours at Garber's home, led and manipulated by Garber. Garber repeatedly steered the conversation to material that could be embarrassing to Wilson or worse. ¶ 146-149, p. 62-63 Wilson Decl.

b) Garber asked Wilson about his previous romances, going through each in detail. He wanted to know if there had been anyone-night stands. He was evidently on a fishing expedition, looking for anything derogatory, any cheating, anything nasty or duplicitous, asking leading questions to identify anything that might be met with rebuke society wide, within certain circles, or from specific individuals should the information be distributed beyond their "private" talk. ¶ 152-156, p. 64-65 Wilson Decl.

c) He asked details about any drug and alcohol use, wanted to know if, or what occasions, Wilson may have drunk too much, who was there, dates, locations, occasions. He asked about whether Wilson had ever attended strip clubs, red light districts, prostitutes; anything that might be compromising, or embarrassing in certain company. With no apparent reason he asked if Wilson was gay, had ever had any gay relationships, or gay friends, and several other questions along similar lines. ¶ 153-154, p. 64 Wilson Decl.

d) Garber asked Wilson whether he had ever gone out with anyone underage. Garber was very persistent and asked about multiple possible scenarios, seeking disclosure or any ambiguity, where there may have been any uncertainty and therefor the possibility something might have occurred. For example, he wanted to know how Wilson could be certain someone might not have been underage, that they might have lied to him, deceived him about their age and so on. In hindsight, Garber sought to establish a link to a label, even if it was only a conceptually possibility; he seemed to be keen to smear Wilson of pedophilia, even the possibility of pedophilia – consistent with FBI approach to damage dissidents that Holmes disclosed to Wilson in 1996 (see 30 August 2022 Declaration). Garber was grasping and unsuccessful, and his intentions completely dishonorable. Reference to, or a record of, these encounters or conversations would be held by the FBI.¶ 153-154, p. 64 Wilson Decl.

e) Around 2004, NYC, Garber explained to Wilson in a separate conversation the FBI aims to tarnish dissidents and others, brand them with some undesirable social label. Anything that they could make stick, that would take a toll. In previous times it was homosexuality. Today it is pedophilia. Holmes similarly told Wilson in 1997 the FBI wants to brand dissidents as sex offenders, because if they end up in jail on some charge or other, they are treated especially harshly by the jail population which dislikes sex offenders. But anything would do, Garber said to Wilson taunting him, anything that goes against the grain, against social norms - substance abuse, deviant activity, sexual misconduct, anything the FBI could get its hands on.

f) Holmes in 2003, NYC asked Wilson if he remembered the 1999 conversation in Prescott in particular with Garber about JFK, Jnr. and then she continued to discuss specific details of it with Wilson. Given Holmes' familiarity with these details years later, Mr. Wilson believes that it seems the FBI holds records, file notes, or similar on Wilson. ¶ 152-156, p. 64-65; 131, p. 58 Wilson Decl. ¶ (Details in Mr. Wilson's 2003 interview transcript available on request).

g) Reference to, or a record of, these encounters and conversations between Wilson and Garber would be held by the FBI.

16) (c) Steve Garber - vicinity of Central Park and Upper West Side, NYC: C.June 2004

Mr. Wilson has stated that:

a) During a walk in Central Park and the Upper West Side, NYC around June 2004 with Wilson, Garber raised details of the strange things, job loss, interference and harassment Wilson had experienced since 1996. Garber was aware of the details of many of these events since publication of Wilson's 12 March 1996 report on Freeport McMoran and described specific details of the interference Wilson had faced to demonstrate his familiarity with it. He asked Wilson about the report and why he had written it. He focused for a while on Freeport McMoran and asked Wilson about the company, what he thought of it, and what he knew of the operations in West Papua, Indonesia. He asked Wilson about Jim Bob Moffett and what he thought of him whether he liked him. ¶ 181, p. 71-72 Wilson Decl.

b) During the walk Garber provided Wilson with intimate and confidential details concerning aspects of Holmes' FBI career, projects and trips, much of which Wilson was already familiar with from his discussion with Holmes years' earlier. ¶ 178, p. 70-71 Wilson Decl.

c) Garber continued talking, disclosing, closely scrutinizing Wilson's reactions as they walked and answering or deflecting Wilson's questions about how he knew these things. At one point when they were sitting down facing each other, Garber glanced down at the inside front of his open neck shirt as if making sure his wire device, if he was wearing one, was not visible to Wilson. ¶ 184, p. 72 Wilson Decl.

Arizona Wiretap

d) Garber raised details and events from Wilson's life – travel, work, personal places in the Southwest he had recently visited, descriptions of people he had met there, details of telephone calls Wilson made from the Roadrunner backpacker hostel in Tucson Wilson frequently stayed at. – knowledge of private matters consistent with an FBI investigation, people Wilson had chatted with from the landline there (before mobile phones were ubiquitous) and for what reason – such as arranging to meet people in Tucson for different outings or change of travel plans. Garber had no reason to know about these things, and provocatively asked Wilson questions taunting him about whether he thought the FBI might be interfering in his life.¶ 35, p. 12 Wilson Decl.

Reference to, or a record of, these encounters and conversations between Wilson and Garber would be held by the FBI.

17) **(d) Steve Garber – vicinity of Union Square, NYC: C.Sept 2004**

Mr. Wilson has stated that Steve Garver provided him information during a meeting the two had. The details, stated by Mr. Wilson, are as follows:

a) Wilson and Garber met again around September 2004 in NYC. They met one evening for a lecture at Tibet House and 15th Street, after which they walked to the Blue Water Grill nearby in Union Square, a seafood bar and restaurant Garber suggested. ¶ 37, p. 12-13 Wilson Decl.

b) While at the Blue Water Grill Wilson asked Garber about the Freeport McMoran – FBI connection insinuated by Garber to Wilson earlier that year when they met in June. Wilson asked Garber directly words to the effect, "You are doing this for the FBI right? To confirm, I've been targeted by the FBI on account of my Freeport McMoran work – is that right?" After a short pause without a response, Wilson repeated the question. He wanted to hear Garber reaffirm definitively that it was the FBI that wa– behind the att"ck on Wilson, and that their reason was Wilson's work on Freeport McMoran as Garber had insinuated. Wilson wanted to leave no doubt, no uncertainty about who Garber was working for and what the reason was for the interference Wilson had been subjected to. Garber nodded and said, nodding his head in agreement, "Yes." ¶ 37, p. 12-13 Wilson Decl.

c) Then, only partially joking, Wilson asked him if the FBI was planning to kill him now that he had made the connection to Freeport. Garber took the question seriously, saying, "No. They don't kill people for this sort of thing...though they might kill criminals," he added solemnly. ¶ 37, p. 12-13 Wilson Decl.

d) Mr. Wilson believes that reference to, or a record of, these encounters and conversations between Wilson and Garber would be held by the FBI.

[Refer to John Wilson 30 August 2022 Declaration, clauses 202-211].

18) **Colorado rafting trip 1997**

All records pertaining to John Wilson concerning his attendance, or discussions with Susan Holmes or Dave Foreman on a raft trip on the Colorado River in July or August 1997. [¶ 113-116, p. 53-54 Wilson Decl.]

19) **Dave Foreman - New York records – 1996-1999**

Background to Holmes, Foreman and the FBI, as stated by Mr. Wilson:

a) Between 1994 and 1997, when they were dating, Holmes told Wilson in response to a question he asked about her work interest in Dave Foreman, "The FBI is no longer concerned about Dave Foreman doing anything wrong, but it's the people attracted to him, associated with him, who they have the interest in. The people attracted to him are the people they are interested in." ¶ 80, p. 25 Wilson Decl.

b) Given her intense and unusual focus on what Wilson thought and knew of Foreman during her 2003, Café Fiorello, NYC interrogation of Wilson while she was evidently recording the conversation, this further substantiated disclosures from Holmes in 2003 and Garber in 2004 to Wilson that the FBI was attempting to set Wilson up by faking his association with Foreman as payback for his work on Freeport McMoran in 1996. To do this, the FBI utilized Holmes' work access to Foreman who she was targeting for the FBI as part of her work focused on environmental extremists and used her to make an introduction between Foreman and Wilson. ¶ 131-133, p. 58-59 Wilson Decl.

c) (Records of Holmes' discussion of Foreman with Wilson in 2003, NYC at Café Fiorello would be held by the FBI and should be provided to Wilson).

d) Late 1997; NYC - Susan Holmes, while they were still dating, asked Wilson to a lecture with her in NYC to hear David Foreman speak at which photos were evidently taken of Wilson in attendance. Holmes and Wilson arrived at and departed from the event together. However, Holmes explained to Wilson she was attending for work and needed to sit separate from him in the audience. This meant Wilson, if photographed as disclosed by Holmes, would have appeared to be attending on his own. Holmes also alluded to photos of Wilson attending the event during the 2003 NYC Café Fiorello interrogation. ¶ 26, p. 8-9 Wilson Decl.

(Mr. Wilson believes that photos and records of Wilson's attendance at the Foreman talk would be held by the FBI and should be provided to Wilson)

20) **Dave Foreman – Colorado River records, Utah and Arizona, circa July 1997**

a) Dave Foreman was investigated by the FBI for various alleged crimes involving what the FBI called "ecoterrorism" and what he called "monkeywrenching". Based on FBI disclosures by Holmes in 2003 and Garber in 2004 to Wilson, the

FBI endeavored to associate Wilson in close contact with David Foreman in mid-1997, a high-profile environmentalist and one of Holme's FBI work targets. Holme's was evidently an unwitting participant in this scheme at this time in 1997 and was used by the FBI to get to Wilson. ¶ 80, p. 25; 109, p. 52 Wilson Decl.

b) Mr. Wilson was invited by Ms. Holmes and went on a fully sponsored raft trip on the Colorado River for 3 days around July 1997 involving primarily about 20 high profile environmentalists and media representatives including Time Magazine ostensibly to advocate for removal of Glen Canyon dam and other dams blocking the Colorado River. ¶ 113-114, p. 53-54 Wilson Decl.

c) During the 2003 Café Fiorello, NYC interrogation of Wilson by Holmes, Holmes told Wilson that she has photos of him with David Foreman including the Colorado rafting trip in 1997 in her "work" FBI files. ¶ 34, p. 11-12; appendix 82, p. 103 Wilson Decl. These photos would be held by the FBI and should be provided to Wilson.

(For more details refer to ¶ 23-24, p. 8; 34, p. 11-12; 113-115, p. 53-54)

B. Documents Withheld Entirely

The FBI has withheld documents from Mr. Wilson, in particular, citing Exemption 7. Exemption 7 of the Freedom of Information Act protects six distinct categories of law enforcement information from disclosure, specifically: "records or information compiled for law enforcement purposes." 5 U.S.C § 552(b)(7) (2018).

In these circumstances, Exemption 7 does not apply. First, there has been no request for records relating to law enforcement techniques. Plaintiff has simply requested records involving himself, and others in his life. Additionally, all requested records date back to many years ago, with most requested records dating back to at least twenty years ago. Some of the individuals referenced have passed away - many others have aged and entered new phases of their lives. These individuals are no longer involved in the same careers, groups, and social circles. There is no tie between the requested documents and current law enforcement operations and purposes.

C. Documents Redacted Inappropriately

In previously provided documents, the FBI redacted documents inappropriately. These documents include:

1) FBI(22-cv-3062)-34
2) FBI(22-cv-3062)-35
3) FBI(22-cv-3062)-1
4) FBI(22-cv-3062)-2
5) FBI(22-cv-3062)-3
6) FBI(22-cv-3062)-5
7) FBI(22-cv-3062)-6
8) FBI(22-cv-3062)-10
9) FBI(22-cv-3062)-11
10) FBI(22-cv-3062)-12
11) FBI(22-cv-3062)-13
12) FBI(22-cv-3062)-14
13) FBI(22-cv-3062)-16
14) FBI(22-cv-3062)-17
15) FBI(22-cv-3062)-18
16) FBI(22-cv-3062)-19
17) FBI(22-cv-3062)-21

18) FBI(22-cv-3062)-22

19) FBI(22-cv-3062)-23

We look forward to working with you to resolve these search and exemption issues.

Best,

C. Peter Sorenson

Sorenson Law Office

Enclosure - Declaration of Mr. John Wilson notarized 30 August 2022

[Note: Minor edits made to the letter for corrections to typos, formatting and clarification.]

* * * * *

II-2   Email trail between DOJ AUSA Moustakas and Pete Sorenson: August 2023

II-2a   Email exchange: AUSA Mr. John Moustakas:

Select emails between DOJ, AUSA John Moustakas, AUSA Tabitha Bartholomew and attorney Pete Sorenson:

August 2023

"Is this the mining expert? Or it that L_____?" – AUSA Moustakas

Exhibit 4: *August 2023.   DOJ, AUSA Moustakas: "Is this the mining expert? Or it that L_____?"*

* * * * *

From: Peter Sorenson <peter@sorensonfoialaw.com>
Sent: Thursday, August 3, 2023 8:45 PM
To: Moustakas, John (USADC) <JMoustakas@usa.doj.gov>; Peter Sorenson <peter@sorensonfoialaw.com>
Subject: [EXTERNAL] Wilson v FBI, 22-3062-ABJ / response to P's 7-11-2023 letter

John,

We sent an extensive letter concerning the search concerns we have. We sent that letter to you on July 11, 2023 and we would like the FBI's response in a timely fashion.

[Redacted]

Pete

* * * * *

From: Moustakas, John (USADC) <John.Moustakas@usdoj.gov>
Sent: Thursday, August 3, 2023 9:23 PM
To: Peter Sorenson <peter@sorensonfoialaw.com>
Subject: [EXTERNAL] Wilson v FBI, 22-3062-ABJ / response to P's 7-11-2023 letter

Have you received any response whatever? Is the search completely done? Is this the mining expert? Or it that L_____?

* * * * *

From: Peter Sorenson <peter@sorensonfoialaw.com>
Sent: Friday, August 4, 2023 2:45 PM
To: Moustakas, John (USADC) <john.moustakas@usdoj.gov>; Peter Sorenson <peter@sorensonfoialaw.com>
Subject: Wilson v FBI, 22-3062-ABJ / response to P's 7-11-2023 letter

No response whatsoever. It's Wilson v FBI.

* * * * *

September 2023

From: Peter Sorenson <peter@sorensonfoialaw.com>
Sent: Tuesday, September 12, 2023 7:15 PM
To: Moustakas, John (USADC) <JMoustakas@usa.doj.gov>; Peter Sorenson <peter@sorensonfoialaw.com>
Subject: [EXTERNAL] Wilson v FBI - another proposed briefing schedule

September 12, 2023

John Moustakas
Assistant United States Attorney
District of Columbia
Washington, DC

re: Wilson v FBI, 22-3062-ABJ / proposed briefing schedule as of today

Dear John,

Thank you for your email about when the FBI would be able to file its Motion for Summary Judgment.

Concerning materials that Defendant will rely upon in support of its Motion for Summary Judgment, are you anticipating that a Vaughn Index and a Search Declaration will be provided? You only mentioned a Vaughn Index. Let me know. I have built additional time into Plaintiff's schedule (see below) for us to study your materials.

The current JSR requires:

"To facilitate their continued effort to productively meet and confer, the parties propose to submit their next Joint Status Report by no later than September 15. 2023."

Thank you for your work on this case. Now that we're moving forward with the briefing schedule, I might suggest we look at specific dates. You suggested, "contingent briefing schedule of 11/29/23 (D's MSJ), 12/28/23 (P's Cross MSJ and Opp to MSJ), 1/18/24 (D's Opp to Cross Mtn and Reply) and 2/1/24 (P/s Reply). . . "

After reviewing vacation and other briefing requirements of Plaintiff and Plaintiff's counsel, I am suggesting the following language and briefing dates:

"The parties met and conferred, and believe that setting a briefing schedule is appropriate at this time. Accordingly, the parties propose the following schedule:

a. Defendant's Motion for Summary Judgment due by December 20, 2023;

b. Plaintiff's Cross-Motion for Summary Judgment and Opposition due by January 24, 2024;

c. Defendant's Opposition and Reply due by February 14, 2024;

and

d. Plaintiff's Reply due by March 6, 2024."

Best,

Pete

C. Peter Sorenson

Sorenson Law LLC

* * * * *

On Tue, Sep 12, 2023 at 11:50 PM Moustakas, John (USADC) <John.Moustakas@usdoj.gov> wrote:

Ok. I would add that we are going to be producing a search declaration before the briefing schedule commences in an effort to see if the issues can be resolved or narrowed. Otherwise, I accept the date. Can you please file. Friday I am interviewing for another position to get the f out of here.

* * * * *

December 2023

On Wed, Dec 20, 2023 at 11:48 AM Moustakas, John (USADC) <John.Moustakas@usdoj.gov> wrote [sent to attorney Peter Sorenson]:

Pete:

Given my imminent departure (and all of the other deadline already in process that need to be completed), I am asking for your consent for a 60-day extension of time for the Gov't Opening Brief in this case so that an orderly transfer of the case may be made and new counsel given sufficient time to get up to speed. Please confirm your consent as I need to file in the next couple of hours.

Many thanks,

John Moustakas
Assistant United States Attorney

District of Columbia

601 D Street, N.W. | Room 7-1513

Washington, D.C. 20530

Office Tel (202) 252-2518

Mobile Tel (202) 815-8576

* * * * *

From: Peter Sorenson <peter@sorensonfoialaw.com>
Sent: Thursday, December 21, 2023 8:11 AM
To: Moustakas, John (USADC) <john.moustakas@usdoj.gov>; Peter Sorenson <peter@sorensonfoialaw.com>
Subject: Wilson v FBI 22-3062 (ABJ)- P Objects to D's Proposed MOET

December 20, 2023

Dear John,

Thank you for your email proposing a two month delay in the government's motion for summary judgment, due today. We negotiated this deadline several months ago, and it is disappointing that you chose the last day that your Motion was due to inform us that you would be leaving and that you would not be filing your motion for summary judgment.

On the day, this motion is due, you suggested that the government be allowed a 60 day extension and did not propose further dates for the other deadlines in the case.

After we asked about other dates, you gave us several dates.

As you know, our client is a resident of Australia and we have had no response to our email and phone call to him concerning your last minute MOET.

Concerning your plan to file the motion today, please indicate that at this time, plaintiff objects to your motion. We will provide our objection in writing at the appropriate time.

Please send us the name and contact information for the attorney that will be substituted for you.

Best,

Pete

C. Peter Sorenson

* * * * *

April 2024

From: Peter Sorenson <peter@sorensonfoialaw.com>
Sent: Thursday, April 4, 2024 10:43 AM
To: John Wilson <████████████████>; Peter Sorenson <peter@sorensonfoialaw.com>; Gianina Spano <gianina@sorensonfoialaw.com>
Subject: Wilson v FBI - update on defendant's MOET

John,

Today I spoke to AUSA Bartholomew, the latest AUSA on the case. As she mentioned she had a tree fall on her house and wants a Motion for Extension of Time (MOET).

She said she'd like our perspective (ie do we oppose or consent) by Friday, April 5. At this point we will likely accept May 10. We will know in about 24 hours.

Best,

Pete

C. Peter Sorenson

Senior Attorney

Sorenson Law LLC

c: Gianina Spano, Associate Attorney, Sorenson Law LLC

* * * * *

Section III

Declarations of John Wilson

Section III

Declarations of John Wilson

III-1. John Wilson Second Declaration - 2022

    a)   Notarized Declaration dated: 30 August 2022.

III-2. John Wilson First Declaration - 2021

    a)   Notarized Declaration dated: 16 November 2021. Appended to John Wilson's 30 August 2022 first Declaration is the second Declaration dated 16 November 2021.

III-1. John Wilson Second Declaration – 2022

III-1a   John Wilson's second Declaration: 30 August 2022

Second notarized Declaration of John Wilson 30 August 2022. (Includes John Wilson's first Declaration 16 November 2021 as an appendix).

* * * * *

Exhibit 5: *30 August 2022.   Second notarized Declaration of John Wilson.*

Declaration of John Wilson – August 2022

I, John Wilson, do hereby declare under penalties of perjury:

1. I submit this declaration based on my personal knowledge in support of my Administrative Appeal of FOIA Request FOIPA No. 1548515-000.

2. This Declaration is comprised of four major components:

    i. <u>Section 1:</u> Overview chronology

    ii. <u>Section 2:</u> Statement of John Wilson re Susan Holmes: Disclosures re Freeport McMoran and the FBI: 1994-2003

    iii. <u>Section 3:</u> Statement of John Wilson re Steve Garber: Disclosures re Freeport McMoran and the FBI: 1994-2004

    iv. <u>Section 4:</u> List of attachments, including Declaration made by the Plaintiff in relation to the FBI dated 16 November 2021; (The Declaration is attached hereto as <u>Exhibit 1</u>.)

3. I am the Plaintiff in this action.

4. I am a dual Australian and USA citizen.

5. I currently live in Sydney, Australia and have a small equity research consultancy business and live with my wife and two young children.

6. I have tertiary education with the following three degrees:

- The Wharton School, University of Pennsylvania, Philadelphia, PA , Master of Business Administration, (Dual Majors in Finance and Management), 1993
- University of Queensland, Australia, Bachelor of Arts (Major in Economics), 1989
- University of Sydney, Australia, Bachelor of Engineering (Major in Mining), 1986

7. After completing an MBA in 1993 at The Wharton School of the University of Pennsylvania, I moved to New York City and from late 1993 to June 1999 lived at 170 W 74th St, Apt 906, New York, NY 10023.

8. Dialogue reported in this affidavit may be paraphrasing of actual conversation.

9. Dialogue, statements and events reported in this Declaration may be selected for relevance and presented for clarity and brevity, but always to give a true and fair rendering of the situation. Additional details, in cases, may be available.

10. The term "agent" here is used in a generic sense, as in someone being an agent of someone else and does not intend any specific title.

11. Given all the information I have provided to the FBI/DOJ over the years in support of my FOIA requests, including all the disclosures to me by agents of the FBI concerning the agency's operation targeting me **– information set out here-in in greater detail and specificity than previously**, it is astonishing that the FBI cannot find records to release to me.

12. I believe that the FBI/DOJ is acting in **"Bad Faith"** as summarized below and set out in this Declaration, that it holds records on me it has not released, and is potentially shielding some or all of these records under falsely claimed FOIA exemptions. There are two for two reasons I believe the DOJ/FBI is acting in "bad faith":

One: Two operatives of the FBI, Susan Holmes (my then long-term girlfriend, who showed me her black background FBI ID card among other affirmations of her work with the FBI, that included pursuing environmental extremists in the eastern half of the USA) and Steven Garber (who confirmed his work for the FBI on my case), informed me, as set out in this Declaration, that I am the target of a vindictive FBI operation following a work report I published 12 March 1996 as a Wall Street analyst covering US mining company Freeport McMoran's activities in West Papua, Indonesia.

According to Holmes and Garber (as set out in the below Declaration), the FBI has falsified evidence to portray me as an environmental extremist, or similar, with an interest in blowing up dams, and having an association with people of interest to the FBI, including high profile environmentalist and co-founder of Earth First! David Foreman (one of Susan Holmes' FBI work targets). Holmes and Garber's disclosure of what amounts to a vindictive and "goofy" FBI setup is evidence of FBI "bad faith".

Two: The DOJ/FBI repeatedly refused to respond to my assertions, and letters from LA attorney Barry Fisher, that Holmes, Garber, and others named are operatives of the FBI, working as independent contractors, or similar, informants, etc. The DOJ/FBI has consistently sidestepped and never answered the claim Holmes and Garber, etc., are operatives.

The agency has repeatedly mis-represented my complaint, incorrectly claiming that Barry Fisher or I have asserted that Holmes, Garber, etc., are "employees" or "Special Agents" and then it denies they are either of these. Despite us pointing this out to the DOJ/FBI and providing clarification to them, they have never answered the claim that Holmes and Garber, etc., are operatives or informants, etc., of the FBI. (Refer to my 16 November 2021 Declaration, clauses 109-112 on pages 24-25; plus exhibit 8 – a letter from my LA attorney Barry Fisher, dated June 5, 2020 -this letter never received a substantive response.)

The DOJ/FBI's repeated refusal to investigate, or respond to, my assertions, and Barry Fisher's, that Holmes, Garber, etc work as independent contractors, or similar, informants, etc, for the FBI, is evidence of agency "bad faith".

The DOJ/FBI's lack of response to our claims is consistent with the strategy Susan Holmes described to me where the DOJ/FBI routinely misrepresent complaints in a deliberate attempt to delay or avert accountability – the strawman tactic. (Refer to my 16 November 2021 Declaration, clause 46).

13. I believe the FBI is operating in "bad faith", has created fake evidence intent to entangle me as an extremist as alluded to by two FBI operatives Holmes and Garber (in 2003 and 2004). In creating fake evidence, the FBI has compromised perfunctory oversight screening mechanisms which do not detect fraud on the part of the FBI and other intelligence or law enforcement agencies. Their methods effectively subvert the review process, presumably including efforts by former Australian Attorney General, Philip Ruddock (details in this Declaration).

I should have the ability to review and respond to the "evidence" held by the FBI on me, that others rely on, and I should have the right to challenge it with the assistance of an attorney.

Section 1

Overview chronology

14. **August-September 1994; NYC; I met Susan Holmes** around August-September 1994 while I was attending a Sierra Club volunteer meeting in NYC and we started dating shortly after. We dated from 1994 till late 1997.

    I met Steve Garber, through Susan Holmes, also at a Sierra Club volunteer event, sometime in the following month or so after meeting Holmes. After Holmes and I started dating, at Garber's instigation, Holmes, Garber and I went for a hike one weekend in Harriman State Park about 1 hours' drive from NYC.

15. **October 1994;** A week or two after this, around October 1994, **Susan Holmes showed me her black FBI ID card.** She told me she worked undercover for the FBI, and that Steve Garber did also. She said that the intention of our walk that day had been for Steve Garber to vet me for the FBI. Evidently, I passed the FBI's vetting.

16. **1994 to 1997; I worked for SG Warburg (and later SBC Warburg)** on Wall Street in New York as an equity analyst covering US listed mining companies. One of the companies I analyzed and published reports on for distribution to fund managers globally was U.S.-based and listed Freeport McMoran which through Freeport Indonesia controls the Grasberg Mine, one of the largest copper and gold mines in the world, situated in West Papua, Indonesia.

17. **March 12, 1996; Report on Freeport McMoran:** I authored a report (hereinafter the "Report") that flagged concerns about Freeport McMoran, which was under investigation by the United States Department of State following eyewitness reports of human rights abuses against indigenous protestors in the region of its massive Grasberg gold and copper mine in West Papua, Indonesia.

18. **March – April 1996; Initial repercussions:** After publication of my Report, Freeport McMoran did not extend the usual invitation to me to attend the annual analyst briefing in New Orleans that year, May 1996, an event I had attended previously and a must attend event for analysts that follow the company. I had to ask three times for an invitation before one was eventually extended. SG Warburg also, following publication of my Report, tightened its research publication protocols to require formal sign off by management prior to release of analyst reports.

19. **May 1996; Threatened in Freeport McMoran's boardroom alcove:** I asked questions about the investigation to the company's CEO and Chairman Jim Bob Moffett at an analyst briefing in New Orleans in May 1996 after which I was threatened in the boardroom alcove by an individual who appears to have been a federal agent. (Details in Declaration 16 November 2021).

20. **Mid 1996; Befriended by Garber:** In mid-1996, after my Report was published and my question to the Freeport McMoran CEO, Steve Garber started to make overtures to me. He began to show up at Sierra Club NYC chapter volunteer events I regularly attended with Susan. In contrast, I had virtually no contact with him in the prior 18 to 24 months or so since our walk in Harriman State Park in late 1994.

21. **Mid-late 1996 - 1999;** Garber invited me to join him on his regular walks after work in Central Park some days to observe different species of migratory birds that visited the large wooded park at different times of the year.

22. **August-September 1996; Irish folk concert and FBI work disclosures – targeting Dave Foreman:** Holmes used her FBI card in front of me around August-September 1996 to gain access past a security point at an Irish folk music concert in NYC. After the concert as we walked to my apartment she disclosed many facets of her FBI work to me. She disclosed aspects of her FBI work to me on numerous occasions during the time we dated from 1994 to

1997. Holmes said her focus for the FBI was on environmental extremists in the eastern half of the USA, though she did other things as well. She mentioned some of the people she targeted for the FBI, including David Foreman, a high profile environmentalist and author, co-founder of Earth First!, and the Wildlands Network. Holmes told me, "The FBI is no longer concerned about Dave Foreman doing anything wrong, but it's the people attracted to him, associated with him, who they have the interest in. The people attracted to him are the people they are interested in."

23. **March 1997; I left my job at Warburg** as a mining analyst and had 5 months off before getting another job, with time out West hiking, rafting and camping.

24. **Circa July 1997; Holmes invited me on a rafting trip down the Colorado River with Dave Foreman** and around 20 others. The FBI had evidently concocted a sting targeting me, and furtively utilising my relationship with Susan Holmes' and targeting her environmental work for the FBI, most notably Dave Foreman and a campaign to remove dams on the Colorado River (discussed in my Declaration 16 November 2021). The trip "organisers" allocated me to Dave Foreman's dory for the duration of the trip of several days. Associating me with David Foreman, a person targeted by the FBI, seemed to be a well-planned and deliberate tactic by the FBI to falsify evidence and subvert oversight screening mechanisms intended to stop agency corruption.

25. **Around August 1997; I started a new job as a mining analyst with Dresdner Kleinwort Benson (DKB)** back on Wall Street.

26. **Late 1997; NYC - Garber intensifies interactions with me. Conversations of explosives and more Dave Foreman photos.** At this time Steve Garber's interest in me stepped up a notch, with frequent calls and requests to meet up. He started calling me regularly at work at DKB in 1997 and 1998. At one point, he asked me numerous ridiculous, oddball questions about big dams, dams like on the Colorado, and how I thought they could be sabotaged or blown up. He

knew I had a degree in mining engineering and experience with explosives in mining operations. He invited me to join him on various day trips, and at one point surreptitiously entered my apartment building. Around this time, Susan Holmes, while we were still dating, asked me to a lecture with her in NYC to hear David Foreman speak at which photos were evidently taken of me attending.

27. **Circa April-May, 1999**: **Warning from Holmes; and a visit to Steve Garber in Prescott, AZ.** When I was out West, I stayed for 2 nights with Garber and his family after they had moved to Prescott, AZ around April-May 1999. Susan Holmes in the weeks before had strongly warned me against visiting him. It turned out to be a trap. Garber apparently recorded our conversation during both evenings I visited him. He covered off on a broad range of topics intended to embarrass, smear or indict, sounding me out on personal or sensitive questions which he evidently recorded for the FBI, something Susan later implied. This would explain why he had lied about the weekend hiking activities – to entice me to come stay. It also explained Susan's imploring me not to go.

28. **June 1999; NYC. Holmes - Wilson FBI "work files" disclosure.** During June, before I left the USA, Holmes and I met up many times when I was back in NYC. She told me that "You would not believe how surprised I was when I saw your name on the work files." Alluding to "work" was a euphemism for the FBI. We were having dinner at the South Sea Port in NYC and she added cryptically, "I'm not going to let them do this to you!". It didn't click with me at the time what she was talking about and she didn't elaborate when I asked her to explain.

29. **June 1999; I moved back to Sydney, Australia.**

30. **Around 2002 or early 2003**, Mark B. Wilson a former school friend from Sydney (an IT specialist, formerly of 50 Ruskin Rowe Avalon Beach, NSW 2107), who, upon information and belief, works for an Australian law enforcement or intelligence agency, one day in

Sydney said that Susan Holmes was in Sydney on a "work" trip and he asked me if she had made contact with me. Indeed, based on Susan Holmes' insights and statements to me in the 2003 interview, it seemed she had travelled to Australia and met with certain people I have known and that she raised in her 2003 NYC interview with me.

31. **Late 2002 or early 2003: Kroll Associates, Inc., NYC.** Around February 2003, Matthew Levey at Kroll offered me a monthly retainer as a part time consultant mining analyst – a role that went for 12-18 months. Levey had a background of working for the State Department and had tracked me down in Sydney in recent months through an introduction from a mutual friend and former work colleague. It was work I could do remotely, based in Sydney. He did not disclose who his client was, but suggested it was a large fund manager.

32. **Kroll had interest in what I knew of Freeport McMoran's operations in West Papua, Indonesia:** At one point, Matthew Levey asked me to use my network of contacts in the US environmental community to call around and speak with activists about environmental and human rights issues in the Indonesian mining sector. Most of my contacts I had met through Susan Holmes. A couple of large US mining companies were operating in the country – most notably Newmont and Freeport McMoran. Levey seemed particularly interested in my work on Freeport McMoran and he asked me in detail about a senior Freeport operation's executive at the Grasberg mine in West Papua, Indonesia – John Macken, including whether I knew him and had ever spoken with him.

33. **May 2003: Holmes subjected me to a series of intense questioning at Cafe Fiorello, 1900 Broadway in New York City** on or around Saturday, May 10th, 2003. During Holmes' invasive interview of me in NYC in 2003, she revealed she had accessed detailed information about my life, myriad specific details spanning many decades, continents, and people – consistent with the investigative reach and powers of the FBI. Indeed, she said that she was conducting the interview at the behest of a US government agency. (Transcript of the interview based on my recollections and notes is available upon request).

34. **In the 2003 interview, Holmes raised details of my Freeport McMoran Report and question to the CEO in 1996**, and insinuated my work on Freeport was the cause of the interference I had been facing. The details she recounted included but were not limited to information regarding: personal conversations with current and former peers and colleagues going back decades; phone calls I had made on my private home phone; minor traffic offenses incurred in Australia; work records from various companies I had worked at over the years; records of school and university grades; records of purchases; records of state tests; medical history; and camping records at US national parks. Holmes also inexplicably had knowledge of specific phone calls I had received or made from my home phone a year or two after we had split up. She mentioned 3 in detail, all around 1998 and 1999, not just meta data, date, time, number, owner of the number - but she knew the content of the call as well and went through each call with me in explicit detail. During the interview, she told me that she has photos of me with David Foreman including the Colorado rafting trip in 1997 in her "work" files. (Further details available in my Declaration of 16 November 2021).

35. **June 2004; Gaber insinuates FBI operation against me,** during a walk in Central Park and the Upper West Side in NYC around June 2004. He provided intimate details about aspects of Holmes' FBI career, projects and trips, much of which I was already somewhat familiar with. Steve raised details and events from my life - travel, work, personal - places in the Southwest I had visited, descriptions of people I had met there, details of private telephone calls from the Roadrunner backpacker hostel in Tucson I frequently stayed at – knowledge of private matters consistent with an FBI investigation. He had no reason to know about these things, and provocatively asked me leading questions, he seemed to be baiting and mocking me about whether I thought the FBI might be interfering in my life.

36. I did not at the time know how, or why, he had so much information about these many and seemingly disparate events in my life. He wouldn't answer the many questions I put back to him in response to his suggestion. I had done nothing illegal and I had no reason to suspect

the FBI would have any plausible concerns for taking an interest in me. The very notion seemed absurd.

37. **September 2004;** Steven Garber confirms to me that I am the subject of an FBI operation as a result of my work on Freeport McMoran in mid-1996 at the Blue Water Grill, Union Square in NYC. He verified and verbally confirmed to me in person that I had been subjected to ongoing FBI interference as payback for my work in 1996 as a Wall Street mining analyst critical of US mining company Freeport McMoran's actions in and around the company's massive Grasberg mine in West Papua, Indonesia. In response to my direct question, he affirmed that he worked for the FBI, and that I was being targeted as a result of my work. I asked him, seeking to confirm his insinuating remarks when we had met earlier in the year – around June 2004, in sum and substance, "You are doing this for the FBI right? To confirm, I've been targeted by the FBI on account of my Freeport McMoran work - is that right?" After a short pause without a response, I clearly and deliberately repeated the question. I wanted to hear him reaffirm that it was the FBI that was behind the attack on me, and that their reason was my Freeport work. I wanted to leave no doubt, no uncertainty about who he was working for and what the reason was for the interference I had been subjected to. Garber nodded and said, "Yes."

38. **2012-13;** Sydney; **I had three one-hour meetings with Philip Ruddock, the former Australian Attorney General** (from October 2003 to December 2007) in his electoral office around 2012-2013 on the topic of FBI, and Australian partnering agencies, interference with me on account of my Freeport McMoran work in 1996. During these meetings I named several Australian operatives who had interfered with me including: Robert Sadleir, son of former ASIO Director General David Sadleir (1992-96); Dr Trent Allen, Sydney, stockbroking analyst; Michael and Claudia Hackman, Sydney business people; Daniel Aitken, Central coast NSW and Boston, USA; Richard Kaan, Sydney, former business consultant; Fabian Babich, Sydney, former

stockbroking analyst. Some of these agents in Sydney have at various times from around 2005 indicated specific knowledge with clear and distinct details from the 2003 interview by Holmes, such as Fabian Babich. A number of agents have revealed detailed knowledge of aspects of the 2003 Holmes interview. Their knowledge is a further indication the FBI holds documents or records on me. The email is attached hereto as <u>Exhibit 3</u>.

39. **2004 – 2020: DOJ/FBI "bad faith": Plaintiff's correspondence since 2004 to DOJ, OIG, FBI met with evasive and/or highly qualified responses**

    The DOJ/OIG/FBI has never investigated the substance of my complaint concerning FBI misconduct. I have named certain FBI operatives, viz., Holmes, Garber and others, which I reported to them repeatedly over the years since 2004 to 2020. The DOJ/OIG/FBI has made only qualified denials and at no point have they provided a narrow, unqualified response.

40. Following Garber's confirmation to me in 2004 that I had faced long term interference from the FBI after publication of my work report on Freeport March 12, 1996 I made persistent and multiple requests for information from 2004 to 2020. Over the years since 2004 I have applied under FOIA to the DOJ/FBI; and I, or my LA attorney, Barry Fisher, have sent complaint letters to the DOJ, OIG and FBI and to some of my elected representatives. The most recent letter sent to the DOJ/OIG/FBI is dated June 5, 2020 by Barry Fisher to which there has been no substantive response (Attached hereto as <u>Exhibit 2.</u> This comprises a selection of correspondence: Letters from John Wilson dated March 9, 2015, and February 23, 2016. Letters from Barry Fisher dated June 24, 2016, and June 5, 2020. Letter from the OIG May 25, 2016. Letter from the FBI June 26, 2020).

41. The DOJ/FBI/OIG have repeatedly mischaracterized and then denied Holmes, Garber or others I named are "employees" or "Special Agents" of the FBI; but they have never responded to, or denied my claim, that they are operatives, contractors, "informants", or suchlike of the FBI.

42. The DOJ, OIG referred my complaint to the FBI, Inspection Division. The FBI (ISS) then tells me or the various correspondents something along the lines of, "Your letter was forwarded [by OIG] to the Internal Investigations Section (IIS), Inspection Division, for review. The IIS is the FBI entity that investigates complaints of criminality and/or serious misconduct against FBI employees." "ISS reviewed the merits of Mr Wilson's claims and determined his allegations did not warrant the initiation of an investigation inasmuch as the information reflected no allegations of misconduct by any FBI personnel." The FBI refused to investigate the substance of the complaint on the grounds its jurisdiction is "employees" of the FBI, and the people I named (Holmes, Garber, etc) are not employees. They do not state whether Holmes, Garber, etc., are some other category of FBI operative, such as independent contractors or such like. The FBI then stated it considers the matter closed, or that it will take no further action.
It seems that the various complaint letters we have sent have gone in a circle between OIG and the FBI, with neither office investigating and responding to the substance of the complaint.

43. The lack of response from the DOJ/OIG/FBI to these allegations is consistent with the agencies' stonewalling tactics Holmes described to me in 1996 in which the DOJ/FBI evade accountability. The motivation apparent in this evasive behaviour is an indication the FBI holds documents or records on me.

Section 2

Susan Holmes: Disclosures re Freeport McMoran and the FBI

1994-2003

Declaration of John Wilson (cont.) – FBI disclosures

I, John Wilson, do hereby declare under penalties of perjury:

44. I submit this declaration based on my personal knowledge in support of my Administrative Appeal of FOIA Request FOIPA No. 1548515-000.

45. I am the Plaintiff in this action.

46. I am a dual Australian and USA citizen.

47. I currently live in Sydney, Australia and have a small equity research consultancy business and live with my wife and two young children.

48. After completing an MBA in 1993 at The Wharton School of the University of Pennsylvania, I moved to New York City and from late 1993 to June 1999 lived at 170 W 74th St, Apt 906, New York, NY 10023.

49. Dialogue reported in this affidavit may be paraphrasing of actual conversation.

50. Dialogue, statements and events reported in this Declaration may be selected for relevance and presented for clarity and brevity, but always to give a true and fair rendering of the situation. Additional details, in cases, may be available.

51. The term "agent" is used here in a generic sense, as in someone being an agent of someone else and does not intend any specific title.

Background

52. Susan Holmes and I dated for three years from 1994 to 1997 when we each lived in New York City. Approximately one and a half years into the relationship the FBI purportedly commenced surveillance and interference operations against me when I worked as a Wall Street mining analyst for British investment bank SG Warburg after I published comments critical of US mining company Freeport McMoran in a 12 March 1996 report. Going by Holmes' detailed disclosures to me about her undercover work for the FBI, and related disclosures, it is evident that at the time of our meeting in 1994 I was not an FBI target.

53. From the subsequent actions and threats made against me, and disclosures from two FBI agents in 2003 and 2004 (Holmes and Garber) the FBI action against me commenced at some point after my 12 March 1996 report was published. (Select details are provided in my Declaration dated 16 November 2021).

54. During the 3 years from late 1994 to late 1997 that Holmes and I were in a relationship, Holmes revealed many details of her FBI work to me. Some of this information is indicated below:

Details of Holmes FBI work disclosures

55. On multiple occasions from 1994 to 1997 when Holmes and I dated, Holmes said she worked undercover for the FBI, and discussed details of her background with the FBI, her role, training, missions and other details.

56. In late 1994, a couple of months after Holmes and I started dating, Holmes, Steve Garber (who turned out to be an FBI colleague of Holmes), and I did a day hike one weekend in Harriman State Park, about 1 hour's drive from NYC. According to Holmes, the walk was arranged at Steve Garber's instigation.

57. **Late 1994, Holmes FBI ID card:** Not long after the walk with Steve Garber, around a week or two after, Susan Holmes showed me her FBI ID card at her apartment. It was a credit card sized plastic card with an image of her face on it and set on a blackish background. I vaguely recall it had the initials F.B.I in large font emblazoned across it and various other information written on it.

58. An hour or so later, Holmes and I had dinner at a neighbourhood restaurant near my place, Citrus, around 75th and Amsterdam. She confirmed that it was her FBI identity card, and that she worked under cover for the FBI. Holmes said the black background of the card was significant as it distinguished those like herself who worked on a contract type arrangement undercover for the FBI from the "regular" FBI employees, people who were employed by the FBI, who carried an FBI ID card with a white background.

59. She said she and Steve Garber worked together at the FBI. She said that the hike the three of us had taken together to Harriman State Park was intended as an opportunity for him to vet me for the FBI as her new boyfriend. On account of her six month posting to Ireland with the FBI in the recent past, and the fact I was a foreigner (though a dual US/Australian citizen) she said it was not unusual for an agent's new partners to be "checked out".

60. Holmes used her FBI ID card in my presence to get access through a security checkpoint in in 1996 to go backstage at an Irish folk music concert in NYC (more details about the ensuing events are included later in this disclosure).

61. I invited Holmes to Australia for 2 weeks over the Christmas holidays in 1994 when I returned to see my family. Holmes said she would need to get permission from the FBI before she could accept the invitation to travel overseas. She subsequently accepted and travelled with me to Australia.

62. Holmes told me she had an FBI issued handgun that she kept in her apartment. She told me she kept the gun and ammunition in separate places and the locations of each.

63. Holmes said she had received firearms training from the FBI and that she regularly attended FBI training programs at Quantico. In discussions with me about her firearms training she recounted that she did target practice and also was assessed in a mock crime scene shoot out on a purpose-built set. During the assessment, she explained, "good guys" and "bad guys" would momentarily appear on set and Holmes would have to assess whether to shoot or hold fire. She indicated that it was not very difficult, it was obvious who the "good guys" were, and there was lots of time to react before deciding what to do. The main thing was to not shoot a "good guy" - by which she meant an innocent bystander.

64. **Holmes' FBI branded clothing and wire recording device:** Holmes showed me her several FBI branded T shirts and other FBI branded clothing items at her apartment in NYC in 1997.

65. Holmes showed me her FBI wire device she used for covert recording, with two flexible wires, one running over each should and joining at the front. She used this on a sting with a suspected tree spiker from Missoula, Montana, James B. Bechtold who was visiting NYC one evening around 1995-96. Tree spiking is a technique used by activists to defend large tracks of forest from logging companies and involves driving metal or ceramic stakes into trees, dangerous to saw mills – potentially damaging saw blades and equipment, and then notifying the relevant companies of the fact to deter them. He was later convicted for tree spiking.

66. Holmes said to me a number of times, including in 1994-95 that as an environmentalist tactic, tree spiking, had been highly successful in protecting large tracts of wilderness.

67. Holmes explained she could access the FBI's internal computer systems from her laptop computer at home, via her keyboard (relatively new and cutting-edge technology at the time in the mid 1990s).

68. Holmes explained that she had no FBI recording devices for her home phone, but used her personal tape recorder, situated near the phone, to record any relevant conversations for the FBI. She said the standard of the recoding was not very high, but good enough.

69. **FBI "contractors" and "informants":** While notionally retained "full time" by the FBI, Holmes explained people retained as she was, hold their normal day jobs at the same time, if they have one, be it priest, nun, housewife, office worker, environmentalist, corporate exec, congressional staffer - whatever. She explained working for the FBI undercover is not their only job, but it only demands a small portion of their time. According to Holmes, people like her can technically be called upon at any time by the FBI, but in practice this usually doesn't happen and the role is more like being a "sleeper" agent, and generally not much is asked of them. It is mainly up to the individual to read briefs and accept the assignments they want. Holmes explained that there are a huge number of people whose services are retained and contracted by the FBI on the same basis as she was. The FBI gets powerful leverage through these extended networks. For example, a daily list of names and maybe photos are circulated to agents, asking if they know any of these persons and, if so, how and what do they know or what have they heard said about any of them? In this way a lot of information can generally be collected quickly and easily on anyone targeted. Despite having "day jobs", agents like Susan Holmes (and Steve Garber) are nonetheless available to attend the needs of the FBI when called upon. Operatives typically disclose their FBI role to their day job employer, and if the FBI needs the operative for an assignment, which may involve travel out of town, the FBI can liaise directly with their employer to negotiate time off. Susan said her employers generally accommodate the needs and requests of the FBI as the employer, while not feeling pressured as such, wants to stay in the good books with the FBI.

70. Holmes explained to me that a large number of people are contracted to, or retained by, the FBI. She said the FBI employs or retains the services of far more people than it reports on its website - the actual number, including the army of what can best be described as undercover operatives, agents like Susan and Steve, and informants and collaborators, is multiples of that she estimated, though she didn't know precise the number. The lowball count on the website is intended to deceive the public as to the extent of its operations.

For clarification, I asked her if she was classified as a "Special Agent" She said "No. That term has a specific meaning and not many people have it." Holmes went on to explain, as with herself, "contractors" are not engaged by the FBI as "employees" nor as "Special Agents". She mentioned the formal title, some arcane term which I no longer recall, and is not commonly known to the public. She added that such persons are deemed something like "independent contractors", some legal arrangement intended to create a separation from, and shield, the FBI from responsibility and liability.

71. According to Holmes, the contracts for these agents are renewed every 5 years, subject to satisfactory performance and passing a lie detector test.

72. Recruits come from a wide variety of backgrounds and locations across the country, are paid a low wage, but combined with their regular income, afford the agent a marginally elevated lifestyle. In the mid 1990s, when we were in a relationship, Susan said the FBI paid her about $60,000 per annum. She explained that around half was paid to her at the time and the other half was escrowed in an account which she could access when she retired or left the FBI, a measure intended to conceal her earnings so as not to alert targets to her otherwise unaccountable financial means.

73. Holmes said she paid tax on her FBI earnings. Special code numbers were used on her tax forms that signalled to the IRS that she received payments from the FBI. The IRS could then look up the relevant numbers and payment amounts to assess her overall tax liability. This way she didn't need to overtly declare the FBI income on her tax filings and potentially alert others who may come across her tax filings to her role with the FBI.

74. As an example of her work Holmes described to me a not uncommon FBI assignment she might typically self-select for. The FBI online "noticeboard" indicated a former criminal was coming to NY, provided his picture and the details of the train and what time he would arrive at Grand Central Station. Susan's task was to blend in with the crowd on the platform and wait for him. She said it is easy to pick people out from the crowd as they walked by on the

platform and when she saw him, she approached him and said something to him. It was nothing significant, just something he would recognise as personally meaningful. It was a way of letting him know he was under surveillance, even though there would be no further contact after that. Then she would disappear into the crowd and that was it. It was a "friendly" warning to the person not to do anything they might regret while in town. In response to my questions Holmes said it was straight forward to know when targeted people of interest were travelling - via credit card transactions, or other means too.

75. Holmes' mother discussed Holmes' role for the FBI with me during our visit to Holmes' family home in Detroit in 1997.

76. Holmes attempted to recruit me to the FBI in 1997. She pitched me in my apartment on 74th and Amsterdam Ave. one afternoon and strongly encouraged me to apply saying the FBI was looking to recruit more people who work on Wall Street.

77. I met other FBI agents in NYC through Holmes. These FBI operatives included Steve Garber, Stephen Chenault, and John Klotz, among others, who, along with Susan Holmes, were volunteers in the Sierra Club NYC Chapter.

78. **Circa Sept 1997; Holmes' discussion of engagement, FBI parent vetting, and invitation to Christmas:** Around September 1997 I received a call while at work at Dresdner Kleinwort Benson (DKB) from Susan Holmes in a joint call with her mother. Together they invited me to the family home in Detroit for Christmas that year. Shortly after, at dinner on the Upper West Side one evening, Susan addressed me saying, "I'm not getting any younger," (we were both in our mid 30s). We had spoken about marriage a number of times over the years and Susan said she was now ready. She explained that if we were going to do it, Christmas would be a good time to announce it and that I would need to have my parents review and sign certain security clearance forms that Susan would give me to pass on from her "work" (FBI). My parents needed to be vetted before Susan could get approval from the FBI to get

married to me, she explained. I asked her if she had brought the forms to dinner that night and she said no, but she would give them to me.

79. **Holmes' focus on environmental extremists and others for the FBI:** Holmes said her focus for the FBI was on environmental extremists in the eastern half - the eastern states of the USA, though she did other things for the FBI as well. She said she occasionally liaised with her counterparts who covered environmental extremists in the Western half of the US. She frequently mentioned the Unabomber case, a high-profile case at the time Holmes and I dated, though she said that was run by her colleagues in the Western half of the country and she wasn't directly involved with it.

80. **Holmes FBI focus on Dave Foreman:** During the time we were together, on several occasions Holmes mentioned a number of her FBI targets to me. These included:

   a) <u>David Foreman:</u> a high profile environmentalist and author, co-founder of Earth First!, and the Wildlands Network; was inspiration for Edward Abbey's environmental protest and sabotage classic novel "The Monkeywrench Gang"; he was investigated but cleared over his alleged involvement in a plot to blow up powerlines in Arizona; and served on the national board of the Sierra Club including for some of the time Holmes was on the board, among other notable roles he's had. In parts of the West especially, and in certain environmental circles, he is revered as a folk hero for his outspoken passion and maverick role in protecting the environment. At some stage, Holmes clarified the reason for the FBI's ongoing interest in Foreman, saying: "The FBI is no longer concerned about Dave Foreman doing anything wrong, but it's the people attracted to him, associated with him, who they are interested in. The people attached to him are the people they are interested in."

b) <u>Paul Winter:</u> a musician, Winter performed at the annual winter solstice concert at The Cathedral of St John the Divine in NYC, an event which Holmes and I attended a couple times. Holmes said that Winter had been a student environmental activist and leader at college many years before.

81. Holmes said the FBI facilitated her campaign for election to the Sierra Club board of directors. The FBI gave her strategic support, helped position her campaign and develop her pitch, among other things. She said the FBI wanted her to be on the board as a way for her to get closer to David Foreman, who was also on the board.

82. Holmes also mentioned David Brower, but not in the context of an FBI target. In the summer of 1997, when Holmes and I were in Detroit, she took me informally on an FBI work trip to meet with David Brower - the high profile and eminent "Archdruid" of the US environmental movement who was visiting nearby. She said the purpose of the meeting was to enhance her visibility and credibility with other members of the Sierra Club board, in particular with David Foreman, to make it easier to get closer to him. The purpose of having me join her in meeting Brower, she said, was that male bonding chemistry may help break the ice and ease the conversation for her with Brower. There may have been other intentions too on the part of the FBI, not disclosed to Holmes, given our long-term relationship. The FBI's secret meddling in my life, and by association in Susan Holmes' life, was purportedly underway following my 12 March 1996 report and questions to Freeport McMoran CEO and Chairman concerning alleged environmental and human rights abuses in West Papua, Indonesia, which was subject to an investigation by the state department. In the context of our meeting with David Brower who had campaigned with great influence over the decades against dams on the Colorado River, the FBI had evidently concocted a sting targeting me, furtively utilising my relationship with Susan Holmes' and her FBI work, to falsely portray me as a close associate of Dave Foreman and supposedly intent on removing dams on the Colorado River by illicit means (discussed in my Declaration 16 November 2021).

83. **Narrative: FBI disclosures by Holmes to me on a walk home: 1996, NYC**

[Note: The below narrative and recounted conversation excerpt is based on my notes and recollections. Dialogue may be paraphrasing of actual conversation.]

Irish folk music drug bust

The second time I saw Holmes' FBI card was around July or August 1996. This time I saw her use her card to get through security at an Irish folk music concert in Midtown she invited me to. After joining the FBI, about 7 years before at the age of 27, Holmes was posted, or seconded, to Ireland for 6 months where she had acquired a taste for the Irish culture, loved the Irish people, and as an avid harp player and singer enthusiastically followed the Irish music scene. She explained that being a young American woman active in the Irish music scene was good cover for seeking out extremists and other persons of potential interest. Closely associating herself with the high profile, popular Irish music scene, she said, afforded her good access to, and influence across, lots of groups in Ireland.

While in Ireland, she had been introduced to some influential and well known people in Irish folk music, including Mary Black, and met a host of accomplished but less established performers. Introductions were arranged through the FBI to help her establish the right cultural credentials and standing in her temporary role. A bit of name-dropping might go a long way in trying to infiltrate or establish a small network of informants she said.

Six or seven years later, she would still occasionally receive a call from a musician as they passed through the NYC. In mid 1996, one such associate, Mary someone, I forget her name now, was playing a gig at a large venue in Midtown. From recollection, the usual venue she would have played at is best known for hosting visiting religious leaders and speakers of all religious faiths, but at the time this was undergoing refurbishment, and so she played at an alternative venue. It was rather Spartan inside but provided a suitable ambience for high-spirited Celtic folk music.

Susan and Mary were ostensibly friends and Susan enjoyed going to her concerts. At Susan's invitation I went with her to attend one of Mary's New York shows, and after it finished Susan said she wanted to go backstage to say hello. However, it was not the social visit I was expecting. It turned out Susan had a different purpose in mind. She had been collecting evidence of Mary's use of soft drugs, something Mary was prosecuted for some months later. It was not Susan's usual work role she said, but was a "favour" from the FBI to NY police. NY police were cracking down on soft drug use and as Susan knew this particular target, Mary, from her time in Ireland, and had already gathered this sort of background material on her, she was able to help out.

At first, the security guard would not let us backstage and blocked the access ramp. Susan, in a manner that was slightly officious and out of character told me to wait behind her, out of the way. She pulled out a card from her wallet and handed it to him. He scrutinised it very intently in the dim light for a good 30 seconds. Satisfied, he waved us through. Susan sped past him, calling back to me impatiently, "Come on, hurry up!"

I followed her down a slightly inclined ramp at the edge of the stage to a locked door that led to a room underneath. Susan had moved quickly down the ramp, half skipping and hurried walking – she seemed to know the venue well. After trying the handle and realising the door was locked she knocked loudly, several times. I had continued at a more leisurely pace and when I caught up to her, I stood with her and waited as she knocked.

Still no answer. She knocked loudly again. We waited. On the third attempt, the door opened and we walked in. The room was silent, there was virtually nobody there. Mary stood in the middle of what was otherwise a very large empty room, maybe three or four other people around her. No big party, not even all the crew was there, let alone other fans.

Susan walked casually over to Mary and said "hello" and introduced me as her boyfriend. Mary stood there looking her in the face and replied caustically, "Hi Susan, your cover is blown." She looked at me and back to Susan to see what her response might be. Susan didn't say anything clear, mumbling something like "Oh" under her breath. It was clear Susan had been caught flat-footed and wasn't sure what to say or do next, as she later confided to me.

Mary broke the awkward silence explaining, "security called down, said there was an FBI agent coming down with a tall blonde guy". I was the only tall blonde guy in the room and Susan and I were the only two people to have come through the door. It was a decisive miscalculation. Susan's cover was indeed blown. A few awkward, stilted pleasantries were exchanged. Clearly Susan wasn't welcome there and we said goodnight after a minute or two and left.

There was no sign of drug use anywhere. As we walked back up the ramp and outside Susan said to me, "That could have been dangerous. I was expecting a lot more people to be there". I asked her what that whole exchange had been about, as she hadn't forewarned me at all. She simply said, "I really am an FBI agent. Mary has been using drugs after her shows and I have been collecting evidence."

In imploring me to accept her previous disclosures about details of her role with the FBI, including showing me her ID card, she was referring to the fact that I had never taken any interest in her FBI work. I had thought working for the FBI, doing the sorts of things the agency does, detracted from her, and I was in some kind of denial of it, hoping the issue would just go away. Susan was a graduate of Dartmouth College around 1984, intelligent, attractive, and sensitive. I felt association with a nefarious agency like the FBI detracted from the wholesome image and esteem with which I held her. It was anathema to me, indeed contradictory, that she would be drawn to work for an agency like the FBI.

I wondered what it was that she feared, what her aspirations were, what had made her susceptible to work for an agency whose domestic counterintelligence operations were akin to that of a secret-police? What was it that she felt she lacked? Indeed, as she explained it, an undercover career with the FBI was not her Plan A. However, a choppy start to professional life had drawn her to the relative stability of the work, which is why she interviewed at the age of 27 after one of her parents' friends gave her the agency pitch. As Susan explained, the agency doesn't pay well, but nor does it ask much of you. You can continue working your regular day job, if you have one, and through the FBI you can develop a second professional network. She also said that one of the other fringe benefits was getting some personal power over others. But one of the things she failed to mention was the job also comes with a second boss, one with unusual access to intrusive tools.

It was late, though a nice, warm summer evening and we decided to walk the 20 or 30 or so minutes back to my place from the concert. Not sure where to start, I asked "Why bother? Is it really worth the effort of pursuing a visiting Irish folk singer for using marihuana backstage. Does anybody really care?"

Susan said sternly, "Well, if they did it in private, maybe so, but they do it in the middle of big parties, right out in the open. They can't do that!"

"Haven't you tried marijuana?" I asked, surprised by her uncharacteristic, strident conservative viewpoint on a matter many regard as a liberal cause. I wondered where her staunch opposition came from.

"Yes, but not flaunting it out in the open. That's asking for trouble. It has to be policed." I couldn't disagree, but nor did I really sympathise.

"Isn't she your friend?" I asked naively.

"Yes, she is a friend, but it is really work. I don't like doing it ….." With that, the conversation trailed off into the summer evening, leaving only the sounds of our footsteps and the late night city traffic. [One evening, in the ensuing 12 months, Susan arrived at my apartment tired and with a migraine. She seemed dejected. I asked her what was wrong and she told me she had been in court all day for a hearing concerning Mary. Mary had been convicted of soft drug use in a Manhattan court and Susan had testified against her.]

On our walk from Midtown to the Upper West Side on that balmy New York evening in 1996, Susan told me a lot about her work at the FBI. We spoke for 15 or 20 minutes or so as we walked up Amsterdam Avenue, hand in hand.

Targeting environmental "extremists" for the FBI

As stated previously Susan's focus for the FBI was targeting environmental extremists. The Unabomber case was high profile at the time. I asked about it, but she said it was outside her jurisdiction. Her turf was the eastern half of the US. The Unabomber investigation was being handled out of the west. As she was in a confessional mood, I asked whether her main career was FBI agent. or environmentalist. She said she was FBI working as an environmentalist but really she was an environmentalist by empathy.

We chatted and walked in casual conversation, with me asking occasional questions as she talked about some of her assignments and other aspects of working for the FBI. A summary of some of that discussion follows.

She told me she had been invited to a party on Adnan Khashoggi's boat when in NY on one occasion. He was a Saudi Arabian businessman and international arms trader implicated in money laundering and the 80's US Iran-contra scandal. Susan was not the only FBI agent in attendance, a handful of other agents had been "invited" to the party as well, mostly young women, she said. The FBI operatives had just shown up as regular guests, mingled, but none of them handed out their "day job" cards; if asked for a card they replied they didn't have one with them, she said. In response to my questions she explained that they did not plant bugs on the boat, that was too risky, they might be found, but they did take note of who was there.

On another occasion, she ventured that she was one of about 30 young female FBI agents in a bar stake out where the son of a crime group target had arranged to meet friends. The FBI knew this through prior surveillance. The intention was that one of the women might successfully bait and strike up an ongoing relationship with the son, as a way of then getting an FBI introduction to the father and the family home. This particular "honey trap" was successful.

Honey traps

On a personal level, the FBI is evidently a job description with a broad remit! Training includes "kissing practice" classes and other teachings about sexual activities that are used to arouse and seduce in order to deceive and compromise their targets – the training of so called "honey traps". Female agents practice undressing in erotic ways, artful, coquettish moves to entice, to pull their targets in, increasing their desire, how to seduce their targets, slowly pulling their tops up over the top of their head to reveal a full profile of their chest, frontal rubbing of her pelvis against a male, and other seductive and erotic moves. Susan explained and demonstrated the movements for illustration. The endgame can be to sleep with the target to compromise them or someone associated with them. The sex is covertly recorded or videoed for the state files.

I learnt some interesting things about the FBI, not only from Susan, but also from Steve Garber and the many other agents I subsequently met over the years. Baiting with "honey traps" is de rigour as one agent told me later, saying, "It is much more common than you think."

Dissidents

Susan and I continued our conversation as we walked. She said that agents spend a lot of time targeting dissidents. I didn't have a clue about such things in the USA. Over the years I had read things about secret police agencies: the Stasi in Eastern Europe, Russia, China, the Nazi's in WWII; I'd had a summer job in Chile when Pinochet was in power terrorising civil society opponents and critics.

"What does the FBI do to them - maybe in extreme cases kill them, jail them?" I asked thinking of the Gulags.

"No," she said. "Mostly they smear them, try to marginalise them, get them blacklisted, turn their personal life upside down to the extent they can."

"How do they do that?" I asked, mindful that we lived in a democracy with purported separation of powers, with supposedly independent oversight and judiciary.

"They find out who their friends and family members are, where they hang out, what they do, and get them to help; to say and do things to them; to attack them verbally and un-befriend them."

"How do they do this?" I again asked. "How can you recruit someone's friend or family and expect them to turn against the person just because you ask them to?"

"There are ways. They generally get the targeted person to say something negative about another person; reveal something, say something that is not nice about them. Whether it is true or not doesn't matter. The FBI secretly records it then shows it, or plays it, to that person to get them onside," she explained.

"And then what?" I asked. "That doesn't sound like much."

"They will video the person doing something sexual. In their bedroom having sex with someone, or masturbating, or whatever and then maybe play it to their friends who have been recruited by the FBI," she said.

"Don't their friend's tell them?" I asked.

"No," she said. "They have been recruited by the FBI, have security clearance and the information they are receiving is classified. They are not allowed to tell. If they did, they would get into serious trouble," she said.

"Well, doesn't this turn people off the FBI, seeing this sort of stuff, seeing the sort of things they do?" I said, a bit surprised.

"No," she said. "In fact many people like to see it. It's part of the payback of the friend who said something bad about them. And it makes it harder for them to do business if they've shown their business colleagues."

"Don't business people just ignore it and get on with things?"

"No," she said. "Once the material had been viewed, whatever its contents, it's very hard to hold that person with the same level of respect or maintain the same level of rapport that had existed before," she explained. "It's very hard to treat someone normally when you've seen them doing this stuff. It's very hard not to let it show in some way."

"Don't tell me anything you shouldn't. I don't want you to tell me anything that might get you in trouble," I said, wondering whether she might be saying more than she ought to be about her work.

"I won't. Don't worry, it's OK," she said.

FBI oversight

Susan's discussion was of a general nature. She once said the friends and family she disclosed her FBI roles to had always shown great interest in her work there. They were intrigued and curious she said and she wondered why I was not more so. My initial instinct had been to run the night she had first told me when we were reading the menus in Citrus on the Upper West Side near my apartment. It was shortly after we had started going out in 1994, and she had shown me her black FBI identification card. I had shown no interest then, but now, given the events of this evening, my interest was piqued.

And so I continued.

"Don't the people they target complain? Aren't there oversight mechanisms that stop this sort of thing from happening?" I asked incredulous at what she had described. It was totalitarian sounding, like something from the Stasi, or out of Orwell.

"Yes. People complain once they realise that the FBI is involved. But a lot of people don't realise, they don't know that something has happened because of the FBI. If they do find out and complain, the FBI delays responding and then misrepresents the complaint they are responding to, when they do eventually respond," she said.

"Don't the people targeted just complain again, or get a lawyer to complain?" I continued.

"Yes. Even so, there are all sorts of ways the FBI can delay responding and mis-frame the complaint," she said matter of fact.

"Like what sort of things can they do?" I asked

"The DOJ and FBI can mis-frame complaints saying the people someone complains about do not work for the FBI, that they are not "employees" for example, when in fact they are contractors. But the FBI or DOJ does not tell the person making the complaint that this is the case and continues to make only limited denials hoping the person making the complaint doesn't notice. In this way the FBI and DOJ refuse to engage with the complaint, or delay doing so, and evade accountability," she said.

"So the person never gets an answer?"

"They normally get one. Eventually. But it might take a very long time," she said.

"So what happens in the meantime. Does the FBI destroy the evidence of their own wrong doing?" I queried.

"No, they are not meant to. Though I suppose they could. But years pass and people forget or information is lost and eventually statutes of limitation kick in," she offered ambivalently, obviously not herself satisfied about the integrity of the process.

Fishing expeditions

"What else does the FBI do to them?" I asked, assuming there must be a lot of things they could do to their targets, things they wouldn't like.

"They try not to do physical things, not leave a physical trail to get the police and courts involved," she said.

"Another thing they do is smear them with sexual assault or complaints of abuse. They undertake a major fishing expedition," she continued. "They look back to peoples' college days - they almost always find something. And if they don't find it there they look wider, they go back through the teen and tween years if need be till something comes up. Somewhere they over stepped the mark, it doesn't need to be rape or anything like that, it doesn't matter how innocent or slight, so long as it was not welcome or out of line. The FBI can find something like this on virtually all men, and even many women."

"You would be surprised," she said continuing, again matter of fact. "Every male has something. The FBI always finds something. They even find something on a lot of females. If it is not in college, they look closely in later years' and also go back to high school years or earlier. They recruit people close to the person in that time period or place they are looking at, find the people and ask them the questions. "Did so and so ever do anything inappropriate to you. Just curious. I heard something, I don't know if it is true, and am just asking around. It doesn't matter, they eventually find someone where something has happened. They can get someone to say something. Anything at all that could be construed as sexual assault; an unwanted kiss, an inappropriate hug, or something more."

"But does this work? What does this do? Does anybody listen or care if it is a minor thing? High school, or puberty age, everyone seems a bit awkward, unsure, looking for boundaries," I responded trying to understand what damage the FBI could do with this tactic.

"Yes. You can always get someone to listen, someone they [the dissident] cares about. It always has an impact somewhere, no matter how small." Susan continued. "If it is college age, 18 or over, it is sexual assault. It is relatively easy to get someone to make a formal complaint about it to the police, even years later. They just encourage them to do it for the record. If it is a relatively minor thing, or at a younger age in high school, or even primary school, it still takes a toll on the target. There can still be a police report, the information leaked or given to people around the target to embarrass them. It still takes a toll, no matter what. But if it is serious, the person could go to jail. If they have done something wrong, they will get them a long sentence, the harshest punishment permissible. And sex offenders are treated as the scum of the scum in jail and prison life is very unsafe and hard for them."

"If they find something to prosecute them for and the matter goes to court, the FBI gets a reporter friendly to the agency to cover the case, someone they are close to, maybe on the payroll, maybe gets preferential treatment from the FBI. They put it in the newspaper, whatever newspapers they can get to carry it, local, state, national - whatever level of coverage they can get for it. It doesn't matter. They try to destroy them in the public eye."

"They try to make the target look like a monster. Find out what they have done to hurt others. They will find out if they ever killed an animal, a bug or insect, did something cruel to someone or something then portray them as sadistic or cruel. Often it is only things they may have done as a young child, an infant, killing ants, pulling wings off flies. Wantonly killing or hurting something. Everyone has done it, but it can be painted to make the target look like a monster. It's not hard to do. It's easy to find out and virtually everyone did something when they were very young to insects or some little creature. They use whatever they have covertly recorded them saying, make them appear evil, describe the person to make them appear like a hideous monster. Didn't you ever kill or hurt something?" She continued.

"Like swatted a fly or mosquito?" I asked for clarification.

"No. Pretty much everyone has done that. When you were a young child, a toddler even. Did you ever pull wings off a bug, stamp all over a line of ants? As a little kid, you probably did, most people have!" she said. Nothing came to mind and I didn't respond.

She continued. "They will try and make the person think they have done something they never did. Hurt someone, done something, have others react to them as though they did something deplorable, despicable."

"It's a big fishing expedition," I remarked indignantly.

"Yes. A witch hunt," Susan confirmed.

"But how do they get away with that," I challenged circling back. "Doesn't the FBI get accused of bullying or unethical behaviour? Isn't there some kind of oversight process?"

"Yes, but it doesn't stop it. So it doesn't look like a witch hunt, the FBI waits till they find some legitimate reason to investigate the target, or can manufacture a reasonably plausible reason, to justify their investigation, make it less obvious that it is vindictive," she said. "Judges don't like witch hunts, and there is a backlash against the agency if this is what it looks like. So they conceal it, try to make it appear legitimate, like a discovery that came out of a routine, impartial investigation. Not a stitch-up. But some judges are motivated by ambition, not integrity, and are complicit."

"How do they tell judges what to say or do?" I asked sceptically wondering if they too were part of this conspiracy to undermine democratic protections and justice.

"Not exactly. You can't tell judges what to say or do, but they can be given certain incentives to do what the agency wants," she said cryptically.

"What do you mean?"

"They are supported by the agency for promotions, appointments or honours, that sort of thing, or something else they want, not a direct bribe or quid pro quo, more subtle than that, but they get rewarded if they do what is wanted. I don't really know exactly how it works, but the agencies have undisclosed access and influence over many decision makers, decision makers whom they can influence in favour of one candidate, or in cases may themselves be agents - one of the hidden army of agents the US has positioned throughout civil society," she said matter of factly. "Once they have identified judges whose integrity is malleable, they work with them whenever they can. They can't select their judge for a particular case, but they can direct the case to a jurisdiction where they have someone groomed and ready, increasing the chances, at least, that they will have one of "their" people appointed to the case."

More on Dissidents

The traffic was thin. Even in Manhattan main streets can be quiet late at night. The occasional car went by, yellow cabs, but it was as if we had the street to ourselves.

"What did these people do?" I asked moving back to the topic of dissidents. "What makes them dissidents?"

She answered, "Dissidents oppose the system. They are bellicose, obnoxious, outspoken, persistent critics and troublemakers who fight against what America stands for. They try to undo all the good things about our country."

"Do they target environmentalists?" I said provocatively, asking for clarification. "What makes someone these things?" I asked. What about free speech for example, or "wholesome disruption", the civil rights movement - was everyone a dissident who disagreed with or was opposed to elements of some government policy, inequality or systemic discrimination?

"No, not environmentalist!" she said. "Dissidents are not good people. They are really bad people. And they deserve what they get."

I continued, "Aren't some of them smart. People like university professors for example. Intellectuals opposed to policy and certain ideologies. Don't a lot of protest movements originate in universities?"

"Some are not educated, though sometimes they are smart people. The FBI generally tries not to target highly intelligent people. They cause too much trouble, create problems for the FBI which then has to spend too much time and effort in dealing with such people and the problems their complaints cause. They do if they feel they don't have a choice. But they try to find people who won't add anything to the economy, or country, whose removal from the system won't really be noticed or missed. They don't want to take out top research academics, people who may be one of a kind, but pretty much anyone else is fair game. The less smart or educated a target is, the less likely they are to figure out what is happening to them and to fight against it. Ideally, they want people who won't know what is happening and won't fight it," she replied.

[Comment: The conversation changed tack and broadened in scope as we continued.

Despite Susan's strident denouncement of "dissidents" that night in 1996 her certainty and attitude stood in stark contrast to her reaction when she found out I had been branded just such a "dissident" or "environmental extremist" or similar, and that she had been caught up in it as well.

Ironically, she had already told me in detail about the FBI's treatment of dissidents, what they do and how, on that night as we walked home. This was an interesting conversation, all the more so on account of how things turned out. It was innocent enough at the time in 1996. Though in fact, it was a chilling foretelling of the strategies and tactics I was to experience firsthand, as was Susan, each of us as victims of the very tactics of the agency we were discussing. I was dispensable by the standards of the FBI.]

A personal relationship: Reconnecting with Susan, 1998-1999

Later in 1998, though we had broken up, we had started to catch up again casually. She was incredulous and defiant, and reassured me in an exasperated tone, if somewhat cryptically on several occasions in 1998 and 1999 when I had no idea of the circumstances behind it.

"I am not going to let them do this to you!" she exclaimed. Holmes continued, "You would not believe how surprised I was when I saw your name on the work files!" Her alluding to "work" was a euphemism for the FBI. On this occasion we were having dinner at the South Street Seaport in Manhattan near Wall Street around June 1999, not long before I moved back to Australia. I asked her what she meant but she refused to explain to me either who the "they" were, or what the "it" was that she was intending to defend me against. She was stonewalling me, and she knew I knew she was, but she did nothing to assuage my concerns beyond that. She didn't know how, or what to do or say next. She was evidently fearful of the repercussions from her employer, the FBI, of disclosing to me what she knew - that I was a target.

Not long after, in late June 1999, on the night before my departure from NYC when I was scheduled to return to Australia, Susan sat on my bed in my apartment. We had been out all evening and she had come back to talk. All the years of our relationship had come to a dramatic crescendo.

Susan and I had been circling around each other now for months, but there was something not quite falling into place. All the strange comments she made about protecting me, the intimacy, but also the aloofness on things she never had been aloof about before, inconsistencies concerning my laptop being smashed, people entering my apartment, Steve Garber's awareness of so many issues about us; it was a muddied and muddled vista. We had seen each other most days for the past week and she had spent the previous night at my place.

She was confused, as was I, and both a little tense. After talking on the bed for a while, she stood up and walked over to the window. I waited expectantly for her to say something. But she didn't say anything, she didn't move, she was looking out and after a time I went over to her. Her response was not what I expected. She snapped sharply, "Stand away!" officiously in a resolute voice as if she were a police officer on duty.

I had delayed my departure on a daily basis for the past week, but I could delay no longer. If I was to arrive for my agreed start date at work I had to take a plane the next morning. It was a definitive move and a big decision as to whether to leave the US after eight years. Six of those years spent in NY, where my social life was centred and my professional life had been.

Susan seemed to be pondering my permanent and imminent departure, as I was, and the impact it would have on what was left of our relationship. A flicker of self doubt must have transited her mind as to whether the new assumptions she held about me, from the FBI's "criminal investigation" file, were indeed right.

"Did you do something illegal?": She asked me a question in great earnestness and I detected an edge of frustration and hostility, "Did you do something illegal?" The question had come out of the blue for me. I was so surprised by it that at first I needed to appraise whether she was being serious or whether it was a light hearted rhetorical question to lighten the mood. Slightly stunned by the intensity and directness of her manner I realised she was absolutely serious.

After a few seconds I repeated aloud, more to myself than to her "Illegal. Illegal?" Then I looked at her and asked, "What do you mean – ever done anything illegal? In my life? "

"No" she replied testily, "I mean recently. At work." I sat in silence. I was absorbed and lost in thought. I was amazed that she was asking this, really asking me. It was a serious question and she was deadly serious. She wanted an answer.

Still surprised, I wracked my brain. "What could I have done? What could she be talking about?!" I thought to myself.

There was absolutely nothing I could think of that came even close. I had walked a straight line at work, shunned impropriety, loathed and detested that aspect of banking culture – the greed that drove and the vanity whereby some people tried to deviously outsmart the system and enrich themselves as if they deserved wealth and the privileges it brings, no matter what the cost, or as if by divine right.

After a long pause, I felt Susan looking at me. She had watched me intently as I sat on the bed fathoming the depths of my mind for an answer to her question. I was searching the possibility that there could have been something I had done, something I had overlooked, anything I might have done unintentionally, in error, anything that was even remotely possible or that I had heard or seen within my small group at work. I could think of nothing that came even close to what she was asking.

I said, "No, nothing. I haven't done anything illegal. I can't think of anything at all! Where did you get that idea from?!"

She was still looking at me intently and her face completely softened. Susan sat down next to me and spoke to me with a tenderness I had not heard from her for some time. She said in a gentle, supportive way, "Well, you seem to be telling the truth". She seemed confused. She was confused.

I waited a moment and then again asked her, "Wherever did you get that idea. Who said I had done something illegal?" But again she didn't answer.

84. **2003, Holmes' NYC interview:** During Holmes' invasive interview of me in NYC in 2003, she revealed she had accessed detailed information about my life, myriad specific details spanning many decades, continents, and people – consistent with the investigative reach and powers of the FBI. Indeed, she said that she was conducting the interview at the behest of a US government agency. The details she recounted included but were not limited to information regarding: personal conversations with current and former peers and colleagues going back decades; calls I had made on my private home phone; minor traffic offenses in Australia; work records from various companies I had worked at over the years; records of school and university grades; records of purchases; records of state tests; medical history; and even camping records at US National Parks. Holmes also, inexplicably, had knowledge of specific phone calls I had received or made from my home phone a year or two after we had split up. She mentioned three in detail, all around 1998 and 1999, not just meta data, viz., date, time, number, owner of the number, but she knew the content of the call as well and went through each call with me in explicit detail (further details available in my Declaration of 16 November 2021).

85. **2003-04, Holmes and Garber link FBI operation to my work on Freeport McMoran:** During the 2003 interview of me in NYC, Holmes strongly intimated that I had been subjected to ongoing FBI interference as payback for my critical 1996 analyst's report on US mining company Freeport McMoran's approach to, and actions in and around, the company's massive Grasberg mine in West Papua, Indonesia.

86. In separate conversations with me, Holmes in 2003 and Garber in June 2004 in separate conversations with me, linked Henry Kissinger, a former board member and advisor to Freeport McMoran, my analyst report from 1996, and insinuated the report embarrassed the company and potentially fuelled shareholder disquiet. Kissinger at around that time was reportedly doing the rounds in Washington endeavouring to have the company's OPIC political risk insurance policy reinstated. I had covered many companies and written many reports during my years as an analyst, but Garber and Holmes both raised this one report with me and focused intently on it. Around this time at least three other people seemingly independently raised this report with me (including Matthew Levey of Kroll, and mining equity sales person Kathleen Walton), or issues at Freeport McMoran's mining operations in West Papua, Indonesia, the environmental and human rights concerns there, and the larger-than-life CEO and Chairman Jim Bob Moffett. These people, on account of their statements and actions, appeared to have a connection to US intelligence/law enforcement agencies.

87. **Circa June 2004, Central Park walk with Steve Garber confirms details of Holmes' FBI work:** Around June 2004, during a walk in Central Park and the Upper West Side of NYC Steve Garber disclosed to me personal details concerning Holmes' "work", many of which I was already familiar with. He revealed to me that he was aware of a number of Holmes assignments, revealing and corroborating multiple details, which he insinuated were undertaken at the behest of the FBI. These included: A Save the Wolf campaign for which she received a $5,000 grant received from the FBI around 1997 to

augment her credibility in environmental circles; a trip to the Kamchatka Peninsula around 1995; a trip to meet with a Californian congressional hopeful in 1996 prior to the US Presidential election which Holmes herself had portrayed as a "honeytrap" meeting; and election to the Sierra Club board of directors.

88. **September 2004, NYC, Garber confirms FBI operation:** In September 2004, Steve Garber and I again met in NYC, this time at the Blue Water Grill in Union Square. In response to my direct question, he affirmed that he worked for the FBI, and that I was being targeted as a result of my work. Here he verified and verbally confirmed to me in person that I had been subjected to ongoing FBI interference as payback for my work in 1996 as a Wall Street mining analyst critical of US mining company Freeport McMoran's actions in and around the company's massive Grasberg mine in West Papua, Indonesia.

    I asked him, seeking to confirm his insinuating remarks when we had met earlier in the year – around June 2004, in sum and substance, "You are doing this for the FBI right? To confirm, I've been targeted by the FBI on account of my Freeport McMoran work - is that right?" After a short pause without a response, I clearly and deliberately repeated the question. I wanted to hear him reaffirm that it was the FBI that was behind the attack on me, and that their reason was my Freeport work. I wanted to leave no doubt, no uncertainty about who he was working for and what the reason was for the interference I had been subjected to. Garber nodded and said, in sum and substance, "Yes."

89. **2012-13**; **Sydney.** I had **three one-hour meetings with Philip Ruddock, the former Australian Attorney General** (from October 2003 to December 2007) in his electoral office around 2012-2013 on the topic of FBI, and Australian partnering agencies, interference with me on account of my Freeport McMoran work in 1996. During these meetings I named several Australian operatives who had interfered with me including: Robert Sadleir, son of former ASIO Director General David Sadleir (1992-96); Dr Trent Allen, Sydney, stockbroking analyst; Michael and Claudia Hackman, Sydney

business people; Daniel Aitken, Central coast NSW and Boston, USA; Richard Kaan, Sydney, former business consultant; Fabian Babich, Sydney, former stockbroking analyst. Some of these agents in Sydney have at various times from around 2005 indicated specific knowledge with clear and distinct details from the 2003 interview by Holmes, such as Fabian Babich. Multiple agents have revealed multiple instances of such detailed knowledge. Their knowledge is a further indication the FBI holds documents or records on me. (The email is attached hereto as Exhibit 3.)

90. I believe the FBI is operating in "bad faith", has created fake evidence on me as alluded to by FBI operatives Holmes and Garber (in 2003 and 2004), and has compromised oversight screening mechanisms. Their methods subvert the review process, presumably including efforts by former Australian Attorney General, Philip Ruddock (detailed in this Declaration).

91. I should have the ability to review and respond to the "evidence" held by the FBI on me, that others rely on, and the right to challenge it with the assistance of an attorney.

Section 3

Steve Garber: Disclosures re Freeport McMoran and the FBI: 1994-2004

Declaration of John Wilson

I, John Wilson, do hereby declare under penalties of perjury:

92. I submit this declaration based on my personal knowledge in support of my Administrative Appeal of FOIA Request FOIPA No. 1548515-000.

93. I am a dual Australian and USA citizen.

94. I currently live in Sydney, Australia and have a small equity research consultancy business and live with my wife and two young children.

95. After completing an MBA in 1993 at The Wharton School of the University of Pennsylvania, I moved to New York City and from late 1993 to June 1999 lived at 170 W 74th St, Apt 906, New York, NY 10023.

96. Dialogue reported in this affidavit may be paraphrasing of actual conversation.

97. Dialogue, statements and events reported in this Declaration may be selected for relevance and presented for clarity and brevity, but always to give a true and fair rendering of the situation. Additional details, in cases, may be available.

98. The term "agent" as I use it here is used in a generic sense, as in someone being an agent of someone else and does not intend any specific title.

1. **1994: Vetted by Steve Garber:**

99. I met Susan Holmes in the second half of 1994 while I was attending a Sierra Club volunteer meeting in NYC and we started dating shortly after. I met Steve Garber, through Susan

Holmes, also at a Sierra Club volunteer event. After Holmes and I started dating, at Garber's instigation, Holmes, Garber and I went for a hike one weekend in Harriman State Park about 1 hours' drive from NYC.

100. A week or two after this, around October 1994, Susan Holmes showed me her black FBI ID card. She told me she worked undercover for the FBI, and that Steve Garber did also. She said that the intention of our walk that day had been for Steve Garber to vet me for the FBI. Evidently, I passed the test.

101. After that, I rarely saw him in the following 18 months to two years, maybe once or twice, and beyond a courteous salutation he made no particular overtures to me. In mid-1996, that changed after my Freeport McMoran work report of 12 March 1996 evidently came to the FBI's attention.

102. A couple of times around 1994 and 1995, Susan told me Garber worked for the FBI. The first time was after showing me her FBI ID card and related disclosures, but I had never cared much nor placed much heed in it. (Garber confirmed his role with the FBI to me, and my targeting, in September 2004 – details later in this Declaration).

103. Steve was around 10 years my senior, in his early 40s at the time, medium height, with still dark though balding hair. He had a PhD in herpetology (study of reptiles and amphibians) published a number of books, including The Urban Naturalist (1987, John Wiley and Sons)[38]. His day job was with the Port Authority of NY where he focused on developing bird strike abatement strategies for JFK airport. Overly rounded, he would have clearly failed his body mass index (BMI) weight test with the FBI if they had bothered with continuous checks after recruitment. He lived with his wife, Andrea, who I met on occasions, on the Upper West Side in Manhattan, which was also my

---

[38] https://www.goodreads.com/book/show/3165868-the-urban-naturalist

neighbourhood. Over the coming years he had two sons, Micah and another whose name I now forget, possibly Jeremiah.

2. Mid-1996: Freeport McMoran report - Garber resurfaces

104. **Background:** From 1994 to 1997 I worked for SG Warburg (and later SBC Warburg) on Wall Street as an equity analyst covering US listed mining companies. One of the companies I analyzed and published reports on for distribution to fund managers globally was U.S.-based and listed Freeport McMoran which through Freeport Indonesia controls the Grasberg Mine, one of the largest copper and gold mines in the world, situated in West Papua, Indonesia.

105. **Report:** On March 12, 1996, I authored a report (hereinafter the "Report") that flagged concerns about Freeport McMoran, which was under investigation by the United States Department of State following eyewitness reports of human rights abuses against indigenous protestors in the region of its massive Grasberg gold and copper mine in West Papua, Indonesia. I asked questions about the investigation to the company's CEO and Chairman Jim Bob Moffett at an analyst briefing in New Orleans in May 1996 after which I was threatened in the boardroom alcove by an individual who appears to have been a federal agent. The company denied any role in human rights abuses and eyewitness reports were never proven in court. (Details in Declaration 16 November 2021).

106. **Befriended by Garber:** In mid-1996, after my Report was published and my question to the Freeport McMoran CEO, Steve Garber started to make overtures to me. He began to show up at Sierra Club NYC chapter volunteer events I regularly attended with Susan.

107. He invited me to join him on his walks after work in Central Park some days to observe different species of migratory birds that visited the large wooded park at different times of the year. On our walks Steve would often come with a pair of binoculars around his neck and his young son in a backpack on his back.

3. 1997: The Colorado River, dams and talk of explosives

108. Susan Holmes told me during the three years we went out (1994-1997) that her focus for the FBI was on environmental extremists. Based on my experience and disclosures from Holmes (in 2003) and Garber (in 2004), the FBI appears to have duplicitously portrayed me as one of her work targets – as an environmental extremist or suchlike, as discussed below. (In 2004, Steven Garber confirmed to me that I was subject of an FBI operation as a result of my work on Freeport McMoran in mid-1996; details later in this Declaration).

109. It appears the FBI endeavoured to associate me in close contact with David Foreman in mid-1997, a high-profile environmentalist and one of Susan's FBI work targets. I believe Susan was an unwittingly participant in this scheme at this time in 1997.

110. **FBI targets our relationship:** Adding credibility to the FBI's purported portrayal of me as an environmental extremist or similar, or perhaps as part of their efforts to turn my life "upside down", the FBI targeted my relationship with Susan, endeavoring to damage and ultimately end it. Susan in 2003 in her NYC interrogation of me indicated our relationship was targeted by the FBI. (A transcript of the 2003 interrogation based on my notes and recollection is available on request; 200+ pages).

111. In this way, the FBI, if it chose, could falsely portray the relationship was part of Susan's work, as opposed to what it was, a heartfelt and genuine romance commencing in 1994. Whether our relationship would have lasted beyond the 3 years it did without their interference is conjecture, but what is clear is that the FBI went to some lengths to sow distrust, confusion and doubt between us. This apparently extended to deleting key phone messages Susan and I left for each other at a sensitive time, among other things, arranging "honey-traps" (sending Susan as a "honey-trap" to California, and baiting me with others), sowed doubt about Susan's loyalty and commitment, and an attempted predatory undercover drug sting speculatively directed at me. (Some of these FBI

undertakings are described in this Declaration, and the Declaration 16 November 2021 I have submitted.)

112. The FBI's intrusions into my life seemed to be part of what Susan had referred to when she told me in 1996 that the FBI goes after dissidents and other targets, to disrupt or otherwise attempt to "turn their lives upside down". Susan neve expected that she would be targeted by her own agency. The FBI targeted her personal life too, one of its own agents, by intruding into her private relationship. She was evidently collateral damage as far as they were concerned. The FBI knew we had been in a long-term relationship since 1994, and that Susan had invited me to her home for Christmas in 1997 with a view to getting engaged and in due course married.

113. **March 1997:** An invitation to raft down the Colorado. Holmes, Foreman and others: In March 1997, I left my job at Warburg as a mining analyst and had 5 months off before getting another job.

114. Around March, before leaving Warburg, I was invited by Holmes to join her on a large environmentalist campaign rafting trip down the Colorado River organised for July 1997. A range of high profile environmentalists and others were involved, including a journalist from Time Magazine, the young Chairman of the Sierra Club, and David Foreman, whose dory I was allocated to in advance by trip organizers. The intention of the trip had been to raise publicity for dismantling of dams on the Colorado. In inviting me, Holmes said all the 20 or so participants domestic partners were invited, however when I showed up there, I realised I was the only one. Dave Foreman was a co-founder of Earth First! and on an FBI watchlist, targeted by Susan Holmes for the FBI she said. He had advocated removal of dams on the Colorado River and reported to have been investigated as part of a group that blew up power lines in Arizona, though he was later exonerated. (Refer to Declaration of 16 November 2021).

115. Holmes said at the interview in 2003 she had photos in her "work files" (a euphemism for the FBI) depicting me in association with David Foreman in the summer of 1997 on the Colorado

River but that she had forgotten to bring them for me to dinner that night. She also alluded to photos from a talk by Dave Foreman I attended later in 1997 in NYC. My attendance at both encounters was by Holmes' invitation.

116. Between 1994 and 1997, Susan had told me in response to a question I asked about her work interest in Dave Foreman, "The FBI is no longer concerned about Dave Foreman doing anything wrong, but it's the people attracted to him, associated with him, who they have the interest in. The people attracted to him are the people they are interested in."" Given her intense and unusual focus on what I thought and knew of Foreman that evening while she was evidently recording the conversation, this seemed further reason to think this to be the category the FBI was now trying to set me up in. (Refer to Declaration of 16 November 2021).

4. Late 1997: Garber intensifies interactions with me after I start work at DKB

117. Around August 1997, I started a new job as a mining analyst with Dresdner Kleinwort Benson (DKB) back on Wall Street.

118. At this time Steve Garber's interest in me stepped up a notch, with frequent calls and requests to meet up. He started calling me regularly at work at DKB in 1997 and 1998. His calls at work were at times odd, he seemed to have taken a heightened interest in my work, my career ambitions, and my relationship with Susan. He frequently asked me questions about my relationship with Susan, what was going on, how I felt. His questions and interest seemed more intense than a passing interest would merit.

119. Garber and I walked in Central Park on 8 or 10 occasions or more around 1997 and 1998. At this time I did not know I was being targeted by the FBI (he later confirmed in 2004 that I was being targeted by the FBI); he was reaching out to me, building trust and empathy. One day he invited me up to his apartment after our walk to meet his wife and show me his library and some of the reports he was working on. He also invited me on a couple of day trips, one up to his mother's place in suburban Connecticut where he was very familiar with the forests and we went looking for tortoises

in the local creek. She wasn't home that day, but he had the key and we went inside for something and he showed me around. I would never remember where it was, if that was a consideration in his exposing family members to one of his targets, no matter how harmless. On another occasion we participated in the Audubon annual Christmas Bird Count in one of the counties in Connecticut. In this way, we spent quite a bit of time together, he would drive and we would talk, then hike and we got to know each other.

120. **Garber secretly enters my apartment building:** His intrusions into my life were pronounced and, at times, odd. Around this time in 1997, shortly after I had started working at DKB, Steven Garber entered my apartment building unannounced. He had accompanied Susan past the concierge/security then once inside the building went to the basement while Susan came up to get me and we went out. Susan and I had given each other keys to our respective apartments early in our relationship for mutual convenience and as a sign of our commitment to each other. However, the light in my apartment which had been off when we went out, something Susan had asked me to double check and confirm as we went out, was on when we got back. The doorman later told me Steve Garber had left the building sometime after we had gone out. When I later asked him, Garber denied he had been in my apartment or that Holmes had given him a key.

121. Around this time, there was also a large article in the NYT on Steve Garber and his day job at the Port Authority of NY where he had worked as a biologist on a bird plane strike avoidance project at JFK airport (15 September 1997). (The article is attached hereto as <u>Exhibit 4</u>.) Susan suggested in 2003 that the FBI planted this article as a means to help build Steve's status and influence with me to support his efforts to build rapport with me.

122. Also, around this time, Garber drove me from Manhattan to a townhall community gathering about 1 hour away near Harriman State Park one evening after work around August-September 1997. It was at his request that I go in his car, despite the fact Susan was going there as well. Susan and I went in separate cars which was unusual and after, back in NYC at my apartment

with Susan, she showed a heightened level of interest as to what Steve Garber's reasons had been I go with him and she pressed me to find out what he had discussed with me.

123. Shortly after this, Susan and I broke up at my behest. I had already accepted her invitation to Christmas that year at her parents' house in Detroit. She had also brought up and discussed with me the "work" documents for security clearance my parents would need to review and sign before we could get engaged. After breaking up, over the next week or so, she asked me on three separate occasions with increasingly impassioned emotion and irritation, "Did Steve Garber say something to you about me? Is he the cause of this?" She was clearly annoyed by his intrusion into our relationship and her social life. It was evident she did not trust him, though she did not explain her reasons and suspicions to me at the time.

124. On one occasion, not long after Susan and I broke up, Garber was quick to introduce me to a woman he knew, a romantic prospect for me he explained, Jennifer, and who Susan, in 2003 in her NYC interview of me, insinuated was a "honey-trap". Susan knew many of the details of our brief encounter and the distinct, unusual details of Jennifer's calls to me at work.

125. During this time Garber and I continued our walks some evenings into Central Park to look for wildlife.

126. **Explosives and blowing up dams:** Late one afternoon around August – September 1997, not long after the rafting trip when I was back in New York with a new job at DKB, I met up with Steve Garber for a bird watching walk in Central Park after work. I thought at the time how odd and bizarre his behaviour seemed, the strange things he was talking to me about, the questions he asked.

127. After an hour or so of general chat, Garber proceeded to ask me about explosives and blowing up dams. It was represented initially by him as an exploratory conversation with me in which I might be able to help him protect dams, etc from threats, troubleshoot potential threats and weaknesses.

128. I worked as a mining engineer for a large Australian multinational mining company, BHP after graduating from The University of Sydney with an engineering degree in the mid-1980s. He knew I had started my career as a mining engineer and also that in that capacity I had some work place experience with explosives and he asked me about it.

129. But his conversation soon took a twist. He asked numerous ridiculous, oddball questions about big dams, dams like on the Colorado, and how I thought they could be sabotaged. It was late afternoon, and he was pressing me to answer his insistent questions, wanting to know how I would blow up a dam wall if I "had" too. I knew nothing of consequence about dams, my experience was in mining. But he was insistent, he wanted an answer. Any answer – "Just say anything," he said. "Blow it up" seemed clear enough – I had seen a few war films over the years – call in the air force or army I suggested light heartedly. But what was meant by if I "had too"? At first, I treated his questions as a joke, and responded with light hearted tongue and cheek. Was conscription back on the government agenda again? I asked him what he meant. He asked, "What if you were a demolition engineer for example?" I said I still had no idea – and I asked him why was he asking all these inane questions about blowing up dams?

130. As time passed his questions became increasingly ludicrous and increasingly seemed to have a personal agenda. He wanted to know if I had ever thought about blowing up a dam, dreamt about it, what mining industry technology could be applied, even hypothetically he prodded. He asked hopefully, just imagine he said, think of anything. It was hypothetical he said but he pushed for firm answers. "Surely there is something you could think of," he insisted eventually in frustration at my having no answer.

131. Having some inkling of his law enforcement background, during the conversation I asked him by way of confirmation, "I assume you're trying to stop this sort of thing," to which he said "Yes". "You're asking about this to try and identify risks and threats - right?". He answered "Yes." Eventually, after a further tedious conversation, thinking he was goofing around, I came up with a

completely implausible, impractical and dismissive response: a Walt Disney "Roadrunner" cartoon style slap stick scenario, to placate him and he seemed satisfied.

Again, jumping forward, some years later at the dinner in NYC at Café Fiorello in 2003, Susan working on duty undercover for a federal agency, presumed to be the FBI, asked me to clarify points on the same topic of blowing up dams and asked me if I remembered the conversation I had with Steve Garber in 1997. She now confirmed that scenario was implausible and asked me for something else, this time more plausible. It seemed as if the FBI had done some research and determined conclusively the scenario "devised" was implausible and impractical – which was the same point on which the conversation with Steve had ended at the time! It seems the conversation may have been recorded or summarised in a file note or similar.

132. **Section summary:** Based on my experience, and disclosures from both Holmes and Garber, my inclusion in the trip down the Colorado River in 1997, and invitation to hear Foreman speak in NYC later in 1997 seems to have been part of a set-up. This seems to extend to my meeting with Susan Holmes and David Brower that summer in Detroit in 1997; and subsequently Steve Garber's bizarre and duplicitous conversation with me about explosives and blowing up dams in late 1997.

133. It now seems Garber's intention was to help the FBI construct a fake dossier of misinformation and fake evidence about me. According to disclosures from Holmes and Garber, associating me with Foreman gave the FBI the photos to create and seemingly support a fake profile about me, to place me on some kind of watch list. Indeed, Susan insinuated this in 2003 during her extended interrogation of me at Café Fiorello in NYC. Garber confirmed in 2004 that the FBI had targeted me as "payback" for my work on Freeport McMoran, (detailed later in this Declaration). It appears that placing me on a list of some description relying on fake evidence to do so, was sufficient to get through any preliminary and perfunctory oversight screens that might otherwise legitimately uncover illicit schemes. (Refer to Declaration of 16 November 2021).

5. 1999: Susan's veiled warning not to visit Steve Garber in Prescott, AZ

134. **1998: Garber moves to Prescott, AZ:** Around late 1998, or early 1999, Garber and his family left NYC and moved to Prescott, AZ for a couple of years. Steve looked terribly stressed prior to leaving NY. His job at the NY Port Authority for some reason had come to an end at about the same time my work at DKB ended. He had put on a lot of weight and looked pale and generally unwell. I had caught up with him in NY prior to his departure and I was surprised at how distressed and worn out he had looked then: very tired, completely frazzled - clearly things had not been going well for him but he didn't want to discuss it.

135. Before he left NYC, he offered me a standing invitation to come stay one weekend if I was out West, which frequently I was, and we could head off for a two or three day hike somewhere.

136. **Reconnecting with Susan:** In the meantime, in late 1998 and early 1999, Susan and I were contemplating getting back together.

137. She had some months before invited me to Boston for her father's birthday, which I attended. And I invited Susan out to Utah in early 1999 for a few days, where I was spending some time and we went backcountry hiking and camping in the lesser visited back canyons of Zion National Park - arguably the most magical national park in the West.

138. We still weren't back together as such, there was something weird going on in the background with Susan and the FBI which was causing us both some issues. Unbeknownst to me at the time, the FBI had shown her my FBI files she later revealed, apparently sometime in 1998.

139. None-the-less we had a good time exploring Zion's back country canyons in their various stages of geological formation, camping out in the desert fields, and walking down through the incredible main canyon into the spectacular valley that opens into a magnificent clearing framed by a sheer rock face that rises nearly 1000 feet. She had come out for an extended weekend and later I dropped her back at the small local airport nearby.

140. After Susan had returned to New York I continued on to the desert town of Moab in Utah. It was in the days before the ubiquitous mobile phone and I called Susan from a public phone box down the road from the backpackers hostel where I was staying.

141. **Holmes warns me not to visit Garber:** In our conversation over the public phone from Moab, she was chatty, friendly and supportive as always, however gave me a strange and cryptic warning; she said no matter what happens, she was not planning on another trip out West in the next week or two, and whatever I did, "Do not go and visit Steve Garber," in Prescott, AZ.

She said cryptically, "Some strange things might happen. Just ignore them. Call me first if you are thinking about going to Steve Garber's. I want you to promise me you will call me first." She was insistent and emphasised the point several times. She told me to promise her that I would talk to her first and not to go to Garber's home. She emphasised this last point several times, "Don't go to Steve Garber's". Intriguingly, she had said a number of times recently, in an abstract sense, refusing to elaborate, "I'm not going to let them do this to you!" It was strange, but at the time I didn't know what she was referring to; and I wasn't going to let an abstract warning govern specific decisions in my life.

142. I called Steve to discuss his plans and whether a time would suit for me to drive over. Intriguingly, he let slip something he said he shouldn't have, that Susan was coming over too for a surprise visit. Odd given Susan had said she definitely wasn't coming over.

143. I called Susan back to clarify; and also because she had told me to speak to her and not make a decision without talking to her first if I was thinking about going to stay at Steve's. But she didn't answer her phone. The whole situation was getting weirder. I was undecided as to what to do and Prescott was not far out of my way as I was heading in that direction anyway. I had not been able to get in touch with Susan despite my efforts, and in the end, I went to stay at Steve's.

144. *[**Comment:** Susan knew some of the FBI's processes and had given me a veiled warning without disclosing specifics of the threat - that this "friendly" catch up with Steve was a trap to be*

avoided, without explaining that I was at risk: targeted in the manner she had once talked so openly about in a general context of the FBI's treatment of dissidents and others.

145. *For all her loyalty to the FBI, through this period of time, I see in hindsight how loyal Susan had also been to me, evidently caught in a tight spot, she had gone out of her way to help me as best she could, giving me the clues and advice she felt she could within the bounds of the law. She didn't seem to have any idea as to why I was on the FBI's radar, a person of interest, they had evidently not given her all the key details; not mentioned the Freeport connection but kept it secret from her for now, presumably out concern for her potential adverse reaction. (Details in this Declaration in the section about Susan Holmes).]*

6. Circa April-May, 1999: A visit to Steve Garber in Prescott, AZ

146. It was around April or May 1999 when I visited Steve, Andrea his wife and their two kids at their home in Prescott for two days. Steve had moved to Prescott a number of months before having taken a teaching job at Embry Riddle Aeronautical University; he said he was lecturing on the local eco-system, a topic of interest to me; and taking students on fieldtrips out into the desert.

147. If the original plan in coming to stay that weekend had been to head off hiking, it was only a ruse. Steve had no intention of heading out into the desert. Instead, we did some short walks in the surrounding neighbourhoods, but otherwise hung around Prescott, reading and looking at a few minor sites.

148. Steve used the evenings to covertly sound me out on personal or sensitive questions which he evidently recorded for the FBI, something Susan later implied. This would explain why he had lied about the weekend hiking activities and possibility Susan might show up unexpectedly – to entice me to come stay. It also explained Susan's imploring me not to go.

*149. [**Comment:** Susan knew the FBI's modus operandi, and what was awaiting me there was evidently a trap with Garber leading and recording our various conversations intended to capture personal disclosures from me that could be the basis of a smear campaign, or worse. Apparently, this trap was his sole purpose in inviting me to stay, and what had so alarmed Susan about my visit to Steve's place. I didn't have much to say to Steve that was personal, let alone incriminating, indeed he seemed to have more to say about himself in the afternoon when presumably the tape recorder wasn't whirring.]*

7. Garber's fishing expedition

150. Steve apparently recorded our conversation during both evenings I visited him in Prescott in early 1999. He covered off on a broad range of topics intended to embarrass, smear or indict.

151. One evening he started on a slight tangent, and asked me about the "California incident" which involved Susan's visit to a Californian congressional candidate prior to the US presidential election in late 1996. This was the election that saw Bill Clinton re-elected. He implied she went there as a "honey-trap". Garber now went on at length about it, he was well informed of the details. He seemed aware of how extreme was her embarrassment when I showed her an article and picture of the congressman in my apartment one evening. He asked prodding, pointedly, wanting to know the details of how she had responded and what I had thought of Susan's reaction. He honed in on it and wanted to know what I had been thinking - always coming back to my thoughts, feelings, reactions. His insistence and persistence in his questions left me feeling a bit baffled.

152. Steve turned the conversation squarely to me. He asked me about my previous romances, going through each in detail. He wanted to know if there had been any one-night stands. He was evidently on a fishing expedition, looking for anything derogatory, asking leading questions to identify anything that might be met with rebuke society wide, within certain circles, or from specific individuals should the information be distributed beyond our "private" talk.

153. He asked details about any drug and alcohol use, wanted to know if, or what occasions, I may have drunk too much, who was there, dates, locations, occasions. He asked about whether I had ever attended strip clubs, red light districts, prostitutes; anything that might be compromising, or embarrassing in certain company. He asked if I was gay, had ever had any gay relationships, or gay friends, and a number of other questions along similar lines.

154. He then asked about whether I had gone out with anyone under age, a category of questioning about which he seemed passionate and became very persistent. It was all so speculative and he was seeking not only any outright admissions from me but also any possible point of uncertainty, any ambiguity. He wanted to know how I could be certain someone might not have been under age, that they might have lied to me, deceived me about their age and so on. He pressed on with this line of questioning, speculating, reaching for any possibility. In hind sight he was pushing hard to establish a link to a label, even if it was only conceptually possibility; he wanted to be able to accuse me of pedophilia or in the absence of that, possible pedophilia. But he was grasping and was unsuccessful. The lengths he went to were absurd and his intentions completely dishonorable.

155. *[**Comment:** Some years later Steve explained to me the FBI aims to tarnish dissidents and others, brand them with some undesirable social label. Anything that they could make stick. In previous times it was homosexuality. Today it is pedophilia. Susan had once said the FBI wants to brand dissidents as sex offenders, because if they end up in jail on some charge or other, they are treated especially harshly by the jail population which dislikes sex offenders. But anything would do, Steve now disclosed taunting me, anything that goes against the grain, against social norms - substance abuse, deviant activity, sexual misconduct, anything the FBI could get its hands on.*

156. I hadn't done anything wrong, why should I be suspicious of the FBI? Why should I think the FBI would come after me? And why would I think that even if they should have some

unforeseen reason to take an interest in me that they would do it in this fashion - trying to destroy my relationships, my career and any semblance of a normal social life?]

8. Circa June, 1999: Back in NYC with Susan Holmes

157. When I subsequently met Susan back in NYC a couple months later, around June 1999, and told her of my visit to Steve's place she was visibly upset. "I told you not to go. And you said you would call me first if you were thinking of going," she said alarmed and a little gloomy. It seems she thought the veiled warning she gave me was enough to keep me out of harm's way.

158. "I did call you but you didn't answer," I said. She sighed, recognising I had tried to speak to her, and seeming to recognise the flaw in her own plan. I asked, "Why does it matter? What difference does it make?" She said optimistically, if a little disparagingly, resigned to what couldn't be changed, "Probably none."

159. At some point around that time, Holmes said to me "You would not believe how surprised I was when I saw your name on the work files." Her alluding to "work" was a euphemism for the FBI. We were having dinner at the South Sea Port in NYC and she added cryptically, "I'm not going to let them do this to you!". It didn't click with me at the time what she was talking about and she didn't elaborate when I asked her to explain.

160. Later in June, one evening back in my apartment, she asked me outright, albeit still cryptically, "Did you do something illegal?" It was evident she had been led to believe by the FBI that I had done something illegal, something criminal. (Refer to this Declaration section on Susan Holmes)

161. The next morning, in late June 1999, I left the USA and moved back to Australia to start a new job in Sydney.

*[**Comment:** In early 1999, Susan seemed to be trying to walk a fine line between rescuing me while at the same time evidently trying to preserve her career and commitments to the FBI. I don't know what was going through her mind, whether she didn't care enough, whether she was too confused and*

conflicted by the FBI's "investigation" of me: She could have told me outright what was happening to ensure there was no room for misinterpretation and misunderstanding, but she didn't. Susan was in a moral bind. Clearly, the FBI had refrained from giving her my file while we were going out; it no doubt foresaw the conflict they had placed Susan in. For now, Susan seemed to be hedging loyalties between me and the FBI.]

9. 5 years' later: June 2004 - A walk with Garber, Central Park, NYC

162. Now 5 years' later, during a brief trip back to NYC around June 2004, I met up with Steve Garber. At different times during the 10 year period that I had known Garber since 1994, I had been told he worked for the FBI, but I had never cared much nor placed much heed in it.

163. Garber and I had spoken on the phone one morning in June 2004 shortly after I had arrived in NYC and he suggested we should catch up and go for a walk in Central Park. Unbeknownst to me, he had a message to deliver from the FBI.

164. Steve Garber picked me up in his car later that day drove us to nearby Central Park. We had gotten to know each other reasonably well since publication of my report on Freeport McMoran in 1996, 8 years' earlier. We found a place to park on Central Park West near the 72nd Street entrance.

165. As we were getting out of the car my phone rang. It was an urgent call from Matthew Levey at Kroll. Steve locked the car and stood on the footpath near me, positioning himself to overhear my end of the conversation.

166. Matthew Levey explained to me that an important opportunity had come up to open an office for Kroll in Australia and there was an urgent need to talk to me about whether I would be interested in the role. He insisted the window of opportunity to talk was strictly limited to the next hour or so, as he said the position was about to be awarded to someone else, a Brazilian, but I was

the preferred candidate. If I wanted to talk, I would need to drop everything right away, whatever I was doing, and come over to his office immediately. Immediately he repeated. That would mean standing Steve up and not continuing with our walk into Central Park.

167. The urgency of Matthew Levey's call was odd and I felt the substance of it lacked credibility. If Kroll had such an important and strategic opportunity to fill, surely it could wait a couple hours till later in the day or early the next morning; and surely, if I was a serious candidate for the role they would have contacted me earlier in the search process. I declined his pressured invitation to drop everything and come straight in – and I'm glad I did. He did not set a firm time to meet later that day nor early the next morning. Indeed, despite my calls back to him, he never followed up with another time to meet.

168. **Background on Kroll:** Matthew Levey was my consulting manager at Kroll Associates, Inc., in NYC. Around February 2003 he had offered me a monthly retainer as a part time consultant mining analyst. Levey had a background of working for the State Department and had tracked me down in Sydney in recent months through an introduction from a mutual friend and former work colleague. He had an anonymous client, Levey told me, and Kroll needed a mining analyst, part time, to work on gold mining related issues. The fact I was in Sydney was fine, I could work remotely, though there would have been any number of suitable candidates living in NY. He did not disclose who his client was, but suggested it was a large fund manager.

169. At one point, Levey also asked me to use my network of contacts in the US environmental community to call around and speak with activists about environmental and human rights issues in the Indonesian mining sector. A number of large US mining companies were operating in the country – most notably Newmont and Freeport McMoran. Levey seemed particularly interested in my work on Freeport McMoran. However, most of my environmental contacts I met through Susan Holmes, so I called her and briefly filled her in on the assignment. With her input I developed a list and called through it, but nothing of note came out of the calls. This seemed to be Matthew Levey's main

interest in my work, and once the call around had been completed, my consulting contract came to an end shortly after.

170. The Kroll assignment was ill defined and ran for 12-18 months. At one point he mentioned a long term senior executive of Freeport McMoran, John Macken, who according to a press release in November 2003, had left the company to go to work for Ivanhoe. What Levey's motive may have been in asking me about Macken is unclear, but the press release said he had a nineteen year career with Freeport that included "13 years with Freeport's operating unit, P.T. Freeport Indonesia (PTFI), culminating in the position of Executive Vice-President and General Manager at Freeport's Grasberg mining complex in [West] Papua," which spoke to a consistent, if unstated, Freeport related theme in Levey's dealings with me. Levey asked me if I knew Macken, had ever met him, or ever spoken with him. His focus on this individual was unusual and from recollection, this was the only operations person he asked me about during the time I worked for him.

171. *[**Comment:** The timing and urgency of Levey's call was odd, as was Steve's response. Indeed, Steve looked more than a little surprised when I got off the phone and told him that it had been someone from Kroll calling to invite me to an urgent meeting that afternoon. His face dropped and he gave me another one of his penetrating, soul searching looks as if he were aware of something that I was not.*

172. *As it turned out, the Kroll connection, my work touching on Freeport McMoran's operations in West Papua, Indonesia, Matthew Levey's call to me and timing, added authenticity and credibility to what Garber was about to tell me that afternoon; and later that year, in September 2004, his confirmation that I had been targeted by the FBI on account of my Freeport McMoran report and questions to the CEO in 1996.]*

173. **Steve drops a bombshell:** After I got off the call from Levey, Steve and I continued with our plan and walked along Central Park West, entered Central Park at the 72nd Street entrance where we had walked numerous times before when I still lived in NY.

174. This afternoon he led the way in. We veered off the footpath adjacent to one of the main roads and walked down to the lake, over the bridge by the boathouse and along a quiet path into the woodlands on the other side.

175. After we walked over the bridge and into the woodlands there was no one else around. The track narrowed and wound its way through dense shrubs, over boulders and skirted in and out around hidden edges of the pond. As we walked, Steve repeated various facts and figures about Central Park he had told me on previous occasions, then he turned the topic to Susan Holmes.

176. He asked me what I knew of Susan's "work"; he seemed to assume I knew little of her work at the FBI, which in a sense was true as I had always tried to block it out, it was something that had repulsed me and I had never really wanted to know about it. Then he proceeded to disclose details about aspects of her FBI career, projects, trips, people much of which I was already somewhat familiar with, though despite her attempts to tell me more than she did, I never had much interest in, nor understood exactly what it was she did for them, her second career that ran in parallel to her real passion - her work as an environmentalist.

177. Steve talked about some of Susan Holmes' assignments, a former role she had had as a Program Officer at the Harriman Institute, a "business trip" to the Kamchatka Peninsula, a mysterious small grant that had suddenly materialised out of nowhere for a "save the wolf" campaign - cover for a volunteer activist program at the Sierra Club in NY, attendance at "training" programs in Washington, the "California" incident, and so on.

178. Steve continued talking, disclosing, always assessing my reactions and answering or deflecting my questions. He asked me rhetorically whether I thought Susan was more loyal to me or to the state; then opined that she was a devoted and obedient FBI agent before all else, that she was a loyal and virtuous agent for the state. He extolled her virtues as such; her motivation and allegiance in all things, first and foremost to the state. He was attempting to drive a wedge into the history and meaning of our relationship, it seemed. In saying these things, things I knew not to be entirely true

about Susan, about us, she who I still felt fondly toward as a friend, Steve was attempting to be a trouble maker. I had known she was an FBI agent, at least she had told me a number of times and shown me her FBI identification card about 2 years before the Freeport note came out, shortly after we had started dating in 1994, and made various disclosures to me. Our relationship had not been an FBI sting operation from the outset as Steve was now at pains to disingenuously suggest. Susan had disclosed to me things no undercover agent would disclose during a sting operation, especially her role as an undercover FBI agent!

179. Garber continued to bait me, "Do you think you will ever be with Susan again?" he said turning to observe how I reacted to his question. "Maybe I already have," I remarked taunting him in return, not answering his question, and now observing his reaction to see if it gave any clues as to why he would ask such a question. A look of surprise crossed his face as if he had just realized something, his faced dropped as though I had suggested something he hadn't contemplated. *Why would he care so much about my answer?* I wondered. His comments were all the more tainted given Susan was now married, and he knew she was pregnant with her first child. It seems his barbs were intended to stir or sting any residual feelings I had for her,

180. This was just the beginning salvo, Steve's groundwork for the bombshell he was about to drop, one that would lead right back to the jungles of West Papua, Indonesia.

181. As we walked, he raised details of the strange things I had been experiencing since 1996. He was aware of the details of many of these things since publication of my 12 March 1996 report on Freeport McMoran in 1996 and described aspects of the interference I had faced in my personal and work life but he did not directly link it to Freeport. He asked me about the report and why I had written it. Steve raised details and events from my life - travel, work, personal - places in the Southwest I had visited, descriptions of people I had met there, details of private telephone calls from the Roadrunner backpacker hostel in Tucson I frequently stayed at – knowledge of private matters consistent with an FBI investigation. He had no reason to know about these things, and

provocatively asked me leading questions, he seemed to be baiting and mocking me about whether I thought the FBI might be interfering in my life. I did not at the time know how, or why, he had so much information about these many and seemingly disparate events in my life. He wouldn't answer the many questions I put back to him in response to his suggestion. I had done nothing illegal and I had no reason to suspect the FBI would have any plausible concerns for taking an interest in me. The very notion seemed absurd.

182.   At one point during the afternoon he asked hypothetically if I would take the proverbial "tap on the shoulder" if ever I was asked – would I join the FBI if asked. I said, "No". It was the same answer I had given Susan years ago in 1997 when she had tried to recruit me in my apartment.

183.   We spent 2 or 3 hours in Central Park talking and walking, then meandered back through the streets of the Upper West Side and eventually made our way into Riverside Park where Steve said he knew a good place we could go for a beer. The park is a thin strip of land along the Hudson River abutted by a boat marina full of sailing boats and cabin cruisers, and a long line of well tended community gardens.

184.   Not far from the gardens, Steve pointed out a small cafe pavilion and directed me up a small hill towards it. We sat down at an outside table with sweeping views over the river, ordered a beer each and continued to talk as it got dark. At one point as Steve lent forward over the table he surreptitiously stole a nervous glance down the inside of his shirt, apparently, I supposed in hindsight, to make sure he wasn't accidentally revealing his microphone, or wire, he apparently used to record the conversation.

185.   We spent the late afternoon and early evening talking. He disclosed a lot of details without connecting everything and without answering my many questions. Innuendo, enough pieces for a puzzle, not a black and white confession. In telling me these things, he had disclosed something significant, something I had not been aware of before from all the facts and insights he had given me:

that the FBI was targeting me - had me under surveillance and was interfering in my life. But the big mystery remained: What did I do; what was its interest in me?! The connection to me was not clear. The pieces of the puzzle Steve had handed me still did not make sense. What was I to make of Susan's role in it; when did she turn on me? For much of the relationship I thought we were set for marriage, and indeed, it was a sentiment she reciprocated, I believe, and invited me to her family home in Detroit for Christmas in 1997 with the expectation we would get engaged.

I was surprised and confused. Steve tactfully had not filled in all the details, but left gaps for me to join the dots: where had he got all his information from, what were his sources, what were their reasons and who were they taking their orders from? How and why did he know so much about personal and private details of my life? Why so much talk of Freeport McMoran, comprehensive details of Susan's work, detailed knowledge of my life, the odd looks, his unusual concern at Matthew Levey's call: what was going on I wondered?

10. June 2004: Kroll – questions focused on Freeport McMoran:

186. I called Matthew Levey back. I tried a few times to get through to him, starting late that afternoon while I was still with Steve and over the next day or so, and left messages. But there was no call back.

187. Several days went by and I met with the mutual friend, Julie who had introduced me to Kroll, where she now worked too, fulltime. Julie and I met for a coffee at a small street cafe near Kroll's midtown office as a prelude to a tentative more formal meeting with Matthew Levey. Julie came down with another Kroll employee but before confirming Matthew Levey's availability to meet, she had some questions for me. She was acting as gatekeeper. During the general chit chat that ensued, out of the blue, out of context to anything else we discussed, she asked me what I thought of Freeport McMoran; what I thought of CEO Jim Bob Moffett; did I think there might be any connection between the new pressures and uncertainties in my life and Freeport she asked me rhetorically. It

echoed Steve Garber's recent disclosures to me in Central Park. Co-incidence? It seemed unlikely. I was surprised. They were strange questions - but at the time I had still not made the connection to Matthew Levey at Kroll and Freeport. A number of people, independently it seemed, were suddenly raising Freeport McMoran with me. Julie then asked me to wait while the two of them went back up to check if he was still available to meet with me.

188. After 10 minutes they remerged and I was ushered up the lift and into Kroll's foyer. Evidently, my naiveté secured my pass upstairs. From there, I was led directly down a corridor and introduced to Kroll himself as we walked by his corner office before I was shown into Levey's office.

189. Matthew Levey was sitting behind his desk ensconced in his work when we walked in seemingly unannounced. Several State Department acknowledgement awards hung prominently on his office wall for some undisclosed endeavours. He dressed carefully, all in trendy black, a black skivvy, slacks and shoes as if out of the set of the popular 1960s kids TV show "Thunderbirds". He was around my age, affable and we chatted for a while.

190. He said he had not been at Kroll that long, and that his management of my assignment had helped him establish his credibility with the firm and show them the sort of thing he was capable of achieving.

191. **June 2004: Reflection on Garber's disclosures:** It wasn't till later that evening that all the pieces of the puzzle fell into place. I came to the realisation my life had been turned upside down by events associated with Freeport McMoran, and years of interference from the FBI! (Steve Garber verbally confirmed this a few months later in September 2004 – details later in this Declaration). Slow to connect the dots perhaps, but to an innocent, a regular citizen as I was, not a veteran agency insider, the dots seemed implausibly far apart. How could I be caught up in something like this? I seemed so remote from the issue; so peripheral. It seemed inconceivable. Steve Garber told me most people have no idea they have been targeted by the FBI, so I shouldn't feel bad on that count.

192. But at the time in June 2004, my immediate response to Garber's disclosure to me in Central Park was to wonder if I might have overlooked something, drawn the wrong conclusion, perhaps I had done something illegal by mistake which I hadn't realised. I also wondered whether it might be possible that the FBI had made a mistake - a case of mistaken identity - in targeting me.

193. However, as Garber was to clearly reaffirm in September 2004, the FBI had targeted me intentionally and Freeport was the reason. From Holmes and Garber's focus on my 12 March 1996 analyst report, the threats I had received in Freeport's boardroom alcove in 1996, the odd occurrences in my personal life and invasions of privacy, the disparate people that had raised details of Freeport with me, nothing else made sense and nothing else came close to explaining and tying everything together, something Steve Garber subsequently confirmed in September 2004.

194. My work on Freeport McMoran emerged as the sole possibility for the FBI's extensive interest in me: Why Freeport, why would the FBI get involved? A friend succinctly summarised the situation: There's so much money at stake; it's a huge US company; the people involved (Kissinger, former US ambassadors, military advisers, intelligence agency personal). That's the sort of thing the FBI is interested in. That's exactly what they do - protect money and power.

195. I was hearing it from the FBI – Holmes and Garber. Others echoed the same: the huge money at stake for Freeport, the killings in West Papua, Indonesia, the people involved, deep connections to Washington. The issues ticked all the right boxes. It was a no brainer to someone who understood the FBI's ways.

196. As I discussed Kroll, I relayed how Matthew Levey had me call around the activist community in the US in 2003 to find those interested in Indonesian mining issues. "That just reaffirms it," my friend said. "These are patient people," they added referring to Kissinger and other Washington types associated with the company. "You don't get into positions of power at the top like that without patience and attention to detail. They are probably just being exceedingly careful, checking every possible angle, just to see on the off-chance if you know someone or something they had overlooked

who could potentially implicate them in this [the killings of indigenous West Papuans around the mine]. They're taking no chances."

197. **The immediate aftermath of the Report:** Events of the recent years came flooding back with a new significance. I remembered the mild rebuke I received at work at SG Warburg after the research report I authored on Freeport in March 1996, the distribution ban that followed - analyst reports could no longer be released without the personal sign-off of the head of research; I then recalled the cold treatment that followed from Freeport McMoran itself which initially denied me an invitation to the analyst briefing in May that year at Freeport's HQ in New Orleans; then the threat I received in the Freeport boardroom alcove after raising the issue again during an analyst briefing about the State Department's investigation of the company for human rights abuses; I remembered the first thing Warburg did when it hired my replacement later that year was to send him on a Freeport McMoran sponsored trip to West Papua, Indonesia to see the controversial but hugely valuable Grasberg mine. In subsequent years I became aware of 7 or 8 other professionals targeted around this time for their work on Freeport McMoran (refer to my Declaration 16 November 2022).

198. **What does the FBI have to hide?** The connection between my work at Warburg, the FBI and Freeport McMoran had been clearly established in the days following my talk with Garber and reconfirmed in September 2004, but there were other questions that remained unanswered. Steve Garber's disclosure to me had set off alarm bells, raised doubts and more questions about the potentially unpalatable role of the US government in West Papua, Indonesia and in backing Freeport.

199. *[**Comment:** If the FBI is doing all this to me to intimidate others to stay away from sensitive issues, then it seems there was something they feared in relation to my report and my question to Jim Bob in Freeport's boardroom about the State Department investigation into the company. But what exactly was it that they were afraid of? If the FBI or Freeport had done nothing wrong, if the eye witness accounts of murder and torture of indigenous protestors coming out of West Papua, Indonesia were wrong, if they had nothing to hide, what was it they were so sensitive about?*

Why so much interest in a young analyst's comments if there was no truth to what was said. But highly sensitive they were.

200. Steve's disclosures had opened Pandora's box - what does it say about what the FBI and/or CIA secretly think or know Freeport McMoran is up to in West Papua, Indonesia; what is the extent of their own involvement in West Papua, Indonesia supporting Freeport; who were the Americans the FBI was attempting to protect - presumably Henry Kissinger, Jim Bob Moffett - but who else? What had been done and what was at stake and for whom? It raised new questions about what was going on in West Papua, Indonesia. (Refer to my Declaration of 16 November 2021 for some background details).

201. It also raised questions about a parallel sphere - issues of civil liberties, privacy and due process, indeed the integrity and health of democracy in America.]

11. September 2004: Another meeting with Steve Garber: The Blue Water Grill

202. A few months passed since Steve Garber had made his chilling revelations to me during the walk in Central Park that the FBI had been interfering in my life for the past 8 years. That was June 2004. It was now September 2004 and I had returned to NY for a conference and I arranged to meet Steve again.

203. I wanted to disclose to him that I had now comprehensively joined the dots, find out whatever else I could about the circumstances, and discuss what he had implied to me in June about the FBI and Freeport. I called Steve and after he checked with his "work" (FBI) before committing, called me back the next morning and offered to meet me at a lecture I was attending at Tibet House that night. The lecture was presented by Columbia University professor Bob Thurman on Buddhist philosophy, a topic I had an interest in.

204. True to the FBI's harassment campaign, Steve arrived late, after the talk had started, and evidently in order to embarrass me in front of people I knew, made a prominent entry, pretended to be drunk, slurring his words with an attendant and swaggered slightly as he walked through the gallery space to take a seat at the back. After the talk, I mentioned to a few people we bumped into as we left that Steve was an undercover FBI agent and he was just affecting a cover. They looked oddly at him but weren't sure what to make of his behaviour or my disclosure. Some people believed it, some didn't, and some were confused - the usual mix of responses I received when exposing details of FBI interference. As Steve and I emerged onto the street and started to walk down 15th street away from the others he promptly "sobered" up, acted completely "normal".

205. We walked to the Blue Water Grill nearby in Union Square, a seafood bar and restaurant he suggested. We took a seat at the plush bar with dimmed light and background music, ordered a drink and watched as an attractive barmaid went about her work. A large mirror behind the bar lined the wall in front us in which various liquors were placed and staff came and went. A few people mingled nearby.

206. **Garber confirms the FBI's operation:** I turned to Steve and got down to business. I asked him about the Freeport - FBI connection. I asked him, seeking to confirm his insinuating remarks made to me when we had met earlier, in June that year, in sum and substance, "You are doing this for the FBI right? To confirm, I've been targeted by the FBI on account of my Freeport McMoran work - is that right?" After a short pause without a response, I repeated the question. I wanted to hear him reaffirm definitively that it was the FBI that was behind the attack on me, and that their reason was my Freeport work as he had insinuated. I wanted to leave no doubt, no uncertainty about who he was working for and what the reason was for the interference I had been subjected to. Garber nodded and said, in sum and substance, "Yes." Then, only partially joking, I asked him if the FBI was planning to kill me now that I had made the connection to Freeport. Steve took the question seriously, saying, "No.

They don't kill people for this sort of thing...though they might kill criminals," he added nonchalantly with an inscrutable poker face.

207. The most consistent thing about him was that he came across as not particularly enthusiastic about his work. He later confided in me that he felt each of his two careers had been very average to date: at the FBI and as a biologist - he expressed a sense of genuine disappointment. The ambiguity between agent, target, companion or friend was pronounced at times, a bond of convoluted emotions. It seemed that with every encounter with the FBI I was learning a little more about the agency, its people and their motivations and I hoped Steve might let something slip that would reveal more about my situation.

208. Steve excused himself from our conversation and went to the men's room. As he came back, from behind, he fixed his gaze on me not mindful I could see him in the mirror. He screwed up his face and drew a deep breath revealing something humane - it looked like he felt some degree of reticence or remorse. Perhaps Steve had not lived up to his own humanist standards in his role with the FBI or in his life.

209. As Steve momentarily stood there silently looking at me, he seemed apprehensive, uncertain, possibly surprised that I had contacted him. I felt he was eyeing the fruits of his labour, a labour undertaken with regrets, as he faced the meaninglessness and challenge to his values of what the FBI directed him to do. I thought he was dealing with issues of his own conscience acting on state orders he evidently didn't always agree with. There was a worn and slightly tired look that comes with years of carrying burdens, surrendering and compromising ones will to the will of others, of using people; a frayed and thwarted conscience that manifests as an indifferent and apathetic attitude to a job that seemingly lacked satisfaction and meaning for him. He had a doctorate in herpetology but now found himself a henchman of the state, Plan-B, a job whose demands were frequently at variance it seemed with his own personal inclinations and judgement, including the political targeting of me, the onetime partner of one of his own agents, a work colleague of his. The FBI must know that the

directives it gives to agents will at times be met with resistance, go against the grain, against a good person's sense of justice and fairness, not legal, and Steve must have been tempted to resist their orders on occasions as did Susan, to be disobedient. Harming the innocent was not his thing it seemed, however, despite whatever reservations he might have had, he had obviously not resigned from the agency.

210. I wondered if Steve had been particularly ambitious and eager to climb through the ranks of the FBI, but he didn't strike me as overly energetic or hard line. He seemed like a normal middle-aged man, a little stressed, facing the pressures of family life, career and mortgage. He followed through on their orders and did as directed, not, it seemed, out of ideological alignment, he was too experienced, he knew enough to know what the game was, but presumably for the money and career, like 99% of the population evidently would if given the chance. He was making a buck out of it. It appeared he just went along looking after his own interest and didn't care enough about the harm he caused others to be deterred. Personal self-gain. He was working for powerful people in a dog-eat-dog world.

211. He took his seat again. Sensing his reservation, I asked him how often he did this sort of work, targeting innocent people as payback for the FBI, turning ordinary citizens' lives upside down. With surprising candidness, he said, "Fortunately not very often." Then he taunted, revealing limits to his empathy, "but if I was ever called to testify in court about this, I would probably lie."

212. **DOJ- False information:** Some years later, I came across a newspaper article, from 2002, the year before this conversation with Steve, in which US judges had found the FBI and the US Department of Justice (DOJ) had deliberately provided "false information" to the courts, with the intention of misleading them in applying for "more than 75 applications for search warrants and

wiretaps"[39]. The FBI and DOJ also improperly shared information with prosecutors the report said.

(The article is attached hereto as Exhibit 5.)

---

[39] T. Kelly, 25 August 2002 Court Reveals FBI Deceit, Sun Herald. Citation in: Andrew Lynch and George Williams, 2006 What Price Security? Taking stock of Australia's anti-terror laws, University of New South Wales Press. p40.

STATUTORY DECLARATION

This record was acknowledged before me on 30th day of August, 2022

by WILLIAM EDGAR KABLE

W E Kable
Notary Public -   Official Stamp

WILLIAM EDGAR KABLE
NOTARY PUBLIC
N.S.W. AUSTRALIA

SIGNED BY:

John Wilson
30 August 2022

Document Description

This certificate is attached to page 81 of a Declaration, dated August 30 2022, consisting of 183 pages.

List of attachments

213. Annexed hereto are true and accurate copies of the following exhibits:

   a. **Exhibit 1:** Declaration of John Wilson, dated November 15, 2021. (Dated 16 November 2021, Sydney, Australia. This is an excerpt in full of an extended composite document. In the process of extracting it, the page numbers have been changed from the original by the PDF program). – – – – – – – – p84

   b. **Exhibit 2:** Selected correspondence between John Wilson, Barry Fisher and DOJ/OIG/FBI: Letters from John Wilson dated March 9, 2015, and February 23, 2016. Letters from Barry Fisher dated June 24, 2016, and June 5, 2020. Letter from the OIG May 25, 2016. Letter from the FBI June 26, 2020 – – – p115

   c. **Exhibit 3:** Email from John Wilson to Philip Ruddock 14 June 2013. – – – p171

   d. **Exhibit 4:** Andrew C. Revkin, September 15, 1997 When Birds of Man and Nature Meet, Falcons Keep Geese and Gulls From Colliding With Jets, The New York Times – – – – – p174

   e. **Exhibit 5:** T. Kelly, 25 August 2002 Court Reveals FBI Deceit, Sun Herald. Citation in: Andrew Lynch and George Williams, 2006 What Price Security? Taking stock of Australia's anti-terror laws, University of New South Wales Press. p40. – – – – p180

Exhibit 1

III-2. John Wilson First Declaration - 2021

III-2a   John Wilson's first Declaration: 16 November 2021

First notarized Declaration of John Wilson 16 November 2021.
(This was also appended as Exhibit 1 to 30 August 2022 Declaration).

* * * * *

Exhibit 6: *16 November 2021.   First notarized Declaration of John Wilson.*

UNITED STATES DISTRICT COURT
SOUTHERN DISTRICT OF NEW YORK

JOHN WILSON,

                                Plaintiff,

    - against -

FEDERAL BUREAU OF INVESTIGATION,

                               Defendant.

No. [_____]

DECLARATION OF
JOHN WILSON
IN OPPOSITION TO DEFENDANT'S
MOTION FOR SUMMARY JUDGMENT

I, John Wilson, do hereby declare under penalties of perjury:

1. I submit this declaration based on my personal knowledge in support of Plaintiff's Opposition to Defendant's Motion for Summary Judgment in the above-captioned case.

2. I am the Plaintiff in this action.

3. I am a dual Australian and USA citizen.

4. I currently live in Sydney, Australia and have a small equity research consultancy business and live with my wife and two young children.

5. After completing an MBA in 1993 at The Wharton School of the University of Pennsylvania, I moved to New York City and from late 1993 to June 1999 lived at 170 W 74th St, Apt 906, New York, NY 10023.

6. Dialogue reported in this affidavit may be paraphrasing of actual conversation.

7. For a period of 3 years from late 1994 to late 1997 I dated Susan Holmes, during which time she disclosed on multiple occasions details of her undercover work for the Federal Bureau of Investigation ("FBI"). Given the detailed revelations to me of her work for the FBI it is clear I was not a target of the FBI from the outset of our relationship, something which she confirmed.

8. From 1994 to 1997 I worked for SG Warburg (and later SBC Warburg) on Wall Street as an equity analyst covering US listed mining companies.

9. One of the companies I analyzed and published reports on for distribution to fund managers globally was U.S.-based and listed Freeport McMoran. It was, and is, one of the world's largest and most valuable copper companies, worth many tens of billions of dollars, and through its subsidiary Freeport Indonesia controls the Grasberg Mine, one of the largest copper and gold mines in the world, situated in West Papua, Indonesia.

10. On March 12, 1996, I authored a report (hereinafter the "Report") that flagged concerns about Freeport McMoran, which was under investigation by the United States Department of State following eyewitness reports of human rights abuses against indigenous protestors in the region of its massive Grasberg gold and copper mine in West Papua, Indonesia. The Report is attached hereto as Exhibit 1. The company denied any role in human rights abuses and eyewitness reports were never proven in court.

11. The Report mentioned the cancellation of the company's OPIC political risk insurance in October 1995 and was critical of the company's approach to resolving civil disputes. It was published and distributed to investors globally by my employer SG Warburg. *See* Exhibit 1 at 1-2.

12. The 1996 events at the Grasberg mine were of significant interest to the U.S. government, as demonstrated by multiple communications sent from the U.S. embassy in Jakarta to Washington revealed in a document produced by the U.S. State Department in 2014 in response to a separate FOIA request than the one at issue in the instant case. The 2013 FOIA request (F-2013-20605) and an excerpt from the WEP 0002A portion of the subsequent 2016 production concerning the State Department investigation are attached hereto as Exhibit 2.

13. After the Report was published, I was notably excluded from Freeport McMoran's invitation list for the May 1996 annual analyst briefing in New Orleans, to which was standard for all mining analysts from mainstream banks to be invited, and to which I had been invited in the past. Only with persistent requests to their investor relations person was I added back to the list and invited to New Orleans to participate in their annual Wall Street analyst briefing that May.

14. Subsequently, I attended the analyst briefing in May 1996 held at Freeport McMoran's headquarters in New Orleans. There, I was threatened after asking Freeport McMoran's Chairman and CEO, Jim Bob Moffett, a question about the State Department's ongoing investigation of the company for alleged human rights abuses. The CEO affirmed that the state department investigation was ongoing and that an interim report had been completed, but appeared flustered by the question and gave a long winded answer during which he became visibly irritated and annoyed.

15. The person who threatened me (who I subsequently assumed to be a federal agent) addressed me by name and earlier had been sitting among the analysts around the boardroom table during the CEO's presentation and analyst question time. He blended in with the analyst community but I did not recall ever having seen him before. When the analyst briefing ended, I moved out into the alcove that was attached to the boardroom and spoke briefly there with Jim Bob Moffett.

16. Oddly, this person stood slightly behind flanking me and after I moved away from Jim Bob the person moved with me and said to me, "John, I respect you for asking that question," referring to my question during the briefing. "But you might wish you hadn't."

17. Ignoring my own surprise that he knew my name, I replied, "So what, what do I care? What can they do to me?"

18. His response came forth firmly, albeit cryptically, "You might not want to find out,". He then moved away.

19. As described later in this affidavit, in early 1996 Freeport McMoran was under enormous pressure in the face of reports and allegations in the international media of human rights

and environmental abuses at the Grasberg Mine in West Papua, the company's embarrassment over the loss of its OPIC political risk insurance in October 1995, and the March 1996 protests over 3 days at its Grasberg Mine. Indonesian President Suharto was furious with the company as events seemed to be spiraling out of control and unhappy with the damaging exposure in the international media. CEO Moffett made an emergency trip to West Papua arriving March 13, 1996, to negotiate with the traditional landowners.

20. The timing and content of my Report touched a nerve. Following the publication of the Report (on March 12, 1996 the day before CEO Moffett arrived in West Papua) and my question to the CEO, I experienced a campaign of interference and harassment by individuals who identified themselves as working for the FBI that eventually were a factor in my moving away from the United States following intense interference with my employment, social and professional networks, and privacy.

21. In addition to my own experiences of FBI harassment, upon information and belief, at least seven other professionals who made disclosures in the mid-1990s related to Freeport McMoran, including academic and journalists, have described similar interference, including being threatened, blacklisted, and in other ways intimidated for their work. The experiences of these other professionals are detailed in Denise Leith's The Politics of Power Freeport in Suharto's Indonesia. The relevant excerpted pages are attached hereto as Exhibit 3.

22. There are several key indications the FBI holds documents on me, as detailed in this affidavit. These include:

a. Steve Garber confirmed to me in 2004 that he worked for the FBI and that I have been the subject of an FBI interference campaign on account of my work on Freeport McMoran in 1996;

b. Susan Holmes, strongly insinuated the same to me in 2003 during an extensive interview she conducted with me at Cafe Fiorello in NYC;

c. Holmes in 2003 and Garber in June 2004 in separate conversations with me, linked Henry Kissinger, a former board member and advisor to Freeport McMoran, my analyst report from

1996, and insinuated the report embarrassed the company and potentially fuelled shareholder disquiet. I had covered many companies and written many reports during my years as an analyst, but they both raised this one report with me and were intently focused on it. Holmes insinuated I had been set up as an extremist and placed on a watchlist of some kind, in retribution for my work on Freeport McMoran;

d. During the 2003 NYC interview Holmes had extensive detailed knowledge of some of my private conversations and revealed many details of information she had from many private records of mine spanning several decades including state, school, university and employment records;

e. Holmes told me in 1999 in NYC that "You would not believe how surprised I was when I saw your name on the work files." Alluding to "work" was a euphemism for the FBI. In 2003 at Cafe Fiorello she told me that she has photos of me with David Foreman in her "work" files;

f. Subsequent to the 2003 interview with Holmes, agents in Australia and the US revealed they had clear and distinct detailed knowledge of things I discussed with her in 2003;

g. From 2004 to 2020, multiple complaint letters from me, my LA lawyer Barry Fisher, and also my congressional representatives, were sent to a number of U.S. agencies, including DOJ Inspectors General and raising specific questions we were responded to with evasive, incomplete and qualified denials which, for example, deny persons were "employees" of the FBI but not deny they were working in some other capacity, for example, as an independent contractor, for, or providing reports to an agency of the U.S.

Holmes' descriptions of her FBI undercover work:

23. From 1993 to 1997, Susan Holmes made many disclosures to me regarding her work on behalf [of] the FBI.

24. Shortly after I met Holmes in 1994 we started going out and dated until late 1997. She told me that in addition to her "day" job she had a second career where she worked undercover for

the FBI. She made detailed revelations of her work to me with the FBI and assured me I was not a target; I believe I was not a target of any FBI investigation at that time.

25. Around November 1994, shortly after introducing me to Steve Garber, Holmes showed me her FBI identification card. The card had a black background, was plasticky in appearance, possibly laminated, and was around the size of a credit card. I vaguely recall, with less clarity, it displayed her face and personal identification details. She then told me that she worked for the FBI. She was then around 32 years old and told me she had worked for the FBI since she was 27, including a period where she was posted to Ireland by the FBI. She also informed me that she worked at the FBI along with another individual, known to me as Steve Garber.

26. A week or two prior to Holmes showing me her FBI identification card, she invited me on a hike with Steve Garber in Harriman State Park. After the hike, Holmes told me the hike had been a chance for Garber to vet me on behalf of the FBI as Holmes's new boyfriend, due to Holmes's recent six-month posting to Ireland with the FBI, and the fact I, a dual US/Australian citizen, was a foreigner.

27. At that time, Holmes informed me that it was not unusual for the new partner of an individual working on behalf of the FBI to be "checked out".

28. When I invited Holmes to Australia over the Christmas holiday period in 1994, Holmes told me she was required to get permission from her "work" (a euphemism for the FBI) before she could accept the invitation to travel overseas.

29. On around ten or more occasions, from 1994 to 1997, Holmes informed me that she worked for the FBI and several times discussed in extensive detail her background with the FBI, including but not limited to her role, training, and past operations. I was present or accompanied her on several FBI related undertakings. Some of these details are described below.

30. On several occasions, Holmes asked me to accompany her on trips and to social gatherings that she later informed me had been part of her FBI assignments. One involved an unofficial Sierra Club volunteers after work drinks gathering around 1995-6 in a restaurant in NYC with

Montanan tree spiking suspect James B. who was subsequently prosecuted, and at which a number of other undercover FBI agents were present.

31. Holmes showed me her FBI wire device used for covert recording, with two leads, one running over each should[er] and joining at the front. She used this on the above gathering with a suspected tree spiker from Missoula, Montana visiting NYC around 1995-96.

32. Holmes told me that she had received firearms training from the FBI, that she had an FBI issued handgun that she kept in her apartment, and that she regularly attended FBI training programs at Quantico.

33. Holmes showed me several T shirts and other clothing items bearing the FBI's initials in large letters at her New York City apartment in and around 1997.

34. Holmes told me several times between 1994 and 1997 that she focused on eco-extremists for the FBI in the eastern half of the U.S.A. She said she was not directly involved with the western half and its handling of the Unabomber case, a high profile case that had been successfully closed in 1996 with the arrest of Ted Kaczynski in Montana, though on occasion she had discussed the matter in general terms with me or in my presence with others.

35. During 1994 to 1997 Holmes mentioned at least two of her FBI work targets. One was Dave Foreman, founder of the Wildlands Network and co-founder of Earth First! who is a high-profile environmentalist and author. The other was Paul Winter, who performs the annual winter solstice concert at The Cathedral of St John the Divine in NYC, which we used to attend annually. Holmes said Winter had been a student environmental activist and leader years before at college.

36. Holmes took me unofficially on an FBI work trip to meet with David Brower - the eminent "Archdruid" of the US environmental movement in the summer of 1997 when we were in Detroit visiting her family and he was visiting nearby. She said the meeting had been arranged through FBI contacts, to bolster her understanding of the Sierra Club Board (which she was on) in order to boost her credibility with other board members, including David Foreman.

37. On a trip to Holmes's family home in Detroit in 1997, Holmes' mother discussed Holmes' role with the FBI with me.

38. Holmes told me she worked with the FBI undercover notionally on a full-time basis though it was more like a sleeper agent arrangement and she was only occasionally required to do agency work. She said herself and others like Steve Garber were not "employees" nor classified as "Special Agents". Instead her role was akin to an independent contractor and she said a lot of undercover agents work for the FBI by a similar arrangement, the term for which was not generally known to the public.

39. Holmes attempted to recruit me to the FBI in 1997. She pitched me in my apartment one afternoon and strongly encouraged me to apply saying the FBI was looking to recruit more people who work on Wall Street.

40. In mid 1996, I watched her use her FBI identification card to gain access past a security point at an Irish folk music concert we were attending in New York City where Holmes' was targeting one of the performers.

41. When we eventually arrived backstage after a delay, Mary said, "Hi Susan, your cover is blown." She looked at me and back to Susan to see what her response might be. Susan didn't say anything clear, mumbling something like "Oh" under her breath. Mary continued, "Security called down, said there was an FBI agent coming down with a tall blonde guy [alluding to me]". There were only a few people in the room, and we were the only ones to come in recently.

42. Afterwards, as we walked home, Holmes told me that she and her FBI colleagues spend a lot of time targeting "dissidents" and others to assist the FBI in smearing, marginalizing, and blacklisting them, and turning their personal life upside down to the extent they can.

43. Holmes mentioned some of her other FBI work assignments as we walked. This included attendance at a party with other young women working on behalf of the FBI on the boat of a well known Saudi Arabian businessman and alleged international arms trader who had been implicated in money laundering and the US Iran-contra scandal.

44. Holmes detailed specific tactics and told me, in sum and substance, "The FBI tries not to do physical things, not leave a physical trail to get the police and courts involved."

45. "How do they do that?" I asked. She responded, "They find out who their friends and family members are, where they hang out, what they do, and get them to help; to say and do things to them; to attack them verbally and un-befriend them."

46. I asked, "Don't people complain?" Holmes said, "Yes, people complain once they realize that the FBI is involved. But a lot of people don't realize, they don't know that something has happened because of the FBI. If they do find out and complain, the FBI delays responding and then misrepresents the complaint they are responding to, when they do eventually respond".

47. Holmes told me in 1999 that "You would not believe how surprised I was when I saw your name on the work files." Her alluding to "work" was a euphemism for the FBI. We were having dinner at the South Sea Port in mid 1999 in NYC and she added cryptically, "I'm not going to let them do this to you!". This and her statement in 2003 (below) of having photos of me with David Foreman in her "work files" indicates the FBI holds documents and records on me.

Background to events at US mining company Freeport McMoran's Grasberg Mine, West Papua around March 1996:

48. Freeport McMoran's Grasberg Mine in West Papua: The project area around the Grasberg mine has had a long history of violence following the deposit's discovery in 1988. A massive expansion of Freeport's land holding in the area was granted in 1994 rising from around 6 million acres to 9 million acres without requirement to compensate the traditional owners. Further, the concessions were granted without stringent environmental controls. The ensuing conflict over the years, starting in 1994, and including the 1994 Christmas Day massacre, resulted in the deaths of hundreds of indigenous protestors. The relevant excerpted pages are attached hereto as <u>Exhibit 4.</u> (Denise Leith, 2003 The Politics of Power Freeport in Suharto's Indonesia, University of Hawai'i Press. p64)

49. Forced relocations were undertaken by the military reportedly with Freeport's material assistance, and the company, or a subsidiary, also directly funded the Indonesian military and certain Indonesian army officers. To assure continued operations at Grasberg, Freeport built its own private security force, frequently recruiting from US forces, the FBI and CIA. The company has also paid for and provided material support to the Indonesian military and police, to the tune of millions of dollars a year, and offered material support to military operations in West Papua. The NYT also reports estimates that the military had killed 160 people in the area of the mine and surrounds between 1975 and 1997. The relevant excerpted pages are attached hereto as <u>Exhibit 5</u>. (Jane Perlez and Raymond Bonner, December 27, 2005 Below a Mountain of Wealth, a River of Waste, The New York Times)

50. It was the Grasberg riots that went from the 10th to the 13th March 1996 that my analyst report of 12 March 1996 commented on, riots that were also commented upon in the international media, and were closely scrutinized by the US embassy in Jakarta - as was revealed subsequently through an FOIA request (F-2013-20605) I made to the State Department. (US State Department response dated 15 December 2016 to F-2013-20605). In March and April 1996 there were multiple communications sent from the US embassy in Jakarta to Washington as indicated in the FOIA response. It is clear from the cables that the US embassy in Jakarta had a very hands-on role assisting Freeport manage the fallout. Cables from the embassy conveyed details of the gravity of the situation to Washington. The authorities were in no mood for dissent either at home in Washington, or in Indonesia. This was the behind-the-scenes, nonpublic, background to which my analyst report was published 12 March 1996. The relevant excerpted pages are attached hereto as <u>Exhibit 6.</u> (A Wall Street Journal News Roundup, Riots in Indonesia quelled; U.S. mine prepares to reopen, Wall Street Journal, Eastern edition, pA15.)

51. At the height of the riots Jim Bob Moffett, Freeport's CEO, under pressure from Suharto, made an emergency trip to Indonesia arriving on 13 March to try to resolve the conflict and placate the traditional owners. He met with the traditional owners' representatives and offered them

new incentives, including a 1% royalty on sales from Grasberg. He also held meetings with Indonesian military commanders. In the aftermath of the riots 3000 to 4000 additional troops were moved into the area and an Indonesian warship was stationed at the port of Amamapere. The relevant excerpted pages are attached hereto as <u>Exhibit 7.</u> (Denise Leith, 2003 The Politics of Power Freeport in Suharto's Indonesia, University of Hawai'i Press. p203-4.)

2003 Interview by Holmes on behalf of the U.S. government

52. On or around Saturday, May 10th, 2003, Holmes subjected me to a series of intense questioning at Cafe Fiorello, 1900 Broadway in New York City

53. During the roughly two and a half hours, Holmes acknowledged to me she was undertaking an interview at the behest of a U.S. government agency.

54. During the interview, Holmes detailed a myriad of specific details of my life spanning many decades, continents, and people.

55. These details included but were not limited to information regarding: personal conversations with current and former peers and colleagues going back decades; phone calls I had made on my private home phone; minor traffic offenses incurred in Australia; work records from various companies I had worked at over the years; records of school and university grades; records of purchases; records of state tests; medical records; and camping records at US national parks.

56. During the interview, Holmes also asked a large number of questions about my background, family, contacts and opinions.

57. She asked me if I remembered the report on Freeport McMoran I had published about the killings, the threat I received in the boardroom alcove, the state department investigation, and loss of OPIC political risk insurance. "Yes, I remember it," I said having to think for a moment to recall it.

58. "What did you think would happen when you published the Freeport note?" she asked.

59. I was surprised she raised the topic, though she had discussed it with me previously and I thought had some personal interest in it. "I thought nothing would happen, possibly someone might say something, maybe reprimand me. If the world were truly evil, I thought I might lose my job over it," I said.

60. She looked at me intently. "You did? You thought you might lose your job? Didn't you care? It was a good job, didn't you want to keep it?" she prodded.

61. "It was fair to raise the Freeport issues - it was a good issue to raise and I thought it was reasonable to do so. Why should indigenous people be killed for their land and nobody say anything? If I lost my job, I thought I could just go find another one," I said.

62. Holmes insinuated that I had been targeted by the FBI on account of my Freeport McMoran work report and subsequent questions to the company.

63. Holmes mentioned specific incidents in detail with individuals she alluded to by name or description and events she was aware of between 1994 and 1997 from my work in NY at Warburg and subsequently 1997-1998 at investment bank Dresdner Kleinwort Benson (DKB) in NYC, which she was aware of through her own sources. These included detailed knowledge of private discussions I had with HR, IT and other specific individuals at both firms. She was aware too of private conversations I had had with certain people at work, whom she alluded to by name or description. For example, re my time at DKB she knew details of someone who had gone through my briefcase and retrieved a book around early 1998; details of my discussion with HR in late 1998; details of Stefan H. odd statement to me as we went to a meeting in NYC around 1998; events and attendees of a lunchtime celebration near work in 1998; reactions of my boss to an IT incident on my computer. There were many more such details she raised across Warburg, DKB and likewise when I moved back to Australia in 1999 to work at Multiplex in Sydney. She was inexplicably aware of specific incidents and conversations with specific individuals at Multiplex.

64. There were lots of little things Holmes knew from my life spanning many decades, including in Australia, USA, and from certain other countries I had travelled which she mentioned and asked me about. Holmes knew and gave the names and/or descriptions of specific people I knew from my past, school peers and friends, university, work colleagues, etc and related incidents. The incidents were trivial in nature, but she had detailed knowledge of them. The information revealed was consistent with someone who had met or spoken with those people she mentioned and suggests the FBI has records or documents on me.

65. Holmes asked me detailed questions about my efforts to travel to West Papua in the mid 1980s for hiking. This is the region where the Grasberg Mine was subsequently located after discovery in 1988.

66. Holmes' told me details about a NY undercover attempted drug sting against me around late 1996 as I walked home from work. The person seemed out of place on the street in front of my apartment building, and I asked him what he wanted after he made eye contact with me - thinking he might be a beggar. But he was selling drugs. I had no interest in that sort of thing nor intention of buying anything, but in the interview in 2003 Holmes relayed comments she said were made by the undercover officer about his interaction with me, and she asked me if I hadn't realized he was an undercover officer. It seems I was inexplicably targeted by him, that the dealer was aware of who I was, and that Holmes was subsequently informed of the interaction through her work. This suggests the FBI holds documents on me.

67. Holmes also inexplicably had knowledge of specific phone calls I had received or made from my home phone a year or two after we had split up. She mentioned 3 in detail, all around 1998 and 1999, not just meta data, date, time, number, owner of the number - but she knew the content of the call as well:

68. "You received a call from some girl asking you if you wanted to go out on a date. A trader. Who was she, how did you know her and why didn't you want to go out?" Susan asked. I tried to recall the conversation from some years before and then answered.

69. Holmes then asked, "You made a call enquiring about possibly joining a yoga class. Who was the person you spoke to - did you know them? Why were they so rude?" It's true, the person was surprisingly rude. I didn't know her, I had never spoken to her before. Who knows!? But again, Susan knew the details of the call.

70. Susan also knew the details of a call I made around June 1999, shortly before I left the US permanently, in the context of "courtesy calls" I made to a few people I didn't know that well but had been loosely associated with to let them know I was leaving. Again, the call had had a distinctive quality, something unexpected, which Susan was aware of and assumed that I would likely remember as she made mention of it.

71. There were lots of other interferences in my various jobs and personal life. These accounts are included in a transcript of around 200 pages based on my notes and recollections of the 2003 interview with Holmes and other events.

72. Furthermore, during the interview, Holmes insinuated to me that Garber was responsible for the interference I had faced in my personal and professional life in the years since 1996. Susan knew of these events from her own sources and asked about or mentioned some to me, such as: an email at DKB I received that someone had interfered with; she was aware from her own sources of specific things certain people had said to me and events at work at Warburg, DKB and Multiplex; and she was aware of surveillance I had been under, including distinctive comments about my walk to work one morning at Warburg in NYC around 1996; a meeting in midtown with a lawyer around 1997; details of an apparent FBI honey trap introduced to me by Steve Garber around 1997-8 while I was at DKB.

73. Susan knew of several intrusions into my apartment during the day while I was at work around 1997-8, including a quarter someone left in the middle of my wooden lounge floor, a cigarette

roach someone left on a saucer in my open kitchen cupboard, small Freeport corporate gifts handed out at briefings like a maglight and other Freeport items stolen from my apartment - but no other items taken, the laptop on my desk moved; and deleted phone messages we left for each other on my home phone and Susan's home phone around the time of our split up in late 1997. (Upon enquiry from me, building management confirmed they had not been in my apartment, nor had any trades people and such like.)

74. Other examples of interference include: Susan's "accident" in the subway with my laptop around 1998 which I lent her briefly after we broke up. She showed up at my apartment one evening covered in dirt and torn jeans after getting off the subway at 72nd St and falling down the stairs she said. But she was not bruised or hurt in any way and the whole story seemed fake. The screen on the laptop was smashed, it was badly damaged and she requested she keep it. At dinner in 2003, Susan asked again why I hadn't let her keep the broken laptop. Around this time in 1997-8 Steven Garber entered my apartment building unannounced. He had accompanied Susan past the concierge/security then once inside went to the basement while Susan came up to get me and we went out. The light in my apartment which had been off when we went out was on when I got back. The doorman later told me Steve Garber had left the building sometime after we had gone out. When I later asked him, Garber denied he had been in my apartment.

75. The large amount of detailed private information Holmes had about many facets of my life, and surprisingly well researched questions she asked, suggests the FBI holds documents on me.

76. By her statements and questions, Holmes insinuated the FBI concocted to paint me as an environmental extremist, or similar, to justify its long term campaign and conceal the connection to my Freeport McMoran work from 1996. If what she indicates is correct, then the FBI has done this intentionally and maliciously to justify interference with me and also to conceal documents from me that I would otherwise be entitled to access under FOIA.

77. In or around 2002 or 2003, Mark W. a former friend from Sydney, who, upon information and belief, works for an Australian law enforcement or intelligence agency, one day in Sydney told me that he was aware Holmes was in Sydney on a work trip and he asked me if she had made contact with me. Indeed, based on Susan Holmes' insights and statements to me in the 2003 interview, it seemed she had travelled to Australia and met with some of the people she talked about. This is another indication the FBI holds documents on me.

FBI disclosures that insinuate misleading FBI classification of Wilson; inappropriate use of FBI FOIA exemptions:

78. Holmes told me during the interview that FBI controls and punishes people who "step out of line" on Wall Street and asked if I was obedient to authority.

79. Holmes asked if I had I ever heard any rumors that the FBI attacked people who were in a position to influence opinion and who spoke out against large US corporations or the government in a way that harmed their interests? "Yes", I said. "What do you know about the FBI's involvement in punishing people who rock the boat, who speak out and embarrassed prominent figures in the public domain? What have you heard?" she asked.

80. Holmes intimated to me in 2003 that I had been set up as an extremist and placed on an FBI watchlist of some kind, in retribution for my analyst report on Freeport McMoran published in 1996. "Do you think it's possible you're on a watch list?" she asked.

81. I was invited by Holmes to join her on a large organised environmentalist campaign rafting trip down the Colorado River in July 1997 with journalists, including from Time Magazine, and David Foreman, whose dory I was allocated to in advance by trip organizers.

82. Holmes said at the interview in 2003 she had photos in her "work files" (a euphemism for the FBI) depicting me in association with David Foreman in the summer of 1997 on the Colorado River but that she had forgotten to bring them for me to dinner that night. She also alluded to photos

from a talk by Dave Foreman I attended later in 1997 in NYC, both encounters were by Holmes' invitation to join her as her partner.

83. Around late 1997, Susan Holmes invited me to hear David Foreman talk in NY after the rafting trip. We went there together and left together, but she said she needed to sit with some other people for "work" reasons in the audience and that I would have to sit on my own, which I did. I vaguely recall someone taking photos of Dave and of the audience.

84. Holmes took me to two other speaking engagements in NY between 1994 to 1997, including to hear the brother of Nigerian environmental activist and poet Ken Saro-Wiwa talk after his 1995 execution by the government and who had stood in opposition to the massive Shell oil development in the Niger Delta.

85. I was invited by Holmes to each of the 3 speaking engagements and we attended together. At the time, I asked Holmes how she knew the talks were on and she said it was through her "work" (euphemism for FBI).

86. At the 2003 dinner at Cafe Fiorello in NY where Holmes covertly interviewed me, she had an intense focus on Dave Foreman, asked me myriad questions about what I knew of him, my opinions of him, and the Colorado rafting trip in 1997 Holmes had invited me on.

87. In the 2003 interview in NYC, Holmes disavowed many details of her personal life revealed during the time we dated for 3 years between late 1994 and late 1997, including denial that I was her guest at the Foreman lecture and denied that I had gone with her as her at her invitation in 1997. Her denial conveys the impression that my attendance at the talk was at my own instigation. In this context, her denials are consistent with the FBI potentially falsely portraying me as associated with a person of interest to them.

88. Between 1994 and 1997, Susan had once told me in response to a question I asked about her work interest in Dave Foreman, "The FBI is no longer concerned about Dave Foreman doing anything wrong, but it's the people attracted to him, associated with him, who they have the interest in. The people attracted to him are the people they are interested in." Given her intense and unusual

focus on what I thought and knew of Foreman that evening this seemed further reason to think this to be the category they were now trying to put me in.

89. At the 2003 dinner interview Holmes asked what I know about handling explosives referring to when I worked with explosives used in the mining industry after graduating with a mining engineering degree from the University of Sydney in 1985. Working on mine sites as a mining engineer was the only time I ever worked with explosives. I had not worked on a mine site as an engineer since 1989, nor ever dealt with explosives in any other capacity.

90. "Could you still wire up a charge?" Holmes asked for example. "Could you blow up a dam?" "Was that the reason you went on a tour group through Hoover Dam when you were out West?" she asked seeming quite serious, referring to one of the multitude of daily tours open to the public which I had gone on one year when I was out West hiking. "Were you scoping the Hoover Dam with the intention of sabotage?!" she demanded to know. I was alarmed by these baseless assertions and loaded questions.

91. "No. What are you talking about. Why would you ask that?!" I responded, not sure whether to even respond to such nonsense.

92. She explored myriad events and innocent tourist visits in this absurd way and presented it with a negative connotation.

93. These questions placed me in fear that Holmes was attempting to create a record casting me, without basis, as a potential ecological extremist. Alarmingly, her questions, implied, without any basis whatsoever I might have an interest in blowing up a dam, or civilian infrastructure. In odd and alarming questions she asked if I had ever planned such an attack on civilian infrastructure.

94. It seemed I was being painted by the FBI as an environmental extremist or terrorist, at least on paper. That would explain why Susan had lied about so many things that evening in 2003, including her invitation to me to hear Dave Foreman talk, her weird questions about explosives and blowing up civilian infrastructure, and her odd emphasis on photos portraying me in close association with Foreman.

95. I had no other links to "environmental extremists" other than through Holmes' FBI work, nor did I ever have any other contact with any such targets than through Holmes.

96. If the FBI chose to do so, it could have drawn on my long term association with Susan Holmes and her role policing aspects of the environmental community for the FBI, to falsely portray me as one of her targets - as an "environmental extremist".

97. Susan Holmes knew me well. We had gone out for three years, and she knew that I would never have anything to do with any of the things she was suggesting. However, that was not the point. The point seemed to be to record the conversation, a conversation she was leading, and which could, in a different context, be used to misconstrue, or mislead and muddy the waters as part of the FBI sting which could falsely substantiate my false listing as an environmental extremist or similar.

98. The FBI, it seems from Holmes' statements and questions, was seeking to create a "plausible" alternative to the Freeport issue to substantiate its interference with me and was attempting to portray me as having close personal ties and association with other people the FBI has, or once had, a "genuine" interest in.

99. Around 1996 I once expressed understanding or empathy for tree spiking, at which time I was evidently caught inadvertently on Holmes' wire which she hadn't told me about at first, but was still recording as we walked home that night from the FBI's sting on Montana activist James B. I didn't know about that sting at the time, but feeling Susan's wire under her shirt as I put my arm around her amorously she told me that it was her recording wire and what that evening with Sierra Club volunteers had really been about from her point of view, as well as a handful of other FBI present.

100. While I didn't endorse the illegal act of tree spiking, my comment echoed Susan's comments that tree spiking had been a very successful means of protecting forests, by warning off logging companies.

101. In 2003, Holmes asked me why I had gone hiking in the Scapegoat Wilderness near Lincoln, Montana in late 1996. Over my work phone at DKB in NY in late 1997, I had reacted to apparent continuing heavy handed surveillance responding to a question from a third party saying sarcastically I

went to Lincoln to see where the Unabomber was from. Seeming to confirm that my work phone was recorded, Holmes around 1997 and then again in 2003 subsequently asked me whether this was really the reason I had gone there hiking. I said no it wasn't the reason; that the reason I had gone there was because of an article in the *New York Times* from that period that quoted an FBI field agent who was involved in the stake out in the mountain forests around Kaczynski's property in the week leading up to his arrest in April 1996. The *New York Times* reported the agent as saying the area was the most beautiful he had seen in America - magnificent - he had commented on the beauty and mentioned seeing and hearing all kinds of wildlife. Later that year in 1996 when I was deciding on a destination for a hiking trip, I chose the destination based on recall of the agent's comments about the majesty of the surrounds near Lincoln and the beauty of the country.

Statements from Holmes and Garber that the FBI targeted me:

102. Across several conversations, Holmes in 2003 and Garber in 2004 independently discussed the Report with me, spoke about then-CEO of Freeport McMoran Jim Bob Moffett and then-board member and company advisor Henry Kissinger, and strongly insinuated the Report was the cause of interference and disruption to my life.

103. In or around June 2004, Garber strongly insinuated I had been targeted by the FBI on account of my 1996 analyst report. He revealed he knew many things, from his own sources, about me.

104. In September 2004, Steve Garber and I again met in NYC at the Blue Water Grill in Union Square. Here, in response to my question, he affirmed that he worked for the FBI, and that I was being targeted as a result of the Report.

105. I asked him, in sum and substance, "You are doing this for the FBI right? To confirm, I've been targeted by the FBI on account of my Freeport McMoran work - is that right?" After a short pause without a response, I repeated the question. I wanted to hear him reaffirm that it was the FBI that was behind the attack on me, and that their reason was my Freeport work.

106. Garber nodded and said, in sum and substance, "Yes."

107. When I asked Garber how often he did this sort of work on behalf of the FBI, Garber said, in sum and substance, "Fortunately not very often," then," But if I was ever called to testify in court about this, I would probably lie."

108. Holmes and Garber's words and actions suggest to me that a substantive paper trail regarding their investigation of me must exist in the FBI's records.

Complaints since 2004 to DOJ, OIG, FBI met with evasive and limited denials

109. The DOJ/OIG/FBI have never investigated the substance of my complaint concerning FBI misconduct which I reported to them repeatedly over the years since 2004 to 2020. They have made only qualified denials based on a partial assessment and at no point have they provided a complete and unqualified response.

110. Following Garber's confirmation to me in 2004 that I had faced long term interference from the FBI after publication of my work report on Freeport March 12, 1996 I made persistent and multiple requests for information to various agencies from 2004 to 2020. Over the years since 2004 I have applied under FOIA to the DOJ/FBI; and I, or my LA attorney, Barry Fisher, have sent complaint letters to the DOJ, OIG and FBI, to my NY representatives - Senator Schumer and Congressman Nadler, and the House Judiciary Committee among others. The most recent letter sent to the DOJ/OIG/FBI is dated June 5, 2020 by Barry Fisher to which there has been no substantive response (Attached as Exhibit 8).

111. The DOJ/FBI/OIG have repeatedly mischaracterized and then denied Holmes, Garber or others named are "employees" or "Special Agents" of the FBI, but not whether they worked in some other capacity for the FBI.

112. The DOJ's repeated misrepresentation of Holmes, Garber, etc as "employees" or "special Agents", and refusal to engage with the full complaint and make unqualified denials is consistent with the tactics described by Holmes to me in 2006 in which they evade accountability and

suggests they are stonewalling me. The motivation apparent in this evasive behavior is an indication the FBI holds documents or records on me.

113. Around 2012-13 I had three one-hour meetings with Philip Ruddock, the former Australian Attorney General (from October 2003 to December 2007) in his electoral office on the topic of FBI, and Australian partnering agencies, interference with me on account of my Freeport McMoran work in 1996. During these meetings I named Australian operatives who had interfered with me. Some of these agents in Sydney have at various times from around 2005 indicated specific knowledge with clear and distinct details from the 2003 interview with Holmes, with multiple instances of such detailed knowledge. Their knowledge is a further indication the FBI holds documents or records on me.

114. Annexed hereto are true and accurate copies of the following exhibits:

a. Exhibit 1: John Wilson's March 12, 1996 Report on Freeport McMoran

b. Exhibit 2: State Department response December 15, 2016 to John Wilson's FOIA request December 11, 2013 (F-2013-20605) re State Department investigation

c. Exhibit 3: Excerpts from Denise Leith, 2003 *The Politics of Power Freeport in Suharto's Indonesia*. University of Hawai'i Press. p7 footnote 10, p262

d. Exhibit 4: Denise Leith, 2003 The Politics of Power Freeport in Suharto's Indonesia, University of Hawai'i Press. p64.

e. Exhibit 5: Jane Perlez and Raymond Bonner, December 27, 2005 Below a Mountain of Wealth, a River of Waste, The New York Times.

f. Exhibit 6: A Wall Street Journal News Roundup, Riots in Indonesia quelled; U.S. mine prepares to reopen, Wall Street Journal, Eastern edition, pA15.

g. Exhibit 7: Denise Leith, 2003 The Politics of Power Freeport in Suharto's Indonesia, University of Hawai'i Press. p203-4.

h. Exhibit 8: Letter from Barry Fisher June 5, 2020 to FBI and others.

Dated: November 16, 2021
Sydney, Australia

Respectfully submitted,

By: _____
John Wilson

Sworn to before me this
16th day of November, 2021

W E Kable
Notary Public

WILLIAM EDGAR KABLE
NOTARY PUBLIC
N.S.W. AUSTRALIA

This is the Annexure ~~marked~~ referred to in the ~~declaration~~ / affidavit of
JOHN WILSON
declared / ~~sworn~~ before me on the 16 day
of NOVEMBER 2021

W E Kable

William Edgar Kable
Notary Public
New South Wales Australia

EXHIBIT 1

FCX: Grasberg Closure Highlights Political Risks
S.G. Warburg & Co. Inc.--RESEARCH NOTES

Subject:	Freeport McMoRan Copper and Gold (FCX--$29)--NYSE	OPINION	
		Current:	ADD
Analyst:	John Wilson, (212) 224-7740		
		Prior:	ADD
Date:	March 12, 1996	Target Price:	32

	Earnings per Share			Cal. P/E 1996E	LT Growth Rate	Yield	Shares O/S (Mil.)	52-Week Range
	12/94	12/95A	12/96E					
NEW	$0.31	$0.98	$1.77	16.4X	25%	3.0%	203	20-30

	Q1/Mar	Q2/Jun	Q3/Sep	Q4/Dec	Total
1994	0.07	0.05	0.07	0.12	0.31
1995A	0.21	0.22	0.30	0.27	0.98
1996E	0.33	0.52	0.45	0.48	1.77
1997E					0.85

o Riots at Grasberg force closure of mine and mill

o Increased military presence highlights potential for escalation of the conflict mid term

o Recommendation under review

Grasberg closure expected to be temporary

Following the reported death (though it is unclear if anyone actually died) of a Dani native on Freeport property last Sunday, Dani villagers rioted forcing the closure of the Freeport mine and mill. After talking with the company, it appears the situation is under control, and currently the expectation is that operations will resume later this week. The military presence in the area has been increased and will remain at higher levels in an attempt to underwrite security. At this stage, we do not anticipate there will be a significant impact to earnings.

Incident points to increased political risk

Our view is that increased military presence poses potential for escalation of the violence in the mid term, heightening the political risk of Freeport's investment in Irian Jaya. Ultimately, Freeport needs to deal with the civil aspects of this situation to allay investors concerns, and possibly also those of the US Department of State. The timing is unfortunate for Freeport as it coincides with the arbitration over whether $100 million in OPIC political risk insurance should be rescinded. The company has increasingly come under scrutiny following reported human rights abuses in the area of the mine and also concerns over its environmental record. The latter was cited by OPIC last November as the basis for withdrawing the $100 million in insurance.

Recommendation under review

Given the declining outlook for copper prices and the increased risk of political unrest at Grasberg, our ADD recommendation is under review.

A version of this note has been prepared for First Call.

S. G. WARBURG & CO. INC. A MEMBER OF THE NEW YORK STOCK EXCHANGE, NASD AND OTHER PRINCIPAL U.S. EXCHANGES. The information herein has been obtained from, and any opinions herein are based upon sources believed reliable, but we do not represent that it is accurate or complete and it should not be relied upon as such. All opinions and estimates herein reflect our judgment on the date of this report and are subject to change without notice. This report is not intended to be an offer, or the solicitation of any offer, to buy or sell the securities referred to herein. From time to time, this firm or its affiliates or the principals or employees of this firm or its affiliates may have a position in the securities referred to herein or hold options, warrants or rights with respect thereto or other securities of such issuers and may make a market or otherwise act as principal in transactions in any of these securities. Any such non-U.S. persons may have purchased securities referred to herein for their own account in advance of release of this report. Further information on the securities referred to herein may be obtained upon request.

EXHIBIT 2

United States Department of State

Washington, D.C. 20520

DEC 1 5 2016

Case No. F-2013-20605
Segment: WEP-0002A

Mr. John C Wilson

Australia

Dear Mr. Wilson:

A Department of State Appeals Review Panel, whose members are listed in an enclosure to this letter, has considered your appeal of February 26, 2015, for the release of two documents withheld in full and 10 withheld in part by the Department in the course of responding to your request under the Freedom of Information Act.

The Panel has carefully considered the grounds on which you based your appeal. It has decided to release in their entirety six documents initially withheld in full or in part. The released material is enclosed.

The Panel has determined that the previously withheld portions of five documents must continue to be withheld. One document must continue to be withheld in its entirety.

The information in one document withheld in full and in the deleted portions of three documents released in part is properly classified in accordance with Executive Order 13526 (National Security Information) despite the passage of time. Its release reasonably could be expected to cause damage to the national security of the United States. It is therefore exempt from disclosure under subsection (b)(1) of the Freedom of Information Act, 5 USC Section 552(b)(1).

The information in the deleted portions of two documents is of such a nature that its release would constitute a clearly unwarranted invasion of personal

- 2 -

privacy. It is therefore exempt from disclosure under subsection (b)(6) of the Freedom of Information Act, 5 USC Section 552(b)(6).

In the case of a document released in part, all non-exempt material that is reasonably segregable from the exempt material has been released.

In your request letter of December 11, 2013, you ask for information concerning a State Department investigation into the activities of Freeport McMoran Copper and Gold and its subsidiary PT Freeport Indonesia in Indonesia. We have searched the State Department Archive System and can find no record of such an investigation.

The Panel's decision represents the final decision of the Department of State. If you wish to seek judicial review of this determination, you may do so under 5 USC Section 552(a)(4).

Sincerely,

Francis Terry McNamara

Chairman, Appeals Review Panel

Enclosures:
List of Panel Members
Six documents

DEPARTMENT OF STATE

APPEALS REVIEW PANEL MEMBERS

Case Control No.: F-2013-20605, WEP-0002A

Chairman:

    Ambassador Francis Terry McNamara

Members:

    Ambassador James F. Mack

    Ambassador William Ryerson

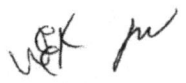

PTQ0053

CONFIDENTIAL PTQ0053

PAGE 01   JAKART 01928 01 OF 02 141045Z
ACTION EAP-01

INFO LOG-00 AID-00 AMAD-01 CA-02 CIAE-00 OASY-00 SRPP-00
      DS-00   EB-01   EUR-01   FBIE-00 H-01   TEDE-00 INR-00
      IO-00   L-01   ADS-00   NSAE-00 NSCE-00 OCS-03   OIC-02
      PRS-00 P-00   SCT-00   SP-00   SSO-00 SS-00   STR-00
      TRSE-00 USIE-00 ASDS-01 DSCC-00 PRM-10 PRME-01 DRL-09
      G-00   /034W
                       ------230F6F 141045Z /38
O 141044Z MAR 96
FM AMEMBASSY JAKARTA
TO SECSTATE WASHDC IMMEDIATE 0637
INFO COMSOCPAC HONOLULU HI IMMEDIATE
USCINCSOC MACDILL AFB FL IMMEDIATE
USCINCPAC HONOLULU HI IMMEDIATE
USMISSION GENEVA
AMEMBASSY CANBERRA
AMEMBASSY PORT MORESBY
AMEMBASSY BONN
AMEMBASSY THE HAGUE
JOINT STAFF WASHDC
SECDEF WASHDC   APPEALS PANEL ACTION: RELEASED IN FULL
JICPAC HONOLULU HI
AMEMBASSY LONDON
DIA WASHDC
JSOC FT BRAGG NC

CONFIDENTIAL SECTION 01 OF 02 JAKARTA 001928

CONFIDENTIAL

CONFIDENTIAL

PAGE 02   JAKART 01928 01 OF 02 141045Z
STATE FOR EAP/PIMBS, DRL/AAA, DS/DSS, DSS/OP/EAP, DSS/ITA, AND
DSS/OP/CC

CINCPAC FOR FPA. AMB. SALMON

E.O. 12958: DECLASSIFY 3/14/2006
TAGS: PHUM, ASEC, CASC, ID

SUBJECT: TRIBAL VIOLENCE IN IRIAN JAYA: SITREP 4: FREEPORT OPERATIONS RESUME

REF: A) JAKARTA 1903 AND PREVIOUS

1. (U) CLASSIFIED BY POLITICAL COUNSELOR BARBARA J. SCHRAGE. REASONS: SEC. 1.5 (B) AND (D).

2. (C) BEGIN SUMMARY: EMBASSY CONSOFF AND ARSO ARE EXPECTED TO ARRIVE IN TIMIKA LATE ON MARCH 14. THE SITUATION IN THE FREEPORT MINING CONCESSION CONTINUES TO RETURN TO NORMAL. THE MINE IS OPEN, MOST FREEPORT WORKERS ARE BACK ON THE JOB, AND THERE HAVE BEEN NO FURTHER OUTBREAKS OF VIOLENCE. ESTIMATES OF THE NUMBERS OF PERSONS INVOLVED IN THE RIOTS HAVE BEEN SCALED BACK. THERE IS NO NEW INFORMATION ON CASUALTIES OR DAMAGE. PRESIDENT SOEHARTO IS REPORTEDLY IRATE THAT THE SITUATION GOT OUT OF CONTROL. FREEPORT SOURCES BELIEVE THERE WILL BE MORE ARRESTS, THAT SENIOR MILITARY FIGURES IN THE AREA WILL BE RELIEVED OF DUTY, AND THAT THERE WILL BE A PERMANENT INCREASE IN TROOP PRESENCE AROUND TIMIKA. A FREEPORT TEAM INCLUDING CEO MOFFETT IS HEARING THE GRIEVANCES OF TRIBAL REPRESENTATIVES IN TIMIKA. FREEPORT BELIEVES THAT "OUTSIDE ELEMENTS" PLAYED A ROLE IN THE INCIDENTS AND HAS PASSED ITS INFORMATION TO MILITARY INTELLIGENCE (BIA) FOR FURTHER ACTION. NGOS GENERALLY BLAME THE DISTURBANCES ON UNDERLYING SOCIO-ECONOMIC INEQUITIES THAT THEY ATTRIBUTE TO FREEPORT'S MASSIVE

CONFIDENTIAL

CONFIDENTIAL

PAGE 03   JAKART 01928 01 OF 02 141045Z
PRESENCE. END SUMMARY.

3. (SBU) CONSOFF AND ARSO DEPARTED JAKARTA 0700 LOCAL TIME MARCH 14 VIA THE DAO'S C-12 AIRCRAFT FOR IRIAN JAYA. ETA TIMIKA IS 1800 MARCH 14. ALTHOUGH WE UNDERSTAND THE AIRPORT IN TIMIKA IS STILL CLOSED TO NORMAL CIVILIAN TRAFFIC UNTIL AT LEAST MARCH 15, THE EMBASSY ARRANGED WITH THE INDONESIAN MILITARY FOR THE C-12 TO LAND.

4. (C) THE SITUATION IN TIMIKA AND TEMBAGAPURA REMAINS CALM, WITH NO FURTHER OUTBREAKS OF VIOLENCE REPORTED. FREEPORT EMPLOYEES HAVE LARGELY RETURNED TO WORK; THE MINE IS NOW BACK IN OPERATION, ACCORDING TO FREEPORT OFFICIALS. ACCORDING TO ONE LOCAL NEWSPAPER, A TOTAL OF SEVEN PEOPLE HAVE BEEN ARRESTED AND 50 WORKERS INJURED. WE HAVE NOT BEEN ABLE TO VERIFY THESE FIGURES; OUR SOURCES HAD NO FURTHER DETAILS OF ARRESTS OR CASUALTIES BEYOND WHAT WAS REPORTED IN REFTEL. THEY DID SAY, HOWEVER, THAT ESTIMATES OF THE NUMBERS OF PERSONS INVOLVED IN THE STRIFE HAD BEEN SCALED DOWN TO NO MORE THAT FIVE TO SIX HUNDRED AT A TIME IN ANY ONE PLACE.

5. (C) FREEPORT SOURCES TELL US THAT FREEPORT HAS GIVEN A REPORT TO MILITARY INTELLIGENCE (BIA) ON THE RIOTING. WE UNDERSTAND THAT BIA, IN TURN, BRIEFED PRESIDENT SOEHARTO. SOEHARTO IS REPORTEDLY

"EXTREMELY IRATE" THAT THE SITUATION GOT OUT OF CONTROL AND BLAMES MILITARY OFFICIALS WHO HAVE RESPONSIBILITY FOR THE REGION. FREEPORT BELIEVES THAT THERE WILL BE MORE ARRESTS, THAT SENIOR MILITARY FIGURES IN THE AREA WILL BE RELIEVED OF DUTY, AND THAT THERE WILL BE A PERMANENT INCREASE IN TROOP PRESENCE IN THE AREA.

6. (C) FREEPORT SOURCES SAY THAT DISCUSSIONS ARE IN PROGRESS BETWEEN A FREEPORT TEAM (INCLUDING CEO MOFFETT) AND A NUMBER OF REPRESENTATIVES NOT ONLY OF THE AMUNGME AND KOMORO TRIBES NATIVE TO THE AREA BUT ALSO

CONFIDENTIAL

PAGE 04   JAKART 01928 01 OF 02 141045Z
OF OUTLYING TRIBES SUCH AS DANI, MONA, AND IKARI. THEY WERE NOT CERTAIN IF GOI AND ABRI REPRESENTATIVES TOOK PART AND DESCRIBED THE MEETING AS ONE IN WHICH FREEPORT WAS BASICALLY SOLICITING THE TRIBESMENS' DEMANDS.

7. (C) THE MOTIVATION BEHIND THE RIOTING REMAINS MURKY. FREEPORT OFFICIALS CLAIM THAT "OUTSIDE FORCES" PLAYED A ROLE IN THE INCIDENTS, AND THEY HAVE PASSED INFORMATION IN THEIR POSSESSION TO BIA FOR FURTHER INVESTIGATION. NGO SOURCES ARE BLAMING THE RECENT RIOTING ON THE SOCIO-ECONOMIC AND POLITICAL SITUATION THAT HAS DEVELOPED SINCE THE ARRIVAL OF FREEPORT IN THE AREA. A NUMBER OF GROUPS, SUCH AS SOME AMUNGME TRIBAL LEADERS WHO WERE IN JAKARTA LAST WEEK TO LOBBY THE PARLIAMENT AND THE HUMAN RIGHTS COMMISSION, ARE CALLING FOR "THREE-PARTY NEGOTIATIONS" BETWEEN FREEPORT, THE GOI, AND THE CONCERNED TRIBES TO REACH A "COMPREHENSIVE SETTLEMENT."

8. (C) FREEPORT HAS RECEIVED WORD THAT THE SAME NGO GROUP THAT STAGED A SMALL DEMONSTRATION AT ITS JAKARTA OFFICES IN SEPTEMBER AT THE TIME THE NATIONAL HUMAN RIGHTS COMMISSION ISSUED ITS REPORT IS PLANNING A SIMILAR ACTION MARCH 15. THEY EXPECT THAT THE DEMONSTRATION MAY BE LARGER THAN THE ONE IN SEPTEMBER BECAUSE OF THE HEIGHTENED PUBLICITY AND EMOTIONS RESULTING FROM THE RECENT

CONFIDENTIAL

UNCLASSIFIED U.S. Department of State Case No. F-2013-20605 Doc No. C05595956 Date: 09/01/2015

NNNNPTQ0054

~~CONFIDENTIAL~~ PTQ0054

PAGE 01   JAKART 01928 02 OF 02 141045Z
ACTION EAP-01

INFO LOG-00 AID-00 AMAD-01 CA-02 CIAE-00 OASY-00 SRPP-00
      DS-00 EB-01 EUR-01 FBIE-00 H-01 TEDE-00 INR-00
      IO-00 L-01 ADS-00 NSAE-00 NSCE-00 OCS-03 OIC-02
      PRS-00 P-00 SCT-00 SP-00 SSO-00 SS-00 STR-00
      TRSE-00 USIE-00 ASDS-01 DSCC-00 PRM-10 PRME-01 DRL-09
      G-00   /034W
                ------------230F72 141045Z /38
O 141044Z MAR 96
FM AMEMBASSY JAKARTA
TO SECSTATE WASHDC IMMEDIATE 0838
INFO COMSOCPAC HONOLULU HI IMMEDIATE
USCINCSOC MACDILL AFB FL IMMEDIATE
USCINCPAC HONOLULU HI IMMEDIATE
USMISSION GENEVA
AMEMBASSY CANBERRA
AMEMBASSY PORT MORESBY
AMEMBASSY BONN
AMEMBASSY THE HAGUE
JOINT STAFF WASHDC
SECDEF WASHDC
JICPAC HONOLULU HI
AMEMBASSY LONDON
DIA WASHDC
JSOC FT BRAGG NC

~~CONFIDENTIAL~~ SECTION 02 OF 02 JAKARTA 001928

~~CONFIDENTIAL~~

~~CONFIDENTIAL~~

PAGE 02   JAKART 01928 02 OF 02 141045Z
STATE FOR EAP/PIMBS, DRL/AAA, DS/DSS, DSS/OP/EAP, DSS/ITA, AND
DSS/OP/CC

CINCPAC FOR FPA. AMB. SALMON

UNCLASSIFIED U.S. Department of State Case No. F-2013-20605 Doc No. C05595956 Date: 09/01/2015

EXHIBIT 3

7. Budiawan, "Human Rights Good for Business," *Jakarta Post*, 2 December 1999.

8. Robert W. Cox, "Global Restructuring: Making Sense of the Changing International Political Economy," *Political Economy and the Changing Global Order*, ed. Richard Stubbs and Geoffrey R. D. Underhill (London: Macmillan, 1994).

9. When referring to the rise of political activism in parties such as the PUDI and PRD in the mid-nineties, Ariel Heryanto ("Indonesia," p. 109) identifies this same phenomenon.

10. Freeport threatened to sue journalists Robert Bryce and Daryl Slusher, university professors Steven Feld, Alan Cline, and Robert Boyer, and environmental activists Lori Udall and Bill Bunch unless they ceased making "false and damaging accusations" about the company, Andrew Duff, "Off the Desk," *Austin Chronicle*, 15-21 December 1995.

11. Greg Earl, "Foreign Miners Warned over Environment," *Australian Financial Review*, 7 December 1995.

12. Formed in 1991, the ICME provides a comprehensive list of its membership <http://206.191.21.210/icme/members.htm>.

13. Eyal Press, "Freeport-McMoRan at Home and Abroad," *The Nation* 261.4 (31 July/7 August 1995): 126; "The Feds Undress Jim Bob: Freeport's Motherlode," *Austin Chronicle*, 10 November 1995, pp. 18-22; and Project Underground, *Risky Business: The Grasberg Gold Mine, An Independent Annual Report on P.T. Freeport Indonesia* (Berkeley, Calif.: Project Underground, 1998).

14. Michael Roe, Seattle Mennonite Church, 2001 FCX shareholder proposal (presented at 2001 Freeport-McMoRan annual general meeting).

15. Gavan Breen, *Let Them Be: West Papua Revisited* (Melbourne; Australian West Papuan Association, 1993), p. 3. The Morning Star hung beside the Dutch flag for eight months until the Indonesians took control.

16. Washington found very little reason to support the dying European power in this dispute. Moreover, the wishes of the indigenous people were irrelevant to the Americans given a number of important strategic and economic factors at the time: Washington wanted to protect its strategic interests in the area by checking what it saw as the growing Soviet influence in Indonesia under Sukarno; needed to protect established economic interests in Indonesia, desired Indonesian support to continue feeding the voracious Japanese appetite for oil and natural resources essential for rebuilding; and believed that if it entered the argument on the side of the Dutch a military conflict would be inevitable—a situation it desperately wanted to avoid with its already growing commitment in Vietnam. Finally, in the belief that it was only a matter of time before Jakarta eventually controlled the island, the United States and its compliant Western allies made the Realpolitik choice of supporting Jakarta.

17. For a comprehensive critique of the New York Agreement and United Nations involvement see Paul W. van der Veur, "The United Nations in West Irian," *International Organization* 18.1 (Winter 1964): 53-73; and John Saltford, "United Nations Involvement with the Act of Self-Determination in West Irian (Indonesia, West New Guinea), 1968 to 1969" (Ph.D. diss., Hull University, 2001).

18. British Embassy, Jakarta, "Confidential Report by Ian Morgan, 3rd Secretary to the British Embassy in Jakarta on visit to West Java and Eastern Indonesia," 28 September-2 October 1968 (London, Public Record Office) FCO 24/444, p. 24.

19. Hans Meijer, interview, Asia/Pacific Program, ABC Radio National (Australia), 17 April 2001. Meijer uncovered Dutch documentation that repeatedly debunks the myth that Holland tried to protect Papuan interests. Aware that, given a free and fair vote, the Papuans would choose independence, Dutch officials turned a blind eye to the illegalities of the Act of Free Choice as "it was not in their interests to fight again with Indonesia because of the Papuans."

20. British Embassy, "Confidential Report by Ian Morgan," p. 24.

21. Reverend Origenes Hokujoku, a participant in the Act of Free Choice and at the time chairperson of the Soekarnopura (Jayapura) City Council, said that the participants were given no choice by the Indonesian military.

Three weeks before the referendum they [those who would vote] were isolated. Instructors continuously pressured them to vote for integration with Indonesia. The electors were given a piece of paper with exact instructions on what to say. There was no way of withdrawing from this sham. If you did there could be serious repercussions against you or your family. I remember we had a final rehearsal to see if we mastered our speeches. One man resisted. He refused to present the obligatory speech. The next morning his body was found in a gorge. My wife was pregnant at the time. Therefore I was given permission to stay home during the weeks preceding the referendum. General Ali Murtopo, the highest officer in Irian, tried to placate me. He had a box of apples imported from Australia to give to my wife, at that time apples cost 3 guilders a piece. We also received towels and transistor radios. We were taken for trips by helicopter. But other times he mocked me. This land belongs to Indonesia, he said. If you want a Free Papua state, then you should ask your god to create an island in the ocean. The Day All Papuans Cried," *Algemeen Dagblad* (The Netherlands), 12 December 1998. E-mail "Kabar-Irian: The Day all Papuans cried" from Evelien van der Broek <brock519@vxs.nl> through KABAR-IRIAN <kabar-irian@nja.org>, December 18 1999).

22. "West Papua: Efforts to Marginalize the People," *Pacific News Bulletin* 9.4 (April 1994): 7.

23. One of the two journalists, Hugh Lunn of the *Courier Mail*, described how he and the Dutch journalist were continually followed by Indonesians to limit their contact with the West Papuans. He states that the Act of Free Choice was the "saddest story" he covered in this thirty years of journalism. "West Papua: An Issue for the South Pacific Forum," *Pacific News Bulletin* 7.3 (March 1992): 6.

24. Ibid. Secret documentation released by the Australian government in late 1999 indicates that although aware that the consensus among the West

EXHIBIT 4

Denise Leith
The Politics of Power

open pit more than 360 meters deep and two kilometers wide filled with green, copper-impregnated water. During its life it had produced approximately thirty-two million tonnes of copper, gold, and silver and had succeeded in generating on average $300 million of revenue annually for the company. In 1988, about 2.2 kilometers away from Ersberg, Freeport announced that it had discovered its El Dorado, Grasberg. There had been rumors of the discovery more than a decade before it was announced. Why the company decided to withhold the announcement of the discovery until 1988 is open to conjecture. Jan van Gruisen, who was Forbes Wilson's Dutch geologist friend, had taken out a concession from the Dutch for the area in 1959 in the name of his company, Oost Borneo Maatschappij (OBM); OBM did not have the finances to join in developing Ersberg, but one of its subsidiaries had retained a 5 percent interest in Freeport Indonesia. It was not until Freeport-McMoRan was able to buy out OBM's interest in Freeport Indonesia that it announced the discovery at Grasberg. Moreover, Freeport did not sign the new contract for Grasberg until the mining laws were amended.[27]

The discovery of Grasberg caused Freeport to sign two new contracts with Jakarta in 1991 and 1994; these effectively gave the company exploration rights for approximately nine million acres and the right to mine any discoveries for a further fifty-year period. The 1991 contract superseded the original 1967 contract and covered not only the existing 24,700 acres (Block A) of the original Ersberg mine but approximately another contiguous 6.5 million acres called Block B, part of which was the new Grasberg site. In 1994 a second contract was signed by a [...] Freeport Indonesia subsidiary, PT IRJA Eastern Minerals Corporation, for another 2.6 million acres. This new contract of work encompassed three separate areas of land, which are referred to as the Eastern Mining Block and are next to Freeport's Block A and Block B. These three blocks gave Freeport a total of nine million acres of exploration leases with guaranteed thirty years of operating and the option of two ten-year extensions. Once again Freeport was not forced to operate under restrictive environmental laws or made to compensate the traditional landowners for loss of land.[28]

The elephant that was Grasberg dwarfed Ersberg in every respect. Not only was it physically more imposing (standing 4,270 meters above sea level, it was 500 meters higher and 2.5 kilometers in diameter), it double the ore recovered from Ersberg during its life. What can be said at Grasberg. In 1999 alone, Grasberg produced more [...] Ersberg's productivity pales into insignificance compared with the phenomenal unearthed at Grasberg. [...] sidered the Grasberg complex.[29] constitutes the world's largest known

deposit of gold (91.4 tonnes of gold compared to its nearest rival, Freegold in South Africa, at 60.44 tonnes).[30] Grasberg also currently holds the world's third-largest open-pit copper reserves (32 million tonnes). At extraction rates of less than 10 cents per pound, it is the lowest-cost copper producer in the world. Estimates of Grasberg's worth continue to increase so that despite all predictions the final worth of the mine is impossible to establish; it is classified as "open at depth," which is a euphemism for a bottomless pit. Grasberg is yielding a greater percentage of gold per tonne the lower the mine goes. While at its peak Ersberg processed 25,000 tonnes per day (tpd) of ore, Grasberg is currently moving approximately 600,000 tpd of earth and rock while discharging about 250,000 tpd of these into the local river system as tailings.[31] The open-pit Grasberg mine is so large and located at such a high altitude that, except for early morning, the site is continually shrouded in cloud; thus satellite tracking of the gigantic mining trucks, which operate twenty-four hours per day than any other mine in the world, is necessary. On current figures Freeport is expected to earn anything from $40 billion to $50 billion from Grasberg over its projected life of more than forty-five years.[32]

Positioned along the ring of fire, the Freeport mining concessions are in one of the highest potential mineralization zones in the world. And while the worth of Grasberg is impossible to establish, so too is the potential of the Freeport concession. Exploration on more than six thousand sites has identified about seventy potential mining sites with drilling commencing on about ten of these. The most recent Freeport estimates are that the concession, which includes a significant new discovery in the old Ersberg Block A area called the Ersberg East Surface (previously referred to as Guru Ridge), will yield 50.9 billion pounds of recoverable copper and 68.7 million ounces of gold. Its proximity to with the surface and already existing mines will mean that this new discovery can be developed in conjunction with existing ore bodies to create yet another massive open-pit/underground complex processing more than five hundred million metric tonnes of ore. Freeport's Moffett realistically believes that the area will eventually produce other Grasbergs, eclipsing the riches of the Panguna, Ok Tedi, Lihir, and Porgera mines in Papua New Guinea. To exploit these minerals Freeport had invested approximately $4.5 billion in West Papua by early 2001.[33] The [...] wealth that is Freeport is, however, only half the story.

Outsiders do not understand the strong emotional attachment that results from working on, and creating, such a mine. This is not to undermine or negate the indigenous peoples' attachment to the land, which is

EXHIBIT 5

December 27, 2005
The Cost of Gold | The Hidden Payroll

Below a Mountain of Wealth, a River of Waste

By JANE PERLEZ and RAYMOND BONNER

JAKARTA, Indonesia - The closest most people will ever get to remote Papua, or the operations of Freeport-McMoRan, is a computer tour using Google Earth to swoop down over the rain forests and glacier-capped mountains where the American company mines the world's largest gold reserve.

With a few taps on a keyboard, satellite images quickly reveal the deepening spiral that Freeport has bored out of its Grasberg mine as it pursues a virtually bottomless store of gold hidden inside. They also show a spreading soot-colored bruise of almost a billion tons of mine waste that the New Orleans-based company has dumped directly into a jungle river of what had been one of the world's last untouched landscapes.

What is far harder to discern is the intricate web of political and military ties that have helped shield Freeport from the rising pressures that other gold miners have faced to clean up their practices. Only lightly touched by a scant regulatory regime, and cloaked in the protection of the military, Freeport has managed to maintain a nearly impenetrable redoubt on the easternmost Indonesian province as it taps one of the country's richest assets.

Months of investigation by The New York Times revealed a level of contacts and financial support to the military not fully disclosed by Freeport, despite years of requests by shareholders concerned about potential violations of American laws and the company's relations with a military whose human rights record is so blighted that the United States severed ties for a dozen years until November.

Company records obtained by The Times show that from 1998 through 2004, Freeport gave military and police generals, colonels, majors and captains, and military units, nearly $20 million. Individual commanders received tens of thousands of dollars, in one case up to $150,000, according to the documents. They were provided by an individual close to Freeport and confirmed as authentic by current and former employees.

Freeport said in a written response to The Times that it had "taken appropriate steps" in accordance with American and Indonesian laws to provide a secure working environment for its more than 18,000 employees and contract workers.

"There is no alternative to our reliance on the Indonesian military and police in this regard," the company said. "The need for this security, the support provided for such security, and the procedures governing such support, as well as decisions regarding our relationships with the Indonesian government and its security institutions, are ordinary business activities."

While mining and natural resource companies sometimes contribute to the costs to foreign governments in securing their operations, payments to individual officers raise questions of bribes, said several people interviewed by The Times, including a former Indonesian attorney general, who said it was illegal under Indonesian law for officers to accept direct payments.

The Times's investigation also found that, according to one current and two former company officials who helped set up a covert program, Freeport intercepted e-mail messages to spy on its environmental opponents. Freeport declined to comment.

More than 30 current and former Freeport employees and consultants were interviewed over the past several months for this article. Very few would speak for attribution, saying they feared the company's retribution.

Freeport's support of the military is one measure of its extraordinary working environment. In the 1960's, when Freeport entered Papua, its explorers were among the very first outsiders ever encountered by local tribesmen swathed only in penis gourds and armed with bows and arrows.

Since then, Freeport has built what amounts to an entirely new society and economy, all of its own making. Where nary a road existed, Freeport, with the help of the San Francisco-based construction company Bechtel, built virtually every stitch of infrastructure over impossible terrain in engineering feats that it boasts are unparalleled on the planet.

That history, Papua's extreme remoteness and the company's long ties to the Indonesian government have given Freeport exceptional sway over a 21st-century version of the old company town, built on a scale unique even by the standards of modern mega-mining.

"If any operation like this was put forward now, it wouldn't be allowed," said Witoro Soelarno, a senior investigator at the Department of Energy and Mineral Resources, who has visited the mine many times. "But now the operation exists, and many people depend on it."

For years, to secure Freeport's domain, James R. Moffett, a Louisiana-born geologist who is the company chairman, assiduously courted Indonesia's longtime dictator, President Suharto, and his cronies, having Freeport pay for their vacations and some of their children's college education, and cutting them in on deals that made them rich, current and former employees said.

It was a marriage of mutual convenience. As Freeport prospered into a company with $2.3 billion in revenues, it also became among the biggest - in some years the biggest - source of revenue for the government. It remains so.

Freeport says that it provided Indonesia with $33 billion in direct and indirect benefits from 1992 to 2004, almost 2 percent of the country's gross domestic product. With gold prices hitting a 25-year high of $540 an ounce this month, the company estimates it will pay the government $1 billion this year.

With Suharto's ouster in 1998, after 30 years of unchallenged power, Freeport's special place was left vulnerable. But its importance to Indonesia's treasury and its carefully cultivated cocoon of support have helped secure it against challenges from local people, environmental groups, and even the country's own Environment Ministry.

Letters and other documents provided to The Times by government officials showed that the Environment Ministry repeatedly warned the company since 1997 that Freeport was breaching environmental laws. They also reveal the ministry's deep frustration.

At one point last year, a ministry scientist wrote that the mine's production was so huge, and regulatory tools so weak, that it was like "painting on clouds" to persuade Freeport to comply with the ministry's requests to reduce environmental damage.

That frustration stems from an operation that, by Freeport's own estimates, will generate an estimated six billion tons of waste before it is through - more than twice as much earth as was excavated for the Panama Canal.

Much of that waste has already been dumped in the mountains surrounding the mine or down a system of rivers that descends steeply onto the island's low-lying wetlands, close to Lorentz National Park, a pristine rain forest that has been granted special status by the United Nations.

A multimillion-dollar 2002 study by an American consulting company, Parametrix, paid for by Freeport and its joint venture partner, Rio Tinto, and not previously made public, noted that the rivers upstream and the wetlands inundated with waste were now "unsuitable for aquatic life." The report was made available to The Times by the Environment Ministry.

Freeport says it strives to mitigate the environmental effect of its mine, while also maximizing the benefits to its shareholders. The Times made repeated requests to Freeport and to the Indonesian government to visit the mine and its surrounding area, which requires special permission for journalists. All were turned down.

Freeport refused to make any official available for an interview and would respond to questions only in writing. A cover letter signed by its legal counsel, Stanley S. Arkin, said that Grasberg is a copper mine, with the gold retrieved as a byproduct, and that many journalists had visited the mine before the government tightened its rules in the 1990's. "Freeport has nothing to hide," Mr. Arkin wrote.

Indeed, at Grasberg, Freeport-McMoRan Copper & Gold mines the world's third-largest copper deposit. The mine also has proven reserves of 46 million ounces of gold, according to the company's 2004 annual report. This year, Mining International, a trade journal, called Freeport's gold mine the biggest in the world.

Social Tensions Erupt

Since Suharto's ouster, Freeport employees say, Mr. Moffett's motto has been "no tall trees," a call to keep as low a profile as possible, for a company that operates on an almost unimaginable scale.

But even before then, the new world that Freeport created was growing smaller. By the mid-1990's, with production in full swing, and the expanding impact of Grasberg's operations ever more apparent, Freeport was beset on all sides.

Environmental groups, able to coordinate more effectively with the Internet, made Freeport a target. Local tribes were more and more restless at seeing little benefit for themselves as vast riches were extracted from their lands. And some military commanders in Papua saw Grasberg's increasing value as ripe for the plucking.

To fortify itself, Freeport, working hand in hand with Indonesian military intelligence officers, began monitoring the e-mail messages and telephone conversations of its environmental opponents, said an employee who worked on the program and read the e-mail messages.

The company also set up its own system to intercept e-mail messages, according to former and current employees, by establishing a bogus environmental group of its own, which asked people to register online with a password. As is often the case, many who registered used the same password for their own messages, which then allowed the company to tap in.

Freeport's lawyers were nervous, a person who was at the company at the time said, but decided that nothing prohibited the company legally from reading e-mail messages abroad.

Social tensions around the mine, meanwhile, were fast growing, as was Papua's population. Papua, mostly animist and Christian after long years of missionary work, is distinct in many ways from the rest of Indonesia, the world's largest Muslim country.

Almost from Indonesia's independence, the province had rumblings of a separatist movement. Throughout Indonesia the military, a deeply nationalist institution, finances itself by setting up legal enterprises like shopping centers and hotels, or illicit ones, like logging. In Papua, the Grasberg mine became a chance for the military not only to profit but also to deepen its presence in a province where it had barely a toehold before Freeport arrived.

For many years Freeport maintained its own security force, while the Indonesian military battled a weak, low-level insurgency. But slowly their security needs became entwined.

"Where Freeport really took it on the chin is the military who came in had no vehicles, and they would commandeer a Freeport bus or a Freeport driver," said the Rev. David B. Lowry, an Episcopal minister hired by Mr. Moffett to oversee social programs. "We had no policies at that time."

No investigation directly linked Freeport to human rights violations, but increasingly Papuans associated it with the abuses of Indonesian military units, in some cases using company facilities.

An Australian anthropologist, Chris Ballard, who worked for Freeport, and Abigail Abrash, an American human rights campaigner, estimated that 160 people had been killed by the military between 1975 and 1997 in the mine area and its surroundings.

Finally, in March 1996, long-simmering anger at the company erupted in rioting when anti-mine sentiment among different groups coalesced into what was perhaps the biggest threat to the company to this day.

The mine and its mill were shut down for three days. Rioters destroyed $3 million of equipment and ransacked offices.

The company intercepted e-mail messages that, according to two persons who read them at the time, suggested that certain military units, the community and environmental groups were working together.

One e-mail exchange, between a community leader and the head of an environmental group, was filled with tactical military intelligence, according to a person who read the messages. In another exchange, an environmental leader urged the group's members to pull out because the demonstrations had turned violent.

Freeport told The Times that local leaders later met with company officials and said "they had provoked the disturbances as a means of expressing their aspiration to receive greater benefits from our operations."

http://www.nytimes.com/2005/12/27/international/asia/27gold.html?pagewanted=print   10/10/2013

In recent interviews, current and former Freeport officials recalled how they were stunned when, among those rioting, they saw men with military haircuts, combat boots and walkie-talkies. They seemed to be directing the rioters, at one point, to a Freeport laboratory, which they ransacked.

It was not long before a worried Mr. Moffett flew out to Indonesia in the company jet.

Freeport refused to comment on the meeting that followed. But a company official who was there recounted that Mr. Moffett met with a group of senior Indonesian military officers at the Sheraton Hotel in the lowland town of Timika, near the mine. The all-powerful Gen. Prabowo Subianto, son-in-law of President Suharto and commander of the Indonesian Special Forces, presided.

"Mr. Moffett, to protect you, to protect your company, you have to help the military here," General Prabowo began, according to the company employee who was present.

Mr. Moffett is said to have replied: "Just tell me what I need to do."

The Cost of Security

Each military service drew up its wish list, current and former company employees said.

In short order, Freeport spent $35 million on military infrastructure - barracks, headquarters, mess halls, roads - and it also gave the commanders 70 Land Rovers and Land Cruisers, which were replaced every few years. Everybody got something, even the Navy and Air Force.

The company had already hired a former C.I.A. operative, and on his recommendation, it now approached a military attaché at the American Embassy in Jakarta, and persuaded him to join the company, according to former and current employees. Two more former American military officers were hired, and a special department, called the Emergency Planning Operation, was set up to handle the company's new relationship with the Indonesian military.

The new department began making direct monthly payments to Indonesian military commanders, while the Security Risk Management office handled the payments to the police, according to company documents and current and former employees.

"They signed a pact with the devil," said an American who was part of Freeport's security operations at the time, and who agreed with the company's decision.

Freeport gave the military and the police in Papua at least $20 million from 1998 to May 2004, according to company documents. In interviews, current and former employees said that at least an additional $10 million was also paid during those years.

Seven years of accounting records were provided to The Times by an individual close to the company. Additional records for three years were provided by Global Witness, a nongovernment organization, which released a report last July, "Paying for Protection," about Freeport's relations with the Indonesian military.

Diarmid O'Sullivan, who works for Global Witness in London, criticized the payments. It may be necessary for a company to help governments with security, he said, but "they should give the money through the proper channels, in a transparent way."

Freeport told The Times, "Our books and records are transparent and accurately reflect the support that we provide."

That support, the company said in its responses, included "mitigating living costs," as well as "infrastructure, catered food and dining hall costs, housing, fuel, travel, vehicle repairs, allowances to cover incidental and administrative costs, and community assistance programs conducted by the military and police."

The company said all of its expenditures were subject to a budget review process.

The records received by The Times showed payments to individual military officers listed under things like "food cost," "administrative services" and "monthly supplement."

Current and former employees said the accounting categories did not reflect what the money was actually used for, and that it was likely that much of the money went into the officers' pockets. The commanders who received the money did not have to sign receipts, current and former employees said.

Asked if there was a reason Freeport would give money directly to military officers, Father Lowry, who retired in March 2004, but remained a consultant to Freeport until June, said, "I can't think of a good one."

The records show that the largest recipient was the commander of the troops in the Freeport area, Lt. Col. Togap F. Gultom.

During six months in 2001, he was given just under $100,000 for "food costs," according to the company records, and more than $150,000 the following year. Freeport gave at least 10 other commanders a total of more than $350,000 for "food costs" in 2002, according to the records.

Colonel Gultom declined to be interviewed.

Those payments were made to individual officers, current and former employees said, even though since the riots Freeport had allowed soldiers to eat in the company's mess and had trucked food to more distant military kitchens. "Three meals a day, seven days a week," a former official said.

Freeport also gave commanders commercial airplane tickets for themselves and their wives and children. Generals flew first or business class and lower ranking officers flew economy, said Brig. Gen. Ramizan Tarigan, who received $14,000 worth of tickets in 2002 for himself and his family.

General Tarigan, who held a senior police post, said that police officers were allowed to accept airplane tickets because their pay was so low - as a general, his base salary was roughly $400 a month - but that it was in violation of police regulations to receive cash payments.

In April 2002, the company gave the senior commander of forces in Papua, Maj. Gen. Mahidin Simbolon, more than $64,000, for what was described in Freeport's books as "fund for military project plan 2002." Eight months later, in December, he was given more than $67,000 for a "humanitarian civic action project." The payments were first reported by Global Witness.

General Simbolon, who is now inspector general of the Indonesian Army, declined requests to be interviewed.

A former Freeport employee who was involved in making those payments said the company could not be certain how much of the money General Simbolon actually spent on those projects.

Unsolved Killings

By 2003, following the Enron scandal and passage of the Sarbanes-Oxley Act, which imposed more rigid accounting practices on companies, Freeport began making payments to military and police units instead of individual officers, according to records and current and former employees.

The company paid police units in Papua slightly under $1 million in 2003, according to the records, listed under items like "monthly supplement payment," "administrative costs" and "administrative support."

Freeport told The Times that "company policies take into account the potential for human rights abuses in determining what types of assistance to provide."

According to the records received by The Times, the police Mobile Brigade, a paramilitary force often cited by the State Department for its brutality, received more than $200,000 in 2003.

In its 2003 annual human rights report, the State Department said soldiers from the Mobile Brigade "continued to commit numerous serious human rights violations, including extrajudicial killings, torture, rape, and arbitrary detention." It cited no specific incidents from Papua.

There was another reason for extra care by the company.

In August 2002, three teachers employed by Freeport, including two Americans, were killed in an ambush on a company road patrolled by the military that Freeport had paid to protect its employees. Three years later, the F.B.I. is still investigating and the reasons for the killings have not been determined. Freeport said that it could not comment on the investigation.

The United States indicted a Papuan, Anthonius Wamang, in 2004. But it has yet to receive the full cooperation of the military, several American officials said.

Freeport employees and American officials said the killings could have been part of a turf war between the military and the police, each of which wanted access to Freeport payments.

An initial report by the Indonesian police pointed to the Indonesia military, and some Freeport and Bush administration officials have said they suspect some level of military involvement.

The police report suggested that the motivation was that Freeport was threatening to cut its support to soldiers. Soldiers assigned to Papua have "high expectations," the report said, but recently, "their perks, such as vehicles, telephones, etc., were reduced."

Questions of Accountability

Freeport has resisted nearly any detailed disclosure of its payments to the military, saying they are legal and even required under Indonesian law.

Marsillam Simanjuntak, who was minister of justice and later attorney general in one of the first governments after the fall of President Suharto, said it was a violation of Indonesian law for soldiers or police officers to accept payments from a company. "Of course, it's illegal," he said.

But many companies do it, he said. The better question to ask, he said, was, "Is it allowed by the laws of the United States?"

This year, the New York City pension funds submitted a shareholder resolution asking Freeport to review its policy on paying the police and military. They argued that it could violate the Foreign Corrupt Practices Act, which forbids American companies from paying bribes to foreign officials. Freeport opposed the resolution.

In 2002, the funds submitted a similar resolution demanding that Freeport disclose how much it was paying to the military. Freeport kept it off the ballot.

In later filings with the Securities and Exchange Commission, Freeport reported that it had paid the military a total of $4.7 million in 2001, and $5.6 million in 2002. The company did not indicate whether the money was paid into commanders' personal accounts, or what the money was used for.

Freeport, in its responses, said it was complying with the Voluntary Principles on Security and Human Rights, a set of guidelines drawn up by the State Department. They recognize that natural resource companies "may be required or expected to contribute to, or otherwise reimburse, the costs of protecting company facilities."

The principles do not address the question of direct payments to individual officers. Nor do they require companies to account for the payments.

Freeport has also said that the payments were required under its Contract of Work, its basic agreement with the government of Indonesia, first signed in 1967 and updated in 1991.

The company declined to provide a copy of the contracts to The Times. A copy of each was provided by Denise Leith, author of "The Politics of Power: Freeport in Suharto's Indonesia." They contained no language requiring payments to the military.

S. Prakash Sethi, head of the International Center for Corporate Accountability, which recently concluded a report on Freeport's development policies in Papua, said that the company had told him that it made "in-kind" contributions to the military, for housing and food, but that he had not been given access to accounting records.

Any direct payments to military officers would be illegal, said Mr. Sethi, an expert on business ethics and corporate social responsibility and a professor at Baruch College. "It's corruption," he said. "It's bribery."

Mine Waste in the Rivers

All the while Freeport sealed its relations with the military, the country's fledgling environment ministry could do little but watch as waste from the mine piled up.

This year Freeport told the Indonesian government that the waste rock in the highlands, 900 feet deep in places, now covers about three square miles.

Down below, nearly 90 square miles of wetlands, once one of the richest freshwater habitats in the world, are virtually buried in mine waste, called tailings, with levels of copper and sediment so high that almost all fish have disappeared, according to environment ministry documents.

The waste, the consistency and color of wet cement, belts down the rivers, and inundates and smothers all in its path, said Russell Dodt, an Australian civil engineer who managed the waste on the wetlands for 10 years until 2004 for Freeport.

About a third of the waste has moved into the coastal estuary, an essential breeding ground for fish, and much of that "was ripped out to sea by the falling tide that acted like a big vacuum cleaner," he said.

But no government, even in Indonesia's new democratic era, has dared encroach on Freeport's prerogatives. The strongest challenge came in 2000, when a feisty politician, Sonny Keraf, who was sympathetic to the Papuans, was appointed environment minister.

Again, Mr. Moffett flew out to Jakarta.

Mr. Keraf initially refused to see the Freeport boss, but eventually agreed, and on the day kept him waiting for an hour and a half. "He came in so arrogant," Mr. Keraf recalled of the meeting in a recent interview, "sitting with his legs crossed."

Freeport refused to comment on the meeting. The American ambassador to Indonesia at the time, Robert Gelbard, said in an interview: "It was a terrible meeting."

Mr. Keraf said that Mr. Moffett had said that his company had never polluted. "I told him that he should spend the money he spent on paying off people not to talk about the mine to properly dispose of the waste," Mr. Keraf said.

Behind the scenes, Mr. Keraf kept up the pressure, angered that the company was using the rivers, forest and wetlands for its mine waste, a process allowed during the Suharto years.

An internal ministry memorandum from 2000 said the mine waste had killed all life in the rivers, and said that this violated the criminal section of the 1997 environmental law.

In January 2001, Mr. Keraf wrote to the coordinating minister for economic affairs, arguing that Freeport should be forced to pay compensation for the rivers, forests and fish that its operations had destroyed.

Six months later, one of his deputies, Masnellyarti Hilman, wrote to Freeport, saying a special environmental commission had recommended that the company stop using the river as a waste chute, and instead build a system of pipes.

She also told Freeport to build sturdier dam-like walls to replace the less solid levees that it used to contain the waste on the wetlands. That practice has continued.

Freeport says that local and regional governments have approved its waste management plans, and that the central government has approved its environmental impact statement and other monitoring plans.

But in a blistering July 2001 letter, Mr. Keraf took the governor of Papua to task for granting Freeport a permit in 1996 to use the rivers for its waste. The governor, Mr. Keraf said, had no authority to grant permits more lenient than the provisions of national laws.

Despite all these efforts, nothing happened. Mr. Keraf was unable to secure the support of other government agencies or his superiors in the cabinet.

In August 2001, a new government came to power, and a less aggressive minister, Nabiel Makarim, replaced Mr. Keraf. At first, he, too, talked publicly of setting stricter limits on Freeport. Soon his efforts petered out.

The Environment Ministry has begun trying to put teeth into its rules where it can. It brought a criminal suit against the world's largest gold company, Newmont Mining Corporation, for alleged pollution, including a charge of not having a permit for disposing of mine waste into the sea. Newmont has fought the charges vigorously.

But in the case of Freeport, the ministry has had no traction. Freeport still does not hold a permit from the national government to dispose of mine waste, as required by the 1999 hazardous waste regulations, according to Rasio Ridho Sani, assistant deputy for toxic waste management at the ministry. Mr. Arkin, Freeport's counsel, said that the company cooperated well with the environment ministry and that Freeport would not otherwise comment.

"Freeport says their waste is not hazardous waste," Mr. Rasio said. "We cannot say it is not hazardous waste." He said his division and Freeport were now in negotiations on how to resolve the permit question.

'A Massive Die-Off'

The environment ministry was not the first to challenge Freeport over how it has disposed of its waste in Papua.

The Overseas Private Investment Corporation, a United States government agency that insures American corporations for political risk in uncertain corners of the world, revoked Freeport's insurance policy in October 1995.

It was a landmark decision, the first time that the agency had cut off insurance to any American company for environmental or human rights concerns.

In doing so, two environmental experts, Harvey Himberg, an official at the agency, and David Nelson, a consultant, after visiting the mine for several days, issued a report critical of Freeport's operations, especially the huge amounts of waste it had sent into rivers, something that would not be allowed in the United States.

http://www.nytimes.com/2005/12/27/international/asia/27gold.html?pagewanted=print   10/10/2013

The company went to court to block the report from being made public, and only a redacted version was later released. A person who thought it should be made public provided an uncensored copy to The Times.

Freeport says the report reached "inaccurate conclusions." The company says it has considered a full range of alternatives for managing and disposing of its waste, instead of using the river, and settled on the best one.

A storage area would not be large enough and would require a tall dam in a region of heavy rainfalls and earthquakes, it said. A waste pipeline, rather than the river, would be too costly, prone to landslides and floods.

To the American auditors, such arguments were not convincing.

Freeport "characterizes engineered alternatives as having the highest potential for catastrophic failure when the project otherwise takes credit for legendary feats," the audit noted, like the pipelines more than 60 miles long down the mountains to carry fuel and copper and gold slurry.

At the time, the waste was jumping the riverbanks, "resulting in a massive die-off of vegetation," the report said.

The company threatened to take the agency to court over the cancellation of its insurance. After protracted negotiations, the policy was reinstated for a few months, as a face-saving gesture to Mr. Moffett, according to the head of the agency then, Ruth Harkin. It was not renewed.

Today, many of the same problems persist, but on a much larger scale. A perpetual worry is where to put all the mine's waste - accumulating at a rate of some 700,000 tons a day.

The danger is that the waste rock atop the mountain will trickle out acids into the honeycomb of caverns and caves beneath the mine in a wet climate that gets up to 12 feet of rain a year, say environmental experts who have worked at the mine.

Stuart Miller, an Australian geochemist who manages Freeport's waste rock, said at a mining conference in 2003 that the first acid runoffs began in 1993.

The company can curb much of it today, he said, by blending in the mountain's abundant limestone with the potentially acid producing rock, which is also plentiful. Freeport also says that the company collects the acid runoff and neutralizes it.

But before 2004, the report obtained by The Times by Parametrix, the consulting company who did the study for Freeport, said that the mine had "an excess of acid-generating material."

A geologist who worked at the mine, who declined to be identified because of fear of jeopardizing future employment, said acids were already flowing into the groundwater. Bright green-colored springs could be seen spouting several miles away, he said, a tell-tale sign that the acids had leached out copper. "That meant the acid water traveled a long way," he said.

Freeport says that the springs are "located several miles from our operations in the Lorentz World Heritage site and are not associated with our operations."

The geologist agreed that the springs probably were in the Lorentz park, and said this showed that acids and copper from the mine were affecting the park, considered a world treasure for its ecological diversity.

In the lowlands, the levees needed to contain the waste will eventually reach more than 70 feet high in some places, the company says.

Freeport says that the tailings are not toxic and that the river it uses for its waste meets Indonesian and American drinking water standards for dissolved metals. The coastal estuary, it says, is a "functioning ecosystem."

The Parametrix report shows copper levels in surface waters high enough to kill sensitive aquatic life in a short time, said Ann Maest, a geochemist who consults on mining issues. The report showed that nearly half of the sediment samples in parts of the coastal estuary were toxic to the sensitive aquatic organisms at the bottom of the food chain, she said.

The amount of sediment presents another problem. Too many suspended solids in water can smother aquatic life. Indonesian law says they should not exceed 400 milligrams per liter.

Freeport's waste contained 37,500 milligrams as the river entered the lowlands, according to an environment ministry's field report in 2004, and 7,500 milligrams as the river entered the Arafura Sea.

Freeport would not comment on the measurements. The company says it spent $30 million on environmental programs in 2004, and planted 50,000 mangrove seedlings last year as part of its reclamation efforts. It says cash crops can be grown on the waste with the addition of nutrients, and has begun demonstration projects.

An Uneasy Coexistence

If the accumulating waste is the despair of critics, for Freeport it signals expanding production. To keep its mine running, the company has increasingly had to play caretaker for the world that it has created.

After the 1996 riots, Freeport began dedicating 1 percent of revenues annually to a development fund for Papua to pay for schools, medical services, roads - whatever the people wanted.

The company built clinics and two hospitals. Other services include programs to control malaria and AIDS and a "recognition" fund for the Kamoro and Amungme tribes of several million dollars which, among other things, gives them shares in the company as part of a compensation package for the lands Freeport is using.

By the end of 2004, Freeport had spent $152 million on the community development fund, the company said.

Mr. Sethi, of the Center for Corporate Accountability, commended Freeport for commissioning the report on the company's development programs, saying that it was the first mining company to do so.

The report, which was released in October, concluded that the company had successfully introduced a human rights training program for its employees and had doubled the number of Papuan employees by 2001. The company was poised to double the number of Papuans in the work force again by 2006, the audit said.

Still, Thom Beanal, the Amungme tribal leader, says the combined weight of the Indonesian government and Freeport has left his people in bad shape. Yes, he said, the company had provided electricity, schools and hospitals, but the infrastructure was built mainly for the benefit of Freeport.

Mr. Beanal, 57, a vocal supporter of independence for Papua, has fought the company from outside and inside. In 2000, he decided that harmony was the better path, and joined the company's advisory board.

In November, he and other Amungme and Komoro tribesmen met with Mr. Moffett at the Sheraton Hotel in Timika. In an interview in Jakarta not long afterward, Mr. Beanal said he told Mr. Moffett that the flood of money from the community fund was ruining people's lives.

When the company arrived, he noted, there were several hundred people in the lowland village of Timika. Now it is home to more than 100,000 in a Wild West atmosphere of too much alcohol, shootouts between soldiers and the police, AIDS and prostitution, protected by the military.

Still more soldiers are on the way. Having negotiated an end to a separatist insurrection this year in another province, Aceh, the government is redeploying soldiers to Papua in a move to defeat the growing enthusiasm for independence, once and for all, and to watch over the province with the world's biggest gold mine. Freeport says its gold ore has 35 years to go.

Mr. Beanal said he was increasingly impatient with the presence of the soldiers and the mine. "We never feel secure there," he said. "What are they guarding? We don't know. Ask Moffett, it's his company."

Evelyn Rusli contributed reporting for this article.

Copyright 2006 The New York Times Company | Home | Privacy Policy | Search | Corrections | | Help | Contact Us | Work for Us | Site Map | Back to Top

http://www.nytimes.com/2005/12/27/international/asia/27gold.html?pagewanted=print   10/10/2013

EXHIBIT 6

Report Information from ProQuest
24 March 2013 19:15
State Library of New South Wales

Table of contents

1. Business and Finance
2. Freeport starts mill after riots
3. Riots in Indonesia quelled; U.S. mine prepares to reopen
4. Business Brief -- FREEPORT-MCMORAN COPPER & GOLD: Indonesian Operations Able To Meet Contract Terms
5. Outside agitators

Document 1 of 5

Riots in Indonesia quelled; U.S. mine prepares to reopen

Publication info: Wall Street Journal, Eastern edition [New York, N.Y] 14 Mar 1996: A15.

ProQuest document link

Abstract:

The army said it restored order in Timika, a remote Indonesian town were rioting on Mar 10 and Mar 12, 1996 between Irian Jaya tribesmen and non-Irianese shop owners forced the closing of a giant US copper mine. At least three people were killed and dozens injured. The huge mine is 82%-owned by Freeport-McMoRan Copper & Gold Inc of New Orleans, which shut the mine as a precautionary measure.

Full text:

JAKARTA, Indonesia -- The army said it restored order in Timika, a remote Indonesian town where rioting Sunday and Tuesday forced the closing of a giant U.S. copper mine. At least three people were killed and dozens injured. Property damage was substantial in the town, though not at the nearby mine, whose closure had driven up copper prices on world markets this week.

Diplomats in Jakarta, Timika residents and local press reports said it was quiet yesterday around Timika and Tembagapura, the town next to the copper and gold mine run by PT Freeport Indonesia in Irian Jaya. In Timika, a town of about 50,000, soldiers patrolled streets while many shops and offices remained closed.

The huge mine is 82%-owned by Freeport-McMoRan Copper & Gold Inc. of New Orleans. After a riot by nearly 200 Irian Jaya tribesmen in Tembagapura on Sunday, Freeport shut the mine as a precautionary measure. Freeport officials said they expected the mine to reopen today. They said there was no damage to the mill or mining operation from the riot.

The extent of property damage in Timika, 40 miles from Tembagapura, wasn't immediately clear. Among the dozens of buildings attacked Tuesday by rioters was the Freeport-built airport. The Associated Press quoted Col. Sutan Iskandar, an armed-forces spokesman, as saying that about 3,000 rioters "practically took over the airport and they damaged some facilities." Aviation officials said the airport will remain closed to commercial traffic until tomorrow.

James Moffett, chairman of Freeport-McMoRan, flew into Timika yesterday. He was expected to meet Indonesian officials and tribal leaders.

Timika residents said the situation remained uneasy. Diplomats and residents said the riot involved fighting between non-Irianese migrants who own shops in the town and Irianese who came into Timika. It wasn't certain what sparked the rioting Sunday and Tuesday. Irianese have been unhappy with Freeport, complaining about loss of traditional lands and not getting jobs at the mine. Freeport has stepped up community education and social programs in recent years.

Through yesterday, reporters haven't been permitted by Indonesian authorities to travel to Timika.

Credit: A Wall Street Journal News Roundup

Subject: Shutdowns; Riots; Mining industry

Location: Indonesia

Company: Freeport-McMoRan Copper & Gold Inc

Publication title: Wall Street Journal, Eastern edition

Pages: A15

Publication year: 1996

Publication date: Mar 14, 1996

Year: 1996

Section: International

Publisher: Dow Jones & Company Inc

Place of publication: New York, N.Y.

Country of publication: United States

Publication subject: Business And Economics--Banking And Finance

ISSN: 00999660

Source type: Newspapers

Language of publication: English

Document type: News

Accession number: 03958325

ProQuest document ID: 398633737

Document URL: http://search.proquest.com/docview/398633737?accountid=13902

Copyright: Copyright Dow Jones & Company Inc Mar 14, 1996

Last updated: 2010-06-26

Database: ABI/INFORM Global

Document 4 of 5

Business Brief -- FREEPORT-MCMORAN COPPER & GOLD: Indonesian Operations Able To Meet Contract Terms

Publication info: Wall Street Journal, Eastern edition [New York, N.Y] 13 Mar 1996: n/a.

ProQuest document link

Abstract:

Freeport-McMoRan Copper & Gold Inc. said its Indonesian operations will still meet contractual obligations despite protests and minor vandalism at its facilities.

Full text:

Freeport-McMoRan Copper & Gold Inc. said its Indonesian operations will still meet contractual obligations despite protests and minor vandalism at its facilities. The New Orleans mining concern said its stockpiles of gold, silver and copper concentrates in the port town of Amamapare will be sufficient to meet its needs. Its mine in Tembagapura, which is about 50 miles north of Timika, remains closed following protests this weekend. The protesters, the island's indigenous people, associate the mining operations with alleged human-rights violations by Indonesia's government. Environmentalists also oppose the mine. In composite trading yesterday on the New York Stock Exchange, Freeport shares closed at $29.75, down $1.375, or 4.4%.

Publication title: Wall Street Journal, Eastern edition

Pages: n/a

Publication year: 1996

Publication date: Mar 13, 1996

Year: 1996

Publisher: Dow Jones & Company Inc

Place of publication: New York, N.Y.

Country of publication: United States

Publication subject: Business And Economics--Banking And Finance

ISSN: 00999660

Source type: Newspapers

Language of publication: English

Document type: NEWSPAPER

ProQuest document ID: 398599229

Document URL: http://search.proquest.com/docview/398599229?accountid=13902

Copyright: (Copyright (c) 1996, Dow Jones & Company, Inc.)

Last updated: 2010-06-26

Database: ABI/INFORM Global

Document 5 of 5

Outside agitators

Author: Anonymous

Publication info: The Progressive 60. 2 (Feb 1996): 11.

ProQuest document link

Abstract:

Freeport-McMoran CEO Jim Bob Moffett counterattacked when environmental and human-rights activists protested his company's operation of a gold mine in Indonesia. He should have kept quiet and kept those profits coming.

Full text:

Pity the giant multinational, having to defend little things like human-rights abuses. Take the case of Freeport-McMoran, a New Orleans-based company that runs the world's biggest gold mine in the rain forests of Indonesia. The government of Indonesia is a 10 percent partner in the mine, and that government has perhaps the worst human-rights record of any government in the world.

In 1965, it wiped out hundreds of thousands of political opponents. In 1975, with the approval of Henry Kissinger and Gerald Ford, it invaded East Timor, resulting in the deaths of 200,000 Timorese-- one-third of the population of that fledgling nation. (Kissinger is now on the board of directors of Freeport.)

In recent years, Indonesia has continued its crack-downs both in East Timor and in Indonesia. Even in the area of the Freeport mine, the Indonesian government has been accused of murdering and torturing separatists. And the mine itself is causing environmental damage.

Environmental and human-rights activists have been protesting Freeport's Indonesian connections, even holding a demonstration outside CEO Jim Bob Moffett's house.

Jim Bob didn't take too kindly to that. "Imagine yourself at home--your kids, your neighbors. It was a terrible, terrible, experience," one of his senior vice presidents said.

Poor Jim Bob. He responded by making a half-hour infomercial defending the company's record in Indonesia, and he bought time on local stations to broadcast it, The Wall Street Journal reported. He also took out a two-page ad in The New York Times, alleging a "smear campaign" by unnamed "foreign interests" funded by the U.S. Agency for International Development.

The cost of this counterattack was just a drop in his bucket, but his friends at The Wall Street Journal think he made a mistake by responding to what it called "a group of postadolescent protesters." Better to have said nothing, and gone on with business as usual, The Journal advised.

That's the credo of the savvy multinational. Just keep quiet, hope the protesters go away, and keep those profits coming. Now if we don't hear from Jim Bob again, we'll know why. You can bet he hasn't pulled out of Indonesia; he's just hired better P.R.

Subject: Multinational corporations; Mining; Human rights; Gold; Environmental impact; Demonstrations & protests

Location: Indonesia

People: Moffett, James R

Company: Freeport-McMoRan Copper & Gold Inc

Publication title: The Progressive

Volume: 60

Issue: 2

Pages: 11

Number of pages: 2

Publication year: 1996

Publication date: Feb 1996

Year: 1996

Publisher: Progressive Incorporated

Place of publication: Madison

Country of publication: United States

Publication subject: Political Science

ISSN: 00330736

CODEN: PRGVB6

Source type: Magazines

Language of publication: English

Document type: Commentary

Accession number: 02689375

ProQuest document ID: 231942276

Document URL: http://search.proquest.com/docview/231942276?accountid=13902

Copyright: Copyright Progressive Incorporated Feb 1996

Last updated: 2010-06-10

Database: ProQuest Political Science; ProQuest Research Library

Contact ProQuest

Copyright © 2012 ProQuest LLC. All rights reserved. - Terms and Conditions

jw sent you the following:

Email 1 of 1

Report Information from ProQuest
24 March 2013 19:08
State Library of New South Wales

Table of contents

1. Business and Finance

2. Freeport starts mill after riots

3. Riots in Indonesia quelled; U.S. mine prepares to reopen

4. Business Brief -- FREEPORT-MCMORAN COPPER & GOLD: Indonesian Operations Able To Meet Contract Terms

5. A fire-breather gets scorched: Two newspapers and a mining giant

Document 1 of 5

Business and Finance

Publication info: Asian Wall Street Journal [Victoria, Hong Kong] 14 Mar 1996: 1.

ProQuest document link

Abstract:

CHINA IS OFFERING to cement $4 billion in orders for commercial jets from Boeing and McDonnell Douglas, provided Washington will delay sanctions in an unrelated softwaretrade dispute, according to government and industry officials. U.S. officials, however, say they won't sawp the plane orders for a freeze on sanctions on a long-term basis.

Section III Appendix - Wilson Declarations 252

Hong Kong shares plunged 3.3% amid the continuing tension between China and Taiwan and uncertainty about the U.S. market. The Hang Seng Index dropped 352.97 points to 10249.48.

Hong Kong mutual funds saw heavy inflows early this year, fueling the market gains that preceded recent declines. In January, net investment in 578 funds tracked rose to $152.4 million, the biggest one-month investment flow ever.

Full text:

CHINA IS OFFERING to cement $4 billion in orders for commercial jets from Boeing and McDonnell Douglas, provided Washington will delay sanctions in an unrelated softwaretrade dispute, according to government and industry officials. U.S. officials, however, say they won't sawp the plane orders for a freeze on sanctions on a long-term basis.

Hong Kong shares plunged 3.3% amid the continuing tension between China and Taiwan and uncertainty about the U.S. market. The Hang Seng Index dropped 352.97 points to 10249.48.

Hong Kong mutual funds saw heavy inflows early this year, fueling the market gains that preceded recent declines. In January, net investment in 578 funds tracked rose to $152.4 million, the biggest one-month investment flow ever.

U.S. shares fell as trading volume declined, but advancers led decliners at midafternoon in New York amid rising technology stocks.

Malaysia is reconsidering the incentives it offers to attract foreign companies to set up wafer plants. The review has temporarily halted a proposed $1.2 billion plant by a Hitachi-Lucky Goldstar joint venture, officials said.

Taiwan Semiconductor picked a Camas, Washington site for a $1.2 billion joint-venture U.S. chip plant, in which it will have a majority stake. The Taiwanese company's stock shot up 3.9% on the Taipei bourse.

Indonesia restored order in Timika, a remote town near a giant Freeport mine, where rioting Tuesday resulted in three deaths, dozens of injuries and substantial property damage.

The dollar eased in midafternoon New York trading, though it seemed to be stabilizing against the mark on news Germany will seek to constrain government spending.

U.S. Treasurys rose, having stabilized after experiencing choppiness for most of the session.

Sapporo's pretax profit rose 3.4% to $122.5 million on a consolidated basis in 1995, despite a slip in sales, which eased 0.2%. The Tokyo-based brewer predicts group pretax profit will rise 16% this year.

Morgan Grenfell advised TVE to reject a takeover offer from the South China Morning Post, questioning the SCMP's ability to manage the company.

An Australian court ruled that Mobil can't send takeover documents to holders of Ampolex. The injunction also prevents the U.S. company from acquiring certain convertible notes in the Sydney oil and gas concern.

Coca-Cola expects its world-wide volume to grow 7% in the first quarter, compared with a 9% increase a year earlier.

Shougang International plans a $55.4 million general offer for shares of Shougang Concord Grand Group after it acquires the 50% stake of Essential Assets it doesn't already own.

GT Chile's shareholders faced concerns amid growing confusion over a plan to give them the option to exit the ailing closed-end fund.

Publication title: Asian Wall Street Journal

Pages: 1

Number of pages: 0

Publication year: 1996

Publication date: Mar 14, 1996

Year: 1996

Column: Business and Finance

Section: What's News

Publisher: Dow Jones & Company Inc

Place of publication: Victoria, Hong Kong

Country of publication: United States

ISSN: 03779920

Source type: Newspapers

Language of publication: English

Document type: NEWSPAPER

ProQuest document ID: 315628987

Document URL: http://search.proquest.com/docview/315628987?accountid=13902

Copyright: Copyright Dow Jones & Company Inc Mar 14, 1996

Last updated: 2011-11-30

Database: ProQuest Asian Business & Reference

Document 2 of 5

Freeport starts mill after riots

Publication info: The Irish Times (1921-Current File) [Dublin, Ireland] 14 Mar 1996: 10.

ProQuest document link

Abstract: None available.

Full text: Not available.

Publication title: The Irish Times (1921-Current File)

First page: 10

Number of pages: 1

Publication year: 1996

Publication date: Mar 14, 1996

Year: 1996

Publisher: The Irish Times Ltd.

Place of publication: Dublin, Ireland

Country of publication: Ireland

Publication subject: General Interest Periodicals--Ireland

Source type: Historical Newspapers

Language of publication: English

Document type: article

ProQuest document ID: 525616847

Document URL: http://search.proquest.com/docview/525616847?accountid=13902

Copyright: Copyright The Irish Times Ltd. Mar 14, 1996

Last updated: 2010-07-09

Database: ProQuest Historical Newspapers: The Irish Times (1859-2011) and The Weekly Irish Times (1876-1958)

Document 3 of 5

Riots in Indonesia quelled; U.S. mine prepares to reopen

Publication info: Wall Street Journal, Eastern edition [New York, N.Y] 14 Mar 1996: A15.

ProQuest document link

Abstract:

The army said it restored order in Timika, a remote Indonesian town were rioting on Mar 10 and Mar 12, 1996 between Irian Jaya tribesmen and non-Irianese shop owners forced the closing of a giant US copper mine. At least three people were killed and dozens injured. The huge mine is 82%-owned by Freeport-McMoRan Copper & Gold Inc of New Orleans, which shut the mine as a precautionary measure.

Full text:

JAKARTA, Indonesia -- The army said it restored order in Timika, a remote Indonesian town where rioting Sunday and Tuesday forced the closing of a giant U.S. copper mine. At least three people were killed and dozens injured. Property damage was substantial in the town, though not at the nearby mine, whose closure had driven up copper prices on world markets this week.

Diplomats in Jakarta, Timika residents and local press reports said it was quiet yesterday around Timika and Tembagapura, the town next to the copper and gold mine run by PT Freeport Indonesia in Irian Jaya. In Timika, a town of about 50,000, soldiers patrolled streets while many shops and offices remained closed.

The huge mine is 82%-owned by Freeport-McMoRan Copper & Gold Inc. of New Orleans. After a riot by nearly 200 Irian Jaya tribesmen in Tembagapura on Sunday, Freeport shut the mine as a precautionary measure. Freeport officials said they expected the mine to reopen today. They said there was no damage to the mill or mining operation from the riot.

The extent of property damage in Timika, 40 miles from Tembagapura, wasn't immediately clear. Among the dozens of buildings attacked Tuesday by rioters was the Freeport-built airport. The Associated Press quoted Col. Sutan Iskandar, an armed-forces spokesman, as saying that about 3,000 rioters "practically took over the airport and they damaged some facilities." Aviation officials said the airport will remain closed to commercial traffic until tomorrow.

James Moffett, chairman of Freeport-McMoRan, flew into Timika yesterday. He was expected to meet Indonesian officials and tribal leaders.

Timika residents said the situation remained uneasy. Diplomats and residents said the riot involved fighting between non-Irianese migrants who own shops in the town and Irianese who came into Timika. It wasn't certain what sparked the rioting Sunday and Tuesday. Irianese have been unhappy with Freeport, complaining about loss of traditional lands and not getting jobs at the mine. Freeport has stepped up community education and social programs in recent years.

Through yesterday, reporters haven't been permitted by Indonesian authorities to travel to Timika.

Credit: A Wall Street Journal News Roundup

Subject: Shutdowns; Riots; Mining industry

Location: Indonesia

Company: Freeport-McMoRan Copper & Gold Inc

Publication title: Wall Street Journal, Eastern edition

Pages: A15

Publication year: 1996

Publication date: Mar 14, 1996

Year: 1996

Section: International

Publisher: Dow Jones & Company Inc

Place of publication: New York, N.Y.

Country of publication: United States

Publication subject: Business And Economics--Banking And Finance

ISSN: 00999660

Source type: Newspapers

Language of publication: English

Document type: News

Accession number: 03958325

ProQuest document ID: 398633737

Document URL: http://search.proquest.com/docview/398633737?accountid=13902

Copyright: Copyright Dow Jones & Company Inc Mar 14, 1996

Last updated: 2010-06-26

Database: ABI/INFORM Global

Document 4 of 5

Business Brief -- FREEPORT-MCMORAN COPPER & GOLD: Indonesian Operations Able To Meet Contract Terms

Publication info: Wall Street Journal, Eastern edition [New York, N.Y] 13 Mar 1996: n/a.

ProQuest document link

Abstract:

Freeport-McMoRan Copper & Gold Inc. said its Indonesian operations will still meet contractual obligations despite protests and minor vandalism at its facilities.

Full text:

Freeport-McMoRan Copper & Gold Inc. said its Indonesian operations will still meet contractual obligations despite protests and minor vandalism at its facilities. The New Orleans mining concern said its stockpiles of gold, silver and copper concentrates in the port town of Amamapare will be sufficient to meet its needs. Its mine in Tembagapura, which is about 50 miles north of Timika, remains closed following protests this weekend. The protesters, the island's indigenous people, associate the mining operations with alleged human-rights violations by Indonesia's government. Environmentalists also oppose the mine. In composite trading yesterday on the New York Stock Exchange, Freeport shares closed at $29.75, down $1.375, or 4.4%.

Publication title: Wall Street Journal, Eastern edition

Pages: n/a

Publication year: 1996

Publication date: Mar 13, 1996

Year: 1996

Publisher: Dow Jones & Company Inc

Place of publication: New York, N.Y.

Country of publication: United States

Publication subject: Business And Economics--Banking And Finance

ISSN: 00999660

Source type: Newspapers

Language of publication: English

Document type: NEWSPAPER

ProQuest document ID: 398599229

Document URL: http://search.proquest.com/docview/398599229?accountid=13902

Copyright: (Copyright (c) 1996, Dow Jones & Company, Inc.)

Last updated: 2010-06-26

Database: ABI/INFORM Global

Document 5 of 5

A fire-breather gets scorched: Two newspapers and a mining giant

Author: Dudley, Steve

Publication info: Columbia Journalism Review 34. 6 (Mar/Apr 1996): 10.

ProQuest document link

Abstract:

Freeport-McMoRan officials disputed an article in the New Orleans "The Times-Picayune" that said the OPIC canceled an insurance policy for the mining firm bcause of the company's environmental damage to an Indonesian mine.

Full text:

two newspapers and a mining giant

At midnight last Halloween, the Overseas Private Investment Corporation (OPIC), a government agency that provides political-risk insurance for American companies operating abroad, canceled the policy of a Louisiana-based multinational mining company called Freeport-McMoRan. Three days later, The TimesPicayune of New Orleans ran a wire-service story reporting that the cancellation was apparently linked to environmental damage at Freeport's gold mine in the remote Indonesian province of Irian Jaya. Freeport's c.e.o., James Robert (Jim Bob) Moffett, was not happy, and he and three employees marched into the offices of the paper the day the story came out, demanding a correction. They contended that OPIC's decision to cancel Freeport's $100 million insurance policy was based on potential rather than actual harm to the environment. "What they're saying," Moffett told the paper's assembled editors and its publisher, "is that a project of this size is going to be very controversial and might - might - create a controversy."

The Times-Picayune listened and quickly began investigating Moffet's claims. But after obtaining OPIC's letter of cancellation, it ran an article refuting much of what Moffett had said. Freeport, the paper reported (quoting OPIC), had "severely degraded the rain forests" in Irian Jaya.

Freeport-McMoRan, which has affiliates in both Indonesia and in Austin, Texas, has constructed a mammoth public relations team and spent a great deal of money and time trying to shape public opinion. But the media in Austin and New Orleans have turned a skeptical eye on a company they see as trying to oversell its virtue.

Freeport-McMoRan's Austin affiliate, FM Properties, develops real estate and the Indonesian affiliate, Freeport-McMoRan Copper & Gold, mines the world's largest gold reserve and runs the third-largest copper mine. Since last spring, the company has been dealing with publicity about the murder and torture of indigenous people in Irian Jaya, first nationally publicized by The Nation magazine. Some environmentalists and human rights activists in the area claim that killings perpetrated by the Indonesian military occurred on Freeport property, and may even have involved Freeport security personnel. The company vehemently denies any involvement, and said so in December in a trio of full-page ads in The New York Times.

The story of Freeport's relationship with the media in New Orleans goes back to 1984. It was then that Times-Picayune environmental reporter Mark Schleifstein discovered documents showing that the Environmental Protection Agency was planning to grant the company an exemption to the Clean Water Act allowing it to dump 25 million pounds of gypsum, a byproduct from the production of fertilizer that contains phosphate and a trace of uranium, directly into the Mississippi river. In some places along the river the gypsum had been stacked as high as forty feet.

Other stories about the gypsum contamination ran on local television news, including one five-day series in the late 1980s by Garland Robinette, then anchor and environmental reporter for WWL, the CBS affiliate in New Orleans. Freeport built a $60 million system to reduce the runoff, a process that even the company's staunchest critics concede has significantly reduced the level of phosphate in the river

It also decided to build a massive public relations machine. Its first hire? Anchorman Robinette. Then came the environmental reporter from the NBC affiliate.

In the end, Freeport had studded its large public relations team with former environmental reporters and activists.

At the same time, the company was donating large sums to local universities and charity events - from charity golf tournaments to hot meals for seniors to $600,000 for an environmental communications chair at Loyola University to train aspiring environmental journalists. And the company rarely missed an opportunity to promote itself. "Jim Bob Moffett spent more money on ads explaining why he was making the playgrounds than on the playgrounds themselves," one local reporter says. According to Robinette, the company bombarded the community with print and television advertising. "We circumvented the [media] industry," Robinette says, "and today Freeport is the most highly thought-of company in Louisiana."

In Austin, Freeport has been under scrutiny for a different reason. Since 1990, the company has been attempting to develop 4,000 acres of land into a residential and commercial area. The development lies upstream from Barton Springs, a large spring-fed swimming pool visited by some 300,000 people a year, and has encountered fierce resistance. In 1992 Austin voted nearly two to one to impose strict development standards in the areas that contribute water to Barton Springs. The company is still trying to move forward with the project.

The vote may have been influenced by relentless and critical coverage in a local alternative weekly, The Austin Chronicle. Two reporters, Daryl Slusher and Robert Bryce, wrote countless articles detailing Freeport's environmental record in both Louisiana and Indonesia. And as in New Orleans, Freeport tried to reshape its image, with heavy print and TV advertising and by hiring former environmental reporters to work on its public relations team. Its spokesman in Austin is Bill Collier, a former environmental reporter for the Austin American-Statesman. According to Collier, the company has donated as much as $42 million to charitable causes. Moffett and his wife personally donated $1 million for a new molecular biology building at the University of Texas at Austin, and Freeport matched the gift.

For years, while the Chronicle was bashing Freeport's environmental record, the American-Statesman consistently seemed to side with the company. The Statesman's publisher, Roger Kintzel, a member and onetime chairman of the Greater Austin chamber of commerce, was sympathetic to suburban development interests, according to the Chronicle's Slusher. At one point, Moffett flew top officials of Austin's chambers of commerce, including Kintzel, in his corporate jet to see his company's operations in New Orleans, a visit the Statesman dutifully covered in its people column.

As in New Orleans, however, Freeport may have placed too much faith in aggressive tactics. Last December, the company threatened to sue three University of Texas professors, two environmental activists, and two reporters (Slusher and Bryce of the Chronicle) for criticizing the company. The threat happened to follow the departure of Kintzel to The Atlanta Journal & Constitution and the arrival of a new editor, Richard Oppel, who had been Washington bureau chief for Knight-Ridder.

Oppel took the opportunity to blast the company, in a December 15 editorial marking what many consider a new era in Statesman coverage. "Corporate leaders today apparently are advised by public relations strategists and Wall Street analysts to strike back furiously, absolutely punishing critics, when drawn into controversy," he wrote. "The results are not pretty." Oppel went on to express his support for those who received the threatening letters.

Oppel again reminded the company, in a February 4 column, of his suggestion that it withdraw the threats against its critics. But by then, in both Austin and New Orleans, some of the tension between Freeport and the press had seemed to ease. Oppel also concluded that evidence directly linking the company to human rights abuse in Indonesia was thin and had been contradicted by other sources, and thus was "no longer an issue," and that "Freeport executives in Indonesia are struggling to contain the environmental damage" from the mines.

The Times-Picayune, meanwhile, weighed in with an impressive four-part series on Freeport's Indonesian operations. Reporter Stewart Yerton explained that the abuses by the Indonesian military are real - including torture and some sixteen murders, mostly in 1995 - and that although some victims blame the company for bringing soldiers to Irian Jaya, a credible human rights observer did not charge it with direct involvement in the abuse. On the environment, as a pageone Times-Picayune subhead put it, "Critics say Freeport has destroyed ancient cultures and rainforests. . . . The company says damage has been minimal. . . . Somewhere in between lies the truth." Freeport's response to the series, unlike its response to earlier reports, has so far been muted and respectful, but it's hard to tell if its fire-breathing days are over.

"The press," says Robinette,

"will communicate maybe a half-dozen times. We'll communicate with the public a couple hundred times."

AuthorAffiliation

Dudley is a free-lance writer based in New York.

Subject: Newspapers; Insurance; Gold mines & mining; Environmental impact

Location: Indonesia

Company: Times-Picayune-New Orleans LA, Overseas Private Investment Corp, OPIC, Freeport-McMoRan Inc

Publication title: Columbia Journalism Review

Volume: 34

Issue: 6

Pages: 10

Number of pages: 4

Publication year: 1996

Publication date: Mar/Apr 1996

Year: 1996

Publisher: Columbia University, Graduate School of Journalism

Place of publication: New York

Country of publication: United States

Publication subject: Journalism

ISSN: 0010194X

CODEN: CJORD7

Source type: Scholarly Journals

Language of publication: English

Document type: Feature

Accession number: 02807068

ProQuest document ID: 230347007

Document URL: http://search.proquest.com/docview/230347007?accountid=13902

Copyright: Copyright Columbia University, Graduate School of Journalism Mar/Apr 1996

Last updated: 2010-06-10

Database: ABI/INFORM Global; ProQuest Research Library

Contact ProQuest

Copyright © 2012 ProQuest LLC. All rights reserved. - Terms and Conditions

EXHIBIT 7

Denise Leith,
The Politics of Power

transported in Freeport buses and security vehicles (presumably with Freeport drivers) and held in Freeport security posts. When questioned directly, Paul Murphy denied any knowledge of long-term human rights abuses but, with regard to the specific incident in Tembagapura, stated that by the time Freeport personnel had heard the gunshots and investigated the source, TNI had left with their prisoners—apparently absolving the company from any responsibility.[50] But according to Munninghoff's report, there was only one gunshot in Tembagapura, and that was seven to eight hours before the detainees were removed from the town, during which time they were held and beaten in Freeport containers at the army post in Tembagapura.[51] Therefore, according to Paul Murphy's account of events, it took about seven hours for the company to investigate the gunshot in a town you could walk around in half an hour. Moreover, if gunshots were heard, it would have been obvious that the first place to investigate would be the army post.

Robert Levin, a Freeport employee, stated that company personnel were aware of incidents occurring on Christmas Day but defended his and others' inaction, arguing that people were afraid to interfere because they really didn't know what was happening and they had their wives and children with them.[52] Levin also stated that Freeport personnel had heard of the killings around the area during the year, but in a region that runs on rumor, it was hard to differentiate fact from fiction. It would appear that one Freeport employee did attempt to pass on the information about the violations during 1994 to an interested party outside the country, but, according to this source, the employee was reprimanded by the company.[53] Moreover, Rumaropen reported to Freeport that he saw road just a few minutes after Rumaropen reported to Freeport that the military, in his opinion shot him, and he believed it to be the military. In his opinion the company was not interested in what he had to say and took no action.

Edward Pressman admitted that, in retrospect, the company had ing in and around the concession or prevent the violations. It also needs Freeport needs to explain why it made no effort to protect Papuans living in and around the concession or prevent the violations. It also needs to explain why it failed to inform anyone about these violations.

died the situation incorrectly; it should have reported the rumors of human rights violations. However, the difficulty the company faced was just who would it report such violations to when the perpetrators were themselves the law enforcers. If the same thing happened again, Pressman hoped that the company would handle the situation better to prevent further loss of lives.[54]

No one, including the company, denies that the violations occurred

Freeport property being used in the torture and killing of people. Freeport has also confirmed that it was responsible for calling in the army after the shooting of Gordon Rumaropen to protect Freeport operations and employees. It would also appear that Freeport personnel were aware of human rights abuses being perpetrated by the military in its area of work during 1994. While Freeport may not have physically been involved in the killings and torture, it cannot expect to operate in West Papua, mine the traditional land of the indigenous peoples, have a contract of work that effectively creates a close working relationship with TNI, rely on TNI to protect its facilities, and have human rights violations perpetrated in its area of work by the group it specifically called in to protect it without accepting some of the responsibility. It cannot, and does not, operate in isolation. While Freeport cannot always control the actions of the military the fact remains that, for as long as the company maintains a close relationship with TNI, it may be argued that it is implicating human rights violations. Moreover, with the U.S. courts recently recognizing the legal ramifications of such associations, the company now has a legal responsibility.

In response to the negative publicity of 1995, TNI announced that it was adopting a humane face: it issued its troops a booklet detailing a human rights code of conduct and, ominously, announced that it was increasing its presence in the region. While the government and the military were making "positive" public utterances, the reality in West Papua bore scant resemblance to the rhetoric. With outside interest abating, the promised bureaucrats failed to arrive, and the military expanded its operations. Using the OPM hostage taking that followed a few months later as justification, Jakarta sealed off the highland region; by April 1996, with the reported arrival of three thousand to four thousand new troops and the stationing of an Indonesian warship at the port of Amamapere, the military presence around the mine had increased dramatically. TNI once again launched a campaign of terror against the indigenous peoples of West Papua who lived near the mine. By December 1997 the military announced that the Freeport concession area was to become the most militarized subdistrict in Indonesia, claiming that the economic importance of the area and the associated need to "safeguard security and deal with any unrest" justified such a move.[55]

On 26 May 1998, the local churches released a report that claimed that between December 1996 and October 1997, rather than an easing of tensions as the government had promised, there had been an army crackdown, led by forces under the command of Lieutenant General

Denise Leith
The Politics of Power

Prabowo Subianto. The report detailed the military's terrorizing of groups of villagers, the extrajudicial killing or disappearance of some thirteen people, the subsequent deaths of many others from disease and malnutrition caused by their fleeing into the jungle to escape persecution, and the destruction of whole villages, churches, homes, livestock, and gardens. As a result at least another 137 people had died. Years later many of the people who fled still choose a difficult nomadic existence in the interior of the island to avoid further contact with the Indonesian military. The church report claimed that these violations were carried out by the military in retaliation for the kidnapping but also in an attempt to destroy the OPM and "to secure the 'vital project' of PT Freeport Indonesia Inc."[56] This time the world paid scant attention, for the events in Jakarta just six days before eclipsed the news from West Papua.

TRANSMIGRATION

While the relationship between Freeport security and TNI implicated the company in human rights abuses, so too does the policy of forced population displacement or transference within the company's concession area, either in the form of *transmigrasi* (transmigration) or *relokasi* (relocation), both of which have led to the loss of traditional lands and culture. The indigenous peoples claim that, without the company's presence, population displacement by either of these methods would simply not have happened. One of the essential elements in the "Indonesianization" of West Papua leading to the violation of human rights in the province has been the transmigration program.

Transmigration was first introduced by the Dutch in 1905 when they moved impoverished Javanese peasants to the less-populated areas to supposedly allow them to start a new life. In reality they represented a supply of cheap labor to foreign-owned plantations. The Suharto regime's transmigration policy, which systematically moved large numbers of migrants from the more crowded islands such as Java and Sulawesi to the outer resource-rich provinces, was not dissimilar. Throughout the history of the New Order government, transmigration was promoted internationally as a socioeconomic program aimed at relieving the population pressure on the densely populated main islands and received extensive financial support from its main donors, the World Bank and the IGGI/CGI.[57] Yet...

families from 1969 to 1994 out of a total population of over two hundred million did little to ease overcrowding.[58]

In practice the Indonesian program was an integral part of the central government's policy of "Indonesianization" or the creation of one kind of Indonesian[59] and focused on incorporating areas resistant to Jakarta's rule, such as East Timor, Aceh, and West Papua. At the same time, transmigration has focused on ensuring a supply of cheap and readily accessible labor to foreign enterprises operating in the most remote regions of the archipelago. Thus, transmigration had a political purpose (the control of the indigenous minorities), a cultural purpose (the alienation and destruction of traditional cultures), and an economic purpose (support for FDI). Given the above, the importance of transmigration to the Suharto government could not be overstated: the 1995 fiscal budget allocated $93 million to the program, making it second in terms of funding only to public works.

Transmigration in West Papua

To secure Indonesian control over West Papua by weakening local resistance and strengthening its border defenses, Jakarta focused on populating strategic regions in the province with transmigrants loyal to the center. Toward this end it encouraged the movement of voluntary transmigrants and financially supported the official government programs of sponsored transmigration (carried out by the government) and assisted-spontaneous transmigration (support by both the government and business). Although Jakarta always denied that the program had a political and security agenda, this association is clearly evident in West Papua in the siting of the settlements. Most are situated along the border with Papua New Guinea to create a cordon sanitaire in a region that always posed a dual security dilemma for the central government. Not only is it an indefensible border shared with an unstable and weak government whose people profess close historical and cultural ties with the inhabitants of West Papua, but the area affords shelter and protection to the OPM. Moreover, much to the embarrassment of Jakarta, OPM and Melanesian asylum seekers routinely cross the border into Papua New Guinea for sanctuary from the Indonesian military. While positioning is an indicator of the settlements' political character, so too is the fact that in the more unstable regions a good percentage of the transmigrants are reputed to be former army personnel.

Through the policy of *relokasi* the Papuan landowners have forcibly been

EXHIBIT 8

	FLEISHMAN & FISHER	
STANLEY FLEISHMAN (1920-1999)	LAWYERS	*PROFESSIONAL CORPORATIONS
BARRY FISHER*	1925 CENTURY PARK EAST, SUITE 2000	ΔOF COUNSEL
DAVID GROSZΔ	LOS ANGELES, CALIFORNIA 90067	CABLE ADDRESS: ARJUNA
MICHAEL B. WEISZΔ	(310) 557-1077 TELECOPIER (310) 557-0770	EMAIL: BFSHR557@GMAIL.COM
HENRY W. McGEE, JR. Δ		
WILLIAM M. KRAMER (1920-2004)		

June 5, 2020

Christopher Wray, Director
Federal Bureau of Investigation
935 Pennsylvania Avenue, N.W.
Washington, D.C. 20535-0001

Re: <u>John C. Wilson</u>

Dear Director Wray:

This firm represents John C. Wilson regarding the conduct of persons causing him harm he has reason to believe were operating on behalf of the FBI. or other element of the United States Department of Justice(DOJ). A history of correspondence over some 3 years resulted solely in a disclaimer that the persons involved were neither F.B.I. special agents nor employees but neither addressed nor denied to date is whether they operated on behalf of the FBI or other DOJ element. The most recent non-response is the 21 March 2020 DOJ - FOIA request denial.

The details at issue are set out in letters I wrote to the US Attorney General, Inspector General of the DOJ, and Director of the FBI June 24, 2016 attaching Mr. Wilson's 23 February 2016 letter, in follow up has not been answered except to tell him that the F.B.I. is the agency of the DOJ he should be addressing. The FBI has not responded.

The crux of Mr. Wilson's complaint is that false intelligence has been disseminated against him by the FBI in the U.S. to partnering agencies in the U.S. and overseas. This follows a work report he published as a Wall Street mining analyst working for SG Warburg (precursor to UBS Warburg) on US mining company Freeport McMoran March 12, 1996 that at the time was under investigation by the State Department following credible and widely reported allegations it was involved in the killing of indigenous protestors at its Grasberg mine in West Papua, Indonesia. He has been denied official acknowledgement of, or access to, any of the FBI's assertions, let alone test any of their claims in court, due to excessive secrecy around what they do. As such, he has endured a deprivation of basic human rights over a period now spanning more than 20 years.

Since then, Mr Wilson has been subjected to a systematic retaliation campaign by persons associated with the FBI involving invasive and aggressive tactics that include targeting his employment, professional, and social networks.

Susan Holmes engendered a personal relationship with Mr. Wilson for 3 years in NYC from 1994 to 1997 during which time she showed him what purported to be her FBI card and made multiple personal disclosures about her work to him. After Mr Wilson's Freeport work note was published 12 March 1996, the FBI commenced interference and disruption tactics across all aspects of his life - professional, social and family networks, surveillance and other intrusions into his life. Descriptions of the FBI intrusions are in the enclosed document "John Wilson Abridged Notes June 2020". This includes details of Susan Holmes' work purporting to be on behalf of the FBI; an overview of a long covert FBI dinner interview in NYC 2003 in which many personal details and personal records spanning many decades and diverse locations from Mr. Wilson's life were revealed (Mr Wilson's transcript of this interview is available upon request); assertions of false intelligence arise from comments made by the FBI and concern the apparent association of Mr Wilson though agent Susan Holmes' work for the FBI with David Foreman, a high profile eco-activist.

In the years following the 1996 publication regarding the Freeport McMoran killings, he had many other contacts with people who at some point revealed themselves as FBI agents and who let him know that he angered important people by the publication. Some of these individuals engendered friendship with him under the auspices of other professional identities and each has interviewed him, two of them extensively, in addition to Susan Holmes' extensive NYC covert interview in 2003. These include- Steven Garber, formerly of New York City, and Livingston Sutro, formerly of Sierra Vista, Arizona.

Aside from these apparent DOJ agents, more than a dozen other people have identified themselves to him as having a high level of familiarity with these circumstances and appear to be FBI agents or associated with agents. A partial list of names of agents has been provided to the FBI and DOJ in the past (the February 23, 2016 letter with list is attached).

The serious allegations of FBI misconduct in this matter have never been investigated, nor has there ever been a response concerning the correct roles of the agents named.

I write to request this matter be thoroughly investigated and hope that this long standing request can now be addressed definitively.

Sincerely yours,

Barry A. Fisher

Christopher Wray, Director
Federal Bureau of Investigation,
935 Pennsylvania Avenue, N.W.
Washington, D.C. 20535-0001

Congressman Jerrold Nadler
2132 Rayburn HOB
Washington, D.C. 20535

White House
600 Pennsylvania Avenue
Washington, D.C. 20530

Michael Evan Horowitz
Inspector General
Department of Justice
950 Pennsylvania Avenue, N.W.
Washington, D.C. 20530-0001

Senator Charles Schumer
Leo O'Brien Building
Room 420
Albay, NY 12207

William P. Barr
Attorney General
Department of Justice
950 Pennsylvania Avenue, N.W.
Washington, D.C. 20530-0001

13 July 2022

Corrections to Declaration

Paragraph 23: 1993; should read 1994
Paragraph 57: OPEC political risk insurance; should read OPIC political risk insurance
Paragraph 112: 2006; should read 1998

[This is Exhibit 2 of the 30 August 2022 John Wilson Declaration]

U.S. Department of Justice

Federal Bureau of Investigation

Washington, D.C. 20535-0001

June 26, 2020

Mr. Barry A Fisher
1925 Century Park East
Suite 2000
Los Angeles, CA 90067

Dear Mr. Fisher:

This letter is in response to your communication which was forwarded to the Federal Bureau of Investigation (FBI), Inspection Division (INSD), Internal Affairs Section (IAS), Initial Processing Unit (IPU). The IAS/INSD is the FBI entity responsible for investigating allegations of misconduct or criminal activity on the part of FBI employees.

IAS/IPU has reviewed your complaint and has determined an Internal Affairs investigation by the FBI is not warranted. This matter was provided to the United States Department of Justice, Office of the Inspector General for its review and any action deemed appropriate. IAS/IPU will take no further action in this matter.

Sincerely,

Initial Processing Unit
Internal Affairs Section
Inspection Division

STANLEY FLEISHMAN (1920-1999)
BARRY FISHER*
DAVID GROSZ△
MICHAEL R. WEISZ△
HENRY W. McGEE, JR. △
WILLIAM M. KRAMER (1929-2004)

FLEISHMAN & FISHER
LAWYERS
1925 CENTURY PARK EAST, SUITE 2000
LOS ANGELES, CALIFORNIA 90067
(310) 557-1077 TELECOPIER (310) 557-0770

*PROFESSIONAL CORPORATIONS
△OF COUNSEL
CABLE ADDRESS: ARJUNA
EMAIL: BFISHR617@GMAIL.COM

June 5, 2020

Christopher Wray, Director
Federal Bureau of Investigation
935 Pennsylvania Avenue, N.W.
Washington, D.C. 20535-0001

Re: John C. Wilson

Dear Director Wray:

This firm represents John C. Wilson regarding the conduct of persons causing him harm he has reason to believe were operating on behalf of the FBI. or other element of the United States Department of Justice(DOJ). A history of correspondence over some 3 years resulted solely in a disclaimer that the persons involved were neither F.B.I. special agents nor employees but neither addressed nor denied to date is whether they operated on behalf of the FBI or other DOJ element. The most recent non-response is the 21 March 2020 DOJ - FOIA request denial.

The details at issue are set out in letters I wrote to the US Attorney General, Inspector General of the DOJ, and Director of the FBI June 24, 2016 attaching Mr. Wilson's 23 February 2016 letter, in follow up has not been answered except to tell him that the F.B.I. is the agency of the DOJ he should be addressing. The FBI has not responded.

The crux of Mr. Wilson's complaint is that false intelligence has been disseminated against him by the FBI in the U.S. to partnering agencies in the U.S. and overseas. This follows a work report he published as a Wall Street mining analyst working for SG Warburg (precursor to UBS Warburg) on US mining company Freeport McMoran March 12, 1996 that at the time was under investigation by the State Department following credible and widely reported allegations it was involved in the killing of indigenous protestors at its Grasberg mine in West Papua, Indonesia. He has been denied official acknowledgement of, or access to, any of the FBI's assertions, let alone test any of their claims in court, due to excessive secrecy around what they do. As such, he has endured a deprivation of basic human rights over a period now spanning more than 20 years.

Since then, Mr Wilson has been subjected to a systematic retaliation campaign by persons associated with the FBI involving invasive and aggressive tactics that include targeting his employment, professional, and social networks.

Susan Holmes engendered a personal relationship with Mr. Wilson for 3 years in NYC from 1994 to 1997 during which time she showed him what purported to be her FBI card and made multiple personal disclosures about her work to him. After Mr Wilson's Freeport work note was published 12 March 1996, the FBI commenced interference and disruption tactics across all aspects of his life - professional, social and family networks, surveillance and other intrusions into his life. Descriptions of the FBI intrusions are in the enclosed document "John Wilson Abridged Notes June 2020". This includes details of Susan Holmes' work purporting to be on behalf of the FBI; an overview of a long covert FBI dinner interview in NYC 2003 in which many personal details and personal records spanning many decades and diverse locations from Mr. Wilson's life were revealed (Mr Wilson's transcript of this interview is available upon request); assertions of false intelligence arise from comments made by the FBI and concern the apparent association of Mr Wilson though agent Susan Holmes' work for the FBI with David Foreman, a high profile eco-activist.

In the years following the 1996 publication regarding the Freeport McMoran killings, he had many other contacts with people who at some point revealed themselves as FBI agents and who let him know that he angered important people by the publication. Some of these individuals engendered friendship with him under the auspices of other professional identities and each has interviewed him, two of them extensively, in addition to Susan Holmes' extensive NYC covert interview in 2003. These include- Steven Garber, formerly of New York City, and Livingston Sutro, formerly of Sierra Vista, Arizona.

mateo

Aside from these apparent DOJ agents, more than a dozen other people have identified themselves to him as having a high level of familiarity with these circumstances and appear to be FBI agents or associated with agents. A partial list of names of agents has been provided to the FBI and DOJ in the past (the February 23, 2016 letter with list is attached).

The serious allegations of FBI misconduct in this matter have never been investigated, nor has there ever been a response concerning the correct roles of the agents named.

I write to request this matter be thoroughly investigated and hope that this long standing request can now be addressed definitively.

Sincerely yours,

Barry A. Fisher

Christopher Wray, Director
Federal Bureau of Investigation,
935 Pennsylvania Avenue, N.W.
Washington, D.C. 20535-0001

Congressman Jerrold Nadler
2132 Rayburn HOB
Washington, D.C. 20535

White House
600 Pennsylvania Avenue
Washington, D.C. 20530

Michael Evan Horowitz
Inspector General
Department of Justice
950 Pennsylvania Avenue, N.W.
Washington, D.C. 20530-0001

Senator Charles Schumer
Leo O'Brien Building
Room 420
Albay, NY 12207

William P. Barr
Attorney General
Department of Justice
950 Pennsylvania Avenue, N.W.
Washington, D.C. 20530-0001

STANLEY FLEISHMAN (1920-1999)
BARRY FISHER*
DAVID GROSZ.
MICHAEL B. WEISZ.
HENRY W. McGEE, JR.
WILLIAM M. KRAMER (1920-2004)

FLEISHMAN & FISHER
LAWYERS
1925 CENTURY PARK EAST, SUITE 2000
LOS ANGELES, CALIFORNIA 90067
(310) 557-1077 TELECOPIER (310) 557-0770

*PROFESSIONAL CORPORATIONS
OF COUNSEL
CABLE ADDRESS: ARJUNA
EMAIL: BFSHR557@GMAIL.COM

June 24, 2016

Loretta Lynch, Attorney General   By Fax: 202-514-4001/616-9881
Department of Justice
950 Pennsylvania Avenue N.W.
Washington, DC 20530-001

Michael E. Horowitz, Inspector General
Department of Justice
950 Pennsylvania Avenue N.W.
Washington, DC 20530

James B. Comey, Director
Federal Bureau of Investigation
935 Pennsylvania Avenue, NW
Washington, D.C. 20535-0001

Re: John C. Wilson:

I represent John C. Wilson who has previously written requesting investigation and clarification regarding personally impacting conduct of persons he has reason to believe were operating on behalf of the F.B.I. or other element of the DOJ. Response was sent to him stating the persons involved were not "employees" of the Department but not addressing the question whether they operated on its behalf.

Mr. Wilson's 23 February 2016 letter, attached, in follow up has not been answered except to tell him that the F.B.I. is the agency of the DOJ he should be be addressing. The F.B.I. has not responded.

I write in hopes that this long standing request can now be address definitely.

Sincerely yours,

Barry A. Fisher

U.S. Department of Justice

Office of the Inspector General

Investigations Division

1425 New York Avenue NW, Suite 7100
Washington, D.C. 20530

May 25, 2016

Barry Fisher, Esq.
Fleishman & Fisher
1925 Century Park East
Suite 2000
Los Angeles, CA 90067

Dear Mr. Fisher:

The purpose of this letter is to acknowledge receipt of your correspondence dated January 28, 2016, February 8, 2016, and February 18, 2016, on behalf of your client, John C. Wilson, alleging misconduct by Federal Bureau of Investigation (FBI) Special Agents.

The Office of the Inspector General (OIG) has received numerous complaints from Mr. Wilson dating back to May 1, 2005. We have reviewed the allegations raised by Mr. Wilson and determined that they were more appropriate for review by the FBI, Inspection Division (INSD), and referred the matter to that office for handling. Mr. Wilson has been advised of this referral and that any further inquiries regarding this matter should be directed to the FBI INSD at 935 Pennsylvania Avenue NW, Washington, D.C. 20035, (202) 324-3000.

This office does not intend to initiate an investigation into Mr. Wilson's allegations and considers this matter to be closed.

Sincerely,

Office of the Inspector General
Investigations Division

166

23 February 2016

Email:

Michael D. McDonald,
Unit Chief
Initial Processing Unit,
Inspection Division
U.S. Department of Justice
Federal Bureau of Investigation
Room 3041,
935 Pennsylvania Avenue, NW
Washington, DC 20535-0001

RE: Complaint concerning FBI abuse

Dear Sir,

I write in response to the letter to me dated 9 February 2016 from Michael D. McDonald, Unit Chief, Initial Processing Unit, Inspection Division, U.S. Department of Justice, Federal Bureau of Investigation, Washington, D.C. concerning my complaint about FBI misconduct I originally sent to the DOJ, Office of the Inspector General dated 9 March 2015.

I am not satisfied with the FBI's response and request the search and investigation be extended. The FBI's response uses the term "employee" exclusively. I want to clarify that those referred to below I believe were working on behalf of the U.S. government, FBI and or other agencies as employees or in other capacities currently or in the past. I did not ask for or suggest that the search be limited solely to employees.

- Michael Mills: the FBI agent who moved into my apartment in NYC and occupied it for several years when I sublet it before my return to Australia.
- Kathleen Walton: former mining analyst at Merrill Lynch in NYC.
- Matthew Levey – Kroll Associates, Inc (New York City midtown office): consulting work case manager 2003 and 2004. Former State Department employee.
- Jeffrey S Robards: corporate finance, formerly Ernst & Young (E&Y) NYC. Now working for C.W. Downer & Co - a boutique M&A firm in Boston. (http://www.cwdowner.com/index.php?option=com_content&view=article&id=42&Itemid=23)
- Susan A. Holmes (formerly resident in New York City in the 1990s)
- Stephan Chenault and John Klotz: volunteers Sierra Club NYC Group since 1990s.
- Ben Worden, Rob Haggerty and Allison Dey (Tucson area): FBI agents involved with Diamond Mountain Buddhist group in southern Arizona and California.
- George Schneider and Livingston Sutro (Sierra Vista, AZ); Jennifer Conner (NYC): Associated with Diamond Mountain Buddhist group in southern Arizona.

167

- Paul Whitby (Tucson): biologist.
- Leigh Freeman – Cherry Creek, Denver based head hunter. Downing Teal. http://www.downingteal.com/Our-People/Downing-Teal-USA
- Robert Schultz – Albuquerque based head hunter. MRC Mining Search. http://www.miningsearch.com/mining-search/our-team/
- Steven D. Garber – (wife Andrea - collaborator) additional details: biologist; lived in Manhattan for much of the 1990s, before taking a two year posting to teach biology at Embry Riddle in Prescott, AZ before returning to the New York area (White Plains). Books authored include The Urban Naturalist (New York. John Wiley and Sons. 1987). PhD in Ecology, Environmental Sciences - Rutgers, The State University of New Jersey-Newark. B.S. in Natural Resources - Cornell University.

For clarification, the nature of my complaint concerning FBI misconduct which I reported in my letter to the DOJ dated 9 March 2015 and request be investigated concerns the FBI's abuse and unwarranted interference with me since 1996 following my report I authored on US mining company Freeport McMoran.

Thank you.

I look forward to your response.

Sincerely,

John Wilson

CC: U.S. Department of Justice
Office of the Inspector General
Investigations Division
950 Pennsylvania Avenue, N.W.
Suite 4706
Washington, D.C. 20530-0001

9 March 2015

Email

U.S. Department of Justice
Office of the Inspector General
Investigations Division
950 Pennsylvania Avenue, N.W.
Suite 4706
Washington, D.C. 20530-0001

Via fax: 202 616 9881

RE: Complaint concerning FBI abuse

Dear Sir/Madam,

My full name is John Christian Wilson. My social security number is   I am a US citizen by birth: my passport number is

I am a mining analyst based in Sydney. I have had ongoing problems with the FBI for the past 18 years since publishing a short report (attached, March 1996) as a Wall Street mining analyst working with SG Warburg (now part of UBS) while I was living and working in New York. The report was on US mining company Freeport McMoran and touched on killings of indigenous protestors at its Grasberg mine in West Papua. Subsequent to publication of the report and a boardroom analyst meeting in New Orleans a couple of months later, I was threatened by an FBI agent and have been subjected to extensive surveillance and interference by the FBI and partnering Australian agencies since then. As a result of intrusive, disruptive and unconstitutional FBI interference I left the USA and moved back to Australia.

The agencies' surveillance and interference with me and more recently my family has been highly intrusive over this period of time to the present.

I believe the agency's activities are unwarranted, abusive and stem from my work as a mining analyst in 1996. It also seems the FBI has made concerted effort to misrepresent material facts of the matter in order to defend its illegitimate decision for surveillance of, and interference with me and to deflect all but a detailed investigation of my allegations, including the court testing of their "evidence" in my file. My then long term girlfriend, was a self disclosed, undercover FBI agent named Susan A. Holmes, based in New York whose work at the FBI involved pursuing environmental radicals on the east coast of the U.S.

In the absence of the agency giving me access to my FBI files I have no way to respond to allegations against me and defend myself in a court. (I am a dual citizen of the USA and Australia and attach what my Australian Member of Parliament Tanya Plibersek said about this matter concerning the FBI's partnering agency in Australia - ASIO; Hansard transcript attached).

By way of further evidence, I list the names of undercover FBI agents and collaborators self-disclosed or that have interfered with me include:

- Michael Milis: the FBI agent who moved into my apartment in NYC and occupied it for several years when I sublet it before my return to Australia.
- Kathleen Walton: former mining analyst at Merrill Lynch in NYC.
- Matthew Levey – Kroll Associates, Inc (New York City midtown office): consulting work case manager 2003 and 2004. Former State Department employee.
- Jeffrey S Robards: corporate finance, formerly Ernst & Young (E&Y) NYC. Now working for C.W. Downer & Co - a boutique M&A firm in Boston. (http://www.cwdowner.com/index.php?option=com_content&view=article&id=42&Itemid=23)
- Susan A. Holmes (formerly resident in New York City in the 1990s)
- Stephan Chenault and John Klotz: volunteers Sierra Club NYC Group since 1990s.
- Ben Worden, Rob Haggerty and Allison Dey (Tucson area): FBI agents involved with Diamond Mountain Buddhist group in southern Arizona and California.
- George Schneider and Livingston Sutro (Sierra Vista, AZ); Jennifer Conner (NYC): Associated with Diamond Mountain Buddhist group in southern Arizona.
- Paul Whitby (Tucson): biologist.
- Leigh Freeman – Cherry Creek, Denver based head hunter. Downing Teal. http://www.downingteal.com/Our-People/Downing-Teal-USA
- Robert Schultz – Albuquerque based head hunter. MRC Mining Search. http://www.miningsearch.com/mining-search/our-team/
- Steven D. Garber – (wife Andrea - collaborator) additional details: biologist; lived in Manhattan for much of the 1990s, before taking a two year posting to teach biology at Embry Riddle in Prescott, AZ before returning to the New York area (White Plains). Books authored include The Urban Naturalist (New York. John Wiley and Sons. 1987). PhD in Ecology, Environmental Sciences - Rutgers, The State University of New Jersey-Newark. B.S. in Natural Resources - Cornell University.

Thank you.

I look forward to your response.

Sincerely,

John Wilson

[This is Exhibit 3 of the 30 August 2022 John Wilson Declaration]

Exhibit 3

From: John Wilson
Sent: Friday, 14 June 2013 5:08 PM
To: 'philip.ruddock.mp@aph.gov.au'
Cc: 'Jackie.Russell@aph.gov.au'
Subject: John Wilson - ASIO

Dear Philip,

Thank you for taking the time to meet with me again several weeks ago concerning the issues I have faced with intrusive ASIO interference. As you recall, this interference has occurred since I published a report as an analyst on Wall Street in 1996 that touched on the killings at the US listed Freeport McMoran's massive Grasberg gold and copper mine in West Papua (note attached).

Following our conversation about Australian intelligence agency misconduct, it is interesting to note the recent media reports of former US National Security Agency (NSA) analyst Edward Snowden who has disclosed the extensive intelligence capability and abuses of the US government in operating an all encompassing communications dragnet domestically and abroad. Associated with this disclosure is that the US is targeting a large number of people everywhere in the world, including Australia, and in turn is sharing this information with its counterparts in foreign agencies, including Australian intelligence agencies.

The possibility of such foreign government intelligence activity in Australia was something we touched on when we spoke. Their direct involvement in Australia obviously makes the need for a warrant from the Australian Attorney General of no consequence in matters where Australian agencies can simply get such information through back door channels – ie, via their US counterparts in this instance. Based on the NSA leaks, there now seems to be little doubt that the US has the capability to bug my phone and all my communications, if they were inclined to do so, without need for the Australian government's direct involvement or consent.

An example of recent media reports quotes Snowden telling the Guardian newspaper, "I, sitting at my desk, certainly had the authority to wiretap anyone, from you or your accountant, to a federal judge, to even the President." (Edward Snowden Search Began Days Before NSA Surveillance Program Reports Went Public, Reuters, posted: 06/12/2013 6:40).

It has also come to my attention, that an ASIO operative, who was aware that I had met with you on two previous occasions in 2011/12 was actively engaging staff at the Environmental Defender's Office (EDO) in mid 2012. This person is active in a local Greenwich community group "Friends of Gore Bay" which is campaigning for the removal of the Shell oil import terminal at Gore Bay on Sydney Harbour and engaged the EDO on the pretext of seeking legal assistance for this campaign. On several occasions this person (not named below), who I know has been actively recruiting for ASIO, has made reference to Kirsty Ruddock and taunted that they were getting to know at least one of her office colleagues well, taking them to lunch, etc – with the intended implication that ASIO was actively recruiting within the EDO's office. Based on this, ASIO, it seems, considers its brief to include the targeting of family members of officials responsible for oversight of the intelligence agencies.

I believe that ASIO is operating without adequate constraints in Australia, that it is operating outside its mandate and abusing its powers. Lawyer Ian Barker, QC has maintained this point of view for some time as outlined in the attached letter I sent to the committee you sit on, the Parliamentary Joint Committee on Intelligence and Security. I attach the letter as a reminder of my experiences with ASIO and my inability to obtain a commitment from any Australian oversight authority to investigate my allegations of intelligence agency abuse in Australia, despite persistent efforts. The current oversight process operates in a way that provides no protection to people subjected to ASIO abuses and offers no outlet that protects the rights and interests of people targeted by ASIO (I have attached Tanya Plibersek's comments to parliament to this effect).

The current revelations about the NSA's conduct and Australia's involvement might serve as the required scandal you referred to as being a necessary catalyst to launch a wide sweeping royal commission into Australia's intelligence agencies. As we discussed, the Hope Royal Commission recommended that there be a mandatory royal commission into the Australian intelligence agencies every eight years or so, but this was never put into effect.

When we met recently, you and I discussed that I would name various ASIO operatives – agents, collaborators and informants active in my case. I have provided you a list of names previously. Operatives I intend to name initially include:

Robert Sadleir, son of former ASIO Director General David Sadleir (1992-96)
Lesa Deleau, staff member of the Green's Senator Rhiannon
Dr Trent Allen, Sydney, stockbroking analyst
Michael and Claudia Hackman, a Sydney businesspeople
Deborah Bye, Melbourne, former lawyer
Daniel Aitken, Central coast NSW and Boston, USA
Richard Kaan, Sydney, former business consultant
Fabian Babich, Sydney, former stockbroking analyst

I would be pleased to discuss with you or provide further information on any of the above. Please let me know if you would like further details.

Best regards,

John Wilson

[This is Exhibit 4 of the 30 August 2022 John Wilson Declaration]

Exhibit 4

The New York Times

https://www.nytimes.com/1997/09/15/nyregion/when-birds-man-nature-meet-falcons-keep-geese-gulls-colliding-with-jets.html

When Birds of Man and Nature Meet; Falcons Keep Geese and Gulls From Colliding With Jets

By Andrew C. Revkin

Sept. 15, 1997

As a Boeing 747 thundered to a landing at Kennedy International Airport, two silver Chevy Blazers raced down a road paralleling the runway, patrolling for intruders.

Spotting movement in the distance, Thomas Cullen, clad in khaki and camouflage, stomped on the brakes and jumped out. But the trespassers, a flock of cowbirds, disappeared before Mr. Cullen could deploy the tools of his trade: a leather gauntlet, half a pigeon carcass and a peregrine falcon named Basil.

In the high-technology world of jets, radio beacons and radar at Kennedy, the 4,000-year-old sport of falconry has become the latest method used to reduce the chances that geese, gulls or other birds will collide with a plane.

Falcons and hawks, whose silhouettes strike fear into almost any other bird, are being flown seven days a week, dawn to dusk, until late November to scare off sea gulls, swallows, Canada geese and other birds that might otherwise be sucked into the engines of airliners.

The birds of prey, trained for hunting ducks and small game, are used to frighten, not kill, with flung pigeon breasts -- bought from a Queens poultry supplier -- acting as a lure. "Just the sight of an actively hunting falcon alone is enough to scare away almost any bird within half a mile," Mr. Cullen said.

Falconry has been tried at a handful of other airports, in Canada, Europe and, most recently, Taiwan. The United States Air Force is testing the technique. But the program at Kennedy, entering its second year, is the biggest. The main reason is that no other airport has a greater potential for bird-airplane collisions, aviation safety officials say, because a major bird sanctuary, the Jamaica Bay National Wildlife Refuge, abuts its busiest runways.

A main target of the falconry program is the laughing gull, which established a giant nesting colony in the protected marshes in the 1980's. That colony has become a source of friction between between aviation safety officials and National Park Service scientists.

In 1989, an international panel of biologists recommended relocating the gull colony. But the Park Service -- saying its mission is to nurture, not repel, birds -- has insisted on conducting more research before anything is done to push the birds from the preserve. In the meantime, efforts have focused on the airport grounds, with booming propane cannons, gull-shooting teams of marksmen, recorded gull distress calls -- and now falcons -- used to cut the collision threat.

Park and airport officials both hope that the falconry patrols will reduce the need to shoot the gulls, which are rebounding after being slaughtered in the 19th century for their feathers.

In doing so, the program could resolve a strange clash of missions. Since laughing gulls first returned to Jamaica Bay, National Park Service biologists have been trying to protect them; but since 1991, just over the property line between preserve and airport, a special wildlife control unit of the United States Department of Agriculture has been shooting thousands of those gulls every summer.

So far, the falconry program appears to be working. Last year -- the first year falconry was tried -- there was a 61 percent decline in the number of birds striking airplanes while falcon flights were under way, compared with the same period in 1995, according to the Port Authority of New York and New Jersey. The number of gulls shot fell to 2,200 from 6,700 between 1995 and 1996. This year, the Port Authority approved a $228,000 contract for the falconers. Airport officials say they expect that falcons will become a fixture, as permanent as the bristling radars and 30-story control tower.

"It's worth spending a little to save major costs from damage to aircraft and, God forbid, loss of life and limb," said Alfred J. Graser, the Port Authority general manager for airport operations and security.

Although it might seem inconsequential to have a one-pound gull or four-pound goose strike a 340,000-pound 747 or other aircraft, such collisions can have deadly consequences. Nationwide in an average year, there are 2,200 reports of birds striking civilian aircraft, said Richard A. Dolbeer, who directs an animal damage control unit at the Agriculture Department. And in a recent analysis, Todd Curtis, an independent aviation safety consultant in Washington State, calculated that there is a 25 percent chance of a deadly collision between bird and airliner in North America in the next 10 years.

The Federal Aviation Administration has estimated that the bill for damage to civilian and military aircraft from collisions with birds is more than $400 million a year in the United States alone. The situation is no better abroad. The Israeli Air Force has lost more planes to birds than to enemy fire, aviation safety officials say. Worldwide, the problem is increasing as conservation efforts are helping to expand bird populations while commercial aircraft flights are also rapidly increasing.

Deadly bird-related accidents occur every few years. In 1995, an American Awacs surveillance jet crashed in Alaska after four geese flew into two engines. Twenty-four people died.

Around New York City, the problem is not limited to Kennedy, with the most recent bird strike occurring on Sept. 4 at Newark International Airport, when a departing Continental Airlines Boeing 737 lost power in one of two engines after striking a sea gull.

But two of the most dramatic close calls were at Kennedy: in June 1995, an arriving Air France Concorde sustained more than $5 million in damage when two engines disintegrated after several geese were struck. And in November 1975, a departing McDonnell Douglas DC-10 crash-landed and burned on the runway after several sea gulls were sucked into an engine. No one was killed in either incident.

The falconry program at Kennedy is by far the most ambitious test yet of this bird-against-bird airport defense, with 6 falconers and 13 birds of prey in rotating shifts. Day after day last week, rain or shine, Mr. Cullen and his team searched for intruding flocks around the 5,200-acre airport, which covers an area the size of Manhattan south of 42d Street.

Each time a gull or other unwanted bird was spotted, one of the falconers removed the custom-made leather hood shielding the eyes of Basil, Sesame or one of the other trained raptors, then flung the bird toward the sky. A piece of pigeon slung in a circle on a string spurred the birds to slice repeatedly through the air at up to 120 miles an hour.

There was something of a lull at Kennedy, Mr. Cullen said, with only sporadic encounters with herring gulls, crows and other species now that the laughing gulls had largely moved on after nesting earlier in the summer. When the laughing gulls were at their peak -- with 3,200 nests in the marshes less than a mile from the runway -- "it was truly a frightening sight," Mr. Cullen said.

But the laughing gulls are only one of dozens of bird species that pass over and around the airport, said Dr. Steven D. Garber, the Port Authority's full-time wildlife biologist. Later this month, Dr. Garber said, dense clouds of tree swallows are expected to pass on their way south, with up to 50,000 birds settling in the north corner of the airport before making their flight south. "There's a new problem every month of the year," he said.

Different birds of prey will be used to ward off the different species of invaders, Dr. Garber said, with small, swift-flying merlins used to harass the swallows. "Merlins are very, very scary to little birds," Mr. Cullen said.

Mr. Cullen and the other falconers also used other tools for driving off birds, including small pistols that shoot firecracker-like shells. But almost all the other deterrents wear thin as birds become inured to the noise, Mr. Cullen said. "The only thing they never tire of is the sight of a raptor," he said.

That was clear on at least one patrol, as Mr. Cullen encountered a flock of about 50 crows. He removed the hood of a male falcon. With the relentless roar of jet engines rumbling in the distance, the yellow-taloned bird rose and then dove to attack the pigeon lure.

In a mass, the crows headed for the horizon.

[This is Exhibit 5 of the 30 August 2022 John Wilson Declaration]

Exhibit 5

180

The Sydney Morning Herald

World

This was published 19 years ago

Court reveals FBI deceit

August 25, 2002 — 10.00am

The FBI and US Justice Department frequently misled a secret American court that approves spying on terrorism suspects, judges have said.

False information was supplied to the court in more than 75 applications for search warrants and wiretaps, including one signed by former FBI director Louis Freeh, according to the Foreign Intelligence Surveillance Court.

"How these misrepresentations occurred remains unexplained to the court," the ruling said.

Authorities had also improperly shared intelligence information with prosecutors in charge of criminal cases on at least four occasions, it said.

The court consists of a rotating panel of judges from around the US. Its ruling was made on May 17 but released only on Friday, the first time any opinion by the court has been announced publicly.

Former National Security Agency general counsel Stewart Baker said it was "a public rebuke" to the Justice Department.

"The message is you need better quality control," he told *The Washington Post*.

"The judges want to ensure that they have information they can rely on implicitly."

The court has refused to grant the Justice Department sweeping new anti-terrorism powers because the judges said this would have effectively allowed the US Government to misuse intelligence information in criminal cases.

The ruling is a major blow to attempts by US Attorney-General John Ashcroft after September 11 to allow terrorism investigators to share more information with criminal investigators.

Mr Ashcroft has appealed against the ruling in the first formal challenge to the court in its 23-year history.

The Justice Department said in a statement: "We believe the court's action unnecessarily narrowed the Patriot Act and limited our ability to fully utilise the authority Congress gave us."

Some legislators have said the law may have hampered the investigation of alleged 20th hijacker Zacarias Moussaoui before the September 11 attacks. Moussaoui, who was arrested six weeks before the attacks, awaits trial on conspiracy charges.

The US wants to prevent enriched uranium from 24 research reactors in 16 countries from falling into the hands of terrorists or rogue nations.

Observers saw a US-sponsored project outside Belgrade, Yugoslavia, on Friday when 48kg of enriched uranium was spirited out of the Vinca research centre to a reprocessing plant in Russia.

The operation took place in an atmosphere of strict co-operation among US, Russian and Yugoslav authorities as a way to place the nuclear fuel under lock and key, avoiding the possibility that it could find its way into the hands of extremist groups or countries looking to build nuclear weapons.

"Project Vinca", as the operation is codenamed, was just a trial run.

Section IV

General Correspondence

Section IV

General Correspondence

IV-1. Correspondence: 2004 to 2011

    a)   FBI/DOJ
    b)   Senator Charles Schumer
    c)   Congressman Jerrold Nadler
    d)   House Judiciary Committee
    e)   UNHRC
    f)   Other

IV-2. Correspondence: 2010 to 2014

    a)   House Judiciary Committee
    b)   Other

IV-3. Correspondence: 2015 to 2019

    a)   FBI/DOJ
    b)   Senator Charles Schumer

IV-4. Correspondence: 2020 to 2023

    a)   FBI/DOJ
    b)   Senator Charles Schumer
    c)   Senator Kirsten Gillibrand
    d)   Congressman Jerrold Nadler

IV-1 Correspondence 2004 to 2010/11

IV-1   Correspondence 2004 to 2011:

FBI/DOJ

* * * * *

Exhibit 7: *17 January 2005.   Letter from John Wilson via Attorney Barry Fisher to DOJ, OIG*

John Christian Wilson   17 January, 2005
c/o Barry A. Fisher
Fleishman & Fisher
1875 Century Park East Suite 2130
Los Angeles, CA 90067
Tel: 310-5571077

Email: ▇▇▇▇▇▇▇▇▇▇▇▇▇▇

US Department of Justice
Office of the Inspector General
950 Pennsylvania Avenue, N.W., Suite 4706
Washington, DC 20530-0001

Dear Sir:

I write because of the oversight responsibilities of your office. I was a mining company equity analyst on Wall Street from 1994 to 1998. I am a citizen of the U.S.A., was born in Australia, and have long lived in the United States, principally in New York and Philadelphia, where I received my MBA degree from Wharton. I am currently visiting family for an extended stay in Australia.

In 1996, in the course of performing my duties, information was leaked to me by a then undisclosed FBI agent who worked undercover as an environmentalist. This person gave me details of a State Department finding into an incident in which 7 people were recently killed in and around the publicly traded Freeport McMoran owned Grasberg mine in Indonesia. The information I received related to a confidential reprimand of the company by the U.S. Department of State for human rights and environmental abuses.

Since then, as set out below, I have been subjected to what appears to be a systematic retaliation campaign by persons associated with the FBI involving invasive and injurious tactics. Among other things, I have faced blacklisting in my industry. I have been unable to gain any employment in the financial services industry despite a recent boom in the mining sector and despite having worked on Wall Street for 6 years, mostly as a senior equity analyst.

For the many years following my 1996 publication regarding the Freeport McMoran killings, I have had many contacts with people who at some point revealed themselves as FBI agents on assignment connected to me, and who let me know that I angered important people by the publication. Some of these individuals engendered friendship with me under the auspices of other professional identities and each has interviewed me, two of them extensively. These include Steven Garber, now of White Plains, New York, formerly of New York City, Susan Holmes, now of Washington, D.C., formerly of New York City, and Livingston Sutro, of Sierra Vista, Arizona.

Aside from these agents, more than a dozen other people have identified themselves to me as having a high level of familiarity with these circumstances and appear to be FBI agents or associated with agents.

Given the fact that the source of the leaked information was itself an FBI agent and given the powerful business interests of Freeport, I am concerned that I am the subject of what appears to be either a case of FBI corruption or incompetence. The agent that passed to me the information about Freeport was a long term friend who targeted environmental extremists, and I am concerned I may have been maliciously profiled to justify the intense scrutiny I have faced.

An FOIA request to the FBI in October, 2004 yielded no information whatsoever.

I look forward to hearing from you. The most convenient means by which to correspond with me are through my attorney (details indicated above), alternatively via email.

Sincerely yours,

John Wilson

* * * * *

Exhibit 8: *16 April 2005.   Letter from John Wilson via Attorney Barry Fisher to DOJ/OIG*

John Christian Wilson
c/o Barry A. Fisher
Fleishman & Fisher
1875 Century Park East Suite 2130
Los Angeles, CA 90067

16 April, 2005

Email: ▮▮▮▮▮▮▮▮▮▮▮▮▮▮

US Department of Justice
Office of the Inspector General
950 Pennsylvania Avenue, N.W., Suite 4706
Washington, DC 20530-0001

Dear Sir:

I write as a follow up to the letter I sent to your office on 17 January, 2005 (copy enclosed). Could you please indicate your expected timing for a response to that letter.

Thank you.

Sincerely yours,

John Wilson

Encl.   Copy of letter sent to your office, dated 17 January, 2005

* * * * *

Exhibit 9: *16 August 2005.   Email from John Wilson to DOJ, Marvin Hernandez*

From: john wilson
Sent: Tuesday, August 16, 2005 10:38 AM
To: bfisher557@aol.com
Subject: DOJ

Hi Barry,

 Details of DOJ: Marvin Hernandez (202 616 4760) in the investigations division dealt with my letter (attached) and forwarded it to the FBI for investigation. I spoke with him early this month and he confirmed that the people identified in the letter were agents and that this was the reason he has taken further action on the matter. He will receive a copy of the repsonse from the FBI and at least in this way, stay involved. The original letter I sent Jan 05 was not in their records when I called, but the April follow up was.

Regards

John

* * * * *

From: BFisher557@aol.com <BFisher557@aol.com>
Sent: Friday, August 26, 2005 3:09 AM
To:
Subject: doj/fbi

spoke to marvin h--he gave me a contact name, number, and doj reference number to follow up at fbi and I will try to contact the person he suggested. B

* * * * *

Exhibit 10: *27 August 2005. Email from Barry Fisher to John Wilson re DOJ, Hernadez.*

From: BFisher557@aol.com <BFisher557@aol.com>
Sent: Saturday, August 27, 2005 1:16 AM
To: [redacted]
Subject: Re: doj/fbi

I spoke to the FBI Inspector General contact Hernandez connected me with. She will look into it and get back to me. Barry

* * * * *

From: john wilson [redacted]
Sent: Saturday, August 27, 2005 9:02 AM
To: BFisher557@aol.com
Subject: Re: doj/fbi

Thanks Barry. Did she give a time frame for getting back to you. Also, did Hernandez verify with you what he verified with me, viz the reason he decided to progress the investigation to the next stage.

rgds

John

* * * * *

Exhibit 11: *10 February 2006. Letter from DOJ to Attorney Barry Fisher.*

U.S. Department of Justice
Federal Bureau of Investigation
Washington, D. C. 20535-0001

February 10, 2006

Mr. Barry A. Fisher
Fleishman and Fisher
1875 Century Park East
Suite 2130
Los Angeles, California 90067

Attention: Mr. John Christian Wilson

Dear Mr. Wilson:

We are in receipt of your letter dated January 17, 2005, to the U.S. Department of Justice (DOJ), Office of Inspector General. DOJ forwarded this correspondence to the Initial processing Unit (IPU), Internal Investigations Section, Inspection Division, Federal Bureau of Investigation (FBI), for our review. The IIS is the FBI entity that provides thorough, high quality, fair, consistent, and timely review and investigation into complaints of criminality and/or serious misconduct against FBI employees.

In the above-referenced letter, you allege that an unidentified Undercover FBI Special Agent (SA) apparently disclosed confidential information to you originating from the U.S. State Department regarding a fatal Grasberg mining accident in Indonesia. You advised that you published an article about the accident at the Freeport McMoran owned Grasberg mine in 1996 and, since its publication, you allege having been contacted by numerous individuals who identified themselves to you as FBI agents, specifically SA Steven Garber, New York; SA Livingston Sutro, Arizona, and SA Susan Holmes, Washington, D.C. A review of our records revealed that the above-named individuals are not employed by the FBI.

Inasmuch as the information provided contains no credible allegations of misconduct by any FBI personnel, IPU has determined that your complaint does not warrant the initiation of an investigation. We consider this matter closed.

Sincerely,

Timothy C. Campbell
Unit Chief
Initial Processing
Inspection Division

* * * * *

Exhibit 12: *22 February 2006.   Email from John Wilson to Barry Fisher re DOJ, Hernandez.*

From: John Wilson
Sent: Wednesday, February 22, 2006 9:20 AM
To: 'BFisher557@aol.com' <BFisher557@aol.com>
Subject: John Wilson

Barry,

I spoke with Marvin this morning. He has not received a copy of the letter you forwarded to me [10 February 2006: DOJ letter to John Wilson via Barry Fisher] and asked that I forward a copy to him. He reconfirmed the process to date as discussed with each of us previously, including confirmation of the people identified in the letter as being agents of the FBI.

Below is a draft of the email I propose to send to Marvin. Please let me know if you have any comments/changes and I will plan to send the final to Marvin later today.

Thanks and regards.

John

Hi Marvin,

Please find the letter from Timothy C. Campbell from the Inspection Division of the FBI dated February 10, 2006 attached.

As reviewed today over the phone with yourself, the process of this inquiry to date has been –

1. I sent a letter to the Department of Justice January 17, 2005
2. You were able to confirm that the people named in the letter were FBI agents
3. On account of the identification of these as FBI agents you forwarded my letter to the FBI for internal investigation
4. I received the above letter from Timothy Campbell which states that the people confirmed as agents by the DOJ are not employed by the FBI. However this letter did not confirm whether at any stage these people had been employed by the FBI or in what capacity. This is in direct conflict with my experience and your advice to myself and my attorney.

I would like to have this matter resolved. In particular, I would appreciate your advice as to what options are available to me to gain official acknowledgement of this near 10 year investigation, how this matter can be resolved most expeditiously, and how I might work with you to this end.

Thank you.

John Wilson

C/o Mr. Barry A. Fisher
Fleishman and Fisher
1875 Century park East
Suite 2130
Los Angeles, California 90067

Telephone: 310 557 1077

* * * *

Exhibit 13: *22 February 2006.   Email from Barry Fisher to John Wilson to re DOJ, Hernandez.*

From: BFisher557@aol.com [mailto:BFisher557@aol.com]
Sent: Wednesday, 22 February 2006 9:34 AM
To: xxxxxxxxxxx@bigpond.com
Subject: Re: John Wilson

did marvin agree that he confirmed persons were agents and if so was it all of the persons-is the list of persons you gave him before the same as in the recent FBI letter? b

* * * *

* * * * *

Exhibit 14: *22 February 2006.   Email from John Wilson to Barry Fisher re DOJ, Hernandez – confirms "they are agents".*

From: John Wilson
Sent: Wednesday, February 22, 2006 9:39 AM
To: 'BFisher557@aol.com' <BFisher557@aol.com>
Subject: RE: John Wilson

It's the same list – the same three people. He implied all three but confirmed only by saying "they are agents".

* * * * *

From: John Wilson
Sent: Wednesday, February 22, 2006 10:55 AM
To: 'BFisher557@aol.com' <BFisher557@aol.com>
Subject: Marvin

Hi Barry,

The number for Marvin Hernandez is 202 616 4760.

John

* * * * *

Exhibit 15: *22 February 2006.   Email from John Wilson to DOJ, Marvin Hernandez – FBI denies agents are "employees", but does not deny they are "contractors".*

From: John Wilson
Sent: Wednesday, February 22, 2006 8:24 PM
To: 'marvin.hernandez@usdoj.gov' <marvin.hernandez@usdoj.gov>
Cc: 'BFisher557@aol.com' <BFisher557@aol.com>
Subject: John Wilson

Hi Marvin,

It was good talking to you today and thanks again for your help to date. Please find the letter from Timothy C. Campbell from the Inspection Division of the FBI dated February 10, 2006 attached.

As reviewed today over the phone with yourself, a summary of the process of this inquiry to date is:

1. It began with a letter I sent to the Department of Justice on January 17, 2005.
2. You were able to confirm with me and again with my attorney Barry Fisher mid last year that the people named in the letter were FBI agents.
3. On account of the identification of these people as FBI agents you forwarded my letter to the FBI for internal investigation.
4. I received the above letter from Timothy Campbell which states that the people confirmed as agents by the DOJ are not employed by the FBI. However this letter did not confirm whether at any stage these people had been employed by the FBI or in what capacity. This is in contrast with my experience and your advice to myself and my attorney.

I am not sure what this means but would be interested in your views of the conflicting advice. I would also appreciate your advice as to what options are available to me to gain official acknowledgement of the reasons for this near 10 year investigation, how this matter can be resolved most expeditiously, and how I might work with you to this end.

Thank you.

John Wilson

C/O Mr. Barry A. Fisher
Fleishman and Fisher
1875 Century Park East
Suite 2130
Los Angeles, California 90067
Telephone: 310 557 1077

* * * * *

Exhibit 16: *8 March 2006.   Email from DOJ, Marvin Hernandez to John Wilson.*

From: Marvin.Hernandez@usdoj.gov [mailto:Marvin.Hernandez@usdoj.gov]
Sent: Wednesday, 8 March 2006 3:14 AM
To: ████████████████████ (Receipt Notification Requested) (IPM Return Requested)
Cc: BFisher557@aol.com (Receipt Notification Requested) (IPM Return Requested)
Subject: RE: John Wilson

Good morning John,

Hope all is well and you had a good weekend.
After further review of your allegations against specific individuals, we have determined that the FBI is correct. The individuals you named are indeed not FBI nor DOJ employees. If you have, any other identifying factors that would help us identify them as DOJ or FBI employees that would be great.

If you have any other further questions, please feel free to contact me.

Thank you

Marvin Hernandez

* * * * *

Exhibit 17: *8 March 2006.   Email from John Wilson to DOJ, Marvin Hernandez.*

From: John Wilson ████████████████████
Sent: Wednesday, March 8, 2006 10:02 PM
To: 'Marvin.Hernandez@usdoj.gov' <Marvin.Hernandez@usdoj.gov>
Cc: 'BFisher557@aol.com' <BFisher557@aol.com>
Subject: RE: John Wilson

Hi Marvin,

Thanks for your email.

Would you able to confirm that the people named were never associated with the FBI (if not currently)?

Thanks again.

John Wilson

* * * * *

From: John Wilson
Sent: Friday, March 24, 2006 7:41 AM
To: 'Marvin.Hernandez@usdoj.gov' <Marvin.Hernandez@usdoj.gov>
Cc: 'BFisher557@aol.com' <BFisher557@aol.com>
Subject: FW: John Wilson

Hi Marvin,

What is your estimate of the likely timing for providing a response to the email below?

Thanks and regards.

John Wilson

* * * * *

Exhibit 18: *11 May 2006.   Email from DOJ, Marvin Hernandez to John Wilson – FBI confirms one agent is an "employee".*

From: Marvin.Hernandez@usdoj.gov [mailto:Marvin.Hernandez@usdoj.gov]
Sent: Thursday, 11 May 2006 4:10 AM
To: jxxxxxxxxxxxx@bigpond.com
Subject: RE: John Wilson

Good afternoon John,

Per our conversation, I wanted to let you know that the FBI, acknowledged on out of the three individuals as being employees. Unfortunately, the other 2 individuals, are not, and have not been employed with the FBI.

I will let you know, what else can be done.

Thank you,

Marvin Hernandez
Investigative Specialist
Department of Justice
Office of the Inspector General
Investigations Division
202-616-4748

This message may contain information that is law enforcement sensitive. If you are not the intended recipient, please immediately (1) advise the sender by reply e-mail that this message was inadvertently transmitted to you, and (2) delete this e-mail from your system. Thank you for your cooperation

* * * * *

Exhibit 19: *11 May 2006.   Email from John Wilson to Barry Fisher re DOJ, Hernandez – DOJ backtracking on agent admission.*

From: John Wilson
Sent: Thursday, May 11, 2006 8:15 AM
To: 'BFisher557@aol.com' <BFisher557@aol.com>
Subject: FW: John Wilson

Hi Barry,

I have attached an email [from above - 11 May 2006] from Marvin Hernandez.

The FBI has acknowledged that one of the people (Susan Holmes according to Hernandez) is an employee. This is in contrast to their letter earlier this year where they said none were. However, the admission is still short of Hernandez's statement last year where he confirmed that at least 2 of the people on the list were agents.

He is trying to get more information and is going to call me back today, though this now looks more likely to be tomorrow.

I will call you Thursday after speaking with Hernandez.

My cell number in the US is 212 595 3886 - I'm currently in AZ.

Thanks and regards
John

* * * * *

Exhibit 20: *19 May 2006.   Email from John Wilson to DOJ, Marvin Hernandez.*

From: John Wilson
Sent: Friday, May 19, 2006 5:34 AM
To: 'Marvin.Hernandez@usdoj.gov' <Marvin.Hernandez@usdoj.gov>
Subject: RE: John Wilson

Hi Marvin,

Just to confirm that it was Jeff Vasey of your office that you suggested I should speak with and also that the FBI has now confirmed that Susan Holmes is the FBI agent you referred to as an employee of the FBI.

Thanks and regards.

John Wilson

* * * * *

Exhibit 21: *14 June 2006.   Email from John Wilson to DOJ, Marvin Hernandez.*

From: John Wilson
Sent: Wednesday, June 14, 2006 4:13 PM
To: 'Marvin.Hernandez@usdoj.gov' <Marvin.Hernandez@usdoj.gov>
Subject: Ongoing harassment

Hi Marvin,

I was wondering whether you had heard anything back from the FBI as a result of your follow-up.

I mentioned to you that I have had contact with many other people appearing familiar with the events I have outlined to you and who appear to be FBI agents or associated with agents. Most recently, I have had problems with someone who I believe is an FBI agent who has been quite aggressive. His name is Ben Worden and gives his address as Bowie AZ. On May 21 2006, he kicked a door in my face, narrowly missing me, though intending either to hit me or intimidate me as he watched my approach before acting. He has also yelled taunts out at repetitively.

Daniel Aitken (who I believe is with ASIO in Australia) and who I have encountered in Arizona is involved in harassment of myself also while in AZ and appears to liaise closely with Ben Worden.

Any assistance you can provide to help resolve this situation is appreciated.

Thanks and regards.

John Wilson

* * * * *

Exhibit 22: *23 August 2006.   Letter from John Wilson via Barry Fisher to DOJ, OIG.*

[Minor typos corrected]

John Christian Wilson   23 August, 2006
c/o Barry A. Fisher
Fleishman & Fisher
1875 Century Park East Suite 2130
Los Angeles, CA 90067

Paul K. Martin
Deputy Inspector General
U.S. Department of Justice
950 Pennsylvania Avenue, N.W., Suite 4706
Washington, D.C. 20530-0001

Dear Mr. Martin:

This is in response to your correspondence of August 9, 2006 to Senator Schumer and copied to myself. I appreciate your response but I believe it is misleading and neither a dependable nor complete review of the allegations raised because it is in fact qualified as set out in point 1 below.

1. The DOJ August 9, 2006 letter claims that the response from the FBI dated February 10, 2006 is accurate in stating that none of the people I mention in my letter to the DOJ April 16, 2005 are FBI agents. But the accuracy of the DOJ statement is subject to the following FBI/DOJ qualifications set out in the letters of February 10 and August 9:

    The FBI denial that the people named are FBI agents is qualified by stating these people are not currently associated (eg., employees, special agents, etc) with the FBI; Or if any of these people are currently associated with the FBI, their activities do not "meet the criteria" such that the FBI/DOJ would consider their activities to constitute harassment.

I will not consider that this matter has been dealt with fully and sincerely by the DOJ until there is a complete and unqualified denial that these people are or have ever been associated with the FBI, irrespective of whether they currently are.

I also request confirmation that there has been no activity conducted by the FBI in relation to myself irrespective of whether or not they agree that the word "harassment" suitably describes those activities.

The DOJ August 9 letter is also not complete, as set out in point 2 below.

2. As mentioned in my letter dated June 13, 2006, the people named have either shown me FBI identification cards or confirmed verbally their status as FBI. The DOJ response of August 9, 2006 makes no account of this.

    Among other things, the people named have shared information with me relating to discussions/interviews conducted by others in the group into the situation I outlined in my letter to DOJ April 16, 2005. These people also have demonstrated they have information that relates to my personal affairs which are of a private nature, including financial records.

If these people are not or have not been associated with the FBI then they have fraudulently represented themselves as agents, a situation which I assume would be of interest to the DOJ. Further, these people are in possession of private records and information relating to myself which I have not authorized them to possess.

To reiterate and expand on details of my letter dated June 13, 2006, I believe the FBI commenced activities against myself as a result of work I undertook as an equity research analyst working for SBC Warburg, the precursor to UBS, on Wall Street in New York in the 1990's.

In early 1996, information was leaked to me by a then undisclosed FBI agent who worked undercover as an environmentalist. This person gave me details of a State Department finding into an incident in which 7 people were recently killed in and around the US publicly traded Freeport McMoran owned Grasberg mine in Indonesia. The information I received related to a confidential reprimand of the company by the U.S. Department of State for human rights and environmental abuses.

Shortly after receiving this information, I published a short analyst note and subsequently I attended the annual analysts briefing at Freeport's head office in New Orleans. During this meeting I asked the then CEO of Freeport, Jim Bob Moffet a question about the investigation into the killings, a question which resulted in him becoming agitated and quite angry. Immediately following this meeting, I received a warning that I would regret having asked this question. Since then, I have been subjected to what appears to be a systematic retaliation campaign by persons associated with the FBI involving invasive and injurious tactics.

Given the powerful business interests and political connections of Freeport, the angry response and the warning I received at the Freeport analyst briefing, and the qualified responses to my letters offered by the DOJ and FBI to date I believe that the central issue of my allegation remains unresolved. I request that the central issue raised by my letters, viz., the issue of FBI interest and activity related to myself stemming from the Freepost incident, be answered without qualification and an explanation given as to the status of the individuals named as FBI.

I respectfully request a response to my allegations concerning the FBI from the OIG/DOJ that is without qualification and that is dependable, accurate and complete.

Sincerely yours,

John Wilson

* * * * *

Exhibit 23: *19 September 2007. Email from John Wilson to Attorney Barry Fisher re ABC reporter.*

From: John Wilson
Sent: Wednesday, September 19, 2007 9:10 AM
To: 'BFisher557@aol.com' <BFisher557@aol.com>
Subject: ABC

Hi Barry,

I have spoken with an Australian TV journalist from the ABC in Sydney – Richard Lindell. He asked if he could speak informally with you by phone. If you are prepared to talk to him I will forward your number to him.

I have passed to him copies of various correspondence, including letters to the Judiciary Committees and the email from Marvin Hernandez at DOJ where he confirmed that one of the people named was an agent of the FBI. I don't know exactly what Richard would want to ask you, but it could include background on the FBI in general.

Please let me know.

Thanks and regards.

John

* * * * *

* * * * *

Exhibit 24: *7 December 2006.   Letter from John Wilson via Attorney Barry Fisher to DOJ, OIG.*

John Christian Wilson
c/o Barry A. Fisher
Fleishman & Fisher
1875 Century Park East Suite 2130
Los Angeles, CA 90067

7 December, 2006

Paul K. Martin
Deputy Inspector General
Office of the Inspector General
U.S. Department of Justice
950 Pennsylvania Avenue, N.W.
Room 1145
Washington, D.C. 20530

RE: Freeport McMoran killings in Indonesia and FBI retaliation against a Wall Street securities analyst

Dear Mr. Martin:

Senator Schumer has forwarded your letter dated October 16, 2006 in response to the letter I sent to the Assistant Attorney General for Office of Legislative Affairs August 31, 2006 (attached).

Your response indicated the issues raised by my letter were not relevant to the Department of Justice, Office of the Inspector General (OIG) and that you would forward my letter to the FBI for handling. For the reasons set out below, I believe that the allegations I raise are relevant to the OIG and that it is not appropriate to forward the letter to the FBI.

Your letter dated October 16, 2006 is inaccurate on key points.

Firstly it states "...we determined the matter was more appropriate for review by the FBI Inspection Division as Mr. Wilson did not identify any specific criminal or administrative misconduct that would require an investigation by the OIG." This statement is not correct for the reason that I have identified FBI harassment of myself, commencing in 1996, apparently in retaliation for equity research work I conducted on Freeport McMoran in 1995/96 as "specific criminal or administrative misconduct" by the FBI.

Secondly, the letter says that "...because he is concerned that these individuals could be fraudulently portraying themselves as FBI agents, we believe that this matter can only be properly addressed by the FBI." This is not correct for the reason that I am not concerned that these individuals may be falsely portraying themselves as FBI agents as I believe they are FBI agents.

In my view, the conduct of the FBI in this matter constitutes the persecution by a US government agency of a Wall Street equities analyst and US citizen.

As previously discussed, I worked as a securities analyst with investment bank SBC Warburg in New York (precursor to UBS Warburg) as a mining analyst. I analyzed US mining company Freeport

McMoran which owns Grasberg, a significant gold/copper mine in Irian Jaya (Indonesia). In the 1990's a series of security related killings occurred at Freeport's Grasberg mine, which according to reports at the time involved killings by company personnel on company property. As an analyst, I consequently asked Jim Bob Moffett (CEO of Freeport McMoran) a question about the subsequent investigation into the killings during an analyst briefing at the company's office in New Orleans in 1996.

Subsequent to raising the issue with Freeport in 1996, I was threatened and have been harassed in a campaign apparently managed by the FBI as outlined in previous letters.

I write to request that this matter be investigated by your office. In addition, to date I have not received a response to the letter forwarded by OIG to the FBI as referred to in your letter of October 16, 2006 and would appreciate your assistance to ensure a timely response (the FBI took over 12 months to respond to my initial inquiry of January 17, 2005 responding February 10, 2006).

Sincerely,

John Wilson

CC: Senator Charles Schumer, U.S. Senator

William E. Moschella, Assistant Attorney General for Office of Legislative Affairs

Attachments: John Wilson letter to William E. Moschella, Assistant Attorney General for Office of Legislative Affairs, dated 31 August, 2006 (not 30 August, 2006 as referred to by the OIG in their letter of October 16, 2006).

Letter forwarded by Senator Schumer from Paul K. Martin, Department of Justice, Office of the Inspector General, dated October 16, 2006.

* * * * *

IV-1b   Correspondence 2004 to 2011

Senator Charles Schumer

* * * * *

Exhibit 25: *22 April 2005.   Letter from John Wilson via Attorney Barry Fisher to Senator Schumer.*

John Christian Wilson
c/o Barry A. Fisher
Fleishman & Fisher
1875 Century Park East Suite 2130
Los Angeles, CA 90067

22 April, 2005

Email: █████████████

Hon. Charles E. Schumer
United States Senate
757 Third Avenue
Suite 17-02
New York, NY 10017

Dear Senator Schumer:

I write because of the oversight responsibilities of your Committee. I was a mining company equity analyst on Wall Street from 1994 to 1998. I am a citizen of the U.S.A., was born in Australia, and have long lived in the United States, principally in New York and Philadelphia, where I received my MBA degree from Wharton. I am currently visiting family for an extended stay in Australia.

In 1996, in the course of performing my duties, information was leaked to me by a then undisclosed FBI agent who worked undercover as an environmentalist. This person gave me details of a State Department finding into an incident in which 7 people were recently killed in and around the publicly traded Freeport McMoran owned Grasberg mine in Indonesia. The information I received related to a confidential reprimand of the company by the U.S. Department of State for human rights and environmental abuses.

Since then, as set out below, I have been subjected to what appears to be a systematic retaliation campaign by persons associated with the FBI involving invasive and injurious tactics. Among other things, I have faced blacklisting in my industry. I have been unable to gain any employment in the financial services industry despite a recent boom in the mining sector and despite having worked on Wall Street for 6 years, mostly as a senior equity analyst.

For the many years following my 1996 publication regarding the Freeport McMoran killings, I have had many contacts with people who at some point revealed themselves as FBI agents on assignment connected to me, and who let me know that I angered important people by the publication. Some of these individuals engendered friendship with me under the auspices of other professional identities and each has interviewed me, two of them extensively. These include Steven Garber, now of White Plains, New York, formerly of New York City, Susan Holmes, now of Washington, D.C., formerly of New York City, and Livingston Sutro, of Sierra Vista, Arizona.

Aside from these agents, more than a dozen other people have identified themselves to me as having a high level of familiarity with these circumstances and appear to be FBI agents or associated with agents.

Given the fact that the source of the leaked information was itself an FBI agent and given the powerful business interests of Freeport, I am concerned that I am the subject of what appears to be either a case of FBI corruption or incompetence. The agent that passed to me the information about Freeport was a long term friend who targeted environmental extremists, and I am concerned I may have been maliciously profiled to justify the intense scrutiny I have faced.

An FOIA request to the FBI in October, 2004 yielded no information whatsoever.

In accordance with the Privacy Act of 1974, you and your staff are hereby authorized to freely discuss any and all aspects of my situation. I look forward to hearing from you. The most convenient means by which to correspond with me are through my attorney (details indicated above), alternatively via email.

Sincerely yours,

John Wilson

* * * * *

Exhibit 24: *25 August 2005.   Email from John Wilson to Senator Schumer.*

From: john wilson
Sent: Thursday, August 25, 2005 11:24 PM
To: steven_crimaldi@schumer.senate.gov
Subject: John Wilson letter

Steven,

Please find letter attached [copy of John Wilson's letter sent to Schumer 22 April 2005] as discussed.

Thank you.

Sincerely

John Wilson

* * * * *

Exhibit 25: *7 September 2005.   Email from John Wilson to Senator Schumer.*

From: john wilson
Sent: Wednesday, September 7, 2005 3:03 PM

To: steven_crimaldi@schumer.senate.gov
Subject: Fw: John Wilson letter

Hi Steven,

Are you able to provide an update on the attached [second copy of John Wilson's letter sent to Schumer 22 April 2005] please.

Thank you.

Sincerely.

John Wilson

* * * * *

Exhibit 26: *25 May 2006.   Letter from John Wilson via Attorney Barry Fisher to Senator Schumer.*

John Christian Wilson   25 May, 2006
c/o Barry A. Fisher
Fleishman & Fisher
1875 Century Park East Suite 2130
Los Angeles, CA 90067

Hon. Charles E. Schumer
United States Senate
757 Third Avenue
Suite 17-02
New York, NY 10017

Attention: Maxine Fields

Dear Maxine:

Further to our conversation last week this serves to document that I have made allegations of harassment by FBI agents in relation to which I contacted the Department of Justice, Office of the Inspector General (OIG) early last year.

Over the past month I have had several conversations and correspondences with Marvin Hernandez, an investigator within OIG. After making initial enquiries last year Marvin Hernandez confirmed to me that people I named in a letter to the OIG 16 April, 2005 (attached) are FBI agents and on that basis he referred the matter to the FBI for internal investigation. I received a reply from the FBI February 10, 2006 (attached) which denied any of the people named were/are FBI agents. Subsequently, on May 11, 2006 Marvin Hernandez confirmed in an email (attached) that one of the people is an FBI agent, which indicates the FBI response is inaccurate and incomplete. Most recently, Marvin

Hernandez has verbally expressed some doubt that the person OIG identified to be an FBI agent is correct.

The responses I have received in relation to this issue have been confused, contradictory and incomplete suggesting the possibility of dishonesty or a cover up. To date, the Department of Justice, Office of the Inspector General has provided no formal, definitive or comprehensive response to the letter I sent 17 January 2005 and (resent) 16 April 2005 in relation to the FBI.

The information I requested relates to harassment and interference by the FBI of myself that apparently commenced as a result of a question I posed when working on Wall St as a securities analyst specializing in the mining sector. I asked the CEO of US mining company Freeport McMoran Copper and Gold at a company briefing for security analysts in 1996 a question about the investigation into the killing of 7 people in a security incident at the company's mine site in Indonesia in 1995.

As detailed in the attached letter, I have been approached by many people appearing to be government agents participating in this harassment, three of whom said they worked for the FBI and one of whom has showed me their FBI identification card.

I would like assistance from you to secure a response to my allegations concerning the FBI from the OIG that is dependable, accurate and complete.

In accordance with the Privacy Act of 1974, you and your staff are hereby authorized to freely discuss any and all aspects of my situation. I look forward to hearing from you. The most convenient means by which to correspond with me are through my attorney (details indicated above), alternatively you can reach me directly by phone on 212 595 3886.

Sincerely yours,

John Wilson

Attachments: Letter to the Department of Justice, OIG January 17, 2005
Letter to the Department of Justice, OIG April 16, 2005
Letter from FBI February 10, 2006
Email from Department of Justice, OIG May 11, 2006

* * * *

Exhibit 27: *9 June 2006.   Email from Barry Fisher to John Wilson.*

From: BFisher557@aol.com <BFisher557@aol.com>
Sent: Friday, June 9, 2006 7:32 AM
To: █████████████████
Subject: contact

heard from Maxine at Shumer's office

(212-486-4430). she raises the question whether you have sufficient contacts with NY for their office to be involved. While you apparently told her you vote in NY, she is concerned you don't have any NY address. she called me because she said she had no way to reach you directly. maybe you want to call her. Barry

* * * *

Exhibit 28: *13 June 2006.   Letter from Senator Schumer to DOJ.*

United States Senate
WASHINGTON, DC 20510

June 13, 2006

Assistant Attorney General for Office of Legislative Affairs
U.S. Department of Justice
950 Pennsylvania Avenue, N.W.
Room 1145
Washington, D.C. 20530

Re: John Christian Wilson
170 West 74th Street
Apt. 906
New York, New York 10023

Dear

I am writing on behalf of John Christian Wilson, who has contacted my office regarding the status of a response from the Department of Justice, Office of the Inspector General, to issues he has been bringing to their attention since April, 2005. I have enclosed for your information a copy of Mr. Wilson's correspondence and it's attachments.

Thank you in advance for reviewing this correspondence. Please direct your written response to the attention of Maxine in my New York City Office.

Sincerely,

Charles E. Schumer
United States Senate

CES/mg
Enclosure

* * * *

Section IV   Appendix - Correspondence   319

* * * * *

Exhibit 29: *20 June 2006.   Email from Barry Fisher to John Wilson.*

From: BFisher557@aol.com <BFisher557@aol.com>
Sent: Tuesday, June 20, 2006 5:42 AM
To: ███████████████
Subject: schumer

some progress---received a copy of a letter schumer has [not (sic)] sent to the justice department on your behalf. basically forwards your letter and says he would like an answer. Barry

* * * * *

Exhibit 30: *9 August 2006.   Letter from the DOJ, OIG to Senator Schumer.*

U.S. Department of Justice

Office of the Inspector General

Washington, D.C. 20530

August 9, 2006

The Honorable Charles Schumer
United States Senator
757 Third Avenue
Suite 1702
New York, New York 10017

Attention: Maxine

Dear Senator Schumer:

    This is in response to your correspondence of June 13, 2006, to William E. Moschella, Assistant Attorney General for the Office of Legislative Affairs, forwarding a letter of concern from your constituent, John Christian Wilson, of New York, New York. Mr. Wilson alleges that he has received conflicting information from the Federal Bureau of Investigation (FBI) and the Office of the Inspector General (OIG) as to whether or not the individuals harassing him are employees of the FBI.

    Please be advised that this office has reviewed Mr. Wilson's allegations and determined that the information contained in the FBI's February 10, 2006, letter to Mr. Wilson is accurate in that there are no FBI employees who meet the criteria described by Mr. Wilson in his complaint. Mr. Wilson alleges that the OIG informed him that one of the individuals named by him is an FBI employee. The OIG has determined that the FBI employs a Special Agent (SA) with the same name as one of the individuals referenced by Mr. Wilson; however, this SA has never been assigned to any of the cities named by Mr. Wilson where the alleged harassment occurred.

The Honorable Charles Schumer
Page 2

I hope this is responsive to your inquiry. If you have further questions concerning this or other matters, please feel free to contact this office again.

Sincerely,

Paul K. Martin
Deputy Inspector General

cc: Mr. John Christian Wilson

* * * * *

Exhibit 31: *15 August 2006.   Email from Barry Fisher to John Wilson*

From: BFisher557@aol.com <BFisher557@aol.com>
Sent: Tuesday, August 15, 2006 3:42 AM
To: ███████████████████
Subject: justice dept letter

John-here is the response to Shumer. not very helpful. Barry

* * * * *

Exhibit 32: *23 August 2006.   Letter from John Wilson via Attorney Barry Fisher to Senator Schumer.*

John Christian Wilson   23 August, 2006
c/o Barry A. Fisher
Fleishman & Fisher
1875 Century Park East Suite 2130
Los Angeles, CA 90067

The Honorable Charles Schumer
United States Senate
757 Third Avenue
Suite 17-02
New York, NY 10017

Attention: Maxine Fields

Dear Senator Schumer:

This is in reference to the letter from the US Department of Justice, dated August 9, 2006.

I appreciate the response of the Deputy Inspector General, Office of the Inspector General, but I believe it is misleading and neither a dependable nor complete review of the allegations raised, for the following reasons:

1. The DOJ letter of August 9, 2006 confirms that the response from the FBI dated February 10, 2006 is accurate in stating that none of the people I mention in my letter to the DOJ April 16, 2005 are FBI agents. The accuracy of this statement is subject to the following FBI/DOJ qualifications:
    a. The FBI denial that the people named are FBI agents is qualified by stating these people are not currently associated (eg., employees, special agents, etc) with the FBI, or
    b. If any of these people are currently associated with the FBI, their activities do not "meet the criteria" such that the FBI/DOJ would consider their activities to constitute harassment.

I will not consider that this matter has been dealt with fully and sincerely by the DOJ until there is a complete and unqualified denial that these people are or have ever been associated with the FBI, irrespective of whether they currently are.

I also require confirmation that there has been no activity conducted by the FBI in relation to myself irrespective of whether or not they agree that the word "harassment" suitably describes those activities.

2. As mentioned in my letter dated June 13, 2006, the people named have either shown me FBI identification cards or confirmed verbally their status as FBI. The DOJ response of August 9, 2006 makes no account of this.

    The people named have also shared information with me relating to discussions/interviews conducted by others in the group into the situation I outlined in my letter to DOJ April 16, 2005. These people also have demonstrated they have information that relates to my personal affairs which are of a private nature, including financial records.

If these people are not or have not been associated with the FBI then they have fraudulently represented themselves as agents, a situation which I assume would be of interest to the DOJ. Further, these people are in possession of private records and information relating to myself which I have not authorized them to posses.

To reiterate and expand on details of my letter dated June 13, 2006, I believe the FBI commenced activities against myself as a result of work I undertook as an equity research analyst working for SBC Warburg, the precursor to UBS, on Wall Street in New York in the 1990's.

In early 1996, information was leaked to me by a then undisclosed FBI agent who worked undercover as an environmentalist. This person gave me details of a State Department finding into an incident in which 7 people were recently killed in and around the US publicly traded Freeport McMoran owned

Grasberg mine in Indonesia. The information I received related to a confidential reprimand of the company by the U.S. Department of State for human rights and environmental abuses.

Shortly after receiving this information I published a short analyst note and subsequently I attended the annual analysts briefing at Freeport's head office in New Orleans. During this meeting I asked the then CEO of Freeport, Jim Bob Moffat a question about the investigation into the killings, a question which resulted in him becoming agitated and quite angry. Immediately following this meeting I received a warning that I would regret having asked this question. Since then I have been subjected to what appears to be a systematic retaliation campaign by persons associated with the FBI involving invasive and injurious tactics.

Given the powerful business interests and political connections of Freeport, the angry response and the warning I received at the Freeport analyst briefing, and the qualified responses to my letters offered by the DOJ and FBI to date I believe that the central issue of my allegation remains unresolved. I request that the central issue raised by my letters, viz., the issue of FBI interest and activity related to myself stemming from the Freepost incident, be answered without qualification and an explanation given as to the status of the individuals named as FBI.

Senator Schumer, I request assistance from you to secure a response to my allegations concerning the FBI from the OIG/DOJ that is without qualification and that is dependable, accurate and complete.

In accordance with the Privacy Act of 1974, you and your staff are hereby authorized to freely discuss any and all aspects of my situation. I look forward to hearing from you. The most convenient means by which to correspond with me are through my attorney (details indicated above).

Sincerely yours,

John Wilson

* * * * *

* * * * *

Exhibit 30: *16 October 2006.   Letter from the DOJ, OIG to Senator Schumer*

[Letter from Paul K. Martin, Deputy Inspector General, DOJ]

U.S. Department of Justice

Office of the Inspector General

October 16, 2006

The Honorable Charles Schumer
United States Senator
757 Third Avenue
Suite 1702
New York, New York 10017

Attention: Maxine

Dear Senator Schumer:

    This is in response to your correspondence of August 30, 2006, to William E. Moschella, Assistant Attorney General for the Office of Legislative Affairs, forwarding a letter of concern from your constituent, John Christian Wilson, of New York, New York. Mr. Wilson states that the Office of the Inspector General's (OIG) correspondence dated August 9, 2006, was unsatisfactory and that he will not consider this matter closed until he receives a "complete and unqualified denial" that the individuals in question are or have never been associated with the Federal Bureau of Investigation (FBI). Additionally, Mr. Wilson requests confirmation that the FBI did not conduct any investigative activity involving him.   He also expresses concern that the individuals in question might be fraudulently representing themselves as FBI agents.

    On May 1, 2005, this office received a complaint from Mr. Wilson involving the same allegations contained in his May 25, 2006, letter to your office, and we determined that the matter was more appropriate for review by the FBI Inspection Division as Mr. Wilson did not identify any specific criminal or administrative misconduct that would require an investigation by the OIG. In a February 10, 2006, letter the FBI Inspection Division, Initial Processing Unit (IPU), informed Mr. Wilson that a review of its records revealed that the individuals in question are not employed by the FBI and that the IPU determined that his complaint did not warrant the initiation of an investigation.

The Honorable Charles Schumer
Page 2

Our August 9, 2006, letter to you explained that the OIG determined that the FBI employs a Special Agent (SA) with the same name as one of the individuals referenced by Mr. Wilson; however, this SA has never been assigned to any of the geographic areas in which Mr. Wilson alleged the harassment occurred. Additionally, the OIG has no reason to dispute the information contained in the FBI's February 10, 2006, letter to Mr. Wilson.

Since Mr. Wilson is now seeking "a complete and unqualified denial" that the individuals in question have never been associated with the FBI and because he is concerned that these individuals could be fraudulently portraying themselves as FBI agents, we believe that this matter can only be properly addressed by the FBI. Therefore, we will forward your August 30, 2006, letter and Mr. Wilson's most recent allegations to the FBI Inspection Division for appropriate handling.

Sincerely,

Paul K. Martin
Deputy Inspector General

cc: Charlene B. Thornton
Assistant Director
Inspection Division
Federal Bureau of Investigation

* * * * *

* * * * *

Exhibit 33: *1 January 2007.   Letter from John Wilson via Attorney Barry Fisher to Senator Schumer.*

John Christian Wilson   January 1, 2007
c/o Barry A. Fisher
Fleishman & Fisher
1875 Century Park East Suite 2130
Los Angeles, CA 90067

Hon. Charles E. Schumer
United States Senate
757 Third Avenue
Suite 17-02
New York, NY 10017
Via fax: 212486 7693

Attention: Maxine Fields

Dear Maxine:

In reference to correspondence with Paul K. Martin, DOJ (7 December 2006 and copied to Senator Schumer) to date there has been no response from Paul K. Martin.

I would appreciate assistance from you to secure a response to my December 7, 2006 correspondence with Paul K. Martin.

In accordance with the Privacy Act of 1974, you and your staff are hereby authorized to freely discuss any and all aspects of my situation. I look forward to hearing from you. The most convenient means by which to correspond with me are through my attorney (details indicated above), alternatively you can reach me directly by phone on 212 595 3886.

Sincerely yours,

John Wilson

Attachments:

* * * * *

* * * * *

Exhibit 34: *20 February 2007.   Letter from John Wilson via Attorney Barry Fisher to Senator Schumer.*

John Christian Wilson
c/o Barry A. Fisher
Fleishman & Fisher
1875 Century Park East Suite 2130
Los Angeles, CA 90067

February 20, 2007

Hon. Charles E. Schumer
United States Senate
757 Third Avenue
Suite 17-02
New York, NY 10017

Attention: Maxine Fields

Dear Maxine:

In reference to recent correspondence with Paul K. Martin, DOJ (7 December 2006 and copied to Senator Schumer) to date there has been no response by the DOJ. There has also been no response from the FBI to a letter Paul K. Martin indicated he would forward to the FBI and referred to in his correspondence to Senator Schumer October 16, 2006.

I would appreciate assistance from you to secure a response to my December 7, 2006 correspondence with Paul K. Martin.

In accordance with the Privacy Act of 1974, you and your staff are hereby authorized to freely discuss any and all aspects of my situation. I look forward to hearing from you. The most convenient means by which to correspond with me are through my attorney (details indicated above), alternatively you can reach me directly by phone on 212 595 3886.

Sincerely yours,

John Wilson

Attachments:

* * * * *

Exhibit 35: *3 April 2007. Letter from Senator Schumer to DOJ.*

CHARLES E. SCHUMER
NEW YORK

COMMITTEES
BANKING
FINANCE
JUDICIARY
RULES

United States Senate
WASHINGTON, DC 20510

April 3, 2007

Eleni Kalisch, Assistant Director of Congressional Affairs
Federal Bureau of Investigation
U.S. Department of Justice
935 Pennsylvania Avenue, N.W., Room 7240
Washington, D.C. 20535-0001

Re: John Christian Wilson
c/o Barry A. Fisher
1875 Century Park East, Suite 2130
Los Angeles, California 90067

Dear Assistant Director Kalisch:

I am writing on behalf of John Christian Wilson, who has contacted my office regarding the status of a response to his correspondence forwarded to the FBI Inspection Division for appropriate handling by the U. S. Department of Justice, Office of the Inspector General. I have enclosed for your information, a copy of Mr. Wilson's correspondence and the October 16, 2006 response from the U. S. Department of Justice, OIG, addressed to my attention.

Thank you in advance for reviewing this correspondence. Please direct your written response to the attention of Maxine in my New York City Office.

Sincerely,

Charles E. Schumer
United States Senate

CES/mg
Enclosure

---

* * * *

Exhibit 36: *7 May 2007.   Letter from the DOJ to Senator Schumer.*

U.S. Department of Justice

Federal Bureau of Investigation

Washington, D.C. 20535-0001

May 7, 2007

Honorable Charles E. Schumer
United States Senator
Suite 1702
757 Third Avenue
New York, New York 10017

MAY 25 2007

Dear Senator Schumer:

  We are in receipt of your letter dated April 3, 2007, addressed to Ms. Eleni Kalisch, Assistant Director, Office of Congressional Affairs, and the enclosed documents which were forwarded to your office by your constituent, Mr. John Wilson.

  Your letter was forwarded to the Internal Investigations Section (IIS), Inspection Division, for review. The IIS is the FBI entity that investigates complaints of criminality and/or serious misconduct against FBI employees.

  IIS reviewed the merits of Mr. Wilson's claims and determined his allegations did not warrant the initiation of an investigation inasmuch as the information reflected no allegations of misconduct by any FBI personnel. This information was previously provided to Mr. Wilson by letter, dated February 10, 2006, addressed to Mr. Barry A. Fisher, Fleishmann and Fisher, Los Angeles, California. However, thank you for bringing this matter to my attention.

Sincerely,

Kevin L. Perkins
Assistant Director
Inspection Division

* * * *

Exhibit 37: *7 June 2007.   Letter from Senator Schumer to DOJ.*

CHARLES E. SCHUMER
NEW YORK

COMMITTEES
BANKING
JUDICIARY
RULES
FINANCE

United States Senate
WASHINGTON, DC 20510

June 7, 2007

William E. Moschella
Assistant Attorney General for Office of Legislative Affairs
U.S. Department of Justice
950 Pennsylvania Avenue, N.W.
Room 1145
Washington, D.C. 20530

Re: John Christian Wilson
c/o Barry A. Fisher
Fleishman & Fisher
1875 Century Park East, Suite 2130
Los Angeles, Calif. 90067

Dear Mr. Moschella:

    I am writing once again, on behalf of John Christian Wilson, who has re-contacted my office regarding a response to him from the Department of Justice, Office of the Inspector General, Paul K. Martin, Deputy Inspector General. Mr. Wilson's correspondence to Paul K. Martin, is dated December 7, 2006 and I have enclosed a copy for your information as well as a copy of Mr. Wilson's recent correspondence to this office.

    Thank you in advance for reviewing the enclosed. Please direct your written response to the attention of Maxine in my New York City Office, 757 Third Avenue, Suite 1702, New York, New York 10017.

Sincerely,

Charles Schumer

Charles E. Schumer
United States Senate

CES/mg
Enclosure

* * * *

* * * * *

Exhibit 38: *7 June 2007.   Letter from John Wilson via Attorney Barry Fisher to Senator Schumer.*

John Christian Wilson
c/o Barry A. Fisher
Fleishman & Fisher
1875 Century Park East Suite 2130
Los Angeles, CA 90067

7 June, 2007

Email: [redacted]

Senator Charles Schumer
United States Senate
Committee Member
Committee on the Judiciary
224 Dirksen Senate Office Building
Washington, DC 20510

RE: FBI harassment of Wall Street Mining Analyst

Dear Sir:

I write because of the oversight responsibilities of the Committee on the Judiciary. I was a mining company equity analyst on Wall Street from 1994 to 1998. I am a citizen of the U.S.A., was born in Australia, and have long lived in the United States, principally in New York and Philadelphia, where I received my MBA degree from Wharton. I am currently visiting family for an extended stay in Australia.

In 1996, in the course of performing my duties, information was leaked to me by a then undisclosed FBI agent who worked undercover as an environmentalist. This person gave me details of a State Department finding into an incident in which 7 people were recently killed in and around the publicly traded Freeport McMoran owned Grasberg mine in Indonesia. The information I received related to a confidential reprimand of the company by the U.S. Department of State following an investigation into human rights and environmental abuses.

Since then, as set out below, I have been subjected to what appears to be a systematic retaliation campaign by persons associated with the FBI involving invasive and injurious tactics. Among other things, I have faced blacklisting in my industry. I have been unable to gain any employment in the financial services industry despite a recent boom in the mining sector and despite having worked on Wall Street for 6 years, mostly as a senior equity analyst.

For the many years following my 1996 publication regarding the Freeport McMoran killings, I have had many contacts with people who at some point revealed themselves as FBI agents on assignment connected to me, and who let me know that I angered important people by the publication. Some of these individuals engendered friendship with me under the auspices of other professional identities and each has interviewed me,

1 of 2

two of them extensively. These include Steven Garber, now of White Plains, New York, formerly of New York City, Susan Holmes, now of Washington, D.C., formerly of New York City, and Livingston Sutro, of Sierra Vista, Arizona.

Aside from these agents, more than a dozen other people have identified themselves to me as having a high level of familiarity with these circumstances and appear to be FBI agents or associated with agents.

Given the fact that the source of the leaked information was itself an FBI agent and given the powerful business interests of Freeport, I am concerned that I am the subject of what appears to be either a case of FBI corruption or incompetence. The agent that passed to me the information about Freeport was a long term friend who targeted environmental extremists, and I am concerned I may have been maliciously profiled to justify the intense scrutiny I have faced.

An FOIA request to the FBI in October, 2004 yielded no information whatsoever.

I look forward to hearing from you. The most convenient means by which to correspond with me are through my attorney (details indicated above), alternatively via my email (above).

Sincerely yours,

John Wilson

CC: Maxine Fields, Case Officer, Senator Schumer's NYC office.

* * * * *

* * * * *

Exhibit 39: *9 August 2007.   Letter from the DOJ to Senator Schumer.*

[Letter from Paul K. Martin, Deputy Inspector General, DOJ]

U.S. Department of Justice

Office of the Inspector General

Washington, D.C. 20530

August 9, 2007

The Honorable Charles Schumer
United States Senator
757 Third Avenue
Suite 1702
New York, New York 10017

Attention: Maxine

Dear Senator Schumer:

    This is in response to your correspondence of June 7, 2007, to William E. Moschella, Assistant Attorney General for the Office of Legislative Affairs, forwarding a letter of concern from your constituent, John Christian Wilson, of New York, New York. In his letter, Mr. Wilson requested your assistance in obtaining a response to his December 7, 2006, letter to Deputy Inspector General Paul K. Martin.

    In an October 16, 2006, letter to your office, we advised that Mr. Wilson's complaint was referred to the Federal Bureau of Investigation (FBI), Inspection Division, for handling. The Office of the Inspector General does not intend to initiate an investigation into Mr. Wilson's allegations and considers this matter to be closed. Any further inquiries regarding this matter should be directed to the FBI Inspection Division.

Sincerely,

Paul K. Martin
Deputy Inspector General

cc: Kevin L. Perkins
       Assistant Director
       Inspection Division
       Federal Bureau of Investigation

* * * * *

* * * * *

Exhibit 40: *6 September 2007. Letter from John Wilson via Attorney Barry Fisher to Senator Schumer.*

John Christian Wilson September 6, 2007
c/o Barry A. Fisher
Fleishman & Fisher
1875 Century Park East Suite 2130
Los Angeles, CA 90067

Hon. Charles E. Schumer
United States Senate
757 Third Avenue
Suite 17-02
New York, NY 10017
Via fax: 212 486 7693

Attention: Maxine Fields

Dear Maxine:

Thank you for forwarding the letter from Paul K. Martin, U.S. Department of Justice, Office of the Inspector General, dated August 9, 2007.

Contrary to statements made in recent correspondence by the DOJ/FBI (Kevin L. Perkins letter of May 7, 2007) I have very clearly and in no uncertain terms made allegations of administrative and personnel misconduct by the FBI. Their denials that my case involves such allegations as justification for not pursuing an investigation is incorrect.

The DOJ/FBI's partial denials of their involvement as alleged have been heavily qualified over the past 3 years as you will note from the correspondence I have provided. Their correspondence has been contradictory, most notably their email confirming FBI status of one of the people I identified (email attached) which they later retracted. Further, statements they have made that avoid responsibility by confusing lines of responsibility are strongly suggestive of cover-up and stonewalling tactics. I would like to reiterate that I have no doubt the FBI is behind the issues I have raised with you.

This matter of FBI harassment of and interference with myself for work I undertook as an analyst in relation to the Freeport McMoran killings (analyst report attached) was recently raised in the Australian Federal Parliament by the main opposition party – the Australian Labor Party (ALP) which had direct responsibility for ASIO (Australian intelligence) when it was the former party in power. The ALP deemed my allegations credible and serious enough to raise in Parliament (Hansard transcript attached – March 28, 2007).

I believe that the FBI has harassed and interfered with me and that allegations behind their conduct should be open to and tested in the courts in the context of all relevant information. As there appears to be no legal remedy to this situation in the USA at present, the political avenue is all that is available to me. As such, I respectfully request that you raise this matter with Senator Schumer requesting that he consider bringing it before the Senate Judiciary Committee. I recently purchased and read Senator

Schumer's book "Positively American: Winning Back the Middle-Class Majority One Family at a Time", and believe that his support for this inquiry would be consistent with his moral and ideological position on transparency, accountability and justice among other things. As you are aware, I have copied you on a letter I also sent to Marco Deleon in Senator Schumer's Washington DC office, dated June 7, 2007. At the very least, I would have thought the Senate Judiciary Committee could definitively establish the participation of the FBI in this matter – with a definitive and unqualified "yes" or "no" response to their involvement.

In the absence of support from my Senator in this matter, the only thing I can do, and have done, is register a protest with the UN Human Rights Commission – an act which does little to represent and defend my rights.

I would appreciate your response to this letter indicating what steps the Senator can take, or has taken, to bring this matter for consideration before the Senate Judiciary Committee.

In accordance with the Privacy Act of 1974, you and your staff are hereby authorized to freely discuss any and all aspects of my situation. The most convenient means by which to correspond with me are through my attorney (details indicated above), alternatively you can reach me directly by phone on 212 595 3886.

Thank you.

Sincerely yours,

John Wilson

Attachments:

1. Email from Office of the Inspector General, Marvin Hernandez, dated May 11, 2006
2. Analyst report on Freeport McMoran by John Wilson, SG Warburg, dated March 12, 1996
3. Australian Federal Parliament House of Representatives proceedings (Hansard) 28 March 2007, speech by Member of Parliament in relation to John Wilson and FBI/ASIO.

* * * * *

Exhibit 41: *27 February 2008.   Letter from John Wilson via Attorney Barry Fisher to Senator Schumer.*

John Christian Wilson　　　　　　　　　　　　　　　　　　　February 27, 2008
c/o Barry A. Fisher
Fleishman & Fisher
1875 Century Park East Suite 2130
Los Angeles, CA 90067

Hon. Charles E. Schumer
United States Senate
c/o Maxine Fields
757 Third Avenue
Suite 17-02
New York, NY 10017

Via fax: 212 486 7693

Dear Senator Schumer:

As you are aware from correspondence and telephone conversations between your office and myself over the past two to three years I was a mining analyst working on Wall St for much of the 1990's and in 1996 published an equity note on US mining company Freeport McMoran that touched on the killings in Indonesia that had been linked to the company and were being investigated by the US State Department. Since publication of the research report I have faced harassment and interference from the FBI, including blacklisting, and interference with my family, social and professional networks.

I have alleged that the FBI is guilty of administrative and personnel misconduct in my case. There are a number of things the DOJ should be able to provide, and which to date has not, including:

1. To date, there has been no definitive denial or affirmation of FBI involvement in this case, and I request a definitive, unqualified statement be provided by the FBI/DOJ OIG of FBI involvement.
2. I would like a definitive response from the FBI/DOJ OIG as to the nature and reason for FBI involvement in this case should point 1 be answered in the affirmative.

As indicated in the letter I sent you September 6, 2007, and to Marco Deleon in your Washington DC office, dated June 7, 2007 my attempts to seek direct resolution through the DOJ and FBI have met with their partial denials of their involvement and their responses have been heavily qualified. Their correspondence has also been contradictory, most notably their email confirming FBI status of one of the people I identified (email from Marvin Hernandez, OIG, May 11, 2006) and which was later retracted. Further, they have made statements that they deny responsibility for investigating the FBI abuses and activities as I have alleged. Letters from Paul K Martin (Deputy Inspector General)

1 of 3

and Kevin L. Perkins (Assistant Director, Inspection Division FBI) confuse and deny their offices' lines of responsibility and consequently they refuse to take action. As a result, my attempts to have this matter resolved through departmental channels have effectively been stonewalled. The repeated and circular buck passing and these gentlemen's apparent confusion as to the facts are strongly suggestive of cover-up tactics. I would like to reiterate that I have no doubt the FBI is behind the issues I have raised with you.

I understand Maxine Fields in your office spoke at length with my attorney, Barry Fisher on Wednesday February 13, 2008. Set out below is the assistance I respectfully request of you as Senator.

I respectfully request as your constituent that you continue to assist in obtaining definitive answers from the DOJ/FBI to questions 1 and 2 listed above. In addition, in your role as a Committee Member of the Senate Judiciary Committee that the following be tended to:

1. That the details of my allegations, including the nature of FBI harassment following publication of my brief research note on killings in Indonesia involving US mining company Freeport McMoran be bought to the attention of the Senate Judiciary Committee. It should be pointed out this note was published in the course of my work as a Wall Street mining analyst employed by SG Warburg (now part of UBS Warburg).

2. That the Committee be informed the Department of Justice (DOJ) acknowledged that my allegations correctly identified an FBI agent. The DOJ subsequently denied the person identified was an FBI agent and DOJ has subsequently been unhelpful, inconsistent, contradictory and erratic in its correspondence with both your office and with me, as previously tendered to you.

3. That the Senate Judiciary Committee investigate my allegations. In this regard I would be pleased to provide evidence or respond to such an inquiry. I would like the opportunity to know the allegations against me and have the right to defend myself in a court against past and ongoing FBI interference.

Ultimately, I would like a definitive and unqualified explanation as to the reasons for, and nature of, FBI involvement in this matter.

I would appreciate your response to this letter indicating what steps you can take, or have taken, to bring this matter for consideration before the Senate Judiciary Committee and in particular, whether you will ask the Committee to open an investigation into my allegations.

In accordance with the Privacy Act of 1974, you and your staff are hereby authorized to freely discuss any and all aspects of my situation. The most convenient means by which to correspond with me are through my attorney (details indicated above), alternatively you can reach me directly by phone on 212 595 3886.

Thank you.

Sincerely yours,

John Wilson

Attachments:

1. Letter to Senator Schumer September 6, 2007, (amended dates added to list of attachments)
2. Letter to Senator Schumer June 7, 2007

* * * * *

* * * * *

Exhibit 42: *12 June 2008.   Letter from John Wilson via Attorney Barry Fisher to Senator Schumer.*

John Christian Wilson
c/o Barry A. Fisher
Fleishman & Fisher
1875 Century Park East Suite 2130
Los Angeles, CA 90067

June 12, 2008

Hon. Charles E. Schumer
United States Senate
c/o Maxine Fields
757 Third Avenue
Suite 17-02
New York, NY 10017

Via fax: 212 486 7693

Dear Senator Schumer:

I refer to my letter to your office dated 27 February 2008 and which subsequently Maxine Fields confirmed had been forwarded to the Senate Judiciary Committee.

I respectfully request an indication from the Senate Judiciary Committee as to whether this is a matter that the Committee intends to investigate and if so, what is the time frame in which I might expect a response. If this is not a matter that the Committee intends to investigate would it be possible to indicate why not.

As outlined in my letter of 27 February 2008, the allegations I made against the FBI in letters sent to the DOJ/FBI have not been answered; replies have been contradictory and highly qualified and are therefore neither forthright nor in "good faith". As such, the central allegations of FBI interference raised in my letters have not been responded to by the DOJ/FBI. Nor has the DOJ/FBI provided unqualified acknowledgement of the roles of Susan Holmes, Steven Garber, and Livingston Sutro.

In accordance with the Privacy Act of 1974, you and your staff are hereby authorized to freely discuss any and all aspects of my situation. The most convenient means by which to correspond with me are through my attorney (details indicated above), alternatively you can reach me directly by phone on 917 569 3475.

Thank you.

Sincerely yours,

John Wilson

1 of 1

* * * * *

IV-1c   Correspondence 2004 to 2011

Congressman Jerrold Nadler

* * * * *

Exhibit 43: *12 June 2007.   Letter from John Wilson via Attorney Barry Fisher to Congressman Nadler.*

John Christian Wilson
c/o Barry A. Fisher
Fleishman & Fisher
1875 Century Park East Suite 2130
Los Angeles, CA 90067
Email:

12 June, 2007

Rep. Jerrold Nadler
201 Varick Street, Suite 669
New York, NY 10014

RE: FBI harassment of Wall Street Mining Analyst

Dear Sir:

I am a constituent of yours, currently registered as a Federal Voter in NYC (former address 170 West 74th St, NY, NY 10023) and currently reside offshore.

I write because of the oversight responsibilities of the Committee on the Judiciary. I was a mining company equity analyst on Wall Street from 1994 to 1998. I am a citizen of the U.S.A., was born in Australia, and have long lived in the United States, principally in New York and Philadelphia, where I received my MBA degree from Wharton. I am currently visiting family for an extended stay in Australia.

In 1996, in the course of performing my duties, information was leaked to me by a then undisclosed FBI agent who worked undercover as an environmentalist. This person gave me details of a State Department finding into an incident in which 7 people were recently killed in and around the publicly traded Freeport McMoran owned Grasberg mine in Indonesia. The information I received related to a confidential reprimand of the company by the U.S. Department of State following an investigation into human rights and environmental abuses.

Since then, as set out below, I have been subjected to what appears to be a systematic retaliation campaign by persons associated with the FBI involving invasive and injurious tactics. Among other things, I have faced blacklisting in my industry. I have been unable to gain any employment in the financial services industry despite a recent boom in the mining sector and despite having worked on Wall Street for 6 years, mostly as a senior equity analyst.

For the many years following my 1996 publication regarding the Freeport McMoran killings, I have had many contacts with people who at some point revealed themselves as FBI agents on assignment connected to me, and who let me know that I angered important people by the publication. Some of these individuals engendered friendship with me under the auspices of other professional identities and each has interviewed me, two of them extensively. These include Steven Garber, now of White Plains, New York, formerly of New York City, Susan Holmes, now of Washington, D.C., formerly of New York City, and Livingston Sutro, of Sierra Vista, Arizona.

Aside from these agents, more than a dozen other people have identified themselves to me as having a high level of familiarity with these circumstances and appear to be FBI agents or associated with agents.

Given the fact that the source of the leaked information was itself an FBI agent and given the powerful business interests of Freeport, I am concerned that I am the subject of what appears to be either a case of FBI corruption or incompetence. The agent that passed to me the information about Freeport was a long term friend who targeted environmental extremists, and I am concerned I may have been maliciously profiled to justify the intense scrutiny I have faced.

An FOIA request to the FBI in October, 2004 yielded no information whatsoever.

I look forward to hearing from you. I will be in NYC for 3 weeks from June 13 and can be contacted on 212 595 3886. Otherwise, the most convenient means by which to correspond with me are through my attorney (details indicated above), alternatively via my email (above).

Sincerely yours,

John Wilson

* * * * *

Exhibit 44: *19 September 2007. Email from John Wilson to Congressman Jerrold Nadler.*

From: John Wilson
Sent: Wednesday, September 19, 2007 7:00 AM
To: 'amy.rutkin@mail.house.gov' <amy.rutkin@mail.house.gov>
Subject: FW: John Wilson correspondence summary for congressman Nadler

Hi Amy,

I am a constituent of Congressman Nadler (Federal Voter status). I am contacting you regards an issue I brought to Ellen Wallach initially on the 13 June 2007 concerning work I undertook as a securities analyst on Wall St and subsequent problems I have had with FBI interference as a result of work I published on Freeport McMoran following their reported involvement in the killing of 7 people in Indonesia.

I am frustrated that no progress appears to have been made by your office despite many assurances by Ellen that she was going to raise the issue with Congressman Nadler "next week".

I am happy to provide any further additional information on this case or discuss it with you. However, I believe there has been a serious misconduct breach by the FBI and would like Congressman Nadler's support to raise this issue with the House Judiciary Committee. I have made repeated attempts to ascertain whether this is a matter Congressman Nadler is prepared to assist me with and I would like confirmation as to whether he will assist and if so when.

Thanks and regards.

John Wilson

* * * * *

* * * * *

Exhibit 45: *2 September 2009.   Letter from John Wilson via Barry Fisher to Rep. Jerrold Nadler.*

John Christian Wilson
c/o Barry A. Fisher
Fleishman & Fisher
1875 Century Park East Suite 2130
Los Angeles, CA 90067

September 2, 2009

Email: ███████████████████

Rep. Jerrold Nadler
201 Varick Street, Suite 669
New York, NY 10014

Attention Ellen Wallach
Ellen.wallach@mail.house.gov

RE: FBI harassment of Wall Street Mining Analyst

Dear Sir:

I am a constituent of yours, currently registered as a Federal Voter in NYC (former address 170 West 74th St, NY, NY 10023) and currently reside offshore.

I am following up on a letter I sent you 12 June 2007 (attached) concerning FBI harassment of myself, a former Wall Street securities analyst, and telephone conversations I had at the time with Ellen Wallach, who also spoke with my attorney Barry Fisher.

I would appreciate assistance to get a response from the House Judiciary Committee following a letter I sent it 26 July 2005 (attached) and subsequent extensive conversations I had with staffers. The House committee staffers Jason Cervanak and Mindy Barry (sp?) spent time interviewing me in 2005 though they have now left, and I have received no official response to my enquiry, nor a record of the interviews, nor the results of their investigations.

The Department of Justice confirmed in an email, from Marvin Hernandez dated 10 May 2006 (attached), that one of the people I identified in the letter was indeed an FBI agent. This person had shown me her FBI identification. The DOJ subsequently retracted the confirmation provided by Mr Hernandez, apparently, in my view, as a cover-up.

In addition to asking for your assistance to secure a response from the House Judiciary Committee, I would appreciate a chance to make an appointment to meet with you briefly to discuss this matter. I will be in NYC from Sunday 27 September to Saturday 3 October 2009 and can be contacted on my cell phone 917 569 3475. Otherwise, the most convenient means by which to correspond with me is via my email (above). Please suggest a time that may be convenient for you to meet.

I look forward to hearing from you.

Sincerely yours,

John Wilson

* * * * *

* * * * *

Email Trail with Congressman Nadler's staffers, NYC – 2009-2011

Exhibit 46: *2009-2011.   Email trail between John Wilson and Rep. Nadler's staffers.*

From: John Wilson [mailto:xxxxxxxxxxxxxxxxxxxxxxxxxxx]
Sent: Wednesday, 2 September 2009 8:14 PM
To: 'ellen.wallach@mail.house.gov'
Subject: Letter attached

Hi Ellen,

Please refer to attached letter [from John Wilson to Congressman Nadler 2 September 2009].

Thanks and regards.

John

* * * * *

Congressman Nadler: No response

* * * * *

From: John Wilson
Sent: Monday, September 07, 2009 8:27 PM
To: Wallach, Ellen
Subject: FW: Letter attached

Hi Ellen,

Please confirm receipt of the below email and whether it may be possible to organise a meeting late September.

Thanks and regards.

John Wilson

* * * * *

From: Mizrahi, Celine [mailto:Celine.Mizrahi@mail.house.gov]
Sent: Thursday, 10 September 2009 12:40 AM
To: jxxxxxxxxxxxx@bigpond.com
Cc: Congressman Nadler (NY office: Wallach, Ellen)
Subject: RE: Letter attached

Hi Mr. Wilson--

Thank you for reaching out to Congressman Nadler. I'm sorry for the delay in getting back to you.

We did receive your email and packet of information last week. I am now looking into what we will be able to do to get some answers for you regarding your situation, and will be back in touch within the week to let you know what we have been able to resolve, or to hopefully schedule a brief appointment for the last week in September to discuss this further.

Best,
Celine Mizrahi

Celine Mizrahi
Manhattan Director
U.S. Congressman Jerrold L. Nadler (NY-08)
201 Varick Street, Suite 669
New York, NY 10014

* * * * *

From: John Wilson
Sent: Tuesday, September 22, 2009 2:12 PM
To: Congressman Nadler (NY office: Mizrahi, Celine)
Cc: Congressman Nadler (NY office: Wallach, Ellen)
Subject: RE: Letter attached

Hi Celine,

I am following up on our recent email correspondence.

Is it possible to provide an update please and potential times to meet if possible?

Thanks and regards.

John Wilson

* * * * *

From: Congressman Nadler (NY office: Mizrahi, Celine)
Sent: Wednesday, 23 September 2009 4:37 AM
To: John Wilson
Cc: Congressman Nadler (NY office: Wallach, Ellen)
Subject: RE: Letter attached

Hi John—

Thanks for your email. I am sorry not to get back to you sooner, but I have been trying to track down someone in DOJ on your behalf just to understand exactly where they left things so that we can determine how to follow up.

I understand that you are in New York next week. Are you free to come into our office for a brief meeting at 2:00 p.m. on Wednesday September 30th? Alternatively, how is 10:00 a.m. on Tuesday October 1st? At that point, I can update you on anything I've been able to find out and we can discuss next steps.

Please let me know which time works best for you,
Celine

Celine Mizrahi
Manhattan Director
U.S. Congressman Jerrold L. Nadler (NY-08)
201 Varick Street, Suite 669
New York, NY 10014

* * * * *

From: John Wilson
Sent: Thursday, September 24, 2009 5:41 AM
To: Congressman Nadler (NY office: Mizrahi, Celine)
Subject: RE: Letter attached

Hi Celine,

Tuesday at 10am would be good. I will see you at 201 Varick Street, Suite 669. Should I ask for you when I arrive?

Thanks and regards.

John Wison

* * * * *

From: Mizrahi, Celine [mailto:Celine.Mizrahi@mail.house.gov]
Sent: Saturday, 26 September 2009 7:16 AM
To: John Wilson
Subject: RE: Letter attached

Forgive my typo in the email below. Just to confirm, we are meeting on Tuesday September 28th at 10 a.m. (not October 1st)? I apologize for the confusion. If you can't meet on Tuesday 9/28, I am free at 1 pm on Thursday 10/1.

And yes, please do ask for me when you arrive. You will need photo ID to get into the building.

Thanks,
Celine

Celine Mizrahi
Manhattan Director
U.S. Congressman Jerrold L. Nadler (NY-08)
201 Varick Street, Suite 669
New York, NY 10014

* * * * *

From: John Wilson
Sent: Thursday, October 08, 2009 3:00 PM
To: 'celine.mizrahi@mail.house.gov'
Subject: Schumer letters

Hi Celine,

Thank you for making the time to meet with me last week.

As discussed, I have attached copies of correspondence to Senator Schumer. Please let me know if you would like further information.

I appreciate your offer for follow up with various parties and graciously accept and offer you whatever further assistance you need from me.

Regards more broadly worded follow up with the FBI/DOJ I can only re-emphasize that I know Susan Holmes was working for the FBI prior to and after the Freeport McMoran killings, and likely still is. She told me on numerous occasions, showed me her FBI ID and her mother even discussed it with me(!). If it is denied, then the agency is either lying, being deceptive or quite possibly it is not required to disclose this information as it may claim to still have me under active "investigation" and to do so would "compromise" its work. Of course, after 13 years and given the circumstances, it is completely unreasonable that it should be able to avoid accountability and prevent disclosure by any such means.

Again thank you.

Best regards.

John Wilson

* * * * *

Congressman Nadler: No response

* * * * *

From: john wilson
Sent: Monday, October 19, 2009 12:52 PM
To: 'ellen.wallach@mail.house.gov'
Cc: 'erin.drinkwater@mail.house.gov'; 'celine.mizrahi@mail.house.gov'
Subject: FW: Schumer letters

Hi Ellen,

Following my meeting with Celine Mizrahi recently in the NY office, she indicated there were a number of steps she intended to take re my complaint against the FBI.

These included:

1. Follow up with the House Judiciary Committee over their staffer's previous interviews with me and records of enquiries they made; ascertaining the Committee's powers and rights with respect to the FBI/DOJ in relation to investigating the specifics of the allegations I have raised; ascertaining the steps/process for further enquiry/investigation.

2. Direct follow up with the FBI/DOJ to broaden the terms of reference.
3. Follow up with Senator Schumer's office to ascertain status of my complaint with regards to the Senate Judiciary Committee.
4. Celine offered to undertake/discuss further action that may be appropriate.

Could you please advise of the continuity and follow up that I might expect on these issues given Celine's leave of absence and who the main point of contact in your office is for this.

Thanks and regards.

John Wilson

* * * * *

Congressman Nadler: No response

* * * * *

From: john wilson
Sent: Wednesday, October 28, 2009 2:36 PM
To: 'ellen.wallach@mail.house.gov'
Subject: FW: Schumer letters

Hi Ellen,

Could you please let me know when I could expect a response to the below email to you.

Thanks and regards.

John Wilson

* * * * *

Congressman Nadler: No response

* * * * *

From: john wilson
Sent: Thursday, November 05, 2009 2:22 PM
To: Wallach, Ellen
Cc: Mizrahi, Celine
Subject: FW: Schumer letters

Hi Ellen,

When I met with your office last month, I had a very positive meeting and Celine expressed support for progressing the matter further, had a number of good ideas and indicated that she would follow up with various parties as outlined in my earlier email below summarizing the meeting action items.

Given Celine's maternity departure shortly after the meeting, I am unclear as to the intentions of your office to follow up with the assistance offered. I assumed Celine was speaking on behalf of the Congressman's office in offering to further assist in my matter and her absence would not affect that position.

Could you please confirm what the position of your office is and whether the offer of assistance made last month by Celine will be followed up in her absence.

Thank you.

John Wilson

* * * * *

From: Mizrahi, Celine [mailto:Celine.Mizrahi@mail.house.gov]
Sent: Wednesday, 10 February 2010 9:23 AM
To: john wilson; Wallach, Ellen
Subject: RE: Schumer letters

Hi Mr. Wilson—

I am now back in the office and happy to follow up with you. I hope all is well. Please see my responses below to the different follow up points. Also, when we ended our meeting, we had said that you should think about how much additional follow up would be useful, if we are unlikely to get significantly different responses from the FBI than you and Senator Schumer received in the past.

I think that the best that we will be able to do to help you is to send another inquiry on your behalf to the FBI/DOJ, making sure that we ask a broadly phrased question to try to capture any possible FBI involvement. As we discussed in the fall, I am doubtful that we will get a significantly different response from the FBI or DOJ than the answer to the narrower question that was asked earlier. Given that, please let me know if you would still like me to proceed.

I can certainly also follow up with Senator Schumer's office to see if there has been any further action on the part of the Senate Judiciary Committee. Unfortunately, there does not seem to be a way to track down the past Judiciary Committee staff's records on this matter. Although the House Judiciary Committee does have oversight over FBI/DOJ, I am not sure there is anything that they will be able to do to further investigate besides to write the kind of letter that we will already be writing on your behalf, and that Senator Schumer wrote.

Thank you for your patience,
Celine Mizrahi

Celine Mizrahi
Manhattan Director
U.S. Congressman Jerrold L. Nadler (NY-08)
201 Varick Street, Suite 669
New York, NY 10014

* * * * *

From: John Wilson
Sent: Thursday, 11 February 2010 8:04 PM
To: 'Mizrahi, Celine'
Subject: RE: Schumer letters

Hi Celine,

Thanks for your email. I trust your maternity leave went well.

I would appreciate your follow through with the FBI/DOJ and the Senate Judiciary Committee. As indicated previously, I believe the FBI is lying or stonewalling, depending on your point of view, by providing qualified and therefore inconclusive responses to my complaint.

In particular I would appreciate your follow through with the House Judiciary Committee. I find it inexplicable that the earlier enquiries and interviews by staffers cannot be located. This alone should send a red flag to the Committee. As discussed, the three FBI agents initially mentioned in my complaint are self disclosed and Susan Holmes had shown me her FBI identity card confirming her FBI credentials. I assume that the Committee has the means and methods to get to the heart of this issue.

Again, thanks for your help.

Best regards.

John Wilson

* * * * *

Congressman Nadler: No response

* * * * *

From: John Wilson
Sent: Wednesday, 10 March 2010 6:12 PM
To: 'Celine.Mizrahi@mail.house.gov'
Subject: FW: Schumer letters

Hi Celine,

I am following up on the below email.

Would it be possible to provide me an update and if possible copies of any correspondence sent or received.

Thanks and regards.

John Wilson

* * * * *

Congressman Nadler: No response

* * * * *

From: John Wilson
To: Mizrahi, Celine
Sent: Mon Mar 15 18:39:03 2010
Subject: FW: Schumer letters

Hi Celine,

Could you please confirm receipt of the below email and if possible indicate the status of any follow up.

Thanks and regards.

John Wilson

* * * * *

From: Mizrahi, Celine [mailto:Celine.Mizrahi@mail.house.gov]
Sent: Tuesday, 16 March 2010 9:47 AM
To: jxxxxxxxxxxx@bigpond.com
Subject: Re: Schumer letters

John:

I received your email and am following up as we discussed. I will email you copies of any letters in the near future, and I will also send you any responses that I receive.

Thank you,
Celine
Celine Mizrahi
Manhattan Director
U.S. Congressman Jerrold L. Nadler (NY-08)
201 Varick Street, Suite 669
New York, NY 10014

* * * * *

From: John Wilson
To: Mizrahi, Celine
Sent: Mon May 17 19:08:47 2010
Subject: john wilson

Hi Celine,

I haven't heard back from you regards my recent emails. Could you please give me some indication where things currently stand, or if preferable let me know and I can call you to discuss.

Thanks and regards.

John

* * * * *

From: Mizrahi, Celine [mailto:Celine.Mizrahi@mail.house.gov]
Sent: Tuesday, 18 May 2010 9:23 AM

To: johnwilson@rcresearch.net
Subject: Re: john wilson

Hi John-

My apologies for the delay. I have sent the letters that we discussed and am waiting for a response. I will follow up to try to expedite things and will let you know soon.

Thanks for your patience,
Celine
Celine Mizrahi
Manhattan Director
U.S. Congressman Jerrold L. Nadler (NY-08)
201 Varick Street, Suite 669
New York, NY 10014

* * * * *

From: John Wilson
Sent: Wednesday, 24 November 2010 6:13 PM
To: 'john.conyers@mail.house.gov'
Cc: 'Celine.Mizrahi@mail.house.gov'
Subject: FW: John Wilson: House Committee on the Judiciary letter - 15 Sept 2010

Dear Sir,

Please find attached my letter to the House Judiciary Committee sent 15 September 2010.

I called the committee to confirm receipt and the office indicated no record of the letter was logged. They suggested I forward it to you directly.

Sincerely,

John Wilson

* * * * *

From: John Wilson
Sent: Wednesday, 24 November 2010 6:19 PM
To: 'Celine.Mizrahi@mail.house.gov'
Subject: FW: John Wilson: House Committee on the Judiciary letter - 15 Sept 2010

Hi Celine,

I have resent the House Judiciary Letter directly to Congressman Conyers (and cc'ed you). As a member of congress is generally required to request the Committee investigate a particular matter, is it possible that Congressman Nadler make such request to the House Judiciary Committee on my behalf regards this matter?

Thanks and regards.

John Wilson

* * * * *

House Judiciary Committee: No response
Congressman Nadler: No response

* * * * *

From: John Wilson
Sent: Monday, November 29, 2010 6:45 PM
To: Mizrahi, Celine
Subject: FW: John Wilson: House Committee on the Judiciary letter - 15 Sept 2010

Hi Celine,

Could you please confirm Congressman Nadler's intention to refer this matter to the House Judiciary Committee for investigation. Is there a time that is good for me to call to discuss?

Thank you.

Regards.

John Wilson

* * * * *

From: Mizrahi, Celine [mailto:Celine.Mizrahi@mail.house.gov]
Sent: Wednesday, 1 December 2010 4:21 AM
To: 'John Wilson'
Subject: RE: John Wilson: House Committee on the Judiciary letter - 15 Sept 2010

Hi John—

Thanks for your email and for sending copies of the letters. Congressman Nadler will discuss this matter with the House Judiciary Staff on your behalf.

Thanks,
Celine

Celine Mizrahi
Manhattan Director
Congressman Jerrold Nadler (NY-08)
201 Varick Street, Suite 669
New York, NY 10014
212.367.7350 (t)
212.367.7356 (f)
celine.mizrahi@mail.house.gov (e)

* * * * *

From: John Wilson
Sent: Thursday, 6 January 2011 10:14 AM
To: 'Mizrahi, Celine'
Subject: RE: John Wilson: House Committee on the Judiciary letter - 15 Sept 2010

Hi Celine,

What is the timing you anticipate for Congressman Nadler to raise the matter as per below email?

Thanks and regards.

John Wilson

* * * * *

From: Mizrahi, Celine [mailto:Celine.Mizrahi@mail.house.gov]
Sent: Thursday, 6 January 2011 7:23 AM
To: John Wilson
Subject: Read: FW: John Wilson: House Committee on the Judiciary letter - 15 Sept 2010

Your message was read on Wednesday, January 05, 2011 3:23:16 PM (GMT-05:00) Eastern Time (US & Canada).

* * * * *

Congressman Nadler: No response

* * * * *

From: John Wilson [mailto:jxxxxxxxxxxxx@bigpond.com]
Sent: Thursday, 27 January 2011 9:52 PM
To: 'Mizrahi, Celine'
Subject: RE: John Wilson: House Committee on the Judiciary letter - 15 Sept 2010

Hi Celine,

Is it possible for any feedback at this point - could I give you a call to discuss? Do you know if Congressman Nadler has had an opportunity to raise or progress this matter with the House Judiciary Staff at this time?

Thanks for your help.

Best regards.

John Wilson

* * * * *

Congressman Nadler: No response

* * * * *

From: John Wilson
Sent: Friday, 4 March 2011 9:17 AM
To: 'Mizrahi, Celine'
Subject: John Wilson

Hi Celine,

I called your office yesterday and today.

Is it possible to receive an update on where things are at with the various letters you sent and approach by Congressman Nadler to the House Judiciary Committee?

Is there a suitable time for me to call you?

Thanks and regards.

John

* * * * *

Congressman Nadler: No response

* * * * *

From: John Wilson
Sent: Thursday, 12 May 2011 10:51 AM
To: 'Mizrahi, Celine'
Subject: FW: John Wilson: House Committee on the Judiciary letter - 15 Sept 2010

Hi Celine,

Are you in a position to be able to confirm the status of the below discussions?

Thanks and regards.

John Wilson

* * * * *

Congressman Nadler: No response

* * * * *

From: John Wilson
Sent: Friday, 15 April 2011 9:46 AM
To: 'Mizrahi, Celine'
Subject: FW: John Wilson

Hi Celine,

I hope you are well and enjoying the Spring.

Would it be possible to let me know whether you are still working on my complaint about FBI interference with me after I published an analyst report while working on Wall Street about US mining company Freeport McMoran that touched on the US State Department's investigation of the company for its alleged role in the killing of indigenous protestors at is mine in West Papua, Indonesia, and also whether you are able to provide me an update on whether there have been responses to the various enquiries previously made on my behalf by yourself?

I appreciate your support in this matter and look forward to hearing from you.

Thanks and regards.

John

* * * * *

Congressman Nadler: No response

* * * * *

From: John Wilson
Sent: Thursday, 6 October 2011 8:47 AM
To: 'Celine.Mizrahi@mail.house.gov'
Subject: FW: John Wilson: House Committee on the Judiciary letter - 15 Sept 2010

Hi Celine,

I will be in NY next Tuesday – Thursday (11-13 Oct). Would it be possible to schedule a meeting with you or Congressman Nadler to discuss the status of my complaint concerning the FBI?

Thanks and regards.

John Wilson

* * * * *

Congressman Nadler: No response

* * * * *

From: John Wilson
Sent: Thursday, 10 November 2011 9:56 PM
To: 'Celine.Mizrahi@mail.house.gov'
Cc: 'Ellen.Wallach@mail.house.gov'
Subject: FW: John Wilson: House Committee on the Judiciary letter - 15 Sept 2010

Hi Celine,

I have not heard back from you since December 2010 – nearly 12 months, despite a number of attempts to contact you. At that time you confirmed that Congressman Nadler, a member of the House Judiciary Committee - a Committee which has oversight responsibility for the FBI, would raise my concerns with staffers at the Committee and you would provide me with feedback.

As a registered Federal Voter in Congressman Nadler's NYC district I initiated dialogue with his NYC office over two years ago. I would like to bring closure to this matter of prolonged FBI interference with myself (ongoing for 15 years) and I seek my Congressman's help in this regard. I am concerned that there has been no further communication from you and would appreciate any clarification of the status of your enquiries into this matter.

Thanks and regards.

John Wilson

* * * * *

IV-1d   Correspondence 2004 to 2011

House Judiciary Committee (HJC)

* * * * *

Exhibit 47: *17 January 2005.   Letter from John Wilson via Attorney Barry Fisher to Rep. Conyers, HJC.*

John Christian Wilson   17 January, 2005
c/o Barry A. Fisher
Fleishman & Fisher
1875 Century Park East Suite 2130
Los Angeles, CA 90067

Email: xxxxxxxxxxxxx@bigpond.com

Hon. John Conyers, Jr.
Judiciary Committee
United States House of Representatives
2464 Rayburn Building
Washington D.C. 20515

Dear Congressman Conyers:

I write because of the oversight responsibilities of your Committee. I was a mining company equity analyst on Wall Street from 1994 to 1998. I am a citizen of the U.S.A., was born in Australia, and have long lived in the United States, principally in New York and Philadelphia, where I received my MBA degree from Wharton. I am currently visiting family for an extended stay in Australia.

In 1996, in the course of performing my duties, information was leaked to me by a then undisclosed FBI agent who worked undercover as an environmentalist. This person gave me details of a State Department finding into an incident in which 7 people were recently killed in and around the publicly traded Freeport McMoran owned Grasberg mine in Indonesia. The information I received related to a confidential reprimand of the company by the U.S. Department of State for human rights and environmental abuses.

Since then, as set out below, I have been subjected to what appears to be a systematic retaliation campaign by persons associated with the FBI involving invasive and injurious tactics. Among other things, I have faced blacklisting in my industry. I have been unable to gain any employment in the financial services industry despite a recent boom in the mining sector and despite having worked on Wall Street for 6 years, mostly as a senior equity analyst.

For the many years following my 1996 publication regarding the Freeport McMoran killings, I have had many contacts with people who at some point revealed themselves as FBI agents on assignment connected to me, and who let me know that I angered important people by the publication. Some of these individuals engendered friendship with me under the auspices of other professional identities and each has interviewed me, two of them extensively. These include Steven Garber, now of White Plains, New York, formerly of New York City, Susan Holmes, now of Washington, D.C., formerly of New York City, and Livingston Sutro, of Sierra Vista, Arizona.

Aside from these agents, more than a dozen other people have identified themselves to me as having a high level of familiarity with these circumstances and appear to be FBI agents or associated with agents.

Given the fact that the source of the leaked information was itself an FBI agent and given the powerful business interests of Freeport, I am concerned that I am the subject of what appears to be either a case of FBI corruption or incompetence. The agent that passed to me the information about Freeport was a long term friend who targeted environmental extremists, and I am concerned I may have been maliciously profiled to justify the intense scrutiny I have faced.

An FOIA request to the FBI in October, 2004 yielded no information whatsoever.

I look forward to hearing from you. The most convenient means by which to correspond with me are through my attorney (details indicated above), alternatively via email.

Sincerely yours,

John Wilson

CC: Hon. Robert C. Scott
        Judiciary Committee
        United States House of Representatives
        2426 Rayburn Building
        Washington D.C. 20515

* * * * *

* * * * *

Exhibit 48: *16 April 2005.   Letter from John Wilson via Barry Fisher to Rep. Conyers, HJC.*

John Christian Wilson   16 April, 2005
c/o Barry A. Fisher
Fleishman & Fisher
1875 Century Park East Suite 2130
Los Angeles, CA 90067
Email: █████████████

Hon. John Conyers, Jr.
Judiciary Committee
United States House of Representatives
2464 Rayburn Building
Washington D.C. 20515

Dear Congressman Conyers:

I write as a follow up to the letter I sent to your office on 17 January, 2005 (copy enclosed). Could you please indicate your expected timing for a response to that letter.

Thank you.

Sincerely yours,

John Wilson

Encl.   Copy of letter sent to your office, dated 17 January, 2005

* * * * *

* * * * *

Exhibit 49: *26 July 2005.   Letter from John Wilson via Attorney Barry Fisher to HJC.*

John Christian Wilson   26 July, 2005
c/o Barry A. Fisher
Fleishman & Fisher
1875 Century Park East Suite 2130
Los Angeles, CA 90067

Email:

U.S. House of Representatives
Committee on the Judiciary
2138 Rayburn House Office Building
Washington, DC 20515

RE: FBI harassment of Wall Street Mining Analyst

Dear Sir:

I write because of the oversight responsibilities of the Committee on the Judiciary. I was a mining company equity analyst on Wall Street from 1994 to 1998. I am a citizen of the U.S.A., was born in Australia, and have long lived in the United States, principally in New York and Philadelphia, where I received my MBA degree from Wharton. I am currently visiting family for an extended stay in Australia.

In 1996, in the course of performing my duties, information was leaked to me by a then undisclosed FBI agent who worked undercover as an environmentalist. This person gave me details of a State Department finding into an incident in which 7 people were recently killed in and around the publicly traded Freeport McMoran owned Grasberg mine in Indonesia. The information I received related to a confidential reprimand of the company by the U.S. Department of State following an investigation into human rights and environmental abuses.

Since then, as set out below, I have been subjected to what appears to be a systematic retaliation campaign by persons associated with the FBI involving invasive and injurious tactics. Among other things, I have faced blacklisting in my industry. I have been unable to gain any employment in the financial services industry despite a recent boom in the mining sector and despite having worked on Wall Street for 6 years, mostly as a senior equity analyst.

For the many years following my 1996 publication regarding the Freeport McMoran killings, I have had many contacts with people who at some point revealed themselves as FBI agents on assignment connected to me, and who let me know that I angered important people by the publication. Some of these individuals engendered friendship with me under the auspices of other professional identities and each has interviewed me, two of them extensively. These include Steven Garber, now of White Plains, New York, formerly of New York City, Susan Holmes, now of Washington, D.C., formerly of New York City, and Livingston Sutro, of Sierra Vista, Arizona.

1 of 2

Aside from these agents, more than a dozen other people have identified themselves to me as having a high level of familiarity with these circumstances and appear to be FBI agents or associated with agents.

Given the fact that the source of the leaked information was itself an FBI agent and given the powerful business interests of Freeport, I am concerned that I am the subject of what appears to be either a case of FBI corruption or incompetence. The agent that passed to me the information about Freeport was a long term friend who targeted environmental extremists, and I am concerned I may have been maliciously profiled to justify the intense scrutiny I have faced.

An FOIA request to the FBI in October, 2004 yielded no information whatsoever.

I look forward to hearing from you. The most convenient means by which to correspond with me are through my attorney (details indicated above), alternatively via email.

Sincerely yours,

John Wilson

* * * * *

* * * * *

Exhibit 50: *14 September 2005. Email from office of Rep. Scott, ranking member of the HJC to Wilson.*

From: Estes-Petty, Randi

To: xxxxxxxxxxxx@bigpond.com

Sent: Wednesday, September 14, 2005 6:20 AM

Subject: Request for assistance

Dear Mr. Wilson:

I regret the delay in my response. However, I wanted Mr. Vassar to review your letter and point me in the right direction.

Unfortunately, in speaking with Mr. Bobby Vassar, Mr. Scott's Legislative Counsel, Congressman Scott neither as the ranking Member on the Judiciary Subcommittee on Crime nor as a single member of Congress has the power to investigate general allegations of harassment by individuals. It has been suggested that you contact the Judiciary Committee's Oversight Counsel, Mindy Barry at 202-225-3951 or Congressman John Conyers Ranking Member on the Judiciary Committee at 202-225-6906 and see what they can do to assist you.

Other than those two options, Mr. Scott can contact the FBI on your behalf and ask them for a response. In which case you will need to contact our Newport News Office at 757-380-1000 and complete a constituent consent form. If you are not interested in the latter, I regret that there is nothing else that we as a congressional office can do.

I hope you find this information of use. I wish that there was more that we could do.

Randi Estes-Petty

Executive Assistant

Office of Robert C. Scott

1201 Longworth House Office Building

Washington, DC 20515

* * * * *

Exhibit 51: *28 September 2005.   Email from John Wilson to Mindy Barry, staffer, HJC.*

From: john wilson ███████████████
Sent: Wednesday, September 28, 2005 7:04 AM
To: mindy.barry@mail.house.gov
Subject: Letter

Mindy,

Please find a copy of the letter mentioned today on the phone. Rep Scott's office referred me to you. I will try and speak with you tomorrow.

Thank you.

John Wilson

* * * * *

IV-1e   Correspondence 2004 to 2011

United Nations Human Rights Committee (UNHRC)

* * * * *

Exhibit 52: *14 April 2007.   Letter from John Wilson via Attorney Barry Fisher to UNHRC.*

John Christian Wilson   14 April, 2007
c/o Barry A. Fisher
Fleishman & Fisher
1875 Century Park East Suite 2130
Los Angeles, CA 90067

Office of the High Commissioner for Human Rights
United Nations Office at Geneva
8-14 Avenue de la Paix
1211 Geneva 10
Switzerland

RE: Political persecution by Australian and US government agencies in relation to Freeport McMoran killings in Indonesia. FBI and ASIO retaliation against a Wall Street securities analyst.

Dear Sir/Madam:

Please find attached copies of two letters containing an outline of that which in my view constitutes the political persecution of a Wall Street equities analyst – myself John Wilson (a dual citizen of Australia and the USA), by US and Australian government agencies. The letters are copies sent to Australia's Green Party Senator Bob Brown.

By way of introduction, I worked as a securities analyst with investment bank SBC Warburg in New York, and analysed US mining company Freeport McMoran which owns the Grasberg mine, a significant gold/copper mine in Irian Jaya (Indonesia). In the 1990's a series of security related killings occurred at the mine, which according to reports at the time involved killings by company personnel on company property. As an analyst, I consequently asked Jim Bob Moffatt (CEO of Freeport McMoran) a question about the US Department of State investigation into the killings during an analyst briefing at the company's office in New Orleans in 1996.

Subsequent to raising the issue with Freeport, I was threatened and have been harassed in a campaign apparently managed by the FBI and later ASIO (Australian intelligence) as outlined in the attached letters.

I have been unable to obtain confirmation from either the Australian Government or the USA Government of their involvement in this matter despite attempts over the past 2.5 years seeking their accountability. In Australia, numerous letters have been sent to, and/or meetings held with various

Australian Members of Parliament and Senators as well as the Parliamentary oversight committee with responsibility for ASIO. Letters I sent or that were forwarded on my behalf to the Australian Attorney General (2 letters) and the Inspector General of Intelligence and Security (IGIS, 4 letters) have effectively met with stonewall responses (see the IGIS letter attached as an example). In the USA, numerous letters sent to the FBI and US Department of Justice oversight offices since 2004 on this issue have also been blocked by stonewall responses. The FBI took over 12 months to respond to my initial inquiry of January 17, 2005 responding February 10, 2006. To date, neither it, nor the Department of Justice has either confirmed or denied their involvement as alleged. Any further supporting documentation required can be supplied upon request.

I am now seeking the assistance of international agencies to register a complaint against the Australian Government and the USA Government. The Government's and their agencies' tactics have been invasive and injurious to me, and the situation is one that I believe is a human rights abuse. I believe the UN Universal Declaration of Human Rights has been breached on Article 10, Article 12, and Article 19 amongst others. Given the situation, I believe I should have a right to know the allegations against me, review the evidence the agencies are relying on, and I should have a right of defence. In Australia, a legal opinion (attached) indicates that ASIO is exempt by law from having to conform with one or more of the above Articles.

I write to inform you of my situation and also to ask for your assistance in relation to the political persecution I face from Australian and US government agencies.

I appreciate any assistance you may be able to offer including the formal registration of my complaint with the UN and making reference to it available in the public record of the UN Human Rights Commission.

Yours faithfully,

John Wilson
1306/183 Kent Street
Sydney, NSW 2000
Australia
Tel: +612 9252 9405
Email:

Attached
1. Letter to Australian Green Party Senator Bob Brown 21 February 2005.
2. Letter to Australian Green Party Senator Bob Brown 31 May 2006.
3. Australian House of Representatives proceedings (Hansard) 28 March 2007, speech by Member of Parliament in relation to John Wilson and ASIO.
4. Tony Hargreaves & Partners Lawyers letter 24 November 2004.
5. Inspector General of Intelligence and Security (IGIS, Australia) letter of response 11 January 2005.
6. Australian Attorney-General letter 18 November 2005.
7. Parliamentary Joint Committee on Intelligence and Security letter 2 December 2005.
8. Tanya Plibersek MP letter 24 August 2006.

9. Inspector General of Intelligence and Security letter 29 August 2006.
10. US Department of Justice letter to John Wilson 10 February, 2006.
11. Partial timeline of events.

* * * * *

Exhibit 53: *24 April 2007.   Letter from UNHRC to John Wilson via Attorney Barry Fisher.*

NATIONS UNIES
HAUT COMMISSARIAT AUX DROITS DE L'HOMME

UNITED NATIONS
HIGH COMMISSIONER FOR HUMAN RIGHTS

Téléfax: (41-22)-917.90.22
Télégrammes: UNATIONS, GENEVE
Télex: 41 29 62
Téléphone: (41-22)-917 000
Internet: www.unhchr.ch
Email: th-petitions@ohchr.org

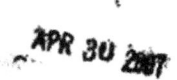

Address:
Palais des Nations
CH-1211 GENEVE 10

REFERENCE: G/SO 215/51 AUS (GEN)

24/04/2007

Dear Mr. Wilson,

After careful consideration of the contents of your petition of 14 April 2007, we sincerely regret having to inform you that the United Nations Office of the High Commissioner for Human Rights is not in a position to assist you in the matter you raise, for the reasons indicated on the back of this letter. Accordingly, your petition is being returned to you.

Please accept our apologies for not replying in a more personal manner. You may understand that, while we appreciate your reasons for writing to us, the existing procedures require that it is ascertained whether certain preliminary criteria are satisfied before proceeding with the examination of a petition.

For information about the procedures for the examination of individual petitions on human rights violations, please consult our website: www.ohchr.org, (direct link http://www.ohchr.org/english/about/publications/docs/fs7.htm). If you have difficulty accessing our website, please write to the UNHCHR, Information Office PW-RS-011, 1211 Geneva 10, and ask for Human Rights Fact Sheets Nos. 7, 12, 15 and 17.

Yours sincerely,

The Petitions Unit

1. ☒ The Human Rights Committee cannot examine petitions alleging violations of the International Covenant on Civil and Political Rights (ICCPR) unless the State is also a party to the Optional Protocol (OP). <u>The United States of America</u> is not a State party to the Optional Protocol.

2. ☐ The Committee against Torture cannot examine petitions alleging violations of the Convention against Torture (CAT) unless the State has made the declaration under article 22 recognizing the Committee's competence to receive and consider petitions. _____ has not made the declaration.

3. ☐ The Committee on the Elimination of Racial Discrimination cannot examine petitions alleging violations of the Convention on the Elimination of Racial Discrimination (CERD) unless the State has made the declaration under article 14 recognizing the Committee's competence to receive and consider petitions. _____ has not made the declaration.

Considering your petition under ___CCPR for your complaint against <u>Australia</u>:

4. ☐ The State party concerned has entered a reservation to the relevant treaty as a result of which your petition cannot be examined.

5. ☐ Your complaint is being examined or has been examined by the European Court of Human Rights, by the Inter-American Commission on Human Rights or by the African Commission on Human and Peoples' Rights.

6. ☐ The object of your petition falls outside the scope of the relevant treaty.

7. ☐ The events complained of occurred prior to the entry into force of the Optional Protocol to the ICCPR, of article 22 CAT or of article 14 CERD for the State concerned.

8. ☒ Domestic judicial/administrative remedies do not appear to have been exhausted, and it has not been substantiated that the application of domestic remedies would be unreasonably prolonged or that the remedies would be otherwise unavailable or ineffective.

9. ☐ The Human Rights Committee is not generally in a position to review the evaluation of facts and evidence by the national courts and authorities, nor can it review the interpretation of domestic legislation.

10. ☐ The Human Rights Committee is not generally in a position to review a sentence imposed by national courts, nor can it review the question of innocence or guilt.

11. ☐ The Committees cannot generally examine disputes between private individuals or alleged violations of human rights that have been committed by non-state actors.

12. ☐ The Committees can only examine individual petitions presented by the alleged victims themselves or by duly authorised representatives. Anonymous petitions cannot be considered.

13. ☒ Your petition does not provide sufficient details as to the facts of your case, and/or as to how your rights under the relevant treaty have been violated.

N.B. Please note that the working languages of the Secretariat are English, French, Russian and Spanish. You are therefore kindly requested to use any of these languages in future correspondence.

* * * * *

* * * *

Exhibit 54: *24 August 2007.   Letter from UNHRC to John Wilson via Attorney Barry Fisher.*

OFFICE DES NATIONS UNIES A GENÈVE
UNITED NATIONS OFFICE AT GENEVA
CH - 1211 GENÈVE 10

PW A-082

PORT PAYÉ
1211 GENÈVE 10

SEP - 4 2007

John Christian Wilson
c/o Barry A. Fisher
Fleishman & Fisher
1875 Century Park East Suite 2130
Los Angeles, CA 90067
U.S.A.

90067+2574 0024

NATIONS UNIES
HAUT COMMISSARIAT AUX DROITS DE L'HOMME

UNITED NATIONS
HIGH COMMISSIONER FOR HUMAN RIGHTS

Téléfax: (41-22)-9179022
Télégrammes: UNATIONS, GENEVE
Télex: 41 29 62
Internet: www.unhchr.ch

SEP - 4 2007

Address:
Palais des Nations
CH-1211 GENEVE 10

REFERENCE: G/SO 215/4

24 August 2007

Dear Sir/Madame,

Thank you for alerting us to your case. We have examined your letter with attention, and it has been put on file.

We nonetheless regret that the United Nations Secretariat is unable to assist you in the circumstances of your case.

Yours sincerely,

Petitions Unit
Treaties and Commission Branch
OHCHR

* * * * *

IV-1f   Correspondence 2004 to 2011

Other

Senator Clinton

* * * * *

Exhibit 55: *2 May 2005.   Letter from John Wilson via Attorney Barry Fisher to Senator Clinton.*

John Christian Wilson   2 May, 2005
c/o Barry A. Fisher
Fleishman & Fisher
1875 Century Park East Suite 2130
Los Angeles, CA 90067
Email:

The Honorable Hillary Rodham Clinton
780 Third Avenue
Suite 2601
New York, NY 10017

Dear Senator Clinton:

I write because of the oversight responsibilities of your Committee. I was a mining company equity analyst on Wall Street from 1994 to 1998. I am a citizen of the U.S.A., was born in Australia, and have long lived in the United States, principally in New York and Philadelphia, where I received my MBA degree from Wharton. I am currently visiting family for an extended stay in Australia.

In 1996, in the course of performing my duties, information was leaked to me by a then undisclosed FBI agent who worked undercover as an environmentalist. This person gave me details of a State Department finding into an incident in which 7 people were recently killed in and around the publicly traded Freeport McMoran owned Grasberg mine in Indonesia. The information I received related to a confidential reprimand of the company by the U.S. Department of State for human rights and environmental abuses.

Since then, as set out below, I have been subjected to what appears to be a systematic retaliation campaign by persons associated with the FBI involving invasive and injurious tactics. Among other things, I have faced blacklisting in my industry. I have been unable to gain any employment in the financial services industry despite a recent boom in the mining sector and despite having worked on Wall Street for 6 years, mostly as a senior equity analyst.

For the many years following my 1996 publication regarding the Freeport McMoran killings, I have had many contacts with people who at some point revealed themselves as FBI agents on assignment connected to me, and who let me know that I angered important people by the publication. Some of these individuals engendered friendship with me under the auspices of other professional identities and each has interviewed me, two of them extensively. These include Steven Garber, now of White Plains, New York, formerly of New York City, Susan Holmes, now of Washington, D.C., formerly of New York City, and Livingston Sutro, of Sierra Vista, Arizona.

Aside from these agents, more than a dozen other people have identified themselves to me as having a high level of familiarity with these circumstances and appear to be FBI agents or associated with agents.

Given the fact that the source of the leaked information was itself an FBI agent and given the powerful business interests of Freeport, I am concerned that I am the subject of what appears to be either a case of FBI corruption or incompetence. The agent that passed to me the information about Freeport was a long term friend who targeted environmental extremists, and I am concerned I may have been maliciously profiled to justify the intense scrutiny I have faced.

An FOIA request to the FBI in October, 2004 yielded no information whatsoever.

I look forward to hearing from you. The most convenient means by which to correspond with me are through my attorney (details indicated above), alternatively via email.

Sincerely yours,

John Wilson

* * * * *

IV-2 Correspondence 2010 to 2014

IV-2a Correspondence 2010 to 2014

House Judiciary Committee (HJC)

* * * * *

Exhibit 56: *15 September 2010.   Letter from John Wilson via Barry Fisher to HJC.*

John Christian Wilson
c/o Barry A. Fisher
Fleishman & Fisher
1875 Century Park East Suite 2130
Los Angeles, CA 90067

15 September, 2010

Email: [redacted]

U.S. House of Representatives
Committee on the Judiciary
2138 Rayburn House Office Building
Washington, DC 20515

RE: FBI harassment of Wall Street Mining Analyst

Dear Sir/Madam:

I am registered as a Federal Voter in NYC (former address 170 West 74th St, NY, NY 10023) and currently reside offshore.

I sent a letter to the House Judiciary Committee 26 July 2005 (attached) concerning intense FBI harassment of myself following an analyst report I published while working on Wall Street that touched on a State Department investigation into US mining company Freeport McMoran. The company was being investigated following allegations of its involvement in the killing of indigenous protestors at its Grasberg copper/gold mine in West Papua, Indonesia in the 1990's.

Following receipt of my letter, House committee staffers Jason Cervanak and Mindy Barry contacted me and extensively interviewed me as to what I knew of the State Department investigation into Freeport, what I knew of Freeport's activities which were the subject of the investigation and the harassment I was experiencing from the FBI. Jason Cervanak, in particular spent considerable time interviewing me in 2005 amounting to 2 to 3 hours by phone. I have made a number of attempts since 2005 to follow up with the House Judiciary Committee on my complaint against the FBI and ascertain the conclusions and details of the House investigators - Cervanak and Barry. I am aware Cervanak and Barry left some years ago, and to date I have received no official response to my enquiry from the House Judiciary Committee, nor a record of the interviews, nor the results of their investigations.

I now respectfully request a response from the House Judiciary Committee as to my initial complaint against FBI harassment which is ongoing to this day and the results of the investigation undertaken in 2005 by House staffers.

I look forward to your response.

Sincerely yours,

John Wilson

CC: Celine Mizrahi, Manhattan Director, U.S. Congressman Jerrold L. Nadler (NY-08), 201 Varick Street, Suite 669, New York, NY 10014

* * * * *

IV-2b   Correspondence 2010 to 2014

Other

United Steelworkers

* * * * *

Exhibit 57: *25 February 2013.   Email from John Wilson to United Steelworkers.*

From: John Wilson [mailto:jxxxxxxxxxxxx@bigpond.com]
Sent: Monday, February 25, 2013 1:51 AM
To: Stack, Barbara White
Subject: Freeport - DOJ action - USW

Hi,

I am a former Wall Street analyst doing some work on Freeport.

Where did your complaint to the DOJ get to concerning the below issue about Freeport? Are there any letters/documents you can share? [See article below]

Mining News: US DOJ investigation.

Grasberg at 5% capacity: report, 7 November 2011

"...... the recent revelations that Freeport made payments to Indonesian police have resulted in a United Steelworkers request for investigations from the US Department of Justice.

"The Indonesian police have recently been quoted in the local media acknowledging that they accepted millions of dollars from Freeport-McMoRan's Indonesian subsidiary PT Freeport to provide security for the miner's operations in Papua, Indonesia," the major US union said.

"The Foreign Corrupt Practices Act bans companies from paying foreign officials to do or omit to do an act in violation of his or her lawful duty."

A spokesman from the US Department of Justice declined to comment on the matter, according to the Wall Street Journal."

http://www.miningnews.net/StoryView.asp?StoryID=2491536Mining News: US DOJ investigation.

Regards.

John Wilson

* * * * *

* * * * *

Exhibit 58: *27 February 2013.   Email from United Steelworkers to John Wilson.*

From: Stack, Barbara White [mailto:bstack@usw.org]
Sent: Wednesday, 27 February 2013 8:54 AM
To: John Wilson
Subject: RE: Freeport - DOJ action - USW

We received an initial response from the DOJ on April 27, 2012 saying that they reviewed the allegations, but "cannot comment publicly on whether we are pursuing a particular matter." The letters also encouraged us to bring the events of October 10, 2011, to the attention of appropriate authorities in Indonesia. That was the last we heard.

* * * * *

IV-3   Correspondence 2015 to 2019

IV-3a   Correspondence 2015 to 2019

FBI/DOJ

* * * * *

Exhibit 59: *9 March 2015.   Letter from John Wilson to DOJ, Office of the Inspector General.*

John C. Wilson   9 March 2015

▮▮▮▮
▮▮▮▮
Australia

Email: ▮▮▮▮

U.S. Department of Justice
Office of the Inspector General
Investigations Division
950 Pennsylvania Avenue, N.W.
Suite 4706
Washington, D.C. 20530-0001

Via fax: 202 616 9881

RE: Complaint concerning FBI abuse

Dear Sir/Madam,

My full name is John Christian Wilson. My social security number ▮▮▮▮. I am a US citizen by birth: my passport number ▮▮▮▮.

I am a mining analyst based in Sydney. I have had ongoing problems with the FBI for the past 18 years since publishing a short report (<u>attached</u>, March 1996) as a Wall Street mining analyst working with SG Warburg (now part of UBS) while I was living and working in New York. The report was on US mining company Freeport McMoran and touched on killings of indigenous protestors at its Grasberg mine in West Papua. Subsequent to publication of the report and a boardroom analyst meeting in New Orleans a couple of months later, I was threatened by an FBI agent and have been subjected to extensive surveillance and interference by the FBI and partnering Australian agencies since then. As a result of intrusive, disruptive and unconstitutional FBI interference I left the USA and moved back to Australia.

The agencies' surveillance and interference with me and more recently my family has been highly intrusive over this period of time to the present.

I believe the agency's activities are unwarranted, abusive and stem from my work as a mining analyst in 1996. It also seems the FBI has made concerted effort to misrepresent material facts of the matter in order to defend its illegitimate decision for surveillance of, and interference with me and to deflect all but a detailed investigation of my allegations, including the court testing of their "evidence" in my file. My then long term girlfriend, was a self disclosed, undercover FBI agent named Susan A. Holmes, based in New York whose work at the FBI involved pursuing environmental radicals on the east coast of the U.S.

In the absence of the agency giving me access to my FBI files I have no way to respond to allegations against me and defend myself in a court. (I am a dual citizen of the USA and Australia and attach what my Australian Member of Parliament Tanya Plibersek said about this matter concerning the FBI's partnering agency in Australia - ASIO; Hansard transcript attached).

By way of further evidence, I list the names of undercover FBI agents and collaborators self-disclosed or that have interfered with me include:

- Michael Mills: the FBI agent who moved into my apartment in NYC and occupied it for several years when I sublet it before my return to Australia.
- Kathleen Walton: former mining analyst at Merrill Lynch in NYC.
- Matthew Levey – Kroll Associates, Inc (New York City midtown office): consulting work case manager 2003 and 2004. Former State Department employee.
- Jeffrey S Robards: corporate finance, formerly Ernst & Young (E&Y) NYC. Now working for C.W. Downer & Co - a boutique M&A firm in Boston. (http://www.cwdowner.com/index.php?option=com_content&view=article&id=42&Itemid=23)
- Susan A. Holmes (formerly resident in New York City in the 1990s)
- Stephan Chenault and John Klotz: volunteers Sierra Club NYC Group since 1990s.
- Ben Worden, Rob Haggerty and Allison Dey (Tucson area): FBI agents involved with Diamond Mountain Buddhist group in southern Arizona and California.
- George Schneider and Livingston Sutro (Sierra Vista, AZ); Jennifer Conner (NYC): Associated with Diamond Mountain Buddhist group in southern Arizona.
- Paul Whitby (Tucson): biologist.
- Leigh Freeman – Cherry Creek, Denver based head hunter. Downing Teal. http://www.downingteal.com/Our-People/Downing-Teal-USA
- Robert Schultz – Albuquerque based head hunter. MRC Mining Search. http://www.miningsearch.com/mining-search/our-team/
- Steven D. Garber – (wife Andrea - collaborator) additional details: biologist; lived in Manhattan for much of the 1990s, before taking a two year posting to teach biology at Embry Riddle in Prescott, AZ before returning to the New York area (White Plains). Books authored include The Urban Naturalist (New York. John Wiley and Sons. 1987). PhD in Ecology, Environmental Sciences - Rutgers, The State University of New Jersey-Newark. B.S. in Natural Resources - Cornell University.

Thank you. I look forward to your response.

Sincerely,

John Wilson

* * * * *

* * * * *

Exhibit 60: *9 March 2015.   Fax from John Wilson to DOJ, Office of the Inspector General.*

[Fax transmission verification report; resent DOJ/OIG letter originally sent 9 March 2015]

```
TRANSMISSION VERIFICATION REPORT

                                    TIME  : 18/06/2015 07:04
                                    NAME  :
                                    FAX   :
                                    SER.# : BROB0F268975

DATE,TIME              18/06 07:02
FAX NO./NAME           001112026169881
DURATION               00:01:54
PAGE(S)                07
RESULT                 OK
MODE                   STANDARD
                       ECM
```

Sydney, Australia
Tel:
Email: [redacted]

facsimile transmittal

To:	U.S. DOJ Inspector General	Fax:	1 202 616 9881
		Tel:	1 (202) 514 3435/(202) 514-3435
From:	John Wilson	Date:	3/9/2015 *Resent 18 June 2015*
Re:	FBI abuse	Pages:	(including header) 7
CC:			

☐ Urgent   ☐ For Review   ☐ Please Comment   ☐ Please Reply   ☐ Please Recycle

Please refer to letter and attachments.

Resending

* * * * *

* * * * *

Exhibit 61: *2 October 2015.   Email from John Wilson to Attorney Barry Fisher re DOJ/FBI.*

From: John Wilson
Sent: Friday, October 2, 2015 4:49 PM
To: 'bfisher557@aol.com' <bfisher557@aol.com>
Subject: DOJ/FBI

Hi Barry,

Some years ago I sent a complaint letter to the DOJ about the FBI (which you helped me with). Earlier this year I tried to send a follow up complaint to the Department of Justice (DOJ), Office of the Inspector General, Investigations Division but they have repeatedly refused to acknowledge receipt. It is a detailed complaint (attached) providing names and details of (some of) the abuses of the FBI and its agents I have been subjected to since publishing the report on Freeport McMoran. I sent a fax on June 18, 2015 and two certified letters, both signed for on delivery by the postal service and confirmed to me as delivered July 17 and July 27, 2015. I also sent the same documents in an unregistered letter and two other faxes. Not one of them has been officially acknowledged as received by the DOJ. They seemed to be deliberately keeping it out of the official complaints system.

Revisiting the previous correspondence from the FBI, upon reflection I think the 2007 letter the FBI sent to Schumer (attached) is playing with semantics - referring specifically to FBI "personnel" as opposed to FBI agents, or other category of people acting at the behest of the FBI - as their reason for not taking the matter further. As I have been continuing to have trouble with the FBI and ASIO (counterparts here in Australia) I am keen to rekindle the complaints process again.

What would you suggest I do at this point? This week I have approached Senator Schumer again to see if he can send the letter through to the DOJ. Is this something you could fax/post to the DOJ/OIG certified mail as well - it might be faster than going through Schumer's office?

Thanks and regards.

John

John Wilson

Managing Director

RCR
Resource Capital Research
www.rcresearch.com.au
T +61 x xxxx xxxx (SYD)

* * * * *

Exhibit 62: *8 February 2016. Fax from Attorney Barry Fisher to DOJ/FBI.*

FLEISHMAN & FISHER
LAWYERS
1925 CENTURY PARK EAST, SUITE 2000
LOS ANGELES, CALIFORNIA 90067
Tel (310) 557-1077 * Fax (310) 557-0770

FAX COVER SHEET

TO: U.S. Dept. Of Justice,
Investigations Division
FAX : 202-616-9881

FROM: BARRY FISHER
RE:
DATE: February 8, 2016

THIS COVER LETTER PLUS __9__ PAGE(S) TRANSMITTED. IF YOU DO NOT RECEIVE ALL PAGES, PLEASE CONTACT   BARRY FISHER   AT THE ABOVE NUMBER.

THIS MESSAGE IS INTENDED FOR THE USE OF THE INDIVIDUAL OR ENTITY TO WHICH IT IS ADDRESSED, AND MAY CONTAIN INFORMATION THAT IS PRIVILEGED, CONFIDENTIAL AND EXEMPT FROM DISCLOSURE UNDER APPLICABLE LAW. IF YOU ARE NOT THE INTENDED RECIPIENT, OR THE EMPLOYEE OR AGENT OF THE INTENDED RECIPIENT, YOU ARE HEREBY NOTIFIED THAT ANY REVIEW, DISSEMINATION, DISTRIBUTION OR COPYING OF THIS COMMUNICATION IS STRICTLY PROHIBITED. IF YOU HAVE RECEIVED THIS COMMUNICATION IN ERROR, PLEASE NOTIFY US AT THE ABOVE. THANK YOU.

STANLEY FLEISHMAN (1920-1999)
BARRY FISHER*
DAVID GROSZ
MICHAEL B. WEISZ
HENRY W. McGEE, JR.
WILLIAM M. KRAMER (1929-2004)

FLEISHMAN & FISHER
LAWYERS
1925 CENTURY PARK EAST, SUITE 2000
LOS ANGELES, CALIFORNIA 90067
(310) 557-1077 TELECOPIER (310) 557-0770

*PROFESSIONAL CORPORATIONS
OF COUNSEL
CABLE ADDRESS: ARJUNA
EMAIL: BFSHR557@GMAIL.COM

February 8, 2016

U.S. Department of Justice
Investigations Division
P (202) 516-4760
F (202) 616-9881

We originally faxed this to the Office of the General Counsel, U.S. Department of Justice, fax number (202) 616-9152 on Friday January 29, 2016. Today, Monday, February 8, 2016, we called the same department at (202) 616-0646 to follow up.

We were told that the department does not handle these matters and whether or not our fax was received was not confirmed. We were told to fax the documents to the Investigations Division.

We will follow up to ensure that the complaint is formally logged into your system. Thank you.

Adrianne Bacci
Assistant to Barry Fisher

FLEISHMAN & FISHER

LAWYERS
1925 CENTURY PARK EAST, SUITE 2000
LOS ANGELES, CALIFORNIA 90067
Tel (310) 557-1077 * Fax (310) 557-0770

FAX COVER SHEET

TO: Michael E. Horowitz
FAX: 202-514-4001

FROM: BARRY FISHER
RE:
DATE: January 28, 2016

THIS COVER LETTER PLUS __7__ PAGE(S) TRANSMITTED. IF YOU DO NOT RECEIVE ALL PAGES, PLEASE CONTACT __BARRY FISHER__ AT THE ABOVE NUMBER.

THIS MESSAGE IS INTENDED FOR THE USE OF THE INDIVIDUAL OR ENTITY TO WHICH IT IS ADDRESSED, AND MAY CONTAIN INFORMATION THAT IS PRIVILEGED, CONFIDENTIAL AND EXEMPT FROM DISCLOSURE UNDER APPLICABLE LAW. IF YOU ARE NOT THE INTENDED RECIPIENT, OR THE EMPLOYEE OR AGENT OF THE INTENDED RECIPIENT, YOU ARE HEREBY NOTIFIED THAT ANY REVIEW, DISSEMINATION, DISTRIBUTION OR COPYING OF THIS COMMUNICATION IS STRICTLY PROHIBITED. IF YOU HAVE RECEIVED THIS COMMUNICATION IN ERROR, PLEASE NOTIFY US AT THE ABOVE. THANK YOU.

STANLEY FLEISHMAN (1920-1999)
BARRY FISHER*
DAVID GROSZ
MICHAEL B. WEISZ
HENRY W. McGEE, JR.
WILLIAM M. KRAMER (1920-2004)

FLEISHMAN & FISHER
LAWYERS
1925 CENTURY PARK EAST, SUITE 2000
LOS ANGELES, CALIFORNIA 90067
(310) 557-1077 TELECOPIER (310) 557-0770

*PROFESSIONAL CORPORATIONS
OF COUNSEL
CABLE ADDRESS: ARJUNA
EMAIL: BFSHR557@GMAIL.COM

January 27, 2016

Michael E. Horowitz, Inspector General

U.S. Department of Justice   By Fax: (202) 514-4001

950 Pennsylvania Avenue, N.W., Suite 4706

Washington, D.C. 20530-0001

Re: John Christian Wilson

Dear Inspector General Horowitz:

I write on behalf on my above referenced client concerning FBI conduct. The details are set out in the accompanying correspondence from Mr. Wilson which was sent to your office directly by him; however he has been unable to confirm receipt and has had no response whatsoever. I trust that you will do so through this office.

Sincerely yours,

Barry A. Fisher

9 March 2015

John C. Wilson

Australia

Email: johncwilson74@bigpond.com.au

U.S. Department of Justice
Office of the Inspector General
Investigations Division
950 Pennsylvania Avenue, N.W
Suite 4706
Washington, D.C. 20530-0001

Via fax: 202 616 9881

RE: Complaint concerning FBI abuse

Dear Sir/Madam,

My full name is John Christian Wilson. My social security number is ███████████ I am a US citizen by birth; my passport number is ███████████

I am a mining analyst based in Sydney. I have had ongoing problems with the FBI for the past 18 years since publishing a short report (attached, March 1996) as a Wall Street mining analyst working with SG Warburg (now part of UBS) while I was living and working in New York. The report was on US mining company Freeport McMoran and touched on killings of indigenous protestors at its Grasberg mine in West Papua. Subsequent to publication of the report and a boardroom analyst meeting in New Orleans a couple of months later, I was threatened by an FBI agent and have been subjected to extensive surveillance and interference by the FBI and partnering Australian agencies since then. As a result of intrusive, disruptive and unconstitutional FBI interference I left the USA and moved back to Australia.

The agencies' surveillance and interference with me and more recently my family has been highly intrusive over this period of time to the present.

I believe the agency's activities are unwarranted, abusive and stem from my work as a mining analyst in 1996. It also seems the FBI has made concerted effort to misrepresent material facts of the matter in order to defend its illegitimate decision for surveillance of, and interference with me and to deflect all but a detailed investigation of my allegations, including the court testing of their "evidence" in my file. My then long term girlfriend, was a self disclosed, undercover FBI agent named Susan A. Holmes, based in New York whose work at the FBI involved pursuing environmental radicals on the east coast of the U.S.

In the absence of the agency giving me access to my FBI files I have no way to respond to allegations against me and defend myself in a court. (I am a dual citizen of the USA and Australia and attach what my Australian Member of Parliament Tanya Plibersek said about this matter concerning the FBI's partnering agency in Australia - ASIO; Hansard transcript attached).

By way of further evidence, I list the names of undercover FBI agents and collaborators self-disclosed or that have interfered with me include:

- Michael Mills: the FBI agent who moved into my apartment in NYC and occupied it for several years when I sublet it before my return to Australia.
- Kathleen Walton: former mining analyst at Merrill Lynch in NYC.
- Matthew Levey – Kroll Associates, Inc (New York City midtown office): consulting work case manager 2003 and 2004. Former State Department employee
- Jeffrey S Robards: corporate finance, formerly Ernst & Young (E&Y) NYC. Now working for C.W. Downer & Co - a boutique M&A firm in Boston. (http://www.cwdowner.com/index.php?option=com_content&view=article&id=42&Itemid=23)
- Susan A. Holmes (formerly resident in New York City in the 1990s)
- Stephan Chenault and John Klotz: volunteers Sierra Club NYC Group since 1990s.
- Ben Worden, Rob Haggerty and Allison Dey (Tucson area) FBI agents involved with Diamond Mountain Buddhist group in southern Arizona and California.
- George Schneider and Livingston Sutro (Sierra Vista, AZ); Jennifer Conner (NYC) Associated with Diamond Mountain Buddhist group in southern Arizona
- Paul Whitby (Tucson): biologist.
- Leigh Freeman – Cherry Creek, Denver based head hunter. Downing Teal http://www.downingteal.com/Our-People/Downing-Teal-USA
- Robert Schultz – Albuquerque based head hunter. MRC Mining Search. http://www.miningsearch.com/mining-search/our-team/
- Steven D. Garber – (wife Andrea - collaborator) additional details: biologist; lived in Manhattan for much of the 1990s, before taking a two year posting to teach biology at Embry Riddle in Prescott, AZ before returning to the New York area (White Plains). Books authored include The Urban Naturalist (New York. John Wiley and Sons. 1987). PhD in Ecology, Environmental Sciences - Rutgers, The State University of New Jersey-Newark. B.S. in Natural Resources - Cornell University.

Thank you.

I look forward to your response.

Sincerely,

John Wilson

Australian Security Intelligence Organisation Surveillance

(Australian federal parliamentary record HANSARD, p 111 HOUSE OF REPRESENTATIVES Wednesday, 28 March 2007, MAIN COMMITTEE.)

Ms PLIBERSEK (Sydney) (10.49 am)—I rise today to speak on an issue that relates to a constituent of mine, a Mr Wilson, who believes that he is the subject of an investigation and of intrusive surveillance by ASIO. I know that members of parliament often hear these stories from constituents and most of the time we are given the unenviable task of explaining to them that it is unlikely that they are the subject of surveillance by ASIO. But in 1996, while living and working as an equity research analyst in the United States for SBC Warburg, Mr Wilson was given details of a confidential US state department report. The person who gave him the report revealed confidential details of the investigation into an incident in which seven people had been killed in and around the Grasberg mine in Indonesia.

The mine is owned by publicly traded Freeport McMoran. According to the information leaked by the United States person, the contents of the state department report noted that the US government had given the mining company a confidential soft reprimand that related to environmental abuses only rather than anything to do with the killings. As part of his duties as a mining analyst, Mr Wilson informed the market with regard to these incidents and suggested that there was an economic and political sensitivity in relation to them. He was subsequently sacked by his employer and black-listed from Wall Street and he believes that for that reason he has been the subject of ongoing surveillance.

I do not know whether it is true that he is the subject of ongoing surveillance. The difficulty for him is that, despite his own contacts with officials in Australia and despite the fact that I have written to the Inspector-General of Intelligence and

Security, he cannot know whether he is or is not the subject of surveillance. If allegations have been made against him, he has had no opportunity to answer those allegations. This has put enormous stress on his family. The reason I am raising this in the parliament is not because I am convinced either way of the truth of his concerns but because we have a situation where an Australian citizen is convinced—he makes a convincing case—and he has no opportunity to know whether there are allegations against him and how he can respond to them.

FCX: Grasberg Closure Highlights Political Risks
S.G. Warburg & Co. Inc.--RESEARCH NOTES

Subject: **Freeport McMoRan Copper and Gold** OPINION
(FCX--$29)--NYSE
Current: ADD

Analyst: John Wilson, (212) 224-7740
Prior: ADD

Date: March 12, 1996 Target Price: 32

	Earnings per Share			Cal. P/E 1996E	LT Growth Rate	Yield	Shares O/S (Mil.)	52-Week Range
	12/94	12/95A	12/96E					
NEW	$0.31	$0.98	$1.77	16.4X	25%	3.0%	203	20-30

	Q1/Mar	Q2/Jun	Q3/Sep	Q4/Dec	Total
1994	0.07	0.05	0.07	0.12	0.31
1995A	0.21	0.22	0.30	0.27	0.98
1996E	0.33	0.52	0.45	0.48	1.77
1997E					0.85

o   Riots at Grasberg force closure of mine and mill

o   Increased military presence highlights potential for escalation of the conflict mid term

o   Recommendation under review

Grasberg closure expected to be temporary

Following the reported death (though it is unclear if anyone actually died) of a Dani native on Freeport property last Sunday, Dani villagers rioted forcing the closure of the Freeport mine and mill. After talking with the company, it appears the situation is under control, and currently the expectation is that operations will resume later this week. The military presence in the area has been increased and will remain at higher levels in an attempt to underwrite security. At this stage, we do not anticipate there will be a significant impact to earnings.

Incident points to increased political risk

Our view is that increased military presence poses potential for escalation of the violence in the mid term, heightening the political risk of Freeport's investment in Irian Jaya. Ultimately, Freeport needs to deal with the civil aspects of this situation to allay investors concerns, and possibly also those of the US Department of State. The timing is unfortunate for Freeport as it coincides with the arbitration over whether $100 million in OPIC political risk insurance should be rescinded. The company has increasingly come under scrutiny following reported human rights abuses in the area of the mine and also concerns over its environmental record. The latter was cited by OPIC last November as the basis for withdrawing the $100 million in insurance.

Recommendation under review

Given the declining outlook for copper prices and the increased risk of political unrest at Grasberg, our ADD recommendation is under review.

A version of this note has been prepared for First Call.

S. G. WARBURG & CO. INC. A MEMBER OF THE NEW YORK STOCK EXCHANGE, NASD AND OTHER PRINCIPAL U.S. EXCHANGES. The information herein has been obtained from, and any opinions herein are based upon sources believed reliable, but we do not represent that it is accurate or complete and it should not be relied upon as such. All opinions and estimates herein reflect our judgment on the date of this report and are subject to change without notice. This report is not intended to be an offer, or the solicitation of any offer, to buy or sell the securities referred to herein. From time to time, this firm or its affiliates or the principals or employees of this firm or its affiliates may have a position in the securities referred to herein or hold options, warrants or rights with respect thereto or other securities of such issuers and may make a market or otherwise act as principal in transactions in any of these securities. Any such non-U.S. persons may have purchased securities referred to herein for their own account in advance of release of this report. Further information on the securities referred to herein may be obtained upon request.

* * * * *

* * * * *

Exhibit 63: *9 February 2016.   Letter from DOJ, FBI to John Wilson.*

U.S. Department of Justice

Federal Bureau of Investigation

Washington, D. C. 20535-0001

February 9, 2016

John Christian Wilson

Australia

Dear Mr. Wilson:

Your complaint directed to United States Senator Charles E. Schumer was forwarded to the Initial Processing Unit (IPU), Internal Investigations Section (IIS), Inspection Division (INSD), Federal Bureau of Investigation (FBI). The IIS/INSD is the FBI entity responsible for investigating allegations of misconduct or criminal activity on the part of FBI employees.

In your complaint, you reported you were unable to access your FBI file. In addition, you stated you are the subject of an investigation by an FBI partnering agency in Australia, the Australian Security Intelligence Organisation.

The purpose of this letter is to inform you the IPU/INSD has reviewed your allegations and has determined this matter does not warrant the initiation of an FBI investigation. Therefore, no further action will be taken by this office. Your request for information should be directed to:

Federal Bureau of Investigation
Attn: FOI/PA Request
Record/Information Dissemination Section
170 Marcel Drive
Winchester, VA 22602-4843

Sincerely,

Michael D. McDonald
Unit Chief
Initial Processing Unit
Inspection Division

* * * * *

* * * * *

Exhibit 64: *23 February 2016.   Letter from John Wilson to DOJ, FBI.*

John C. Wilson

Australia

Email:

23 February 2016

Michael D. McDonald,
Unit Chief
Initial Processing Unit,
Inspection Division
U.S. Department of Justice
Federal Bureau of Investigation
Room 3041,
935 Pennsylvania Avenue, NW
Washington, DC 20535-0001

RE: Complaint concerning FBI abuse

Dear Sir,

I write in response to the letter to me dated 9 February 2016 from Michael D. McDonald, Unit Chief, Initial Processing Unit, Inspection Division, U.S. Department of Justice, Federal Bureau of Investigation, Washington, D.C. concerning my complaint about FBI misconduct I originally sent to the DOJ, Office of the Inspector General dated 9 March 2015.

I am not satisfied with the FBI's response and request the search and investigation be extended. The FBI's response uses the term "employee" exclusively. I want to clarify that those referred to below I believe were working on behalf of the U.S. government, FBI and or other agencies as employees or in other capacities currently or in the past. I did not ask for or suggest that the search be limited solely to employees.

- Michael Mills: the FBI agent who moved into my apartment in NYC and occupied it for several years when I sublet it before my return to Australia.
- Kathleen Walton: former mining analyst at Merrill Lynch in NYC.
- Matthew Levey – Kroll Associates, Inc (New York City midtown office): consulting work case manager 2003 and 2004. Former State Department employee.
- Jeffrey S Robards: corporate finance, formerly Ernst & Young (E&Y) NYC. Now working for C.W. Downer & Co - a boutique M&A firm in Boston. (http://www.cwdowner.com/index.php?option=com_content&view=article&id=42&Itemid=23)
- Susan A. Holmes (formerly resident in New York City in the 1990s)
- Stephan Chenault and John Klotz: volunteers Sierra Club NYC Group since 1990s.
- Ben Worden, Rob Haggerty and Allison Dey (Tucson area): FBI agents involved with Diamond Mountain Buddhist group in southern Arizona and California.
- George Schneider and Livingston Sutro (Sierra Vista, AZ); Jennifer Conner (NYC): Associated with Diamond Mountain Buddhist group in southern Arizona.

- Paul Whitby (Tucson): biologist.
- Leigh Freeman – Cherry Creek, Denver based head hunter. Downing Teal.
http://www.downingteal.com/Our-People/Downing-Teal-USA
- Robert Schultz – Albuquerque based head hunter. MRC Mining Search.
http://www.miningsearch.com/mining-search/our-team/
- Steven D. Garber – (wife Andrea - collaborator) additional details: biologist; lived in Manhattan for much of the 1990s, before taking a two year posting to teach biology at Embry Riddle in Prescott, AZ before returning to the New York area (White Plains). Books authored include The Urban Naturalist (New York. John Wiley and Sons. 1987). PhD in Ecology, Environmental Sciences - Rutgers, The State University of New Jersey-Newark. B.S. in Natural Resources - Cornell University.

For clarification, the nature of my complaint concerning FBI misconduct which I reported in my letter to the DOJ dated 9 March 2015 and request be investigated concerns the FBI's abuse and unwarranted interference with me since 1996 following my report I authored on US mining company Freeport McMoran.

Thank you.

I look forward to your response.

Sincerely,

John Wilson

CC: U.S. Department of Justice
Office of the Inspector General
Investigations Division
950 Pennsylvania Avenue, N.W.
Suite 4706
Washington, D.C. 20530-0001

* * * *

* * * * *

Exhibit 65: *25 May 2016.   Letter from DOJ, OIG to John Wilson's Attorney Barry Fisher.*

U.S. Department of Justice

Office of the Inspector General

Investigations Division

1425 New York Avenue NW, Suite 7100
Washington, D.C. 20530

May 25, 2016

Barry Fisher, Esq.
Fleishman & Fisher
1925 Century Park East
Suite 2000
Los Angeles, CA 90067

Dear Mr. Fisher:

The purpose of this letter is to acknowledge receipt of your correspondence dated January 28, 2016, February 8, 2016, and February 18, 2016, on behalf of your client, John C. Wilson, alleging misconduct by Federal Bureau of Investigation (FBI) Special Agents.

The Office of the Inspector General (OIG) has received numerous complaints from Mr. Wilson dating back to May 1, 2005. We have reviewed the allegations raised by Mr. Wilson and determined that they were more appropriate for review by the FBI, Inspection Division (INSD), and referred the matter to that office for handling. Mr. Wilson has been advised of this referral and that any further inquiries regarding this matter should be directed to the FBI INSD at 935 Pennsylvania Avenue NW, Washington, D.C. 20035, (202) 324-3000.

This office does not intend to initiate an investigation into Mr. Wilson's allegations and considers this matter to be closed.

Sincerely,

Office of the Inspector General
Investigations Division

* * * * *

* * * * *

Exhibit 66: *24 June 2016.*   *Letter from Attorney Barry Fisher to the US Attorney General, DOJ and FBI.*

FLEISHMAN & FISHER
LAWYERS

STANLEY FLEISHMAN (1920-1999)

BARRY FISHER*

DAVID GROSZ∆

MICHAEL B. WEISZ∆

HENRY W. McGEE, JR. ∆

WILLIAM M. KRAMER (1920-2004)

1925 CENTURY PARK EAST, SUITE 2000

LOS ANGELES, CALIFORNIA 90067

(310) 557-1077 TELECOPIER (310) 557-0770

*PROFESSIONAL CORPORATIONS

∆OF COUNSEL

CABLE ADDRESS: ARJUNA

EMAIL: XXXXXXXX@GMAIL.COM

June 24, 2016

By Fax: 202-514-4001/616-9881

Loretta Lynch, Attorney General
Department of Justice
950 Pennsylvania Avenue N.W.
Washington, DC 20530-001

Michael E. Horowitz, Inspector General
Department of Justice
950 Pennsylvania Avenue N.W.
Washington, DC 20530

James B. Comey, Director
Federal Bureau of Investigation
935 Pennsylvania Avenue, NW
Washington, D.C. 20535-0001

Re: John C. Wilson:

I represent John C. Wilson who has previously written requesting investigation and clarification regarding personally impacting conduct of persons he has reason to believe were operating on behalf of the F.B.I. or other element of the DOJ. Response was sent to him stating the persons involved were not "employees" of the Department but not addressing the question whether they operated on its behalf.

Mr. Wilson's 23 February 2016 letter, attached, in follow up has not been answered except to tell him that the F.B.I. is the agency of the DOJ he should be be addressing. The F.B.I. has not responded.

I write in hopes that this long standing request can now be address definitely.

Sincerely yours,

Barry A. Fisher

* * * * *

IV-3b   Correspondence 2015 to 2019

Senator Charles Schumer

* * * * *

Exhibit 67: *14 March 2016.   Online Casework Request from John Wilson to Senator Schumer.*

Casework Request | Mar 14 2016 05:03:04 | Mr. john wilson - 1 of 3

Charles E. SCHUMER
UNITED STATES SENATOR FOR NEW YORK

Federal agencies are prohibited from releasing information concerning an individual to a third party under the Privacy Act of 1974. Please complete and sign this form, which will allow information regarding your concern to be released to the office of Senator Schumer.

Your Contact Information
Mr. john wilson
Gender:
male
Date of Birth:
▇▇▇▇▇
Phone:
▇▇▇▇▇
Email:
▇▇▇▇▇▇▇▇
Residential Address
▇▇▇▇▇▇▇

Case Details
Federal Agency Involved:
DOJ/FBI
Social Security No.:
▇▇▇▇▇
Contacted another congressional office?
No
Court of Law?
No

Your Request
The DOJ has declined to consider the issues I raised in my complaint letter sent initially March 2015 where I named FBI agents that have been interfering with me - illegally I believe, following a report I published as a Wall Street securities analyst working for a major investment bank (now part of UBS) that touched on issues concerning US mining company Freeport McMoran and a US State Department investigation into the company's human rights record at its Grasberg mine in West Papua. The DOJ refused to acknowledge receipt of my complaint initially sent 9 March 2015 though I had fax confirmation receipts and postal service receipts of proof of subsequent delivery. I previously contacted Senator Schumer's office 1 October 2015 about my complaint with the DOJ and requested help in having the DOJ acknowledge receipt of it and to garner a response. I was assigned Angela Morel in Senator Schumer's office as my case worker and I received initial

Casework Request | Mar 14 2016 05:03:04 | Mr. john wilson - 1 of 3 assistance for which I am grateful. However, the case was closed by Angela Morel after receiving the initial, incomplete response from the DOJ 9 March 2016. I believe the case was closed prematurely and requested the case remain open. I sent back a reply letter to the DOJ/FBI dated 23 February 2016 outlining an error in the DOJ's response and asked if Senator Schumer's office (email to Angela Morel dated 24 February 2016) could forward it in reply to the DOJ/FBI but she has not responded to my emails for confirmation. I hope to receive satisfactory resolution to the issues I raised with the DOJ/FBI - that the people named work or worked in some capacity for the DOJ/FBI, not necessarily as employees. I now respectfully request that the case be reopened or a new case opened to follow up on the initial response received from the DOJ/FBI dated 9 March 2016 and forward my letter dated 23 February 2016 to the DOJ/FBI. The problem, as stated in my follow up letter to the DOJ/FBI dated 23 February 2016 is: The FBI's response uses the term "employee" exclusively. I want to clarify that those referred to below I believe were working on behalf of the U.S. government, FBI and or other agencies as employees or in other capacities currently or in the past. I did not ask for or suggest that the search be limited solely to employees. - Michael Mills: the FBI agent who moved into my apartment in NYC and occupied it for several years when I sublet it before my return to Australia. - Kathleen Walton: former mining analyst at Merrill Lynch in NYC. - Matthew Levey – Kroll Associates, Inc (New York City midtown office): consulting work case manager 2003 and 2004. Former State Department employee. - Jeffrey S Robards: corporate finance, formerly Ernst & Young (E&Y) NYC. Now working for C.W. Downer & Co - a boutique M&A firm in Boston. (http://www.cwdowner.com/index.php?option=com_content&view=article&id=42&Itemid=23) - Susan A. Holmes (formerly resident in New York City in the 1990s) - Stephan Chenault and John Klotz: volunteers Sierra Club NYC Group since 1990s. - Ben Worden, Rob Haggerty and Allison Dey (Tucson area): FBI agents involved with Diamond Mountain Buddhist group in southern Arizona and California. - George Schneider and Livingston Sutro (Sierra Vista, AZ); Jennifer Conner (NYC): Associated with Diamond Mountain Buddhist group in southern Arizona. - Paul Whitby (Tucson): biologist. - Leigh Freeman – Cherry Creek, Denver based head hunter. Downing Teal. http://www.downingteal.com/Our-People/Downing-Teal-USA - Robert Schultz – Albuquerque based head hunter. MRC Mining Search. http://www.miningsearch.com/mining-search/our-team/ - Steven D. Garber – (wife Andrea - collaborator) additional details: biologist; lived in Manhattan for much of the 1990s, before taking a two year posting to teach biology at Embry Riddle in Prescott, AZ before returning to the New York area (White Plains). Books authored include The Urban Naturalist (New York. John Wiley and Sons. 1987). PhD in Ecology, Environmental Sciences - Rutgers, The State University of New Jersey-Newark. B.S. in Natural Resources - Cornell University. For clarification, the nature of my complaint concerning FBI misconduct which I reported in my letter to the DOJ dated 9 March 2015 and request be investigated concerns the FBI's abuse and unwarranted interference with me since 1996 following my report I authored on US mining company Freeport McMoran.

Is there anything else that Senator Schumer or his staff needs to know?

I am now registered as a federal voter living overseas - former address 170 West 74th street NY NY 10023. I can provide copies of letters other documents upon request. My reply letter to the DOJ/FBI dated 23 February 2016 is attached to the fax.

I authorize the Office of Senator Chuck Schumer to address the matter described above on my behalf and to receive any relevant information the Senator and his staff may need in their efforts to provide assistance to me:

Signature:_____ date: March 14, 2016
           (Required)

Please complete and mail or fax this form to:

    Senator Chuck Schumer
    780 Third Avenue Suite 2301
    New York, NY 10017
    Fax: (202) 228-2838

* * * *

* * * * *

Exhibit 68: *9 February 2017.   Online and faxed Casework Request from John Wilson to Sen. Schumer.*

TRANSMISSION VERIFICATION REPORT

```
                                    TIME  : 09/02/2017 13:47
                                    NAME  :
                                    FAX   :
                                    SER.# : BROB0F268975
```

```
DATE,TIME           09/02  13:45
FAX NO./NAME        001112022282838
DURATION            00:02:39
PAGE(S)             12
RESULT              OK
MODE                STANDARD
                    ECM
```

Sydney, Australia
Tel:
Email:

facsimile transmittal

To:	Senator Schumer	Fax:	1 202 228 2838
		Tel:	1 212 486 4430
From:	John Wilson	Date:	2/9/2017
Re:	DOJ/FBI/AG follow up correspondence	Pages:	(including header) 12
CC:			

☐ Urgent   ☐ For Review   ☐ Please Comment   ☐ Please Reply   ☐ Please Recycle

Please refer to casework request and letter.

Section IV   Appendix - Correspondence   400

Charles E. SCHUMER
UNITED STATES SENATOR FOR NEW YORK

Federal agencies are prohibited from releasing information concerning an individual to a third party under the Privacy Act of 1974. Please complete and sign this form, which will allow information regarding your concern to be released to the office of Senator Schumer.

Your Contact Information

Mr. john christian wilson

Gender:
male

Date of Birth:
[redacted]

Phone:
[redacted]

Secondary Phone:
[redacted]

Email:
[redacted]

Residential Address

federal voter overseas (formerly) 170 west 74th street
Apt 906
ny, NY 10023

Mailing Address

[redacted]

Case Details

Federal Agency Involved:
FBI/DOJ/AG

Social Security No.:
[redacted]

Contacted another congressional office?
No

Court of Law?
No

Your Request

Dear Sir: I would appreciate assistance from you to secure a response to my February 23, 2016 correspondence with the DOJ and FBI (attached) which has gone unanswered. I would also appreciate assistance from you to secure a response to my attorney's follow up correspondence to the DOJ, FBI and Attorney General June 24, 2016 (attached) which has also gone unanswered. To date, no response has been received to either complaint from any of the entities to whom correspondence was sent. As explained in the attached correspondence, I have requested that these agencies extend their search term to go beyond "employees" as stated in our letters; and I also request that they extend their search to all sources, not limited to the electronic databases or index searches previously specified by them. In accordance with the Privacy Act of 1974, you and your staff are hereby authorized to freely discuss any and all aspects of my situation. I am now registered as a federal voter living overseas - former address 170 West 74th street NY NY 10023. My social security number ▓▓▓▓. My current postal address is John Wilson, ▓▓▓▓ Australia. Telephone number: ▓▓▓▓ Email address: ▓▓▓▓ I look forward to hearing from you. The most convenient means by which to correspond with me are through my attorney (details indicated above), alternatively you can reach me directly by phone in Sydney on ▓▓▓▓ Please copy all correspondence to me. Sincerely yours, John Wilson Attachments (sent to you via fax): 1. John Wilson letter February 23, 2016 sent to U.S. DOJ Inspector General with cc to the FBI, Inspection Division. Fax delivery confirmation included. 2. John Wilson's attorney Barry Fisher's letter June 24, 2016 sent to: Loretta Lynch, Attorney General; Michael E. Horowitz, Inspector General, Department of Justice; James B. Comey, Director, Federal Bureau of Investigation.

Charles E. SCHUMER
UNITED STATES SENATOR FOR NEW YORK

I authorize the Office of Senator Chuck Schumer to address the matter described above on my behalf and to receive any relevant information the Senator and his staff may need in their efforts to provide assistance to me:

Signature: _____ date: **February 08, 2017**
(Required)

Please complete and mail or fax this form to:

Senator Chuck Schumer
780 Third Avenue Suite 2301
New York, NY 10017
Fax: (202) 228-2838

[Privacy Act agreement for Senator Schumer Caseworker Request: John Wilson registered as a Federal Voter in NYC, currently living in Australia]

Name: John Wilson
Street Address: (Formerly) 170 West 70th St, Ap 806
City, State Zip: NY NY 10023
Email: ███

Senator Charles E. Schumer
780 Third Avenue, Suite 2301
New York, NY 10017

I am registered as a federal voter now living overseas.
███
Australia

Dear Senator Schumer:

In accordance with the Privacy Act of 1974, you and your staff are hereby authorized to freely discuss any and all aspects of my situation.

Sincerely,

Signature: [signed]

Date of Birth: ███
Social Security Number: ███
Home Telephone Number: ███

Do you currently have a case pending before a local, state, or federal court pertaining to this matter?
Yes ○   No ☑

John Christian Wilson
c/o Barry A. Fisher
Fleishman & Fisher
1925 Century Park East Suite 2000
Los Angeles, CA 90067

February 9, 2016

Senator Charles E. Schumer
United States Senate
757 Third Avenue
Suite 2301
New York, NY 10017

Via fax: (202) 228-2838

Dear Sir:

I would appreciate assistance from you to secure a response to my February 23, 2016 correspondence with the DOJ and FBI (attached) which has gone unanswered.

I would also appreciate assistance from you to secure a response to my attorney's follow up correspondence to the DOJ, FBI and Attorney General June 24, 2016 (attached) which has also gone unanswered.

To date, no response has been received to either complaint from any of the entities to whom correspondence was sent.

As explained in the attached correspondence, I have requested that these agencies extend their search term to go beyond "employees" as stated in our letters; and I also request that they extend their search to all sources, not limited to the electronic databases or index searches previously specified by them.

In accordance with the Privacy Act of 1974, you and your staff are hereby authorized to freely discuss any and all aspects of my situation.

I am now registered as a federal voter living overseas - former address 170 West 74th street NY NY 10023. My social security number is ▮▮▮▮▮. My current postal address is John Wilson, ▮▮▮▮▮ Australia. Telephone number: +▮▮▮▮▮ Email address: ▮▮▮▮▮

I look forward to hearing from you. The most convenient means by which to correspond with me are through my attorney (details indicated above), alternatively you can reach me directly by phone in Sydney on ▮▮▮▮▮

Please copy all correspondence to me.

1 of 2

Sincerely yours,

[signature]

John Wilson

Attachments:
1. John Wilson letter February 23, 2016 sent to U.S. DOJ Inspector General with cc to the FBI, Inspection Division. Fax delivery confirmation included.
2. John Wilson's attorney Barry Fisher's letter June 24, 2016 sent to: Loretta Lynch, Attorney General; Michael E. Horowitz, Inspector General, Department of Justice; James B. Comey, Director, Federal Bureau of Investigation.

CC: c/o Barry A. Fisher
Fleishman & Fisher
1925 Century Park East Suite 2000
Los Angeles, CA 90067

John C. Wilson   23 February 2016

[REDACTED]
Australia

Email: [REDACTED]

Michael D. McDonald,
Unit Chief
Initial Processing Unit,
Inspection Division
U.S. Department of Justice
Federal Bureau of Investigation
Room 3041,
935 Pennsylvania Avenue, NW
Washington, DC 20535-0001

RE: Complaint concerning FBI abuse

Dear Sir,

I write in response to the letter to me dated 9 February 2016 from Michael D. McDonald, Unit Chief, Initial Processing Unit, Inspection Division, U.S. Department of Justice, Federal Bureau of Investigation, Washington, D.C. concerning my complaint about FBI misconduct I originally sent to the DOJ, Office of the Inspector General dated 9 March 2015.

I am not satisfied with the FBI's response and request the search and investigation be extended. The FBI's response uses the term "employee" exclusively. I want to clarify that those referred to below I believe were working on behalf of the U.S. government, FBI and or other agencies as employees or in other capacities currently or in the past. I did not ask for or suggest that the search be limited solely to employees.

- Michael Mills: the FBI agent who moved into my apartment in NYC and occupied it for several years when I sublet it before my return to Australia.
- Kathleen Walton: former mining analyst at Merrill Lynch in NYC.
- Matthew Levey – Kroll Associates, Inc (New York City midtown office): consulting work case manager 2003 and 2004. Former State Department employee.
- Jeffrey S Robards: corporate finance, formerly Ernst & Young (E&Y) NYC. Now working for C.W. Downer & Co - a boutique M&A firm in Boston. (http://www.cwdowner.com/index.php?option=com_content&view=article&id=42&Itemid=23)
- Susan A. Holmes (formerly resident in New York City in the 1990s)
- Stephan Chenault and John Klotz: volunteers Sierra Club NYC Group since 1990s.
- Ben Worden, Rob Haggerty and Allison Dey (Tucson area): FBI agents involved with Diamond Mountain Buddhist group in southern Arizona and California.
- George Schneider and Livingston Sutro (Sierra Vista, AZ); Jennifer Conner (NYC): Associated with Diamond Mountain Buddhist group in southern Arizona.

- Paul Whitby (Tucson): biologist.
- Leigh Freeman – Cherry Creek, Denver based head hunter. Downing Teal. http://www.downingteal.com/Our-People/Downing-Teal-USA
- Robert Schultz – Albuquerque based head hunter. MRC Mining Search. http://www.miningsearch.com/mining-search/our-team/
- Steven D. Garber – (wife Andrea - collaborator) additional details: biologist; lived in Manhattan for much of the 1990s, before taking a two year posting to teach biology at Embry Riddle in Prescott, AZ before returning to the New York area (White Plains). Books authored include The Urban Naturalist (New York. John Wiley and Sons. 1987). PhD in Ecology, Environmental Sciences - Rutgers, The State University of New Jersey-Newark. B.S. in Natural Resources - Cornell University.

For clarification, the nature of my complaint concerning FBI misconduct which I reported in my letter to the DOJ dated 9 March 2015 and request be investigated concerns the FBI's abuse and unwarranted interference with me since 1996 following my report I authored on US mining company Freeport McMoran.

Thank you.

I look forward to your response.

Sincerely,

John Wilson

CC: U.S. Department of Justice
Office of the Inspector General
Investigations Division
950 Pennsylvania Avenue, N.W.
Suite 4706
Washington, D.C. 20530-0001

	FLEISHMAN & FISHER	
STANLEY FLEISHMAN (1920-1999)		*PROFESSIONAL CORPORATIONS
BARRY FISHER*	LAWYERS	ΔOF COUNSEL
DAVID GROSZΔ	1925 CENTURY PARK EAST, SUITE 2000	CABLE ADDRESS: ARJUNA
MICHAEL B. WEISZΔ	LOS ANGELES, CALIFORNIA 90067	EMAIL: BFSHR557@GMAIL.COM
HENRY W. McGEE, JR. Δ	(310) 557-1077 TELECOPIER (310) 557-0770	
WILLIAM M. KRAMER (1920-2004)		

June 24, 2016

Loretta Lynch, Attorney General By Fax: 202-514-4001/616-9881
Department of Justice
950 Pennsylvania Avenue N.W.
Washington, DC 20530-001

Michael E. Horowitz, Inspector General
Department of Justice
950 Pennsylvania Avenue N.W.
Washington, DC 20530

James B. Comey, Director
Federal Bureau of Investigation
935 Pennsylvania Avenue, NW
Washington, D.C. 20535-0001

Re: John C. Wilson:

I represent John C. Wilson who has previously written requesting investigation and clarification regarding personally impacting conduct of persons he has reason to believe were operating on behalf of the F.B.I. or other element of the DOJ. Response was sent to him stating the persons involved were not "employees" of the Department but not addressing the question whether they operated on its behalf.

Mr. Wilson's 23 February 2016 letter, attached, in follow up has not been answered except to tell him that the F.B.I. is the agency of the DOJ he should be be addressing. The F.B.I. has not responded.

I write in hopes that this long standing request can now be address definitely.

Sincerely yours,

Barry A. Fisher

* * * *

* * * *

Exhibit 69: *15 March 2017.   Letter from John Wilson to Senator Schumer re Casework Request.*

```
                    TRANSMISSION VERIFICATION REPORT

                                        TIME   : 15/03/2017 10:19
                                        NAME   :
                                        FAX    :
                                        SER.#  : BROB0F268975

        DATE,TIME              15/03  10:18
        FAX NO./NAME           001112022283027
        DURATION               00:00:35
        PAGE(S)                01
        RESULT                 OK
        MODE                   STANDARD
```

Sydney, Australia
Tel: +
Email:

facsimile transmittal

To:	Senator Schumer	Fax:	1 (202) 228-3027
		Tel:	1 (202) 224-6542 (DC)
			1 (212) 486-4430 (NYC)
From:	John Wilson	Date:	3/15/2017
Re:	DOJ/FBI/AG follow up	Pages:	(including header) 1
	Casework request # 186451C		
CC:			

☐ Urgent   ☐ For Review   ☐ Please Comment   ☐ Please Reply   ☐ Please Recycle

Dear Senator Schumer,

I am a constituent registered as a federal voter in NYC. I submitted a casework request to your office 8 February 2017 and was informed 22 February 2017 it has been assigned case number #186451C.

I have been unable to ascertain from the NYC office handling my case its status. Neither I, nor my attorney, despite numerous attempts have been unable to get through by phone to reach the assigned caseworker or supervisor in NYC. Nor have my email enquiries (confirmed received at casework_schumer@schumer.senate.gov) been answered in which I requested a status update. Would it be possible to provide me a status update please (by return email to

Sydney, Australia
Tel: +
Email:

facsimile transmittal

To:	Senator Schumer	Fax:	1 (202) 228-3027
		Tel:	1 (202) 224-6542 (DC)
			1 (212) 486-4430 (NYC)
From:	John Wilson	Date:	3/15/2017
Re:	DOJ/FBI/AG follow up: Casework request # 186451C	Pages:	(including header) 1
CC:			

☐ Urgent ☐ For Review ☐ Please Comment ☐ Please Reply ☐ Please Recycle

Dear Senator Schumer,

I am a constituent registered as a federal voter in NYC. I submitted a casework request to your office 8 February 2017 and was informed 22 Februrary 2017 it has been assigned case number #186451C.

I have ben unable to ascertain from the NYC office handling my case its status. Neither I, nor my attorney, despite numerous attempts have been unable to get through by phone to reach the assigned caseworker or supervisor in NYC. Nor have my email enquiries (confirmed received at casework_schumer@schumer.senate.gov) been answered in which I requested a status update. Would it be possible to provide me a status update please (by return email to johnwilson@rcresearch.net); and if there is a specific person to speak to provide a full name and direct phone number.

Thank you.

Sincerely,

John Wilson

* * * * *

* * * * *

Email Trail with Senator Schumer's staffers, NYC – 2017-2021.
Seeking Senator Schumer's assistance with DOJ/FBI accountability.

Exhibit 70: *2017-2021.   Email trail: John Wilson, Attorney Barry Fisher and Senator Schumer.*

2017

On Thu, Feb 9, 2017 at 12:35 PM, John Wilson <johnwilson@rcresearch.net> wrote:

Hi Barry,

I have sent a fax to Schumer (attached) requesting assistance from a case worker to get a response to your letters, and mine, sent to the DOJ/FBI and AG.

Regards.

John

John Wilson

Managing Director

Resource Capital Research
www.rcresearch.com.au
T +61 x xxxx xxxx (SYD)

* * * * *

From: Barry Fisher [mailto:xxxxxxxx@gmail.com]
Sent: Friday, 10 February 2017 7:42 AM
To: John Wilson
Subject: Re: Schumer request

looks good John. he is now senate minority leader and should be listened to. Barry

* * * * *

From: John Wilson
Sent: Friday, February 10, 2017 7:55 AM

To: 'Barry Fisher' <xxxxxxxx@gmail.com>
Subject: RE: Schumer request

Let's see how responsive Schumer's staff are. I may need you to follow up with them at some point.

John Wilson

Managing Director

Resource Capital Research
www.rcresearch.com.au
T +61 x xxxx xxxx (SYD)

* * * * *

From: John Wilson mailto:johnwilson@rcresearch.net
Sent: Thursday, 23 February 2017 10:18 AM
To: 'casework_schumer@schumer.senate.gov'
Subject: John Wilson Case # 186451C

ATTN: Angela

Hi Angela,

I understand you are the caseworker assigned my case - # 186451C - request for assistance for a response to my letter, and my attorney's letter, to the FBI, DOJ, and attorney general.

Are you able to give me an update please on the status of my case?

Thank you.

Best regards.

John Wilson

Managing Director

Resource Capital Research
www.rcresearch.com.au
T +61 x xxxx xxxx (SYD)

* * * * *

From: John Wilson
Sent: Saturday, February 25, 2017 8:53 AM

To: 'casework_schumer@schumer.senate.gov' <casework_schumer@schumer.senate.gov>
Subject: ATTN:Angela - Case # 186451C

Hi Angela,

Is it possible to provide a status update on my case please (#186451C) to let me know if you have, or will, send correspondence to the agencies concerned or indicate the nature of the assistance you may be able to offer.

Thank you.

Regards.

John Wilson

Managing Director

RCR
Resource Capital Research
www.rcresearch.com.au
T +61 x xxxx xxxx (SYD)

* * * * *

From: John Wilson
Sent: Tuesday, February 28, 2017 1:33 PM
To: 'Barry Fisher' <xxxxxxxx@gmail.com>
Subject: FW: Schumer request

Hi Barry,

Would you or Adrianne be able to contact Schumer's staff in NY and assess the progress of my complaint. I can rarely get through to them - their phone normally rings out towards the end of the day when I am able to call. They confirmed a case office had been assigned when I spoke to the switch board about 1 week ago - but I haven't been able to speak to the person directly (Angela).

My case number is 186451C; case officer is Angela; NYC switch tel 212 486 4430.

I would like confirmation from her that she has sent correspondence to each of the agencies we sent letters to and that she has requested that they respond to us/Schumer.

Thanks Barry.

John Wilson

Managing Director

RCR
Resource Capital Research
www.rcresearch.com.au
T +61 x xxxx xxxx (SYD)

* * * * *

From: John Wilson [mailto:johnwilson@rcresearch.net]
Sent: Wednesday, 1 March 2017 3:01 PM
To: 'casework_schumer@schumer.senate.gov'
Cc: 'Barry Fisher'
Subject: FW: ATTN:Angela - Case # 186451C

ATTN: Angela

Hi Angela,

Barry Fisher, my attorney, will give you a call Wednesday to discuss my case.

Thank you.

Best regards.

John

John Wilson

Managing Director

RCR
Resource Capital Research
www.rcresearch.com.au
T +61 x xxxx xxxx (SYD)

* * * * *

From: Barry Fisher <xxxxxxxx@gmail.com>
Sent: Wednesday, March 1, 2017 3:41 AM
To: John Wilson
Subject: Re: FW: Schumer request

just tried calling at 11:40 am new york time--phone number rang and rang, no pick up, no answer machine. have another number?

* * * * *

On Thu, Mar 2, 2017 at 12:41 PM, John Wilson johnwilson@rcresearch.net wrote:

Hi Barry,

Any luck getting through to Schumer's office? Is this something Adrianne might persist with on a daily basis till she gets through to Angela?

Thanks and regards.

John

John Wilson

Managing Director

Resource Capital Research
www.rcresearch.com.au
T +61 x xxxx xxxx (SYD)

* * * * *

From: Barry Fisher [mailto:xxxxxxxx@gmail.com]
Sent: Friday, 3 March 2017 8:50 AM
To: John Wilson
Subject: Re: FW: ATTN:Angela - Case # 186451C

called number you gave me last week, no answer, no machine to leave message. what number should I use to call angela?

* * * * *

From: John Wilson
Sent: Tuesday, March 7, 2017 8:38 AM
To: 'Barry Fisher' <xxxxxxxx@gmail.com>
Subject: schumer

Hi Barry,

I spoke to schumer's office, but Angela was not available. She has responded to non of the emails, not taken any of my calls.

Would you email her and cc me perhaps?

Regards.

John

John Wilson

Managing Director

Resource Capital Research
www.rcresearch.com.au
T +61 x xxxx xxxx (SYD)

* * * * *

On Thu, Mar 9, 2017 at 3:08 PM, John Wilson johnwilson@rcresearch.net wrote:

Hi Barry,

Any luck getting through to Schumer? Will you keep trying? Maybe the office has a manager we can speak to? Alternatively, is it worth you approaching your senator in CA requesting assistance for a response. After all the agencies have not responded to your letters either - something your rep may be able to rectify, even if mine won't.

Could we agree to a firm plan Barry - as otherwise I feel this matter is not getting the attention and push it needs: If we don't hear from the agencies by March 22 in response to the issues raised in our letters, that we commence legal proceedings to force a response. Are you onboard with this approach, or suggest alternative please.

Thanks and regards.

John

John Wilson

Managing Director

Resource Capital Research
www.rcresearch.com.au
T +61 x xxxx xxxx (SYD)

* * * * *

From: Barry Fisher [mailto:xxxxxxxx@gmail.com]
Sent: Saturday, 11 March 2017 3:09 AM
To: John Wilson
Subject: Re: FW: ATTN:Angela - Case # 186451C

tried both new york and washington phone numbers multiple times today. sometimes after waiting line disconnected, few times message try later, one time after waiting got a ring to an office then went dead. suggest you try a fax to following washington schumer number: (*202*) 228-3027 just say you are constituent, that provided information, given a case number(list date or about when given this number) but unable to get thru by phone to reach anyone at NY or DC offices to find out status. if there is a specific person to speak to what full name and direct phone number.   worth trying this. maybe don't refer to angela but focus on inquiry, case number and inability to reach anyone by phone or even to know who exactly working on it and a direct number given extreme difficulty to get thru to any main office number by phone.

* * * * *

On Tue, Mar 14, 2017 at 5:41 PM, John Wilson <johnwilson@rcresearch.net> wrote:

Hi Barry,

I assume you have had no further luck getting through to NYC office. I sent the attached fax as you suggested to DC. Fax and confirmation attached.

If still no response, I would like to commence litigation against fbi/doj forthwith. Can you tell me what will be involved with this, and cost. I intend to proceed with this next week.

Thanks and regards.

John

John Wilson

Managing Director

RCR
Resource Capital Research
www.rcresearch.com.au
T +61 x xxxx xxxx (SYD)

* * * * *

From: Barry Fisher [mailto:xxxxxxxx@gmail.com]
Sent: Wednesday, 15 March 2017 12:46 PM

To: John Wilson
Subject: Re: FW: ATTN:Angela - Case # 186451C

let me know if anything happens with fax

* * * * *

* * * * *

2019

Exhibit 71: *1 March 2019.   Emails: John Wilson and Senator Schumer's office re OGIS.*

From: John Wilson [mailto:jxxxxxxxxxxx@bigpond.com]
Sent: Friday, 1 March 2019 8:03 AM
To: 'casework_schumer@schumer.senate.gov'
Subject: John Wilson - casework; ATTN: Susan

ATTN: Susan - casework

Hi Susan,

I just left a voice message for you re OGIS. (I faxed a follow up request for casework assistance to your office dated 17 January 2019 in relation to OGIS). OGIS shut down my request for mediation assistance to the FBI in which I requested assistance to obtain my files/records/etc - both general held by the agency and also I mentioned in my request details pertaining to a specific event from about 20 years' ago in NYC. OGIS shut my case (case number 2017-03007) after making me wait nearly 2 years for an answer from OGIS without making any representation to the FBI or offering me any mediation regards access to my files/records/etc.

I would appreciate assistance from you in approaching OGIS to request they keep my case open and make due representations on my behalf to the FBI to release the requested items to me under FOI.

I am based in Sydney Australia, and am registered as a Federal Voter in NYC. The easiest way to contact me is via reply email.

Thank you.

Best regards.

John Wilson

* * * * *

From: John Wilson [mailto:jxxxxxxxxxxx@bigpond.com]
Sent: Saturday, 2 March 2019 9:08 AM
To: 'casework_schumer@schumer.senate.gov'
Subject: FW: John Wilson - casework; ATTN: Susan

Hi Susan,

Could you please confirm receipt of below? Will you be able to follow up on this - would you like me to give you a call to discuss any questions you might have?

Thank you.

Best regards.

John Wilson

* * * * *

From: John Wilson <mailto:jxxxxxxxxxxxx@bigpond.com>
Sent: Thursday, 7 March 2019 10:38 AM
To: 'casework_schumer@schumer.senate.gov'
Subject: FW: John Wilson - casework; ATTN: Susan - re OGIS (case number 2017-03007)

Hi Susan,

I have tried a number of times to reach you by phone (and email) but have not been able to reach you. Most of the time the call to the NYC office reception rings out and goes straight to voicemail.

Could you please confirm re the below whether this is a case you will assist with by following up with OGIS on my behalf, or if it is something you will not be assisting with. Please let me know either way so that I can consider in an informed way what my best options may be for attempting to move things forward with OGIS/FBI.

Thank you.

Regards.

John Wilson

* * * * *

From: John Wilson <mailto:jxxxxxxxxxxxx@bigpond.com>
Sent: Saturday, 9 March 2019 9:09 AM
To: 'casework_schumer@schumer.senate.gov'
Subject: FW: John Wilson - casework; ATTN: Susan - re OGIS (case number 2017-03007)

Hi Susan,

I spoke to your office today and they indicated my request for assistance was incomplete and asked me to send in a separate privacy waiver form. Please find the original fax submission confirmation 17 Jan 2019 attached and separate privacy waiver signed and attached 9 March 2019.

Please acknowledge receipt and confirm if you will be able to assist me.

Thank you.

Regards.

John Wilson

* * * * *

From: John Wilson <jxxxxxxxxxxxx@bigpond.com>
Sent: Monday, March 25, 2019 7:26 PM
To: Schumer,Casework (Schumer) <Casework_Schumer@schumer.senate.gov>
Subject: FW: John Wilson - casework; ATTN: Susan - re OGIS (case number 2017-03007)

Hi Susan,

I have been unable to contact your office by phone despite several attempts over the past week - your phone keeps ringing into voicemail at the main reception.

Could you confirm by reply email what action you may take on my behalf re the below OGIS complaint/assistance please so I know whether your office is assisting me with this or not. Otherwise I have no way of knowing if it is being acted upon, and in a timely manner.

Thank you for your understanding.

Best regards.

John Wilson

* * * * *

From: Orlove, Suzan (Schumer) <Suzan_Orlove@schumer.senate.gov> **On Behalf Of** Schumer,Casework (Schumer)
Sent: Wednesday, March 27, 2019 3:05 AM
To: John Wilson
Subject: RE: John Wilson - casework; ATTN: Susan - re OGIS (case number 2017-03007)

We will not be taking any action.

* * * * *

IV-4 Correspondence 2020 to 2023

IV-4a   Correspondence 2020 to 2023

FBI/DOJ

* * * * *

Exhibit 72: *5 June 2020.   Letter from Attorney Barry Fisher to FBI, Director Wray.*

[cc'd to Rep Jerrold Nadler, Michael Horowitz – IG, DOJ, Sen. Schumer, William Barr – US Attorney General, White House].

STANLEY FLEISHMAN (1920-1999)
BARRY FISHER*
DAVID GROSZ△
MICHAEL B. WEISZ△
HENRY W. McGEE, JR. △
WILLIAM M. KRAMER (1920-2004)

FLEISHMAN & FISHER
LAWYERS
1925 CENTURY PARK EAST, SUITE 2000
LOS ANGELES, CALIFORNIA 90067
(310) 557-1077 TELECOPIER (310) 557-0770

*PROFESSIONAL CORPORATIONS
△OF COUNSEL
CABLE ADDRESS: ARJUNA
EMAIL: BFSHR557@GMAIL.COM

June 5, 2020

Christopher Wray, Director
Federal Bureau of Investigation
935 Pennsylvania Avenue, N.W.
Washington, D.C. 20535-0001

Re: John C. Wilson

Dear Director Wray:

This firm represents John C. Wilson regarding the conduct of persons causing him harm he has reason to believe were operating on behalf of the FBI. or other element of the United States Department of Justice(DOJ). A history of correspondence over some 3 years resulted solely in a disclaimer that the persons involved were neither F.B.I. special agents nor employees but neither addressed nor denied to date is whether they operated on behalf of the FBI or other DOJ element. The most recent non-response is the 21 March 2020 DOJ - FOIA request denial.

The details at issue are set out in letters I wrote to the US Attorney General, Inspector General of the DOJ, and Director of the FBI June 24, 2016 attaching Mr. Wilson's 23 February 2016 letter, in follow up has not been answered except to tell him that the F.B.I. is the agency of the DOJ he should be addressing. The FBI has not responded.

The crux of Mr. Wilson's complaint is that false intelligence has been disseminated against him by the FBI in the U.S. to partnering agencies in the U.S. and overseas. This follows a work report he published as a Wall Street mining analyst working for SG Warburg (precursor to UBS Warburg) on US mining company Freeport McMoran March 12, 1996 that at the time was under investigation by the State Department following credible and widely reported allegations it was involved in the killing of indigenous protestors at its Grasberg mine in West Papua, Indonesia. He has been denied official acknowledgment of, or access to, any of the FBI's assertions, let alone test any of their claims in court, due to excessive secrecy around what they do. As such, he has endured a deprivation of basic human rights over a period now spanning more than 20 years.

Since then, Mr Wilson has been subjected to a systematic retaliation campaign by persons associated with the FBI involving invasive and aggressive tactics that include targeting his employment, professional, and social networks.

Susan Holmes engendered a personal relationship with Mr. Wilson for 3 years in NYC from 1994 to 1997 during which time she showed him what purported to be her FBI card and made multiple personal disclosures about her work to him. After Mr Wilson's Freeport work note was published 12 March 1996, the FBI commenced interference and disruption tactics across all aspects of his life - professional, social and family networks, surveillance and other intrusions into his life. Descriptions of the FBI intrusions are in the enclosed document "John Wilson Abridged Notes June 2020". This includes details of Susan Holmes' work purporting to be on behalf of the FBI; an overview of a long covert FBI dinner interview in NYC 2003 in which many personal details and personal records spanning many decades and diverse locations from Mr. Wilson's life were revealed (Mr Wilson's transcript of this interview is available upon request); assertions of false intelligence arise from comments made by the FBI and concern the apparent association of Mr Wilson though agent Susan Holmes' work for the FBI with David Foreman, a high profile eco-activist.

In the years following the 1996 publication regarding the Freeport McMoran killings, he had many other contacts with people who at some point revealed themselves as FBI agents and who let him know that he angered important people by the publication. Some of these individuals engendered friendship with him under the auspices of other professional identities and each has interviewed him, two of them extensively, in addition to Susan Holmes' extensive NYC covert interview in 2003. These include- Steven Garber, formerly of New York City, and Livingston Sutro, formerly of Sierra Vista, Arizona.

Aside from these apparent DOJ agents, more than a dozen other people have identified themselves to him as having a high level of familiarity with these circumstances and appear to be FBI agents or associated with agents. A partial list of names of agents has been provided to the FBI and DOJ in the past (the February 23, 2016 letter with list is attached).

The serious allegations of FBI misconduct in this matter have never been investigated, nor has there ever been a response concerning the correct roles of the agents named.

I write to request this matter be thoroughly investigated and hope that this long standing request can now be addressed definitively.

Sincerely yours,

Barry A. Fisher

Christopher Wray, Director
Federal Bureau of Investigation,
935 Pennsylvania Avenue, N.W.
Washington, D.C. 20535-0001

Congressman Jerrold Nadler
2132 Rayburn HOB
Washington, D.C. 20535

White House
600 Pennsylvania Avenue
Washington, D.C. 20530

Michael Evan Horowitz
Inspector General
Department of Justice
950 Pennsylvania Avenue, N.W.
Washington, D.C. 20530-0001

Senator Charles Schumer
Leo O'Brien Building
Room 420
Albay, NY 12207

William P. Barr
Attorney General
Department of Justice
950 Pennsylvania Avenue, N.W.
Washington, D.C. 20530-0001

* * * * *

Exhibit 73: *26 June 2020.   Letter from FBI to Attorney Barry Fisher.*

U.S. Department of Justice

Federal Bureau of Investigation

Washington, D.C. 20535-0001

June 26, 2020

Mr. Barry A Fisher
1925 Century Park East
Suite 2000
Los Angeles, CA 90067

Dear Mr. Fisher:

　　This letter is in response to your communication which was forwarded to the Federal Bureau of Investigation (FBI), Inspection Division (INSD), Internal Affairs Section (IAS), Initial Processing Unit (IPU). The IAS/INSD is the FBI entity responsible for investigating allegations of misconduct or criminal activity on the part of FBI employees.

　　IAS/IPU has reviewed your complaint and has determined an Internal Affairs investigation by the FBI is not warranted. This matter was provided to the United States Department of Justice, Office of the Inspector General for its review and any action deemed appropriate. IAS/IPU will take no further action in this matter.

Sincerely,

Initial Processing Unit
Internal Affairs Section
Inspection Division

* * * *

Exhibit 74: *18 March 2022.   Letter from John Wilson to US Attorney General Garland.*

Attorney General
Merrick B. Garland
U.S. Department of Justice
950 Pennsylvania Avenue, NW
Washington, DC 20530-0001

Department of Justice Main Switchboard: 202-514-2000

March 18, 2022

Dear Sir,

RE: FBI abuse of John Wilson SS#

My complaint to you concerns FBI abuse. The details are summarized in the below statement of facts prepared November 2021 by my NYC based lawyer, David Rankin for a separate matter concerning an FOIA lawsuit I am taking against the FBI. The issues summarized below contained in my affidavit concerns FBI abuses and are the subject of my request to you for assistance, however are not themselves the subject of any court case. The affidavit is publicly available and provides more detail of the abuses (attached).

The FBI and DOJ/Inspector General have repeatedly failed to deal with my complaint by stating that the people I complained about are not "employees" even though they are operating on behalf of the FBI in some other official capacity, such as independent contractor or such like. At least one of the individuals complained about, Susan Holmes, carries a black background FBI identity card confirming her identity and authority to act on behalf of the FBI.

With your assistance I would like your office to launch an investigation into the details of the FBI's misconduct in this matter.

Statement of facts: Mr. Wilson is a former Wall Street mining analyst who served as an employee of SG Warburg from 1994 to 1997. Affidavit of John Wilson (Wilson), Declaration of Katherine Q Adams (Adams) Exh. A., at ¶ 4. In March of 1996, Mr. Wilson authored a report (the Report) that flagged concerns about the U.S. based mining company Freeport McMoran, including that the company was under investigation by the United States Department of State following the deaths of indigenous protestors at its Grasberg Mine in West Papua, Indonesia, among other human rights concerns. Wilson at ¶ 9; the Report, Wilson Exh. A. The 1996 allegations against Freeport McMoran were of significant interest to the U.S. government, as demonstrated by documents produced by the U.S. State Department (DOS) in 2014 in response to a FOIA request not presently at issue in the instant case. Wilson at 10, see also 2014 DOS FOIA Request and Subsequent Production on the Grasberg Mine, Wilson Exh. B.

Following the publication of Mr. Wilson s report, Mr. Wilson experienced a campaign of interference and harassment by individuals who identified themselves as working for the FBI, which was eventually a factor in Mr. Wilson s moving away from the United States following interference with his employment, social and professional networks, and privacy. Wilson at ¶14.

The individuals representing themselves to Mr. Wilson as working with or on behalf of the FBI gave Mr. Wilson the strong impression, and even directly told him on one occasion, that he was the subject of an FBI investigation due to the Report. Wilson at ¶¶ 38, 43, 51, and 52. One of the individuals subjected Mr. Wilson to intense questioning and represented that the interview was being undertaken at the behest of a U.S. government agency. Wilson at ¶¶ 54-55. The individual had a large amount of detailed private information on Mr. Wilson that suggested extensive research and investigation beyond the capacity of an individual in the late 1990s and early 2000s. Wilson at ¶ 97.

I am a dual citizen of Australia and USA. My SS# is ▇▇▇▇, and I currently reside at ▇▇▇▇ ▇▇▇▇, Australia. I am registered as a Federal Voter at my former address Apt 906, 170 West 74th Street, New York, NY 10023. My preferred means of communication is via email and I can be reached at ▇▇▇▇.

I look forward to your response.

Thank you.

Sincerely yours,

John Wilson

▇▇▇▇
Australia

[I am registered as a Federal Voter at my former address:
Apt 906, 170 West 74th Street,
New York, NY 10023]

* * * * *

IV-4b   Correspondence 2020 to 2023

Senator Charles Schumer

* * * * *

Email Trail with Senator Schumer's staffers, NYC – 2021-2022

Exhibit 75: *2021-2022.   Various emails between John Wilson, attorneys and Senator Schumer.*

2021

* * * * *

On Mon, Nov 22, 2021 at 2:27 PM John Wilson <jxxxxxxxxxxx@bigpond.com> wrote:

Hi Barry,

I've been thinking about going back to Schumer and Nadler with the affidavit, etc - I think it does a good job of setting out the various issues and concerns about the FBI's conduct in this matter.

I don't see what the benefit might be of waiting for the government's response - I suspect it will continue to be evasive and string us along for time. Irrespective of whether it does or doesn't, if it concedes anything I'm sure it will be minimal and in its own interest. Going to Schumer and Nadler, in the best case, could see more pressure applied, independence - at least potentially get the wheels of that process in motion; and in the worst case I'm not sure what harm it does - I could update them with the government's response in due course.

What do you think? I am happy to pay you to take this next step now if you feel the timing is appropriate.

Best regards.

John

* * * * *

From: Barry Fisher <xxxxxxxx@gmail.com>
Sent: Tuesday, November 23, 2021 1:59 PM
To: John Wilson
Subject: Re: Schumer and Nadler

could make sense to consider any modification of the declaration based on the gov response which would mean some, but given the history and longevity of the dispute, might really be worth it. consider it.b

* * * * *

2022

[At the suggestion of Barry Fisher I retained an FOIA attorney, David Rankin of BLHNY, who represented me in my first FOIA lawsuit against the FBI – circa 2020-2022. The emails below are background to further outreach to Senator Schumer's office outlining the political nature of the FBI/DOJ's abusive conduct and "bad faith" conduct in this matter forwarding my Declaration and select other material from the FOIA case.]

* * * * *

From: Katherine "Q" Adams <QAdams@BLHNY.COM>
Sent: Saturday, 22 January 2022 2:32 AM
To: John Wilson <jxxxxxxxxxxxx@bigpond.com>
Cc: David B. Rankin <DRankin@BLHNY.COM>
Subject: Defendant's Reply to Summary Judgment

Mr. Wilson,

We received Defendant's reply papers to the summary judgment motion; please find them attached. We will draft a reply and file it to the docket on February 3.

I can also confirm that we did receive the hard copy of your declaration. Thank you again for sending it.

Best,

Q

Q Adams (She/Her/Hers) | Associate
Beldock Levine & Hoffman LLP
99 Park Avenue, PH/26th Fl. | New York, NY 10016
Tel: (212) 277-5824 | Fax: (212) 277-5880
QAdams@blhny.com | http://www.blhny.com

* * * * *

On Fri, Jan 21, 2022 at 1:36 PM John Wilson <jxxxxxxxxxxxx@bigpond.com> wrote: [Time difference between Sydney and NYC and LA account for the apparent email date and time stamp discrepancies]

Hi Barry,

Attached is the FBI's response. {FOIA judicial review of FOIA]

I will forward you my comments to David Rankin. What do you think we should do from here – it seems there is no quick fix. It may be time now to go back to Schumer with my affidavit etc and ask for his assistance – is that something you could again assist with preparing if you think it appropriate?

Thanks and regards.

John

* * * * *

From: Barry Fisher <xxxxxxxx@gmail.com>
Sent: Saturday, 22 January 2022 1:20 PM
To: John Wilson <jxxxxxxxxxxx@bigpond.com>
Subject: Re: FW: Defendant's Reply to Summary Judgment

try to get your lawyers to send a draft of their brief and to send it to you with enough time for you to comment and for them to take your comments into account. very important

* * * * *

From: John Wilson <jxxxxxxxxxxx@bigpond.com>
Sent: Wednesday, January 26, 2022 9:16 AM
To: 'Barry Fisher' <xxxxxxx@gmail.com>
Subject: RE: FW: Defendant's Reply to Summary Judgment

Thanks Barry. I've asked them for what you suggest below and also to update me on the significance of the FBI's filing last week. Unfortunately, I don't get much feedback from David and have heard nothing in response concerning the FBI's filing nor anything about our strategy to reply.

Irrespective, I think this may now be a good time to go back to Schumer and Nadler, and/or others. What do you think and would you be available to prepare a cover letter in follow up with them (I assume we would attach my affidavit and any other relevant supporting documents). Let me know and an estimate of the fees and I can transfer the funds.

Thanks and regards.

John

* * * * *

From: Dennis-Intern, Alexus (Schumer) <Alexus_Dennis-Intern@schumer.senate.gov>
Sent: Wednesday, 20 April 2022 12:35 AM
To: johnwilson@rcresearch.com.au
Subject: Inquiry Update

Good morning Mr. Wilson,

Thank you for contacting the office of U.S. Senator Charles Schumer in regards to your request for assistance.

While we sympathize with the circumstances you have described, with respect to such matters, we are unable to intervene. Due to the nature of your problem, it appears that an attorney would be better equipped to assess the legal implications of the issues involved. If you have not done so already, we suggest that you consult a private attorney or your local legal services agency for assistance.

We hope that your situation is resolved in a timely and judicious manner.

Best regards,

OFFICE OF SENATOR CHARLES E. SCHUMER

780 Third Ave, Suite 2301

New York, NY 10017

Phone: (212) 486-4430 Fax: (202) 228-2838

* * * * *

From: john wilson@rcresearch.com.au <johnwilson@rcresearch.com.au>
Sent: Wednesday, 20 April 2022 9:38 AM
To: 'Dennis-Intern, Alexus (Schumer)' <Alexus_Dennis-Intern@schumer.senate.gov>
Subject: RE: Inquiry Update

Hi Alexus,

Thanks for your email.

The issue is the DOJ/FBI has not responded to my letters, nor those of my already appointed private attorney, to confirm that the people I named, (and who in cases confirmed to me they work for the FBI, including showing me ID), and who have been interfering with me, are indeed working on behalf of the FBI. It is a question of official accountability at this stage. Despite various attempts by me and my attorney to have the DOJ/FBI definitely confirm this, they obfuscate or avoid answering the question. In doing so, they deny me the evidence I need to commence legal action. Without this confirmation, I cannot start legal action. Hence my approach to Senator Schumer, and through him the Senate Judiciary Committee, to have the agencies definitively clarify their relationship to the people I have named. The power to compel the agencies to respond resides in political oversight. I do not, nor does the legal system, hold that power. It is a question of holding the executive accountable at this stage.

I hope you will be able to follow up on my request to have the DOJ/FBI to respond and confirm what their relationship is to the people I have named in the correspondence (attached). The DOJ/FBI has merely said the people named are not "employees" or "special agents", but they have not addressed if they work for them in some other capacity, such as for example, but not limited to, independent contractors. The attached letters, from myself and my attorney, clearly set out the issue at hand. [Email attachments (included elsewhere in this volume): Letter from attorney Barry Fisher to the FBI 5 June 2020; letter from Barry Fisher to the US Attorney General Lynch, DOJ Inspector general Horowitz; and FBI Director Comey, 24 June 2016; letter from John Wilson to FBI 23 February 2016].

Thank you. I look forward to your response.

Best regards.

John Wilson

* * * * *

From: John Wilson ████████████
Sent: Tuesday, May 3, 2022 8:35 AM
To: 'Schumer,Casework (Schumer)' <Casework_Schumer@schumer.senate.gov>
Subject: FW: Inquiry Update

Hi Alexus,

I have not heard back from you re the below. Do you have a manager I could take this up with - could you let me know their contact details please.

I think you have misunderstood the nature of the matter I requested help with from the Senator. To reiterate, I have had a long term problem with a federal agency, the FBI/DOJ that has repeatedly failed to respond, or nor responded, to the question asked about the status of people who claim to represent the agency. The agency is meant to clarify the relationship they have to these people, but it refuses to do so.

I see from other representatives websites this is a standard constituent request for help with a non-responsive, or slow to respond, federal agency, and for which caseworkers are employed to handle such requests. You have not explained why you will not assist me with what I think is my reasonable request for help, and hence I would like clarification, and hopefully rectification, by your manager. While there are others representatives I can potentially turn to going forward who may be more responsive, I have approached Senator Schumer in the first instance and would appreciate your help or understanding what aspect of my request lies outside your standard requirements for constituent assistance.

Thank you. I look forward to your reply.

Sincerely,

John Wilson

Registered as a Federal Voter,

Formerly domiciled at:

Apartment 906,

170 West 74th Street,

New York, NY 10023-2354

* * * * *

IV-4c Correspondence 2020 to 2023

Senator Kirsten Gillibrand

* * * * *

Exhibit 76: *25 May 2022.   Online Caseworker Request from John Wilson to Senator Gillibrand.*

Help With A Federal Agency | May 25 2022 05:05:38 | Wilson, John - 1 of 2

Case Authorization and Privacy Release Form

The Privacy Act of 1974 is a federal law designed to protect you from any unauthorized use or exchange of personal information by federal agencies. Any information that a federal agency has on file regarding your dealings with the United States Government may not (with limited exceptions) be given to another agency or Member of Congress without your written permission.

Your Information

Name:
Mr. John Wilson

Address:
170 West 74th Street, #906 New York, NY 10023

DOB: [redacted]

SSN: [redacted]

Gender:
Male

Email: [redacted]

Alt Phone: [redacted]

Request Details

What can I assist you with
Other

Request Details

Do you currently have a case pending before a local, state, or federal court pertaining to this matter?
No

Please briefly explain your problem
RE: FBI/DOJ I am registered as a Federal Voter formerly residing at 170 West 74th Street, NY, NY 10023 (and currently reside in Sydney at [redacted] Australia). I was a securities analyst working for an investment bank covering the mining sector on Wall Street in the 1990s. One of the companies I followed was NYSE listed US mining company Freeport McMoran which at the time was under investigation following eye witness reports it was involved with the killing, and other human rights abuses, of indigenous protestors at its massive Grasberg copper and gold mine in West Papua, Indonesia. After writing a report that touched on this and later asking the company's chairman a question about it, I found I had the FBI breathing down my back, a matter subsequently confirmed by two FBI agents - Steve Garber and my long term friend Susan Holmes. Based on what they told me, and some of the things I experienced, including threats made to me around the time the report was published, I believe the FBI has set me up in retribution to make it appear as though I am an environmental extremist, or at least associate with people who are, or have been, considered environmental extremists by the FBI. These comprise people introduced to me by Holmes, as her FBI targets Paul Winter and David Foreman, among others, people whom I had no contact with otherwise. I have since experienced gross interference with my professional and social networks, intrusive surveillance, and violation of my personal privacy amongst other things. There are two things you may be able to do to assist me. The first is I seek help with getting a response from the DOJ/FBI to my allegations of their retribution and intrusions into my life, as confirmed by two of its agents, namely Steve Garber and

Help With A Federal Agency | May 25 2022 05:05:38 | Wilson, John - 2 of 2

Susan Holmes. I sent the Attorney General, Merrick B. Garland a letter via email 18 March 2022 outlining the details and circumstances of my allegations and requested his office investigate the alleged FBI misconduct. To date, the Attorney General has not responded to my letter and I would appreciate your help in obtaining an explanation from him in which the substance of my complaint is addressed. The second way you may assist me is to refer this matter to the Senate Judiciary Committee for investigation. I will forward you the emailed letter I sent to the AG 18 March 2022 - to casework@gillibrand.senate.gov. I thank you respectfully for your assistance in advance. Best regards. John Wilson

---

I hereby request the assistance of Senator Kirsten Gillibrand. I authorize Senator Gillibrand and her staff to make inquiries into my personal records and/or files as necessary to assist me in the matter that I have presented to her office. The information I have provided is true and accurate to the best of my knowledge.

Signature: _____ Date: 25 / May 2022

Please sign, date, and return this form to my office:

E-mail: casework@gillibrand.senate.gov
Fax: 866-824-6340
Mail: Office of US Senator Kirsten Gillibrand
780 Third Avenue, 2601
New York, NY 10017

Please feel free to attach additional information and documentation and instead: Add: If there are <u>relevant</u> documents that you feel are necessary to support your request, you may also send them to my office.

[Note: In 2022, Senator Gillibrand was the junior federal senator from New York].

* * * * *

* * * * *

Email Trail with Senator Gillibrand's staffers, NYC – 2022

Exhibit 77: *2022.   Various emails from John Wilson to Senator Gillibrand.*

* * * * *

From: John Wilson
Sent: Friday, June 10, 2022 8:05 AM
To: casework@gillibrand.senate.gov
Subject: FW: Attn: Senator Gillibrand: John Wilson - casework request - re DOJ/FBI

Hi,

Could you please give me an update on the below request for casework assistance.

Thank you.

Regards.

John Wilson

* * * * *

From: John Wilson   jxxxxxxxxxxx@bigpond.com
Sent: Wednesday, 15 June 2022 10:28 AM
To: 'casework@gillibrand.senate.gov' <casework@gillibrand.senate.gov>
Subject: FW: Attn: Senator Gillibrand: John Wilson - casework request - re DOJ/FBI

Hi,

What is the expected timing to review and respond to the below request for casework assistance?

Thank you.

Regards.

John Wilson

* * * * *

From: John Wilson
Sent: Tuesday, June 21, 2022 10:59 AM
To: casework@gillibrand.senate.gov
Subject: FW: Attn: Senator Gillibrand: John Wilson - casework request - re DOJ/FBI

Hi,

I am following up on the below - could you please provide a status update.

Thank you.

Regards.

John Wilson

* * * * *

IV-4d   Correspondence 2020 to 2023

Congressman Jerrold Nadler

* * * * *

Exhibit 78: *26 May 2022.   Copy of online Casework Request from John Wilson to Jerrold Nadler.*

RE: FBI/DOJ

I am registered as a Federal Voter formerly residing at 170 West 74th Street, NY, NY 10023 (and currently reside in Sydney ███████████████████████████, Australia).

I was a securities analyst working for a large British investment bank (SG Warburg, now part of UBS Warburg) covering the mining sector on Wall Street in the 1990s. One of the companies I followed was NYSE listed US mining company Freeport McMoran which at the time was under investigation following eye witness reports it was involved with the killing, and other human rights abuses, of indigenous protestors at its massive Grasberg copper and gold mine in West Papua, Indonesia. After writing a report that touched on this and later asking the company's chairman a question about it, I found I had the FBI breathing down my neck, a matter subsequently confirmed by two FBI agents - Steve Garber, and my long term friend Susan Holmes. Based on what they told me, and some of the things I experienced, including threats made to me around the time the report was published and in the Freeport boardroom alcove following an analyst briefing, I believe the FBI has set me up in retribution to make it appear as though I am an environmental extremist, or at least associate with people who are, or have been, considered environmental extremists by the FBI and placed me on some kind of list, amongst other things. These environmental activists and extremists comprise people introduced to me by agent Susan Holmes, as her FBI targets, targets of her work for the FBI, Paul Winter and David Foreman, among others, people whom I had no other contact with otherwise. I have since experienced gross interference with my professional and social networks, intrusive surveillance, and violation of my personal privacy amongst other things - which I understand is all due to the FBI.

There are two things that come to mind that you may be able to do that would assist me. The first is I seek help with getting a response from the DOJ/FBI to my allegations of their retribution and intrusions into my life, as confirmed by the two FBI agents, namely Steve Garber and Susan Holmes. To this end, I sent the Attorney General, Merrick B. Garland a letter via email 18 March 2022 outlining the details and circumstances of my allegations and requested his office investigate the alleged FBI misconduct. To date, the Attorney General has not responded to my letter and I would appreciate your help in obtaining an explanation from him in which the substance of my complaint is addressed.

The second way you may assist me is to refer this matter to the House Judiciary Committee for investigation.

I will forward you the emailed letter I sent to the AG 18 March 2022 - please let me know the best email address.

I thank you respectfully for your assistance in advance.

Best regards.

John Wilson

I am a US citizen registered as a Federal Voter in the USA formerly residing at 170 West 74th Street, NY, NY 10023 (and currently reside in Sydney █████████████████████████, Australia). The best way to contact me is via email at █xxxxxxxxxxx@bigpond.com█.

* * * * *

Exhibit 79: *26 May 2022.   Automated email response from Congressman Nadler to John Wilson.*

From: noreply@mail.house.gov <noreply@mail.house.gov>

Sent: Thursday, 26 May 2022 12:51 PM

To: ████████████████████

Subject: Rep. Nadler Request Received

Thank you for submitting your casework request to the office of Congressman Jerrold Nadler. This is an automated message confirming receipt of your request. You will be contacted by a caseworker as soon as possible.

Please note that our response time is approximately 2 weeks. However, due to the COVID-19 pandemic, the volume of casework requests we receive has increased significantly, and our response time is slightly longer than usual.

It is also important to note that we are cognizant of the urgent nature of the inquires we receive. Therefore, our Constituent Services team reviews each casework request as it is received, and we prioritize emergency requests that require immediate action.

Please review our Casework FAQ in the interim. Thank you again.

* * * * *

[Note: My subsequent emails and calls to Congressman Nadler's office to follow up on the Caseworker request went unreturned.]

Section V

FBI - Freedom of Information (FOIA)

Section V

Freedom of Information Requests (FOIA)

V-1. FOIA Requests: 2004 to 2005

    FBI/DOJ
- a. FOIPA Request No.: 1006988-000; Appeal No.: 05-0661

V-2. FOIA Requests: 2013 to 2014

    FBI/DOJ
- a. 14 June 2013 FOIPA No.: 1224169-000 [Sobel]; Appeal No.: AP-2014-01140
- b. 14 June 2013: FOIPA No.: 1250235-000; Appeal No. N/A
- c. 26 March 2014: FOIPA No.: 1250235-001; Appeal No.: AP-2015-00491
- d. OGIS mediation: Appeal No.: AP-2014-01140 and AP-2015-00491

V-3. FOIA Requests: 2019 to 2020

    FBI/DOJ
- a. FOIPA Request No.: 1450535 [Rankin]; Appeal No.: A-2020-00197

V-4. FOIA Requests: 2022 and after

    FBI/DOJ
- a. FOIPA Request No.: 1548515-000 [Sorenson]; Appeal No.: A-2022-02028

V-1   FOIA requests, appeals and OGIS mediation: 2004 to 2005

V-1a FOIA requests, appeals and mediation: 2004 to 2005

FBI/DOJ

FOIPA Request No.: 1006988- 000

Appeal No.: 05-0661

Schedule of key correspondence

Letter dated 12 October 2004 FOIPA Request from John Wilson's employment attorney Rachel Minter to FBI.

Letter dated 25 October 2004, FBI assigns FOIPA Request No. 1006988- 000 and responds to search – no records.

Letter dated 19 December 2004 from John Wilson's personal attorney Barry Fisher requests administrative appeal to DOJ, OIP.

Letter dated 30 December 2004, DOJ, OIP assigns Appeal No.: 05-0661.

Letter 6 September 2005, DOJ,OIP responds to appeal – no records.

* * * * *

Exhibit 80: *12 October 2004.   FOIA letter from Attorney Rachel Minter to FBI.*

October 12, 2004

FOIPA Section
Federal Bureau of Investigation
Department of Justice
935 Pennsylvania Avenue, N.W.
Washington, D.C. 20535

Re: **FREEDOM OF INFORMATION REQUEST**
John Christian Wilson
Date of Birth:
Place of Birth: Sydney, Australia

Dear Sirs:

This office represents the above-referenced person in connection with his request for certain records believed to be in the custody of or maintained by the Federal Bureau of Investigation. Enclosed please find a Form DOJ-361 which has been executed by my client.

On behalf of Mr. Wilson, we hereby request copies of any and all records, files, reports and other like or related documents, whether produced, reproduced or stored on paper, electronically or on any other media, regarding any investigation, surveillance, inquiries or other like or related information-gathering procedures from 1993 to date

(a) of which Wilson is the subject;

(b) containing any reference to or information about Wilson;

(c) concerning Wilson's prior employment at SBC Warburg;

(d) reflecting Wilson's contacts with any employees of the Federal Bureau of Investigation and/or the Department of Justice

All replies should be directed to this office.

Sincerely,

Rachel J. Minter

RJM/tbh

Enc.

* * * * *

Exhibit 81: *25 October 2004.   FOIA letter from FBI to Attorney Rachel Minter.*

U.S. Department of Justice

Federal Bureau of Investigation

Washington, D.C. 20535

October 25, 2004

RACHEL J MINTER ESQ
SUITE 4710
EMPIRE STATE BUILDING
350 FIFTH AVENUE
NEW YORK, NY 10118

Request No.: 1006988-000
Subject: WILSON, JOHN CHRISTIAN

Dear Ms. Minter:

This is in response to your Freedom of Information-Privacy Acts (FOIPA) request noted above.

Based on the information furnished, a search of the automated indices to the central records system files at FBI Headquarters located no records responsive to your FOIPA request to indicate the subject of your request has ever been of investigatory interest to the FBI. The automated indices is an index to all records created since January 1, 1958, in security, applicant, and administrative matters, as well as to all records created since January 1, 1973, in criminal matters.

If you have reason to believe records responsive to your request exist prior to the above dates, you will have to request another search. In order to respond to our many requests in a timely manner, our focus is to identify responsive records in the automated indices that are indexed as main files. A main index record carries the names of subjects of FBI investigations.

Although no main file records responsive to your FOIPA request were located in our automated indices, we are required to inform you that you are entitled to file an administrative appeal if you so desire. Appeals should be directed in writing to the Co-Director, Office of Information and Privacy, U. S. Department of Justice, Suite 570, Flag Building, Washington, D. C. 20530, within 60 days from the date of this letter. The envelope and the letter should be clearly marked "Information Appeal." Please cite the FOIPA request number assigned to your request so that it may easily be identified.

Sincerely yours,

David M. Hardy
Section Chief,
Record/Information
  Dissemination Section
Records Management Division

* * * * *

Exhibit 82: *19 December 2004.   FOIA appeal letter from John Wilson to FBI, cc Barry Fisher.*

John Christian Wilson   19 December, 2004

Australia

Co-Director

Office of Information and Privacy

United States Department of Justice

Suite 570, Flag Building

Washington, D.C. 20530

RE: Notice of Information Appeal, FOIPA Request No.: 1006988- 000

Dear Co-Director:

I hereby notice my appeal the results of the FOIPA requested search. For reasons set out below, it is very unlikely that there are no documents on me.

I was an equity analyst on Wall Street from 1994 to 1998, where I worked as a mining analyst. In the course of performing my duties, I came across information in 1996 that drew the interest of the FBI.

Unknown to me at the time, information was a leaked to me by an undercover FBI agent who worked as an environmentalist. This person gave me details of a State Department finding regarding an incident in which 7 people were killed in and around the Freeport McMoran-owned Grasberg mine in Indonesia in the mid 90's. The information I received related to a confidential reprimand of the company by the US Department of State, for reasons concerning environmental and, from recollection, human rights abuses.

For a number of years following that, I have had contact with people who have revealed themselves to me to be FBI agents. These people have indicated that I have been the subject of FBI interest, suggesting that the catalyst was the note I published on the State Department finding on Freeport in 1996. These individuals engendered friendship with me under the auspices of other professional identities and each has interviewed me, two of them extensively. These include- Steven Garber, now of White Plains, NewYork, formerly of New York City, Susan Holmes, now of Washington, D.C., formerly of New York City, and Livingston Sutro, of Sierra Vista, Arizona.

Given these facts it seems improbable that there are no records.

Sincerely,

John Wilson

(Please copy my attorney on correspondence).

Cc: Barry A. Fisher

Fleishman & Fisher

1875 Century Park East Suite 2130

Los Angeles, CA 90067

* * * *

* * * * *

Exhibit 83: *30 December 2004.   FOIA appeal letter from FBI to John Wilson.*

U.S. Department of Justice

Office of Information and Privacy

Telephone: (202) 514-3642   Washington, D.C. 20530

DEC 3 0 2004

Mr. John Wilson

AUSTRALIA

Re: Request No. 1006988-000

Dear Mr. Wilson:

This is to advise you that your administrative appeal from the action of the Federal Bureau of Investigation on your request for information from the files of the Department of Justice was received by this Office on December 22, 2004.

The Office of Information and Privacy, which has the responsibility of adjudicating such appeals, has a substantial backlog of pending appeals received prior to yours. In an attempt to afford each appellant equal and impartial treatment, we have adopted a general practice of assigning appeals in the approximate order of receipt. Your appeal has been assigned number **05-0661**. Please mention this number in any future correspondence to this Office regarding this matter.

We will notify you of the decision on your appeal as soon as we can. The necessity of this delay is regretted and your continuing courtesy is appreciated.

Sincerely,

Priscilla Jones
Administrative Specialist

* * * * *

* * * * *

Exhibit 84: *16 April 2005.   FOIA appeal letter from FBI to John Wilson.*

John Christian Wilson   16 April, 2005

c/o Barry A. Fisher

Fleishman & Fisher

1875 Century Park East Suite 2130

Los Angeles, CA 90067

Email: ███████████████████

Co-Director

Office of Information and Privacy

United States Department of Justice

Suite 570, Flag Building

Washington, D.C. 20530

RE: Notice of Information Appeal, FOIPA Request No.: 1006988- 000

Appeal No.: 05-0661

Dear Co-Director:

I write as a follow up to your letter dated 30 December, 2004. Could you please indicate, based on current expectations, what your likely timing will be for a response to the appeal.

Thank you.

Sincerely yours,

John Wilson

* * * *

* * * * *

Exhibit 85: *6 September 2005.   FOIA appeal letter from FBI to John Wilson.*

U.S. Department of Justice

Office of Information and Privacy

Telephone: (202) 514-3642   Washington, D.C. 20530

SEP 0 6 2005

Mr. John Christian Wilson

AUSTRALIA

Re: Appeal No. 05-0661
Request No. 1006988
RLH:ADW:JTR

Dear Mr. Wilson:

You appealed from the action of the Headquarters Office of the Federal Bureau of Investigation on your request for access to records concerning you.

After carefully considering your appeal, I have decided to affirm the FBI's action on your request.

The FBI informed you that it could locate no records responsive to your request. It has been determined that the FBI's response is correct. The FBI conducted another search of its automated indices for main files and cross-references responsive to your request, but it did not locate any records.

If you are dissatisfied with my action on your appeal, you may seek judicial review in accordance with 5 U.S.C. § 552(a)(4)(B).

Sincerely,

Richard L. Huff
Co-Director

* * * * *

V-2 FOIA requests, appeals and OGIS mediation: 2013 to 2014

V-2a   FOIA Requests: 2013 to 2014

FBI/DOJ

FOIPA Request No.: 1224169-000 – Sobel

Appeal No.: AP-2014-01140

Schedule of key correspondence

Emailed FBI standard form dated 14 June 2013 FOIPA Request to FBI.

Email dated 17 June 2013, FBI acknowledges receipt of FOIPA request.

Letter dated 20 November 2013, FBI assigns FOIPA Request No. 1224169-000 and responds to search – no records.

Letter dated 23 December 2013, John Wilson's FOIA attorney David Sobel requests administrative appeal to DOJ, OIP.

Letter dated [no correspondence available], DOJ, OIP assigns Appeal No.: AP-2014-01140.

Letter 25 February 2014, DOJ,OIP responds to appeal AP-2014-01140 – no records.

* * * * *

Exhibit 86: *14 June 2013.   FOIA letter from John Wilson to FBI.*

From: John Wilson
Sent: Friday, June 14, 2013 7:37 PM
To: FOIPARequest
Subject: Attn: FBI FOI/PA Request

Attn: FBI FOI/PA Request

FBI FOI/PA Request attached

[REDACTED]
Australia

June 14, 2013

Federal Bureau of Investigation
Records/Information Dissemination Section
170 Marcel Drive
Winchester, VA 22602-4843

FREEDOM OF INFORMATION ACT / PRIVACY ACT REQUEST

Dear Sir or Madam:

This is a request for records under the provisions of the Freedom of Information Act and the Privacy Act. Please process this request under both statutes to release the maximum number of records.

I request copies of all files, correspondence, or other records concerning myself. To assist you with this search I am providing the following information about myself:

   My full name: John Christian Wilson
   Other names used: _____
   My date of birth: [REDACTED]
   My place of birth: Sydney, NSW Australia
   My Social Security number: [REDACTED]

Please search both your automated indices and the older general (manual) indices, as well as all Field Offices.

This is an individual request for research and study purposes, and I agree that I will pay up to $30 for fees, if necessary. Please notify me in advance if fees are expected to exceed that amount. If the file is likely to result in more than 250 pages, I would appreciate receiving a digital copy of the file on a CD-ROM rather than in paper form.

If you have any questions, please call me at +612 [REDACTED]

Under penalty of perjury, I hereby declare that I am the person named above and I understand that any falsification of this statement is punishable under the provisions of Title 18, United States Code (U.S.C.), Section 1001 by a fine of not more than $10,000 or by imprisonment of not more than five years, or both; and that requesting or obtaining any record(s) under false pretenses is punishable under the provisions of Title 5, U.S.C., Section 552a(i)(3) as a misdemeanor and by a fine of not more than $5,000.

Sincerely,

[signature]
John Christian Wilson

Former US address
170 West 74th St
New York, NY 10023

* * * * *

* * * * *

Follow up emails between John Wilson and FBI FOIA liaison David Sobonya; DOJ letters; and - correspondence with FOIA attorney David Sobel – 2013

* * * * *

Exhibit 87: *Jul-Nov 2013.   Emails between Wilson, FBI - Sobonya; and FOIA Attorney David Sobel.*

From: Sobonya, David P. [mailto:David.Sobonya@ic.fbi.gov]
Sent: Monday, 17 June 2013 11:08 PM
To: John Wilson
Subject: RE: Attn: FBI FOI/PA Request

Dear Mr. Wilson,

The FBI has received your Freedom of Information Act/Privacy (FOIPA) request and it will be forwarded to Initial Processing for review. Your request will be processed under the provisions of FOIPA and a response will be mailed to you at a later date.

Requests for fee waivers and expedited processing will be addressed once your request has been assigned an FOIPA request number. You will receive written notification of the FBI's decision.

Information regarding the Freedom of Information Act/Privacy is available at http://www.fbi.gov/ or http://www.fbi.gov/foia/. If you require additional assistance please contact the Public Information Officer.

Thank you,

David P. Sobonya
Public Information Officer/Legal Admin. Specialist
Record/Information Dissemination Section (RIDS)
FBI-Records Management Division
170 Marcel Drive, Winchester, VA 22602-4843
PIO: (540) 868-4593
Direct: (540) 868-4286
Fax: (540) 868-4391/4997

* * * * *

From: John Wilson
Sent: Thursday, July 18, 2013 7:33 PM
To: 'sobel@eff.org' <sobel@eff.org>
Subject: FOIA

Hi David,

I understand you specialise in FOIA requests (I recently read an article on wired.com that you secured documents in relation to Aaron Swartz).

I have had problems securing any documents or acknowledgement from the FBI of long term interference with myself since I published a report in 1996 as a Wall Street analyst that touched on the killing of indigenous protestors at US mining company Freeport McMoran's Grasberg copper and gold mine in West Papua.

I have been the subject of a vindictive campaign by the FBI since then. I applied for FOI in 2005. They replied there were no documents but the response was qualified. I appealed their decision but to no effect – documents attached. I also sent a letter to the House Judiciary Committee (26 July 2005, attached) – also ultimately to no effect.

I know the FBI is involved with me in this matter and that their response is a deceptive denial. My former long term girlfriend was an undercover FBI agent – and I know with certainty that the FBI is directly responsible and involved in this elaborate reprisal.

I recently (June 2013) filed new FOIA's with the FBI, and also with the CIA (for the first time) – both attached.

I am writing to possibly engage your services to assist with my FOIA as I assume I will continue to face hurdles with this most recent round of applications. Could you let me know the terms on which you might be able to assist.

I am a dual US/Australian citizen and currently reside in Sydney.

Thanks you.

Sincerely.

John Wilson

John Wilson

Managing Director

RCR
Resource Capital Research
www.rcresearch.com.au
T +61 x xxxx xxxx (SYD)

* * * * *

From: David Sobel [mailto:sobel@eff.org]
Sent: Friday, 19 July 2013 11:09 PM
To: johnwilson@rcresearch.net
Subject: Re: FOIA

John -

Thanks for your message. I would be glad to consider assisting you with your requests. For work at the administrative level, my fee is $300/hour; for litigation, it is $450/hour. At this point, it seems like you just need to wait a while until the agencies respond to your request (or don't). While a lawsuit can be filed as soon as 30 days after an agency's receipt of a request, the reality is that it takes much longer, which is to say that even if a lawsuit is filed, the court will allow the agency many additional months in which to respond to a request. So there's really no point in acting quickly. One thing I can suggest at this point is that you might want to submit requests directly to the FBI field offices you believe are most likely to possess relevant files. A request to FBI HQ does not extend to the field offices (even though your request asks them to treat it as such).

Glad to provide additional info that might help put you in a posture to proceed further after a decent amount of time has passed.

Best,

- D.

* * * * *

From: John Wilson [mailto:jxxxxxxxxxxx@bigpond.com]
Sent: Monday, August 12, 2013 8:24 AM
To: Sobonya, David P.
Subject: RE: Attn: FBI FOI/PA Request

Dear sir,

Could you please provide an update as to the status of my below FOI/PA request.

Thank you.

Regards.

John Wilson

* * * * *

From: Sobonya, David P. [mailto:David.Sobonya@ic.fbi.gov]
Sent: Monday, 12 August 2013 10:42 PM
To: John Wilson
Subject: RE: Attn: FBI FOI/PA Request

Dear Mr. Wilson,

Requests are processed in the order that they are received. The request is waiting to be opened, at which time it will be assigned a FOIPA request number and correspondence will be mailed to you. Upon receipt of the correspondence, you will be able to check the status of your request online at http://www.fbi.gov/foia/.

Please remember that the FBI receives a voluminous amount of requests on a daily, weekly, monthly and annual basis.

Please contact me if you require further assistance.

Thank you,

David P. Sobonya
Public Information Officer/Legal Admin. Specialist

Record/Information Dissemination Section (RIDS)
FBI-Records Management Division
170 Marcel Drive, Winchester, VA 22602-4843
PIO: (540) 868-4593
Direct: (540) 868-4286
Fax: (540) 868-4391/4997

* * * * *

From: John Wilson
Sent: Tuesday, August 13, 2013 9:48 AM
To: 'David Sobel' <sobel@eff.org>
Subject: FW: Attn: FBI FOI/PA Request

Hi David,

We corresponded a month or so ago.

Below I forward a status update re my FOI from the FBI. It is nearly 2 months since they received my request.

I will be guided by you as to whether now is the time to engage you to commence a parallel FOI process (such as approaching regional FBI offices with an FOI) or whether I should give the folks in DC a few more months to process the existing FOI request. Please let me know.

Thanks and regards.

John Wilson

* * * * *

From: John Wilson
Sent: Wednesday, November 20, 2013 3:32 PM
To: 'Sobonya, David P.' <David.Sobonya@ic.fbi.gov>
Subject: RE: Attn: FBI FOI/PA Request

Dear sir,

Could you please provide an update as to the status of my below FOI/PA request. My understanding was that the agency has 1 month to fulfil and respond to FOIA requests and it is now over 6 months since you acknowledged receipt of my request.

Thank you.

Regards.

John Wilson

* * * * *

From: Sobonya, David P. [mailto:David.Sobonya@ic.fbi.gov]
Sent: Thursday, 21 November 2013 6:44 AM
To: John Wilson
Subject: RE: Attn: FBI FOI/PA Request

Dear Mr. Wilson,

The above FOIPA was closed on this date and a NO RECORD response has been placed in the mail.

Thank you,

David P. Sobonya
Public Information Officer/Legal Admin. Specialist
Record/Information Dissemination Section (RIDS)
FBI-Records Management Division
170 Marcel Drive, Winchester, VA 22602-4843
PIO: (540) 868-4593
Direct: (540) 868-4286
Fax: (540) 868-4391/4997

* * * * *

From: John Wilson
Sent: Thursday, November 21, 2013 7:59 AM
To: 'Sobonya, David P.' <David.Sobonya@ic.fbi.gov>
Subject: RE: Attn: FBI FOI/PA Request

Dear Sir,

Is it possible to provide an estimate of the likely time till a response is provided? For example, can you indicate, based on the duration of the current delay, whether the time required is more likely to be in the order of years or is it several more months? An approximate indication would be appreciated.

Thank you.

John Wilson

* * * * *

From: Sobonya, David P. [mailto:David.Sobonya@ic.fbi.gov]
Sent: Thursday, 21 November 2013 8:01 AM
To: John Wilson
Subject: RE: Attn: FBI FOI/PA Request

Dear Mr. Wilson,

Correspondence was mailed to you on this date by way of the U. S. Postal Service.

Thank you,

David P. Sobonya
Public Information Officer/Legal Admin. Specialist
Record/Information Dissemination Section (RIDS)
FBI-Records Management Division
170 Marcel Drive, Winchester, VA 22602-4843
PIO: (540) 868-4593
Direct: (540) 868-4286
Fax: (540) 868-4391/4997

* * * * *

From: John Wilson ██████████████
Sent: Thursday, November 21, 2013 8:25 AM
To: 'Sobonya, David P.' <David.Sobonya@ic.fbi.gov>
Subject: RE: Attn: FBI FOI/PA Request

Dear Sir,

I find your response surprising.

What options do I have to appeal your findings?

Regards.

John Wilson

* * * * *

* * * * *

Exhibit 88: *20 November 2013.   Letter from FBI to John Wilson (received circa December 2013).*

U.S. Department of Justice

Federal Bureau of Investigation
Washington, D.C. 20535

November 20, 2013

JOHN CHRISTIAN WILSON

AUSTRALIA

FOIPA Request No.: 1224169-0
Subject: WILSON, JOHN CHRISTIAN

Dear Mr. Wilson:

This is in response to your Freedom of Information/Privacy Acts (FOIPA) request.

Based on the information you provided, we conducted a search of the Central Records System. We were unable to identify main file records responsive to the FOIPA. If you have additional information pertaining to the subject that you believe was of investigative interest to the Bureau, please provide us the details and we will conduct an additional search.

In accordance with standard FBI practice and pursuant to FOIA exemption (b)(7)(E)/ Privacy Act exemption (j)(2) [5 U.S.C. § 552/552a (b)(7)(E)/(j)(2)], this response neither confirms nor denies the existence of your subject's name on any watch lists.

For your information, Congress excluded three discrete categories of law enforcement and national security records from the requirements of the FOIA. See 5 U.S.C. § 552(c) (2006 & Supp. IV (2010). This response is limited to those records that are subject to the requirements of the FOIA. This is a standard notification that is given to all our requesters and should not be taken as an indication that excluded records do, or do not, exist.

You may file an appeal by writing to the Director, Office of Information Policy (OIP), U.S. Department of Justice, 1425 New York Ave., NW, Suite 11050, Washington, D.C. 20530-0001, or you may submit an appeal through OIP's eFOIA portal at http://www.justice.gov/oip/efoia-portal.html. Your appeal must be received by OIP within sixty (60) days from the date of this letter in order to be considered timely. The envelope and the letter should be clearly marked "Freedom of Information Appeal." Please cite the FOIPA Request Number in any correspondence to us for proper identification of your request.

Enclosed for your information is a copy of the FBI Fact Sheet and Explanation of Exemptions.

Sincerely,

David M. Hardy
Section Chief,
Record/Information
  Dissemination Section
Records Management Division

Enclosure(s)

* * * * *

* * * * *

From: John Wilson ███████████████████
Sent: Thursday, November 21, 2013 8:23 AM
To: 'sobel@eff.org' <sobel@eff.org>
Subject: FW: Attn: FBI FOI/PA Request

Hi David,

I corresponded with you a number of months ago about my FBI FOIA request and provided you with some documents.

The FBI is denying me access to any records and according to the below email has mailed me a "no record" letter.

I believe they hold extensive records on me and that they are not releasing them. What options do I have for taking this further?

Thank you.

Regards.

John Wilson

* * * * *

From: John Wilson ███████████████████
Sent: Friday, November 22, 2013 8:54 AM
To: 'sobel@eff.org' <sobel@eff.org>
Subject: FW: FOIA

Hi David,

I am resending my email to you from July with background documents, after yesterday sending you notification from the FBI that they will be providing a "no records" response to my FOIA request.

Is this something you can help me pursue and if so, how would we proceed? I would be keen to progress this to the next level.

Regards.

John Wilson
Tel: +61 ██████████

* * * * *

* * * * *

Exhibit 89: *23 December 2013.   Appeal letter from John Wilson FOIA Attorney David Sobel to FBI.*

David L. Sobel
Attorney-at-Law

Suite 410
1818 N Street, N.W.
Washington, DC 20036

(202) 246-6180 (voice)
(202) 237-7727 (fax)
sobel@att.net (e-mail)

December 23, 2013

BY CERTIFIED MAIL -- 70123050000135142323

Melanie Pustay
Director
Office of Information Policy
U.S. Department of Justice
1425 New York Ave., N.W.
Suite 11050
Washington, DC 20530-0001

Re: **Freedom of Information/ Privacy Acts Appeal;**
        FBI FOIPA Request No. 1224169-0

Dear Ms. Pustay:

This letter constitutes an administrative appeal under the Freedom of Information Act ("FOIA"), 5 U.S.C. § 552, and the Privacy Act, 5 U.S.C. § 552a, and is submitted on behalf of my client, John Christian Wilson.

By letter to the Federal Bureau of Investigation ("FBI") dated June 14, 2013 (attached hereto), Mr. Wilson sought access to "all files, correspondence, or other records" relating to him. He provided his date and place of birth, Social Security Number, and his current and former addresses. He specifically requested that the FBI search "both your automated indices and the older general (manual) indices, as well as all Field Offices."

By letter from David M. Hardy dated November 20, 2013 (attached hereto), Mr. Wilson was advised that "[b]ased on the information [he] provided, [the Bureau] conducted a search of the Central Records System" and was "unable to identify main file records responsive to the FOIPA." Mr. Wilson was advised of his right to submit an appeal of that determination to your office.

We believe that the Bureau's failure to locate responsive records was likely the result of conducting too narrow a search. I note that while Mr. Hardy stated that the FBI was "unable to identify main file records," Mr. Wilson's request was not limited to "main file records." Rather, he expressly requested "*all* files, correspondence, or other records" (emphasis added), and his request clearly was not limited to a search of the Central Records System.

Melanie Pustay
Director, OIP
December 23, 2013
Page two

Through this appeal, Mr. Wilson requests that the FBI be directed to perform a complete and thorough search of all filing systems and locations for all records maintained by the Bureau pertaining to him. Such a search should include, but not be limited to, files and documents captioned in (or whose captions include) his name in the title. The FBI should search the Central Records System, Electronic Surveillance Records (ELSUR), and Electronic Case File (ECF). Further, Mr. Wilson specifically requests that the Bureau conduct a text search of the ECF to identify all potentially responsive main and cross-reference files. The FBI's comprehensive search should include "main" files and "see references." In addition, appropriate field offices (certainly New York) should be tasked to conduct searches. In short, Mr. Wilson requests that the agency conduct a thorough search reasonably calculated to locate "all files, correspondence, or other records" about him, as his initial request clearly stated.

To assist the Bureau in conducting a comprehensive search, Mr. Wilson provides some relevant background information. He was a mining company equity analyst on Wall Street from 1994 to 1998. He is a citizen of the United States, was born in Australia, and lived in the United States for many years, principally in New York and Philadelphia, where he received an MBA degree from Wharton. Mr. Wilson currently resides in Australia.

In 1996, in the course of performing his duties as a mining industry analyst for SG Warburg (which subsequently became part of SBC Warburg, thence UBS Warburg), Mr. Wilson published information pertaining to an extended shutdown of the NYSE publicly traded U.S. mining company Freeport McMoran owned Grasberg mine in Indonesia. According to press reports at the time and other sources, the company was under investigation by the U.S. Department of State following eyewitness allegations it had been involved in the killing of indigenous protestors. A confidential source told Mr. Wilson there had been a confidential reprimand of the company by the U.S. Department of State following completion of an interim investigation into human rights and environmental abuses.

For the many years following his 1996 publication of information regarding the Freeport McMoran killings, Mr. Wilson has had contacts with several individuals who indicated that they were associated with the FBI and who made reference to the Freeport McMoran matter. As a result, Mr. Wilson believes it is likely that the Bureau maintains information about him stemming from the 1996 report, and potentially other matters.

Melanie Pustay
Director, OIP
December 23, 2013
Page three

Your consideration of this appeal is appreciated, and Mr. Wilson and I stand ready to provide any additional information that might assist you. As the law requires, I will anticipate a decision on the appeal within twenty working days.

Sincerely,

David L. Sobel

enclosures

* * * * *

* * * * *

From: David Sobel <sobel@eff.org>
Sent: Friday, January 3, 2014 3:56 AM
To: John Wilson
Subject: FOIA appeal received

John -

Happy new year! Just to let you know that the appeal letter to DOJ (attached [23 December 2013]) was received by the agency on Dec. 30. So you can either wait for a reply to the appeal (which will likely take several months), or (by the end of this month) you would be entitled to file a lawsuit. I believe you previously expressed a preference for the former, so I'll assume we'll be waiting to hear from DOJ before taking any further action.

Best,

- D.

* * * * *

From: David Sobel <sobel@eff.org>
Sent: Thursday, February 27, 2014 1:57 AM
To: John Wilson
Subject: Appeal response re FBI request

John -

I received the attached response to the appeal to DOJ on the FBI request. As you see, they have endorsed the FBI's action. Given that your initial request was fairly bare-bones, you might want to submit a new request providing some, if not most, of the info they suggest.

Glad to follow-up if you need more guidance.

Best,

- D.

* * * * *

* * * * *

Exhibit 90: *25 February 2014.   Appeal letter from FBI to Attorney David Sobel.*

U.S. Department of Justice
Office of Information Policy
Suite 11050
1425 New York Avenue, NW
Washington, DC 20530-0001

Telephone: (202) 514-3642

February 25, 2014

David L. Sobel, Esq.
Suite 410
1818 N Street, NW
Washington, DC 20036
sobel@att.net

Re: Appeal No. AP-2014-01140
     Request No. 1224169
     SRO:CDT

VIA: E-mail

Dear Mr. Sobel:

You appealed on behalf of your client, John Christian Wilson, from the action of the Federal Bureau of Investigation on your client's request for access to records concerning himself.

After carefully considering your appeal, I am affirming the FBI's action on your client's request. The Freedom of Information Act provides for disclosure of many agency records. At the same time, Congress included in the FOIA nine exemptions from disclosure that provide protection for important interests such as personal privacy, privileged communications, and certain law enforcement activities. To the extent that your client's request seeks access to records that would either confirm or deny an individual's placement on any government watch list, the FBI properly refused to confirm or deny the existence of any records responsive to your client's request because the existence of such records is protected from disclosure pursuant to 5 U.S.C. § 552a(j)(2) and 5 U.S.C. § 552(b)(7)(E). FOIA Exemption (b)(7)(E) concerns records or information compiled for law enforcement purposes the release of which would disclose techniques and procedures for law enforcement investigations or prosecutions. This response should not be taken as an indication that records do or do not exist. Rather, this is the standard response made by the FBI.

As to any other records, the FBI informed your client that it could locate no main file records subject to the FOIA in its files. I have determined that the FBI's response was correct and that it conducted an adequate, reasonable search for records responsive to your request. Please note that the FBI's search encompassed all of its automated indices in all field offices. Further, the FBI did not search its manual indices because the manual indices only contain records created before 1959, well before your client's date of birth.

I note that in your appeal letter you ask that the FBI conduct a search for electronic surveillance records and any cross-references. Please be advised that your client will need to submit a new request asking specifically that an ELSUR search be performed. Regarding your client's request for a cross-reference search, please be advised that you need to provide information sufficient to enable the FBI to determine with certainty that any cross-references it

- 2 -

locates are identifiable to the subject of your client's request. This information may include the following:

1) the specific circumstances in which the subject of your request had contact with the FBI;
2) the date(s) of such contact;
3) the location(s) of such contact;
4) the full name (first, middle, and last) as well as any prior names or aliases used by the subject of your client's request;
5) Social Security number, date of birth, place of birth, and home address of the subject of your client's request;
6) names of associates of the subject of your client's request the mention of whom might aid in the identification of responsive records; and
7) other references of the subject of your client's request in media, such as books, articles, websites, etc.

You should provide this information to the FBI directly. Please note that the FBI may not be able to identify responsive cross-references despite the additional information you provide. You may appeal any future adverse determination made by the FBI.

Please be advised that this Office's decision was made only after a full review of this matter. Your appeal was assigned to an attorney with this Office who thoroughly reviewed and analyzed your appeal, your client's underlying request, and the action of the FBI in response to your client's request.

If your client is dissatisfied with my action on your appeal, the FOIA permits him to file a lawsuit in federal district court in accordance with 5 U.S.C. § 552(a)(4)(B).

For your information, the Office of Government Information Services (OGIS) offers mediation services to resolve disputes between FOIA requesters and Federal agencies as a non-exclusive alternative to litigation. Using OGIS services does not affect your client's right to pursue litigation. The contact information for OGIS is as follows: Office of Government Information Services, National Archives and Records Administration, Room 2510, 8601 Adelphi Road, College Park, Maryland 20740-6001; e-mail at ogis@nara.gov; telephone at 301-837-1996; toll free at 1-877-684-6448; or facsimile at 301-837-0348.

Sincerely,

Sean R. O'Neill
Chief
Administrative Appeals Staff

* * * * *

V-2b FOIA Requests: 2013 to 2014

FBI/DOJ

FOIPA Request No.: 1250235-000
Appeal No.: N/A

Schedule of key correspondence

[The FBI in error responded twice to my 14 June 2013 FOIPA Request was responded to twice by the FBI and assigned two FOIPA Request No's: 1224169-000 on 20 November 2013 and 1250235-000 on29 January 2014].

Emailed FBI standard form dated 14 June 2013 FOIPA Request to FBI.

Email dated [no correspondence available], FBI acknowledges receipt of FOIPA request.

Letter dated 29 January 2014, FBI assigns FOIPA Request No. 1250235-000 and responds to search – no records.

No request made for administrative appeal to DOJ, OIP.

* * * * *

Exhibit 91: *14 June 2013.   FOIA letter from John Wilson to FBI.*

From: John Wilson
Sent: Friday, June 14, 2013 7:37 PM
To: FOIPARequest
Subject: Attn: FBI FOI/PA Request

Attn: FBI FOI/PA Request

FBI FOI/PA Request attached

Australia

June 14, 2013

Federal Bureau of Investigation
Records/Information Dissemination Section
170 Marcel Drive
Winchester, VA 22602-4843

FREEDOM OF INFORMATION ACT / PRIVACY ACT REQUEST

Dear Sir or Madam:

This is a request for records under the provisions of the Freedom of Information Act and the Privacy Act. Please process this request under both statutes to release the maximum number of records.

I request copies of all files, correspondence, or other records concerning myself. To assist you with this search I am providing the following information about myself:

My full name: John Christian Wilson
Other names used:
My date of birth:
My place of birth: Sydney, NSW Australia
My Social Security number:

Please search both your automated indices and the older general (manual) indices, as well as all Field Offices.

This is an individual request for research and study purposes, and I agree that I will pay up to $30 for fees, if necessary. Please notify me in advance if fees are expected to exceed that amount. If the file is likely to result in more than 250 pages, I would appreciate receiving a digital copy of the file on a CD-ROM rather than in paper form.

If you have any questions, please call me at +612

Under penalty of perjury, I hereby declare that I am the person named above and I understand that any falsification of this statement is punishable under the provisions of Title 18, United States Code (U.S.C.), Section 1001 by a fine of not more than $10,000 or by imprisonment of not more than five years, or both; and that requesting or obtaining any record(s) under false pretenses is punishable under the provisions of Title 5, U.S.C., Section 552a(i)(3) as a misdemeanor and by a fine of not more than $5,000.

Sincerely,

John Christian Wilson

Former US address
170 West 74th St
New York, NY 10023

[Note: The FBI in error responded twice to my 14 June 2013 FOIPA Request was responded to twice by the FBI and assigned two FOIPA Request No's: 1224169-000 on 20 November 2013 and 1250235-000 on29 January 2014].

* * * * *

* * * * *

Exhibit 92: *29 January 2014.   FOIA letter from FBI to John Wilson.*

U.S. Department of Justice

Federal Bureau of Investigation
Washington, D.C. 20535

January 29, 2014

MR. JOHN CHRISTIAN WILSON

AUSTRALIA

FOIPA Request No.: 1250235-000
Subject: WILSON, JOHN CHRISTIAN

Dear Mr. Wilson:

This is in response to your Freedom of Information/Privacy Acts (FOIPA) request.

Based on the information you provided, we conducted a search of the Central Records System. We were unable to identify main file records responsive to the FOIPA. If you have additional information pertaining to the subject that you believe was of investigative interest to the Bureau, please provide us the details and we will conduct an additional search.

In accordance with standard FBI practice and pursuant to FOIA exemption (b)(7)(E)/ Privacy Act exemption (j)(2) [5 U.S.C. § 552/552a (b)(7)(E)/(j)(2)], this response neither confirms nor denies the existence of your subject's name on any watch lists.

For your information, Congress excluded three discrete categories of law enforcement and national security records from the requirements of the FOIA. See 5 U.S.C. § 552(c) (2006 & Supp. IV (2010). This response is limited to those records that are subject to the requirements of the FOIA. This is a standard notification that is given to all our requesters and should not be taken as an indication that excluded records do, or do not, exist.

You may file an appeal by writing to the Director, Office of Information Policy (OIP), U.S. Department of Justice, 1425 New York Ave., NW, Suite 11050, Washington, D.C. 20530-0001, or you may submit an appeal through OIP's eFOIA portal at http://www.justice.gov/oip/efoia-portal.html.   Your appeal must be received by OIP within sixty (60) days from the date of this letter in order to be considered timely. The envelope and the letter should be clearly marked "Freedom of Information Appeal." Please cite the FOIPA Request Number in any correspondence to us for proper identification of your request.

Enclosed for your information is a copy of the FBI Fact Sheet and Explanation of Exemptions.

Sincerely,

David M. Hardy
Section Chief,
Record/Information
   Dissemination Section
Records Management Division

Enclosure(s)

FBI FACT SHEET

- The primary functions of the FBI are national security and law enforcement.

- The FBI does not keep a file on every citizen of the United States.

- The FBI was not established until 1908 and we have very few records prior to the 1920s.

- **FBI files generally contain reports** of FBI investigations of a wide range of matters, including counterterrorism, counter-intelligence, cyber crime, public corruption, civil rights, organized crime, white collar crime, major thefts, violent crime, and applicants.

- **The FBI does not issue clearances or non-clearances for anyone other than its own personnel or persons having access to FBI facilities.** Background investigations for security clearances are conducted by many different Government agencies. Persons who received a clearance while in the military or employed with some other government agency should contact that entity. Most government agencies have websites which are accessible on the internet which have their contact information.

- **A criminal history summary check or "rap sheet" is NOT the same as an "FBI file."** It is a listing of information taken from fingerprint cards and related documents submitted to the FBI in connection with arrests, federal employment, naturalization or military service. The subject of a "rap sheet" may obtain a copy by submitting a written request to FBI, Criminal Justice Information Services (CJIS) Division, Record Request, 1000 Custer Hollow Road, Clarksburg, West Virginia 26306. Along with a specific written request, the individual must submit a new full set of his/her fingerprints in order to locate the record, establish positive identification, and ensure that an individual's records are not disseminated to an unauthorized person. The fingerprint submission must include the subject's name, date and place of birth. There is a required fee of $18 for this service, which must be submitted by money order or certified check made payable to the Treasury of the United States. A credit card payment option is also available. Forms for this option and additional directions may be obtained by accessing the FBI Web site at www.fbi.gov/about-us/cjis/background-checks/background_checks.

- **The National Name Check Program (NNCP)** conducts a search of the FBI's Universal Index (UNI) to identify any information contained in FBI records that may be associated with an individual and provides the results of that search to a requesting federal, state or local agency. Names are searched in a multitude of combinations and phonetic spellings to ensure all records are located. The NNCP also searches for both "main" and "cross reference" files. A main file is an entry that carries the name corresponding to the subject of a file, while a cross reference is merely a mention of an individual contained in a file. The results from a search of this magnitude can result in several "hits" and "idents" on an individual. In each instance where UNI has identified a name variation or reference, information must be reviewed to determine if it is applicable to the individual in question.

- **The Record/Information Dissemination Section (RIDS)** searches for records and provides copies of FBI files responsive to Freedom of Information or Privacy Act (FOIPA) requests for information. RIDS provides responsive documents to requesters seeking "reasonably described information." For a FOIPA search, the subject's name, event, activity, or business is searched to determine whether there is an associated investigative file. This is called a "main file search" and differs from the **NNCP** search.

FOR GENERAL INFORMATION ABOUT THE FBI, VISIT OUR WEBSITE AT
www.fbi.gov

1/6/14

EXPLANATION OF EXEMPTIONS

SUBSECTIONS OF TITLE 5, UNITED STATES CODE, SECTION 552

(b)(1)   (A) specifically authorized under criteria established by an Executive order to be kept secret in the interest of national defense or foreign policy and (B) are in fact properly classified to such Executive order;

(b)(2)   related solely to the internal personnel rules and practices of an agency;

(b)(3)   specifically exempted from disclosure by statute (other than section 552b of this title), provided that such statute(A) requires that the matters be withheld from the public in such a manner as to leave no discretion on issue, or (B) establishes particular criteria for withholding or refers to particular types of matters to be withheld;

(b)(4)   trade secrets and commercial or financial information obtained from a person and privileged or confidential;

(b)(5)   inter-agency or intra-agency memorandums or letters which would not be available by law to a party other than an agency in litigation with the agency;

(b)(6)   personnel and medical files and similar files the disclosure of which would constitute a clearly unwarranted invasion of personal privacy;

(b)(7)   records or information compiled for law enforcement purposes, but only to the extent that the production of such law enforcement records or information (A) could reasonably be expected to interfere with enforcement proceedings, (B) would deprive a person of a right to a fair trial or an impartial adjudication, (C) could reasonably be expected to constitute an unwarranted invasion of personal privacy, (D) could reasonably be expected to disclose the identity of confidential source, including a State, local, or foreign agency or authority or any private institution which furnished information on a confidential basis, and, in the case of record or information compiled by a criminal law enforcement authority in the course of a criminal investigation, or by an agency conducting a lawful national security intelligence investigation, information furnished by a confidential source, (E) would disclose techniques and procedures for law enforcement investigations or prosecutions, or would disclose guidelines for law enforcement investigations or prosecutions if such disclosure could reasonably be expected to risk circumvention of the law, or (F) could reasonably be expected to endanger the life or physical safety of any individual;

(b)(8)   contained in or related to examination, operating, or condition reports prepared by, on behalf of, or for the use of an agency responsible for the regulation or supervision of financial institutions; or

(b)(9)   geological and geophysical information and data, including maps, concerning wells.

SUBSECTIONS OF TITLE 5, UNITED STATES CODE, SECTION 552a

(d)(5)   information compiled in reasonable anticipation of a civil action proceeding;

(j)(2)   material reporting investigative efforts pertaining to the enforcement of criminal law including efforts to prevent, control, or reduce crime or apprehend criminals;

(k)(1)   information which is currently and properly classified pursuant to an Executive order in the interest of the national defense or foreign policy, for example, information involving intelligence sources or methods;

(k)(2)   investigatory material compiled for law enforcement purposes, other than criminal, which did not result in loss of a right, benefit or privilege under Federal programs, or which would identify a source who furnished information pursuant to a promise that his/her identity would be held in confidence;

(k)(3)   material maintained in connection with providing protective services to the President of the United States or any other individual pursuant to the authority of Title 18, United States Code, Section 3056;

(k)(4)   required by statute to be maintained and used solely as statistical records;

(k)(5)   investigatory material compiled solely for the purpose of determining suitability, eligibility, or qualifications for Federal civilian employment or for access to classified information, the disclosure of which would reveal the identity of the person who furnished information pursuant to a promise that his/her identity would be held in confidence;

(k)(6)   testing or examination material used to determine individual qualifications for appointment or promotion in Federal Government service he release of which would compromise the testing or examination process;

(k)(7)   material used to determine potential for promotion in the armed services, the disclosure of which would reveal the identity of the person who furnished the material pursuant to a promise that his/her identity would be held in confidence.

FBI/DOJ

*   *   *   *

V-2c   FOIA Requests: 2013 to 2014

FBI/DOJ

FOIPA Request No.: 1250235-001
Appeal No.: AP-2015-00491

Schedule of key correspondence

Emailed letter dated 26 March 2014 FOIPA Request to FBI.

Email dated 26 March 2014, FBI acknowledges receipt of FOIPA request.

Latter dated 6 May 2014 from FBI to John Wilson assigns FOIPA Request No. 1250235-001.

Letter dated 25 September 2014, FBI responds to search – reviewed 21 pages, and released 10 in full or part.

Letter dated 6 November 2014, John Wilson requests administrative appeal to DOJ, OIP.

Letter dated 6 November 2014, DOJ, OIP assigns Appeal No.: AP-2015-00491.

Letter 23 February 2015, DOJ,OIP responds to appeal AP-2014-01140 – no further records.

* * * * *

Exhibit 93: *20-25 March 2014.   Emails between John Wilson and Attorney David Sobel.*

From: David Sobel <sobel@eff.org>
Sent: Thursday, March 20, 2014 12:27 PM
To: John Wilson
Subject: Re: FW: FW: Appeal response re FBI request

John -

Apologies for my delay in responding. I am attaching a draft request that would be appropriate to submit to the FBI. I think you need to submit this as a new request, as that is what the DOJ said you must do in response to the appeal.

Let me know if you have questions. Once you submit the request, please send me a copy of the final version.

Best,

- D.

* * * * *

From: David Sobel <sobel@eff.org>
Sent: Tuesday, March 25, 2014 3:12 AM
To: John Wilson
Subject: Re: FW: FW: Appeal response re FBI request

John –

Your letter looks fine. However, I'm not sure where you found the email address for the FBI you've included in the letter. The FBI website gives this address for submission of requests: foiparequest@ic.fbi.gov

You can include my name and phone number (202-246-6180) as a contact if they have questions, but I doubt they will contact me.

I'm about to leave for Europe for the remainder of the week and will likely be difficult to reach. But the letter looks good and you can submit it.

Best,

- D.

* * * * *

* * * * *

Exhibit 94: *26 March 2014.   FOIA Request email from John Wilson to FBI.*

From: John Wilson
mailto:jxxxxxxxxxxxxx@bigpond.com
Sent: Tuesday, March 25, 2014 3:58 PM
To: Sobonya, David P.
Cc: FOIPARequest; sobel@eff.org
Subject: FOI request - John Wilson

Please find FOI request attached for JOHN CHRISTIAN WILSON.

[Attachment: 26 March 2014   FOIA Request email from John Wilson to FBI.]

Date 26 March 2014

Federal Bureau of Investigation
Att'n: FOI/PA Request
Record/Information Dissemination Section
170 Marcel Drive
Winchester, VA 22602-4843

VIA EMAIL: foiparequest@ic.fbi.gov

<u>**Re: Freedom of Information Act Request**</u>

Dear Sir or Madam:

This letter constitutes a request under the Freedom of Information Act ("FOIA"), 5 U.S.C. § 552.

I request disclosure of all agency records concerning, naming, or relating to me. I specifically request that the FBI perform a complete and thorough search of all filing systems and locations for all records maintained by the Bureau pertaining to me. Such a search should include, but not be limited to, files and documents captioned in (or whose captions include) my name in the title. The FBI should search the Central Records System, Electronic Surveillance Records (ELSUR), and Electronic Case File (ECF). Further, I specifically request that the Bureau conduct a text search of the ECF to identify all potentially responsive main and cross-reference files. The FBI's search should include "main" files and "see references."

In the event that you determine that some responsive material might be exempt from disclosure under FOIA, please indicate the specific exemption or exemptions upon which the agency relies. I agree to incur legally assessable processing fees not to exceed $100.

To assist the Bureau in conducting a comprehensive search, I provide some relevant background information. My full name is JOHN ▇▇▇▇▇ WILSON. I was born in ▇▇▇▇▇▇ Australia on ▇▇▇▇▇. My social security number is ▇▇▇▇. My US passport number is: ▇▇▇▇.

I was a mining company equity analyst on Wall Street from 1994 to 1998. I am a citizen of the United States, and lived in the United States for many years, principally in New York and Philadelphia, where I received an MBA degree from Wharton. Currently I reside in Australia.

In 1996, in the course of performing my duties as a mining industry analyst for SG Warburg (which subsequently became part of SBC Warburg, thence UBS Warburg), the company published one of my reports containing information pertaining to an extended shutdown of the NYSE publicly traded U.S. mining company Freeport McMoran owned Grasberg mine in Indonesia. According to press reports at the time and other sources, the company was under investigation by the U.S. Department of State following eyewitness allegations it had been involved in the killing of indigenous protestors. A source indicated to me that there had been a confidential reprimand of the company by the U.S. Department of State following completion of an interim investigation into human rights and environmental abuses.

For the many years following the 1996 publication of information regarding the Freeport McMoran killings, I have had contact with multiple individuals who indicated that they were associated with the FBI and some who made reference to the Freeport McMoran matter. As a result, I believe it is likely that the Bureau maintains information about me stemming from the 1996 report, related and potentially other matters. I have been approached by undercover agents/employees/others that work for or on behalf of the FBI and which include multiple meetings with each during various periods between 1996 and 2010. In particular:

- Michael Mills: the FBI agent who moved into my apartment in NYC and occupied it for several years when I sublet it before my return to Australia.

- Kathleen Walton: former mining analyst at Merrill Lynch in NYC.

- Matthew Levey - Kroll Associates, Inc (New York City midtown office): consulting work case manager 2003 and 2004. Former State Department employee.

- Jeffrey S Robards: corporate finance, formerly Ernst & Young (E&Y) NYC. Now working for C W Downer & Co - a boutique M&A firm in Boston. (http://www.cwdowner.com/index.php?option=com_content&view=article&id=42&Itemid=23)

- Stephan Chenault and John Klotz: volunteers Sierra Club NYC Group since 1990s.

- Ben Worden, Rob Haggerty and Allison Dey (Tucson area): FBI agents involved with Diamond Mountain Buddhist group in southern Arizona and California.

- George Schneider and Livingston Sutro (Sierra Vista, AZ); Jennifer Conner (NYC): Associated with Diamond Mountain Buddhist group in southern Arizona.

- Paul Whitby (Tucson): biologist.

- Robert Schultz - Albuquerque based head hunter, MRC Mining Search. http://www.miningsearch.com/mining-search/our-team/

- Steven D. Garber - (wife Andrea - collaborator) additional details: biologist, lived in Manhattan for much of the 1990s, before taking a two year posting to teach biology at Embry Riddle in Prescott, AZ. Books authored include The Urban Naturalist (New York

John Wiley and Sons. 1987). PhD in Ecology, Environmental Sciences - Rutgers, The State University of New Jersey-Newark. B.S. in Natural Resources - Cornell University.

- Susan Ackerson Holmes (born 1962) - extensive interview in New York in 2003, former board member of the Sierra Club and subsequently an employee of the Sierra Club. Susan Holmes showed me her FBI identification card and identified herself as working for the FBI.

As the FOIA requires, I will anticipate your response to this request within twenty working days. Please feel free to contact me at the e-mail address or telephone number indicated below if you wish to discuss this request. Alternatively, my FOI attorney David Sobel can be contacted at Electronic Frontier Foundation, phone number in Washington D.C. (202-246-6180).

Under penalty of perjury, I hereby declare that I am the person named above and I understand that any falsification of this statement is punishable under the provisions of Title 18, United States Code (U.S.C.), Section 1001 by a fine of not more than $10,000 or by imprisonment of not more than five years, or both; and that requesting or obtaining any record(s) under false pretenses is punishable under the provisions of Title 5, U.S.C., Section 552a(i)(3) as a misdemeanor and by a fine of not more than $5,000.

Sincerely,

John Wilson

Australia

E:
T:

* * * * *

* * * * *

From: Sobonya, David P. <David.Sobonya@ic.fbi.gov>
Sent: Wednesday, March 26, 2014 7:00 AM
To: John Wilson
Subject: RE: FOI request - John Wilson

Dear Mr. Wilson,

The FBI has received your Freedom of Information Act/Privacy (FOIPA) request. Before we can process your request you must complete and submit the **U. S. Department of Justice (*Certification of Identity*) Form DOJ-361.** Privacy Act requests (records about yourself); requires an original and legible signature, and the "penalty of perjury statement" which is included on the Form DOJ-361.

If you do not wish to use the Form DOJ-361, your request must be accompanied by a notarized signature or a statement signed under penalty of perjury stating that you are the person that you say you are. The statement should be above your signature and state, "I declare under penalty of perjury that the foregoing is true and correct. Executed on [date]."

The Form DOJ-361 is available at http://www.fbi.gov/ under the **Freedom of Information Act/Privacy** link, or http://www.fbi.gov/foia/. The form may be mailed or faxed to the FBI at the address/number below. A scanned copy is acceptable if sent by electronic means but the FBI does not accept electronic signatures. You may submit an attachment listing additional information that may aid in locating responsive records. **Please place your name and contact information on the attachment.**

If you are requesting a copy or wish to challenge your Criminal History Summary Check often referred to as a (Rap Sheet) or a Criminal Background Check, please contact the FBI's Criminal Justice Information Services Division (CJIS) at (304) 625-2000 or write to: FBI, CJIS Division, Attention: Record Request, 1000 Custer Hollow Road, Clarksburg, WV 26306.

If you require additional assistance please contact me.

Thank you,

David P. Sobonya

Public Information Officer/Legal Admin. Specialist

Record/Information Dissemination Section (RIDS)

FBI-Records Management Division

170 Marcel Drive, Winchester, VA 22602-4843

PIO: (540) 868-4593

Direct: (540) 868-4286

Fax: (540) 868-4391/4997

* * * * *

From: John Wilson
Sent: Tuesday, March 25, 2014 4:26 PM
To: Sobonya, David P.

Cc: sobel@eff.org; FOIPARequest
Subject: RE: FOI request - John Wilson

Hi David,

Please find revised FOI request and signed privacy statement attached.

Regards.

John Wilson

* * * * *

From: Sobonya, David P. <David.Sobonya@ic.fbi.gov>
Sent: Wednesday, March 26, 2014 9:45 PM
To: John Wilson
Subject: RE: FOI request - John Wilson

Dear Mr. Wilson,

The FBI has received your Freedom of Information Act/Privacy (FOIPA) request and it will be forwarded to Initial Processing for review. Your request will be processed under the provisions of FOIPA and a response will be mailed to you at a later date.

Requests for fee waivers and expedited processing will be addressed once your request has been assigned an FOIPA request number. You will receive written notification of the FBI's decision.

Information regarding the Freedom of Information Act/Privacy is available at http://www.fbi.gov/ or http://www.fbi.gov/foia/. If you require additional assistance please contact the Public Information Officer.

Thank you,

David P. Sobonya
Public Information Officer/Legal Admin. Specialist
Record/Information Dissemination Section (RIDS)
FBI-Records Management Division
170 Marcel Drive, Winchester, VA 22602-4843
PIO: (540) 868-4593
Direct: (540) 868-4286
Fax: (540) 868-4391/4997

* * * * *

From: John Wilson [mailto:jxxxxxxxxxxxx@bigpond.com]
Sent: Friday, 25 April 2014 7:53 AM
To: 'Sobonya, David P.'
Cc: 'sobel@eff.org'
Subject: RE: FOI request - John Wilson

ATTN: FBI FOIA

Dear Mr Sobonya,

Could you please confirm whether the FBI will comply with the mandatory 20 day response time for the below FOIA request and anticipated timing of the FBI response.

Thank you.

John Wilson

* * * * *

From: John Wilson [mailto:jxxxxxxxxxxxx@bigpond.com]
Sent: Wednesday, April 30, 2014 2:14 AM
To: Sobonya, David P.
Cc: sobel@eff.org
Subject: FW: FOI request - John Wilson

Dear Mr Sobonya,

I am not sure if you received the below email. Could you please confirm whether the FBI will comply with the mandatory 20 day response time for the below FOIA request and anticipated timing of the FBI response.

Thank you.

John Wilson

* * * * *

From: Sobonya, David P. [mailto:David.Sobonya@ic.fbi.gov]
Sent: Thursday, 1 May 2014 2:21 AM
To: John Wilson
Subject: RE: FOI request - John Wilson

Dear Mr. Wilson,

The above FOIPA request (#1250235-000) was closed and a NO RECORD response letter was mailed to you on 1-29-2014.

Thank you,

David P. Sobonya
Public Information Officer/Legal Admin. Specialist
Record/Information Dissemination Section (RIDS)
FBI-Records Management Division
170 Marcel Drive, Winchester, VA 22602-4843
PIO: (540) 868-4593
Direct: (540) 868-4286
Fax: (540) 868-4391/4997

[NOTE: The FBI appears to be confusing the 26 March 2014 FOIA Request with a previous FOIA Request I made 14 June 2013. The FBI appears to have responded twice to the same 14 June 2013 request; once on 20 November 2013 with FOIA No. 1224169-000 (appealed by attorney David Sobel 23 December 2013); and again, 29 January 2014 with FOIA No. 1250235-000]

* * * * *

* * * * *

From: John Wilson
Sent: Thursday, May 1, 2014 8:01 AM
To: 'sobel@eff.org' <sobel@eff.org>
Subject: FW: FOI request - John Wilson

Hi David,

As you can see from the below email trail (I cc'd you on the communications), I don't seem to be making much headway with the FBI FOIA process. Is this something we can discuss how you might help from here, what to do, options, etc?

Please let me know.

Thanks and regards.

John

* * * * *

From: John Wilson [mailto:jxxxxxxxxxxxx@bigpond.com]
Sent: Thursday, 1 May 2014 7:55 AM
To: 'Sobonya, David P.'
Cc: 'sobel@eff.org'
Subject: RE: FOI request - John Wilson

Dear Mr Sobonya,

You will see your email to me below of 26 March 2014 acknowledging receipt of the revised FOIA request. I am asking whether this revised FOIA which provides further details as requested will be processed within the mandatory 20 day period by the FBI.

Please confirm.

Thank you.

John Wilson

* * * * *

From: John Wilson
Sent: Friday, May 2, 2014 1:41 PM
To: 'sobel@eff.org' <sobel@eff.org>
Subject: FW: FOI request - John Wilson

Hi David,

I would be keen to progress my FOI with the FBI if you think there is any point in proceeding. It could be that the FOI process, particularly in relation to the FBI, is too broken to bother with!?

What would make sense do you think from your point of view in relation to this? Is it easier if I call you to discuss where things might go from here, what your ongoing interest might be, and the likely cost of different options that could exist. For instance, is the option of taking the FBI to court still a possibility?

Thanks and regards.

John Wilson

* * * * *

From: David Sobel <sobel@eff.org>
Sent: Friday, May 2, 2014 11:07 PM
To: John Wilson
Subject: Re: FW: FOI request - John Wilson

Hi John -

I'm not at all surprised that the FBI has not yet responded to your recent request. As I think I mentioned early on, requests to the Bureau are never processed within the "required" time limit. Instead, it generally takes several months to receive a final reply. Filing suit does not speed things up, as the agency can file what's known as an "Open America" motion and the court will allow it more time to complete processing.

So at this point, I don't think there's really any alternative to waiting a few months and see what you hear. All of this must also be tempered by my frequently stated belief that it's unlikely the FBI even has responsive records.

Sorry not to be more encouraging.

Best,

- D.

* * * * *

From: John Wilson
Sent: Saturday, May 3, 2014 3:29 PM
To: 'David Sobel' <sobel@eff.org>
Subject: RE: FW: FOI request - John Wilson

Thanks David.

The FBI in its latest email I forwarded you said they consider the FOI request closed. I assume then they will treat this one submitted 26 March 2014 as a new request and open to reviewing it.

It sounds like you are of the view the FBI holds all the cards and I am basically powerless to do anything (which is probably correct)? If they incorrectly list me as a terrorist for example, or whatever they have me down as, I have no rights to be told this, let alone to challenge it. It is inexplicable but it seems the FOIA is my only avenue for advancing this situation. As I have said to you before, I am happy to pay to explore/advance alternative legal options, if there are any. I assume FBI held records that are not responsive become so at a certain point in time; are there any time limits or other ways of challenging the FBI's categorisation of such records? For my part, I have no doubt they are holding files on me.

Thanks and regards.

John

* * * * *

Exhibit 95: *6 May 2014.   Letter assigning FOIA No. from FBI to John Wilson.*

U.S. Department of Justice

Federal Bureau of Investigation
Washington, D.C. 20535

May 6, 2014

MR. JOHN CHRISTIAN WILSON
27 MANNS AVENUE
GREENWICH, NSW 2065
AUSTRALIA

FOIPA Request No.: 1250235-001
Subject: WILSON, JOHN CHRISTIAN

Dear Mr. Wilson:

This acknowledges receipt of your Freedom of Information/Privacy Acts (FOIPA) request to the FBI.

☑ Your request has been received at FBI Headquarters for processing.

☐ Your request has been received at the [_____ Resident Agency / _____ Field Office] and forwarded to FBI Headquarters for processing.

☑ We are searching the indices to our Central Records System for the information responsive to this request. We will inform you of the results in future correspondence.

☐ Your request for a fee waiver is being considered and you will be advised of the decision at a later date.

☑ Please check for the status of your FOIPA request at www.fbi.gov/foia.

The FOIPA Request number listed above has been assigned to your request. Please use this number in all correspondence concerning your request. Your patience is appreciated.

Sincerely,

David M. Hardy
Section Chief,
Record/Information
   Dissemination Section
Records Management Division

* * * * *

* * * * *

From: David Sobel <sobel@eff.org>
Sent: Wednesday, May 7, 2014 12:54 AM
To: John Wilson
Subject: Re: FW: FOI request - John Wilson

John -

I think there are a few separate issues at play here. First, with respect to timing, the FBI never responds to a request within the statutory time limit of 20 working days, and efforts to have a court require them to do so are not successful. The FBI is almost always given at least several months to answer requests, so any litigation at this point would be premature.

Assuming (as I do) that the Bureau will eventually respond and tell you they don't have any records, you could certainly challenge that in court (after filing an administrative appeal). You could file suit 20 working days after filing the appeal -- no need to wait on that part of the process. What I have said from the outset is that I haven't seen any evidence from you that would overcome their claim that they don't have records about you. Claims by people you dealt with that they were affiliated with the FBI are hearsay -- they carry no weight in court. So my concern has always been that you have nothing to present other than your suspicions based upon what other people said.
That's a significant problem.

Another issue is that the FBI filing system is organized in a way that doesn't always lend itself to a name of an individual being found. So if your name was incidentally mentioned in a document, but it is not "indexed" under your name, it would not be located. If (despite the other problem I mentioned) you want to aggressively pursue the "indexing" issue, I might recommend that you consult another FOIA attorney here in DC, a guy who spent many years as an FBI lawyer and knows the records system better than I do. Let me know if you'd like me to put you in touch with him.

In the meantime, I think you'll need to wait a couple of months longer before litigation is a feasible option.

I hope that clarifies things a bit.

Best,

- D.

* * * * *

From: John Wilson
Sent: Wednesday, May 7, 2014 7:11 AM
To: 'David Sobel' <sobel@eff.org>
Subject: RE: FW: FOI request - John Wilson

Hi David,

I would be interested in talking with the lawyer you mention if you think he might have an angle on this, though it sounds to me like FOIA is not a reliable tool by any means - too many ways for the FBI to get around it on these sorts of issues.

Regards.

John

* * * * *

From: John Wilson [███████████████████████]
Sent: Friday, 9 May 2014 6:13 AM
To: 'David Sobel'
Subject: RE: FW: FOI request - John Wilson

Hi David,

The other issue is whether there is any way to challenge the FBI's classification of non responsive/responsive records? If they have misclassified my files, unintentionally or otherwise, is there no way of reviewing/challenging this? Or is that the internal inspector general's job? Would that be the only alternative avenue to FOIA? I suspect the IG is a captive entity of the FBI/DOJ and would be a waste of time dealing with from my point of view?

Regards.

John

* * * * *

From: John Wilson ███████████████████████
Sent: Tuesday, May 13, 2014 9:00 AM
To: 'David Sobel' <sobel@eff.org>
Subject: FW: FW: FOI request - John Wilson

Hi David,

Further to below, re challenging the FBI's potential for for mis-classification of non-exempt files, are there other options that I can pursue. Would you be prepared to write a letter to the inspector general for instance setting out my complaint?

Regards.

John Wilson

* * * * *

From: David Sobel <sobel@eff.org>
Sent: Wednesday, May 14, 2014 3:51 AM
To: John Wilson ███████████████████████
Subject: Re: FW: FW: FOI request - John Wilson

John -

The lack of evidence problem, which I discussed previously, will hamper any effort to show that there was "mis-classification" or any other improper activity, whether before a court or the IG. I just don't see how you are going to be able to demonstrate that.

I had mentioned an attorney who previously worked at the FBI on FOIA matters, and I checked in with him re your request. He said he would be glad to have you contact him. He is Scott Hodes <infoprivacylaw@yahoo.com>. He has seen the appeal I submitted on your behalf and DOJ's response, so he is somewhat familiar with the matter. Check in with him and see if he has a more positive sense of this than I do. If he requests a fee, I can transfer to him the balance of what you wired to me, approximately $500. Let me know how you'd like to proceed.

Best,

- D.

* * * * *

From: John Wilson
Sent: Wednesday, 14 May 2014 6:36 AM
To: 'David Sobel'
Subject: RE: FW: FW: FOI request - John Wilson

Thanks David. I'll have a chat to him though I assume he would have mentioned any untried options to you.

Re the lack of evidence issue and the IG - I thought that's what they were meant to do: investigate and collect the information outsiders don't have access to. From the IG's point of view, my knowing the names of so many agents, what they do for the FBI and the Freeport McMoran connection ought to make it clear to him I have been targeted, whether rightly or not. If the IG is not independent then his involvement will make no difference. If he is independent he might look into my claims. That's why sending a letter might be worth while?

Regards.

John

* * * * *

From: John Wilson
Sent: Friday, May 16, 2014 9:31 AM
To: 'David Sobel' <sobel@eff.org>
Subject: FW: FW: FW: FOI request - John Wilson

Hi David,

Could you draft a letter for IG outlining my complaint and request for enquiry please? Can it be sent under your letterhead?

Regards.

John

* * * * *

From: David Sobel <sobel@eff.org>
Sent: Saturday, May 17, 2014 3:08 AM
To: John Wilson
Subject: Re: FW: FW: FW: FOI request - John Wilson

John -

I don't feel comfortable going to the IG with this for a couple of reasons. First, your updated (and more descriptive) request is still pending at the FBI, so it seems premature to claim that there has been some sort of misconduct with respect to its handling. Since you opted to follow OIP's guidance and submit a new, more detailed request, you need to let that play out.

The second, more substantive, issue is the one I've now raised a couple of times. While you might suspect that files exist, you have no evidence of that. The legal standard on this is very clear: an agency is obligated to perform a reasonable search and, once they have done so, the results can be challenged only with "positive indications" of overlooked material. You simply cannot make that showing, and that presents an insurmountable obstacle whether you're dealing with the IG or the court.

With respect to a lawsuit, assuming the FBI either sends you another "no records" response or fails to respond within another month or two, I have tried from the outset to lower your expectations as to what is likely to happen. The first thing I told you is that, sometimes, filing a lawsuit can prompt an agency to be more careful about the search it conducts, as the matter gets elevated above the usual intake staff at the agency. I have had the experience of an agency locating material after a suit is filed when they initially said they couldn't find anything. But that does not mean that, if they continue to insist after being sued that they have no records, that there is a valid basis to challenge that claim. Although we are not at that point yet, I want to reiterate that should I file a suit on your behalf, I would only be prepared to do so with the understanding that I would not challenge a post-lawsuit claim by the FBI that they have no records.

While I take my obligation to you aa a client seriously, I am also obligated to only pursue legal claims in court that I believe have merit. Unless I have some evidence that I have not yet seen, I would thus feel obligated not to challenge a "no records" claim reiterated by the FBI after a suit was filed.

I would fully understand it if you elect to have another attorney pursue this further than I am prepared to do. That is why I suggested you might want to contact Scott Hodes to see if, given his intimate knowledge of FBI practices and procedures, he might feel more strongly about the likelihood of showing that something has been overlooked.

I'm about to go out of town until May 28, but would be glad to discuss this by phone when I return, if you'd like.

Best,

- D.

* * * * *

* * * * *

From: John Wilson
Sent: Saturday, 17 May 2014 7:24 AM
To: 'David Sobel'
Subject: RE: FW: FW: FW: FOI request - John Wilson

Hi David,

With regard to the IG, my complaint would revolve around the issue of FBI harassment since 1996 stemming from my analyst report on the Freeport McMoran related killings in West Papua, not the failure to provide records requested through the FOIA. As you have indicated, even if FBI records exist, they in all likelihood are exempt from having to be released.

My understanding is the IG was established to deal with exactly these sort of citizen complaints about FBI misconduct. The IG can take my allegations and confirm them, if he is sufficiently independent to do so. Depending on how 'deep' he chooses to investigate will determine what sort of evidence of wrongdoing he turns up. This is not a court procedure and the burden of evidence doesn't exist at the level required by the court. Nor is it a complaint about the FOIA. It is a complaint about the FBI and a dozen or more agents, whose names I have provided, and it is being put forward to the IG as a weighty allegation worthy of his attention.

Regards.

John

* * * * *

From: John Wilson
Sent: Tuesday, June 3, 2014 7:35 AM
To: 'David Sobel' <sobel@eff.org>
Subject: FW: FW: FW: FW: FOI request - John Wilson

Hi David,

Just seeing if you are now back. I would be interested in sending a letter to the IG - as per below. Can you help with this?

Thanks and regards.

John Wilson

* * * * *

From: David Sobel <sobel@eff.org>
Sent: Wednesday, June 4, 2014 3:06 AM
To: John Wilson
Subject: Re: FW: FW: FW: FW: FOI request - John Wilson

John -

For the reasons I previously explained, I don't feel comfortable submitting a complaint to the IG.

It is now apparent that we have divergent views of the relevant issues surrounding your FOIA request. As I have said since the outset, I do not believe it is likely the FBI has any files about you. You, on the other hand, seem convinced that they do. In light of that difference, I don't think I could adequately represent you in any litigation concerning your FOIA request. As I mentioned, you might explore further possibilities with Scott Hodes and see if he has a different impression of the situation.

Although I have spent a bit of time assisting you with this, I am prepared to send you a full refund of the $1000 retainer you sent several months ago. As I previously mentioned, I could also transfer funds to Mr. Hodes if he is prepared to represent you. Please let me know how you'd like to proceed.

Thanks.

- D.

* * * * *

From: John Wilson
Sent: Wednesday, June 4, 2014 7:27 AM
To: 'David Sobel' <sobel@eff.org>
Subject: RE: FW: FW: FW: FW: FOI request - John Wilson

Hi David,

I have to say I cannot understand why you would not be prepared to assist with taking my underlying complaint about FBI misconduct to the IG as this seems a standard route for complaints about the FBI. The matters I would want to raise with the IG have nothing to do with the FOIA request I made but only with the underlying complaint of FBI abuse of me following the research report I published on Wall Street. Nor do I understand your confidence that the FBI has had no part in this matter as I allege - of course, I understand that files might not be forthcoming, but that is a different issue.

That said, if you are reluctant to proceed with this matter further I would be grateful for the refund.

Thanks and regards.

John Wilson

* * * * *

From: David Sobel <sobel@eff.org>
Sent: Tuesday, June 10, 2014 5:40 AM
To: John Wilson
Subject: Re: FW: FW: FW: FW: FOI request - John Wilson

John -

Please provide me with your wire transfer info. I will be sending you US$950, which takes into account transfer fees.

Good luck with your efforts.

- D.

* * * * *

From: John Wilson ███████████████
Sent: Thursday, June 12, 2014 5:26 PM
To: 'David Sobel' <sobel@eff.org>
Subject: RE: FW: FW: FW: FW: FOI request - John Wilson

Hi David,

Account details are:

Name: ███
BSB: ███
Account number: ███
Routing Number: ███
Swift Code: ███
Bank ███
Branch: ███

David - your name and contact details are on my current FOI request to the FBI as my FOIA lawyer contact. They are unlikely to contact you but its remains a possibility.

Regards.

John

* * * * *

From: David Sobel [mailto:sobel@eff.org]
Sent: Tuesday, 17 June 2014 2:15 AM
To: John Wilson
Subject: Re: FW: FW: FW: FW: FOI request - John Wilson

John -

My bank expressed some concern about their ability to ensure a reliable transfer with the info I provided (not sure why). To be cautious, I had them cut a cashier's check payable to you. What is the best postal address to which it should be sent?

If I receive any contacts concerning your request, I will certainly let you know immediately.

Best,

- D.

* * * * *

* * * * *

From: John Wilson
Sent: Tuesday, June 17, 2014 6:04 AM
To: 'David Sobel' <sobel@eff.org>
Subject: RE: FW: FW: FW: FW: FOI request - John Wilson

Hi David,

Address is:

John Wilson

Australia

Thanks and regards.

John

* * * * *

From: John Wilson
Sent: Thursday, October 16, 2014 10:20 AM
To: 'infoprivacylaw@yahoo.com' <infoprivacylaw@yahoo.com>
Subject: DOJ FOIA appeal

ATTN: Scott Hodes

Hi Scott, David Sobel mentioned he had passed details of my matter to you earlier this year. I would be interested in lodging an appeal to the attached FOIA response from the FBI. Is this something you could assist me with? Please let me know.

Thank you.

John Wilson
Managing Director

Resource Capital Research
www.rcresearch.com.au
T +61 x xxxx xxxx (SYD)

* * * * *

From: John Wilson mailto:jxxxxxxxxxxx@bigpond.com
Sent: Tuesday, August 05, 2014 9:43 PM
To: Sobonya, David P.
Subject: RE: FOI request - John Wilson

Hi David,

Could you give me a status update on the below FOIA request [26 March 2014] please.

Regards.

John Wilson

* * * * *

From: Sobonya, David P. <David.Sobonya@ic.fbi.gov>
Sent: Wednesday, August 6, 2014 10:06 PM
To: John Wilson
Subject: RE: FOI request - John Wilson

Dear Mr. Wilson,

[THIS EMAIL WAS BLANK]

David P. Sobonya
Public Information Officer/GIS
Record/Information Dissemination Section (RIDS)
FBI-Records Management Division
170 Marcel Drive, Winchester, VA 22602-4843
PIO: (540) 868-4593
Direct: (540) 868-4286
Fax: (540) 868-4391/4997

* * * * *

From: John Wilson [mailto:jxxxxxxxxxxxx@bigpond.com]
Sent: Friday, August 22, 2014 4:16 PM
To: Sobonya, David P.
Subject: RE: FOI request - John Wilson

Hi David,

Could you provide a status update on the below FOIPA request [26 March 2014] and expected timing for a response.

Thank you.

John Wilson

* * * * *

From: Sobonya, David P. <David.Sobonya@ic.fbi.gov>
Sent: Monday, August 25, 2014 10:50 PM
To: John Wilson
Subject: RE: FOI request - John Wilson

Dear Mr. Wilson,

The estimated date of completion which the FBI will complete action on the request is October 24, 2014.

Please contact me If you require further assistance.

NOTE: Interim releases that generally equal approximately 500 pages are made for medium and large track cases.

Thank you,

David P. Sobonya
Public Information Officer/GIS
Record/Information Dissemination Section (RIDS)
FBI-Records Management Division
170 Marcel Drive, Winchester, VA 22602-4843
PIO: (540) 868-4593
Direct: (540) 868-4286
Fax: (540) 868-4391/4997

* * * * *

* * * * *

Exhibit 96: *25 September 2014.   Letter and disc of released documents from FBI to John Wilson.*

[Note: The FBI indicates it reviewed 21 pages and 10 pages are being released].

FEDERAL BUREAU OF INVESTIGATION
FOIA RELEASE

FOIA # 1250235-001

Subject: WILSON, JOHN CHRISTIAN

General Instructions TO VIEW CD: (Windows)
- Install Acrobat Reader on your computer
- Place CD into your CD-ROM drive
- Double click on MY COMPUTER icon (located on your desktop)
- Double click on the drive for your CD-ROM
- Double click on any folder icon to view its contents
- Double click on a PDF icon within a folder to view its contents

U.S. Department of Justice

Federal Bureau of Investigation
Washington, D.C. 20535

September 25, 2014

MR. JOHN CHRISTIAN WILSON

FOIPA Request No.: 1250235-001
Subject: WILSON, JOHN CHRISTIAN

Dear Mr. Wilson:

The enclosed documents were reviewed under the Freedom of Information/Privacy Acts (FOIPA), Title 5, United States Code, Section 552/552a. Deletions have been made to protect information which is exempt from disclosure, with the appropriate exemptions noted on the page next to the excision. In addition, a deleted page information sheet was inserted in the file to indicate where pages were withheld entirely. The exemptions used to withhold information are marked below and explained on the enclosed Explanation of Exemptions:

Section 552
- ☐ (b)(1)
- ☐ (b)(2)
- ☐ (b)(3)
- _____
- _____
- ☐ (b)(4)
- ☐ (b)(5)
- ☒ (b)(6)

- ☐ (b)(7)(A)
- ☐ (b)(7)(B)
- ☒ (b)(7)(C)
- ☐ (b)(7)(D)
- ☐ (b)(7)(E)
- ☐ (b)(7)(F)
- ☐ (b)(8)
- ☐ (b)(9)

Section 552a
- ☐ (d)(5)
- ☒ (j)(2)
- ☐ (k)(1)
- ☐ (k)(2)
- ☐ (k)(3)
- ☐ (k)(4)
- ☐ (k)(5)
- ☐ (k)(6)
- ☐ (k)(7)

21 pages were reviewed and 10 pages are being released.

☐ Document(s) were located which originated with, or contained information concerning, other Government agency(ies) [OGA].

☐ This information has been referred to the OGA(s) for review and direct response to you.

☐ We are consulting with OGA(s). The FBI will correspond with you regarding this information when the consultation is finished.

☒ In accordance with standard FBI practice and pursuant to FOIA exemption (b)(7)(E) and Privacy Act exemption (j)(2) [5 U.S.C. § 552/552a (b)(7)(E)/(j)(2)], this response neither confirms nor denies the existence of your subject's name on any watch lists.

For your information, Congress excluded three discrete categories of law enforcement and national security records from the requirements of the FOIA. See 5 U.S.C. § 552(c) (2006 & Supp. IV (2010). This response is limited to those records that are subject to the requirements of the FOIA. This is a standard notification that is given to all our requesters and should not be taken as an indication that excluded records do, or do not, exist. Enclosed for your information is a copy of the Explanation of Exemptions.

☑ You have the right to appeal any denials in this release. Appeals should be directed in writing to the Director, Office of Information Policy (OIP), U.S. Department of Justice,1425 New York Ave., NW, Suite 11050, Washington, D.C. 20530-0001, or you may submit an appeal through OIP's eFOIA portal at http://www.justice.gov/oip/efoia-portal.html. Your appeal must be received by OIP within sixty (60) days from the date of this letter in order to be considered timely. The envelope and the letter should be clearly marked "Freedom of Information Appeal." Please cite the FOIPA Request Number assigned to your request so that it may be easily identified.

☐ The enclosed material is from the main investigative file(s) in which the subject(s) of your request was the focus of the investigation. Our search located additional references, in files relating to other individuals, or matters, which may or may not be about your subject(s). Our experience has shown when ident. references usually contain information similar to the information processed in the main file(s). Because of our significant backlog, we have given priority to processing only the main investigative file(s). If you want the references, you must submit a separate request for them in writing, and they will be reviewed at a later date, as time and resources permit.

☑ See additional information which follows.

Sincerely,

David M. Hardy
Section Chief
Record/Information
   Dissemination Section
Records Management Division

Enclosure(s)

In response to your Freedom of Information/Privacy Acts (FOIPA) request submitted to the Records Management Division at Winchester, VA, enclosed is a processed copy of the responsive FBI Headquarters document.

The enclosed responsive document represents the final release of information responsive to your Freedom of Information Act (FOIA) request.

The enclosed documents responsive to your request are exempt from disclosure in their entirety pursuant to the Privacy Act, Title 5, United States Code, Section 552(a), subsection (j)(2). However, these records have been processed pursuant to the Freedom of Information Act, Title 5, United States Code, Section 552, thereby affording you the greatest degree of access authorized by both laws.

This material is being provided to you at no charge.

EXPLANATION OF EXEMPTIONS

SUBSECTIONS OF TITLE 5, UNITED STATES CODE, SECTION 552

(b)(1) (A) specifically authorized under criteria established by an Executive order to be kept secret in the interest of national defense or foreign policy and (B) are in fact properly classified to such Executive order;

(b)(2) related solely to the internal personnel rules and practices of an agency;

(b)(3) specifically exempted from disclosure by statute (other than section 552b of this title), provided that such statute (A) requires that the matters be withheld from the public in such a manner as to leave no discretion on issue, or (B) establishes particular criteria for withholding or refers to particular types of matters to be withheld;

(b)(4) trade secrets and commercial or financial information obtained from a person and privileged or confidential;

(b)(5) inter-agency or intra-agency memorandums or letters which would not be available by law to a party other than an agency in litigation with the agency;

(b)(6) personnel and medical files and similar files the disclosure of which would constitute a clearly unwarranted invasion of personal privacy;

(b)(7) records or information compiled for law enforcement purposes, but only to the extent that the production of such law enforcement records or information (A) could reasonably be expected to interfere with enforcement proceedings, (B) would deprive a person of a right to a fair trial or an impartial adjudication, (C) could reasonably be expected to constitute an unwarranted invasion of personal privacy, (D) could reasonably be expected to disclose the identity of confidential source, including a State, local, or foreign agency or authority or any private institution which furnished information on a confidential basis, and, in the case of record or information compiled by a criminal law enforcement authority in the course of a criminal investigation, or by an agency conducting a lawful national security intelligence investigation, information furnished by a confidential source, (E) would disclose techniques and procedures for law enforcement investigations or prosecutions, or would disclose guidelines for law enforcement investigations or prosecutions if such disclosure could reasonably be expected to risk circumvention of the law, or (F) could reasonably be expected to endanger the life or physical safety of any individual;

(b)(8) contained in or related to examination, operating, or condition reports prepared by, on behalf of, or for the use of an agency responsible for the regulation or supervision of financial institutions; or

(b)(9) geological and geophysical information and data, including maps, concerning wells.

SUBSECTIONS OF TITLE 5, UNITED STATES CODE, SECTION 552a

(d)(5) information compiled in reasonable anticipation of a civil action proceeding;

(j)(2) material reporting investigative efforts pertaining to the enforcement of criminal law including efforts to prevent, control, or reduce crime or apprehend criminals;

(k)(1) information which is currently and properly classified pursuant to an Executive order in the interest of the national defense or foreign policy, for example, information involving intelligence sources or methods;

(k)(2) investigatory material compiled for law enforcement purposes, other than criminal, which did not result in loss of a right, benefit or privilege under Federal programs, or which would identify a source who furnished information pursuant to a promise that his/her identity would be held in confidence;

(k)(3) material maintained in connection with providing protective services to the President of the United States or any other individual pursuant to the authority of Title 18, United States Code, Section 3056;

(k)(4) required by statute to be maintained and used solely as statistical records;

(k)(5) investigatory material compiled solely for the purpose of determining suitability, eligibility, or qualifications for Federal civilian employment or for access to classified information, the disclosure of which would reveal the identity of the person who furnished information pursuant to a promise that his/her identity would be held in confidence;

(k)(6) testing or examination material used to determine individual qualifications for appointment or promotion in Federal Government service the release of which would compromise the testing or examination process;

(k)(7) material used to determine potential for promotion in the armed services, the disclosure of which would reveal the identity of the person who furnished the material pursuant to a promise that his/her identity would be held in confidence.

FBI/DOJ

* * * * *

* * * * *

Exhibit 97: *25 September 2014.   Disc contents - released documents from FBI to John Wilson.*

```
FEDERAL BUREAU OF INVESTIGATION
FOI/PA
DELETED PAGE INFORMATION SHEET
FOI/PA# 1250235-1

Total Deleted Page(s) = 11
Page 10 ~ b6; b7C;
Page 12 ~ b6; b7C;
Page 13 ~ b6; b7C;
Page 14 ~ b6; b7C;
Page 15 ~ b6; b7C;
Page 17 ~ Duplicate;
Page 18 ~ Duplicate;
Page 19 ~ Duplicate;
Page 20 ~ Duplicate;
Page 21 ~ Duplicate;
Page 22 ~ Duplicate;

                          XXXXXXXXXXXXXXXXXXXXXXXX
                          X   Deleted Page(s)    X
                          X   No Duplication Fee X
                          X   For this Page      X
                          XXXXXXXXXXXXXXXXXXXXXXXX
```

February 10, 2006

Mr. Barry A. Fisher
Fleishman and Fisher
1875 Century Park East
Suite 2130
Los Angeles, California 90067

Attention: Mr. John Christian Wilson

Dear Mr. Wilson:

    We are in receipt of your letter dated January 17, 2005, to the U.S. Department of Justice (DOJ), Office of Inspector General. DOJ forwarded this correspondence to the Initial processing Unit (IPU), Internal Investigations Section, Inspection Division, Federal Bureau of Investigation (FBI), for our review. The IIS is the FBI entity that provides thorough, high quality, fair, consistent, and timely review and investigation into complaints of criminality and/or serious misconduct against FBI employees.

    In the above-referenced letter, you allege that an unidentified Undercover FBI Special Agent (SA) apparently disclosed confidential information to you originating from the U.S. State Department regarding a fatal Grasberg mining accident in Indonesia. You advised that you published an article about the accident at the Freeport McMoran owned Grasberg mine in 1996 and, since its publication, you allege having been contacted by numerous individuals who identified themselves to you as FBI agents, specifically SA [redacted] New York; SA [redacted] Arizona, and SA [redacted] Washington, D.C. A review of our records revealed that the above-named individuals are not employed by the FBI.   b6 b7C

    Inasmuch as the information provided contains no credible allegations of misconduct by any FBI personnel, IPU has determined that your complaint does not warrant the initiation of an investigation. We consider this matter closed.

Sincerely,

[redacted]   b6 b7C
Unit Chief
Initial Processing Unit
Inspection Division

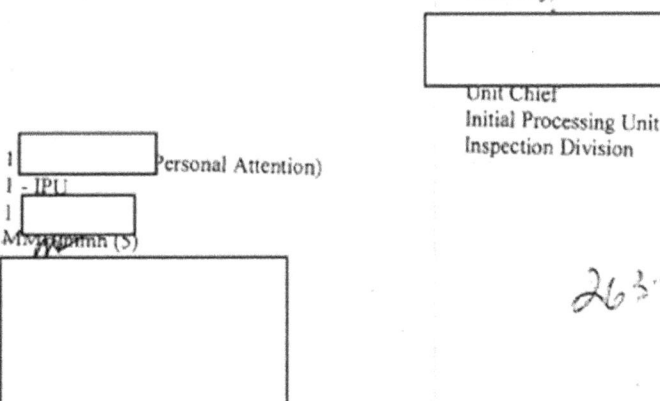

1 - [redacted] (Personal Attention)
1 - IPU
1 - [redacted] (S)

```
From:                    [redacted] (INSD) (FBI)
                         [redacted] (OPR) (FBI)
Sent:    Wednesday, February 08, 2006 4:39 PM
To:      [redacted] (INSD) (FBI)
Cc:      [redacted] (INSD) (FBI)
Subject: RE: Hey it's the new guy
```

UNCLASSIFIED
NON-RECORD

[redacted] - First I saw of this was when [redacted] brought it to me with you--- I think I forwarded [redacted] another one. Anyway, it appears that the Complainant (Wilson) never got a copy of any letter from IPU advising him that he failed to identify any FBI employees who have engaged in misconduct. I will ask [redacted] to draft a letter to send to OCA to send to Mr. Wilson (Complainant).

[redacted] - I put the paperwork I had in your in-box with refernce to Complaint# 1245. We will address this tomorrow morning [redacted]

```
-----Original Message-----
From:    [redacted] (INSD) (FBI)
Sent:    Wednesday, February 08, 2006 1:35 PM
To:      [redacted] (INSD) (FBI)
Cc:      [redacted] (OPR) (FBI)
Subject: RE: Hey it's the new guy
```

UNCLASSIFIED
NON-RECORD

[redacted] did you say you put this complaint o[n] [redacted] desk?

```
-----Original Message-----
From:    [redacted] (INSD) (FBI)
Sent:    Wednesday, February 08, 2006 12:35 PM
To:      [redacted] (INSD) (FBI)
Subject: Hey it's the new guy
```

UNCLASSIFIED
NON-RECORD

Do you have the hardcopy paperwork for complaint # 1245 [redacted] ecelved a call from Congressional Affairs (CA) on this matter. When you are available, may I come over and close the loop on this. I spoke to the CA a few minutes ago and they advised what information they are seeking. I am sure you already know what they want.

Thanks,

[redacted]

UNCLASSIFIED

UNCLASSIFIED

UNCLASSIFIED

U.S. Department of Justice

Office of the Inspector General

Washington, D.C. 20530

DATE: July 27, 2005

TO: Charlene B. Thornton
Assistant Director
Inspection Division
Federal Bureau of Investigation

FROM: *Glenn G. Powell*
Glenn G. Powell
Special Agent in Charge
Investigations Division

SUBJECT: OIG Complaint No. 2005005905
Subject: ███████ et al.
New York Division
FBI No. OIG Initiated

☒ We consider this a management matter. The information is being provided to you for whatever action you deem appropriate in accordance with your agency's policy and regulations. A copy of your findings and/or final action is not required by the OIG.

☐ This matter is referred to your agency for investigation. Please provide the OIG with a copy of your final report on this matter.

☐ This complaint will be investigated by the OIG.

IMPORTANT NOTICE

Identifying information may have been redacted from the attached OIG Report/Referral pursuant to § 7 of the IG Act or because an individual has (a) requested confidentiality or (b) expressed a fear of reprisal. If you believe that it is necessary that redacted information be made available to your Agency, you may contact the Assistant Inspector General for Investigations.

Please be advised that, where adverse action is not contemplated, the subject of an investigation does not have a right to have access to an OIG Report/Referral or to the identities of complainants or witnesses, and that, in all cases, complainants and witnesses are entitled to protection from reprisal pursuant to the Inspector General Protection Act.

Attachment

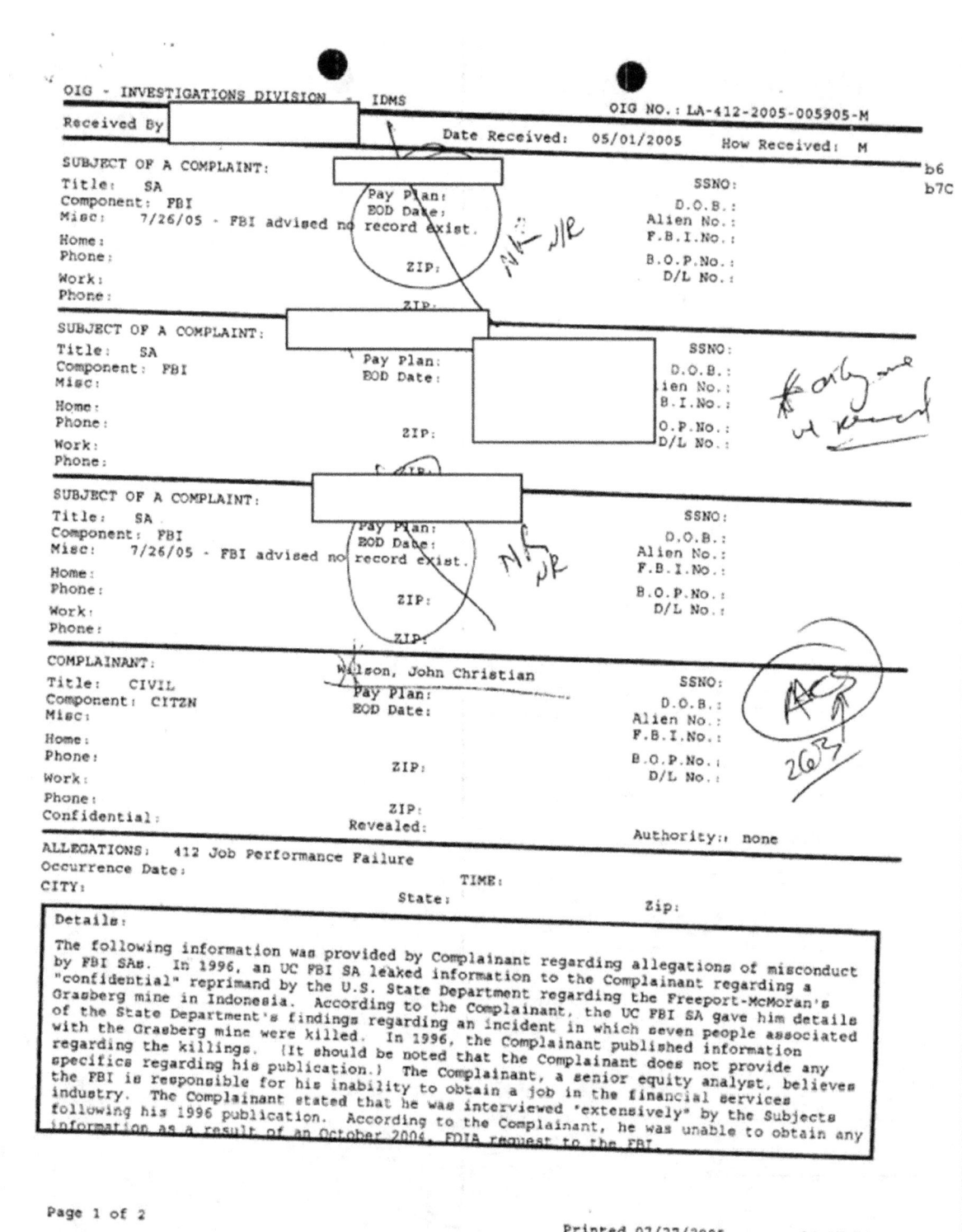

OIG - INVESTIGATIONS DIVISION - IDMS   OIG NO.: LA-412-2005-005905-M
Received By   Date Received: 05/01/2005   How Received: M

SUBJECT OF A COMPLAINT:
Title: SA   SSNO:
Component: FBI   Pay Plan: D.O.B.:
Misc: 7/26/05 - FBI advised no record exist.   Alien No.:
                            EOD Date: F.B.I.No.:
Home:
Phone: B.O.P.No.:
                                ZIP: D/L No.:
Work:
Phone: ZIP:

SUBJECT OF A COMPLAINT:
Title: SA   SSNO:
Component: FBI   Pay Plan: D.O.B.:
Misc: EOD Date: Alien No.:
                                                       B.I.No.:
Home:
Phone: O.P.No.:
                                ZIP: D/L No.:
Work:
Phone:

SUBJECT OF A COMPLAINT:
Title: SA   SSNO:
Component: FBI   Pay Plan: D.O.B.:
Misc: 7/26/05 - FBI advised no record exist.   Alien No.:
                            EOD Date: F.B.I.No.:
Home:
Phone: B.O.P.No.:
                                ZIP: D/L No.:
Work:
Phone:

COMPLAINANT: Wilson, John Christian
Title: CIVIL   Pay Plan: SSNO:
Component: CITZN   EOD Date: D.O.B.:
Misc: Alien No.:
                                                       F.B.I.No.:
Home:
Phone: B.O.P.No.:
                                ZIP: D/L No.:
Work:
Phone: ZIP:
Confidential: Revealed: Authority: none

ALLEGATIONS: 412 Job Performance Failure
Occurrence Date:
CITY: State: TIME: Zip:

Details:
The following information was provided by Complainant regarding allegations of misconduct by FBI SAs. In 1996, an UC FBI SA leaked information to the Complainant regarding a "confidential" reprimand by the U.S. State Department regarding the Freeport-McMoran's Grasberg mine in Indonesia. According to the Complainant, the UC FBI SA gave him details of the State Department's findings regarding an incident in which seven people associated with the Grasberg mine were killed. In 1996, the Complainant published information regarding the killings. (It should be noted that the Complainant does not provide any specifics regarding his publication.) The Complainant, a senior equity analyst, believes the FBI is responsible for his inability to obtain a job in the financial services industry. The Complainant stated that he was interviewed "extensively" by the Subjects following his 1996 publication. According to the Complainant, he was unable to obtain any information as a result of an October 2004 FOIA request to the FBI.

Page 1 of 2   Printed 07/27/2005   12:16:17

OIG - INVESTIGATIONS DIVISION - IDMS   OIG NO.: LA-412-2005-005905-M

DISPOSITION DATA: Date: 07/26/2005   Disposition: M   Approval: POWELL, GLENN G
Referred to Agency: Component: CITZN
Civil Rights: N   Sensitive: N
Component Number: Consolidated Case Number:

Remarks:

7/27/05 - Acknol letter sent to the Complainant advising him that the matter was forwarded to the FBI, Inspection Division. (yht)

7/27/05 - Management referral to AD Thornton, FBI Inspection Division. (yht)

John Christian Wilson
c/o Barry A. Fisher
Fleishman & Fisher
1875 Century Park East Suite 2130
Los Angeles, CA 90067

16 April, 2005

Email:

US Department of Justice
Office of the Inspector General
950 Pennsylvania Avenue, N.W., Suite 4706
Washington, DC 20530-0001

Dear Sir:

I write as a follow up to the letter I sent to your office on 17 January, 2005 (copy enclosed). Could you please indicate your expected timing for a response to that letter.

Thank you.

Sincerely yours,

John Wilson

Encl. Copy of letter sent to your office, dated 17 January, 2005

John Christian Wilson
c/o Barry A. Fisher
Fleishman & Fisher
1875 Century Park East Suite 2230
Los Angeles, CA 90067
Tel: 310-5571077

Email:

17 January, 2005

US Department of Justice
Office of the Inspector General
950 Pennsylvania Avenue, N.W., Suite 4706
Washington, DC 20530-0001

Dear Sir:

I write because of the oversight responsibilities of your office. I was a mining company equity analyst on Wall Street from 1994 to 1998. I am a citizen of the U.S.A., was born in Australia, and have long lived in the United States, principally in New York and Philadelphia, where I received my MBA degree from Wharton. I am currently visiting family for an extended stay in Australia.

In 1996, in the course of performing my duties, information was leaked to me by a then undisclosed FBI agent who worked undercover as an environmentalist. This person gave me details of a State Department finding into an incident in which 7 people were recently killed in and around the publicly traded Freeport McMoran owned Grasberg mine in Indonesia. The information I received related to a confidential reprimand of the company by the U.S. Department of State for human rights and environmental abuses.

Since then, as set out below, I have been subjected to what appears to be a systematic retaliation campaign by persons associated with the FBI involving invasive and injurious tactics. Among other things, I have faced blacklisting in my industry. I have been unable to gain any employment in the financial services industry despite a recent boom in the mining sector and despite having worked on Wall Street for 6 years, mostly as a senior equity analyst.

For the many years following my 1996 publication regarding the Freeport McMoran killings, I have had many contacts with people who at some point revealed themselves as FBI agents on assignment connected to me, and who let me know that I angered important people by the publication. Some of these individuals engendered friendship with me under the auspices of other professional identities and each has interviewed me, two of them extensively. These include Steven Garber, now of White Plains, New York, formerly of New York City, Susan Holmes, now of Washington, D.C., formerly of New York City, and Livingston Sutro, of Sierra Vista, Arizona.

1 of 2

Aside from these agents, more than a dozen other people have identified themselves to me as having a high level of familiarity with these circumstances and appear to be FBI agents or associated with agents.

Given the fact that the source of the leaked information was itself an FBI agent and given the powerful business interests of Freeport, I am concerned that I am the subject of what appears to be either a case of FBI corruption or incompetence. The agent that passed to me the information about Freeport was a long term friend who targeted environmental extremists, and I am concerned I may have been maliciously profiled to justify the intense scrutiny I have faced.

An FOIA request to the FBI in October, 2004 yielded no information whatsoever.

I look forward to hearing from you. The most convenient means by which to correspond with me are through my attorney (details indicated above), alternatively via email.

Sincerely yours,

John Wilson

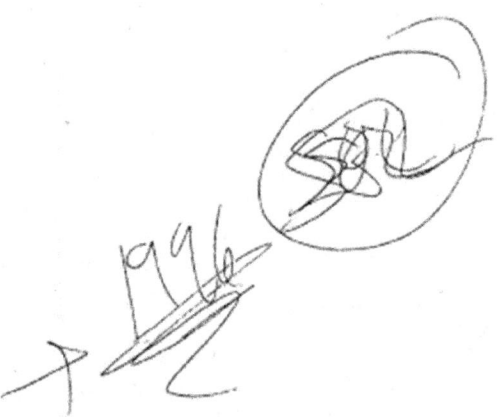

```
End of Data
02/10/06                       List Summary Response
13:19:29                                                                UNI050MK
Type X, x, or / to view Full Response, then press Enter.

    Name: WILSON, JOHN, CHRISTIAN
    M/R : M  Case ID: HQ 263-0                    Serial: 8636
    Race: U  Sex: M  DOB/Event:           ID Info:
    Misc: NO ACTION
                                    Entry Date: 10/13/2005 Class Level: SN




Command . . > ............................................................. +
F1=Help,F3=Exit,F4=Prompt,F12=Cancel
4AÛ                                                                      06,002
```

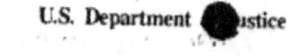 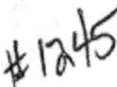

U.S. Department of Justice

Office of the Inspector General

Washington, D.C. 20530

DATE: July 27, 2005

TO: Charlene B. Thornton
Assistant Director
Inspection Division
Federal Bureau of Investigation

FROM: *Glenn G. Powell* (signature)
Glenn G. Powell
Special Agent in Charge
Investigations Division

SUBJECT: OIG Complaint No. 2005005905
Subject: ████████
New York Division
FBI No. OIG Initiated

b6
b7C

☒ We consider this a management matter. The information is being provided to you for whatever action you deem appropriate in accordance with your agency's policy and regulations. A copy of your findings and/or final action is not required by the OIG.

☐ This matter is referred to your agency for investigation. Please provide the OIG with a copy of your final report on this matter.

☐ This complaint will be investigated by the OIG.

IMPORTANT NOTICE

Identifying information may have been redacted from the attached OIG Report/Referral pursuant to § 7 of the IG Act or because an individual has (a) requested confidentiality or (b) expressed a fear of reprisal. If you believe that it is necessary that redacted information be made available to your Agency, you may contact the Assistant Inspector General for Investigations.

Please be advised that, where adverse action is not contemplated, the subject of an investigation does not have a right to have access to an OIG Report/Referral or to the identities of complainants or witnesses, and that, in all cases, complainants and witnesses are entitled to protection from reprisal pursuant to the Inspector General Protection Act.

Handwritten notes: No Action - None of the individuals names are FBI employees. Unsubstantiated 10-4-05/S

263-0-8636

* * * * *

* * * * *

Exhibit 98: *6 November 2014.   FOIA Request Appeal letter from John Wilson to FBI.*

Date 6 November 2014

Director, Office of Information Policy (OIP),

U.S. Department of Justice,

1425 New York Ave., NW,

Suite 11050,

Washington, D.C. 20530-0001

<u>Re: Freedom of Information Act Request Appeal</u>

<u>FOIPA Request No.: 1250235-001</u>

<u>Subject: WILSON, JOHN CHRISTIAN</u>

Dear Sir or Madam:

This letter constitutes an appeal request relating to FOIPA Request No.: 1250235-001

I request disclosure of all agency records concerning, naming, or relating to me.

I specifically request that the FBI/DOJ perform a complete and thorough search of all filing systems and locations for all records maintained by the Bureau/DOJ pertaining to me. Such a search should include, but not be limited to, files and documents captioned in (or whose captions include) my name in the title. The FBI/DOJ should search the Central Records System, Electronic Surveillance Records (ELSUR), and Electronic Case File (ECF). Further, I specifically request that the Bureau conduct a text search of the ECF to identify all potentially responsive main and cross-reference files. The FBI's/DOJ search should include "main" files and "see references."

In the event that you determine that some responsive material might be exempt from disclosure under FOIA, please indicate the specific exemption or exemptions upon which the agency relies. I agree to incur legally assessable processing fees not to exceed $100.

To assist the Bureau/DOJ in conducting a comprehensive search, I provide some relevant background information. My full name is JOHN CHRISTIAN WILSON. I was born in Sydney, NSW Australia ███████. My social security number is ███████. My US passport number is: ███████.

I was a mining company equity analyst on Wall Street from 1994 to 1998. I am a citizen of the United States, and lived in the United States for many years, principally in New York and Philadelphia, where I received an MBA degree from Wharton. Currently I reside in Australia.

In 1996, in the course of performing my duties as a mining industry analyst for SG Warburg (which subsequently became part of SBC Warburg, thence UBS Warburg), the company published one of my reports containing information pertaining to an extended shutdown of the NYSE publicly traded U.S. mining company Freeport McMoran owned Grasberg mine in Indonesia. According to press reports at the time and other sources, the company was under investigation by the U.S. Department of State following eyewitness allegations it had been involved in the killing of indigenous protestors. A source indicated to me that there had been a confidential reprimand of the company by the U.S. Department of State following completion of an interim investigation into human rights and environmental abuses.

For the many years following the 1996 publication of information regarding the Freeport McMoran killings, I have had contact with multiple individuals who indicated that they were associated with the FBI and some who made reference to the Freeport McMoran matter. As a result, I believe it is likely that the Bureau maintains information about me stemming from the 1996 report, related and potentially other matters. I have been approached by undercover agents/employees/others that work for or on behalf of the FBI and which include multiple meetings with each during various periods between 1996 and 2010. In particular:

- Michael Mills: the FBI agent who moved into my apartment in NYC and occupied it for several years when I sublet it before my return to Australia.

- Kathleen Walton: former mining analyst at Merrill Lynch in NYC.

- Matthew Levey - Kroll Associates, Inc (New York City midtown office): consulting work case manager 2003 and 2004. Former State Department employee.

- Jeffrey S Robards: corporate finance, formerly Ernst & Young (E&Y) NYC. Now working for C.W. Downer & Co - a boutique M&A firm in Boston. (http://www.cwdowner.com/index.php?option=com_content&view=article&id=42&Ite mid=23)

- Stephan Chenault and John Klotz: volunteers Sierra Club NYC Group since 1990s.

- Ben Worden, Rob Haggerty and Allison Dey (Tucson area): FBI agents involved with Diamond Mountain Buddhist group in southern Arizona and California.

- George Schneider and Livingston Sutro (Sierra Vista, AZ); Jennifer Conner (NYC): Associated with Diamond Mountain Buddhist group in southern Arizona.

- Paul Whitby (Tucson): biologist.

- Robert Schultz - Albuquerque based head hunter. MRC Mining Search. http://www.miningsearch.com/mining-search/our-team/

- Steven D. Garber - (wife Andrea - collaborator) additional details: biologist; lived in Manhattan for much of the 1990s, before taking a two year posting to teach biology at Embry Riddle in Prescott, AZ. Books authored include The Urban Naturalist (New York. John Wiley and Sons. 1987). PhD in Ecology, Environmental Sciences - Rutgers, The State University of New Jersey-Newark. B.S. in Natural Resources - Cornell University.

- Susan Ackerson Holmes (born 1962) - extensive interview in New York in 2003, former board member of the Sierra Club and subsequently an employee of the Sierra Club. Susan Holmes showed me her FBI identification card and identified herself as working for the FBI.

Please feel free to contact me at the e-mail address or telephone number indicated below if you wish to discuss this request.

Under penalty of perjury, I hereby declare that I am the person named above and I understand that any falsification of this statement is punishable under the provisions of Title 18, United States Code (U.S.C.), Section 1001 by a fine of not more than $10,000 or by imprisonment of not more than five years, or both; and that requesting or obtaining any record(s) under false pretenses is punishable under the provisions of Title 5, U.S.C., Section 552a(i)(3) as a misdemeanor and by a fine of not more than $5,000.

Sincerely,

John Wilson

▮▮▮▮▮▮▮▮

▮▮▮▮▮▮▮▮

Australia

E: ▮▮▮▮▮▮▮▮
T: ▮▮▮▮

* * * * *

* * * * *

Exhibit 99: *6 November 2014.   FOIA Appeal letter from FBI to John Wilson.*

U.S. Department of Justice

Office of Information Policy

Telephone: (202) 514-3642   *Washington, D.C. 20530*

November 6, 2014

Mr. John Wilson

AUSTRALIA

Re: Request No. 1250235-001

Dear Mr. Wilson:

    This is to advise you that your administrative appeal from the action of the Federal Bureau of Investigation was received by this Office on November 3, 2014.

    The Office of Information Policy has the responsibility of adjudicating such appeals. In an attempt to afford each appellant equal and impartial treatment, we have adopted a general practice of assigning appeals in the approximate order of receipt. Your appeal has been assigned number AP-2015-00491. Please mention this number in any future correspondence to this Office regarding this matter. Please note that if you provide an e-mail address or another electronic means of communication with your request or appeal, this Office may respond to your appeal electronically even if you submitted your appeal to this Office via regular U.S. Mail.

    We will notify you of the decision on your appeal as soon as we can. If you have any questions about the status of your appeal, you may contact me at the number above. If you have submitted your appeal through this Office's online electronic appeal portal, you may also obtain an update on the status of your appeal by logging into your portal account.

Sincerely,

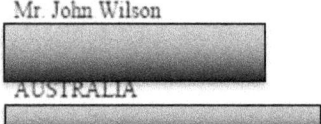

Priscilla Jones
Supervisory Administrative Specialist

* * * * *

* * * * *

Exhibit 100: *23 February 2015. FOIA Appeal decision letter from FBI to John Wilson.*

U.S. Department of Justice
Office of Information Policy
Suite 11050
1425 New York Avenue, NW
Washington, DC 20530-0001

Telephone: (202) 514-3642

Mr. John C. Wilson

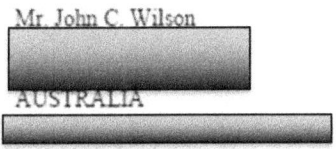

AUSTRALIA

Re: Appeal No. AP-2015-00491
Request No. 1250235-001
CDT:MTC

VIA: Appeal Portal

Dear Mr. Wilson:

You appealed from the action of the Federal Bureau of Investigation on your request for access to records concerning yourself.

After carefully considering your appeal, I am affirming the FBI's action on your request. In order to provide you with the greatest possible access to responsive records, your request was reviewed under both the Privacy Act of 1974 and the Freedom of Information Act. I have determined that the records responsive to your request are exempt from the access provision of the Privacy Act. See 5 U.S.C. § 552a(j)(2); see also 28 C.F.R. § 16.96 (2014). For this reason, I have reviewed your appeal under the FOIA.

The FOIA provides for disclosure of many agency records. At the same time, Congress included in the FOIA nine exemptions from disclosure that provide protection for important interests such as personal privacy, privileged communications, and certain law enforcement activities. The FBI properly withheld certain information because it is protected from disclosure under the FOIA pursuant to:

5 U.S.C. § 552(b)(6), which concerns material the release of which would constitute a clearly unwarranted invasion of the personal privacy of third parties; and

5 U.S.C. § 552(b)(7)(C), which concerns records or information compiled for law enforcement purposes the release of which could reasonably be expected to constitute an unwarranted invasion of the personal privacy of third parties.

Furthermore, to the extent that your request seeks access to records that would either confirm or deny an individual's placement on any government watch list, the FBI properly refused to confirm or deny the existence of any records responsive to your request because the existence of such records is protected from disclosure pursuant to

- 2 -

5 U.S.C. § 552a(j)(2) & 5 U.S.C. § 552 (b)(7)(E). FOIA Exemption 7(E) concerns records or information compiled for law enforcement purposes the release of which would disclose techniques and procedures for law enforcement investigations or prosecutions. This response should not be taken as an indication that records do or do not exist. Rather, this is the standard response made by the FBI.

Finally, as to your appeal concerning the adequacy of the FBI's search for responsive records subject to the FOIA, I have determined that the FBI's response was correct and that it conducted an adequate, reasonable search for such records.

Please be advised that this Office's decision was made only after a full review of this matter. Your appeal was assigned to an attorney with this Office who thoroughly reviewed and analyzed your appeal, your underlying request, and the action of the FBI in response to your request.

If you are dissatisfied with my action on your appeal, the FOIA permits you to file a lawsuit in federal district court in accordance with 5 U.S.C. § 552(a)(4)(B).

For your information, the Office of Government Information Services (OGIS) offers mediation services to resolve disputes between FOIA requesters and Federal agencies as a non-exclusive alternative to litigation. Using OGIS services does not affect your right to pursue litigation. The contact information for OGIS is as follows: Office of Government Information Services, National Archives and Records Administration, Room 2510, 8601 Adelphi Road, College Park, Maryland 20740-6001; e-mail at ogis@nara.gov; telephone at 202-741-5770; toll free at 1-877-684-6448; or facsimile at 202-741-5769.

Sincerely,

2/23/2015

X *[signature]*

Christina D. Troiani, Attorney-Advisor for
Sean O'Neill, Chief, Administrative Appeals Staff
Signed by: CHRISTINA TROIANI

* * * * *

V-2d   FOIA Requests: 2013 to 2018

FBI/DOJ

OGIS mediation for Appeal No.: AP-2014-01140 and AP-2015-00491

* * * * *

Emails between John Wilson, Barry Fisher and OGIS - 2017-2019.

2017-2018

* * * * *

Exhibit 101: *May 2017 - Nov 2018.   Emails between Wilson, Barry Fisher and OGIS – 2017-2019.*

From: John Wilson <redacted>
Sent: Thursday, May 11, 2017 7:33 AM
To: 'Barry Fisher' <xxxxxxxx@gmail.com>
Subject: FW: FW: FBI FOIA appeal

Hi Barry,

Your thoughts about where to from here please.

Thanks and regards.

John Wilson
Managing Director

RCR
Resource Capital Research
www.rcresearch.com.au
T +61 x xxxx xxxx (SYD)

* * * * *

From: Barry Fisher [mailto:xxxxxxxx@gmail.com]
Sent: Thursday, 11 May 2017 7:36 AM
To: John Wilson
Subject: Re: FW: FW: FBI FOIA appeal

awaiting responses to items below. and if not response to 2014 foia request, why no followup by you? also seems odd if was received since seems there is a set of automatic responses agencies make to foia requests.

2- No. 2--where this come from? From your attachment no. 3 or what?

I will need to see if I can find any other details relating to this - date 25 September 2014 from DOJ to JW [FOIPA 1250235-001]. Also now added to chronology.

3--item 4 is your new foia request 3/26/14—don't see any gov response, decision or appeal on chron or in documents-please clarify

As far as I am aware, they have not responded.

* * * * *

From: John Wilson
Sent: Thursday, May 11, 2017 8:16 AM
To: 'Barry Fisher' <xxxxxxxx@gmail.com>
Subject: RE: FW: FW: FBI FOIA appeal

Hi Barry,

Item 2: fbi/doj sent me a disc - summary and two docs contained attached.
item 3: No response from them. They may claim they never received it...in any event, I'm not sure their response would be any different to how they have responded previously...

John Wilson
Managing Director

RCR
Resource Capital Research
www.rcresearch.com.au
T +61 x xxxx xxxx (SYD)

* * * * *

From: John Wilson
Sent: Thursday, May 11, 2017 8:38 AM
To: 'Barry Fisher' <xxxxxxxx@gmail.com>
Subject: RE: FW: FW: FBI FOIA appeal

Hi Barry,

Item 2: fbi/doj sent me a disc - summary and two docs contained attached.

disc sent when? no cover letter or connected to any writing they sent to you?

29 Sept 2014 - attached. Also date is on one of the documents. Just the disc and summary slip.

item 3: No response from them. They may claim they never received it...in any event, I 'm not sure their response would be any different to how they have responded previously...

the difference it makes goes to possible statute of limitiation, not following thru after told could go to court--arguable a new and separate foia request with new time periods. also first request not raise issue about specific survaillance/persons so following up on what they never answered thru foia procedures instead of arguments that just never correctly responded to letter send not part of a law procedure requiring response --is a difference. curious just never following thru on the 2nd foia request.

I came to you at this point for help. It is more like the 4th foia request over the years. What is the statute of limitation on the existing foia appeal - 3 years, 6 years?

John Wilson
Managing Director

RCR
Resource Capital Research
www.rcresearch.com.au
T +61 x xxxx xxxx (SYD)

* * * * *

From: Barry Fisher <xxxxxxxx@gmail.com>
Sent: Friday, May 12, 2017 2:48 AM
To: John Wilson
Subject: Re: FW: FW: FBI FOIA appeal

may be 6 years, have not done any full research. maybe worth you following up on the 2014 foia request resending and demanding statutorily required acknowledgement and processing.

* * * * *

On Thu, May 11, 2017 at 2:24 PM, John Wilson < ███████ > wrote:

Hi Barry,

Yes - may be a waste of time of course, but I can send a follow up request. What will you do to advance my case in the meantime? Are you now prepared to take it to court.

John

* * * * *

From: Barry Fisher <xxxxxxxx@gmail.com>
Sent: Friday, May 12, 2017 7:41 AM
To: John Wilson
Subject: Re: FW: FW: FBI FOIA appeal

any case here needs expert foia counsel involved in washington as I have been saying. over the last weeks I have been trying to help the matter get clarified and organize, also trying to figure out what has been raised and denied. the unresponded 2014 foia request seems to most clearly set out what you want and the little time needed to send letter with copy of it appears merited and I recommend you do so. the earlier one asked for any documents and they sort of say there are none-an appeal would have to show they have or much have things. the documents that came on a disc omit certain information and possible to challenge redactions, but would have to have some credible argument that they were wrongfully redacted.

these last weeks going over emails and attachments, and the back and forth has been time consuming and if I were to help further organize and try to help connect with foia litigation counsel in washington would need to be compensated.

* * * * *

From: John Wilson <
Sent: Friday, May 12, 2017 11:30 AM
To: 'Barry Fisher' <xxxxxxxx@gmail.com>
Subject: RE: FW: FW: FBI FOIA appeal

Hi Barry,

A few possibilities:

1. Would you follow up on the appeal for me (AP-2015-00491)? If they don't respond promptly (say within 20-30 days) does this open an avenue for court action?

26 March 2014: JW FBI new FOIA request sent
25 September 2014: DOJ to JW FOIA request; disc sent by doj with two pdf attachments - [FOIPA 1250235-001]
6 November 2014: DOJ to JW - appeal received confirmation [1250235-001; AP-2015-00491].

2. What about follow up on your 2016 fax? (No point do you think, they won't respond and there is no legal leverage to force a response??)

3. Any point in providing additional information/commencing court action as per 25 February 2014: FBI responds to David Sobel foia appeal [AP-2014-01140].? There are/were definitely fbi files on me; whether they have been destroyed or transferred elsewhere, or classified in an obscure way - court action seems a promising way to try to get to the bottom of it??

Could you give me a cost estimate, or tell me how much of a retainer I should send you please; and specify what you would do at this point to advance my case. I would like to get my FBI file/get official confirmation of the FBI's interference with me. How best to achieve this is the issue.

Thanks and regards.

John

John Wilson
Managing Director

Resource Capital Research
www.rcresearch.com.au
T +61 x xxxx xxxx (SYD)

* * * * *

From: John Wilson
Sent: Tuesday, May 23, 2017 9:47 PM
To: 'ogis@nara.gov' <ogis@nara.gov>
Cc: 'Barry Fisher' <xxxxxxxx@gmail.com>
Subject: John Wilson - FBI FOIA dispute resolution Appeal No. AP-2014-01140

Office of Government Information Services,

National Archives and Records Administration, Room 2510,

8601 Adelphi Road,

College Park, Maryland 20740-6001

Dear Sir/Madam,

RE: Appeal No. AP-2014-01140

    Request No. 1224169

The DOJ FOI appeal dated 25 February 2014 (attached) in response to my request failed to provide any records.

I believe records exist as per the two letters attached above: one from my lawyer Barry Fisher dated 24 June 2016; the other from myself dated 23 February 2016 - neither of which has received a response.

I would appreciate your assistance to resolve and procure said records.

Thank you, I look forward to your response.

Sincerely.

John Wilson
Managing Director

Resource Capital Research

www.rcresearch.com.au
T +61 x xxxx xxxx (SYD)

* * * * *

From: OGIS <OGIS+noreply@nara.gov>
Sent: Tuesday, May 23, 2017 9:48 PM
To: John Wilson
Subject: Re: John Wilson - FBI FOIA dispute resolution Appeal No. AP-2014-01140

Thank you for contacting the Office of Government Information Services (OGIS) This email confirms our receipt of submission.

Due to an increase in demand for our services, there may be a delay in our response to your email. We apologize for any inconvenience this may cause. We will contact you regarding your submission as soon as possible.

In the meantime, to learn more about our mediation program, visit
https://ogis.archives.gov/mediation-program/about-mediation-program.htm

To learn more about requesting OGIS assistance, visit https://ogis.archives.gov/mediation-program/request-assistance.htm

Best regards,
OGIS Staff

--
OFFICE OF GOVERNMENT INFORMATION SERVICES National Archives and Records Administration
8601 Adelphi Road (OGIS)
College Park, MD 20740-6001
Email: ogis@nara.gov
Phone: 202-741-5770
Fax: 202-741-5769
Website: https://ogis.archives.gov/
Blog: http://foia.blogs.archives.gov/

* * * * *

From: John Wilson
Sent: Thursday, May 25, 2017 2:08 PM
To: 'OGIS' <OGIS+noreply@nara.gov>
Cc: 'Barry Fisher' <xxxxxxxx@gmail.com>
Subject: RE: John Wilson - FBI FOIA dispute resolution Appeal No. AP-2014-01140

Dear OGIS Staff,

Please find further documents attached pursuant to my request for mediation RE: John Wilson - FBI FOIA dispute resolution Appeal No. AP-2014-01140.

I have outlined my concerns of FBI interference, including listing the names of people associated with the FBI. The names of the FBI associated people listed are not necessarily "employees" or "special agents" but have an association with the agency, the formal title of which I am not privy.

I would appreciate your assistance to resolve and procure said records.

Thank you, I look forward to your response.

Sincerely.

John Wilson
Managing Director
Resource Capital Research
www.rcresearch.com.au
T

* * * * *

From: OGIS <OGIS+noreply@nara.gov>
Sent: Thursday, May 25, 2017 2:18 PM
To: John Wilson <
Subject: Re: FW: John Wilson - FBI FOIA dispute resolution Appeal No. AP-2014-01140

Thank you for contacting the Office of Government Information Services (OGIS) This email confirms our receipt of submission.

Due to an increase in demand for our services, there may be a delay in our response to your email. We apologize for any inconvenience this may cause. We will contact you regarding your submission as soon as possible.

In the meantime, to learn more about our mediation program, visit https://ogis.archives.gov/mediation-program/about-mediation-program.htm

To learn more about requesting OGIS assistance, visit https://ogis.archives.gov/mediation-program/request-assistance.htm

Best regards,
OGIS Staff

--
OFFICE OF GOVERNMENT INFORMATION SERVICES National Archives and Records Administration
8601 Adelphi Road (OGIS)
College Park, MD 20740-6001
Email: ogis@nara.gov
Phone: 202-741-5770
Fax: 202-741-5769
Website: https://ogis.archives.gov/
Blog: http://foia.blogs.archives.gov/

* * * * *

Exhibit 102: *8 June 2017.   Email from OGIS to John Wilson: Assigned case no. 201703007.*

From: OGIS <OGIS@nara.gov>
Sent: Thursday, June 8, 2017 4:10 AM
To: OGIS <OGIS@nara.gov>
Cc: ogis@nara.gov; xxxxxxxx@gmail.com;
Subject: Re: John Wilson - FBI FOIA dispute resolution Appeal No. AP-2014-01140

Dear Mr. Wilson

Please see attached Acknowledgment letter for your request to OGIS. [from May 23, 2017]

Regards,

OGIS team

OFFICE of GOVERNMENT INFORMATION SERVICES

June 7, 2017--Sent via email

Mr. John Wilson

Re: Case No. 201703007

NATIONAL ARCHIVES and RECORDS ADMINISTRATION

8601 ADELPHI ROAD
COLLEGE PARK, MD
20740-6001

web: www.ogis.archives.gov
e-mail: ogis@nara.gov
phone: 202-741-5770
toll-free: 1-877-684-6448
fax: 202-741-5769

Dear Mr. Wilson:

Thank you for contacting the Office of Government Information Services (OGIS). We will assign your request for assistance to an OGIS facilitator who will contact you directly.

Due to an increase in demand for our services, there may be a delay in our response to your request for assistance. We apologize for any inconvenience this may cause.

For tracking purposes, we assigned your request for assistance the case number listed above. Please cite this case number in all communications to our office regarding this matter.

Sincerely,

The OGIS Staff

NATIONAL ARCHIVES

* * * * *

From: John Wilson
Sent: Wednesday, June 14, 2017 10:11 AM
To: 'OGIS' <OGIS@nara.gov>
Cc: bfisher557@aol.com (bfisher557@aol.com) <bfisher557@aol.com>
Subject: John Wilson - FBI FOIA dispute resolution Appeal No. AP-2015-00491

Office of Government Information Services,
National Archives and Records Administration, Room 2510,
8601 Adelphi Road,
College Park, Maryland 20740-6001

Dear Sir/Madam,

RE: **Appeal No. AP-2015-00491**
     Request No. 1250235-001

The DOJ FOI appeal dated 23 February 2015 (attached) in response to my request I believe failed to provide a complete set of records.

Please find documents attached pursuant to my request for mediation dispute resolution regards FBI FOIA Appeal No. AP-2015-00491.

I have outlined my concerns of FBI interference, including listing the names of people associated with the FBI. The names of the FBI associated people listed are not necessarily "employees" or "special agents" but have an association with the agency, the formal title of which I am not privy.

I believe additional records exist as per the two letters attached above: one from my lawyer Barry Fisher dated 24 June 2016; the other from myself dated 23 February 2016 - neither of which has received a response.

I would appreciate your assistance to resolve and procure said records.

Please note my contact details:

John Wilson

Australia

Tel:
email:

Thank you, I look forward to your response.

Sincerely.

John Wilson
Managing Director

Resource Capital Research
www.rcresearch.com.au
T +61 x xxxx xxxx (SYD)

* * * * *

From: OGIS <OGIS+noreply@nara.gov>
Sent: Wednesday, June 14, 2017 10:14 AM
To: John Wilson
Subject: Re: John Wilson - FBI FOIA dispute resolution Appeal No. AP-2015-00491

Thank you for contacting the Office of Government Information Services (OGIS) This email confirms our receipt of submission.

Due to an increase in demand for our services, there may be a delay in our response to your email. We apologize for any inconvenience this may cause. We will contact you regarding your submission as soon as possible.

In the meantime, to learn more about our mediation program, visit https://ogis.archives.gov/mediation-program/about-mediation-program.htm

To learn more about requesting OGIS assistance, visit https://ogis.archives.gov/mediation-program/request-assistance.htm

Best regards,
OGIS Staff

--
OFFICE OF GOVERNMENT INFORMATION SERVICES National Archives and Records Administration
8601 Adelphi Road (OGIS)
College Park, MD 20740-6001
Email: ogis@nara.gov
Phone: 202-741-5770
Fax: 202-741-5769
Website: https://ogis.archives.gov/
Blog: http://foia.blogs.archives.gov/

* * * * *

From: OGIS <OGIS+noreply@nara.gov>
Sent: Saturday, July 1, 2017 8:25 AM
To: John Wilson
Subject: Re: RE: John Wilson - FBI FOIA dispute resolution Appeal No. AP-2014-01140

Thank you for contacting the Office of Government Information Services (OGIS) This email confirms our receipt of submission.

Due to an increase in demand for our services, there may be a delay in our response to your email. We apologize for any inconvenience this may cause. We will contact you regarding your submission as soon as possible.

In the meantime, to learn more about our mediation program, visit
https://www.archives.gov/ogis/mediation-program

To learn more about requesting OGIS assistance, visit https://www.archives.gov/ogis/mediation-program/request-assistance

Best regards,
OGIS Staff

--
OFFICE OF GOVERNMENT INFORMATION SERVICES National Archives and Records Administration
8601 Adelphi Road (OGIS)
College Park, MD 20740-6001
Email: ogis@nara.gov
Phone: 202-741-5770
Fax: 202-741-5769
Website: https://ogis.archives.gov/
Blog: http://foia.blogs.archives.gov/

* * * * *

From: OGIS <OGIS+noreply@nara.gov>
Sent: Wednesday, July 26, 2017 8:15 AM
To: John Wilson
Subject: Re: RE: John Wilson - FBI FOIA dispute resolution Appeal No. AP-2014-01140

Thank you for contacting the Office of Government Information Services.

If you requested our assistance with resolving a Freedom of Information Act (FOIA) dispute and have not done so already, please send us a brief description of your dispute and copies of your FOIA request, the agency's response to your request, your appeal letter (if you filed an appeal), and the agency's response to your appeal (if received a response).

You may send these documents to OGIS by email, fax, or mail. Our contact information is below in the signature block.

Due to an increase in the demand for our services, there may be a delay in our response. We apologize for any inconvenience this may cause and look forward to assisting you.

Sincerely,
The OGIS Staff

--
OFFICE OF GOVERNMENT INFORMATION SERVICES National Archives and Records Administration
8601 Adelphi Road (OGIS)
College Park, MD 20740-6001
Email: ogis@nara.gov
Phone: 202-741-5770
Fax: 202-741-5769
Website: https://www.archives.gov/ogis

* * * * *

From: John Wilson
Sent: Thursday, August 3, 2017 8:30 AM
To: 'OGIS' <OGIS+noreply@nara.gov>
Cc: 'Barry Fisher' <xxxxxxxx@gmail.com>
Subject: RE: John Wilson - FBI FOIA dispute resolution Appeal No. AP-2015-00491

Hi,

I put in separate requests for mediation on the 2 appeals shown below:
1) John Wilson - FBI FOIA dispute resolution Appeal No. AP-2014-01140, and also,
2) John Wilson - FBI FOIA dispute resolution Appeal No. AP-2015-00491.

You provided me with an acknowledgement letter on 8 June 2017 for AP-2014-01140; when do you expect to send me a response and acknowledgement letter for Appeal No. AP-2015-00491.

Also, can you provide me a schedule with anticipated timing to commence mediation with both appeals?

Thanks and regards.

John Wilson
Managing Director
Resource Capital Research
www.rcresearch.com.au
T

* * * * *

From: Barry Fisher <xxxxxxxx@gmail.com>
Sent: Tuesday, August 8, 2017 12:51 AM
To: ogis@nara.gov
Cc: John Wilson
Subject: OGIS Case No. 201703007

I phoned your offices to learn the status of the above matter, but was able to neither reach an operator or leave a message. Please inform me of the status of this matter.
Barry A. Fisher
Attorney for John Wilson
Fleishman & Fisher
1925 Century Park East Suite 2000
Los Angeles CA 90067
310-557-1077

* * * * *

* * * * *

Exhibit 103: *16 August 2017.   Email from OGIS to John Wilson: Assigned case no. 201703993.*

From: OGIS <OGIS@nara.gov>
Sent: Wednesday, August 16, 2017 5:48 AM
To: OGIS <OGIS@nara.gov>
Cc: ogis@nara.gov; ███████████████; xxxxxxxx@gmail.com
Subject: Acknowledgement Letter

Good afternoon.

Thank you for contacting the Office of Government Information Services.

Please see the attached acknowledgement letter.

Thank you,

OGIS
[Attachment]

OFFICE of GOVERNMENT INFORMATION SERVICES

August 15, 2017--Sent via e-mail

Re: Case No. 201703993

NATIONAL
ARCHIVES
and RECORDS
ADMINISTRATION

8601 ADELPHI ROAD
COLLEGE PARK, MD
20740-6001

web: www.ogis.archives.gov
e-mail: ogis@nara.gov
phone: 202-741-5770
toll-free 1-877-684-6448
fax: 202-741-5769

Dear Mr. Fisher:

Thank you for contacting the Office of Government Information Services (OGIS), the Freedom of Information Act (FOIA) Ombudsman. Your assistance request is assigned the tracking case number listed above. Please reference this number in all communications with our office regarding this matter.

An OGIS facilitator will review your request for assistance and any materials you have submitted and determine what assistance we can provide. Due to an increase in demand for our services, there may be a delay in our response. We apologize for any inconvenience this may cause, but we assure you that your request will be addressed as soon as possible.

If you have reached the stage in the agency's FOIA process where you are able to file an appeal, we strongly encourage you to do so. By filing an appeal, you preserve your administrative rights and give the agency a chance to look at the request anew and carefully review and reconsider every part of the initial response. If we are able to assist you in resolving your dispute with the agency, you may withdraw your FOIA appeal at any time. Please note that not all requesters who seek OGIS assistance have reached the stage in the FOIA process in which they have been given appeal rights.

We look forward to assisting you.

Sincerely,

The OGIS Staff

* * * * *

* * * * *

From: Barry Fisher <xxxxxxx@gmail.com>
Sent: Saturday, August 19, 2017 1:53 AM
To: John Wilson
Subject: Re: FW: Senator Rhiannon speech - re John Wilson revised submission to the inquiry into whistleblower protections in the corporate, public and not-for-profit sectors

thanks John-look forward to ready the 2 attachments. hard put to see options except maybe court action in washington. B

* * * * *

On Fri, Aug 18, 2017 at 3:55 AM, John Wilson wrote:

Hi Barry,

For your interest, my federal senator in Australia raised my ASIO/FBI issues in parliament earlier this week (speech attached). It was in the context of a submission I made to a current parliamentary inquiry into whistleblowers. The committee refused to accept either my initial compliant submission nor my revised compliant submission (the revised submission is attached). Furthermore, the committee provided no reasons for rejecting the revised submission. It also refused to consider any further correspondence from me on the issue. It appears to me that the committee rejected my submission on the grounds that the submission is critical of ASIO. I brought their strange response to the attention of Senator Lee Rhiannon.

I note that none of the committee members, including the chairman Mr. Steve Irons, MP, nor any of the members' staff whose advice members may depend on, has any requirement to disclose any association they may have with ASIO, nor whether they receive any financial payments or other incentives from ASIO. Therefore each member is potentially conflicted in the way they represent their constituents on this committee and likewise, may be conflicted in their reasons for rejecting my submission.

It's the same problem in the US - the FBI/intel agencies have essentially undermined the separation of powers.

I know, with your assistance we tried to get Schumer and Nadler interested and also the house and senate judiciary committees. Indeed, you spoke with the house judiciary staffers about my case and their interview with me - Mindy Barry, Jason Cervanac (Sp?) - but the house judiciary committee now seems to have no records of any of that!?

I would be interested in considering any options with you that might succeed in having my matter properly/independently reviewed by the authorities in the US, or ways to apply pressure for that to occur.

Thanks and regards.

John

* * * * *

From: Barry Fisher [mailto:xxxxxxxx@gmail.com]
Sent: Tuesday, 24 October 2017 2:49 AM
To: John Wilson
Subject: OGIS

Barry Fisher <xxxxxxxx@gmail.com> Aug 7

[to ogis, John]

I phoned your offices to learn the status of the above matter, but was able to neither reach an operator or leave a message. Please inform me of the status of this matter.
Barry A. Fisher
Attorney for John Wilson
Fleishman & Fisher
1925 Century Park East Suite 2000
Los Angeles CA 90067
310-557-1077

8:29 AM (19 minutes ago)

Office of Government Information Services

[to me]

Dear Mr. Fisher,

Thank you for your message concerning the status of your pending Office of Government Information Services (OGIS) case, OGIS case No. 201703007.

Your case is in our queue pending assignment. An increase in demand for our dispute resolution services has delayed our responses to requests for assistance. We apologize for any inconvenience this may cause. Once we assign your case to an OGIS facilitator, the facilitator will contact you directly.

If you have reached the stage in the agency's FOIA process where the agency has informed you that you are able to file an appeal, we strongly encourage you to do so. By filing an appeal, you preserve your administrative rights and give the agency a chance to look at the request anew and carefully review and reconsider every part of the initial response. If we are able to assist you in resolving your dispute with the agency, you may withdraw your FOIA appeal at any time. Please contact us if you are able to resolve your concerns directly with the agency.

Sincerely,

The OGIS Staff

OFFICE OF GOVERNMENT INFORMATION SERVICES
National Archives and Records Administration
8601 Adelphi Road (OGIS)
College Park, MD 20740-6001
Email: ogis@nara.gov
Phone: 202-741-5770
Fax: 202-741-5769

Website: https://www.archives.gov/ogis
Blog: http://foia.blogs.archives.gov/

* * * * *

From: John Wilson
Sent: Tuesday, October 24, 2017 7:01 AM
To: 'Barry Fisher' <xxxxxxxx@gmail.com>
Subject: RE: OGIS

Barry,
I received this from you today. Is this an update, or is one available?
john

John Wilson
Managing Director

RCR
Resource Capital Research
www.rcresearch.com.au
T +61 x xxxx xxxx (SYD)

* * * * *

From: Barry Fisher <xxxxxxxx@gmail.com>
Sent: Tuesday, October 24, 2017 7:51 AM
To: John Wilson
Subject: Re: OGIS

I received this today as a response to my email and call months ago.

* * * * *

On Wed, Oct 25, 2017 at 10:11 PM, John Wilson <johnwilson@rcresearch.com.au> wrote:

Hi OGIS staff,

To clarify - I have two outstanding requests to you for mediation services with the numbers assigned as set out below (details attached). As indicated today in your email to me, Barry Fisher corresponded with you concerning Case No. 201703007.

(Please confirm the case number for my second request for mediation (number 2 below) Appeal No. AP-2015-00491 is correctly stated as per below).

1. RE: Appeal No. AP-2014-01140

Request No. 1224169

John Wilson request to OGIS for mediation services sent 23 May 2017

Assigned OGIS Case No. 201703007

OGIS email confirmation dated: 8 June 2017

Barry Fisher email and phone correspondence with OGIS confirmed by OGIS email 26 Oct 2017.

2. RE: Appeal No. AP-2015-00491

Request No. 1250235-001

John Wilson request to OGIS for mediation services sent via email 14 June 2017

Assigned OGIS Case No. 201703993

OGIS email confirmation dated: 15 August 2017

Can you provide clarity around your anticipated timing to commence the above mediation and dispute resolution services.

Thanks and regards.

John Wilson

Managing Director

RCR
Resource Capital Research
www.rcresearch.com.au
T +61 x xxxx xxxx (SYD)

* * * * *

Exhibit 104: *2 November 2017.   Email from OGIS to John Wilson: Apology from OGIS for delays and confusion - Case no. "sent in error".*

From: Office of Government Information Services [mailto:ogis@nara.gov]
Sent: Thursday, 2 November 2017 12:34 AM
To: john_wilson@rcresearch.com.au
Cc: Barry Fisher
Subject: Re: John Wilson OGIS mediation request

Dear Mr. Wilson,

Your OGIS mediation case number for FOIA appeal No. AP-2014-01140 and AP-2015-00491 is 201703007. As noted in previous responses to your inquiries about the case numbers, the acknowledgement letter that cited 201703993 was sent in error.

OGIS case No. 201703007, which includes **both** of your FOIA disputes with FBI (i.e., AP-2014-01140 and AP-2015-00491) is in our complex queue pending assignment. An increase in demand for our dispute resolution services has delayed our responses to requests for assistance. We apologize for any inconvenience this may cause. Once we assign your case to an OGIS facilitator, the facilitator will contact you directly.

We hope this information is helpful and clears up any confusion our error has caused.

Sincerely,

The OGIS Staff

OFFICE OF GOVERNMENT INFORMATION SERVICES

National Archives and Records Administration

8601 Adelphi Road (OGIS)

College Park, MD 20740-6001
Email: ogis@nara.gov

Phone: 202-741-5770
Fax: 202-741-5769

Website: https://www.archives.gov/ogis

Blog: http://foia.blogs.archives.gov/

* * * * *

From: John Wilson ███████████████
Sent: Saturday, February 10, 2018 9:16 AM
To: 'Barry Fisher' <xxxxxxxx@gmail.com>
Subject: Intelgate

Barry,

The Nunes memo and rising profile of "Intelgate" and rising public distrust of the processes intended to contain the intelligence agencies may open new avenues for my complaints to be heard/reviewed. Your thoughts? Are there enquiries or other opportunities for submissions I might make (possibly with your assistance) in the current climate? What about to senate judiciary committee (again) or the administration/White House directly - is there a process for filing a complaint of FBI abuse directly with the administration (POTUS and his administration seem to be experiencing the same FBI style abuses as myself).

Thanks and regards.

John

* * * * *

From: John Wilson [mailto:johnwilson@rcresearch.com.au]
Sent: Tuesday, 27 March 2018 1:20 PM
To: 'Office of Government Information Services'
Cc: 'Barry Fisher'
Subject: RE: John Wilson OGIS mediation request

Hi,

Can you please provide an update as to anticipated timing for commencement of the mediation process as per below?

Thank you.

Regards.

John Wilson

Managing Director

RCR
Resource Capital Research
www.rcresearch.com.au
T +61 x xxxx xxxx (SYD)

* * * * *

From: OGIS <OGIS+noreply@nara.gov>
Sent: Tuesday, March 27, 2018 1:20 PM
To: John Wilson
Subject: Re: RE: John Wilson OGIS mediation request

Thank you for contacting the Office of Government Information Services. This is an auto reply message.

If you requested our assistance with resolving a Freedom of Information Act (FOIA) dispute and have not done so already, please send us a brief description of your dispute and copies of your FOIA request, the agency's response to your request, your appeal letter (if you filed an appeal), and the agency's response to your appeal (if received a response).

Send these documents to OGIS by email, fax, or mail. Our contact information is below in the signature block.

Due to an increased demand for our services, there may be a delay in our response. We apologize for any inconvenience and look forward to assisting you.

Sincerely,
The OGIS Staff

OFFICE OF GOVERNMENT INFORMATION SERVICES National Archives and Records Administration
8601 Adelphi Road (OGIS)
College Park, MD 20740-6001
Email: ogis@nara.gov
Phone: 202-741-5770
Fax: 202-741-5769
Website: https://www.archives.gov/ogis

* * * * *

From: John Wilson [mailto:johnwilson@rcresearch.com.au]
Sent: Thursday, 29 March 2018 7:45 AM
To: 'Office of Government Information Services'
Cc: 'Barry Fisher'
Subject: FW: John Wilson OGIS mediation request

Hi OGIS,

Please confirm receipt of below [to John Wilson's email request 27 March 2018].

Regards.

John Wilson

Managing Director

RCR
Resource Capital Research
www.rcresearch.com.au
T +61 x xxxx xxxx (SYD)

* * * * *

From: OGIS <OGIS+noreply@nara.gov>
Sent: Thursday, March 29, 2018 7:45 AM
To: John Wilson
Subject: Re: FW: John Wilson OGIS mediation request

Thank you for contacting the Office of Government Information Services. This is an auto reply message.

If you requested our assistance with resolving a Freedom of Information Act (FOIA) dispute and have not done so already, please send us a brief description of your dispute and copies of your FOIA request, the agency's response to your request, your appeal letter (if you filed an appeal), and the agency's response to your appeal (if received a response).

Send these documents to OGIS by email, fax, or mail. Our contact information is below in the signature block.

Due to an increased demand for our services, there may be a delay in our response. We apologize for any inconvenience and look forward to assisting you.

Sincerely,
The OGIS Staff

--
OFFICE OF GOVERNMENT INFORMATION SERVICES National Archives and Records Administration
8601 Adelphi Road (OGIS)
College Park, MD 20740-6001
Email: ogis@nara.gov
Phone: 202-741-5770
Fax: 202-741-5769
Website: https://www.archives.gov/ogis

* * * * *

From: John Wilson [mailto:johnwilson@rcresearch.com.au]
Sent: Friday, 6 April 2018 7:07 AM
To: 'Office of Government Information Services'
Subject: FW: John Wilson OGIS mediation request - OGIS mediation case number for FOIA appeal No. AP-2014-01140 and AP-2015-00491 is 201703007.

Please provide a status update on the OGIS mediation case number for FOIA appeal No. AP-2014-01140 and AP-2015-00491 of 201703007.

John Wilson

Managing Director

Resource Capital Research
www.rcresearch.com.au
T +61 x xxxx xxxx (SYD)

* * * * *

On Mon, Apr 9, 2018 at 2:04 PM, John Wilson <johnwilson@rcresearch.com.au> wrote:

Hi Barry,

Would you be able to call OGIS tomorrow to request an update on the below please - they are not responding to my emails?

Thanks and regards.

John

John Wilson

Managing Director

Resource Capital Research
www.rcresearch.com.au
T +61 x xxxx xxxx (SYD)

* * * * *

From: Barry Fisher [mailto:xxxxxxxx@gmail.com]
Sent: Tuesday, 10 April 2018 7:51 AM
To: John Wilson
Subject: Re: FW: John Wilson OGIS mediation request - OGIS mediation case number for FOIA appeal No. AP-2014-01140 and AP-2015-00491 is 201703007.

[n]ever possible to reach someone by phone??and if live person, someone knoweldgeable or simply registering concern? phone number, name, case reference?

* * * * *

On Mon, Apr 9, 2018 at 3:09 PM, John Wilson johnwilson@rcresearch.com.au wrote:

Thanks Barry.

OGIS case No. 201703007, which includes **both** of your FOIA disputes with FBI (i.e., AP-2014-01140 and AP-2015-00491) is in our complex queue pending assignment.

The general number is 202 741 5770; or

Alina M. Semo

Director

E-mail: alina.semo@nara.gov

Phone: 202-741-5771

John Wilson

Managing Director

Resource Capital Research

www.rcresearch.com.au
T +61 x xxxx xxxx (SYD)

* * * * *

From: John Wilson
Sent: Tuesday, April 10, 2018 7:11 AM
To: 'alina.semo@nara.gov' <alina.semo@nara.gov>; 'sheela.portonovo@nara.gov' <sheela.portonovo@nara.gov>; 'carrie.mcguire@nara.gov' <carrie.mcguire@nara.gov>
Cc: 'Barry Fisher' <xxxxxxxx@gmail.com>
Subject: FW: John Wilson OGIS mediation request - OGIS mediation case number for FOIA appeal No. AP-2014-01140 and AP-2015-00491 is 201703007.

Hi - is it possible to receive an update please as to progress of the below case?

Thank you.

John Wilson
Managing Director

RCR
Resource Capital Research
www.rcresearch.com.au
T +61 x xxxx xxxx (SYD)

* * * * *

From: Barry Fisher [mailto:xxxxxxxx@gmail.com]
Sent: Thursday, 12 April 2018 2:09 AM

To: John Wilson
Subject: Re: FW: John Wilson OGIS mediation request - OGIS mediation case number for FOIA appeal No. AP-2014-01140 and AP-2015-00491 is 201703007.

left phone message with the director at number you provided. B

* * * * *

On Mon, Jun 11, 2018 at 5:28 PM, John Wilson johnwilson@rcresearch.com.au> wrote:

Hi Barry,

This has FOIA appeal review has now been sitting with OGIS for over a year - one could reasonably wonder if there is any real hope of resolution here....

Given the long history of attempting to get resolution on my abuse by the FBI through multiple channels, all to no avail, is this now a case you could take to court - possibly through the Inter-American Commission on Human Rights? I think there is also scope, I seem to recall seeing somewhere, to provide additional details I have of FBI interactions with me, through a parallel process while waiting for OGIS?

Thanks and regards.

John

John Wilson

Managing Director

Resource Capital Research
www.rcresearch.com.au
T +61 x xxxx xxxx (SYD)

* * * * *

From: Barry Fisher [mailto:xxxxxxxx@gmail.com]
Sent: Sunday, 17 June 2018 2:38 AM
To: John Wilson
Subject: Re: FW: John Wilson OGIS mediation request - OGIS mediation case number for FOIA appeal No. AP-2014-01140 and AP-2015-00491 is 201703007.

what additional details do you have John?

* * * * *

On Sat, Jun 16, 2018 at 9:19 PM, John Wilson <johnwilson@rcresearch.com.au> wrote [to Barry Fisher]:

For this, the complaint is shifting from FBI abuse, to lack of any viable means for individuals abused by which the FBI can be held accountable, ie oversight channels compromised or ineffective - based on loss of my complaints, interview records and files by the House Judiciary Committee (you spoke with a couple people there at one point about my case); no access to records via FOI; inordinate delays (in the vicinity of 12 months) in their correspondence and refusal to address the substance of complaints; year/s in delays to address appeals; no follow through from congressman (Nadler) and senators (Schumer) in seeking accountability. You have been involved in much of this over the years and know firsthand the number of avenues we have tried and the nature of meaningless or incorrect answers and in cases no response at all. There is probably more I could add, but this gives you the gist of it.

Whether the channels lack independence, are compromised or underfunded is not the point. It is that they are not effective - in effect system leaves people in my position without any rights regards justice/fairness, etc.

John Wilson

Managing Director

Resource Capital Research
www.rcresearch.com.au
T +61 x xxxx xxxx (SYD)

* * * * *

From: Barry Fisher <xxxxxxxx@gmail.com>
Sent: Tuesday, June 19, 2018 3:52 AM
To: John Wilson <
Subject: Re: FW: John Wilson OGIS mediation request - OGIS mediation case number for FOIA appeal No. AP-2014-01140 and AP-2015-00491 is 201703007.

yes, corrupt system. inspector general horowitz justice department jumps to trump/republican requests but connected to you, others, including imprisoned oppressed client of mine, a dead ear, unmoving hand. and getting worse

* * * * *

From: John Wilson <
Sent: Tuesday, June 19, 2018 8:56 AM
To: 'Barry Fisher' <xxxxxxxx@gmail.com>
Subject: RE: FW: John Wilson OGIS mediation request - OGIS mediation case number for FOIA appeal No. AP-2014-01140 and AP-2015-00491 is 201703007.

Hi Barry, can you make a case out of the facts of my situation regards ineffective oversight and lack of FBI accountability to take to the Inter-American Commission on Human Rights do you think? John

John Wilson

Managing Director

Resource Capital Research
www.rcresearch.com.au
T +61 x xxxx xxxx (SYD)

* * * * *

From: John Wilson <
Sent: Friday, August 3, 2018 12:02 PM
To: 'Barry Fisher' <xxxxxxxx@gmail.com>; bfisher557@aol.com (bfisher557@aol.com) <bfisher557@aol.com>
Subject: letter 25 Feb 2014

Hi Barry,

No response from OGIS appeal request yet...well into the second year of waiting. I will bring the delay to Schumer's attention.

The attached letter 25 Feb 2014 says I can file an ELSUR directly with the FBI and provide further information (excerpted below) for the cross reference search. I can provide details of the 2003 FBI covert interview with me in NYC with Susan Holmes to assist with the cross reference search. We have discussed this before.

Are you able to assist me break through this impasse? One or more of the following all raised in the attached letter seem possible courses of action you could take on my behalf:

1. filing the ELSUR;

2. providing the details of the 2003 fbi interview to aid their cross-reference search;

3. file a lawsuit in federal district court in accordance with 5 U.S.C. § 552(a)(4)(B)

Excerpt from attached:

I note that in your appeal letter you ask that the FBI conduct a search for electronic

surveillance records and any cross-references. Please be advised that your client will need to

submit a new request asking specifically that an ELSUR search be performed. Regarding your client's request for a cross-reference search, please be advised that you need to provide information sufficient to enable the FBI to determine with certainty that any cross-references it locates are identifiable to the subject of your client's request. This information may include the following:

1) the specific circumstances in which the subject of your request had contact

with the FBI;

2) the date(s) of such contact;

3) the location(s) of such contact;

4) the full name (first, middle, and last) as well as any prior names or aliases used by the subject of your client's request;

5) Social Security number, date of birth, place of birth, and home address of the subject of your client's request;

6) names of associates of the subject of your client's request the mention of whom might

aid in the identification of responsive records; and

7) other references of the subject of your client's request in media, such as books,

articles, websites, etc.

You should provide this information to the FBI directly. Please note that the FBI may not be able to identify responsive cross-references despite the additional information you provide. You

may appeal any future adverse determination made by the FBI.

Thanks and regards.

John Wilson

Managing Director

RCR
Resource Capital Research
www.rcresearch.com.au
T +61 x xxxx xxxx (SYD)

* * * * *

From: OGIS <OGIS@nara.gov>
Sent: Wednesday, December 19, 2018 5:37 AM
To: OGIS <OGIS@nara.gov>
Cc: ;
Subject: OGIS request for assistance 201703007

December 18, 2018

Dear Mr. Wilson,

Please see the attached response to your inquiry with OGIS.

* * * * *

* * * *

Exhibit 105: 18 December 2018.   OGIS mediation FOIA Appeal decision letter to John Wilson re case no. 201703007.

NATIONAL ARCHIVES and RECORDS ADMINISTRATION
8601 ADELPHI ROAD - OGIS | COLLEGE PARK, MD 20740-6001
www.archives.gov/ogis | ogis@nara.gov | o: 202.741.5770 | f: 202.741.5769 | t: 877.684.6448

December 18, 2018 — Sent via email

John Wilson   Re: Case No. 2017-03007

Dear Mr. Wilson:

This responds to your May 23, 2017 request to the Office of Government Information Services (OGIS), which we received via email. Your request for assistance concerns your Freedom of Information Act (FOIA) request to the Federal Bureau of Investigation (FBI). We apologize for our delay in responding to your submission—requests for our assistance have dramatically increased, and we are doing our best to respond to the demand for our services as quickly as we can. Thank you for your patience as we handled your case.

You submitted two FOIA requests to the FBI. The first, request No. 1224169, sought access to records relating to yourself. The FBI responded that they could locate no responsive records. You appealed that response, and the Department of Justice Office of Information Policy (OIP) affirmed the FBI's action on your request. OIP also provided you with further information about how to specifically request ELSUR and cross-reference searches. You submitted a second FOIA request, No. 1250235-001 with the FBI, requesting a cross-reference search and providing additional information including the names and identifying information of specific individuals. The FBI responded by releasing 10 pages with redactions and withholding 11 pages in full pursuant to FOIA Exemptions 6 and 7(C), 5 U.S.C. §§ 552(b)(6) and (b)(7)(C). You appealed the FBI's response, and OIP affirmed the FBI's action on your request. Finally, on February 23, 2016, you sent a fax to the Department of Justice Office of Inspector General (OIG) disputing the FBI's response arguing that you did not limit your request to a search to FBI employees. You asked for OGIS's assistance with this matter since you had not received a response to the February 2016 fax.

Congress created OGIS to complement existing FOIA practice and procedure; we strive to work in conjunction with the existing request and appeal process. Our goal is to allow, whenever practical, the requester to exhaust his or her remedies within the agency, including the appeal process. OGIS has no investigatory or enforcement power, nor can we compel an agency to release documents. OGIS serves as the Federal FOIA Ombudsman and our jurisdiction is limited to assisting with the FOIA process. OGIS cannot intervene regarding complaints submitted to OIGs as this, although related to your FOIA request, is a separate investigative action outside of the FOIA appeal process.

In your submission to OGIS, you assert your belief that the FBI has not released responsive records.

In reviewing your submission, we noted that information about yourself was released to you The information still withheld relates to 3rd parties who are mentioned in the file. This information was withheld under FOIA Exemptions 6 and 7(C). Exemptions 6 and 7(C) protect personal privacy interests, the latter specifically in law enforcement records. FOIA Exemption 6 protects information about individuals in "personnel and medical files and similar files" when the disclosure of such information "would constitute a clearly unwarranted invasion of personal privacy." FOIA Exemption 7(C) is limited to information compiled for law enforcement purposes and protects personal information when disclosure "could reasonably be expected to constitute an unwarranted invasion of personal privacy."

FOIA Exemptions 6 and 7(C) protect the vast majority of information about any individuals mentioned in government records other than yourself. However, the protections of Exemption 6 and 7(C) can be overcome if you are able to provide a consent or privacy waiver from the individual about whom you seek records; proof of death of the individual who is the subject of the information; or a strong showing by you that there is an overriding public interest in the information because release would shed light on the operations of the government.

We hope that this information is useful. Thank you for bringing this matter to OGIS. At this time, it appears that there is no further assistance OGIS can offer and we will close your case.

Sincerely,

ALINA M. SEMO
Director

* * * * *

* * * * *

From: John Wilson ████████████████████████
Sent: Wednesday, December 19, 2018 5:11 PM
To: 'OGIS' <OGIS@nara.gov>
Subject: RE: OGIS request for assistance 201703007

ATTN: Alina M. Semo

Dear Ms Semo,

Thank you for your email and letter to me dated 18 December 2018.

Could you confirm the dates of the information released to me by the FBI/DOJ please that you reference in your letter. Do you have a copy of the records released to me that you can email me too please?

By way of further explanation regards my FOIA appeal and subsequent approach to OGIS for assistance, my concern is there have been numerous instances of people operating at the directive of the FBI who have interfered with me, or otherwise associated with me and none of these have been mentioned in the records released, nor have transcripts from these occasions been provided to me. I request that these records by released to me.

I do not know the formal title of these operatives, that is whether they are classified as employee, agent, or whatever - only that they are operating at the direction of the FBI and they have been issued FBI identity cards. I request all records be provided relating to me in relation to contact by Susan Holmes - an operative of the FBI - which occurred in New York City in 2003 when she conducted a lengthy interview of me at Cafe Fiorello one evening. In 2004, there was further contact by Steven Garber with me, another operative of the FBI, near my apartment at 74th and Amsterdam in NYC one afternoon, followed by an extensive interview and discussion with him in Central Park. I request all records of these meetings be provided to me.

Thank you.

Regards.

John Wilson

* * * * *

From: OGIS <OGIS+noreply@nara.gov>
Sent: Wednesday, December 19, 2018 5:12 PM
To: John Wilson ████████████████████████
Subject: Re: RE: OGIS request for assistance 201703007

Thank you for contacting the Office of Government Information Services. This is an auto reply message.

If you requested our assistance with resolving a Freedom of Information Act (FOIA) dispute and have not done so already, please send us a brief description of your dispute and copies of your FOIA request, the agency's response to your request, your appeal letter (if you filed an appeal), and the agency's response to your appeal (if received a response).

Send these documents to OGIS by email, fax, or mail. Our contact information is below in the signature block.

Due to an increased demand for our services, there may be a delay in our response. We apologize for any inconvenience and look forward to assisting you.

Sincerely,
The OGIS Staff

--
OFFICE OF GOVERNMENT INFORMATION SERVICES National Archives and Records Administration
8601 Adelphi Road (OGIS)
College Park, MD 20740-6001
Email: ogis@nara.gov
Phone: 202-741-5770
Fax: 202-741-5769
Website: https://www.archives.gov/ogis

* * * * *

* * * * *

Emails between John Wilson, Barry Fisher and OGIS - 2017-2019.

2019

* * * * *

From: John Wilson <jxxxxxxxxxxx@bigpond.com>
Sent: Friday, 18 January 2019 2:20 PM
To: 'OGIS@nara.gov'
Subject: FW: OGIS request for assistance 201703007

ATTN: OGIS

Further to your correspondence to me concerning my request for arbitration, I believe you closed the matter prematurely in a prejudicial way against my rights and interests without due consideration of the chief reason I approached your agency to request assistance, as outlined in the email below.

Could you respond please to the below and let me know a good time to contact you. Calls to your office go unanswered and messages and emails unreturned.

Thank you.

Regards.

John Wilson

* * * * *

On Saturday, March 30, 2019 at 4:57:54 AM UTC-4, John Wilson wrote:

Hi,

Could you confirm whether my request for arbitration assistance by OGIS will be reviewed and re-considered in relation to the below.

Thank you.

Regards.

John Wilson

* * * * *

* * * * *

Exhibit 106: *12 April 2019.   Email letter from OGIS to John Wilson: Closing case no. 201703007.*

From: OGIS [mailto:OGIS@nara.gov]
Sent: Friday, 12 April 2019 11:09 PM
To: OGIS
Cc: jxxxxxxxxxxxx@bigpond.com
Subject: Re: FW: OGIS request for assistance 201703007

April 12, 2019

OGIS Case 201703007

Dear Mr. Wilson,

Please see attached OGIS' response to your emails below as well as the FBI release letter and released documents referenced in our previous correspondence.

Sincerely,

OGIS Staff

[Attachment: 12 April 2019.   OGIS mediation FOIA Appeal decision review letter to John Wilson.]

NATIONAL ARCHIVES and RECORDS ADMINISTRATION
8601 ADELPHI ROAD · OGIS | COLLEGE PARK, MD 20740-6001
www.archives.gov/ogis | ogis@nara.gov | o: 202.741.5770 | f: 202.741.5769 | t: 877.684.6448

April 12, 2019 – sent via email

John Wilson

Re: Case No. 201703007

Dear Mr. Wilson:

This responds to your December 19, 2018, January 18, 2019, and March 30, 2019 emails requesting further assistance from the Office of Government Information Services (OGIS) in connection with your Freedom of Information Act (FOIA) requests to the Federal Bureau of Investigation (FBI).

In our December 18, 2018 correspondence closing your OGIS case (case no. 201703007), we attempted to address the issues you raised. However, in your recent submission to OGIS, you explain that you remain dissatisfied with the FBI's search for responsive records relating to yourself, and you ask for OGIS's continued assistance with this matter.

In response to your correspondence, we contacted the FBI to discuss your requests and the FBI's responses. The FBI affirmed its responses to your requests, explaining that it conducted a proper and sufficient search for records responsive to your request.

It may be helpful to explain the process by which OGIS approaches requests for assistance. OGIS provides mediation services to resolve disputes between FOIA requesters and Federal agencies. OGIS advocates for neither the requester nor the agency, but for the FOIA process to work as intended. After opening a case, OGIS gathers information from the requester and the agency to learn more about the nature of the dispute. This process helps us gather necessary background information, assess whether the issues are appropriate for mediation, and determine the willingness of the parties to engage in our services. Mediation is a voluntary and collaborative process in which OGIS — as a neutral third party — works with the parties to help find a mutually agreeable solution within the confines of the FOIA statute. The voluntary nature of mediation means that *both* the requester and the agency willingly participate in the process. We do not make determinations or dictate resolutions to disputes, nor do we compel agencies to release documents.

In cases such as yours in which the agency is firm in its position, OGIS does not have the authority to demand that the agency change its position. What OGIS can do is provide information regarding the FOIA process and suggest possible next steps. In our communications with the FBI, OGIS staff inquired about the specific third-party names you included with your request. While the FBI affirmed that it conducted a proper search, FOIA staff noted that you did not include the proper authorizations to permit the FBI to conduct a search for records related to third parties. In order to protect an individual's personal privacy, the FBI will not release information about a third party without their written consent, proof of their death or a showing of an overriding public interest in disclosure of the information.

April 11, 2019
Page 2

Please know that these third-party protections also apply if someone were to request records from an agency that pertain to *you*.

Finally, in your December 19, 2018 email you asked: "Could you confirm the dates of the information released to me by the FBI/DOJ please that you reference in your letter. Do you have a copy of the records released to me that you can email me too please?" For your reference, we are attaching both the FBI's letter responding to your request and the released documents referenced in our previous correspondence.

Thank you for bringing this matter to OGIS. Although this may not be the outcome you anticipated, I hope you find this information useful. At this time, however, there is no further assistance OGIS can offer, and as a result, we will close your case.

Sincerely,

ALINA M. SEMO
Director

cc: FBI FOIA
Enclosures

* * * * *

From: John Wilson
Sent: Monday, April 29, 2019 3:31 PM
To: 'OGIS' <OGIS@nara.gov>
Subject: RE: FW: OGIS request for assistance 201703007

Dear Ms Semo,

Thank you for your response below, dated 12 April 2019, to my 19 December 2018 email to you in which I provided additional details of the FBI operatives and records in question.

In your reply to me you make the erroneous statement:

"In our communications with the FBI, OGIS staff inquired about the specific third-party names you included with your request. While the FBI affirmed that it conducted a proper search, FOIA staff noted that you did not include the proper authorizations to permit the FBI to conduct a search for records related to third parties. In order to protect an individual's personal privacy, the FBI will not release information about a third party without their written consent, proof of their death or a showing of an overriding public interest in disclosure of the information."

I do not agree with your assessment that the individuals whose names I provided to you, viz Susan Holmes and Steven Garber, are "third parties" and as you assert are unrelated to the FBI. Indeed, they carry formal FBI identification cards which I have seen used to gain access from security personnel in order to carry out FBI surveillance and operations. To say that these individuals, and the operations they conducted in relation to myself as detailed in my correspondence to you, are not related to the FBI is a flawed conclusion on the part of OGIS. There is no doubt they were operating for the FBI. I believe your office should be able to at least definitively ascertain this and identify the location of the requested records.

I do not know the formal title of these operatives, that is whether they are classified as employee, agent, or whatever - only that they are operating at the direction of the FBI and they have been issued FBI identity cards. In particular, I request all records be provided relating to me in relation to contact by Susan Holmes - an operative of the FBI - which occurred in New York City in 2003 when she conducted a lengthy interview of me at Cafe Fiorello one evening. In 2004, there was further contact by Steven Garber with me, another operative of the FBI, near my apartment at 74th and Amsterdam in NYC one afternoon, followed by an extensive interview and discussion with him in Central Park. I request all records of these meetings be provided to me.

Would you please re-approach the FBI on my behalf to resolve the above and seek release of the requested files.

Thank you.

Regards.

John Wilson

* * * * *

From: OGIS [mailto:OGIS@nara.gov]
Sent: Friday, 3 May 2019 2:35 AM
To: OGIS
Cc: xxxxxxxxxxxx@bigpond.com
Subject: Re: FW: OGIS request for assistance 201703007

May 2, 2019

OGIS request 201703007

Dear Mr. Wilson,

The term "3rd party" references any individual named in the files who is not you. We did not mean to suggest that they were unrelated to the FBI, simply that they were individuals other than yourself.

The FBI stood firm in its determination, so there is no further assistance that OGIS can provide at this time.

Sincerely,

OGIS Staff

* * * * *

On Tuesday, May 7, 2019 at 12:12:23 AM UTC-4, John Wilson wrote:

Dear Ms Semo,

Thank you for your response of May 2, 2019 and attachments.

The FBI response of September 25, 2014 indicates the FBI is withholding release of information to me based on various exemptions. The FBI has indicated which specific exemptions it has used to

withhold information and provided a generic Explanation of Exemptions:

One of the exemptions it claims is Section 552a (j)(2), viz:

552a (j)(2) material reporting investigative efforts pertaining to the enforcement of criminal law including efforts to prevent, control, or reduce crime or

apprehend criminals;

I find this a surprising claim on their part and frankly unbelievable. Are you able to request more information from them in relation to their claim, or is that the domain of judicial review and the courts? I believe they are lying.

Thank you.

Best regards.

John Wilson

* * * * *

From: OGIS [mailto:OGIS@nara.gov]
Sent: Wednesday, 8 May 2019 5:54 AM
To: OGIS
Cc: xxxxxxxxxxxx@bigpond.com
Subject: Re: FW: OGIS request for assistance 201703007

May 7, 2019

OGIS request 201703007

Dear Mr. Wilson,

5 U.S.C. § 552a of the U.S. Code is the The Privacy Act of 1974. This citation was used by the FBI to explain that the system of records in which the records you requested may be filed are exempt from the disclosure provisions of the Privacy Act. The Office of Government Information Services

(OGIS) does not have statutory authority for the Privacy Act, as we do for the Freedom of Information Act (FOIA).

I hope this information is helpful.

Sincerely,

OGIS Staff

*   *   *   *   *

From: John Wilson [mailto:jxxxxxxxxxxxx@bigpond.com]
Sent: Wednesday, 8 May 2019 10:34 AM
To: 'OGIS'
Subject: RE: FW: OGIS request for assistance 201703007

Thank you for your response.

The implication of 552a (j)(2) appears to be that I am or have been a suspect or investigated by the FBI for some possible or alleged crime - is that correct? If so, how do I find out what it is the FBI has suspected me of, or investigated me for?

Sincerely,

John Wilson

*   *   *   *   *

From: John Wilson <jxxxxxxxxxxxx@bigpond.com>
Sent: Thursday, May 9, 2019 8:43 AM
To: 'Barry Fisher' <xxxxxxx@gmail.com>
Subject: FW: FW: OGIS request for assistance 201703007

Barry,

Can I re-engage your services to help with a renewed effort to get to the bottom of whether I am a suspect or have been "legitimately" investigated by the FBI for some possible or alleged crime? It is now over 20 years since the interference began, and over 5 years since the last FOI request was responded to (in 2014). The implication of 552a (j)(2) in the FBI FOI response appears to be that I am or have been a suspect or investigated by the FBI for some possible or alleged crime - is that correct? How do I find out what it is the FBI has suspected me of, or investigated me for?

As you are aware FOI requests went nowhere and previous requests to the internal inspector general at DOJ provided no useful information.

Recent OGIS emails re my request for arbitration are below - but ultimately the process went nowhere.

Thanks Barry.

Regards.

John Wilson

*   *   *   *   *

* * * * *

From: Barry Fisher [mailto:xxxxxxxx@gmail.com]
Sent: Friday, 10 May 2019 4:54 AM
To: John Wilson
Subject: Re: FW: FW: OGIS request for assistance 201703007

I think there may be investigator specialists, former fbi or cia types, or lawyer with specialized experience, that might be helpful. don't know any off hand, but think they exist and some google search efforts might be fruitful to see how hold him/her self out to be such a person. some vetting could be done after. B

* * * * *

From: John Wilson
Sent: Friday, May 10, 2019 8:30 AM
To: 'Barry Fisher' <xxxxxxxx@gmail.com>
Subject: RE: FW: FW: OGIS request for assistance 201703007

Hi Barry,

Are you able to make an enquiry through your network to find someone with requisite experience/expertise?

Regards.

John

* * * * *

From: Barry Fisher [mailto:xxxxxxxx@gmail.com]
Sent: Friday, 10 May 2019 8:55 AM
To: John Wilson
Subject: Re: FW: FW: OGIS request for assistance 201703007

Could try, couple hours time

* * * * *

From: John Wilson
Sent: Friday, May 10, 2019 3:10 PM
To: 'Barry Fisher' <xxxxxxxx@gmail.com>
Subject: RE: FW: FW: OGIS request for assistance 201703007

Hi Barry,

You once referred me to Ali Beydoun a D.C. lawyer and law professor as someone who has worked with international human rights and other matters, with much experience in foia, including state secret issues. Tel: (202) 277-4552. He sounds like someone I should try again to engage now...

Do you have a view re the implication of 552a (j)(2) for me - are they indicating documents/records are being withheld on account that I have been/ or am under some kind of criminal investigation? That seems to me to be what it is saying - do you agree that seems to be what they are saying - is that something you can comment on off the cusp?

I am also thinking of filing a more formal complaint against Henry Kissinger (at various times a Freeport advisor and board member) given a number of factors - mainly that the FBI in 2003 strongly insinuated he was the link behind my "listing" and subsequent problems I have had with the agencies. Not sure if that is something I would work on with you or speak to Ali about too?

Thanks and regards.

John

* * * * *

From: John Wilson
Sent: Friday, May 10, 2019 7:02 PM
To: 'aalibeydoun@hotmail.com' <aalibeydoun@hotmail.com>; 'Ali Beydoun' <misterbeydoun@gmail.com>
Cc: 'Barry Fisher' <xxxxxxxx@gmail.com>
Subject: FW: OGIS request for assistance 201703007

Hi Ali,

We spoke and corresponded in 2016 following an introduction from Barry Fisher. I have had unacknowledged problems with the FBI since working on Wall Street and publishing an investor report in 1996 on US mining company Freeport McMoran which at the time was under investigation by the state department for human rights violations in West Papua, Indonesia.

Can I engage your services to help with a renewed effort to get to the bottom of whether I am a suspect or have been "legitimately" investigated by the FBI for some possible or alleged crime? It is now over 20 years since the interference began, and over 5 years since my last FOI request was responded to (in 2014). The implication of 552a (j)(2) in the FBI FOI response (attached) appears to be that I am or have been a suspect or investigated by the FBI for some possible or alleged crime - is that correct? How do I find out what it is the FBI has suspected me of, or investigated me for - is this something you can help me with?

As I discussed with you in 2016 my FOI requests went nowhere and previous requests to the internal inspector general at DOJ provided no useful information.

Recent OGIS emails re my request for arbitration are below - but ultimately the process has gone nowhere.

Thanks Ali.

Best regards.

John Wilson

* * * * *

From: ali beydoun [mailto:misterbeydoun@gmail.com]
Sent: Sunday, 12 May 2019 9:36 PM
To: John Wilson
Subject: Re: FW: OGIS request for assistance 201703007

Hi John. Sorry for the delay in responding. Because of other work commitments I am unable to take your case. I really wish that I could, but given my current situation is is not feasible.

Sorry about that,

Ali

* * * * *

From: John Wilson [mailto:jxxxxxxxxxxxx@bigpond.com]
Sent: Monday, 13 May 2019 8:47 AM
To: 'ali beydoun'
Subject: RE: FW: OGIS request for assistance 201703007

Thanks Ali. Can you recommend others with suitable experience/qualifications I might be able to approach?

Thank you.

Best regards.

John Wilson

* * * * *

From: Barry Fisher <xxxxxxxx@gmail.com>
Sent: Wednesday, May 15, 2019 2:54 AM
To: John Wilson
Subject: Re: FW: FW: OGIS request for assistance 201703007

ali referrals could be useful. ask him for some names,contact info.b

* * * * *

From: John Wilson
Sent: Thursday, June 20, 2019 10:29 AM
To: 'Barry Fisher' <xxxxxxxx@gmail.com>
Subject: FW: state/doj

Hi Barry,

Did anyone ever send you a response to your letter from June 2016 to the AG, DOJ and FBI (attached)?

Is this something you can follow up for me? I can transfer funds to you if so - please let me know how much.

Thanks and regards.

John

* * * * *

From: Barry Fisher [mailto:xxxxxxxx@gmail.com]
Sent: Friday, 21 June 2019 1:01 AM
To: John Wilson
Subject: Re: FW: state/doj

don't recall ever received written response, only contact thru "lori" years ago in obama administration justice department. what do you think might be productive?barry

* * * * *

On Thu, Jun 20, 2019 at 3:59 PM John Wilson <johnwilson@rcresearch.net> wrote:

Hi Barry,

Follow up letters I suppose, also to the FBI OIG. Other? No doubt they will still not respond - but I suppose it is potential ammunition for my senator/congressman to follow up with, or possibly at some point one of the judiciary committees.

What are your thoughts? (Are there other regulators/committees/politicians/etc also worth approaching possibly?)

best regards.

John Wilson

* * * * *

From: Barry Fisher [mailto:xxxxxxxx@gmail.com]
Sent: Saturday, 22 June 2019 7:47 AM
To: John Wilson
Subject: Re: FW: state/doj

between trump running justice dept and all its elements, fbi etc, and the congress/trump battles, hard to see where any attention would be given to this.

* * * * *

On Fri, Jun 21, 2019 at 6:23 PM John Wilson <johnwilson@rcresearch.net> wrote:

Hi Barry,

Expectations have never been too high re accountability. none the less, better it comes from you than me - I'm happy to transfer funds to you, especially for follow up/letter to FBI OIG re their misrepresentation of the FBI operatives I am complaining about as "Special Agents" "employees"

Regards.

John Wilson

Managing Director

RCR
Resource Capital Research
www.rcresearch.com.au
T +61 x xxxx xxxx (SYD)

* * * * *

From: Barry Fisher [mailto:xxxxxxxx@gmail.com]
Sent: Saturday, 22 June 2019 12:22 PM
To: John Wilson
Subject: Re: FW: state/doj

please send the the letters which should be referenced and attached to any inquiry.

* * * * *

On Sun, Jun 23, 2019 at 6:28 PM John Wilson <johnwilson@rcresearch.net> wrote:

Hi Barry,

I suppose best to follow up on your letter of 24 (?tbc) June 2016 (attached).

The FBI, DOJ and AG never responded to your letter dated 24 June 2016. (Barry - your letter 24 June 2016 points out their constant misclassification of my complaint as pertaining to "employee" [and in other correspondence from them to "Special Agent"], a matter which they have never addressed, viz. whether the people I named operated on the DOJ/FBI's behalf.) I don't think it makes any difference but you may want to add in any cover letter the term "Special Agent" as well as "employee" as constant mis-statements used by the agencies to dodge responding to the essence of my complaint.

I've attached some of the historical correspondence from the FBI/DOJ for your convenience and as a reminder of the repeated and long history of their intentional strategy of misclassifying the people I named - constantly misnaming them as "employees" or "Special Agents".

    - The FBI's IPU/IIS/INSD letter sent addressed to you 10 Feb 2006 refers to "employees" and also "Special Agents", says the matter is closed.

    - The FBI's IPU/IIS/INSD letter sent addressed to me 9 Feb 2016 refers to "employees", says the matter does not warrant investigation and refers me to the FOIA process.

    - The FBI's IPU/IIS/INSD letter sent addressed to Barry Fisher 25 May 2016 refers to "Special Agents", says the matter does not warrant investigation and it considers the matter closed. (It references a number of letters from me, including one that says 18   February 2016 - not sure what this is - possible error on their part for my letter dated 23 February 2016).

Could a letter also be sent to others? For example, does the White House have a complaints section for constituent problems with federal agencies; An integrity/ethics related congressional committee? (Previous efforts on my part to get Schumer and Nadler involved led to only partial assistance from them but never did they follow through to a definitive conclusion and get a definitive answer despite my best efforts to have them do so).

Thanks Barry.

Regards.

John Wilson

* * * * *

From: Barry Fisher [mailto:xxxxxxxx@gmail.com]
Sent: Tuesday, 25 June 2019 12:49 AM
To: John Wilson
Subject: Re: FW: state/doj

Hi John-yes, letters could now be sent but without optimism we will get responses. I could work on this upon transfer of $1500 funds. Let me know. thanks, Barry

* * * * *

On Mon, Jun 24, 2019 at 4:01 PM John Wilson <johnwilson@rcresearch.net> wrote:

Barry,

Are there any legal avenues for pursuing the agencies/escalating my complaint if they are being evasive - it seems all the political/executive channels are compromised? On the issue of the letter, who else do you think you might send it to?

Thanks and regards.

John Wilson

Managing Director

Resource Capital Research
www.rcresearch.com.au
T +61 x xxxx xxxx (SYD)

* * * * *

From: Barry Fisher [mailto:xxxxxxxx@gmail.com]
Sent: Wednesday, 26 June 2019 12:47 AM
To: John Wilson
Subject: Re: FW: state/doj

the judicial and legislatiive branches of the government are the only separate one that might look at what the executive branch, DOJ, State etc., have or have not done.nothing has resulted from direct complaints to the executive and legislative branches. perhaps if there was implication of clinton and/or obama administrations, this executive regime or the republican controlled senate might take interest. otherwise the judicial branch.

* * * * *

On Tue, Jun 25, 2019 at 3:44 PM John Wilson <johnwilson@rcresearch.net> wrote:

Is there any opening for legal action here based on the executive's refusal to respond to the essence of the question we have put to the FBI/DOJ? Do I have a right to know the information requested, and if they don't respond is that a matter I can take them to court over, or to an administrative tribunal or similar?

John Wilson

* * * * *

From: Barry Fisher <xxxxxxxx@gmail.com>
Sent: Wednesday, June 26, 2019 9:13 AM
To: John Wilson <
Subject: Re: FW: state/doj

we've talked about court follow up and efforts were made to get D.C. counsel. yes, a preliminary question is what is possible in court, a question don't know if you addressed with Ali.

* * * * *

From: John Wilson <████████>
Sent: Wednesday, June 26, 2019 5:14 PM
To: 'Barry Fisher' <xxxxxxx@gmail.com>
Subject: RE: FW: state/doj

Hi Barry,

I addressed FOIA court potential with Ali - though he never pursued that option with me beyond an initial discussion.

This would now be a different matter with the FBI/DOJ - not FOIA, but still concerns my rights to the information requested and their requirement to provide aspects of it or confirm their involvement. Perhaps I should raise this with Ali too. He has not responded to my various attempts to progress my FOIA through him (I cc'd you on some of the recent emails earlier this year) - so that leaves me to think he is not interested in assisting me. I'm not sure what to do...if you think it worthwhile, I could try him again.

Thanks and regards.

John Wilson

* * * * *

From: John Wilson ████████
Sent: Thursday, June 27, 2019 11:36 AM
To: 'ali beydoun' <misterbeydoun@gmail.com>
Cc: 'aalibeydoun@hotmail.com' <aalibeydoun@hotmail.com>; 'Barry Fisher' <xxxxxxx@gmail.com>
Subject: fbi/doj rquest

Hi Ali,

I have a follow up request for your assistance.

You and I previously discussed my FOIA request and mediation with the FBI/DOJ. However, there is a second issue now - one we haven't discussed. That is, the FBI/DOJ never responded to my or Barry Fisher's requests asking them to confirm if the people we have identified to them are operatives. They either do not respond to requests for confirmation or they respond with a misleading misrepresentation of our request, limiting their answer to specific categories of operative such as "employee" or "Special Agent" but never have they answered the question as to whether these people are operatives despite our concerted efforts to have them do so.

For example, the FBI, DOJ and AG never responded to Barry Fisher's letter dated 24 June 2016 (attached); also as per my letter 23 February 2016 (attached).

I believe I have a right to know if the people named are operatives working at the FBI's behest. Do the agencies and their operatives have a requirement to disclose, if asked, if the operatives are working at the behest of the FBI/DOJ? If they refuse to answer the question, is there some legal avenue by which to force the agency to respond, eg., via court action, administrative appeal, or similar?

I've attached some of the historical correspondence from the FBI/DOJ which shows the long history of their intentional strategy of misclassifying the people I named - constantly misnaming them as "employees" or "Special Agents".

- The FBI's IPU/IIS/INSD letter sent addressed to you 10 Feb 2006 refers to "employees" and also "Special Agents", says the matter is closed.
- The FBI's IPU/IIS/INSD letter sent addressed to me 9 Feb 2016 refers to "employees", says the matter does not warrant investigation and refers me to the FOIA process.
- The FBI's IPU/IIS/INSD letter sent addressed to Barry Fisher 25 May 2016 refers to "Special Agents", says the matter does not warrant investigation and it considers the matter closed. (It references a number of letters from me, including one that says 18 February 2016 - not sure what this is - possible error on their part for my letter dated 23 February 2016).

Could you let me know what legal options I might have from here please to pursue this? I am happy to pay a retainer if you would let me know an estimate of time and cost and I can transfer the funds to you.

Thanks Ali.

Best regards.

John Wilson
Managing Director

RCR
Resource Capital Research
www.rcresearch.com.au
T +61 x xxxx xxxx (SYD)

* * * * *

From: ali beydoun <aalibeydoun@hotmail.com>
Sent: Friday, June 28, 2019 2:51 AM
To: John Wilson <███████████████████> 'ali beydoun' <misterbeydoun@gmail.com>
Cc: 'Barry Fisher' <xxxxxxxx@gmail.com>
Subject: Re: fbi/doj rquest

Hi John,

I am sorry that I cannot help you any further with this matter. I am afraid that my current career position and work commitments do not allow me to offer you any legal advice or assistance.

Sincerely,
Ali

* * * * *

From: John Wilson <██████████████>
Sent: Friday, June 28, 2019 9:07 AM
To: 'Barry Fisher' <xxxxxxxx@gmail.com>
Subject: FW: fbi/doj rquest

Hi Barry,

Sounds like Ali is a dead end for taking this matter further with review of legal options.

I think sending the additional letters is still a good idea, but I would also like to know if there is a legal angle here whereby we can force the agencies to respond to a court order or similar. Is the legal aspect of this something you can ascertain?

Thanks and regards.

John Wilson

* * * * *

V-3   FOIA requests, appeals and OGIS mediation: 2019 to 2020

V-3a FOIA Requests 2019 to 2020

FBI/DOJ

FOIPA Request No.: 1450535 - 000

Appeal No.: A-2020-00197

Schedule of key FOIA correspondence

Website form application dated 23 October 2019 FOIPA Request to FBI.

Letter dated 29 October 2019, FBI acknowledges receipt of FOIPA request, assigns FOIPA Request No. 1450535 - 000, and responds to search – no records.

Email dated 18 February 2020, John Wilson requests administrative appeal to DOJ, OIP.

Email letter dated 20 February 2020, DOJ, OIP acknowledges appeal request.

Email letter dated 21 February 2020, DOJ,OIP assigns Appeal No.: A-2020-00197; responds to appeal – no records.

[Litigation: Note –FOIPA litigation subsequently commenced 8 December 2020. Filed in the United States district court for the Southern District of New York by David Rankin of Beldock Levine & Hoffman LLP (BLHNY). (See section VI).

16 February 2022. Judge Stewart D. Aaron US Magistrate Judge filed the Report and Recommendation to Hon. Lewis A. Kaplan senior US District Judge. The Defendant's motion was granted in part and denied in part and the Plaintiff's cross-motion was granted in part and denied in part.]

* * * * *

Exhibit 107: *23 October 2019.   Website FOIA Request from John Wilson to FBI.*

[This is the first of two requests to the FBI submitted 23 October 2019. It was submitted prematurely in error and incomplete. A second was submitted shortly after but not acknowledged by the FBI].

----START MESSAGE---- Subject: eFOIA Request Received Sent: 2019-10-23T23:50:56.186728+00:00 Status: pending Message:

Individual Information

Prefix	Mr.
First Name	john
Middle Name	christian
Last Name	wilson
Suffix	
Email	[redacted]
Phone	
Location	Outside United States

Non-Domestic Address

Address Line 1	[redacted]
Address Line 2	
City	
State	
Postal	
Country	Australia

Agreement to Pay

1/2

Section V — Appendix - FOIA Requests

How you will pay	I am willing to pay additional fees and will enter the maximum amount I am willing to pay in the box below
Allow up to $	10

Privacy Act

US Citizen	True
Prefix	Mr.
First Name	john
Middle Name	christian
Last Name	wilson
Suffix	
Date of Birth	▮▮▮▮
Place of Birth	▮▮▮▮▮▮ FRCP 5.2
Additional Information	SS: ▮▮▮▮

**

Please be advised that efoia@subscriptions.fbi.gov is a no-reply email address. Questions regarding your FOIA request may be directed to foipaquestions@fbi.gov. If you have received a FOIPA request number, please include this in all correspondence concerning your request. Please note eFOIPA requests are processed in the order that they are received. If you have not received a FOIPA request number, your request is in the process of being opened at which time it will be assigned a FOIPA request number and correspondence will be forthcoming.

**

Upon receipt of your FOIPA request number, you may check the status of your FOIPA request on the FBI's electronic FOIA Library (The Vault) on the FBI's public website, http://vault.fbi.gov by clicking on the 'Check Status of Your FOI/PA Request tool' link. Status updates are performed on a weekly basis. If you receive a comment that your FOIPA request number was not located in the database, please check back at a later date.

----END MESSAGE----

* * * * *

* * * * *

Exhibit 108: *29 October 2019.   FOIA Response from FBI to John Wilson.*

U.S. Department of Justice

Federal Bureau of Investigation

Washington, D.C. 20535

October 29, 2019

MR. JOHN CHRISTIAN WILSON

AUSTRALIA

FOIPA Request No.: 1450535-000
Subject: WILSON, JOHN CHRISTIAN

Dear Mr. Wilson:

This is in response to your Freedom of Information/Privacy Acts (FOIPA) request. Please see the paragraphs below for relevant information specific to your request as well as the enclosed FBI FOIPA Addendum for standard responses applicable to all requests.

Records regarding your subject were previously reviewed and released to you pursuant to the FOIPA. An additional search was conducted, and no additional records were located. Therefore, your request is being administratively closed.

Please refer to the enclosed FBI FOIPA Addendum for additional standard responses applicable to your request. **"Part 1"** of the Addendum includes standard responses that apply to all requests. **"Part 2"** includes additional standard responses that apply to all requests for records on individuals. **"Part 3"** includes general information about FBI records that you may find useful. Also enclosed is our Explanation of Exemptions.

For questions regarding our determinations, visit the www.fbi.gov/foia website under "Contact Us." The FOIPA Request number listed above has been assigned to your request. Please use this number in all correspondence concerning your request.

You may file an appeal by writing to the Director, Office of Information Policy (OIP), United States Department of Justice, Sixth Floor, 441 G Street, NW, Washington, D.C. 20001, or you may submit an appeal through OIP's FOIA online portal by creating an account on the following website: https://www.foiaonline.gov/foiaonline/action/public/home. Your appeal must be postmarked or electronically transmitted within ninety (90) days from the date of this letter in order to be considered timely. If you submit your appeal by mail, both the letter and the envelope should be clearly marked "Freedom of Information Act Appeal." Please cite the FOIPA Request Number assigned to your request so it may be easily identified.

You may seek dispute resolution services by contacting the Office of Government Information Services (OGIS). The contact information for OGIS is as follows: Office of Government Information Services, National Archives and Records Administration, 8601 Adelphi Road-OGIS, College Park, Maryland 20740-6001, e-mail at ogis@nara.gov; telephone at 202-741-5770; toll free at 1-877-684-6448; or facsimile at 202-741-5769. Alternatively, you may contact the FBI's FOIA Public Liaison by emailing foipaquestions@fbi.gov. If you submit your dispute resolution correspondence by email, the subject heading should clearly state "Dispute Resolution Services." Please also cite the FOIPA Request Number assigned to your request so it may be easily identified.

Sincerely yours,

David M. Hardy
Section Chief,
Record/Information
 Dissemination Section
Information Management Division

Enclosure

FBI FOIPA Addendum

As referenced in our letter responding to your Freedom of Information/Privacy Acts (FOIPA) request, the FBI FOIPA Addendum includes information applicable to your request. Part 1 of the Addendum includes standard responses that apply to all requests. Part 2 includes additional standard responses that apply to all requests for records on individuals. Part 3 includes general information about FBI records. For questions regarding Parts 1, 2, or 3, visit the www.fbi.gov/foia website under "Contact Us." Previously mentioned appeal and dispute resolution services are also available at the web address.

Part 1: The standard responses below apply to all requests:

(i) **5 U.S.C. § 552(c).** Congress excluded three categories of law enforcement and national security records from the requirements of the FOIA [5 U.S.C § 552(c) (2006 & Supp. IV (2010)]. FBI responses are limited to those records subject to the requirements of the FOIA. Additional information about the FBI and the FOIPA can be found on the www.fbi.gov/foia website.

(ii) **National Security/Intelligence Records.** The FBI can neither confirm nor deny the existence of national security and foreign intelligence records pursuant to FOIA exemptions (b)(1), (b)(3), and PA exemption (j)(2) as applicable to requests for records about individuals [5 U.S.C. §§ 552/552a (b)(1), (b)(3), and (j)(2); 50 U.S.C § 3024(i)(1)]. The mere acknowledgment of the existence or nonexistence of such records is itself a classified fact protected by FOIA exemption (b)(1) and/or would reveal intelligence sources, methods, or activities protected by exemption (b)(3) [50 USC § 3024(i)(1)]. This is a standard response and should not be read to indicate that national security or foreign intelligence records do or do not exist.

Part 2: The standard responses below apply to all requests for records on individuals:

(i) **Requests for Records about any Individual—Watch Lists.** The FBI can neither confirm nor deny the existence of any individual's name on a watch list pursuant to FOIA exemption (b)(7)(E) and PA exemption (j)(2) [5 U.S.C. §§ 552/552a (b)(7)(E), (j)(2)]. This is a standard response and should not be read to indicate that watch list records do or do not exist.

(ii) **Requests for Records for Incarcerated Individuals.** The FBI can neither confirm nor deny the existence of records which could reasonably be expected to endanger the life or physical safety of any incarcerated individual pursuant to FOIA exemptions (b)(7)(E), (b)(7)(F), and PA exemption (j)(2) [5 U.S.C. §§ 552/552a (b)(7)(E), (b)(7)(F), and (j)(2)]. This is a standard response and should not be read to indicate that such records do or do not exist.

Part 3: General Information:

(i) **Record Searches.** The Record/Information Dissemination Section (RIDS) searches for reasonably described records by searching those systems or locations where responsive records would reasonably be found. A reasonable search normally consists of a search for main files in the Central Records System (CRS), an extensive system of records consisting of applicant, investigative, intelligence, personnel, administrative, and general files compiled and maintained by the FBI in the course of fulfilling law enforcement, intelligence, and administrative functions. The CRS spans the entire FBI organization and encompasses the records of FBI Headquarters (FBIHQ), FBI Field Offices, and FBI Legal Attaché Offices (Legats) worldwide and includes Electronic Surveillance (ELSUR) records. For additional information about our record searches visit www.fbi.gov/services/information-management/foipa/requesting-fbi-records.

(ii) **FBI Records.** Founded in 1908, the FBI carries out a dual law enforcement and national security mission. As part of this dual mission, the FBI creates and maintains records on various subjects; however, the FBI does not maintain records on every person, subject, or entity.

(iii) **Requests for Criminal History Records or Rap Sheets.** The Criminal Justice Information Services (CJIS) Division provides Identity History Summary Checks – often referred to as a criminal history record or rap sheets. These criminal history records are not the same as material in an investigative "FBI file." An Identity History Summary Check is a listing of information taken from fingerprint cards and documents submitted to the FBI in connection with arrests, federal employment, naturalization, or military service. For a fee, individuals can request a copy of their Identity History Summary Check. Forms and directions can be accessed at www.fbi.gov/about-us/cjis/identity-history-summary-checks. Additionally, requests can be submitted electronically at www.edo.cjis.gov. For additional information, please contact CJIS directly at (304) 625-5590.

(iv) **The National Name Check Program (NNCP).** The mission of NNCP is to analyze and report information in response to name check requests received from federal agencies, for the purpose of protecting the United States from foreign and domestic threats to national security. Please be advised that this is a service provided to other federal agencies. Private citizens cannot request a name check.

EXPLANATION OF EXEMPTIONS

SUBSECTIONS OF TITLE 5, UNITED STATES CODE, SECTION 552

(b)(1)   (A) specifically authorized under criteria established by an Executive order to be kept secret in the interest of national defense or foreign policy and (B) are in fact properly classified to such Executive order;

(b)(2)   related solely to the internal personnel rules and practices of an agency;

(b)(3)   specifically exempted from disclosure by statute (other than section 552b of this title), provided that such statute (A) requires that the matters be withheld from the public in such a manner as to leave no discretion on issue, or (B) establishes particular criteria for withholding or refers to particular types of matters to be withheld;

(b)(4)   trade secrets and commercial or financial information obtained from a person and privileged or confidential;

(b)(5)   inter-agency or intra-agency memorandums or letters which would not be available by law to a party other than an agency in litigation with the agency;

(b)(6)   personnel and medical files and similar files the disclosure of which would constitute a clearly unwarranted invasion of personal privacy;

(b)(7)   records or information compiled for law enforcement purposes, but only to the extent that the production of such law enforcement records or information (A) could reasonably be expected to interfere with enforcement proceedings, (B) would deprive a person of a right to a fair trial or an impartial adjudication, (C) could reasonably be expected to constitute an unwarranted invasion of personal privacy, (D) could reasonably be expected to disclose the identity of confidential source, including a State, local, or foreign agency or authority or any private institution which furnished information on a confidential basis, and, in the case of record or information compiled by a criminal law enforcement authority in the course of a criminal investigation, or by an agency conducting a lawful national security intelligence investigation, information furnished by a confidential source, (E) would disclose techniques and procedures for law enforcement investigations or prosecutions, or would disclose guidelines for law enforcement investigations or prosecutions if such disclosure could reasonably be expected to risk circumvention of the law, or (F) could reasonably be expected to endanger the life or physical safety of any individual;

(b)(8)   contained in or related to examination, operating, or condition reports prepared by, on behalf of, or for the use of an agency responsible for the regulation or supervision of financial institutions; or

(b)(9)   geological and geophysical information and data, including maps, concerning wells.

SUBSECTIONS OF TITLE 5, UNITED STATES CODE, SECTION 552a

(d)(5)   information compiled in reasonable anticipation of a civil action proceeding;

(j)(2)   material reporting investigative efforts pertaining to the enforcement of criminal law including efforts to prevent, control, or reduce crime or apprehend criminals;

(k)(1)   information which is currently and properly classified pursuant to an Executive order in the interest of the national defense or foreign policy, for example, information involving intelligence sources or methods;

(k)(2)   investigatory material compiled for law enforcement purposes, other than criminal, which did not result in loss of a right, benefit or privilege under Federal programs, or which would identify a source who furnished information pursuant to a promise that his/her identity would be held in confidence;

(k)(3)   material maintained in connection with providing protective services to the President of the United States or any other individual pursuant to the authority of Title 18, United States Code, Section 3056;

(k)(4)   required by statute to be maintained and used solely as statistical records;

(k)(5)   investigatory material compiled solely for the purpose of determining suitability, eligibility, or qualifications for Federal civilian employment or for access to classified information, the disclosure of which would reveal the identity of the person who furnished information pursuant to a promise that his/her identity would be held in confidence;

(k)(6)   testing or examination material used to determine individual qualifications for appointment or promotion in Federal Government service the release of which would compromise the testing or examination process;

(k)(7)   material used to determine potential for promotion in the armed services, the disclosure of which would reveal the identity of the person who furnished the material pursuant to a promise that his/her identity would be held in confidence.

FBI/DOJ

* * * *

* * * * *

Exhibit 109: *18 February 2020.   FOIA Request Appeal from John Wilson to FBI.*

From: John Wilson
Sent: Tuesday, February 18, 2020 1:00 PM
To: doj.oip.foia@usdoj.gov
Subject: Freedom of Information Act Appeal - FOIPA Request No.: 1450535-000

Freedom of Information Act Appeal - FOIPA Request No.: 1450535-000

Hi,

I am appealing the above FOIA response.

The response, and previous responses to me from the FBI/DOJ have made no mention of the existence of interviews with me dating to 2003 and 2004 despite agents working for the FBI interviewing me in NYC, as well as at other times and locations. One of the agents involved in the 2003 interview in NYC, Susan Ackerson Holmes, showed me her FBI identity card, a NYC resident whom I am aware worked for the FBI from at least the early 1990s. I don't remember the name of her title. Dr Steve Garber of the FBI also interviewed me in NYC, among other occasions in 2004. Nor do I know the name of his title

I have previously named these individuals to the FBI/DOJ and the circumstances of their engagement with me. The FBI's response to my complaint and claims has always involved their misstatement of these people's identity as "employees" or "Special Agents". As such, the FBI and DOJ have never responded to my complaint about these people, as they repeatedly misclassify them and on that erroneous basis deny responsibility for or association with them. I have challenged them repeatedly on this previously and they failed to respond in all cases.

Never has the FBI or DOJ acknowledged or addressed the fact these people worked for them under different titles or job descriptions. And never has acknowledgement of these interviews been made evident through my FOIA requests which now the subject of my appeal.

The FBI/DOJ has withheld this information as requested in my FOIA and not acknowledged its existence. Nor have they claimed any exemption for doing so. I request that details of these interviews or more broadly the encounters between me and the identified individuals above and as identified in my FOIA request be provided to me - including confirmation of dates, locations and purpose.

Thank you.

Sincerely,

John Wilson

* * * * *

* * * * *

Exhibit 110: *21 February 2020.   FOIA Appeal confirmation letter to John Wilson from FBI, OIP.*

From: Administrator Email <noreplies@micropact.com>
Sent: Friday, February 21, 2020 1:44 PM
To: John Wilson
Subject: Acknowledgment of FOIA Appeal A-2020-00197

The Office of Information Policy has received your FOIA Appeal. Please see the attached acknowledgment letter.

[Attached]

U.S. Department of Justice
Office of Information Policy
Sixth Floor
441 G Street, NW
Washington, DC 20530-0001

Telephone: (202) 514-3642

February 20, 2020

Dear John Wilson:

This is to advise you that the Office of Information Policy (OIP) of the U.S. Department of Justice received your administrative appeal from the action of the FBI regarding Request No. 1450535 on 02/17/2020.

In an attempt to afford each appellant equal and impartial treatment, OIP has adopted a general practice of assigning appeals in the approximate order of receipt. Your appeal has been assigned number A-2020-00197 . Please refer to this number in any future communication with OIP regarding this matter. Please note that if you provided an email address or another electronic means of communication with your request or appeal, this Office may respond to your appeal electronically even if you submitted your appeal to this Office via regular U.S. Mail.

We will notify you of the decision on your appeal as soon as we can. If you have any questions about the status of your appeal, you may contact me at (202) 514-3642. If you have submitted your appeal through FOIA STAR, you may also check the status of your appeal by logging into your account.

Sincerely,

Priscilla Jones
Supervisory Administrative Specialist

* * * * *

* * * * *

Exhibit 111: *21 March 2020. FOIA Appeal decision review letter to John Wilson from FBI, OIP.*

From: Administrator Email <noreplies@micropact.com>
Sent: Saturday, March 21, 2020 5:09 AM
To: John Wilson
Subject: Response to FOIA Appeal A-2020-00197

The Office of Information Policy has made its final determination on your FOIA Appeal Number A-2020-00197. A copy of this determination is enclosed for your review, along with any enclosures, if applicable. Thank you.

[Attached]

U.S. Department of Justice
Office of Information Policy
Sixth Floor
441 G Street, NW
Washington, DC 20530-0001

Telephone: (202) 514-3642

John Wilson

Re: Appeal No. A-2020-00197
Request No. 1450535
CDT:PJA

VIA: Email

Dear John Wilson:

You appealed from the action of the Federal Bureau of Investigation on your Freedom of Information Act request for access to records concerning yourself. I note that your appeal concerns the adequacy of the FBI's search for records responsive to your FOIA request.

After carefully considering your appeal, I am affirming FBI's action on your request. The FBI informed you that it could locate no other responsive main file records subject to the FOIA other than those previously provided to you by letter dated September 25, 2014. I have determined that the FBI's action was correct and that it conducted an adequate, reasonable search for such records.

Please be advised that this Office's decision was made only after a full review of this matter. Your appeal was assigned to an attorney with this Office who thoroughly reviewed and analyzed your appeal, your underlying request, and the action of the FBI in response to your request.

If you are dissatisfied with my action on your appeal, the FOIA permits you to file a lawsuit in federal district court in accordance with 5U.S.C. 552(a)(4)(B).

For your information, the Office of Government Information Services (OGIS) offers mediation services to resolve disputes between FOIA requesters and Federal agencies as a non-exclusive alternative to litigation. Using OGIS services does not affect your right to pursue litigation. The contact information for OGIS is as follows: Office of Government Information Services, National Archives and Records Administration, Room 2510, 8601 Adelphi Road, College Park, Maryland 20740-6001; email at ogis@nara.gov; telephone at 202-741-5770; toll free at 1-877-684-6448; or facsimile at 202-741-5769. If you have any questions regarding the action this Office has taken on your appeal, you may contact this Office's FOIA Public Liaison for your appeal. Specifically, you may speak with the undersigned agency official by calling (202) 514-3642.

Sincerely,

X_____
Christina D. Troiani

Associate Chief, for
Matthew Hurd, Acting Chief, Administrative Appeals Staff

* * * * *

V-4   FOIA requests, appeals and OGIS mediation: 2021 to 2023

V-4a   FOIA Requests 2021 to 2023:

FBI/DOJ

FOIPA Request No.: 1548515 - 000

Appeal No.: A-2022-02028

Schedule of key FOIA correspondence

Letter dated 20 May 2022 FOIPA Request to FBI by John Wilson's FOIA attorney Pete Sorenson.

Letter dated 13 June 2022, FBI acknowledges receipt of FOIPA request, assigns FOIPA Request No. 1548515 – 000, and responds to search – no records.

Letter dated 1 September 2022, John Wilson's attorney Pete Sorenson requests administrative appeal to DOJ, OIP.

Letter dated 1 September 2022, DOJ, OIP assigns Appeal No.: A-2022-02028.

No response to Appeal prior to commencing litigation 8 October 2022.

[Litigation: Note –second FOIPA litigation subsequently filed 8 October 2022, in the United States District Court for the district of Columbia by John Wilson's attorney Pete Sorenson. (See section VI).

FOIA response – "litigation release" letter dated 28 April 2023 received from DOJ, FBI. The FBI states 35 pages were reviewed of which 26 pages were released.

Litigation ongoing as at publication date of this volume.]

* * * * *

Exhibit 112: *20 May 2022. FOIA Request from Attorney Pete Sorenson for John Wilson to the FBI.*

Sorenson Law Office
FOIA LAW

May 20, 2022

FBI Records Information Dissemination Section
Attn: FOIPA request
170 Marcel Drive
Winchester, VA 22602-4843

SENT CERTIFIED MAIL/RETURN RECEIPT REQUESTED MAIL
7018 2290 0000 7703 2006

RE: Freedom of Information Act (FOIA) Request of John Christian Wilson

Dear Federal Bureau of Investigation FOIA Officer,

I, C. Peter Sorenson, am writing on behalf of our law firm's client, John Christian Wilson. Our law firm address is PO Box 10836, Eugene, Oregon 97440 and Mr. Wilson's address is ▓▓▓ ▓▓▓▓▓▓▓▓▓▓▓▓▓▓▓▓▓▓▓▓▓ Australia. My email address is: ▓▓▓▓▓▓▓▓▓▓▓▓▓▓▓▓▓▓▓▓. My phone number is 541-606-9173.

Mr. Wilson has asked me to represent him on the matter of making this FOIA request. His Declaration authorizing me to make the request is attached.

A. REQUEST

John Christian Wilson requests, pursuant to the Freedom of Information Act (hereafter FOIA):

1) All records, documents, or communications prepared by, received by or maintained by the FBI which mention the following terms:
John Christian Wilson
John C. Wilson
John Wilson

2) All records describing FBI informant or FBI agent contacts with

1

John Christian Wilson
John C. Wilson
John Wilson

3) All records describing FBI contractors, or others operating on behalf of the FBI or other DOJ element, contacts with
John Christian Wilson
John C. Wilson
John Wilson

4) The 1996 securities analyst report on NYSE listed U.S. mining company Freeport McMoran Copper and Gold Inc (which trades on the NYSE under the symbol FCX) written by John Wilson. This report is entitled, "FCX: Grasberg Closure Highlights Political Risks." Mr. Wilson wrote the report as an analyst working for S.G. Warburg & Co. Inc. and the report was dated March 12, 1996.

5) All records describing the attendance of John Wilson at the Freeport McMoran Copper and Gold Inc. May 1996 annual analyst briefing at Freeport McMoran Copper and Gold Inc's headquarters in New Orleans, Louisiana. In particular, records are sought concerning n interaction between John Wilson and James R. Moffett (known as Jim Bob), CEO and Chairman of Freeport McMoran Copper and Gold Inc, in the boardroom alcove after the analyst question period that was held in Freeport McMoran's boardroom.

6) All records describing an interaction between John Wilson and an unnamed person, apparently a federal agent or FBI operative, also in Freeport's boardroom alcove after the analyst question period in Freeport's boardroom mentioned above at the Freeport headquarters in New Orleans, Louisiana in May 1996.

7) All records describing or documenting interactions between John Wilson and people operating on behalf of the FBI or other DOJ element, in particular by Steve Garber.

8) All records, including notes, recordings or transcripts of interviews, made by Steve Garber in early 1999 during the several days when Mr. Wilson visited Garber at his home in Prescott, AZ.

9) All records, including notes, recordings or transcripts, of a discussion or interview involving Mr. Wilson and Steve Garber in June 2004 in New York, New York.

10) All records, including notes, recordings or transcripts, of a discussion or interview involving Mr. Wilson and Steve Garber in September 2004, including at Tibet House, and also the Blue Water Grill both in the vicinity of the Union Square neighborhood of New York, New York.

11) All records of the attendance involving John Wilson in connection with a presentation that Dave Foreman gave in New York, New York in late 1997. David Foreman (usually referred to as Dave) is a well-known American environmental activist and co-founder of environmental group Earth First! Dave Foreman was a subject of Susan Holmes for her work for the FBI.

12) All records pertaining to John Wilson concerning his attendance, or discussions with Susan Holmes or Dave Foreman on, a raft trip on the Colorado River in July or August 1997 with journalists, including a reporter for Time Magazine, Ms. Holmes and Mr. Foreman.

13) All records of discussions between John Wilson and Susan Ackerson Holmes. All records describing or documenting interactions between John Wilson and people operating on behalf of the FBI or other DOJ element, in particular Susan Ackerson Holmes.

14) All records of discussions between John Wilson and Susan Holmes during the three years that they dated in New York, New York, calendar years 1994, 1995, 1996 and 1997.

15) All records of discussions between John Wilson and Susan Holmes in a May 10, 2003 (on or about) dinner conversation between Susan Holmes and John Wilson in New York, New York.

16) All telephone wiretaps on telephones used by John Wilson.

17) All records showing any applications for surveillance or wiretaps of telephones used by John Wilson.

18) All records showing any applications for search warrants for properties owned or leased by John Wilson.

19) All records showing any applications for surveillance of John Wilson.

B. TIME FRAME OF THIS REQUEST

The time frame for this request includes records created or received on or after January 1, 1994 to present.

C. INFORMATION HELPFUL TO THE FBI IN FULFILLING THIS REQUEST

My client, John Christian Wilson, was a securities expert and was based in New York, New York. His work was involved in international mining finance, with a focus on equity research. He later worked in Australia, where he now lives.

My client has signed DOJ Form 361 and has signed a Declaration of John Christian Wilson. These documents are attached to and made part of this request.

Mr. Wilson was working for S.G. Warburg & Co. in 1996. He wrote a report "FCX: Grasberg Closure Highlights Political Risks" The report was dated March 12, 1996.

As part of Mr. Wilson's request, records about his analyst report March 12, 1996 on U.S. mining company Freeport McMoran Copper and Gold Inc and attendance at Freeport's annual analyst briefing in New Orleans in May 1996 are pertinent. Mr. Wilson was a securities analyst in 1996. As part of his duties, he traveled from New York to New Orleans to attend the annual analysts briefing of Freeport McMoran Copper and Gold Inc. The meeting was held in May 1996. Mr. Wilson asked, during the analyst question time, a question of Jim Bob Moffet, Freeport McMoran's Chairman and CEO. The question was about the next phase of the U.S. State Department's investigation into Freeport, following eyewitness allegations the company was involved in the killing of indigenous protestors and other human rights violations in the vicinity of its massive copper and gold mine, the Grasberg mine, in West Papua, Indonesia. Mr. Wilson alluded to a recent New York Times article that stated that an interim report had been completed by the State Department, although it had not been publicly released. Jim Bob Moffett acknowledged the existence of the State Department investigation into the company and completion of the interim report. Mr. Wilson asked the CEO of Freeport McMoran, "What can investors expect?" After the meeting a shadowy figure who had been sitting among the analysts but whom Mr. Wilson did not recall having ever seen before and did not know, approached Mr. Wilson and suggested he not ask more questions on this subject and threatened him.

Mr. Wilson visited Steve Garber early in 1999 in Prescott, AZ. Mr. Wilson believes, by Mr. Garber's own admission, and as attested by Susan Holmes, that Mr. Garber worked for the FBI as an undercover operative, co-operating with the FBI in some capacity such as an FBI contractor, informant or in some other capacity. Mr. Wilson wants records from the report or recording that may have been made.

Mr. Wilson visited New York, New York in June 2004. He went on a long walk, through Central Park and the Upper West Side with Steve Garber. During this time Mr. Wilson said Steve Garber strongly insinuated that Mr. Wilson had been targeted by the FBI on account of Mr. Wilson's 1996 analyst report. Mr. Garber revealed many things that he knew about Mr. Wilson's background, from his own sources.

Mr. Wilson visited New York in September 2004. He again met with Steve Garber, this time at Tibet House and they walked to the Blue Water Grill, a restaurant in the Union Square neighborhood of New York, New York. Mr. Garber confirmed in this discussion that he worked for the FBI and that Mr. Wilson was being targeted for the report that Mr. Wilson published on Freeport McMoran Copper and Gold Inc. Mr. Wilson asked Mr. Garber if the FBI was responsible for the attack (comprising aggressive intrusions and interference in Mr. Wilson's life) on Mr. Wilson and Mr. Garber said yes. Mr. Garber said he occasionally did this type of work for the FBI and would likely deny the existence of his work.

On around ten or more occasions, from 1994 to 1997, the period in which Holmes and Wilson dated, Holmes informed Wilson that she worked for the FBI and several times discussed in extensive detail her background work for the FBI, including but not limited to her role, training, and past operations. Mr. Wilson was present or accompanied her on several FBI related undertakings. Some of these details are described below.

On several occasions, Holmes asked Mr. Wilson to accompany her on trips and to social gatherings that she later informed him had been part of her FBI assignments. One involved an unofficial Sierra Club volunteers after work drinks gathering around 1995-6 in a restaurant in NYC with a Montana tree spiking suspect James B. who was subsequently prosecuted, and at which a number of other undercover FBI agents were present.

Holmes showed Mr. Wilson her FBI wire device used for covert recording, with two leads, one running over each shoulder and joining at the front. She used this on the above gathering with a suspected tree spiker from Missoula, Montana visiting NYC around 1995-96.

Holmes told Wilson that she had received firearms training from the FBI, that she had an FBI issued handgun that she kept in her apartment, and that she regularly attended FBI training programs at Quantico.

Holmes showed Wilson several T-shirts and other clothing items bearing the FBI's initials in large letters at her New York City apartment in and around 1997.

Holmes told Wilson several times between 1994 and 1997 that she focused on eco-extremists for the FBI in the eastern half of the U.S.A. She said she was not directly involved with the western half and its handling of the Unabomber case, a high-profile case that had been successfully closed in 1996 with the arrest of Ted Kaczynski in Montana, though on occasion she had discussed the matter in general terms with him or in his presence with others, mainly her FBI peers.

During 1994 to 1997, the period in which Holmes and Wilson dated, Holmes disclosed and discussed at least two of her FBI work targets. One was Dave Foreman, founder of the Wildlands Network and co-founder of Earth First! who is a high-profile environmentalist and author. The other was Paul Winter, who performs the annual winter solstice concert at The Cathedral of St John the Divine in NYC, which at Holmes invitation, they used to attend annually. Holmes said Winter had been a student environmental activist and leader years before at college. Ms. Holmes invited Mr. Wilson to a presentation by Dave Foreman in New York, New York. This presentation was made in 1997. Mr. Wilson had no contact or association with any of these individuals on any occasion who were subjects of Holmes FBI work, other than through Ms. Holmes FBI work.

Mr. Wilson, in 1997, went on a rafting trip on the Colorado River, with Ms. Susan Holmes. Holmes was Mr. Wilson's girlfriend at the time, and introduced Mr. Wilson to Dave Foreman, a famous environmental activist and, a onetime person of interest to the FBI and subject of Holmes' work. There were about 20 or so people on the raft trip. Journalists were part of the rafting party, including a reporter from Time Magazine. Mr. Wilson had been invited by Holmes on the pretext everyone's partners were invited to attend. However, Mr. Wilson was surprised to find later when he arrived for the trip that of all the participants, he was the only domestic partner invited. The trip organizers arranged to have Mr. Wilson placed in the same raft with Mr. Foreman.

Mr. Wilson has had a lot of contact with persons who were aware of many of his private personal details and appeared to be undercover FBI agents. His former girlfriend, Susan Holmes, told Mr. Wilson that she worked as an undercover agent. She showed Mr. Wilson her black FBI identification card. She apparently said she was not an employee or a special agent of the agency. Rather her work for the FBI was on a contract basis more akin to an independent contractor. She told Mr. Wilson that the color of the ID card was significant, hers being black, whereas the regular day to day FBI employees have white background ID cards. Depending on her work capacity for the FBI, this may have some bearing as to which of the FBI databases the information is held in and that should be searched.

On or around Saturday, May 10th, 2003, Susan Holmes subjected Mr. Wilson to a series of intense questioning at Cafe Fiorello, 1900 Broadway, in New York City. During the roughly two and a half hours, Holmes acknowledged to Mr. Wilson that she was undertaking an interview at the behest of a U.S. government agency. During the interview, Holmes detailed a myriad of specific details of Mr. Wilson's life spanning many decades, continents, and people. These details included but were not limited to information regarding: personal conversations of Wilson's with current and former peers and colleagues going back decades; content of phone calls Mr. Wilson had had on his private home phone; minor traffic offenses incurred in Australia; work records from various companies Mr. Wilson had worked at over the years; records of school and university grades; records of purchases; records of state tests; medical history; and camping records at US national parks. During the interview, Holmes also asked a large number of questions about Mr. Wilson's background, family members, contacts and opinions including seeking information on any crimes or misdemeanors – a systematic interrogation. Of all the analyst reports that Mr. Wilson had published over the years, the only one she asked about was concerning Freeport McMoran published 12 March 1996. Ms. Holmes asked if Mr. Wilson remembered the report on Freeport McMoran he had published about the killings, the threat that Mr. Wilson received in the boardroom alcove, the state department investigation, and loss of OPIC political risk insurance and subsequent interactions experienced by Mr. Wilson in relation to the report and analyst meeting.

D. HOW RESPONSIVE RECORDS SHOULD BE PROVIDED

My client requests copies of the responsive records for this FOIA request be provided in a digital format, either via email, or stored on a thumb drive, CD or other electronic data storage device. See 5 U.S.C. §552 (a)(3) B). Providing these records in an electronic format will save agency staff processing time, as well as reducing the cost of making paper copies of all responsive records.

E. PROCESSING FEES

My client is pre-authorizing payments up to $30 for the processing of this request but only if the FBI complies with all statutory deadlines in FOIA. Congress amended FOIA in 2007. An effect of the 2007 Amendments was to impose consequences on agencies that fail to comport with FOIA's requirements. See S.Rep. No. 110-59. To underscore Congress's belief in the importance of the statutory time limit, the 2007 Amendments declare that "[a]n agency shall not assess search fees ... if the agency fails to comply with any time limit" of FOIA. § 552(a)(4)(A)(viii) (emphasis added). Bensman v National Park Service, 806 F.Supp.2d 31 (DCD 2011).

F. POLICY AND LEGAL DIRECTION FOR OPEN GOVERNMENT

Disclosure of the above referenced agency records are also sought in order to promote government transparency, and to reflect the Administration's policy to support our nation's fundamental commitment to open government. As the Supreme Court has observed, "virtually every document generated by an agency is available in one form or another, unless it falls within one of the Act's nine exemptions." NLRB v. Sears, Roebuck & Co., 421 U.S. 132, 136 (1975). FOIA was designed to "pierce the veil of administrative secrecy and to open agency action to the light of public scrutiny," see, e.g., Dept. of the Air Force v. Rose, 425 U.S. 352, 361 (1976), and in order "to ensure an informed citizenry, vital to the functioning of a democratic society, needed to check against corruption and to hold the governors accountable to the governed." NLRB v. Robbins Tire & Rubber Co., 437 U.S. 214, 242 (1978); see also Judicial Watch, Inc. v. Rossotti, 326 F.3d 1309, 1310 (D.C. Cir. 2003); United States Dept. of Justice v. Reporters Comm. for Freedom of the Press, 489 U.S. 749, 773 (1989).

The above-described agency records are subject to disclosure under FOIA, and are not otherwise exempt from disclosure pursuant to FOIA's nine statutory exemptions. See 5 U.S.C. § 552(b)(1) - (9). To the extent that a determination is made by your FOIA office staff that any limited portions of the records listed above will be withheld from disclosure for this request, FOIA expressly requires all agencies to disclose "[a]ny reasonably segregable portion of a record ...after deletion of the portions of the record which are exempt." 5 U.S.C. §552(b). See, e.g., Oglesby v. U.S. Dept. of Army, 79 F.3d 1172, 1178 (D.C. Cir. 1996); see also Abdelfattah v. U.S. Dept. Of Homeland Security, 488 F.3d 178, 186-187 (3rd Cir).

The 2007 Openness Promotes Effectiveness in our National Government Act amendments to FOIA (the "OPEN Government Act") requires identification of the amount of any material withheld, the location of any withholdings, a direct reference to the specific statutory exemption supporting each withholdings asserted, and if technically possible, also require that this information shall "be indicated at the place in the record where such deletion is made." See 5 U.S.C. § 552(b). Therefore, I would appreciate your assistance in expressly identifying any exempt responsive records (or portions thereof) and the applicable FOIA exemptions for any responsive materials withheld for this FOIA request.

Please inform my office in writing if there are any "unusual circumstances" that will cause delay in responding to this FOIA request, or providing the records which are requested, and in addition, please provide the approximate date that you anticipate a final response will be provided.

G. AUTHORIZATION

Attached to this request is a Declaration of John Christian Wilson and the DOJ Form 361 signed by John Christian Wilson.

The declaration, in particular, authorizes C. Peter Sorenson and the Sorenson Law Office to make this request and to receive records on behalf of John Christian Wilson. The declaration expressly waives privacy rights – as they may apply to C. Peter Sorenson and the Sorenson Law Office – relating to this FOIA request and any records that the FBI has in response to this request. Furthermore, the declaration establishes that John Christian Wilson is willing and able to sign any forms the agency may require to formalize the waiver of privacy rights to C. Peter Sorenson and the Sorenson Law Office.

H. ESTIMATED DATE OF COMPLETION REQUESTED

The Sorenson Law Office, on behalf of our client, specifically requests the agency to provide an estimated date of completion for this request.

I. CONTACT

Please provide a receipt for this request and provide a tracking number so that we may inquire about the status of this request.

If you have any questions regarding this FOIA request or need help locating documents, or if I can be of any other assistance, please feel free to contact me at (541) 606-9173, or via email to: peter@sorensonfoialaw.com.

Thank you in advance for your assistance.

Best,

C. Peter Sorenson
Sorenson Law Office
PO Box 10836
Eugene, Oregon 97440

Attachments: 1) Declaration of John Christian Wilson; 2) DOJ Form 361 signed by John Christian Wilson.

* * * * *

* * * * *

Exhibit 113: *13 June 2022.   FOIA response from the FBI to Pete Sorenson re John Wilson.*

U.S. Department of Justice

Federal Bureau of Investigation

Washington, D.C. 20535

June 13, 2022

C. PETER SORENSON
SORENSON LAW OFFICE
POST OFFICE BOX 10836
EUGENE, OR 97440

FOIPA Request No.: 1548515-000
Subject: WILSON, JOHN CHRISTIAN
(From October 28, 2019 to June 6, 2022)

Dear C. Sorenson:

This is in response to your Freedom of Information/Privacy Acts (FOIPA) request. Please see the paragraphs below for relevant information specific to your request as well as the enclosed FBI FOIPA Addendum for standard responses applicable to all requests.

Records regarding your subject were previously reviewed and released to you pursuant to the FOIPA. An additional search was conducted for main entity records, and no additional records subject to the FOIPA were located. Therefore, your request is being administratively closed. For more information about records searches and the standard search policy, see the enclosed FBI FOIPA Addendum General Information Section.

Please refer to the enclosed FBI FOIPA Addendum for additional standard responses applicable to your request. "**Part 1**" of the Addendum includes standard responses that apply to all requests. "**Part 2**" includes additional standard responses that apply to all requests for records about yourself or any third party individuals. "**Part 3**" includes general information about FBI records that you may find useful. Also enclosed is our Explanation of Exemptions.

For questions regarding our determinations, visit the www.fbi.gov/foia website under "Contact Us." The FOIPA Request number listed above has been assigned to your request. Please use this number in all correspondence concerning your request.

If you are not satisfied with the Federal Bureau of Investigation's determination in response to this request, you may administratively appeal by writing to the Director, Office of Information Policy (OIP), United States Department of Justice, 441 G Street, NW, 6th Floor, Washington, D.C. 20530, or you may submit an appeal through OIP's FOIA STAR portal by creating an account following the instructions on OIP's website: https://www.justice.gov/oip/submit-and-track-request-or-appeal. Your appeal must be postmarked or electronically transmitted within ninety (90) days of the date of my response to your request. If you submit your appeal by mail, both the letter and the envelope should be clearly marked "Freedom of Information Act Appeal." Please cite the FOIPA Request Number assigned to your request so it may be easily identified.

You may seek dispute resolution services by contacting the Office of Government Information Services (OGIS). The contact information for OGIS is as follows: Office of Government Information Services, National Archives and Records Administration, 8601 Adelphi Road-OGIS, College Park, Maryland 20740-6001, e-mail at ogis@nara.gov; telephone at 202-741-5770; toll free at 1-877-684-6448; or facsimile at 202-741-5769. Alternatively, you may contact the FBI's FOIA Public Liaison by emailing foipaquestions@fbi.gov. If you submit your dispute resolution correspondence by email, the subject heading should clearly state "Dispute Resolution Services." Please also cite the FOIPA Request Number assigned to your request so it may be easily identified.

Sincerely,

Michael G. Seidel
Section Chief
Record/Information
 Dissemination Section
Information Management Division

Enclosures

FBI FOIPA Addendum

As referenced in our letter responding to your Freedom of Information/Privacy Acts (FOIPA) request, the FBI FOIPA Addendum provides information applicable to your request. Part 1 of the Addendum includes standard responses that apply to all requests. Part 2 includes standard responses that apply to requests for records about individuals to the extent your request seeks the listed information. Part 3 includes general information about FBI records, searches, and programs.

Part 1: The standard responses below apply to all requests:

(i) **5 U.S.C. § 552(c).** Congress excluded three categories of law enforcement and national security records from the requirements of the FOIPA [5 U.S.C. § 552(c)]. FBI responses are limited to those records subject to the requirements of the FOIPA. Additional information about the FBI and the FOIPA can be found on the www.fbi.gov/foia website.

(ii) **Intelligence Records.** To the extent your request seeks records of intelligence sources, methods, or activities, the FBI can neither confirm nor deny the existence of records pursuant to FOIA exemptions (b)(1), (b)(3), and as applicable to requests for records about individuals, PA exemption (j)(2) [5 U.S.C. §§ 552/552a (b)(1), (b)(3), and (j)(2)]. The mere acknowledgment of the existence or nonexistence of such records is itself a classified fact protected by FOIA exemption (b)(1) and/or would reveal intelligence sources, methods, or activities protected by exemption (b)(3) [50 USC § 3024(i)(1)]. This is a standard response and should not be read to indicate that any such records do or do not exist.

Part 2: The standard responses below apply to all requests for records on individuals:

(i) **Requests for Records about any Individual—Watch Lists.** The FBI can neither confirm nor deny the existence of any individual's name on a watch list pursuant to FOIA exemption (b)(7)(E) and PA exemption (j)(2) [5 U.S.C. §§ 552/552a (b)(7)(E), (j)(2)]. This is a standard response and should not be read to indicate that watch list records do or do not exist.

(ii) **Requests for Records about any Individual—Witness Security Program Records.** The FBI can neither confirm nor deny the existence of records which could identify any participant in the Witness Security Program pursuant to FOIA exemption (b)(3) and PA exemption (j)(2) [5 U.S.C. §§ 552/552a (b)(3), 18 U.S.C. 3521, and (j)(2)]. This is a standard response and should not be read to indicate that such records do or do not exist.

(iii) **Requests for Records for Incarcerated Individuals.** The FBI can neither confirm nor deny the existence of records which could reasonably be expected to endanger the life or physical safety of any incarcerated individual pursuant to FOIA exemptions (b)(7)(E), (b)(7)(F), and PA exemption (j)(2) [5 U.S.C. §§ 552/552a (b)(7)(E), (b)(7)(F), and (j)(2)]. This is a standard response and should not be read to indicate that such records do or do not exist.

Part 3: General Information:

(i) **Record Searches and Standard Search Policy.** The Record/Information Dissemination Section (RIDS) searches for reasonably described records by searching systems, such as the Central Records System (CRS), or locations where responsive records would reasonably be found. The CRS is an extensive system of records consisting of applicant, investigative, intelligence, personnel, administrative, and general files compiled by the FBI per its law enforcement, intelligence, and administrative functions. The CRS spans the entire FBI organization, comprising records of FBI Headquarters, FBI Field Offices, and FBI Legal Attaché Offices (Legats) worldwide; Electronic Surveillance (ELSUR) records are included in the CRS. The standard search policy is a search for main entity records in the CRS. Unless specifically requested, a standard search does not include a search for reference entity records, administrative records of previous FOIPA requests, or civil litigation files.

   a. *Main Entity Records* – created for individuals or non-individuals who are the subjects or the focus of an investigation
   b. *Reference Entity Records* – created for individuals or non-individuals who are associated with a case but are not known subjects or the focus of an investigation

(ii) **FBI Records.** Founded in 1908, the FBI carries out a dual law enforcement and national security mission. As part of this dual mission, the FBI creates and maintains records on various subjects; however, the FBI does not maintain records on every person, subject, or entity.

(iii) **Requests for Criminal History Records or Rap Sheets.** The Criminal Justice Information Services (CJIS) Division provides Identity History Summary Checks – often referred to as a criminal history record or rap sheet. These criminal history records are not the same as material in an investigative "FBI file." An Identity History Summary Check is a listing of information taken from fingerprint cards and documents submitted to the FBI in connection with arrests, federal employment, naturalization, or military service. For a fee, individuals can request a copy of their Identity History Summary Check. Forms and directions can be accessed at www.fbi.gov/about-us/cjis/identity-history-summary-checks. Additionally, requests can be submitted electronically at www.edo.cjis.gov. For additional information, please contact CJIS directly at (304) 625-5590.

EXPLANATION OF EXEMPTIONS

SUBSECTIONS OF TITLE 5, UNITED STATES CODE, SECTION 552

(b)(1) (A) specifically authorized under criteria established by an Executive order to be kept secret in the interest of national defense or foreign policy and (B) are in fact properly classified to such Executive order;

(b)(2) related solely to the internal personnel rules and practices of an agency;

(b)(3) specifically exempted from disclosure by statute (other than section 552b of this title), provided that such statute (A) requires that the matters be withheld from the public in such a manner as to leave no discretion on issue, or (B) establishes particular criteria for withholding or refers to particular types of matters to be withheld;

(b)(4) trade secrets and commercial or financial information obtained from a person and privileged or confidential;

(b)(5) inter-agency or intra-agency memorandums or letters which would not be available by law to a party other than an agency in litigation with the agency;

(b)(6) personnel and medical files and similar files the disclosure of which would constitute a clearly unwarranted invasion of personal privacy;

(b)(7) records or information compiled for law enforcement purposes, but only to the extent that the production of such law enforcement records or information (A) could reasonably be expected to interfere with enforcement proceedings, (B) would deprive a person of a right to a fair trial or an impartial adjudication, (C) could reasonably be expected to constitute an unwarranted invasion of personal privacy, (D) could reasonably be expected to disclose the identity of confidential source, including a State, local, or foreign agency or authority or any private institution which furnished information on a confidential basis, and, in the case of record or information compiled by a criminal law enforcement authority in the course of a criminal investigation, or by an agency conducting a lawful national security intelligence investigation, information furnished by a confidential source, (E) would disclose techniques and procedures for law enforcement investigations or prosecutions, or would disclose guidelines for law enforcement investigations or prosecutions if such disclosure could reasonably be expected to risk circumvention of the law, or (F) could reasonably be expected to endanger the life or physical safety of any individual;

(b)(8) contained in or related to examination, operating, or condition reports prepared by, on behalf of, or for the use of an agency responsible for the regulation or supervision of financial institutions; or

(b)(9) geological and geophysical information and data, including maps, concerning wells.

SUBSECTIONS OF TITLE 5, UNITED STATES CODE, SECTION 552a

(d)(5) information compiled in reasonable anticipation of a civil action proceeding;

(j)(2) material reporting investigative efforts pertaining to the enforcement of criminal law including efforts to prevent, control, or reduce crime or apprehend criminals;

(k)(1) information which is currently and properly classified pursuant to an Executive order in the interest of the national defense or foreign policy, for example, information involving intelligence sources or methods;

(k)(2) investigatory material compiled for law enforcement purposes, other than criminal, which did not result in loss of a right, benefit or privilege under Federal programs, or which would identify a source who furnished information pursuant to a promise that his/her identity would be held in confidence;

(k)(3) material maintained in connection with providing protective services to the President of the United States or any other individual pursuant to the authority of Title 18, United States Code, Section 3056;

(k)(4) required by statute to be maintained and used solely as statistical records;

(k)(5) investigatory material compiled solely for the purpose of determining suitability, eligibility, or qualifications for Federal civilian employment or for access to classified information, the disclosure of which would reveal the identity of the person who furnished information pursuant to a promise that his/her identity would be held in confidence;

(k)(6) testing or examination material used to determine individual qualifications for appointment or promotion in Federal Government service the release of which would compromise the testing or examination process;

(k)(7) material used to determine potential for promotion in the armed services, the disclosure of which would reveal the identity of the person who furnished the material pursuant to a promise that his/her identity would be held in confidence.

FBI/DOJ

U.S. Department of Justice
Federal Bureau of Investigation
200 Constitution Drive
Winchester, VA 22602-4693

Official Business
Penalty for Private Use $300

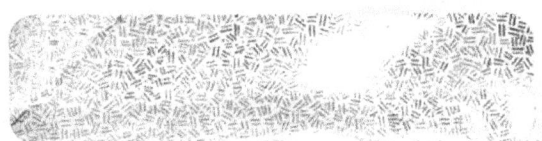

9744032836 B025

* * * * *

* * * * *

Exhibit 114: *1 September 2022.   FOIA Administrative Appeal to the OIP, DOJ from Pete Sorenson.*

[Attachments appended to the appeal to the Office of Information Policy (OIP), DOJ include John Wilson's notarized Declaration of 30 August 2022 (184 pages) reproduced in full earlier in this volume.]

Sorenson Law Office
PO Box 10836
Eugene, Oregon 97440

September 1, 2022

Director
Office of Information Policy (OIP)
U.S. Department of Justice
441 G Street, NW, 6th Floor
Washington, D.C. 20530

SENT VIA PORTAL AT: https://www.justice.gov/oip/submit-and-track-request-or-appeal

RE: Administrative Appeal of FOIA Request FOIPA No. 1548515-000

I. FACTUAL BACKGROUND

On May 20, 2022, our law firm, on behalf of our law firm's client, John Christian Wilson, submitted a FOIA request to the Federal Bureau of Investigation (FBI) that sought:

> 1) All records, documents, or communications prepared by, received by or maintained by the FBI which mention the following terms:
> > John Christian Wilson
> > John C. Wilson
> > John Wilson
>
> 2) All records describing FBI informant or FBI agent contacts with
> > John Christian Wilson

John C. Wilson
John Wilson

3) All records describing FBI contractors, or others operating on behalf of the FBI or other DOJ element, contacts with
John Christian Wilson
John C. Wilson
John Wilson

4) The 1996 securities analyst report on NYSE listed U.S. mining company Freeport McMoran Copper and Gold Inc (which trades on the NYSE under the symbol FCX) written by John Wilson. This report is entitled, "FCX: Grasberg Closure Highlights Political Risks." Mr. Wilson wrote the report as an analyst working for S.G. Warburg & Co. Inc. and the report was dated March 12, 1996.

5) All records describing the attendance of John Wilson at the Freeport McMoran Copper and Gold Inc. May 1996 annual analyst briefing at Freeport McMoran Copper and Gold Inc's headquarters in New Orleans, Louisiana. In particular, records are sought concerning n interaction between John Wilson and James R. Moffett (known as Jim Bob), CEO and Chairman of Freeport McMoran Copper and Gold Inc, in the boardroom alcove after the analyst question period that was held in Freeport McMoran's boardroom.

6) All records describing an interaction between John Wilson and an unnamed person, apparently a federal agent or FBI operative, also in Freeport's boardroom alcove after the analyst question period in Freeport's boardroom mentioned above at the Freeport headquarters in New Orleans, Louisiana in May 1996.

7) All records describing or documenting interactions between John Wilson and people operating on behalf of the FBI or other DOJ element, in particular by Steve Garber.

8) All records, including notes, recordings or transcripts of interviews, made by Steve Garber in early 1999 during the several days when Mr. Wilson visited Garber at his home in Prescott, AZ.

9) All records, including notes, recordings or transcripts, of a discussion or interview involving Mr. Wilson and Steve Garber in June 2004 in New York, New York.

10) All records, including notes, recordings or transcripts, of a discussion or interview involving Mr. Wilson and Steve Garber in September 2004, including at Tibet House, and

also the Blue Water Grill both in the vicinity of the Union Square neighborhood of New York, New York.

11) All records of the attendance involving John Wilson in connection with a presentation that Dave Foreman gave in New York, New York in late 1997. David Foreman (usually referred to as Dave) is a well-knownAmerican environmental activist and co-founder of environmental group Earth First! Dave Foreman was a subject of Susan Holmes for her work for the FBI.

12) All records pertaining to John Wilson concerning his attendance, or discussions with Susan Holmes or Dave Foreman on a raft trip on the Colorado River in July or August 1997 with journalists, including a reporter for Time Magazine, Ms. Holmes and Mr. Foreman.

13) All records of discussions between John Wilson and Susan Ackerson Holmes. All records describing or documenting interactions between John Wilson and people operating on behalf of the FBI or other DOJ element, in particular Susan Ackerson Holmes.

14) All records of discussions between John Wilson and Susan Holmes during the three years that they dated in New York, New York, calendar years 1994, 1995, 1996 and 1997.

15) All records of discussions between John Wilson and Susan Holmes in a May 10, 2003 (on or about) dinner conversation between Susan Holmes and John Wilson in New York, New York.

16) All telephone wiretaps on telephones used by John Wilson.

17) All records showing any applications for surveillance or wiretaps of telephones used by John Wilson.

18) All records showing any applications for search warrants for properties owned or leased by John Wilson.

19) All records showing any applications for surveillance of John Wilson.

The time frame for this request includes records created or received on or after January 1, 1994 to present. A form DOJ-361 signed by John Christian Wilson was included that allowed release of the records. Ex. 1.

On June 6, 2022, the FBI responded to Mr. Wilson's request and numbered it FOIPA No. 1548515-000. The response is attached as Ex. 2.

II. THE FREEDOM OF INFORMATION ACT

The purpose of FOIA is to "open agency action to the light of public scrutiny." *Dep't of the Air Force v. Rose*, 425 U.S. 352, 372 (1976). Former President Obama reinforced FOIA's strong presumption of disclosure with regard to all FOIA decisions. *See* Presidential Memorandum for Heads of Executive Departments and Agencies Concerning the Freedom of Information Act, 74 Fed. Reg. 4683 (Jan. 21, 2009) (directing agencies to administer FOIA under a presumption that, "[i]n the face of doubt, openness prevails"). Former Attorney General Eric Holder issued FOIA guidelines that reinforce a commitment to open government, encouraging federal agencies to both "make discretionary releases of information" and to "make partial disclosures" when an agency determines full disclosure is not possible. *See* Former Attorney General Eric Holder's Memorandum for Heads of Executive Departments and Agencies (Mar. 19, 2009).

In his memo, the Former Attorney General also announced a "foreseeable harm" standard for defending agency decisions to withhold information under FOIA. *See id.* Thus, the DOJ will defend an agency's denial of a FOIA request "only if (1) the agency reasonably foresees that disclosure would harm an interest protected by one of the statutory exemptions, or (2) disclosure is prohibited by law." *Id.* These authorities have not been changed by the current Administration and remain in effect.

FOIA "mandates a policy of broad disclosure of government documents" and carries a strict disclosure mandate that requires federal agencies to expeditiously disclose requested records to requesters. *See* 5 U.S.C. § 552, *Church of Scientology v. Dep't of the Army*, 611 F.2d 738, 741 (9th Cir. 1980). Consequently, any inquiry under FOIA brings with it a "strong presumption in favor of disclosure." *U.S. Dep't of State v. Ray*, 502 U.S. 164, 173 (1991). To that end, nothing in FOIA should be read to "authorize withholding of information or limit the availability of records to the public, except as specifically stated." *See* 5 U.S.C. § 552(c). Congress recognized that in certain limited instances, records may be exempt from FOIA's broad disclosure mandate, and thus created nine categories of exemptions. § 552(b). These exemptions, however, "must be narrowly construed in light of FOIA's dominant objective of disclosure, not secrecy." *Maricopa Audubon Soc'y. v. U.S. Forest Serv.*, 108 F.3d 1082, 1085 (9th Cir. 1996).

Accordingly, because FOIA carries a presumption in favor of disclosure, and indeed, because, "FOIA requesters face an information asymmetry given that the agency possesses the requested information and decides whether it should be withheld or disclosed," *COMPTEL v. U.S. Federal Comm'n.*, 910 F. Supp. 2d 100, 111 (D.D.C. 2012) (internal citations omitted), agencies bear the burden of justifying the withholding of any records that are responsive to a FOIA request. 5 U.S.C. §552 (a)(4). An agency must provide "a relatively detailed justification, specifically identifying the reasons why a particular exemption is relevant and correlating those claims with the particular part of a withheld document to which they apply." *See King v. Dept. of Justice*, 830 F.2d 210, 219 (D.C. Cir. 1987) (agency must provide); *see also Coastal States Gas Corp. v. Dep't of Energy*, 617 F.2d 854, 861 (D.C. Cir. 1980) (holding an agency's disclosure of "who wrote the [document], to whom it was addressed, its date, and a brief description" was "patently inadequate" to establish exemption under FOIA).

Under the FOIA Improvement Act of 2016, agencies are prohibited from denying requests for information under FOIA unless the agency reasonably believes release of the information will harm an interest that is protected by the exemption. *See* FOIA Improvement Act of 2016 (Public Law No. 114-185), codified at 5 U.S.C. § 552(a)(8)(A).

III. FOIA REQUIRES AGENCIES CONDUCT A SEARCH WHEN REQUESTERS REASONABLY DESCRIBE THE RECORDS SOUGHT

FOIA requires that a requester "reasonably describe" the records sought in sufficient detail that an agency professional familiar with the subject matter can locate the records with a "reasonable amount of effort." *Ferri v. DOJ*, 573 F. Supp. 852, 859 (W.D. Pa. 1983). After a valid request has been made to the agency, that agency must "make reasonable efforts to search for records." 5 U.S.C. § 552 (a)(3)(A)(C). The term "search" here means "to review, manually *or* by automated means, agency records for the purpose of locating those records which are responsive to a request." *Id.* § (a)(3)(A)(D) (emphasis added).

On June 13, 2022, FBI stated "Records regarding your subject were previously reviewed and released to you pursuant to the FOIPA. An additional search was conducted for main entity records, and no additional records subject to the FOIPA were located. Therefore, your request is being administratively closed." Ex. 3.

From 1994 to 1997 Mr. Wilson worked for SG Warburg (and later SBC Warburg) on Wall Street as an equity analyst covering US listed mining companies. Ex. 4.

One of the companies Mr. Wilson analyzed and published reports on, for distribution to fund managers globally, was U.S.-based Freeport McMoran. It was, and is, one of the world's largest and most valuable copper companies, worth many tens of billions of dollars. Through its subsidiary, Freeport Indonesia, Freeport McMoran controls the Grasberg Mine, one of the largest copper and gold mines in the world, situated in West Papua, Indonesia. *Id.*

On March 12, 1996, Mr. Wilson authored a report that flagged concerns about Freeport McMoran, which was under investigation by the United States Department of State following eyewitness reports of human rights abuses against indigenous protestors in the region of its massive Grasberg gold and copper mine in West Papua, Indonesia. The Report mentioned the cancellation of the company's OPIC political risk insurance in October 1995 and was critical of the company's approach to resolving civil disputes. It was published and distributed to investors globally by Mr. Wilson's employer SG Warburg. *Id.*

Mr. Wilson was threatened in the Freeport McMoran (a mining company based in Phoenix, AZ) boardroom alcove in 1996 by an undisclosed person, presumably a federal agent, who seemed to know a lot about Mr. Wilson and the retribution Mr. Wilson was to face for his Freeport McMoran work, associating Mr. Wilson with people of interest to the FBI (and targets of agent Holmes FBI work, including David Foreman). *Id.*

Mr. Wilson believes the FBI to have requested records they failed to disclose. In part, Mr. Wilson believes this because Mr. Wilson visited Steve Garber early in 1999 in Prescott, AZ. Mr. Wilson believes, by Mr Garber's own admission, and as attested by Susan Holmes, that Mr. Garber worked for the FBI as an undercover operative, co-operating with the FBI in some capacity such as an FBI contractor, informant or in some other capacity. *Id.* Mr. Wilson wants records from the report or recording that may have been made.

Further, Mr. Wilson visited New York, New York in June 2004. He went on a walk with Steve Garber. During this time Steve Garber strongly insinuated to Mr. Wilson that Mr. Wilson had been targeted by the FBI on account of Mr. Wilson's 1996 analyst report. Mr. Garber revealed many things that he knew about Mr. Wilson's background, from his own sources.

Mr. Wilson again visited New York, New York in September 2004. He again met with Steve Garber. Mr. Garber confirmed in this discussion that he worked for the FBI and that Mr. Wilson was being targeted for the report that Mr. Wilson published on Freeport McMoran Copper and Gold Inc. Mr. Wilson asked Mr. Garber if the FBI was responsible for the attack (comprising aggressive intrusions and interference in Mr. Wilson's life) on Mr. Wilson and Mr. Garber said yes. Mr. Garber said he occasionally did this type of work for the FBI and the FBI would likely deny the existence of his work. *Id.*

From 1994 to 1997 Ms. Susan Holmes and Mr. Wilson dated. On approximately ten or more occasions, Ms. Holmes informed Mr. Wilson that she worked for the FBI and several times discussed in extensive detail her background work for the FBI, including but not limited to her role, training, and past operations. Ms. Holmes showed Mr. Wilson her FBI ID card at her NYC apartment. It was late 1994. It was a credit card sized plastic card with an image of her face on it and set on a blackish background. *Id.* Ms. Holmes used her FBI card in front of Mr. Wilson in 1996 to gain access past a security point at an Irish folk music concert in NYC. *Id.*

Ms. Holmes focused on environmental extremists for the FBI. *Id.*

Mr. Wilson was present or accompanied her on several FBI related undertakings. On several occasions, Ms. Holmes asked Mr. Wilson to accompany her on trips and to social gatherings that she later informed him had been part of her FBI assignments. One involved an unofficial Sierra Club volunteers after work drinks gathering around 1995-6 in a restaurant in NYC with a Montana tree spiking suspect James B. who was subsequently prosecuted, and at which a number of other undercover FBI agents were present. Id.

Ms. Holmes showed Mr. Wilson her FBI wire device used for covert recording, with two leads, one running over each shoulder and joining at the front. She used this on the above gathering with a suspected tree spiker from Missoula, Montana visiting NYC around 1995 -96. Id.

Ms. Holmes told Mr. Wilson that she had received firearms training from the FBI, that she had an FBI issued handgun that she kept in her apartment, and that she regularly attended FBI training programs at Quantico. Id.

Ms. Holmes told Mr. Wilson several times between 1994 and 1997 that she focused on eco-extremists for the FBI in the eastern half of the U.S.A. Id.

The DOJ/FBI have consistently sidestepped the claim that Ms. Holmes and Mr. Garber were operatives despite their admissions to the fact. The DOJ/FBI refusal to respond to assertions that Ms. Holmes and Mr. Garber were operatives of the FBI is evidence of agency "bad faith".

The FBI has vindictively investigated Mr. Wilson because of his Freeport McMoran work in 1996.

Mr. Wilson has knowledge that the FBI had a case concerning him. Mr. Wilson demands to know what the case was about, when did it start/close, and why all of the information concerning the investigation of him is being withheld.

Mr. Wilson demands to know why and when information on him was collected by the FBI.

For these reasons, Mr. Wilson believes that the FBI has records, which he lawfully requested under FOIPA, and which have not been provided to Mr. Wilson by the FBI.

VI. CONCLUSION

As described above, the FBI has failed to conduct a reasonable search in response to a FOIA request that specifically describes the documents sought.

Accordingly, the FBI must conduct an adequate search for responsive records and produce all responsive records by a certain date. In so doing, the FBI must also provide an estimated date of completion of its release of the records. 5 U.S.C. § 552 (a)(7)(B).

Please notify me of the date you receive this FOIA Appeal and the number you assign to identify this FOIA Appeal. I expect your timely resolution of this matter. Do not hesitate to contact me with any questions regarding this appeal. Please contact me at peter@sorensonfoialaw.com or Sorenson Law Office, PO Box 10836, Eugene, Oregon 97440.

C. Peter Sorenson
Sorenson Law Office
PO Box 10836
Eugene, Oregon 97440

Enclosures:

- Ex. 1 Mr. Wilson's FOIA request dated May 20, 2022.
- Ex. 2 FBI response dated June 6, 2022.
- Ex. 3 FBI response dated June 13, 2022.
- Ex. 4 Declaration of Mr. John Christian Wilson.

* * * * *

* * * * *

Exhibit 115: *1 September 2022.   FOIA Admin. Appeal receipt from the OIP, DOJ to Pete Sorenson.*
Administrative Appeal assigned case number A-2022-02028 by OIG,FBI.

U.S. Department of Justice
Office of Information Policy
Sixth Floor
441 G Street, NW
Washington, DC 20530-0001

Telephone: (202) 514-3642

September 01, 2022

peter@sorensonfoialaw.com

Dear C. Sorenson:

    This is to advise you that the Office of Information Policy (OIP) of the U.S. Department of Justice received your administrative appeal from the action of the FBI regarding Request No. 1548515-000 on 09/01/2022.

    In an attempt to afford each appellant equal and impartial treatment, OIP has adopted a general practice of assigning appeals in the approximate order of receipt. Your appeal has been assigned number A-2022-02028. Please refer to this number in any future communication with OIP regarding this matter. Please note that if you provided an email address or another electronic means of communication with your request or appeal, this Office may respond to your appeal electronically even if you submitted your appeal to this Office via regular U.S. Mail.

    We will notify you of the decision on your appeal as soon as we can. If you have any questions about the status of your appeal, you may contact me at (202) 514-3642. If you have submitted your appeal through FOIA STAR, you may also check the status of your appeal by logging into your account.

Sincerely,

Priscilla Jones

Priscilla Jones
Supervisory Administrative Specialist

* * * * *

* * * * *

Exhibit 116: *28 April 2023.   FOIA "litigation release" letter and disc sent to Attorney Pete Sorenson.*

["Litigation release letter" Civil Action No.:22-cv-3062 filed 8 October 2022 (for details see section VI). The FBI response states 35 pages were reviewed of which 26 pages were released – the disc contents are attached below.]

U.S. Department of Justice

Federal Bureau of Investigation
Washington, D.C. 20535

April 28, 2023

C. PETER SORENSON
SORENSON LAW OFFICE
POST OFFICE BOX 10836
EUGENE, OR 97440

John Christian Wilson v. FBI
Civil Action No.: 22-cv-3062
FOIPA Request No.: 1548515-000
Subject: WILSON, JOHN CHRISTIAN

Dear C. Peter Sorenson:

The FBI has completed its review of records subject to the Freedom of Information/Privacy Acts (FOIPA) that are responsive to your request. The enclosed documents were reviewed under the FOIPA, Title 5, United States Code, Section 552/552a. Below you will find checked boxes under applicable statutes for the exemptions asserted to protect information exempt from disclosure. The appropriate exemptions are noted on the processed pages next to redacted information. In addition, a deleted page information sheet was inserted to indicate where pages were withheld entirely pursuant to applicable exemptions. An Explanation of Exemptions is enclosed to further explain justification for withheld information.

Section 552
- ☐ (b)(1)
- ☐ (b)(2)
- ☐ (b)(3)
- _____
- _____
- _____
- ☐ (b)(4)
- ☐ (b)(5)
- ☑ (b)(6)

- ☐ (b)(7)(A)
- ☐ (b)(7)(B)
- ☑ (b)(7)(C)
- ☐ (b)(7)(D)
- ☑ (b)(7)(E)
- ☐ (b)(7)(F)
- ☐ (b)(8)
- ☐ (b)(9)

Section 552a
- ☐ (d)(5)
- ☐ (j)(2)
- ☐ (k)(1)
- ☑ (k)(2)
- ☐ (k)(3)
- ☐ (k)(4)
- ☐ (k)(5)
- ☐ (k)(6)
- ☐ (k)(7)

35 pages were reviewed and 26 pages are being released.

Please see the paragraphs below for relevant information specific to your request and the enclosed FBI FOIPA Addendum for standard responses applicable to all requests.

Based on the information you provided, we conducted a main and reference entity record search of the Central Records System (CRS) per our standard search policy. For more information about records searches and the standard search policy, see the enclosed FBI FOIPA Addendum General Information Section.

This is the final release of information responsive to your FOIPA request. This material is being provided to you at no charge.

The enclosed documents responsive to your request are exempt from disclosure in their entirety pursuant to the Privacy Act, Title 5, United States Code, section 552(a), subsection (k)(2). However, these records have been processed pursuant to the Freedom of Information Act, Title 5, United States Code, Section 552, thereby affording you the greatest degree of access authorized by both laws.

Duplicate copies of the same document were not processed.

Additional material potentially responsive to your request was located regarding civil suits and/or administrative claims. If you would like this material processed pursuant to the FOIPA, please advise the FBI at your earliest convenience.

For your information, a search of the indices to our Central Records System reflected there were additional records potentially responsive to your Freedom of Information/Privacy Acts (FOIPA) request. We have attempted to obtain this material so it could be reviewed to determine whether it was responsive to your request. We were advised that the potentially responsive records were not in their expected location and could not be located after a reasonable search. Following a reasonable waiting period, another attempt was made to obtain this material. This search for the missing records also met with unsuccessful results.

The appropriate redactions were made by the Department of State (DOS) and the Department of Justice-Office of the Inspector General (DOJ-OIG).

Please refer to the enclosed FBI FOIPA Addendum for additional standard responses applicable to your request. "Part 1" of the Addendum includes standard responses that apply to all requests. "Part 2" includes additional standard responses that apply to all requests for records about yourself or any third party individuals. "Part 3" includes general information about FBI records that you may find useful. Also enclosed is our Explanation of Exemptions.

Although your request is in litigation, we are required by law to provide you the following information:

If you are not satisfied with the Federal Bureau of Investigation's determination in response to this request, you may administratively appeal by writing to the Director, Office of Information Policy (OIP), United States Department of Justice, 441 G Street, NW, 6th Floor, Washington, D.C. 20530, or you may submit an appeal through OIP's FOIA STAR portal by creating an account following the instructions on OIP's website: https://www.justice.gov/oip/submit-and-track-request-or-appeal. Your appeal must be postmarked or electronically transmitted within ninety (90) days of the date of my response to your request. If you submit your appeal by mail, both the letter and the envelope should be clearly marked "Freedom of Information Act Appeal." Please cite the FOIPA Request Number assigned to your request so it may be easily identified.

You may seek dispute resolution services by emailing the FBI's FOIA Public Liaison at foipaquestions@fbi.gov. The subject heading should clearly state "Dispute Resolution Services." Please also cite the FOIPA Request Number assigned to your request so it may be easily identified. You may also contact the Office of Government Information Services (OGIS). The contact information for OGIS is as follows: Office of Government Information Services, National Archives and Records Administration, 8601 Adelphi Road-OGIS, College Park, Maryland 20740-6001, e-mail at ogis@nara.gov; telephone at 202-741-5770; toll free at 1-877-684-6448; or facsimile at 202-741-5769.

Please direct any further inquiries about this case to the Attorney representing the Government in this matter. Please use the FOIPA Request Number and/or Civil Action Number in all correspondence or inquiries concerning your request.

Sincerely,

Joseph E. Bender, Jr.
Acting Section Chief
Record/Information Dissemination Section
Information Management Division

Enclosure(s)

FBI FOIPA Addendum

As referenced in our letter responding to your Freedom of Information/Privacy Acts (FOIPA) request, the FBI FOIPA Addendum provides information applicable to your request. Part 1 of the Addendum includes standard responses that apply to all requests. Part 2 includes standard responses that apply to requests for records about individuals to the extent your request seeks the listed information. Part 3 includes general information about FBI records, searches, and programs.

Part 1: The standard responses below apply to all requests:

(i) **5 U.S.C. § 552(c).** Congress excluded three categories of law enforcement and national security records from the requirements of the FOIPA [5 U.S.C. § 552(c)]. FBI responses are limited to those records subject to the requirements of the FOIPA. Additional information about the FBI and the FOIPA can be found on the www.fbi.gov/foia website.

(ii) **Intelligence Records.** To the extent your request seeks records of intelligence sources, methods, or activities, the FBI can neither confirm nor deny the existence of records pursuant to FOIA exemptions (b)(1), (b)(3), and as applicable to requests for records about individuals, PA exemption (j)(2) [5 U.S.C. §§ 552/552a (b)(1), (b)(3), and (j)(2)]. The mere acknowledgment of the existence or nonexistence of such records is itself a classified fact protected by FOIA exemption (b)(1) and/or would reveal intelligence sources, methods, or activities protected by exemption (b)(3) [50 USC § 3024(i)(1)]. This is a standard response and should not be read to indicate that any such records do or do not exist.

Part 2: The standard responses below apply to all requests for records on individuals:

(i) **Requests for Records about any Individual—Watch Lists.** The FBI can neither confirm nor deny the existence of any individual's name on a watch list pursuant to FOIA exemption (b)(7)(E) and PA exemption (j)(2) [5 U.S.C. §§ 552/552a (b)(7)(E), (j)(2)]. This is a standard response and should not be read to indicate that watch list records do or do not exist.

(ii) **Requests for Records about any Individual—Witness Security Program Records.** The FBI can neither confirm nor deny the existence of records which could identify any participant in the Witness Security Program pursuant to FOIA exemption (b)(3) and PA exemption (j)(2) [5 U.S.C. §§ 552/552a (b)(3), 18 U.S.C. 3521, and (j)(2)]. This is a standard response and should not be read to indicate that such records do or do not exist.

(iii) **Requests for Confidential Informant Records.** The FBI can neither confirm nor deny the existence of confidential informant records pursuant to FOIA exemptions (b)(7)(D), (b)(7)(E), and (b)(7)(F) [5 U.S.C.§ § 552 (b)(7)(D), (b)(7)(E), and (b)(7)(F)] and Privacy Act exemption (j)(2) [5 U.S.C.§ 552a (j)(2)]. The mere acknowledgment of the existence or nonexistence of such records would reveal confidential informant identities and information, expose law enforcement techniques, and endanger the life or physical safety of individuals. This is a standard response and should not be read to indicate that such records do or do not exist.

Part 3: General Information:

(i) **Record Searches and Standard Search Policy.** The Record/Information Dissemination Section (RIDS) searches for reasonably described records by searching systems, such as the Central Records System (CRS), or locations where responsive records would reasonably be found. The CRS is an extensive system of records consisting of applicant, investigative, intelligence, personnel, administrative, and general files compiled by the FBI per its law enforcement, intelligence, and administrative functions. The CRS spans the entire FBI organization, comprising records of FBI Headquarters, FBI Field Offices, and FBI Legal Attaché Offices (Legats) worldwide; Electronic Surveillance (ELSUR) records are included in the CRS. The standard search policy is a search for main entity records in the CRS. Unless specifically requested, a standard search does not include a search for reference entity records, administrative records of previous FOIPA requests, or civil litigation files.

 a. *Main Entity Records* – created for individuals or non-individuals who are the subjects or the focus of an investigation
 b. *Reference Entity Records* - created for individuals or non-individuals who are associated with a case but are not known subjects or the focus of an investigation

(ii) **FBI Records.** Founded in 1908, the FBI carries out a dual law enforcement and national security mission. As part of this dual mission, the FBI creates and maintains records on various subjects; however, the FBI does not maintain records on every person, subject, or entity.

(iii) **Foreseeable Harm Standard.** As amended in 2016, the Freedom of Information Act provides that a federal agency may withhold responsive records only if: (1) the agency reasonably foresees that disclosure would harm an interest protected by one of the nine exemptions that FOIA enumerates, or (2) disclosure is prohibited by law (5 United States Code, Section 552(a)(8)(A)(i)). The FBI considers this foreseeable harm standard in the processing of its requests.

(iv) **Requests for Criminal History Records or Rap Sheets.** The Criminal Justice Information Services (CJIS) Division provides Identity History Summary Checks – often referred to as a criminal history record or rap sheet. These criminal history records are not the same as material in an investigative "FBI file." An Identity History Summary Check is a listing of information taken from fingerprint cards and documents submitted to the FBI in connection with arrests, federal employment, naturalization, or military service. For a fee, individuals can request a copy of their Identity History Summary Check. Forms and directions can be accessed at www.fbi.gov/about-us/cjis/identity-history-summary-checks. Additionally, requests can be submitted electronically at www.edo.cjis.gov. For additional information, please contact CJIS directly at (304) 625-5590.

EXPLANATION OF EXEMPTIONS

SUBSECTIONS OF TITLE 5, UNITED STATES CODE, SECTION 552

(b)(1) (A) specifically authorized under criteria established by an Executive order to be kept secret in the interest of national defense or foreign policy and (B) are in fact properly classified to such Executive order;

(b)(2) related solely to the internal personnel rules and practices of an agency;

(b)(3) specifically exempted from disclosure by statute (other than section 552b of this title), provided that such statute (A) requires that the matters be withheld from the public in such a manner as to leave no discretion on issue, or (B) establishes particular criteria for withholding or refers to particular types of matters to be withheld;

(b)(4) trade secrets and commercial or financial information obtained from a person and privileged or confidential;

(b)(5) inter-agency or intra-agency memorandums or letters which would not be available by law to a party other than an agency in litigation with the agency;

(b)(6) personnel and medical files and similar files the disclosure of which would constitute a clearly unwarranted invasion of personal privacy;

(b)(7) records or information compiled for law enforcement purposes, but only to the extent that the production of such law enforcement records or information (A) could reasonably be expected to interfere with enforcement proceedings, (B) would deprive a person of a right to a fair trial or an impartial adjudication, (C) could reasonably be expected to constitute an unwarranted invasion of personal privacy, (D) could reasonably be expected to disclose the identity of confidential source, including a State, local, or foreign agency or authority or any private institution which furnished information on a confidential basis, and, in the case of record or information compiled by a criminal law enforcement authority in the course of a criminal investigation, or by an agency conducting a lawful national security intelligence investigation, information furnished by a confidential source, (E) would disclose techniques and procedures for law enforcement investigations or prosecutions, or would disclose guidelines for law enforcement investigations or prosecutions if such disclosure could reasonably be expected to risk circumvention of the law, or (F) could reasonably be expected to endanger the life or physical safety of any individual;

(b)(8) contained in or related to examination, operating, or condition reports prepared by, on behalf of, or for the use of an agency responsible for the regulation or supervision of financial institutions; or

(b)(9) geological and geophysical information and data, including maps, concerning wells.

SUBSECTIONS OF TITLE 5, UNITED STATES CODE, SECTION 552a

(d)(5) information compiled in reasonable anticipation of a civil action proceeding;

(j)(2) material reporting investigative efforts pertaining to the enforcement of criminal law including efforts to prevent, control, or reduce crime or apprehend criminals;

(k)(1) information which is currently and properly classified pursuant to an Executive order in the interest of the national defense or foreign policy, for example, information involving intelligence sources or methods;

(k)(2) investigatory material compiled for law enforcement purposes, other than criminal, which did not result in loss of a right, benefit or privilege under Federal programs, or which would identify a source who furnished information pursuant to a promise that his/her identity would be held in confidence;

(k)(3) material maintained in connection with providing protective services to the President of the United States or any other individual pursuant to the authority of Title 18, United States Code, Section 3056;

(k)(4) required by statute to be maintained and used solely as statistical records;

(k)(5) investigatory material compiled solely for the purpose of determining suitability, eligibility, or qualifications for Federal civilian employment or for access to classified information, the disclosure of which would reveal the identity of the person who furnished information pursuant to a promise that his/her identity would be held in confidence;

(k)(6) testing or examination material used to determine individual qualifications for appointment or promotion in Federal Government service the release of which would compromise the testing or examination process;

(k)(7) material used to determine potential for promotion in the armed services, the disclosure of which would reveal the identity of the person who furnished the material pursuant to a promise that his/her identity would be held in confidence.

FBI/DOJ

* * * * *

* * * * *

Exhibit 117: *28 April 2023.   Disc contents - released documents from FBI to John Wilson.*

```
FEDERAL BUREAU OF INVESTIGATION
FOI/PA
DELETED PAGE INFORMATION SHEET
FOI/PA# 22-cv-3062

Total Deleted Page(s) = 9
Page 21 ~ Duplicate;
Page 26 ~ Duplicate;
Page 27 ~ Duplicate;
Page 28 ~ Duplicate;
Page 29 ~ Duplicate;
Page 30 ~ Duplicate;
Page 31 ~ Duplicate;
Page 32 ~ b6 - -1; b7C - -1;
Page 33 ~ Duplicate;

               XXXXXXXXXXXXXXXXXXXXXXX
               X   Deleted Page(s)   X
               X   No Duplication Fee X
               X   For this Page     X
               XXXXXXXXXXXXXXXXXXXXXXX
```

February 21, 2006

Mr. [redacted]
United States Department of State
Office of the Legal Adviser
Law Enforcement and Intelligence
Washington, D.C. 20520

b6 per DOS

RE: Complaint of John Christian Wilson

Dear [redacted]

b6 per DOS

We are in receipt of your letter dated December 23, 2006, to Ms. Candice M. Will, Assistant Director, Office of Professional Responsibility (OPR), Federal Bureau of Investigation (FBI) and the corresponding attachments that you forwarded to our office on behalf of the above-captioned complainant. OPR forwarded this correspondence to the Initial Processing Unit (IPU), Internal Investigations Section, Inspection Division for our review. The IIS is the FBI entity that provides thorough, high quality, fair, consistent, and timely review and investigation into complaints of criminality and/or serious misconduct against FBI employees.

A letter dated January 17, 2005, from John Christian Wilson to the U.S. Department of Justice (DOJ), Office of Inspector General was forwarded IPU for our review. Mr. Wilson's letter alleged potential misconduct by FBI personnel however, a review of our records revealed that the individuals named by Mr. Wilson are not employed by the FBI.

We responded to Mr. Wilson by letter dated February 10, 2006, advising him that inasmuch as the information he provided contained no credible allegations of misconduct by any FBI personnel, IPU determined that his complaint does not warrant the initiation of an investigation and that the FBI considers this matter closed. A copy of our response to Mr. Wilson is being forwarded for your information. If you need additional information, please contact me at [redacted]

Sincerely,

/s/

[redacted]
Unit Chief
Initial Processing Unit
Inspection Division

b6 -1
b7C -1
b7E -3

Enclosure

1 - Ms. Kalisch (Personal Attention)
1 - IPU
1 - [redacted] (5)

8893

b6 -1
b7C -1

FBI(22-cv-3062)-1

February 21, 2006

Mr. [redacted]
United States Department of State
Office of the Legal Adviser
Law Enforcement and Intelligence
Washington, D.C. 20520

b6 per DOS

RE: Complaint of John Christian Wilson

Dear [redacted]

b6 per DOS

We are in receipt of your letter dated December 23, 2006, to Ms. Candice M. Will, Assistant Director, Office of Professional Responsibility (OPR), Federal Bureau of Investigation (FBI) and the corresponding attachments that you forwarded to our office on behalf of the above-captioned complainant. OPR forwarded this correspondence to the Initial Processing Unit (IPU), Internal Investigations Section, Inspection Division for our review. The IIS is the FBI entity that provides thorough, high quality, fair, consistent, and timely review and investigation into complaints of criminality and/or serious misconduct against FBI employees.

A letter dated January 17, 2005, from John Christian Wilson to the U.S. Department of Justice (DOJ), Office of Inspector General was forwarded IPU for our review. Mr. Wilson's letter alleged potential misconduct by FBI personnel however, a review of our records revealed that the individuals named by Mr. Wilson are not employed by the FBI.

We responded to Mr. Wilson by letter dated February 10, 2006, advising him that inasmuch as the information he provided contained no credible allegations of misconduct by any FBI personnel, IPU determined that his complaint does not warrant the initiation of an investigation and that the FBI considers this matter closed. A copy of our response to Mr. Wilson is being forwarded for your information. If you need additional information, please contact me at [redacted]

Sincerely,

[redacted signature]

Unit Chief
Initial Processing Unit
Inspection Division

b6 -1
b7C -1
b7E -3

Enclosure

1 - Ms. Kalisch (Personal Attention)
1 - IPU
1 - [redacted] (5)

b6 -1
b7C -1

FBI(22-cv-3062)-2

United States Department of State

Washington, D.C. 20520
www.state.gov

December 23, 2005

Ms. Candice M. Will
Assistant Director
Office of Professional Responsibility
Federal Bureau of Investigation
Suite PA - 444
935 Pennsylvania Avenue, N.W.
Washington, DC 20535

Re: Complaint of John Christian Wilson

Dear Ms. Will:

Enclosed please find a diplomatic note from the Government of Australia describing the concerns of an Australian citizen, John Christian Wilson, regarding alleged mistreatment at the hands of the Federal Bureau of Investigation.

The Government of Australia has also provided a copy of a letter that may have been sent to your office regarding this case.

I am forwarding this matter to you for appropriate handling, and will inform the Government of Australia that I have done so. If there is a further appropriate response you wish communicated to that government, please do not hesitate to contact me and I can arrange for it to be communicated.

Thank you very much.

Very truly yours,

[redacted] b6 per DOS

Office of the Legal Adviser
Law Enforcement and Intelligence

b6 -1 per FBI
b7C -1 per FBI

REC'D OPR FRONT OFFICE
2006 JAN -5 P 1:52

1/2005 (Cons)

The Consulate-General of Australia, New York, presents its compliments to the Department of State and has the honour of bringing to the attention of the Department of State a matter concerning an Australian citizen, Mr. John Christian Wilson.

Mr. Wilson has informed the Consulate the he is the subject of what appears to be a systematic retaliation campaign by persons associated with the FBI involving, as Mr. Wilson states, invasive and injurious tactics. Mr. Wilson advised that he was employed as a mining company equity analyst on Wall Street from 1994 to 1998. In 1996, he states that an undercover FBI agent working undercover as an environmentalist provided him with details of a Department of State finding regarding the Freeport McMoran owned Grasberg mine, located in Indonesia. Mr. Wilson completed a FOIA with the FBI in October, 2004 and advises that he has had no response or information to date.

With Mr. Wilson's agreement, the Consulate attaches, for the information of the Department of State, a copy of a letter forwarded by Mr. Wilson to the Consulate, in which Mr. Wilson describes the circumstances of his case under which he believes he is being treated unjustly. The letter clearly details Mr. Wilson's allegations and indicates that his matter with regards to his FOIA request has not progressed with the FBI.

Mr. Wilson has requested that the Consulate assist with determining the reason behind the original and ongoing investigations alleged by Mr. Wilson and to why it has been going on for so long.

In expressing its interest in the welfare of Mr. Wilson, the Consulate would be grateful if the Department of State would examine the claims of Mr. ☐ and keep the Consulate informed of developments.

b6 -3
b7C -3

The Consulate-General of Australia in New York avails itself of this opportunity to convey to the Department of state the assurance of its highest consideration.

FBI(22-cv-3062)-5

DEC. 9.2005 11:14AM   AUSTRALIAN CG NYC 212 351 6501   NO.108   P.3

John Christian Wilson   16 April, 2005
c/o
Fleishman & Fisher   b6 -3
1875 Century Park East Suite 2130   b7C -3
Los Angeles, CA 90067
Tel: 310-5571077

Email:

Office of Professional Responsibility
Federal Bureau of Investigation
U.S. Department of Justice
935 Pennsylvania Avenue, N.W.
Washington, D.C. 20535-0001

Dear Sir:

I write because of the oversight responsibilities of your office. I was a mining company equity analyst on Wall Street from 1994 to 1998. I am a citizen of the U.S.A., was born in Australia, and have long lived in the United States, principally in New York and Philadelphia, where I received my MBA degree from Wharton. I am currently visiting family for an extended stay in Australia.

In 1996, in the course of performing my duties as a mining analyst, information was leaked to me by a then undisclosed FBI agent who worked undercover as an environmentalist. This person gave me details of a State Department finding into an incident in which 7 people were recently killed in and around the publicly traded Freeport McMoran owned Grasberg mine in Indonesia. The information I received related to a confidential reprimand of the company by the U.S. Department of State for human rights and environmental abuses.

Since then, as set out below, I have been subjected to what appears to be a systematic retaliation campaign by persons associated with the FBI involving invasive and injurious tactics. Among other things, I have faced blacklisting in my industry. I have been unable to gain any employment in the financial services industry despite a recent boom in the mining sector and despite having worked on Wall Street for 6 years, mostly as a senior equity analyst.

For the many years following my 1996 publication regarding the Freeport McMoran killings, I have had many contacts with people who at some point revealed themselves as FBI agents on assignment connected to me, and who let me know that I angered important people by the publication. Some of these individuals engendered friendship with me under the auspices of other professional identities and each has interviewed me, two of them extensively. These include Steven Garber, now of White Plains, New York, formerly of New York City, Susan Holmes, now of Washington, D.C., formerly of New York City, and Livingston Sutro, of Sierra Vista, Arizona.

Aside from these agents, more than a dozen other people have identified themselves to me as having a high level of familiarity with these circumstances and appear to be FBI agents or associated with agents.

Given the fact that the source of the leaked information was itself an FBI agent and given the powerful business interests of Freeport, I am concerned that I am the subject of what appears to be either a case of FBI corruption or incompetence. The agent that passed to me the information about Freeport was a long term friend who targeted environmental extremists, and I am concerned I may have been maliciously profiled to justify the intense scrutiny I have faced.

1 of 2

FBI(22-cv-3062)-6

An FOIA request to the FBI in October, 2004 yielded no information whatsoever.

I look forward to hearing from you. The most convenient means by which to correspond with me are through my attorney (details indicated above), alternatively via email.

Sincerely yours,

John Wilson

REC'D OPR FRONT OFFICE
2006 JAN -4 P 3:08

FBI(22-cv-3062)-9

ExecSec (RMD)

From: ExecSec (RMD)
Sent: Friday, April 13, 2007 12:47 PM
To: KAISER, KENNETH W. (INSD) (FBI); [redacted] (INSD) (FBI); [redacted]
Cc: [redacted] (OCA) (FBI); [redacted] (OCA) (FBI); [redacted] (OCA) (FBI)
Subject: CONGRESSIONAL / TRIM Document : 07/DO/2879 : Congressional on behalf of John Christian Wilson requesting a response from the FBI regarding his allegations that he is being harassed by persons identifying themselves as FBI agents.

b6 -1
b7C -1
b7E -3

[PDF icon] Congressional on behalf of Joh...

ACTION OFFICE: INSP

The above division, designated as the action office, is assigned the attached correspondence for preparation of a final response over the signature of YOUR AD or DEPUTY AD by the due date shown below. The original will be forwarded to your division's point of contact. An information only copy is also being sent to the Office of Congressional Affairs (OCA).

If this matter needs to be reassigned to another entity, the FBI ExecSec should be advised immediately (within 2 days of e-mail receipt). The ExecSec will need to know to whom the request should be reassigned to, together with a point of contact (if known), and the original correspondence will need to be returned to ExecSec, Room 6236.

ACTION OFFICE INSTRUCTIONS: (Failure to comply with the following instructions will delay the closing of pending action and will result in the correspondence appearing on the overdue report)

A. Preparation of Response:

1. Prepare the following:

    -Two post-dated (allow at least 5 days for processing) letterhead copies,
    -An envelope or mailing label,
    -A blocked yellow post-dated file copy, attaching the original incoming correspondence to the yellow file copy, and a copy of the incoming to each designated "courtesy copy" (cc), as appropriate. The yellow copy mail room block must be checked and initialed.

2. At a minimum, the copy count must include a copy for the appropriate congressional file number:[redacted] and the following copy designations:

b7E -3

    1 - OCA, Rm 7240 - Enc (s).
    1 - FBI ExecSec, Room 6236 (Trim #07/DO/XXXX)
    1 - (Your confirmation white copy, if desired)

3. Save your final response letter to a disk. The disk must be labeled with the appropriate classification (i.e. unclassified, confidential, etc.), and if you would like the disk returned to your office, it must include a your name, division, room number, and extension.

4. To assist you in preparing a response and disk, please see the ExecSec web site: [redacted] and specific samples responses for:

    Representatives: [redacted]

b7E -3

Senators:

Senate Chairman of a Committee: b7E -3

House Chairman of a Committee:

B. Routing of the Final Response Package:

1. Route your final response package and disk in a plastic envelope, to the FBI ExecSec, Room 6236, who will ensure that the package is delivered to the OCA, Room 7240, for review/approval. FBI policy requires that all Congressional responses be approved by the OCA prior to mailing.

2. Upon approval by OCA, the FBI ExecSec will forward the completed package to the Records Management Centers Unit (RMCU) for uploading into ACS and routing to the mailroom. If you want your disk returned and/or plastic envelope, clearly label the disk with a name, division, room number, and extension. These procedures are outlined on our web site at: b7E -3

If you have any questions, comments, suggestions, or require the attached correspondence to be sent to another division/office for action or information, please contact the Executive Secretariat, [ ] Ext [ ], [ ] Ext [ ] or by e-mail to [ ]

b6 -1
b7C -1
b7E -3

Thursday, January 18, 2006   b7E -3

------< TRIM Record Information >------

Date Due   : 5/7/2007
Action Office   : AD-Inspection (Action Office)
Current Action   : PREPARE RESPONSE PER INSTRUCTIONS (Responsibility of: Secretariat, Executive, Due in 15 Days, 7 Hours, 25 Minutes)
All Contacts   : AD-Inspection (Action Office); Office of Congressional Affairs (Info)
Access DB or Workflow :
From   : SCHUMER, CHARLES E.
Constituent   : WILSON, JOHN CHRISTIAN
Title (Free Text Part) : Congressional on behalf of John Christian Wilson requesting a response from the FBI regarding his allegations that he is being harassed by persons identifying themselves as FBI agents.
Date of Communication : Tuesday, April 03, 2007
Notes :
Related Records : 06/DO/3875: Ltr on behalf of John Christian Wilson, New York, NY, alleging that information that he rec'd from the OIG is inconsistent with information that he rec'd from the FBI on whether or not the individuals that he has identified as FBI agents are in fact FBI (Related to); 06/DO/5270: Writing further on behalf of John Christian Wilson, New York, NY, regarding his continued concern that he was the victim of harassment by an FBI agent or fraud by an individual claiming to be an FBI agent. See WF 1020111. (PS) (Related to)

2

FBI(22-cv-3062)-11

CHARLES E. SCHUMER
NEW YORK

United States Senate
WASHINGTON, DC 20510

COMMITTEES:
BANKING
FINANCE
JUDICIARY
RULES

April 3, 2007

Eleni Kalisch, Assistant Director of Congressional Affairs
Federal Bureau of Investigation
U.S. Department of Justice
935 Pennsylvania Avenue, N.W., Room 7240
Washington, D.C. 20535-0001

Re: John Christian Wilson
c/o [redacted]
1875 Century Park East, Suite 2130
Los Angeles, California 90067

b6 -3
b7C -3

Dear Assistant Director Kalisch:

    I am writing on behalf of John Christian Wilson, who has contacted my office regarding the status of a response to his correspondence forwarded to the FBI Inspection Division for appropriate handling by the U. S. Department of Justice, Office of the Inspector General. I have enclosed for your information, a copy of Mr. Wilson's correspondence and the October 16, 2006 response from the U. S. Department of Justice, OIG, addressed to my attention.

    Thank you in advance for reviewing this correspondence. Please direct your written response to the attention of [redacted] in my New York City Office.

b6 -5
b7C -5

Sincerely,

Charles E. Schumer
United States Senate

CES [redacted]
Enclosure

b6 -3
b7C -3

FBI(22-cv-3062)-12
07100/2879

John Christian Wilson
c/o ▌▌▌▌▌▌
Fleishman & Fisher
1875 Century Park East Suite 2130
Los Angeles, CA 90067

February 20, 2007

b6 -3
b7C -3

Hon. Charles E. Schumer
United States Senate
757 Third Avenue
Suite 17-02
New York, NY 10017

Attention: ▌▌▌▌▌▌

Dear ▌▌▌▌

b6 -5
b7C -5

In reference to recent correspondence with Paul K. Martin, DOJ (7 December 2006 and copied to Senator Schumer) to date there has been no response by the DOJ. There has also not been a response to a letter Paul K. Martin indicated he would forward to the FBI and referred to in his correspondence to Senator Schumer October 16, 2006.

I would appreciate assistance from you to secure a response to my December 7, 2006 correspondence with Paul K. Martin.

In accordance with the Privacy Act of 1974, you and your staff are hereby authorized to freely discuss any and all aspects of my situation. I look forward to hearing from you. The most convenient means by which to correspond with me are through my attorney (details indicated above), alternatively you can reach me directly by phone on 212 595 3886.

Sincerely yours,

[signature]

John Wilson

Attachments:

U.S. Department of Justice

Office of the Inspector General

Mailed 10/25/06

October 16, 2006

The Honorable Charles Schumer
United States Senator
757 Third Avenue
Suite 1702
New York, New York 10017

Attention: [redacted]

b6 -5
b7C -5

Dear Senator Schumer:

    This is in response to your correspondence of August 30, 2006, to William E. Moschella, Assistant Attorney General for the Office of Legislative Affairs, forwarding a letter of concern from your constituent, John Christian Wilson, of New York, New York. Mr. Wilson states that the Office of the Inspector General's (OIG) correspondence dated August 9, 2006, was unsatisfactory and that he will not consider this matter closed until he receives a "complete and unqualified denial" that the individuals in question are or have never been associated with the Federal Bureau of Investigation (FBI). Additionally, Mr. Wilson requests confirmation that the FBI did not conduct any investigative activity involving him. He also expresses concern that the individuals in question might be fraudulently representing themselves as FBI agents.

    On May 1, 2005, this office received a complaint from Mr. Wilson involving the same allegations contained in his May 25, 2006, letter to your office, and we determined that the matter was more appropriate for review by the FBI Inspection Division as Mr. Wilson did not identify any specific criminal or administrative misconduct that would require an investigation by the OIG. In a February 10, 2006, letter the FBI Inspection Division, Initial Processing Unit (IPU), informed Mr. Wilson that a review of its records revealed that the individuals in question are not employed by the FBI and that the IPU determined that his complaint did not warrant the initiation of an investigation.

FBI(22-cv-3062)-14

The Honorable Charles Schumer
Page 2

Our August 9, 2006, letter to you explained that the OIG determined that the FBI employs a Special Agent (SA) with the same name as one of the individuals referenced by Mr. Wilson; however, this SA has never been assigned to any of the geographic areas in which Mr. Wilson alleged the harassment occurred. Additionally, the OIG has no reason to dispute the information contained in the FBI's February 10, 2006, letter to Mr. Wilson.

Since Mr. Wilson is now seeking "a complete and unqualified denial" that the individuals in question have never been associated with the FBI and because he is concerned that these individuals could be fraudulently portraying themselves as FBI agents, we believe that this matter can only be properly addressed by the FBI. Therefore, we will forward your August 30, 2006, letter and Mr. Wilson's most recent allegations to the FBI Inspection Division for appropriate handling.

Sincerely,

Paul K. Martin
Deputy Inspector General

cc: Charlene B. Thornton
 Assistant Director
 Inspection Division
 Federal Bureau of Investigation

FBI(22-cv-3062)-15

May 1, 2007

Honorable Charles E. Schumer
United States Senator
Suite 1702
757 Third Avenue
New York, New York 10017

Dear Senator Schumer:

    We are in receipt of your letter dated April 3, 2007, addressed to Ms. Eleni Kalisch, Assistant Director, Office of Congressional Affairs, and the enclosed documents which were forwarded to your office by your constituent, Mr. John Wilson.

    Your letter was forwarded to the Internal Investigations Section (IIS), Inspection Division, for review. The IIS is the FBI entity that investigates complaints of criminality and/or serious misconduct against FBI employees.

    IIS reviewed the merits of Mr. Wilson's claims and determined his allegations did not warrant the initiation of an investigation inasmuch as the information reflected no allegations of misconduct by any FBI personnel. This information was previously provided to Mr. Wilson by letter, dated February 10, 2006, addressed to [redacted] Fleishmann and Fisher, Los Angeles, California. However, thank you for bringing this matter to my attention.

                                         Sincerely yours,

                                         Kenneth W. Kaiser
                                         Assistant Director
                                         Inspection Division

1 - ExecSec, DOJ, Room 4400-Encs.
1 - FBI ExecSec, Room 6236 (Trim Doc # 07/DO/2879)-Encs.
1 - OLA, DOJ, Room 1338-Encs.
1 - OCA, Room 7240-Encs.
   [redacted] (6)

February 10, 2006

[redacted]
Fleishman and Fisher
1875 Century Park East
Suite 2130
Los Angeles, California 90067

Attention: Mr. John Christian Wilson

Dear Mr. Wilson:

We are in receipt of your letter dated January 17, 2005, to the U.S. Department of Justice (DOJ), Office of Inspector General. DOJ forwarded this correspondence to the Initial processing Unit (IPU), Internal Investigations Section, Inspection Division, Federal Bureau of Investigation (FBI), for our review. The IIS is the FBI entity that provides thorough, high quality, fair, consistent, and timely review and investigation into complaints of criminality and/or serious misconduct against FBI employees.

In the above-referenced letter, you allege that an unidentified Undercover FBI Special Agent (SA) apparently disclosed confidential information to you originating from the U.S. State Department regarding a fatal Grasberg mining accident in Indonesia. You advised that you published an article about the accident at the Freeport McMoran owned Grasberg mine in 1996 and, since its publication, you allege having been contacted by numerous individuals who identified themselves to you as FBI agents, specifically SA Steven Garber, New York; SA Livingston Sutro, Arizona, and SA Susan Holmes, Washington, D.C. A review of our records revealed that the above-named individuals are not employed by the FBI.

Inasmuch as the information provided contains no credible allegations of misconduct by any FBI personnel, IPU has determined that your complaint does not warrant the initiation of an investigation. We consider this matter closed.

Sincerely,

[redacted]
Unit Chief
Initial Processing Unit
Inspection Division

1 - Ms. Kalisch (Personal Attention)
1 - IPU
1 - [redacted] (5)

U.S. Department of Justice

Office of the Inspector General

#1245

Washington, D.C. 20530

DATE: July 27, 2005

TO: Charlene B. Thornton
Assistant Director
Inspection Division
Federal Bureau of Investigation

FROM: *Glenn G. Powell* (signature)
Glenn G. Powell
Special Agent in Charge
Investigations Division

SUBJECT: OIG Complaint No. 2005005905
Subject: [redacted] et al.
New York Division
FBI No. OIG Initiated

b6 -3
b7C -3

☒ We consider this a management matter. The information is being provided to you for whatever action you deem appropriate in accordance with your agency's policy and regulations. A copy of your findings and/or final action is not required by the OIG.

☐ This matter is referred to your agency for investigation. Please provide the OIG with a copy of your final report on this matter.

☐ This complaint will be investigated by the OIG.

IMPORTANT NOTICE

Identifying information may have been redacted from the attached OIG Report/Referral pursuant to § 7 of the IG Act or because an individual has (a) requested confidentiality or (b) expressed a fear of reprisal. If you believe that it is necessary that redacted information be made available to your Agency, you may contact the Assistant Inspector General for Investigations.

Please be advised that, where adverse action is not contemplated, the subject of an investigation does not have a right to have access to an OIG Report/Referral or to the identities of complainants or witnesses, and that, in all cases, complainants and witnesses are entitled to protection from reprisal pursuant to the Inspector General Act and the Whistleblower Protection Act.

```
OIG - INVESTIGATIONS DIVISION  -  IDMS            OIG NO.: LA-412-2005-005905-M
```

b6 per DOJ-OIG
b7C per DOJ-OIG

Received By: [redacted]   Date Received: 05/01/2005   How Received: M

SUBJECT OF A COMPLAINT: [redacted]   SSNO: b6 -3
Title: SA   Pay Plan: D.O.B.:   b7C -3
Component: FBI   EOD Date: Alien No.:
Misc: 7/26/05 - FBI advised no record exist.   F.B.I.No.:
Home: B.O.P.No.:
Phone: ZIP: D/L No.:
Work:
Phone: ZIP:

SUBJECT OF A COMPLAINT: [redacted]   SSNO: b6 -3
Title: SA   Pay Plan: D.O.B.:   b7C -3
Component: FBI   EOD Date: Alien No.:
Misc: F.B.I.No.:
Home: B.O.P.No.:
Phone: ZIP: D/L No.:
Work:
Phone: ZIP:

SUBJECT OF A COMPLAINT: [redacted]   SSNO: b6 -3
Title: SA   Pay Plan: D.O.B.:   b7C -3
Component: FBI   EOD Date: Alien No.:
Misc: 7/26/05 - FBI advised no record exist.   F.B.I.No.:
Home: B.O.P.No.:
Phone: ZIP: D/L No.:
Work:
Phone: ZIP:

COMPLAINANT: Wilson, John Christian   SSNO:
Title: CIVIL   Pay Plan: D.O.B.:
Component: CITZN   EOD Date: Alien No.:
Misc: F.B.I.No.:
Home: B.O.P.No.:
Phone: ZIP: D/L No.:
Work:
Phone: ZIP:
Confidential: Revealed: Authority: none

ALLEGATIONS: 412 Job Performance Failure
Occurrence Date: TIME:
CITY: State: Zip:

Details:

The following information was provided by Complainant regarding allegations of misconduct by FBI SAs. In 1996, an UC FBI SA leaked information to the Complainant regarding a "confidential" reprimand by the U.S. State Department regarding the Freeport-McMoran's Grasberg mine in Indonesia. According to the Complainant, the UC FBI SA gave him details of the State Department's findings regarding an incident in which seven people associated with the Grasberg mine were killed. In 1996, the Complainant published information regarding the killings. (It should be noted that the Complainant does not provide any specifics regarding his publication.) The Complainant, a senior equity analyst, believes the FBI is responsible for his inability to obtain a job in the financial services industry. The Complainant stated that he was interviewed "extensively" by the Subjects following his 1996 publication. According to the Complainant, he was unable to obtain any information as a result of an October 2004 FOIA request to the FBI.

OIG - INVESTIGATIONS DIVISION - IDMS   OIG NO.: LA-412-2005-005905-M

DISPOSITION DATA: Date: 07/26/2005   Disposition: M   Approval: POWELL, GLENN G
Referred to Agency: Component: CITZN
Civil Rights: N   Sensitive: N
Component Number: Consolidated Case Number:

Remarks:

7/27/05 - Acknol letter sent to the Complainant advising him that the matter was forwarded to the FBI, Inspection Division.

b6 per DOJ-OIG
b7C per DOJ-OIG

7/27/05 - Management referral to AD Thornton, FBI Inspection Division.

John Christian Wilson
c/o [redacted]
Fleishman & Fisher
1875 Century Park East Suite 2130
Los Angeles, CA 90067

16 April, 2005

b6 -3
b7C -3

Email: [redacted]

US Department of Justice
Office of the Inspector General
950 Pennsylvania Avenue, N.W., Suite 4706
Washington, DC 20530-0001

Dear Sir:

I write as a follow up to the letter I sent to your office on 17 January, 2005 (copy enclosed). Could you please indicate your expected timing for a response to that letter.

Thank you.

Sincerely yours,

[signature]

John Wilson

Encl. Copy of letter sent to your office, dated 17 January, 2005

John Christian Wilson
c/o [redacted]
Fleishman & Fisher
1875 Century Park East Suite 2130
Los Angeles, CA 90067
Tel: 310-5571077

Email: [redacted]

17 January, 2005

US Department of Justice
Office of the Inspector General
950 Pennsylvania Avenue, N.W., Suite 4706
Washington, DC 20530-0001

Dear Sir:

I write because of the oversight responsibilities of your office. I was a mining company equity analyst on Wall Street from 1994 to 1998. I am a citizen of the U.S.A., was born in Australia, and have long lived in the United States, principally in New York and Philadelphia, where I received my MBA degree from Wharton. I am currently visiting family for an extended stay in Australia.

In 1996, in the course of performing my duties, information was leaked to me by a then undisclosed FBI agent who worked undercover as an environmentalist. This person gave me details of a State Department finding into an incident in which 7 people were recently killed in and around the publicly traded Freeport McMoran owned Grasberg mine in Indonesia. The information I received related to a confidential reprimand of the company by the U.S. Department of State for human rights and environmental abuses.

Since then, as set out below, I have been subjected to what appears to be a systematic retaliation campaign by persons associated with the FBI involving invasive and injurious tactics. Among other things, I have faced blacklisting in my industry. I have been unable to gain any employment in the financial services industry despite a recent boom in the mining sector and despite having worked on Wall Street for 6 years, mostly as a senior equity analyst.

For the many years following my 1996 publication regarding the Freeport McMoran killings, I have had many contacts with people who at some point revealed themselves as FBI agents on assignment connected to me, and who let me know that I angered important people by the publication. Some of these individuals engendered friendship with me under the auspices of other professional identities and each has interviewed me, two of them extensively. These include Steven Garber, now of White Plains, New York, formerly of New York City, Susan Holmes, now of Washington, D.C., formerly of New York City, and Livingston Sutro, of Sierra Vista, Arizona.

1 of 2

Aside from these agents, more than a dozen other people have identified themselves to me as having a high level of familiarity with these circumstances and appear to be FBI agents or associated with agents;

Given the fact that the source of the leaked information was itself an FBI agent and given the powerful business interests of Freeport, I am concerned that I am the subject of what appears to be either a case of FBI corruption or incompetence. The agent that passed to me the information about Freeport was a long term friend who targeted environmental extremists, and I am concerned I may have been maliciously profiled to justify the intense scrutiny I have faced.

An FOIA request to the FBI in October, 2004 yielded no information whatsoever.

I look forward to hearing from you. The most convenient means by which to correspond with me are through my attorney (details indicated above), alternatively via email.

Sincerely yours,

John Wilson

```
End of Data
04/24/07                    List Summary Response                    UNI050MK
14:20:04
Type X, x, or / to view Full Response, then press Enter.

    .   Name: WILSON, JOHN, CHRISTIAN
        M/R : M  Case ID: HQ 263-0                    Serial: 8636
        Race: U  Sex: M  DOB/Event:         ID Info:
        Misc: NO ACTION                     Entry Date: 10/13/2005 Class Level: SN

    .   Name: WILSON, JOHN, CHRISTIAN
        M/R : R  Case ID: HQ 263-0                    Serial: 8893
        Race: U  Sex: M  DOB/Event:         ID Info:
        Misc:                               Entry Date: 05/17/2006 Class Level: SN




Command . . > ................................................................. +
F1=Help,F3=Exit,F4=Prompt,F12=Cancel

 4AÛ                                                            06,002
```

(Rev. 01-31-2003)

FEDERAL BUREAU OF INVESTIGATION

Precedence: ROUTINE   Date: 05/03/2007

To: Los Angeles   Attn: ADIC (Personal Attention)

From: Inspection
      Initial Processing Unit/Room 3041
      Contact:

Approved By:

Drafted By:

Case ID #: 263-HQ-0-8636

Title: JOHN CHRISTIAN WILSON;
       COMPLAINANT
       INFORMATION CONCERNING

Synopsis: The Initial Processing Unit (IPU), Internal Investigations Section (IIS), Inspection Division (INSD), is forwarding the enclosed correspondence regarding Mr. John Christian Wilson to Los Angeles Field Office (LAFO) for information only.

Enclosure(s): Letter dated 04\03\2007 from Charles E. Schumer, United States Senator from New York State, to Assistant Director (AD) Eleni Kalisch, with appropriate attachments and responding letter dated 05\01\2007 drafted by IPU in response which is currently under review by the FBI Executive Secretariat; letter dated 07\27\2005 from Glenn G. Powell, Office of the Inspector General (OIG), Department of Justice, to AD Charlene Thornton, with appropriate attachments; letter dated 02\10\2007, from IPU to John Christian Wilson; letter dated 12\23\2005 from [   ] Department of State to AD Candice Will with appropriate attachments; and letter dated 02\21\2006 from IPU to [   ].

Details: IPU acknowledges receipt of the enclosed documentation which reflects several letters directed to the FBI on behalf of John Christian Wilson.

Wilson alleged that an unidentified undercover FBI Special Agent apparently disclosed confidential information to him originating from the U.S. State Department regarding a fatal Grasberg mining accident in Indonesia. Wilson apparently published an article about the accident at the Freeport McMoran owned Grasberg mine in 1996 and, since its publication, he claims

To: Los Angeles   From: Inspection
Re: 263-HQ-0-8636, 05/03/2007

that he has been harassed by individuals who identified themselves to him as FBI agents. The specific individuals named by Wilson, [redacted] New York; [redacted] Arizona; and [redacted] Washington, D.C., were determined by IIS not to be FBI personnel. Wilson has directed his complaints to various government entities, including the OIG and Senator Charles Schumer. IPU has responded to this issue on several occasions and notified Wilson by letter dated 02\10\2006, addressed to Wilson in care of [redacted] Fleishmann and Fisher, Los Angeles, California, that IIS determined his allegations did not warrant the initiation of an investigation inasmuch as the information reflected no allegations of misconduct by any FBI personnel.

IPU has concluded that this matter does not warrant any further administrative action and considers this matter closed. IPU is forwarding the enclosed documents to LAFO for information only.

b6 -3
b7C -3

Section VI

FBI - FOIA Judicial Review

Section VI

FBI - FOIA Judicial Review

VI-1. First FOIA Judicial Review filed 8 December 2020

    a)   FBI/DOJ - Complaint
           Filed in the United States District Court for the Southern District of New York. Case 1:20-cv-10324. [Attorney David Rankin re FOIPA NO.: 125

VI-2. Second FOIA Judicial Review filed 8 October 2022

    a)   FBI/DOJ
           Filed in the United States District Court for the District of Columbia. Case 1:22-cv-03062. [Attorney Pete Sorenson re FOIPA No.: 1548515-000]

VI-1　First FBI - FOIA Judicial Review - BLHNY: 8 December 2020

VI-1a First FBI - FOIA Judicial Review 2020:

Complaint

Case 1:20-cv-10324

United States District Court for the Southern District of New York

8 December 2020

Schedule of key dates

8 December 2020: First FOIA litigation filed in the United States District Court for the Southern District of New York by David Rankin of Beldock Levine & Hoffman LLP (BLHNY).

16 February 2022: Judge Stewart D. Aaron United States Magistrate Judge filed the Report and Recommendation to Hon. Lewis A. Kaplan senior United States District Judge. [The Judge recommend that Defendant's motion be GRANTED IN PART and DENIED IN PART and that Plaintiff's cross-motion be GRANTED IN PART and DENIED IN PART.]

* * * * *

Exhibit 118: *8 December 2020.   Complaint: First FOIA litigation filed in the US District Court for the Southern District of New York by Attorney David Rankin.*

FOIA litigation filed in the United States District Court for the Southern District of New York by David Rankin of Beldock Levine & Hoffman LLP (BLHNY).

Case 1:20-cv-10324   Document 1   Filed 12/08/20   Page 1 of 5

UNITED STATES DISTRICT COURT
SOUTHERN DISTRICT OF NEW YORK
---x
JOHN WILSON,

                   Plaintiff,   No. _____

                 -against-   COMPLAINT

FEDERAL BUREAU OF INVESTIGATION,

                   Defendant.
---x

Plaintiff John Wilson, by his attorney David B. Rankin of Beldock, Levine & Hoffman, LLP for his complaint, does hereby state and allege:

<u>Preliminary Statement</u>

1. This is an action under the Freedom of Information Act ("FOIA"), 5 U.S.C. §§552 *et seq.*, seeking the production of agency records improperly searched for by Defendant United States Department of Justice ("DOJ"), specifically its component the Federal Bureau of Investigation ("FBI") ("Defendant"), in response to requests properly made by Plaintiff.

2. Plaintiff seeks an injunction requiring defendant to release the requested records.

<u>Jurisdiction and Venue</u>

3. This Court has subject matter jurisdiction of the FOIA claim and personal jurisdiction over the parties pursuant to 5 U.S.C. § 552(a)(4)(b). This Court also has jurisdiction over this action pursuant to 28 U.S.C. § 1331.

4. Venue is proper as the records exist on databases within this district.

5. The FBI has partially responded to Plaintiff's request and denied Plaintiff's appeal. Plaintiff has exhausted all administrative remedies pursuant to 5 U.S.C. § 522(a)(6)(c).

Parties

6. John Wilson ("Plaintiff") is a United States citizen and the requester of the records.

7. Defendant FBI is a department of the executive branch of the U.S. government and an agency within the meaning of 5 U.S.C. §§ 551(1) & 552(f)(1). Defendant FBI is a component of DOJ.

Factual Background

8. On March 26, 2014, Plaintiff submitted a FOIA request to the Federal Bureau of Investigation via email for a copy of all agency records concerning, naming, or relating to Plaintiff, including but not limited to all potentially responsive main and cross-reference files. The request is attached hereto as Exhibit 1.

9. On September 25, 2014, Plaintiff received a response from David M. Hardy, Section Chief, Record/Information Dissemination Section, Records Management Division of the FBI. Hardy indicated that 21 pages were reviewed and released 10 pages with redactions. The response is attached hereto as Exhibit 2.

10. The pages included a February 10, 2006 letter from the Initial Processing Unit, Internal Investigations Section, Inspection Division of the FBI, to counsel for Plaintiff, responding to Plaintiff's January 17, 2005 letter alleging misconduct by FBI personnel. Other pages include intra-agency emails on the topic of Plaintiff's letter and the resulting investigation; OIG's letter to Charlene B. Thornton, Assistant Director, Inspection Division of the FBI with their conclusions regarding the OIG complaint; a letter from Plaintiff following up on his January 17, 2005 letter; Plaintiff's original January 17, 2005 letter; and a list summary response entry for Mr. Wilson's complaint. Attached hereto as Exhibit 3.

11. The defendant's production in response to the Plaintiff's request was inadequate. Defendant explained their limited production by stating that they did not find records that the named agents listed in the request were employees of the FBI. Plaintiff has had prior conversations with the named individual in which they told Plaintiff that they were employed by the FBI and in one case showed Plaintiff an FBI identification.

12. Defendant incorrectly limited their search to special agents of the FBI. A proper and adequate search by the FBI would have returned records of the employment or contracts or contacts with the named individuals or records of communications with these named individuals, person who were operating on behalf of the FBI or others in the Department of Justice.

13. The search ran by the defendant did not search all the available databases for references to Mr. Wilson.

14. On November 6, 2014, Plaintiff appealed the FBI's September 25, 2014 production, disputing the adequacy of the FBI's search for records responsive to his FOIA request. Attached hereto as Exhibit 4.

15. On February 23, 2015, Christina D. Troiani, Attorney-Advisor for Sean O'Neill, Chief, Administrative Appeals Staff, Office of Information Policy, U.S. Department of Justice responded to Plaintiff's appeal and affirmed the FBI's actions on Plaintiff's FOIA request. Ms. Troiani of the Administrative Appeals Staff stated she had determined the FBI had conducted an adequate and reasonable search for records responsive to Mr. Wilson's FOIA request. The letter is attached hereto as Exhibit 5.

16. On October 24, 2019, Plaintiff submitted a new FOIA request to the FBI through their online portal, again seeking a copy of all agency records concerning, naming, or relating to

Plaintiff. Plaintiff does not possess a copy of this request as it was submitted directly through the FBI's online portal for such FOIA requests.

17. On October 29, 2019, David M. Hardy, Section Chief, Record/Information Dissemination Section, Information Management Decision, Federal Bureau of Investigation, U.S. Department of Justice responded to Plaintiff's request. Mr. Hardy stated that the FBI had released all relevant records to Mr. Wilson in response to his previous request, and that no additional records could be located. Attached hereto as Exhibit 6.

18. On Feb 18, 2020, Plaintiff appealed the FBI's October 26, 2019 conclusions, again disputing the adequacy of the FBI's search for records responsive to his FOIA request. Attached hereto as Exhibit 7.

19. On March 21, 2020, Christina D. Troiani, Associate Chief, for Matthew Hurd, Acting Chief, Administrative Appeals Staff, Office of Information Policy, U.S. Department of Justice responded to Plaintiff's appeal and affirmed the FBI's actions on Plaintiff's FOIA request. Ms. Troiani of the Administrative Appeals Staff stated she had determined the FBI had conducted an adequate and reasonable search for records responsive to Mr. Wilson's FOIA request. The letter is attached hereto as Exhibit 8.

Cause of Action

20. Defendant's failure to conduct an adequate search for the records sought by the Request violates the FOIA, 5 U.S.C. § 522(a)(3)(A)-(D), and defendant's corresponding regulations.

Request for Relief

WHEREFORE, Plaintiff respectfully requests that this Court:

A. Order Defendant to conduct a thorough search for all records responsive to Plaintiff's Request and demonstrate that it employed search methods reasonably calculated to uncover all records responsive to Plaintiff's Request;

B. Issue a declaration that Plaintiff is entitled to disclosure of the records responsive to Plaintiff's Request;

C. Order Defendant to disclose all non-exempt records responsive to Plaintiff's Request in its entirety, as well as all non-exempt portions of responsive records;

D. Order defendant to promptly provide an index pursuant to *Vaughn v. Rosen*, 484 F.2d 820 (D.C. Cir. 1973), and its progeny, inventorying all responsive records and itemizing and justifying all withholdings of responsive documents;

E. Enjoin Defendant from continuing to withhold any and all non-exempt records or portions thereof responsive to Plaintiff's Request;

F. Immediately process all records responsive to the Request;

G. Award plaintiff reasonable attorneys' fees and costs pursuant to incurred in this action; and 5 U.S.C. § 552(a)(4)(E);

H. Grant such other relief as the Court may deem just and proper

Dated: December 8, 2020
New York, New York

Respectfully submitted,

By: _____
David B. Rankin
Beldock, Levine & Hoffman, LLP
99 Park Avenue, PH/26th Fl.
New York, New York 10016
t: 212-277-5825
e: DRankin@blhny.com

Katherine "Q" Adams
e: QAdams@blhny.com

* * * * *

* * * *

Exhibit 119: *16 February 2022.   Report and Recommendation.*

Judge's Report and Recommendation

Judge Stewart D. Aaron United States Magistrate Judge filed the Report and Recommendation to Hon. Lewis A. Kaplan senior United States District Judge. [The Judge recommend that Defendant's motion be GRANTED IN PART and DENIED IN PART and that Plaintiff's cross-motion be GRANTED IN PART and DENIED IN PART.]

Case 1:20-cv-10324-LAK-SDA   Document 44   Filed 02/16/22   Page 1 of 16

UNITED STATES DISTRICT COURT
SOUTHERN DISTRICT OF NEW YORK

John Wilson,

        Plaintiff,

-against-

Federal Bureau of Investigation,

        Defendant.

1:20-cv-10324 (LAK) (SDA)

REPORT AND RECOMMENDATION

STEWART D. AARON, UNITED STATES MAGISTRATE JUDGE.

TO THE HONORABLE LEWIS A. KAPLAN, UNITED STATES DISTRICT JUDGE:

Plaintiff John Wilson ("Plaintiff" or "Wilson") brings this action under the Freedom of Information Act ("FOIA"), 5 U.S.C. § 552, against the Federal Bureau of Investigation ("Defendant" or "FBI") seeking the disclosure and release of all agency records pertaining to him. (*See* Compl., ECF No. 1.) Presently before the Court are Defendant's motion for summary judgment (Def.'s Mot., ECF No. 35) and Plaintiff's cross-motion for summary judgment. (Pl.'s Cross-Mot., ECF No. 38.) For the reasons set forth below, I respectfully recommend that Defendant's motion be GRANTED IN PART and DENIED IN PART and that Plaintiff's cross-motion be GRANTED IN PART and DENIED IN PART.

BACKGROUND

Wilson, a former Wall Street mining analyst, is a dual citizen of the United States and Australia, who currently resides in Sydney, Australia. (*See* Wilson Decl., ECF No. 40-1, ¶¶ 3-4.) From June 2013 to October 2019, he submitted three FOIA requests to the FBI seeking the disclosure of the agency's records pertaining to him. (*See* Compl., ¶¶ 8, 16; Adams Decl., Ex. B, ECF No. 40-2; Adams Decl., Ex. D, ECF No. 40-4; Adams Decl., Ex. H, ECF No. 40-8.) According to

Wilson, in March 1996, he had authored a report that flagged concerns about the U.S.-based mining company Freeport McMoran, including that the company was under investigation by the U.S. Department of State following the deaths of indigenous protestors at its Grasberg Mine in West Papua, Indonesia, among other human rights concerns. (*See* Wilson Decl. ¶¶ 9-10.) Wilson contends that he submitted his FOIA requests following decades of harassment and interference by persons holding themselves out to be acting on behalf of the FBI, which occurred after publication of his report. (*See id.* ¶ 20; Pl.'s Mem., ECF No. 39, at 1.)

Certain documents were produced to Wilson by the FBI. (*See* Compl. ¶¶ 9-10.) However, he alleges that the FBI conducted insufficient searches in response to his FOIA requests and that the FBI improperly withheld seven documents. (*See id.* ¶ 20; Pl.'s Mem. at 9-10.)

After exhausting his agency appeals, Wilson commenced this action on December 8, 2020. (*See* Compl.) On March 31, 2021, the parties appeared for a telephone conference with the Court, at which time counsel for the FBI informed the Court that the FBI would be making a revised production to Plaintiff in response to his FOIA request in early April 2021. (*See* 4/26/21 Joint Ltr., ECF No. 17.) On April 2, 2021, the FBI made such production. (*See* Adams Decl., Ex. J, ECF No. 40-10.) After Plaintiff reviewed the revised production, counsel for Plaintiff informed counsel for the FBI that, notwithstanding the revised production, Plaintiff still intended to challenge the adequacy of the FBI's search, and the parties agreed to proceed to motion practice. (*See* 4/26/21 Joint Ltr.)

This report and recommendation addresses the parties' pending cross-motions for summary judgment.

LEGAL STANDARDS

FOIA was enacted "to ensure an informed citizenry, vital to the functioning of a democratic society, needed to check against corruption and to hold the governors accountable to the governed." *NLRB v. Robbins Tire & Rubber Co.*, 437 U.S. 214, 242 (1978). "In order to prevail on a motion for summary judgment in a FOIA case, the defending agency has the burden of showing that its search was adequate and that any withheld documents fall within an exemption to the FOIA." *Carney v. U.S. Dep't of Just.*, 19 F.3d 807, 812 (2d Cir. 1994) (citing 5 U.S.C. § 552(a)(4)(B)).

I. Adequacy Of Search

In measuring adequacy, courts ask "whether the search was reasonably calculated to discover the requested documents, not whether it actually uncovered every document extant." *Grand Cent. P'ship, Inc. v. Cuomo*, 166 F.3d 473, 489 (2d Cir. 1999) (citation omitted); *accord Schoenman v. FBI*, 764 F. Supp. 2d 40, 45 (D.D.C. 2011) (agency "must show beyond material doubt . . . that it has conducted a search reasonably calculated to uncover all relevant documents" (citing *Weisberg v. U.S. Dep't of Just.*, 705 F.2d 1344, 1351 (D.C. Cir. 1983)).[1]

Adequacy "may be established solely on the basis of the Government's relatively detailed, non-conclusory affidavits that are submitted in good faith," *Adamowicz v. I.R.S.*, 552 F. Supp. 2d 355, 361 (S.D.N.Y. 2008), "setting forth the search terms and the type of search performed, and averring that all files likely to contain responsive materials . . . were searched."[2]

---

[1] The Second Circuit recognizes that the D.C. Circuit is "something of a specialist" in adjudicating FOIA disputes, "given the nature of much of its caseload." *Whitaker v. Dep't of Com.*, 970 F.3d 200, 206 n.25 (2d Cir. 2020) (citation omitted).

[2] Agency submissions are "accorded a presumption of good faith such that discovery relating to the agency's search . . . generally is unnecessary if the agency's submissions are adequate on their face." *Junk*

Iturralde v. Comptroller of Currency, 315 F.3d 311, 314-15 (D.C. Cir. 2003) (citation omitted). "Conversely, summary judgment in the agency's favor is inappropriate 'where the agency's response raises serious doubts as to the completeness of the agency's search, where the agency's response is patently incomplete, or where the agency's response is for some other reason unsatisfactory.'" *NAACP Legal Def. & Educ. Fund, Inc. v. U.S. Dep't of Just.*, 463 F. Supp. 3d 474, 483 (S.D.N.Y. 2020) (quoting *Nat'l Day Laborer Org. Network v. U.S. Immigr. & Customs Enf't Agency*, 877 F. Supp. 2d 87, 96 (S.D.N.Y. 2012)). In such cases, a district court may "direct the defendant to conduct additional searches," *Immigr. Def. Project v. U.S. Immigr. & Customs Enf't Agency*, 208 F. Supp. 3d 520, 527 (S.D.N.Y. 2016), conduct an *in camera* review, "elicit[ ] additional detail from the government" or permit further discovery, where appropriate. *Assadi v. U.S. Citizenship & Immigr. Servs.*, No. 12-CV-01374 (RLE), 2015 WL 1500254, at *2 (S.D.N.Y. Mar. 31, 2015).

"There is no requirement that an agency search every record system in response to a FOIA request." *Brunetti v. F.B.I.*, 357 F. Supp. 2d 97, 103 (D.D.C. 2004) (citing *Meeropol v. Meese*, 790 F.2d 942, 952-53 (D.C. Cir. 1986)). However, the agency must identify, and search, each record system in which responsive documents are likely to be found. *See Oglesby v. U.S. Dep't of Army*, 920 F.2d 57, 68 (D.C. Cir. 1990).

II. <u>Withholdings Pursuant To FOIA Exemptions</u>

The Court reviews the applicability of a particular FOIA exemption *de novo*. *See Azmy v. U.S. Dep't of Def.*, 562 F. Supp. 2d 590, 597 (S.D.N.Y. 2008). The exemptions are construed

---

v. Bd. of Governors of Fed. Rsrv. Sys., No. 19-3125-CV, 2022 WL 363776, at *1 (2d Cir. Feb. 8, 2022) (cleaned up).

narrowly, see *Bloomberg, L.P. v. Bd. of Governors of the Fed. Rsrv. Sys.*, 601 F.3d 143, 147 (2d Cir. 2010) ("To implement [the] presumption for disclosure, FOIA exemptions 'have been consistently given a narrow compass.'") (quoting *U.S. Dep't of Just. v. Tax Analysts*, 492 U.S. 136, 151 (1989)), and "doubts as to the applicability of [an] exemption must be resolved in favor of disclosure." *Florez v. Cent. Intell. Agency*, 829 F.3d 178, 182 (2d Cir. 2016).

"[A]n agency is entitled to summary judgment when it has . . . articulated reasonably detailed explanations why any withheld documents fall within an exemption." *Kuzma v. U.S. Dep't of Just.*, No. 13-CV-00675 (WMS), 2016 WL 9446868, at *3 (W.D.N.Y. Apr. 18, 2016), *aff'd sub nom. Kuzma v. U.S. Dep't of Just.*, 692 F. App'x 30 (2d Cir. 2017) (citing *Carney*, 19 F.3d at 812). Conversely, "[a] plaintiff is entitled to summary judgment in a FOIA case 'when an agency seeks to protect material which, even on the agency's version of the facts, falls outside the proffered exemption.'" *Id.* (quoting *New York Times Co. v. U.S. Dep't of Def.*, 499 F. Supp. 2d 501, 509 (S.D.N.Y. 2007)).

To carry its burden, an agency may rely on declarations/affidavits that describe "with reasonable specificity the nature of the documents at issue and the justification for nondisclosure." *See Kuzma*, 2016 WL 9446868, at *3 (citing *Lesar v. U.S. Dep't of Just.*, 636 F.2d 472, 481 (D.C. Cir. 1980)). "[T]he description provided in the affidavits must show that the information logically falls within the claimed exemption." *Id.*

Agency affidavits are presumed to have been made in good faith. *See Carney*, 19 F.3d at 812. "Thus, the agency's justification is sufficient if it appears logical and plausible." *Am. Civil Liberties Union v. U.S. Dep't of Def.*, 901 F.3d 125, 133 (2d Cir. 2018), *as amended* (Aug. 22, 2018). "If the agency's submissions are facially adequate, summary judgment is warranted unless the plaintiff can make a showing of bad faith on the part of the agency or present evidence that the exemptions claimed by the agency should not apply." *Garcia v. U.S. Dep't of Just., Off. of Info. & Priv.*, 181 F. Supp. 2d 356, 366 (S.D.N.Y. 2002) (citing *Carney*, 19 F.3d at 812); *see also Ctr. for Const. Rts. v. C.I.A.*, 765 F.3d 161, 166 (2d Cir. 2014) (agency declarations "are accorded a presumption of good faith," and "when such declarations are 'not controverted by either contrary evidence in the record nor by evidence of agency bad faith,' summary judgment for the government is warranted.") (citing *Wilner v. Nat'l Sec. Agency*, 592 F.3d 60, 73 (2d Cir. 2009))).

DISCUSSION

I. <u>Adequacy Of Defendant's Search</u>

As discussed below, the Court finds that the FBI has carried its burden of showing its search was adequate, except in one respect. On June 14, 2013, Plaintiff sent his first FOIA request seeking "all files, correspondence or other records concerning [him]self." (*See* Adams Decl., Ex. B.) According to the FBI's first Declaration, in response to Plaintiff's first request, its Record/Information Dissemination Section ("RIDS") conducted a Central Records System ("CRS")[3] index search for potentially responsive records, employing in the Automated Case Support system ("ACS")[4] the automated Universal Index ("UNI") application, using the search terms "John C Wilson" and "John Wilson." (*See* First Seidel Decl. ¶ 40.) As a result of this search effort, RIDS

---

[3] The CRS, which spans the entire FBI organization, is a system of records consisting of applicant, investigative, intelligence, personnel, administrative and general files compiled and maintained by the FBI in the course of fulfilling its mission and integrated functions. (*See* First Seidel Decl., ECF No. 37, ¶ 21.)

[4] ACS is an electronic, integrated case management system designed to enable the FBI to locate, retrieve and maintain information in its files. (*See* First Seidel Decl. ¶ 25.)

located one reference file, but did not produce it, ostensibly due to RIDS's policy.[5] (*See id.*) This reference file, however, was produced in response to Plaintiff's second request, discussed below.

On March 26, 2014, Plaintiff sent his second FOIA request seeking "disclosure of all agency records concerning, naming, or relating to [him]." (*See* Adams Decl., Ex. D.) In his second request, Plaintiff provided additional information and "specifically request[ed]" that the FBI "identify all potentially responsive main and cross-reference files." (*See id.*) According to the FBI's first Declaration, in response to Plaintiff's second request, RIDS conducted a CRS index search for potentially responsive records employing the UNI application of ACS using the search terms "John Christian Wilson," "John C Wilson" and "John Wilson." (*See* First Seidel Decl. ¶ 41.) As a result of this search effort, the FBI located the same reference file discussed above, but this time it was produced because "Plaintiff asked for the identification of both main and reference files and because he provided additional information that allowed RIDS to assess the responsiveness of the reference file." (*See id.*)

On October 23, 2019, Plaintiff submitted his third FOIA request through the FBI's eFOIPA portal seeking all agency records concerning himself. (*See* Adams Decl., Ex. H.) According to the FBI's Declaration, in response to the third request, RIDS conducted a CRS index search for potentially responsive records employing the Sentinel indices and ACS indices available through

---

[5] According to Seidel, "RIDS policy, generally, is to identify only main files responsive to a request at the administrative stage," and not reference files. (*See* First Seidel Decl. ¶ 40.)

Sentinel[6] using the search term "John Wilson." (*See* First Seidel Decl. ¶ 42.) As a result of this search effort, RIDS did not locate any additional records. (*See id.*)

Upon Plaintiff's filing of the Complaint in this action, the FBI conducted a new search of the CRS and reviewed all responsive records previously located in response to Plaintiff's three requests. (*See* First Seidel Decl. ¶ 20.) As set forth in the Background Section above, the FBI made a supplemental production on April 2, 2021. (*See* Adams Decl., Ex. J.)

In total, the searches the FBI performed in response to the three requests and after the Complaint was filed identified one reference file resulting in the review of 22 pages of records, of which the FBI released 15 pages in whole or in part. (*See* First Seidel Decl. ¶¶ 41, 45.) The reference file located concerned a complaint that Plaintiff had made to the Department of Justice's Office of the Inspector General ("OIG").[7] (*See id.* ¶ 45.)

Based upon its review of the two Seidel Declarations submitted by Defendant, the Court finds that Defendant has made the required showing regarding the adequacy of its search, except in one respect — *i.e.*, Defendant's failure to search the Delta record-keeping system, which is addressed below. Putting the Delta record-keeping system to the side, the issues raised by Plaintiff regarding the adequacy of Defendant's search are easily disposed:

- Plaintiff asserts that, in response to the first search, the reference file should have been produced. (*See* Pl.'s Mem. at 7-8.) However, Plaintiff admits that the reference

---

[6] Sentinel, the FBI's next generation case management system that became effective FBI-wide on July 1, 2012, provides a web-based interface to FBI users and includes the same automated applications that were utilized in ACS. (*See* First Seidel Decl. ¶ 27.)

[7] The OIG had forwarded Plaintiff's allegation of misconduct by FBI employees to the FBI's Inspection Division ("INSD"), which reviews and investigates allegations of criminal behavior and other types of misconduct of FBI employees. (*See* First Seidel Decl. ¶ 45.)

file was produced in response to Plaintiff's second request (*see id.* at 9), thereby curing any defect in the first search.

- Plaintiff asserts that, in response to the first and second requests, Defendant failed to search the Sentinel database. (*See* Pl.'s Mem. at 8-9.) However, Plaintiff admits that Defendant searched the Sentinel database in response to his third request (*see id.* at 9), thereby curing any defect in the first two searches regarding use of the Sentinel database.

- Plaintiff asserts that Defendant failed to search electronic surveillance (referred to as "ESLUR") indices. (*See* Pl.'s Mem. at 9.) However, as Defendant explained, it expected that searches of the CRS would locate records relating to electronic surveillance. (*See* First Seidel Decl. ¶ 31; Second Seidel Decl., ECF No. 42, ¶ 22.) In any event, Defendant conducted a search of the ESLUR indices in response to Plaintiff's second request, and that search produced no results. (*See* Second Seidel Decl. ¶ 22.)

- Plaintiff asserts that Defendant failed to search its so-called 137 and 210 files. (*See* Pl.'s Mem. at 9.) As a part of its Confidential Human Source ("CHS") program, the FBI maintains CRS file classification numbers 137 and 270 for purposes of compiling law enforcement records, which contain the identity of confidential sources and cooperating witnesses, the information furnished by confidential sources or cooperating witnesses, and information regarding law enforcement techniques, procedures and guidelines related to the CHS program. (*See* Second Seidel Decl. ¶ 6.) The FBI's second Declaration states that, if 137 or 270 file classifications existed concerning or mentioning Plaintiff, those files would have been indexed to Plaintiff, either as a main entry or a reference entry, and would have been located within the CRS indices via the searches conducted in response to Plaintiff's requests.[8] (*See id.* ¶ 5.) Thus, there was no need for Defendant to separately search these files.

The search of Defendant's Delta record-keeping system requires further discussion. Plaintiff asserts that Defendant improperly failed to search its Delta record-keeping system. (*See* Pl.'s Mem. at 9.) Delta is the FBI's official electronic record-keeping system for the management of confidential human sources, *i.e.*, informants. (*See* Second Seidel Decl. ¶ 12.) Defendant admittedly did not search the Delta record-keeping system. (*See* Def.'s Reply Mem., ECF No. 41, at 7.) In its second Declaration, Defendant states that Plaintiff "provided no justification for the FBI to search Delta." (*See* Second Seidel Decl. ¶ 23.) However, this is not the case. Defendant itself notes in its reply memorandum the justification provided by Plaintiff for searching Delta: "Plaintiff claims that Defendant should have searched Delta because he claims that third-party individuals discussed information with him, including their employment with the FBI in a possible informant capacity."[9] (Def.'s Reply Mem. at 7 (citing Pl.'s Mem. at 8-9).) Thus, contrary to Defendant's assertion, Plaintiff has provided a justification for searching the Delta system.

In addition, Defendant asserts that "the FBI found no clear lead indicating that . . . a search [of Delta] was warranted," and that the information provided by Plaintiff and the "results of the

---

[8] The Court has reviewed the opinion of former FBI agent Jennifer Coffindaffer that "137 and 270 files contain information not discoverable through CRS, ACS and Sentinel searches." (*See* Adams Decl., Ex. K-1, at 4.) This opinion, however, is not inconsistent with the sworn statement made by the FBI's current Section Chief of RIDS's Information Management Division, which is presumed to have been made in good faith, that if 137 or 270 file classifications existed concerning or mentioning Plaintiff, those files would have been indexed to Plaintiff and located within the CRS. (*See* Second Seidel Decl. ¶ 5.)

[9] In his second request, Plaintiff stated: "I have been approached by undercover agents/employees/others that work for or on behalf of the FBI and which include multiple meetings with each during various periods between 1996 and 2010." (*See* Adams Decl., Ex. D, at PDF p. 3.)

CRS index search were insufficient to lead the FBI to believe that records would exist in Delta." (*See* Second Seidel Declaration ¶¶ 17, 23.) However, Defendant does not provide any explanation for why the information and search results are insufficient. Notably, Defendant does not state, as it did with respect to the 137 or 270 file classifications, that information in the Delta system would be located or referenced in the CRS. In these circumstances, the Court finds Defendant's response regarding search of the Delta system to be unsatisfactory. Accordingly, the Court recommends that Defendant be ordered to search the Delta system for responsive information.

II. **Defendant's Withholdings**

Defendant's searches in response to Plaintiff's requests identified 22 pages of records. (*See* First Seidel Decl. ¶ 4.) Of those, eight pages were released in their entirety, seven pages were released in part and withheld in part, and seven pages were withheld in full (with two of those seven amounting to duplicates of pages accounted for elsewhere). (*See id.*) Defendant's withholdings were premised upon FOIA Exemptions (b)(6) ("Exemption 6") and (b)(7)(C) ("Exemption 7(C)"). (*See id.* ¶ 20.) Plaintiff belatedly challenges Defendant's withholdings.[10]

Exemption 6 exempts from disclosure "personal and medical files and similar files the disclosure of which would constitute a clearly unwarranted invasion of personal privacy." 5 U.S.C. § 552(b)(6). To determine whether identifying information may be withheld pursuant to

---

[10] Plaintiff had led Defendant to believe that he only was challenging the adequacy of Defendant's search. (*See* First Seidel Decl. ¶ 5 ("By electronic mail . . . dated July 27, 2021, Plaintiff's counsel represented to the United States Attorney's Office for the Southern District of New York that Plaintiff would not challenge the FBI's withholdings of records or portions of information within records.").) Nevertheless, in his memorandum in support of his cross-motion for summary judgment, Plaintiff took the position that "[t]he FBI has provided no basis on which it has withheld the records under these [FOIA Exemptions (b)(6) and (b)(7)(C)]." (*See* Pl.'s Mem. at 11.) This change in position required Defendant to provide in the Second Seidel Declaration the basis for each of its withholdings. (*See* Second Seidel Decl. ¶¶ 27-40.)

Exemption 6, the court "must: (1) determine whether the identifying information is contained in 'personnel and medical files and similar files;' and (2) balance the public need for the information against the individual's privacy interest in order to assess whether disclosure would constitute a clearly unwarranted invasion of personal privacy." *Associated Press v. U.S. Dep't of Def.*, 554 F.3d 274, 291 (2d Cir. 2009) (quoting *Wood v. F.B.I.*, 432 F.3d 78, 86 (2d Cir. 2005)). "The determination of whether Exemption 6 applies requires balancing an individual's right to privacy against the preservation of FOIA's basic purpose of opening agency action to the light of public scrutiny." *Id.* (citing *Dep't of the Air Force v. Rose*, 425 U.S. 352, 372 (1976)). "Only where a privacy interest is implicated does the public interest for which the information will serve become relevant and require a balancing of the competing interests." *Id.* (quoting *Fed. Lab. Rels. Auth. v. U.S. Dep't of Veterans Affs.*, 958 F.2d 503, 509 (2d Cir. 1992)). To prevail over the public interest in disclosure, "[a]n invasion of more than a *de minimis* privacy interest protected by Exemption 6 must be shown to be 'clearly unwarranted.'" *Id.* "Under Exemption 6, therefore, the government's burden in establishing the required invasion of privacy is heavier than the burden in establishing invasion of privacy under Exemption 7(C)." *Id.* (citing *U.S. Dep't of State v. Ray*, 502 U.S. 164, 172 (1991)).

Exemption 7(C) similarly exempts from disclosure "records or information compiled for law enforcement purposes, but only to the extent that the production of such law enforcement records or information . . . (C) could reasonably be expected to constitute an unwarranted invasion of personal privacy." 5 U.S.C. § 552(b)(7)(C). Exemption 7(C) may be invoked where no public interest would be served by disclosure of information that implicates privacy interests. *See U.S. Dep't of Just. v. Rptrs. Comm. for Freedom of Press*, 489 U.S. 749, 775 (1989) "[W]hether disclosure of a private document under Exemption 7(C) is warranted must turn on the nature of the requested document and its relationship to the basic purpose of the Freedom of Information Act to open agency action to the light of public scrutiny, rather than on the particular purpose for which the document is being requested." *Id*. at 772 (cleaned up).

Defendant explains that the five non-duplicate pages that were withheld in full are FBI records check documents containing personal identifiable information of an FBI special agent, such as his or her name, date of birth, social security number, FBI employment history, FBI personnel file number, GS classification, salary, promotion history, level of security clearance, assigned field office, building location, work phone number, office room number and squad name. (*See* Second Seidel Decl. ¶¶ 38-39.) The special agent plainly has a privacy interest in these documents. *See Long v. Off. of Pers. Mgmt.*, 692 F.3d 185, 191 (2d Cir. 2012) ("the bar is low: 'FOIA requires only a measurable interest in privacy to trigger the application of the disclosure balancing tests'" (citation omitted)). Disclosure of the names of federal law enforcement personnel, like the special agent in this case, "could permit the targeting of [them] and their families outside the workplace" and subject them to "an increased risk of harassment or attack." *See id*. at 192.

Under Exemption 6, the special agent's privacy interest "must be weighed against the public interest that would be advanced by disclosure." *See Long*, 692 F.3d at 193 (citation omitted). "The only public interest cognizable under FOIA is the public 'understanding of the operations or activities of the government.'" *Id*. (quoting *Rptrs. Comm. for Freedom of Press*, 489 U.S. at 775). The Court finds that disclosure of the name and personal identifying information of the special agent in this case will not further public understanding of the operations or activities of the government. Such an understanding can be discerned from the documents already produced to Plaintiff, which reflect the INSD investigation that was done of the complaint he filed with the OIG. (*See* Adams Decl., Ex. J.)

Defendant's withholding of the subject records also was appropriate under the lower threshold of Exemption 7(C). The records were compiled for law enforcement purposes. *See Pagan v. Treasury Inspector Gen. for Tax Admin.*, 231 Fed. App'x 99, 100 (2d Cir. 2007) ("[I]t is settled law in this Court that an Inspector General of a federal government agency engages in law enforcement activities within the meaning of FOIA.") (internal citation and quotation omitted). And, again, disclosing the records would not add to the public's understanding of how the government functions. *See Garcia*, 181 F. Supp. 2d at 374 (upholding invocation of Exemption 7(C) to protect identities of FBI special agents).[11]

Finally, Plaintiff invites the Court to conduct an *in camera* review of the withheld records. (*See* Pl.'s Mem. at 10-11; Pl.'s Reply Mem., ECF No. 43, at 9-10.) "If an agency affidavit or declaration is conclusory, contradicted in the record, or there is evidence in the record of agency bad faith, then summary judgment is not appropriate and a court may grant *in camera* review as a last resort." *Khatchadourian v. Def. Intel. Agency*, 453 F. Supp. 3d 54, 76 (D.D.C. 2020) (cleaned up) (citing *Hayden v. Nat'l Sec. Agency/Cent. Sec. Serv.*, 608 F.2d 1381, 1387 (D.C. Cir. 1979)). "A reviewing court has broad discretion to decide whether *in camera* review is necessary." *Id.* (cleaned up) (citing *100Reporters LLC v. U.S. Dep't of Just.*, 248 F. Supp. 3d 115, 166 (D.D.C. 2017)). The Court, in its discretion, declines to conduct an *in camera* review. The Second Seidel

---

[11] The Court also finds that Defendant has satisfied its obligation under FOIA to provide reasonably segregable portions of the redacted records to Plaintiff. (*See* Def.'s Reply at 17-18.)

Declaration provides reasonable specificity as to the nature of the documents at issue and the justification for nondisclosure.

CONCLUSION

For the foregoing reasons, I respectfully recommend that Defendant's motion for summary judgment be GRANTED IN PART and DENIED IN PART and that Plaintiff's cross-motion for summary judgment be GRANTED IN PART and DENIED IN PART. Specifically, I recommend that Defendant only be compelled to conduct a search of its Delta record-keeping system for records responsive to Plaintiff's requests.

Dated: New York, New York
February 16, 2022

STEWART D. AARON
United States Magistrate Judge

* * *

NOTICE OF PROCEDURE FOR FILING OBJECTIONS TO THIS REPORT AND RECOMMENDATION

The parties shall have fourteen (14) days (including weekends and holidays) from service of this Report and Recommendation to file written objections (to those portions other than with respect to the motion to strike), pursuant to 28 U.S.C. § 636(b)(1) and Rule 72(b) of the Federal Rules of Civil Procedure. *See also* Fed. R. Civ. P. 6(a), (d) (adding three additional days when service is made under Fed. R. Civ. P. 5(b)(2)(C), (D) or (F)). A party may respond to another party's objections within fourteen days after being served with a copy. Fed. R. Civ. P. 72(b)(2). Such objections, and any response to objections, shall be filed with the Clerk of the Court. *See* 28 U.S.C. § 636(b)(1); Fed. R. Civ. P. 6(a), 6(d), 72(b). Any requests for an extension of time for filing objections must be addressed to Judge Kaplan.

FAILURE TO OBJECT WITHIN FOURTEEN (14) DAYS WILL RESULT IN A WAIVER OF OBJECTIONS AND WILL PRECLUDE APPELLATE REVIEW. *See* 28 U.S.C. § 636(b)(1); Fed. R. Civ. P. 6(a), 6(d), 72(b); *Thomas v. Arn,* 474 U.S. 140 (1985).

* * * * *

VI-2 Second FBI - FOIA Judicial Review - Sorenson: 8 October 2022

VI-2a   Second FBI - FOIA Judicial Review 2022:

Complaint

Case 1:22-cv-03062

United States District Court for the District of Columbia

8 October 2022

Schedule of key dates

8 October 2022: Second FOIA litigation filed in the United States District Court for the district of Columbia by John Wilson's attorney Pete Sorenson.

Litigation ongoing as at publication date of this volume.

* * * * *

Exhibit 120: *8 October 2022. Complaint: Second FOIA litigation filed in the United States District Court for the District of Columbia by Attorney Pete Sorenson.*

Case 1:22-cv-03062   Document 1   Filed 10/08/22   Page 1 of 7

UNITED STATES DISTRICT COURT
FOR THE DISTRICT OF COLUMBIA

JOHN CHRISTIAN WILSON,

██████████ Australia

Plaintiff,

v.

FEDERAL BUREAU OF INVESTIGATION,
935 Pennsylvania Avenue, NW
Washington, DC 20535

Defendant.

Civil Action No. 22-3062

COMPLAINT

1. Plaintiff ("Plaintiff" or "Mr. Wilson") brings this Freedom of Information Act ("FOIA") judicial review against Defendant Federal Bureau of Investigation ("Defendant" or "FBI") to compel Defendant to produce the responsive records relating to Mr. Wilson's FOIPA Request No.: 1548515-000. Defendant has violated FOIA by 1) by failing to conduct a reasonable search, and 2) by failing to produce the responsive, non-exempt records.

PARTIES

2. Plaintiff is a resident of Greenwich, Australia and he is a dual citizen of the Commonwealth of Australia and the United States of America. Plaintiff made a FOIA request to Defendant on May 20, 2022.

3. Defendant is a federal agency subject to the Freedom of Information Act, 5 U.S.C. § 552.

JURISDICTION AND VENUE

4. This case is brought against a Federal Defendant under 28 U.S.C. § 1346 which is a Federal agency under 5 U.S.C. § 552(a)(4)(B). This case presents a federal question under 28 U.S.C. § 1331. These statutes confer jurisdiction on this Court.

5. The venue is proper under 5 U.S.C. § 552(a)(4)(B).

PLAINTIFF'S MAY 20, 2022 FOIA REQUEST

6. On May 20, 2022 Plaintiff submitted a FOIA request to FBI for the following:

    a. All records, documents, or communications prepared by, received by or maintained by the FBI which mention the following terms:

        i. John Christian Wilson

        ii. John C. Wilson

        iii. John Wilson

    b. All records describing FBI informant or FBI agent contacts with:

        i. John Christian Wilson

        ii. John C. Wilson

        iii. John Wilson

c. All records describing FBI contractors, or others operating on behalf of the FBI or other United States Department of Justice ("DOJ") element, contacts with:
   i. John Christian Wilson
   ii. John C. Wilson
   iii. John Wilson

d. The 1996 securities analyst report on NYSE listed U.S. mining company Freeport McMoran Copper and Gold Inc (which trades on the NYSE under the symbol FCX) written by John Wilson. This report is entitled, "FCX: Grasberg Closure Highlights Political Risks." Mr. Wilson wrote the report as an analyst working for S.G. Warburg & Co. Inc. and the report was dated March 12, 1996.

e. All records describing the attendance of John Wilson at the Freeport McMoran Copper and Gold Inc. May 1996 annual analyst briefing at Freeport McMoran Copper and Gold Inc's headquarters in New Orleans, Louisiana. In particular, records are sought concerning an interaction between John Wilson and James R. Moffett (known as Jim Bob), CEO and Chairman of Freeport McMoran Copper and Gold Inc, in the boardroom alcove after the analyst question period that was held in Freeport McMoran's boardroom.

f. All records describing an interaction between John Wilson and an unnamed person, apparently a federal agent or FBI operative, also in Freeport's boardroom alcove after the analyst question period in Freeport's boardroom mentioned above at the Freeport headquarters in New Orleans, Louisiana in May 1996.

g. All records describing or documenting interactions between John Wilson and people operating on behalf of the FBI or other DOJ element, in particular by Steve Garber.

h. All records, including notes, recordings or transcripts of interviews, made by Steve Garber in early 1999 during the several days when Mr. Wilson visited Garber at his home in Prescott, AZ.

i. All records, including notes, recordings or transcripts, of a discussion or interview involving Mr. Wilson and Steve Garber in June 2004 in New York, New York.

j. All records, including notes, recordings or transcripts, of a discussion or interview involving Mr. Wilson and Steve Garber in September 2004, including at Tibet House, and also the Blue Water Grill both in the vicinity of the Union Square neighborhood of New York, New York.

k. All records of the attendance involving John Wilson in connection with a presentation that Dave Foreman gave in New York, New York in late 1997. David Foreman (usually referred to as Dave) is a well-known American environmental activist and co-founder of environmental group Earth First! Dave Foreman was a subject of Susan Holmes for her work for the FBI.

l. All records pertaining to John Wilson concerning his attendance, or discussions with Susan Holmes or Dave Foreman on, a raft trip on the Colorado River in July or August 1997 with journalists, including a reporter for Time Magazine, Ms. Holmes and Mr. Foreman.

m. All records of discussions between John Wilson and Susan Ackerson Holmes. All records describing or documenting interactions between John Wilson and people operating on behalf of the FBI or other DOJ element, in particular Susan Ackerson Holmes.

n. All records of discussions between John Wilson and Susan Holmes during the three years that they dated in New York, New York, calendar years 1994, 1995, 1996 and 1997.

o. All records of discussions between John Wilson and Susan Holmes in a May 10, 2003 (on or about) dinner conversation between Susan Holmes and John Wilson in New York, New York.

p. All telephone wiretaps on telephones used by John Wilson.

q. All records showing any applications for surveillance or wiretaps of telephones used by John Wilson.

r. All records showing any applications for search warrants for properties owned or leased by John Wilson.

s. All records showing any applications for surveillance of John Wilson.

Ex. 1.

7. The time frame for this request includes records created or received on or after January 1, 1994 to present. Ex. 1.

8. Defendant acknowledged receipt of the request on June 6, 2022. Ex. 2.

9. Defendant assigned FOIPA Request No: 1548515-000 to Plaintiff's request. Ex. 2.

10. On June 13, 2022, Defendant sent a denial letter and provided no records. Ex. 3.

11. The time frame of Defendant's search was from October 28, 2019 to June 6, 2022. Ex. 3.

12. Plaintiff filed his administrative appeal on September 1, 2022. His administrative appeal, not including exhibits thereto, is attached as Ex. 4.

13. Defendant acknowledged Plaintiff's administrative appeal on September 1, 2022. Ex. 5.

14. As of this date, there has been no decision on Plaintiff's administrative appeal. Ex. 6.

15. Plaintiff has constructively exhausted his administrative remedies.

16. Plaintiff has retained the services of a law firm, including attorneys, law clerks and paralegals to represent him in this judicial review.

17. As of the date of this filing, the FBI has not complied with FOIA and has failed to release records responsive to Plaintiff's request.

COUNT I – DEFENDANT'S FAILURE TO CONDUCT A REASONABLE SEARCH

18. The above paragraphs are incorporated by reference.

19. FBI has failed to conduct a reasonable search for records responsive to the request.

COUNT II – DEFENDANT'S FAILURE TO PRODUCE RECORDS

20. The above paragraphs are incorporated by reference.

21. FBI has failed to release records responsive to the request.

WHEREFORE, PLAINTIFF respectfully requests the Court to:

  i. order FBI to conduct a reasonable search for records;

  ii. order FBI to promptly produce all non-exempt responsive records or portions of records;

  iii. enjoin FBI from withholding non-exempt public records under FOIA;

  iv. award Plaintiff's reasonable attorneys' fees and costs; and,

  v. award such other relief the Court considers appropriate.

Dated: October 8, 2022

RESPECTFULLY SUBMITTED,

/s/ C. Peter Sorenson
Attorney for Plaintiff
C. Peter Sorenson, DC Bar #438089
Sorenson Law Office
PO Box 10836
Eugene, OR 97440
(541) 606-9173
peter@sorensonfoialaw.com

* * * * *

Exhibit 121: *17 March 2014.   Summary Declaration of John Wilson*

Summary Declaration of John Wilson

Case 1:22-cv-03062-ABJ   Document 16-2   Filed 03/21/24   Page 1 of 15

UNITED STATES DISTRICT COURT
FOR THE DISTRICT OF COLUMBIA

JOHN CHRISTIAN WILSON,

Plaintiff,

v.

FEDERAL BUREAU OF INVESTIGATION,

Defendant.

Civil Action No. 22-3062 (ABJ)

SECOND DECLARATION OF JOHN CHRISTIAN WILSON

I, John Christian Wilson, do declare, subject to the penalties of perjury, that the following statements are true and correct to the best of my knowledge and belief.

1. I am the Plaintiff in this action. If I were to testify at a deposition or at a trial, I would testify to the facts I am including in this Declaration.

2. This Declaration is intended to be a summary of the most relevant facts to assist the Court.

3. I submitted a much lengthier Declaration and Exhibits to the Federal Bureau of Investigation ("FBI") as an attachment to my Freedom of Information Act ("FOIA") Administrative Appeal of my Request No. 1548515-000, at issue in this case. Defendant has filed a copy of that Declaration, titled "Declaration of Mr. John Wilson," [ECF No. 15-13] at 54-165, and the attached Exhibits, *id.* at 166-28. I again attest to the truthfulness of my statements made in that Declaration. I respectfully refer the Court's

attention to that Declaration for further factual support indicating the existence of records responsive to my FOIA request and bad faith on the part of the FBI in responding to my FOIA request.

BACKGROUND

4. I am a resident of Greenwich, New South Wales, Australia. I am a citizen of the United States of America.

5. I completed my MBA in 1993, at The Wharton School of the University of Pennsylvania.

6. Following my graduation from Wharton, I worked on Wall Street for a major British investment bank, S.G. Warburg (now part of UBS Warburg), as a securities analyst covering mining companies based in the United States.

7. On March 12, 1996, I authored a report flagging concerns about New York Stock Exchange ("NYSE") listed Freeport McMoran Copper and Gold Inc. ("Freeport"), one of the world's largest and most valuable copper companies. At the time, Freeport owned the Grasberg copper and gold mine in West Papua, Indonesia, and was under investigation by the U.S. Department of State following eyewitness allegations that Freeport was involved in the killing of indigenous protesters and other human rights abuses.

8. An article in the New York Times from March 1996 indicated an interim investigation of Freeport had been completed by the State Department and further investigations were underway or planned. The article mentioned that a U.S. mining company operating a large mine in West Papua, Indonesia was being investigated by the State Department. The article stated an interim report had been completed and investigations by the State Department were ongoing. The article was posted in an early edition of the New York

Times. The early edition of the New York Times is neither archived nor kept by the New York Times, mainstream U.S. libraries, nor any news service terminals accessible to me or any research consultants I retained. However, the State Department human rights investigation of Freeport's activities in West Papua at this time was referenced in at least two other sources. *See* Robert Bryce, *U.S. Cancels Indonesian Mine's Insurance By Robert Bryce*, New York Times (Nov. 2, 1995), https://www.nytimes.com/1995/11/02/business/international-business-us-cancels-indonesian-mine-s-insurance.html?smid=url-share; *see also* Ralph K. M. Haurwitz, *U.S. finds no evidence of abuses by Freeport*, Austin American-Statesman (Texas) (January 20, 1996).

9. I also received verbal confirmation of both the existence of the human rights investigation into Freeport McMoran and a report by the U.S. Department of State on two separate occasions:

   a. In May 1996, the Freeport McMoran chairman, James R. Moffett (known as Jim Bob), confirmed the existence of the State Department's investigation and report during a briefing to Wall Street analysts at Freeport McMoran's headquarters in New Orleans, LA.

   b. On March 12, 1996, in New York City, FBI operative Susan Holmes confirmed the existence of the State Department's investigation into, and report on Freeport.

10. Following the publication of my report flagging concerns about Freeport, *see supra* ¶ 7, which touched on human rights issues and Freeport's loss of the Overseas Private Investment Corporation ("OPIC") political risk insurance, I received backlash from Freeport, my employer S.G. Warburg, and the Federal Bureau of Investigation.

11. By way of contextual background, Freeport lost its $100 million OPIC political risk

insurance policy in October 1995. This was an embarrassing issue for Freeport – management found its international reputation and $2-4 billion investment in West Papua, Indonesia in jeopardy.

12. OPIC possessed highly regarded expertise and cited environmental abuses in West Papua, Indonesia as the ostensible reason for Freeport's loss of the OPIC political risk insurance. Whispers on Wall Street, and FBI sources, suggested the key reason for Freeport's loss of insurance was that the U.S. government was sending Freeport a message – a "slap on the wrist" for all the bad publicity concerning the reported human rights abuses in West Papua, Indonesia in the vicinity of the Grasberg mine.

13. In an attempt to overturn OPIC's decision and have the policy reinstated, Henry Kissinger (former US secretary of state) and James Woolsey (former CIA director), who were advisers to Freeport in 1996 (Kissinger was also on the Board of Directors), were aggressively lobbying in Washington, D.C. through much of 1996. *See* Denise Leith, The Politics of Power, 177-78 (2003).

14. Further killings of indigenous protestors in the vicinity of Freeport's Grasberg mine in West Papua, Indonesia were reported in early March 1996, and the mine was closed for three days due to strikes. Freeport was on the backfoot, the Indonesian President at the time, Suharto, was angry, and on March 12, 1996, (the same day my report came out) the Freeport Chairman and CEO was flying to West Papua, Indonesia for emergency talks. The Chairman/CEO Jim Bob Moffett arrived in West Papua on March 13, 1996, on an emergency trip. Freeport was under intense pressure to resolve the conflict and silence embarrassing adverse publicity, under mounting pressure from both the Indonesian President Suharto and U.S. leaders to quell unrest to solve the problem.

15. Kissinger and Woolsey would have known the screening mechanisms used by the FBI and other intelligence agencies, and could have subverted these mechanisms, if they chose, to retaliate against myself and others like me, and to silence us. Kissinger and Woolsey were retained to advise and help Freeport, which was highly sensitive to negative media coverage, Freeport's potential link to environmental and human rights abuses in West Papua, Indonesia, and the cancellation of Freeport's OPIC political risk insurance. Woolsey, Kissinger, and Freeport were making great efforts to have the policy reinstated. *See id.*

16. I attest that the FBI has targeted me, based on disclosures made to me by two FBI operatives involved in my case – Susan Holmes and Steve Garber.

17. The FBI's interest in me, starting in 1996, has been confirmed by these FBI operatives and is further evidenced by interactions, relationships, and events in my personal life. The FBI and partnering agencies interfered in my career, professional, social, and family networks, and attempted to entrap me in a failed drug sting, DUI, and other offenses.

18. At least seven other professionals who made disclosures related to Freeport McMoran in the mid-1990s, including academics and journalists, have described similar backlash, including being threatened, blacklisted, and in other ways intimidated for their work. For example, journalist Robert Bryce, who wrote about Freeport's loss of OPIC political risk insurance, was one of the people targeted. *See supra* ¶ 8. The experiences of these other professionals are detailed in Denise Leith's book, "The Politics of Power: Freeport in Suharto's Indonesia."

19. I gained detailed knowledge of the FBI's interest in me through my long-term relationship with Ms. Susan Holmes. Ms. Holmes disclosed her role working undercover

for the FBI, which she said was in a capacity like an independent contractor. She explained that this was a standard legal arrangement for a large number of undercover FBI operatives. Ms. Holmes showed me her black background FBI identification card on multiple occasions, as well as other evidence of her work for the FBI.

20. Susan Holmes, my long-term girlfriend from 1994 to 1997, informed me on many occasions that she worked in some capacity for the FBI, and provided details of her work for the FBI. Ms. Holmes stated that she targeted environmental activists and extremists in the eastern half of the United States, including the founder of Earth First! Dave Foreman, while her FBI counterpart in the western United States targeted the Unabomber. It should be noted that Dave Foreman died on September 19, 2022.

21. Around July 1997, I was introduced to Dave Foreman (now deceased). Ms. Holmes, who targeted environmental activists and extremists for the FBI, introduced me to Mr. Foreman.

22. In 1997, I was invited by Ms. Holmes on a rafting trip down the Colorado River. Myself, Ms. Holmes, and Mr. Foreman, were all present on this trip, along with around 20 other people, mainly high-profile U.S. environmentalists, as well as media personnel.

23. My inclusion on the trip, and placement in Dave Foreman's dory, was evidently part of the FBI ploy to portray me as a close associate of Dave Foreman to create the appearance of the FBI's justified interest in me. By making it appear that I was an associate of Dave Foreman, the FBI sought to subvert the screening process intended to keep innocent people off FBI watchlists, investigations, etc.

24. In 2003, Ms. Holmes confirmed the FBI's interest in me, and this was verified by agent Steve Garber in 2004. I was told that the FBI's interest in me was on account of my

report and work on Freeport McMoran. Furthermore, Ms. Holmes subjected me to an extended detailed interview in 2003 in NYC. During this interview, Ms. Holmes revealed many private details about me, going back decades, indicative of surveillance. These details include private phone conversations, including from my home in NYC, details of my credit card purchases, private details of school and university records, personal details of friends and associates, details of minor traffic offenses, and details of workplace records and assignments, among many other details indicating surveillance by the FBI.

25. I had multiple conversations and connections with Steve Garber, who began befriending me following publication of my March 12, 1996, work report on Freeport McMoran. In 2004, Steve Garber confirmed in NYC that I was the subject of an FBI investigation as a result of my earlier report and work on Freeport McMoran.

26. Since 1996, I have been targeted, investigated, and interfered with by the FBI, evidenced by disclosures from FBI agents Holmes and Garber, consistent with the timing of threats made to me and interference experienced.

FOIA Request No. 1548515-000.

27. I now seek records held by the FBI relating to me, as well as confirmation and an explanation from the FBI as to the reasons for, and instances in which, FBI operatives have targeted me.

28. To assist with my Freedom of Information Act ("FOIA") request, I retained C. Peter Sorenson, my attorney, and his staff at Sorenson Law Office, now known as Sorenson Law LLC.

29. With the assistance of counsel, I submitted a FOIA request to the FBI on May 20, 2022.

[ECF No. 1-5]. I requested:

1) All records, documents, or communications prepared by, received by or maintained by the FBI which mention the following terms:

John Christian Wilson

John C. Wilson

John Wilson

2) All records describing FBI informant or FBI agent contacts with

John Christian Wilson

John C. Wilson

John Wilson

3) All records describing FBI contractors, or others operating on behalf of the FBI or other DOJ element, contacts with

John Christian Wilson

John C. Wilson

John Wilson

4) The 1996 securities analyst report on NYSE listed U.S. mining company Freeport McMoran Copper and Gold Inc (which trades on the NYSE under the symbol FCX) written by John Wilson. This report is entitled, "FCX: Grasberg Closure Highlights Political Risks." Mr. Wilson wrote the report as an analyst working for S.G. Warburg & Co. Inc. and the report was dated March 12, 1996.

5) All records describing the attendance of John Wilson at the Freeport McMoran Copper and Gold Inc. May 1996 annual analyst briefing at Freeport McMoran

Copper and Gold Inc's headquarters in New Orleans, Louisiana. In particular, records are sought concerning n [sic] interaction between John Wilson and James R. Moffett (known as Jim Bob), CEO and Chairman of Freeport McMoran Copper and Gold Inc, in the boardroom alcove after the analyst question period that was held in Freeport McMoran's boardroom.

6) All records describing an interaction between John Wilson and an unnamed person, apparently a federal agent or FBI operative, also in Freeport's boardroom alcove after the analyst question period in Freeport's boardroom mentioned above at the Freeport headquarters in New Orleans, Louisiana in May 1996.

7) All records describing or documenting interactions between John Wilson and people operating on behalf of the FBI or other DOJ element, in particular by Steve Garber.

8) All records, including notes, recordings or transcripts of interviews, made by Steve Garber in early 1999 during the several days when Mr. Wilson visited Garber at his home in Prescott, AZ.

9) All records, including notes, recordings or transcripts, of a discussion or interview involving Mr. Wilson and Steve Garber in June 2004 in New York, New York.

10) All records, including notes, recordings or transcripts, of a discussion or interview involving Mr. Wilson and Steve Garber in September 2004, including at Tibet House, and also the Blue Water Grill both in the vicinity of the Union Square neighborhood of New York, New York.

11) All records of the attendance involving John Wilson in connection with a

presentation that Dave Foreman gave in New York, New York in late 1997. David Foreman (usually referred to as Dave) is a well-known American environmental activist and co-founder of environmental group Earth First! Dave Foreman was a subject of Susan Holmes for her work for the FBI.

12) All records pertaining to John Wilson concerning his attendance, or discussions with Susan Holmes or Dave Foreman on, a raft trip on the Colorado River in July or August 1997 with journalists, including a reporter for Time Magazine, Ms. Holmes and Mr. Foreman.

13) All records of discussions between John Wilson and Susan Ackerson Holmes. All records describing or documenting interactions between John Wilson and people operating on behalf of the FBI or other DOJ element, in particular Susan Ackerson Holmes.

14) All records of discussions between John Wilson and Susan Holmes during the three years that they dated in New York, New York, calendar years 1994, 1995, 1996 and 1997.

15) All records of discussions between John Wilson and Susan Holmes in a May 10, 2003 (on or about) dinner conversation between Susan Holmes and John Wilson in New York, New York.

16) All telephone wiretaps on telephones used by John Wilson.

17) All records showing any applications for surveillance or wiretaps of telephones used by John Wilson.

18) All records showing any applications for search warrants for properties owned or leased by John Wilson.

19) All records showing any applications for surveillance of John Wilson.

30. The time frame for my request includes records created or received on or after January 1, 1994, to present.

31. Defendant acknowledged receipt of my request on June 6, 2022, and assigned FOIPA Request No. 1548515-000. [ECF No. 1-6].

32. On June 13, 2022, Defendant issued a determination, closed my request, and provided no records. [ECF No. 1-7]. Defendant's determination letter stated "[r]ecords regarding your subject were previously reviewed and released to you pursuant to the FOIPA. An additional search was conducted for main entity records, and no additional records subject to the FOIPA were located." *Id.*

Administrative Appeal

33. I filed an administrative appeal on September 1, 2022, with the assistance of counsel. My administrative appeal, although not including exhibits thereto, can be found at ECF No. 1-8.

34. Defendant acknowledged my administrative appeal on September 1, 2022. [ECF No. 1-9].

35. Twenty working days from the date that Defendant acknowledged my appeal passed on September 30, 2022.

36. Having constructively exhausted my administrative remedies, I directed my attorney, Mr. Sorenson, to file a complaint with this Court. I felt that commencing litigation against the FBI was my only option to obtain the records I requested.

Judicial Review

37. My Complaint was filed on October 8, 2022. Complaint [ECF No. 1].

38. On December 8, 2022, the Department of Justice notified me that it was closing my administrative appeal since "an appeal ordinarily will not be acted upon by this Office if the FOIA request becomes the subject of litigation." Defendant's Exhibit F [ECF No. 15-3 at 239].

39. On April 28, 2023, the FBI released 26 pages of responsive records. The FBI's release letter stated that "35 pages were reviewed and 26 pages are being released." Many of the released records contained redactions. The FBI asserted exemptions under § 552 (b)(6), § 552 (b)(7)(C), § 552 (b)(7)(E), and § 552a (k)(2). The FBI has also issued a *Glomar* response. The FBI stated that it had completed its review of records. Defendant's Exhibit G [ECF No. 15-3 at 241].

40. The FBI has failed to perform an adequate search and has improperly issued a *Glomar* response.

41. The FBI states that it searched only for "Wilson, John" and "John Wilson." Declaration of Michael G. Seidel ("Seidel Decl.") ¶ 22 [ECF No. 15-2]. The FBI did not search for records using other variations of my name included in the request: "John Christian Wilson" and "John C. Wilson."

42. Likewise, the FBI did not search for records under any of the other names listed in my request including Jame R Moffett (known as Jim Bob), Susan Ackerson Holmes, Dave Foreman, and Steve Garber.

43. Defendant did not search for any other terms stated in my request.

44. The FBI produced only documents or communications despite the language of my request seeking "all records."

45. I have provided extensive evidence of the existence of records responsive to my request.

In its Motion for Summary Judgment, [ECF No. 15] and attachments, [ECF Nos. 15-1 - 15-4], Defendant does not address the factual evidence of records that I have provided.

The FBI's Failure to Act in Good Faith

46. As detailed below, The FBI, as an agency within the DOJ, has improperly targeted me and has disregarded its obligations under FOIA. The agency is acting in bad faith in its claims of the adequacy of its search, its assertion of the *Glomar* response, and in its failure to produce all records responsive to my request.

47. On May 11, 2006, Marvin Hernandez of the DOJ confirmed in an email to me that an individual I had interacted with was an agent or employee of the FBI. Mr. Hernandez did not name names, but he did confirm that one of the individuals I had named was in fact an agent or employee of the FBI. Mr. Hernandez's statement, while later retracted by him, warrants further explanation. I was advised by Mr. Hernandez that the DOJ management had revoked his authority to communicate with me about anything. Mr. Hernandez was correct in making his original disclosure to me and his subsequent retraction is unreliable.

48. The FBI has been disingenuous in repeatedly misclassifying the people named as FBI operatives – misclassifying them in categories of employees or special agents – but never including contractors or other categories of FBI operatives in their denials. Myself and attorneys have made repeated requests to the FBI and DOJ to correct their misclassifications, provide clarification, and respond more broadly to the assertion that people named as FBI operatives are working as contractors or under some other arrangement with the FBI. However, in a sign of bad faith, neither the FBI nor the DOJ have ever responded to this request for a broader search and response.

49. I have many letters, to and from the DOJ and the FBI, where the agencies have repeatedly misclassified the FBI's association with Garber, Holmes, and others, and have avoided answering the substance of my complaint.

50. This repeated misclassification of the FBI's association with Garber, Holmes, and others, is an act of bad faith on the part of the FBI and DOJ. This bad faith behavior is consistent with disclosures to me by FBI agent Holmes in 1997, concerning techniques used by the FBI and the DOJ to evade transparency and accountability. Further, the FBI, during the period in question, has a history of deliberately deceiving regulators. *See Court Reveals FBI Deceit*, Sydney Morning Herald, (August 25, 2002) https://www.smh.com.au/world/court-reveals-fbi-deceit-20020825-gdfkne.html (detailing FBI and DOJ deceit in falsifying more than 75 applications for search warrants and wiretaps in prior years).

51. The evidence indicates that the FBI has engaged in surveillance of me and holds detailed records concerning my telephone communications, metadata, details of the conversations, and national electronic payment transactions data, but has refused to produce such records, as required under FOIA.

52. The FBI has failed to address whether Ms. Holmes, Mr. Garber, and others have worked for the FBI in some form. With respect to my FOIA request, the FBI has evaded answering this question and has therefore skirted its obligation to consult with these personnel in fulfilling the agency's obligations under FOIA. In the absence of verifying the role of these operatives with the FBI, the FBI is failing to include them and request information from them as part of its search commitments under FOIA. The FBI is expected to consult with personnel who may have knowledge of the requested

information.

53. The FBI has targeted me for my work on Freeport McMoran. The FBI is deliberately withholding responsive records I am entitled to under FOIA and should be ordered to conduct an adequate search, to release all responsive records, and should not be permitted to hide behind an improperly invoked *Glomar* response.

In accordance with 28 U.S.C. § 1746, I declare under penalty of perjury, under the laws of the United States of America, that the foregoing is true and correct.

Dated this 17th day of March 2024 at Greenwich, New South Wales, Australia.

/s/ John Christian Wilson
John Christian Wilson

* * * * *

Exhibit 122: *17 March 2024.   Independent Expert's Report: Jennifer Coffindaffer - a 25 year veteran of the FBI.*

Expert Witness Report: 25-year veteran of the FBI—Jennifer Coffindaffer

Case 1:22-cv-03062-ABJ   Document 16-3   Filed 03/21/24   Page 1 of 14

UNITED STATES DISTRICT COURT
FOR THE DISTRICT OF COLUMBIA

JOHN CHRISTIAN WILSON,

Plaintiff,

v.

FEDERAL BUREAU OF INVESTIGATION,

Defendant.

Civil Action No. 22-3062 (ABJ)

DECLARATION OF JENNIFER LYNNE COFFINDAFFER

I, Jennifer Lynne Coffindaffer, do declare, subject to the penalties of perjury, that the following statements are true and correct to the best of my knowledge and belief.

1. I provide expert witness consulting services through Eagle Security Group, Inc.

2. I was retained by counsel for the Plaintiff to review and evaluate the totality of the records provided by the Federal Bureau of Investigation ("FBI") pursuant to Mr. Wilson's Freedom of Information Act ("FOIA") Request No. 1548515-000 and to give my expert opinions thereafter as to the adequacy of the search conducted by the FBI and any Exemptions asserted by the FBI with respect to the records requested.

3. In developing my opinions, I have relied on my knowledge, training, skill, education and experience developed during my 25 years as FBI Special Agent, Senior Supervisory Resident Agent ("SSRA") and Supervisory Special Agent ("SSA") with the FBI,

including specific experience in the areas of conducting electronic searches, and finding and retrieving documents within the FBI's databases, including: the Central Records System ("CRS"), Automated Case Support system ("ACS"), Sentinel Electronic Surveillance files ("ELSUR"), Informant Databases ("DELTA") as well as other FBI databases. I have also relied on the experience of fellow agents and clerks in the FBI related to searches within the same FBI databases.

4. The materials I reviewed are as follows:

   a. Litigation Release Letter from the FBI and 10 pages of released records on Request No. 1250235-001 (September 25, 2014)

   b. Report and Recommendation from Magistrate Judge Stewart D. Aaron in *John Wilson v Federal Bureau of Investigation*, 1:20-cv-10324 (LAK) (SDA) (S.D.N.Y 2022)

   c. Complaint and Exhibits (in this case, No. 22-3062) [ECF Nos. 1, 1-5 – 1-10]

   d. Answer (in this case, No. 22-3062) [ECF No. 7]

   e. Litigation Release Letter from the FBI and 26 pages of released records in Request No. 1548515-000 (the subject of this case) (April 28, 2023)

   f. Letter from C. Peter Sorenson to Assistant United States Attorney John Moustakas (in this case, No. 22-3062) (July 11, 2023)

   g. Declaration of Michael G. Seidel (in this case, No. 22-3062) (Ex. 1) [ECF No. 15-2]

   h. Second Declaration of Michael G. Seidel (in this case, No. 22-3062) (Ex. 2) [ECF No. 15-4]

   i. Exemption Application Index (in this case, No. 22-3062) (Ex. H) [ECF No. 15-3]

j. Declaration of Susan C. Weetman (in this case, No. 22-3062) (Ex. I) [ECF No. 15-3]

k. Declaration of Deborah M. Waller (in this case, No. 22-3062) (Ex. J) [ECF No. 15-3]

l. FOIA request the FBI received from the Plaintiff dated June 14, 2013

m. FOIA request the FBI received from the Plaintiff dated March 26, 2014

n. FOIA request the FBI received from the Plaintiff dated November 6, 2014

o. FOIA request the FBI received from the Plaintiff dated May 20, 2022 [ECF No. 1-5]

p. FBI response to Plaintiff's first FOIA request dated January 29, 2014

q. FBI response to Plaintiff's second FOIA request

r. FBI response to Plaintiff's third FOIA request dated April 2, 2021

s. *John Wilson v Federal Bureau of Investigation*, 1:20-cv-10324 (LAK) (SDA) (S.D.N.Y) - Complaint filed December 8, 2020

t. *John Wilson v Federal Bureau of Investigation*, 1:20-cv-10324 (LAK) (SDA) (S.D.N.Y) - Declaration of Michael G. Seidel, filed September 13, 2021

u. Declaration of David M. Hardy in *Watkins Law & Advocacy, PLLC v Department of Veterans Affairs, et al.*, 17-cv-01974 (ABJ) (D.D.C. December 10, 2018)

v. Memorandum Opinion in *Cato Institute v FBI*, 20-cv-3338 (JEB) (D.D.C. Jan 9, 2024)

HISTORY OF FOIA REQUESTS SUBMITTED TO THE FBI BY THE PLAINTIFF

5. To date, the Plaintiff has submitted FOIA requests to the FBI for records pertaining to himself. On each of the FOIA requests, the FBI searched the Central Records System using the Sentinel case-management system and the Automated Case Support case-management system, but in my opinion has failed to provide responsive records to the Plaintiff.

6. Listed below are the details regarding four requests and the FBI's responses:

    a. The Plaintiff submitted **FOIA Request Number 1** on June 14, 2013, requesting "all files, correspondence, and other records" concerning the Plaintiff. The Plaintiff provided specific identifying information concerning himself including his date of birth, place of birth, and his social security number to aid in the FBI's search. In response to this request, the FBI produced no records, inaccurately claiming the Plaintiff did not provide identifying information and that the Plaintiff did not ask for "reference" files, dismissing the fact that the Plaintiff asked for "all files".[1,2,3]

    b. The Plaintiff submitted **FOIA Request Number 2** on March 26, 2014, requesting "all files, correspondence, and other records" concerning the Plaintiff. Like the first request, the Plaintiff provided specific identifying information concerning himself. In response to the Plaintiff's second request the FBI reviewed 21 pages, 10 of which the FBI indicated were responsive. The FBI withheld a total of 11

---

[1] Plaintiff's FOIA request dated June 14, 2013
[2] Declaration of Michael G. Seidel dated January 9, 2014
[3] Declaration of Michael G. Seidel dated September 13, 2021

pages citing legal exemptions from Section 552 (b)(6) and (b)(7)(C) and Section 552a (j)(2) as well as FOIA, GLOMAR and Privacy Act exemptions. The FBI claimed they produced this record because the Plaintiff provided identifying information and asked for the main and reference files to be searched. These assertions were inaccurate because in fact, the Plaintiff provided the same information on both the first and in the second request. The record was not located in the first search, and in my opinion, that was because the FBI did not conduct a responsive, good faith search.[4][5]

c. The Plaintiff submitted **FOIA Request Number 3** on November 6, 2014, requesting "all files, correspondence, and other records" concerning the Plaintiff. Like the first and second request, the Plaintiff provided specific identifying information concerning himself. In response to the Plaintiff's third request, the FBI produced 15 pages of the 22 pages of records the FBI indicated were responsive to the Plaintiff's third FOIA request. The FBI withheld in total 7 pages citing legal exemptions concerning "law enforcement purposes."

d. The Plaintiff submitted **FOIA Request Number 4** to the FBI on May 20, 2022, concerning himself. [ECF No. 1-5]. This is the request at issue in this case. The time frame for the request included records created or received on or after January 1, 1994 to present. Plaintiff requested:

❖ All records, documents, or communications prepared by, received by or maintained by the FBI which mention the following terms:

John Christian Wilson

---
[4] Plaintiff's FOIA request dated March 26, 2014
[5] Declaration of Michael G. Seidel dated September 13, 2021

John C. Wilson

John Wilson

- All records describing FBI informant or FBI agent contacts with

    John Christian Wilson

    John C. Wilson

    John Wilson

- All records describing FBI contractors, or others operating on behalf of the FBI or other DOJ elements, contacts with

    John Christian Wilson

    John C. Wilson

    John Wilson

- The 1996 securities analyst report on the New York Stock Exchange (NYSE) listed U.S. mining company Freeport McMoran Copper and Gold Inc (which trades on the NYSE under the symbol FCX) written by John Wilson. This report is entitled, "FCX: Grasberg Closure Highlights Political Risks." Mr. Wilson wrote the report as an analyst working for S.G. Warburg & Co. Inc. and the report was dated March 12, 1996.

- All records describing the attendance of John Wilson at the Freeport McMoran Copper and Gold Inc. May 1996 annual analyst briefing at Freeport McMoran Copper and Gold Inc's headquarters in New Orleans, Louisiana. In particular, records are sought concerning interaction between John Wilson and James R. Moffett (known as Jim Bob), CEO and Chairman of Freeport McMoran Copper and Gold Inc, in the boardroom alcove after the analyst question period that was held in Freeport McMoran's boardroom.

- All records describing an interaction between John Wilson and an unnamed person, apparently a federal agent or FBI operative, also in Freeport's boardroom alcove after the analyst question period in Freeport's boardroom mentioned above at the Freeport headquarters in New Orleans, Louisiana in May 1996.
- All records describing or documenting interactions between John Wilson and people operating on behalf of the FBI or other DOJ element, in particular by Steve Garber.
- All records, including notes, recordings or transcripts of interviews, made by Steve Garber in early 1999 during the several days when Mr. Wilson visited Garber at his home in Prescott, AZ.
- All records, including notes, recordings or transcripts, of a discussion or interview involving Mr. Wilson and Steve Garber in June 2004 in New York, New York.
- All records, including notes, recordings or transcripts, of a discussion or interview involving Mr. Wilson and Steve Garber in September 2004, including at Tibet House, and also the Blue Water Grill both in the vicinity of the Union Square neighborhood of New York, New York.
- All records of the attendance involving John Wilson in connection with a presentation that Dave Foreman gave in New York, New York in late 1997. David Foreman (usually referred to as Dave) is a well-known American environmental activist and co-founder of environmental group Earth First! Dave Foreman was a subject of Susan Holmes for her work for the FBI.
- All records pertaining to John Wilson concerning his attendance, or discussions with Susan Holmes or Dave Foreman on, a raft trip on the

Colorado River in July or August 1997 with journalists, including a reporter for Time Magazine, Ms. Holmes and Mr. Foreman.

- All records of discussions between John Wilson and Susan Ackerson Holmes. All records describing or documenting interactions between John Wilson and people operating on behalf of the FBI or other DOJ element, in particular Susan Ackerson Holmes.
- All records of discussions between John Wilson and Susan Holmes during the three years that they dated in New York, New York, calendar years 1994, 1995, 1996 and 1997.
- All records of discussions between John Wilson and Susan Holmes in a May 10, 2003 (on or about) dinner conversation between Susan Holmes and John Wilson in New York, New York.
- All telephone wiretaps on telephones used by John Wilson.
- All records showing any applications for surveillance or wiretaps of telephones used by John Wilson.
- All records showing any applications for search warrants for properties owned or leased by John Wilson.
- All records showing any applications for surveillance of John Wilson.

7. In response to the Plaintiff's FOIA request assigned Request No. 1548515-000 (the request that is the subject of this litigation), the FBI advised via a letter dated June 13, 2022, that the FBI completed a new search and found no additional records responsive to the FOIA request.

8. Then, on April 28, 2023, after litigation was filed in the Federal District Court, District of Columbia, the FBI advised the Plaintiff that they found additional records.

Specifically, the FBI advised they had processed 35 pages of responsive records. Of these pages, the FBI released 7 pages in full, 19 pages in part, and withheld 9 pages in full citing that the pages were exempt pursuant to applicable FOIA Exemption(s) or that the pages were duplicates.

LEGAL ACTIONS TAKEN BY PLAINTIFF CONCERNING HIS FOIA REQUESTS

9. On December 8, 2020, the Plaintiff commenced a legal action against the FBI in Federal District Court, Southern District of New York seeking disclosure and release of all agency records pertaining to him. The FBI disclosed to the New York court that they located 22 pages responsive to the Plaintiff's FOIA requests. The FBI indicated they released 8 pages in their entirety, 7 pages in part and withheld 7 pages in full (2 of those pages being duplicates). After reviewing the case, the Honorable U.S. Magistrate Judge, Stewart D. Aaron recommended that the FBI be compelled to search its "Delta record-keeping system" for records responsive to the Plaintiffs requests.[6] The Honorable Lewis A. Kaplan, United States District Judge, adopted the Report and Recommendation on April 4, 2022.

10. On October 8, 2022, the Plaintiff commenced a legal action against the FBI in the United States District Court for the District of Columbia (this case).

11. Listed Below, in table format, is a synopsis of records produced by the FBI to the Plaintiff. The FBI initially provided 0 records responsive to the Plaintiff's first FOIA request and now, after four FOIA requests and two civil complaints, the FBI has processed 35 records in response to the Plaintiff's FOIA request. In short, the FBI

---

[6] USDC, SDNY, Report and Recommendations dated February 16, 2022

provided four separate productions of records despite the fact that the Plaintiff asked for all records pertaining to him in each request.

FBI Production in Response to FOIA Requests by Plaintiff

FOIA Request	Date of FOIA Request	Date of FOIA Response	FBI Production of Records Provided to Plaintiff
FOIA Request Number 1	June 14, 2013	January 29, 2014	No records produced
FOIA Request Number 2 - No. 1250235-001	March 26, 2014	September 25, 2014	21 pages, 10 pages released in full or in part, and 11 pages withheld
FOIA Request Number 3	November 6, 2014	April 2, 2021	22 pages, 15 pages released in full or in part, and 7 pages withheld
FOIA Request Number 4 - No. 1548515-000 (the subject of this judicial review)	May 20, 2022	June 13, 2022	No records produced
	May 20, 2022	April 28, 2023	35 pages, 7 pages released in full, 19 pages in part, and 9 pages withheld

FBI Production in Response to litigation filed by Plaintiff

District and Civil Action Number	Date Complaint	Date of Court Order	Court Order Details	Date and Documents Produced by the FBI

	was Filed by Plaintiff			
Southern District of New York 1:20-CV-10324	December 8, 2020	February 16, 2022	Court recommended that the FBI search DELTA Database	April 2, 2021: 22 pages, 15 pages released in whole or in part
District of Columbia 22-3062 (ABJ)	October 8, 2022	Pending	Pending	April 28, 2023: 35 pages, 26 pages released in full or in part

CONCLUSION AND OPINIONS

12. The opinions below are based upon my review of the materials cited herein, my knowledge of the FBI's computer systems including Sentinel, ACS, CRS, ELSUR, DELTA, training, education, and experience as a special agent with the Federal Bureau of Investigation and use of these systems throughout my 25 years as an FBI Agent and are all centered upon a reasonable degree of probability based on my experience in these areas.

13. In conducting their search on Request No. 1548515-000, the subject of this judicial review, the FBI searched only for "Wilson, John" and "John Wilson." Declaration of Michael G. Seidel ("Seidel Decl.") ¶ 22 [ECF No. 15-2]. The FBI did not search using the other variations of Plaintiff's name listed in the request ("John Christian Wilson" and "John C. Wilson") in their search of Sentinel. This could result in flawed search results unresponsive to the Plaintiff's FOIA request. In my professional opinion, the FBI did not

undertake an adequate search for records when they did not search Sentinel for "John Christian Wilson" and "John C. Wilson."

14. The Plaintiff has provided information for the FBI to reasonably conclude that responsive records may reside outside the CRS. Specifically, responsive records may reside in the DELTA Database. The FBI DELTA Database contains files pertaining to confidential informant and cooperating witness records. There are records maintained in the DELTA Database that are not maintained in the CRS. For this reason, the DELTA Database should be searched. Furthermore, the Honorable U.S. Magistrate Judge Aaron, in his 16-page review of the Southern District of New York case, rendered a recommendation supporting the opinion that the FBI should be "compelled" to Search the DELTA Database. The Honorable Lewis A. Kaplan, United States District Judge, adopted the Report and Recommendation on April 4, 2022. In my professional opinion, the FBI did not undertake an adequate search for records when they did not search the DELTA Database in response to Request No. 1548515-000.

15. The Plaintiff has also provided information for the FBI to reasonably conclude that responsive records may reside in ELSUR files. The ELSUR files contain files pertaining to electronic surveillance. There are records maintained in the ELSUR files that are not maintained in the CRS. For this reason, the ELSUR files should be searched.

16. In my professional opinion, the FBI did not justify its assertion of a GLOMAR response to Plaintiff's request for records. Specifically, the FBI broadly used the GLOMAR responses in a general and overarching way to excuse them from providing records that are responsive to the Plaintiff's FOIA requests. The GLOMAR responses are not relevant to the Plaintiff's requests. The FBI has used boiler plate GLOMAR language and

indicated that it applies to the Defendant's requests when such an assertion is patently inaccurate. The GLOMAR assertions have been used, yet seem to have been abandoned when the FBI provided some documents to the Plaintiff. In my professional opinion, GLOMAR is being asserted to shield production of the requested records when GLOMAR exceptions do not apply.

17. In this case, the FBI claims that law enforcement activities will be imperiled if the requested documents are provided. This, in my professional opinion, is not accurate. The events described in the FOIA requests and contained in the limited documents that the FBI released are approximately 20 to 30 years old. All of the statutes of limitations on the crimes that could possibly have been prosecuted have expired. In addition, there are no on-going law enforcement activities concerning the documents requested.

18. In addition, it should be noted that there are no national security issues presented, nor are there any "Watch List" concerns. This is evidenced not only by the nature of the records requested, but by the records produced to the Plaintiff by the FBI. Most of the records produced precede the creation of the FBI's Watch List and are not related to international terrorism. In addition, the records requested also have no nexus to the witness security program. Moreover, to date, the documents produced to the Plaintiff by the FBI indicate Office of Professional Responsibility ("OPR") file numbers. OPR cases are not criminal cases, international terrorism cases, or substantive investigative cases. OPR cases are, in fact, internal affairs cases involving employee conduct.

19. Concerning possible confidential source information, if such documents are located pursuant to a search of the DELTA Database, identifying and/or singular information could be withheld from production or redacted. However, it is my professional opinion

that if the FBI does not search the DELTA database, they will remain unresponsive to the Plaintiff's FOIA request.

20. In short, there is no reason for any records to remain hidden more than 20 years after the documents were created and using GLOMAR as an excuse to not produce the records undermines the legitimate use of GLOMAR to withhold records under FOIA.

21. Based on the FBI's track record of unresponsiveness concerning the production of records regarding the Plaintiff's FOIA responses, and a court ordered recommendation, it is my opinion that the FBI's assertion that they have acted in "Good Faith" and have been responsive is not accurate. Specifically, initially the FBI responded they had no records. Then, the FBI responded they had one record. Then the FBI responded they had 22 records but provided limited production of the 22 records. Then the FBI asserted they had 35 records, yet again limited the production. With each request, the FBI's answer has changed.

22. Based on each of the points cited above, it is my opinion that the FBI has not in good faith conducted responsive searches pertaining to the Plaintiff's FOIA requests.

In accordance with 28 U.S.C. § 1746, I declare under penalty of perjury, under the laws of the United States of America, that the foregoing is true and correct.

Dated this 17th day of March 2024 at Jacksonville, Florida.

/s/ Jennifer Lynne Coffindaffer
Jennifer Lynne Coffindaffer

INDEX

A

Attorneys
- Fisher, Barry 51, 52, 53, 54, 90, 125, 134, 204, 220, 221, 299, 300, 302, 303, 304, 305, 306, 308, 309, 311, 312, 314, 316, 318, 320, 321, 326, 327, 331, 334, 336, 339, 340, 343, 358, 360, 361, 365, 367, 369, 371, 374, 381, 382, 395, 396, 412, 413, 414, 415, 416, 417, 418, 419, 423, 426, 429, 430, 431, 432, 443, 446, 447, 449, 516, 517, 518, 519, 520, 521, 524, 527, 529, 530, 531, 532, 533, 534, 535, 537, 538, 539, 540, 547, 553, 554, 555, 556, 557, 558, 559, 560, 561, 562, 563
- Rankin, David (BLHNY) 56, 58, 430, 441, 565, 633, 635, 636
- Sobel, David (EFF) 56, 441, 452, 454, 455, 457, 462, 465, 466, 474, 480, 482, 484, 485, 486, 487, 488, 489, 490, 491, 519
- Sorenson, Pete 7, 46, 47, 56, 59, 66, 68, 85, 87, 112, 114, 441, 578, 579, 587, 591, 599, 600, 633, 658, 659

Australian intelligence operatives

Aitken, Daniel	49, 133, 164, 309
Allen, Trent	49, 133, 163
Babich, Fabian	49, 101, 133, 134, 164
Bye, Deborah	49
Cropper, Charlie	49, 95
Hackman, Michael	49, 133, 163
Kaan, Richard	49, 133, 164
Maish, Richard	49, 97
Sadleir, Robert	49, 133, 163
Wilson, Mark B. (formerly of Avalon Beach)	49, 95, 130

C

CIA - former Director

Woolsey, James	10, 15

D

Department of Justice (DOJ)
- Hernandez, Marvin, (Investigative Specialist) 53, 90, 301, 302, 303, 304, 305, 306, 307, 308, 309, 311, 316, 317, 335
- Horowitz, Michael E. (Inspector General) 57, 396, 423, 432
- Martin, Paul K. (Deputy Inspector General, OIG) 25, 31, 95, 101, 309, 310, 312, 313, 324, 326, 327, 333, 334
- Moustakas, John (AUSA)3, 46, 47, 48, 56, 66, 67, 68, 69, 84, 85, 87, 114
- Sobonya, David (Public Information Officer) 454, 456, 457, 458, 459, 475, 478, 479, 480, 481, 491, 492, 493

F

FBI Director

Comey, James B.	396, 432
Wray, Christopher	423

FBI operatives

Chenault, Stephan	50, 142, 379, 511
Conner, Jennifer	50, 379, 511
Dey, Allison	50, 379, 511

- Garber, Steve 8, 10, 11, 15, 16, 33, 34, 40, 46, 47, 50, 51, 53, 56, 66, 67, 68, 69, 78, 79, 80, 89, 90, 91, 92, 93, 94, 105, 106, 107, 108, 109, 110, 123, 125, 126, 127, 128, 129, 130, 133, 134, 135, 137, 138, 140, 142, 150, 159, 162, 163, 164, 165, 166, 167, 168, 170, 171, 172, 174, 175, 176, 177, 178, 181, 183, 185, 188, 189, 190, 191, 192, 203, 205, 207, 213, 214, 219, 220, 300, 303, 315, 341, 359, 372, 379, 437, 446, 512, 545, 551, 572

Haggerty, Rob	50, 379, 511

- Holmes, Susan 10, 15, 21, 46, 48, 49, 50, 51, 53, 56, 59, 66, 67, 68, 69, 88, 89, 90, 91, 92, 93, 94, 95, 96, 97, 98, 99, 100, 101, 102, 103, 104, 105, 106, 107, 108, 109, 110, 123, 124, 125, 126, 127, 128, 129, 130, 131, 132, 134, 135, 136, 137, 138, 139, 140, 141, 142, 143, 144, 145, 158, 161, 162, 163, 164, 165, 166, 168, 169, 170, 171, 174, 176, 177, 180, 182, 184, 189, 201, 203, 204, 205, 206, 207, 208, 210, 211, 212, 213, 214, 215, 216, 217, 218, 219, 220, 221, 300, 303, 308, 315, 341, 347, 350, 359, 372, 379, 437, 447, 512, 541, 545, 551, 572

Klotz, John	50, 142, 379, 511
Levey, Matthew	50, 93, 131, 162, 181, 182, 183, 187, 188, 189, 379, 511
Mills, Michael	50, 379, 511
Robards, Jeffrey	50, 379, 511
Schneider, George	50, 379, 511
Schultz, Robert	50, 379, 512
Sutro, Livingston	50, 51, 53, 90, 300, 303, 315, 341, 359, 372, 379, 447, 511
Walton, Kathleen	50, 93, 162, 379, 511
Whitby, Paul	50, 379, 511
Worden, Ben	16, 50, 309, 379, 511

FBI targets
- Foreman, Dave 51, 59, 67, 69, 89, 91, 99, 106, 109, 110, 125, 128, 129, 130, 132, 143, 144, 168, 169, 170, 174, 204, 206, 208, 215, 216, 217, 437

Winter, Paul	144, 206, 437

FBI techniques

"Dissidents" and cancel culture	15, 16, 28, 51, 107, 150, 157, 158, 169, 177, 179, 207
Abuse of power	46, 48, 67, 75
Entrapment	46, 47, 48, 74, 75
Evasive and misleading responses	46
Gaslighting	48, 100

Honey traps 150
Inflict a toll 24, 52, 107, 154
Lack of "good faith" 46
Misuse of surveillance powers 46, 48
Planted evidence 46
Smear campaigns 52, 107, 130, 151, 153, 178
Suppression of dissent 46, 48, 66
Tainted records 46

Freeport-McMoRan - former Directors
Kissinger, Henry 8, 10, 11, 14, 15, 23, 24, 28, 37, 45, 162, 189, 191, 203, 219, 555
Moffett, Jim Bob 66, 92, 105, 108, 128, 162, 167, 187, 191, 202, 203, 209, 219, 313

Freeport-McMoRan - West Papua, Indonesia
Grasberg mine 45, 55, 66, 88, 92, 127, 131, 133, 162, 163, 167, 183, 190, 201, 203, 208, 209, 210, 212, 299, 303, 310, 313, 314, 323, 340, 358, 365, 371, 375, 378, 437, 446, 455, 511

H

House Judiciary Committee (HJC)
Correspondence 53, 358, 360, 361, 363, 364, 374

O

Office of Government Information Services (OGIS)
Correspondence 56, 57, 58, 419, 420, 421, 441, 516, 521, 522, 523, 524, 525, 526, 527, 528, 530, 531, 532, 533, 534, 535, 536, 537, 538, 539, 540, 541, 542, 545, 546, 547, 548, 550, 551, 552, 553, 554, 555, 556

Overseas Private Investment Corporation (OPIC) 6, 9, 10, 11, 18, 19, 45, 88, 162, 201, 203, 210

R

Royal Commission into Australian intelligence agencies
Hope Royal Commission 49
Ruddock, Philip (former Australian Attorney General)
49, 126, 133, 163, 164, 221

U

United States Attorney General
Barr, William 423
Garland, Merrick B. 427, 437
Lynch, Loretta 396

United States Congressmen
Nadler, Jerrold (New York City) 45, 53, 54, 55, 57, 220, 297, 340, 341, 342, 343, 344, 345, 346, 347, 348, 349, 350, 351, 352, 353, 354, 355, 356, 357, 429, 431, 437, 438, 529, 539, 559

United States Department of State *5, 7, 8, 9, 11, 12, 14, 27, 45, 46, 50, 59, 80, 88, 92, 127, 131, 167, 182, 188, 190, 201, 202, 209, 221, 299, 303, 310, 314, 322, 323, 340, 356, 358, 365, 371, 379, 446, 511*

United States senators
Clinton, Hillary 54, 58, 75, 178, 371
Gillibrand, Kirsten (New York) 54, 297, 434, 435, 436
Schumer, Chuck (New York) 45, 53, 54, 57, 220, 297, 310, 312, 313, 314, 315, 316, 319, 320, 321, 322, 323, 324, 326, 327, 328, 329, 330, 331, 333, 334, 335, 336, 339, 346, 347, 348, 349, 350, 351, 381, 397, 400, 410, 412, 413, 414, 415, 416, 417, 419, 420, 421, 429, 430, 431, 432, 433, 529, 539, 541, 559

United Steelworkers
Correspondence 55, 375, 376

www.ingramcontent.com/pod-product-compliance
Lightning Source LLC
Chambersburg PA
CBHW080321080526
44585CB00021B/2421